THE POETRY OF SCOTLAND

In memoriam Alexander Scott
(1920–1989)

THE POETRY OF SCOTLAND

Gaelic, Scots and English 1380–1980

Edited and Introduced by

Roderick Watson

EDINBURGH UNIVERSITY PRESS

© Copyright of poems resides with the individual poets; the acknowledgements on pp. 712–14 constitute an extension of this copyright page.

Edinburgh University Press Ltd
22 George Square, Edinburgh

Typeset in Linotron Goudy
by Nene Phototypesetters Ltd, Northampton, and
printed and bound in Finland
by Werner Söderström OY

A CIP record for this book is available from the British Library

ISBN 0 7486 0607 6

The Publisher acknowledges subsidy from the Scottish Arts Council towards the publication of this volume.

The Publisher acknowledges an award from the Deric Bolton Poetry Trust towards the publication of this volume.

Contents

The Gude and Godlie Ballatis

The Ballad Tradition

Scots Songs in the 18th and 19th Centuries

Vernacular Scots Poetry

Table of Contents by Theme

The Common Folk

War

Life at Court

The Life of Women

Love

In the City

Landscape and the Seasons

Satire

Celebration

Writing

Lament and Exile

Death

Introduction

Anthologists beware. What was 'forgotten' yesterday may well be reassessed today, and who is to say what will strike us afresh tomorrow? We cannot escape our human tendency to see or to seek patterns in the world around us, and it is not possible to exercise choice without invoking some kind of agenda. The only agenda-free anthology of Scottish poetry would be a project worthy of Borges's notion of the universal library, for it would contain every poem ever written in Scotland, or by a Scot. Every selection entails omission, and each omission will have a reader to plead its case. And such acts of choice, re-valuation and downright disagreement are to be welcomed, for they are what keep us and our culture alive. But the question must still be asked as to whose choice is being exercised, and to what end? In other words, what are anthologies for?

It seems to me that the clear agenda in almost all Scottish anthologies and literary histories has been to sustain, imply, construct or seek a version of ourselves through what we have written and what we have read over the years. After all, the main 'state' left to a 'stateless nation' may well be its state of mind, and in that territory it is literature which maps the land.

It is no coincidence that the first anthology-maps in the self-conscious construction of a Scottish identity were made after the psychic and political trauma of the Union of Parliaments in 1707, nor that these volumes played a part in the rise of Scottish popular publishing. The ground was laid by Watson's *Choice Collection* (1706–11), followed by Ramsay's *Tea Table Miscellany* (1724–32), and two volumes of older poetry, *The Ever Green* (1724), 'wrote by the ingenuous before 1600' and largely selected from the Bannatyne manuscript. It cannot be denied, of course, that this vernacular revival was at least partly motivated by sentimental rusticism and antiquarian patriotism. But another part of it really did seem to speak for the common people, as well as for experience outside the metropolitan centre, and for varieties of language and intimacies of address which the more formal tones of a newly developing administrative English could not gain access to, or admit.

In other words, just as the concept of a unified and imperial Great Britain was being formed, Scots writers and anthologists were taking steps to sustain an account of themselves which spoke for cultural and linguistic (if not always political) *difference*. In this respect Scotland seems to me to have anticipated many later movements in the history of 'English literature', not least the attempts to define what 'American' identity and literature might be, in the aftermath of the Declaration of Independence in 1776.

In the same way, I think that the twentieth-century revival of the 'Modern Scottish Renaissance' will be seen as an early shift in the same post-colonial cultural devolution which has made space for writing in English from Ireland, India, Pakistan and Africa, not to mention the separate development of literatures in Canada, Australia and New Zealand, and the status of 'new Englishes' from black writers in Britain, the Caribbean and further afield. Questions of identity and pluralism, of linguistic, and also of *social* difference, can no longer be excluded from any discussion of contemporary culture and, as Robert Crawford's *Devolving English Literature* has proposed, these issues are now every bit as relevant to historians of 'English' literature as they have been (for years) to specifically Scottish scholars.

But what we see in any landscape depends on where we stand, and it is only natural that our view should change as the miles roll by. My own reading of Scottish literature has undoubtedly been coloured by what I take to be its continuing concern with the demotic voice and common experience – from Henryson's fable of the two mice to Robert Garioch's confrontation with brither worm; from Gavin Douglas's defence of Scots to Tom Leonard's poem 'right inuff / ma language is disgraceful'. In these and many other works I delight to find 'the tongue of the people in the mouth of the scholar' – a phrase used by Robert Lowell to define what he took to be the most effective literary style.[1]

I believe that Scottish literature shows a long-standing and unique intercourse between 'scholars' and 'people' in this respect – for our 'high art' has seldom lost touch with the expressive vigour of the vernacular and folk tradition and its utterance has been constantly refreshed by this forceful contact. Why this should be so is another question, but Scotland has had a long history of belief in its own democratic and egalitarian values, not least in education, and even if such beliefs are no more than 'mythology', they have still been active in how we think of ourselves, and hence in making us what we are in what is still, after all, a small country.

This view is certainly part of what I see in looking back over the landscape of Scottish literature. The demotic spirit can be usefully traced in verse from Rauf Coilyear to Blind Hary, through Henryson, Lindsay, Fergusson, Burns, Tannahill, Thomson, Davidson, MacDiarmid, George Bruce, Robert Garioch, Hamish Henderson, Alastair Mackie, Liz Lochhead and Tom Leonard. Its most influential modern realisation has probably been in working- class drama from Joe Corrie, Roddy McMillan, John McGrath's 7:84

Company, Bill Bryden, John Byrne and many others, carried forward and developed in its turn by prose writers such as Carl MacDougall, James Kelman, Agnes Owens, Janice Galloway, Gordon Legge and Duncan McLean, and spiced, too, by singers and writers like Morris Blythman, Michael Mara, Ricky Ross and many others. These seem to me to be among the most telling figures and forces which must be located in the landscape of Scottish literature from any viewpoint in the 1990s.

But there's another trail to be traced back I think, to what might be called the 'metaphysical' outlook to be found in 'The Dreme of Schir David Lyndesay', 'The Cherrie and the Slae' and Hogg's 'Kilmeny'; and then again in 'The City of Dreadful Night' from James Thomson, and in John Davidson's 'Fleet Street' and the poetry of Hugh MacDiarmid, Sorley Maclean, Norman MacCaig, W. S. Graham, Edwin Morgan and Iain Crichton Smith. Nor is there an easy distinction here between 'high art' and the democratic tradition, for all of these writers have been part of that spirit, too, however abstruse or 'difficult' their poetry might have become. Among contemporary prose writers it is Alasdair Gray who brings all these factors most strikingly together in his work – 'the tongue of the people in the mouth of the scholar', indeed.

So if there is an 'agenda' in this present selection of Scottish poems, it would certainly include a recognition of what I have here called the 'demotic' and the 'metaphysical' strains in our literature and how they have been interrelated. Note that this is *not* that combination of opposites (wild fantasy and coarse realism) which Gregory Smith proposed in his study *Scottish Literature: Character and Influence* (1919), known ever since as the 'Caledonian antisyzygy'. Driven by Hugh MacDiarmid's determination to look in the glass of Scottish letters and to see his own face, this concept was undoubtedly influential in its time, but its binary simplifications must be resisted, for there are paradoxes, antagonisms and silences within the field which cannot simply be wished away by reference to a national penchant for self-contradiction. The most striking example of this – of how complex the Scottish literary and social scene has really been – relates to the mutual status of Scots and Gaelic, and to the relationships between these two cultures.

We have to recognise that while the case for linguistic and cultural difference was being made so vividly by writers of the eighteenth-century vernacular revival, the most prominent figures of the 'Scottish Enlighten-ment' favoured distinctly second-rate neoclassical writing in English and, with the help of Aberdeen's Professor of Moral Philosophy James Beattie, were looking to remove all 'Scotticisms' from their speech and writing. In fact Beattie was only worried about 'those Scotch idioms, which, in this country, are liable to be mistaken for English', adding that 'with respect to broad Scotch words I do not think any caution requisite, as they are easily known, and the necessity of avoiding them is obvious'. One could not ask for a clearer expression of monological authoritarianism, and of the new imperialism's reductive and centralising spirit, than these lines from Beattie's little book:

> There is a time, when languages, as well as men, arrive
> at maturity; and, when that time is past, alterations are
> commonly for the worse . . . Every unauthorised word
> and idiom, which has of late been, without necessity,
> introduced into it, tends to its debasement: and every
> attempt to discredit such words and idioms will be
> praised, or at least pardoned, by the judicious critick.
>
> (*Scoticisms, arranged in Alphabetical*
> *Order, designed to correct Improprieties*
> *of Speech and Writing*, Edinburgh, 1787)

On the other hand, we may look in vain for any substantial acknowledgement of Gaelic poetry from those who wrote in Scots. Ramsay, Fergusson, Burns and Scott were familiar enough with Highland life and traditions, and after all, James Macpherson's 'translation' of Ossian had taken Scotland and Europe by storm when *Fragments of Ancient Poetry* appeared in 1760. Yet Duncan Bàn Macintyre was actually living in Edinburgh by 1768, and his Gaelic poems were published there that year (along with those of Duguld Buchanan). This was only a few years before the appearance of Mackenzie's *The Man of Feeling* and Fergusson's *Poems* (1773), and yet these two strands of Scottish culture never seem to have impinged on each other in any way, despite the fact that Gaelic culture in the Lowlands had its own presence and its own events, such as the piping and poetry competition organised annually at Falkirk by the London Highland Society in the 1780s.

Given the long and sophisticated literary tradition of the Highlands, and the strength of the Gaelic vernacular revival in the eighteenth century, with poets and tradition-bearers such as Alasdair MacMhaighstir Alasdair, John MacCodrum, Rob Donn Mackay, Duncan Bàn and William Ross, it is not an entirely comfortable experience to read Fergusson's comments on Highlanders in 'Hallow-Fair', or to confront the linguistic and cultural stereotypes of Hogg's 'Donald MacDonald'. It would seem that the Scots vernacular poets were as ignorant of the cultural riches on their own doorsteps as any representatives of the 'Honourable Company' in their dealings with 'the natives' in India.

So no anthology of 'Scottish poetry' can be quite complete without recognising the parallel voice of Gaelic culture, just as it would be unthinkable to give an account of Scottish geography without mentioning the Highlands. And yet if there was a gulf between the two cultures, in terms of what Lowland Scots actually *knew* about Gaelic poetry, there have been, over the years, many fruitful points of contact, contrast and influence as well. Thus it was that the extended natural descriptions of James Thomson's 'Seasons' influenced Alasdair MacMhaighstir Alasdair's 'Song to Summer', while MacMhaighstir Alasdair and Duncan Bàn in their turn influenced Hugh MacDiarmid's conception of 'the Gaelic idea' which would give a Scottish provenance for long catalogue poems such as *In Memoriam James Joyce*. The works of Robert Burns and his Gaelic contemporary William Ross take on new perspectives when they appear side by side, and especially when their love poems are compared. The Lowland drawing-room taste for songs of melancholy exile and Jacobite regret in the early nineteenth century must be seen against the more ferocious edge of John MacCodrum's 'Song to the Fugitives' or Duncan Bàn's 'Song to the Foxes'. As a counterbalance to the overtly male bonding which has characterised so many expressions of Scottish culture, we need to recognise the honoured role that was available to women poets in traditional Gaelic society, and the extent to which the 'border ballads' in Lowland Scots evolved and were transmitted through female tradition bearers such as Anna Brown of Falkland (1747–1810) and in more recent years Jeannie Robertson (1908–75) and her daughter Lizzie Higgins. Then again, the tradition of radical protest in Davidson's 'Thirty Bob a Week' and in Ellen Johnston's poetry cannot be separated from the part played in the cause of land reform by Mary Macpherson's 'Incitement of the Gaels', or the spirit of Iain MacGhillEathain's 'The Poet in Canada', and these works in turn must be seen to link with the (com)passionate political convictions of modern writers such as MacDiarmid, Maclean, George Campbell Hay and Hamish Henderson.

By now it should be clear that the 'Scottish poetic tradition' is a much more complex, interactive, rich, many-stranded and fulfilling thing than any simple opposition between 'Highland' and 'Lowland'; 'fantasy' and 'realism'; 'English', 'Scots' or 'Gaelic' can sustain. Indeed, there's no reason why each of us should not plot our own preferred paths across the literary landscape, and the table of themes which follows the chronological table of contents is one way of encouraging readers to do just this.

But of course choices have already been made, and there are many poems and poets whose tracks do not appear in this book. Anthologies such as William Donaldson's *The Language of the People: Scots Prose from the Victorian Revival*, Tom Leonard's *Radical Renfrew*, James Allison's *Poetry of Northeast Scotland*, Tom Hubbard's *The New Makars* and Hilda Spear's *Sword and Pen: Poems of 1915 from Dundee and Tayside* have all shown different ways forward, I think, at a time when many people are uncomfortable with the notion of a single fixed canon of 'great works'. Such misgivings can certainly be overcome, or at least sidestepped, by compiling anthologies like the above books which offer invaluable accounts of 'culture' and literary production from several different perspectives.

Yet major poets remain, not least for their ability to offer different facets of their many-sided inspiration to new readers, so that each generation can find something fresh and of specific interest and lasting value in the work. A culture, after all, must sustain itself by 'remembering' the landscape of its own past, as well as by re-evaluating and 'forgetting' the old and too familiar paths. It is in this spirit that the present selection has been made.

These are not the only Scottish poets of note, nor is this the only face of Scottish poetry. But no educated person could claim to know Scottish poetry well without having made contact with at least most of the names enclosed within these pages. By the same token I have tried to give a big enough selection of each writer's work for the reader to come to know their 'voice' and to find out for themselves how they see the world. This includes extracts from longer poems, for a collection of only lyric verse cannot reflect the strength of a tradition in which poetry once had narrative, moral or chronicling functions, and in which social, philosophical and political issues can still find a place. A different sort of anthology – like Dunn and Heaney's *Rattle Bag*, perhaps, or John Buchan's *Northern Muse* – could offer a larger mix of single poems and poets, linked by themes, or just by the delights of sheer surprise. But the aim of this volume is to make the major figures and the major poems in our literary history more accessible to both the student and the general reader, with a substantial selection of selected writers from the modern (but not the immediately contemporary) period. The poets are arranged in chronological order by date of birth, and this method has its own unexpected insights and contrasts, but on occasion I have grouped a larger selection of single poems and poets under a generic heading, such as 'The Asloan, Bannatyne and Maitland Collections'; 'The Ballad Tradition'; 'Scots Songs' and 'Vernacular Scots Poetry'. I took a similar approach in *The Literature of Scotland* because I think it can reflect a proper variety without losing overall coherence. The preliminary biographies, marginal glosses and the textual notes are offered in the same spirit.

I am glad to acknowledge a very considerable debt to the editors, lexicographers and scholars who have gone before me, not least to the many publications of the Scottish Text Society and the Scottish Gaelic Text Society. In particular I must thank Professor Derick Thomson, first of all for his seminal *Introduction to Gaelic Poetry*, and next for the translations which he has allowed me to use in this edition. 'Translation' is a contentious process, and each generation will have different priorities in what it understands the translator's proper task to be. Furthermore, English idiom changes from one decade to the next, and what passes for 'poetic' language in 1910 will seem rather less convincing in 1990. So I have tried, whenever possible, to use modern translations of older Gaelic poetry, commissioning work, or using translations already made by contemporary scholars and poets. In this regard I owe a debt of gratitude to the scholarship of the late Ian Grimble and William Matheson, and the same debt with particularly warm personal thanks to Derick Thomson, Iain Crichton Smith and especially to William Neill. It is no coincidence that these last three translators are such fine poets in their own right.

For poetry in older Scots, I have chosen to change old forms of spelling as little as possible, though 3 and β have been replaced, and the commonly interchanged letters of u, v and w have been normalised. I have followed the texts of the best editions, but on one or two rare occasions I have favoured a variant reading. The marginal glosses may well offer different accounts of the same word on different pages, but this is perfectly appropriate, since of course a word's meaning will vary according to the context of the line. I have tried to keep notes to a minimum, but difficulties of reference or allusion are just as likely to occur in modern poems as in medieval verses, and my hope is that this anthology will help to make something of the wealth of our country's poetry accessible to readers furth of Scotland.

Finally, I must acknowledge a debt to the late Alexander Scott, well-known as a poet and as head of the Department of Scottish Literature during its early and most formative years at the University of Glasgow. In the first instance this book was Alec Scott's initiative, but he died before it got beyond the planning stage, and I was approached by the publisher then involved to see if I would take up the project. I was glad to do this, not least in memory of a man whom I was proud to know as a friend. The selection of poems, however, along with the glossary, the endnotes, the decision to include Gaelic poetry, and the choice of that poetry, all these were entirely my own, and I must take responsibility for that. Let Alec have the last word on how the local meets with the universal in all the best poetry, and on matters of forgetting, and also remembering.

> I' the water o Leith (as the Water o Lethe)
> I'd neither drink nor droun nor dee,
> But turn frae its wanhope awa til the warld
> And leave it alane to get tint i the sea.
>
> (Alexander Scott, 1920–89)

NOTE
1. Lowell's phrase was first cited in a Scottish context by the late Alexander Scott in his essay on 'Hugh MacDiarmid and the Scots Tradition'.

THE POETRY OF SCOTLAND

Numbers in the left-hand margin refer to line and stanza numbers. In most cases there is only one number, which indicates the line number. Where there are two numbers separated by a full stop, the first number is the stanza number; the second the line number.

John Barbour (1320?–1395)

John Barbour first appears in the records as archdeacon of Aberdeen in 1357. He studied in Oxford and Paris before gaining the post of clerk and auditor to the Exchequer of Robert II. In recognition of this, and of his epic poem about the present King's uncle's father, he was awarded a royal pension. Written around 1375, and dealing with historical events which took place only sixty years before, *The Bruce* is the earliest long poem to have survived in Scots. It combines many of the actual details of Bruce's life and campaigns with the romance values of chivalric combat and noble, if simplified, fortitude. Yet it also speaks for the common folk, and a new concept of patriotism and individual freedom in what was otherwise a narrowly dynastic and feudal age. This is the significance of the tale of the camp followers whose intervention was said to have helped turn the tide at Bannockburn.

from The Bruce
Book I: a Preface[1]

1 Storys to rede ar delitabill	delightful
Suppos that thai be nocht bot fabill,	
Than suld storys that suthfast wer	true
And thai war said on gud maner	providing that
Have doubill plesance in heryng.	
The fyrst plesance is the carpyng,	telling
And the tother the suthfastnes	
That schawys the thing rycht as it wes,	
And suth thyngis that ar likand	acceptable
Tyll mannys heryng ar plesand.	pleasing
Tharfor I wald fayne set my will	
Giff my wyt mycht suffice thartill	If
To put in wryt a suthfast story	
That it lest ay furth in memory	
Swa that na tyme of lenth it let	fade
Na gar it haly be foryet.	Nor cause; forgotten
For auld storys that men redys	
Representis to thaim the dedys	
Of stalwart folk that lyvyt ar	

---

1. The poem, almost 14,000 lines long, was divided into 20 books in Pinkerton's 1790 edition.

Rycht as thai than in presence war.
And certis thai suld weill have prys   *certainly; praise*
That in thar tyme war wycht and wys,   *brave*
And led thar lyff in gret travaill,   *hardship*
And oft in hard stour off bataill   *strife*
Wan gret price off chevalry   *glory for*
And war voydyt off cowardy,   *completely free*
As wes king Robert off Scotland
That hardy wes off hart and hand,   *bold*
And gud Schyr James off Douglas
That in his tyme sa worthy was
That off hys price and hys bounte   *praise; goodness*
In ser landis renownyt wes he.   *several*
Off thaim I thynk this buk to ma,   *make*
Now God gyff grace that I may swa
Tret it and bryng it till endyng
That I say nocht bot suthfast thing.

Quhen Alexander the king wes deid
That Scotland haid to steyr and leid,   *steer and lead*
The land sex yer and mayr perfay
Lay desolat aftyr hys day
Till that the barnage at the last   *baronage*
Assemblyt thaim and fayndyt fast   *attempted*
To cheys a king thar land to ster   *choose; steer (guide)*
That off auncestry cummyn wer
Off kingis that aucht that reawte   *possessed; royal blood*
46   And mayst had rycht thair king to be.

                    *   *   *

179 Quhen Schyr Edward the mychty king
     Had on this wys done his likyng
     Off Jhone the Balleoll, that swa sone
     Was all defautyt and undone,[1]
     To Scotland went he than in hy,   *haste*
     And all the land gan occupy   *did*
     Sa hale that bath castell and toune   *thoroughly*
     War in-till his possessioune
     Fra Weik anent Orknay   *Wick opposite*
     To Mullyr snuk in Gallaway,   *the Mull of Galloway*
     And stuffyt all with Inglis-men.
     Schyrreffys and bailyeys maid he then,
     And alkyn other officeris

1. Edward I overthrew John Balliol ('Toom Tabard') and stormed through Scotland from Castleton to Elgin and back in 1296, sacking towns, killing over 7,000 people and establishing English governors before returning to England with the Stone of Destiny.

That for to govern land afferis
He maid off Inglis nation,
That worthyt then sa rych fellone   *became; very cruel*
And sa wykkyt and covatous
And swa hawtane and dispitous   *haughty and fierce*
That Scottis-men mycht do na thing
That ever mycht pleys to thar liking.
Thar wyffis wald thai oft forly   *wives; rape*
And thar dochtrys dispitusly
And gyff ony of thaim thar-at war wrath   *angry*
Thai watyt hym wele with gret scaith,   *set upon them; harm*
For thai suld fynd sone enchesone   *soon find a reason*
To put hym to destruccione.
And gyff that ony man thaim by   *near them*
Had ony thing that wes worthy,
As hors or hund or other thing
That war plesand to thar liking,
With rycht or wrang it have wald thai,
And gyf ony wald thaim withsay
Thai suld swa do that thai suld tyne   *lose*
Othir land or lyff or leyff in pyne,   *either; live in torment*
For thai dempt thaim efter thar will,   *condemned*
Takand na kep to rycht na skill.   *heed; right or reason*
A! quhat thai dempt thaim felonly,   *how; cruelly*
For gud knychtis that war worthy
For litill enchesoune or than nane   *reason*
Thai hangyt be the nekbane.
Alas that folk that ever wes fre,
And in fredome wount for to be,
Throw thar gret myschance and foly   *Through; misfortune*
War tretyt than sa wykkytly
That thar fays thar jugis war,   *foes; judges*
Quhat wrechitnes may man have mar.

A! fredome is a noble thing,
Fredome mays man to haiff liking,   *makes; choice*
Fredome all solace to man giffis,
He levys at es that frely levys.   *ease*
A noble hart may haiff nane es
Na ellys nocht that may him ples
Gyff fredome failye, for fre liking   *fail; free choice*
Is yharnyt our all other thing.   *yearned for over*
Na he that ay has levyt fre   *Nor; always*
May nocht knaw weill the propyrte
The angyr na the wrechyt dome   *affliction; fate*
That is couplyt to foule thyrldome,   *thralldom*

	Bot gyff he had assayit it.	Unless; tried
	Than all perquer he suld it wyt,	by heart; know
	And suld think fredome mar to prys	more to praise
	Than all the gold in warld that is.	
	Thus contrar thingis ever-mar	
	Discoveryngis off the tother ar,	
	And he that thryll is has nocht his.	serf
	All that he has enbandounyt is	subjected
	Till hys lord quhat-ever he be.	
	Yheyt has he nocht sa mekill fre	nothing so very free
	As fre wyll to leyve or do	live
249	That at hys hart hym drawis to.	Whatever

Book VII: the King and the Gud-wif

233	The king went furth way and angri	
	Menand his man full tenderly	remembering
	And held his way all him allane,	
	And rycht towart the hous is gan	
	Quhar he set tryst to meit his mell.	promised to engage in battle
	It wes weill inwyth nycht be then,	
	He come sone in the hous and fand	
	The howswyff on the benk sittand	bench
	That askit him quhat he was	
	And quhen he come and quhar he gais.	whence
	'A travailland man dame,' said he,	
	'That travaillys her throu the contre.'	
	Scho said, 'All that travailland er	
	For saik of ane ar welcum her.'	one
	The king said, 'Gud dame quhat is he	
	That gerris yow haiff sik specialte	makes; preference
	To men that travaillis.' 'Schyr perfay,'	by my faith
	Quod the gud-wyff, 'I sall yow say,	Said
	The King Robert the Bruys is he,	
	That is rycht lord off this countre.	
	His fayis now haldis him in thrang,	foes; battle
	Bot I think to se or ocht lang	before very long
	Him lord and king our all the land	over
	That na fayis sall him withstand.'	
	'Dame luffis yow him sa weil,' said he.	
	'Yea schyr,' said scho, 'sa God me se.'	
	'Dame,' sayd he, 'hym her ye by,	
	For ik am he, I say ye soithly,	
	Yea certis dame.' 'And quhar ar gane	
	Your men quhen ye ar thus allane.'	
	'At this tyme dame ik haiff no ma.'	

Scho said, 'It may na wys be swa.										no way be so
Ik haiff twa sonnys wycht and hardy,										valiant; bold
Thai sall becum your men in hy.'										straight away
As scho divisyt thai haiff done,										said
His sworn men become thai sone.
The wyff syn gert him syt and ete,										then made him
Bot he has schort quhile at the mete
Syttyn quhen he hard gret stamping
About the hous, then but letting										without delay
Thai stert up the hous for to defende,
Bot sone eftre the king has kend										recognised
James off Douglas. Than wes he blyth										happy
And bad oppyn the the durris swyth										quickly
And thai come in all that thar war.
Schyr Edward the Bruce wes thar,
And James alsua off Douglas
That wes eschapyt fra the chace										pursuit
And with the kingis brother met,
Syn to the tryst that thaim wes set										Then; rendezvous
Thai sped thaim with thar cumpany
That wer ane hunder and weile fyfty.
And quhen that thai haiff sene the king
Thai war joyfull of thar meting
And askyt how that he eschapyt was,
And he thaim tauld all hale the cas.
How the fyve men him pressyt fast,
And how he throw the water past,
And how he met the thevis thre										three robbers
And how he slepand slane suld be
Quhen he waknyt throw Goddis grace,
And how his foster brodyr was
Slayne he tauld thaim all haly.
Than lowyt thai God commounly									got on their knees to
That thar lord wes eschapyt swa,
Than spak thai wordis to and fra
Till at the last the king gan say,
'Fortoun us travaillyt fast today									(for) us worked true
That scalyt us sa sodanly.										scattered
Our fayis to-nycht sall ly traistly									sleep trustingly
For thai trow we so scalit ar										believe
And fled to-waverand her and thar									all trembling
That we sall nocht thir dayis thre										these
All to-giddir assemblit be.
Tharfor this nycht thai sall trastly
But wachys tak thar ese and ly.'										Without guards

Book XII: the second day at Bannockburn

409   The Scottis-men quhen it wes day
    Thar Mess devotly gert thai say   Mass devoutly did
    Syne tuk a sop and maid thaim yar,   sup; ready
    And quhen thai all assemblyt war
    And in thar bataillis all purvayit   battalions; equipped
    With thar braid baneris all displayit
    Thai maid knychtis, as it afferis   behoves
    To men that usys thai mysteris.   arts
    The king maid Walter Stewart knycht
    And James of Douglas that wes wycht,   brave
    And other als of gret bounte   also; goodness
    He maid ilkane in thar degre.   each one
    Quhen this wes done that I yow say
    Thai went all furth in gud aray
    And tuk the plane full apertly,   openly
    Mony gud man wicht and hardy
    That war fulfillyt of gret bounte   full of
    In-till thai routis men mycht se.   companies
    The Inglismen on other party
    That as angelis schane brychtly
    War nocht arayit on sic maner   drawn up; such
    For all thar bataillis samyn wer   together
    In a schilthrum, bot quheyer it was close squadron of spearmen; whether
    Throw the gret stratnes of the place   narrowness
    That thai war in to bid fechting   remain
    Or that it was for abaysing   dismay
    I wate nocht, bot in a schiltrum   know
    It semyt thai war all and sum,
    Outane the avaward anerly   Except for the vanguard only
    That rycht with a gret cumpany
    Be thaim-selvyn arayit war.
    Quha had bene by mycht have sene thar   Anyone nearby
    That folk ourtak a mekill feild   take over; big
    On breid quhar mony a schynand scheld Spread out
    And mony a burnyst brycht armur
    And mony man off gret valur
    And mony a brycht baner and schene   fair
    Mycht in that gret schiltrum be sene.
    And quhen the king of Ingland
    Saw the Scottis swa tak on hand
    Takand the hard feyld sa opynly
    And apon fute he had ferly   wonder
    And said, 'Quhat will yone Scottis fycht.'
    Yea sekyrly schir,' said a knycht,   certainly
    Schyr Ingrame the Umfravill hat he, was called

And said, 'Forsuth now schyr I se
It is the mast ferlyfull sycht   wondrous
That evyre I saw quhen for to fycht
The Scottismen has tane on hand
Agayne the mycht of Ingland
In plane hard feild to giff bataile.
Bot and ye will trow my consaill   But if only you will believe
Ye sall discomfy thaim lychtly.   defeat; quickly
Withdrawys yow hyne sodandly   hence
With bataillis and with penownys   battalions and standards
Quhill that we pas our pailyownys,   Until; tents
And ye sall se alsone that thai
Magre thar lordys sall brek aray   Despite
And scaile thaim our harnays to ta.   break ranks; armour; take
And quhen we se thaim scalit swa
Prik we than on thaim hardely   Ride
And we sall haf thaim wele lychtly,
For than sall nane be knyt to fycht   closely arrayed to fight
That may withstand your mekill mycht.'
'I will nocht,' said the king, 'perfay
Do sa, for thar sall na man say
That I sall eschew the bataill   avoid
Na withdraw me for sic rangaile.'   rabble
Quhen this wes said that er said I
The Scottis-men comounaly
Knelyt all doune to God to pray
And a schort prayer thar maid thai
To God to help thaim in that fycht,
And quhen the Inglis king had sycht
Off thaim kneland he said in hy,   haste
'Yone folk knelis to ask mercy.'
Schyr Ingrahame said, 'Ye say suth now,   speak the truth
Thai ask mercy bot nane at yow,
For thar trespas to God thai cry.
I tell yow a thing sekyrly,   one thing; certainly
That yone men will all wyn or de,   die
For doute of dede thai sall nocht fle.'   fear of death
'Now be it sa,' than said the king,
And than but langer delaying   without
Thai gert trump till the assemble.   did trumpet
On ather sid men mycht than se   either
Mony a wycht man and worthi   brave
Redy to do chevalry.
Thus war thai boune on ather sid,   ready
And Inglis-men with mekill prid
That war in-till thar avaward   vanguard

To the bataill that schyr Edward
Governyt and led held straucht thar way.
The hors with spuris hardnyt thai   urged on
And prikyt apon thaim sturdely,   spurred
And thai met thaim rycht hardely   courageously
Swa that at thar assemble thar
Sic a fruschyng of speris war   clattering
507   That fer away men mycht it her.   hear

Book XIII: the camp followers tip the balance

203   Than mycht men ther enseyneis cry   war-cries shout
And Scottis-men cry hardely,   boldly
'On thaim! On thaim! On thaim, thai faile!'
With that sa hard thai gan assaile
And slew all that thai mycht ourta,   overtake
And the Scottis archeris alswa
Schot amang thaim sa deliverly   nimbly
Engrevand thaim sa gretumly   Angering; greatly
That quhat for thaim that with thaim faucht   That what with those …
That swa gret rowtis to thaim raucht   blows; struck
And pressyt thaim full egrely,   eagerly
And quhat for arowis that felly   fiercely
Mony gret woundis gan thaim ma   did them make
And slew fast off thar hors alswa,   quickly slew their horses too
That thai wandyst a litill wei.   retreated; way
Thai dred sa gretly then to dey   feared
That thar covyn wes wer and wer,   company (fared) worse and worse
For thaim that fechtand with thaim wer
Set hardyment and strenth and will   boldness
And hart and corage als thar-till
And all thar mayne and all thar mycht
To put thaim fully to flycht.

In this tyme that I tell off her
At that bataill on this maner   That that
Wes strykyn quhar on ather party   was engaged; either side
Thai war fechtand enforcely;   mightily
Women and swanys and poveraill   attendants; poor-folk
That in the park to yeme vittaill   field; attend to food
War left, quhen thai wist but lesing   realised without doubt (lying)
That thar lordis with fell fechting   cruel
On thar fayis assemblyt wer,   had joined battle
Ane off thaim-selvyn that war thar
Capitane of thaim all thai maid,   leader of them all
And schetis that war sumdele brad   sheets; somewhat broad
Thai festnyt in steid off baneris

Apon lang treys and speris,   *poles*
And said that thai wald se the fycht
And help thar lordis at thar mycht.
Quhen her-till all assentyt wer   *agreed*
In a rout thai assemblit er   *troop*
Fyften thousand thai war or ma,
And than in gret hy gan thai ga   *haste did they go*
With thar baneris all in a rout
As thai had men bene styth and stout.   *As if; strong*
Thai come with all that assemble   *assembly*
Rycht quhill thai mycht the bataill se,
Than all at anys thai gave a cry,   *once*
'Slay! Slay! Apon thaim hastily,'
And thar-with-all cumand war thai.
Bot thai war yete wele fer away.
And Inglis-men that ruschyt war   *were harried*
Throuch fors of fycht as I said ar   *fierceness of the fight; before*
Quhen thai saw cummand with sic a cry
Towart thaim sic a cumpany
That thaim thocht wele als mony war
As that wes fechtand with thaim thar,
And thai befor had nocht thaim sene,
Than wit ye weill with-outyn wene   *you may well understand; doubt*
Thai war abaysit sa gretumly   *dismayed; greatly*
That the best and the mast hardy   *bold*
That war in-till thar ost that day   *host*
Wald with thar mensk haf bene away.   *honour*

The King Robert be thar relyng   *reeling*
Saw thai war ner at discomfiting   *discouragement*
And his ensenye gan hely cry,   *battle-cry; proudly*
Than with thaim off his cumpany
Hys fayis he pressyt sa fast that thai   *foes*
War in-till sa gret effray   *fear*
That thai left place ay mar and mar,   *lost ground still more and more*
For all the Scottis-men that thar war
Quhen thai saw thaim eschew the fycht   *avoid*
Dang on thaim with all thar mycht   *smote*
That thai scalyt thaim in troplys ser   *scattered; several small groups*
And till discomfitur war ner.   *defeat; were near*
And sum off thaim fled all planly,
Bot thai that wycht war and hardy   *brave; bold*
That schame lettyt to ta the flycht   *forbade; take*
At gret myscheiff mantenyt the fycht   *To great destruction*
And stythly in the stour gan stand.   *strongly; battle*
And quhen the King of Ingland

Saw his men fley in syndry place,
And saw his fayis rout that was   the troop of his foes
Worthyn sa wycht and sa hardy   Doing so valiantly
That all his folk war halyly   wholly
Sa stonayit that thai had na mycht   So confounded
To stynt thar fayis in the fycht,   stop
He was abaysyt sa gretumly
That he and his cumpany
Fyve hunder armyt all at rycht
In-till a frusch all tok the flycht   dash
293   And to the castell held thar way.

King James I (1394–1437)

The boy James Stewart was abducted at sea by the English in 1406 and spent the next eighteen years under guard in the Tower and other fortified places in the South. *The Kingis Quair* (the king's book) comes to us as a manuscript from the 1490s, ascribed to James and scarcely known until its publication in 1783. Certainly the circumstances of the poem could fit the experience of the King during his long exile, as the poet reflects on the cruelty of fortune, on his isolation and captivity, and on the sweeter (but no less painful) captivity of love. A dream vision on courtly love after the style of Chaucer, and a meditation on free will after Boethius, the poem still sustains a fresh and personal voice as the earliest expression of lyrical feeling in Scots. If James did write it, there was nothing melancholic or gentle about the way he set about pacifying the Scots lords and the Gaelic chieftains when he regained his throne in 1424.

from The Kingis Quair

176
Quhare as in ward full oft I wold bewaille	
My dedely lyf, full of peyne and penance,	
Saing ryght thus, quhat have I gilt to faille	done wrong; lose
My fredome in this warld and my plesance?	happiness
Sen every wight has thereof suffisance,	
That I behold, and I a creature	
Put from all this – hard is myn aventure!	experience
The bird, the beste, the fisch eke in the see,	also
They lyve in fredome everich in his kynd;	according to his nature
And I a man, and lakkith libertee;	
Quhat schall I seyne, quhat resoun may I fynd,	
That fortune suld do so? Thus in my mynd	
My folk I wold argewe, bot all for noght;	debate with
Was non that myght, that on my peynes rought.	paid attention (to)
Than wold I say, 'Gif God me had devisit	devised
To lyve my lyf in thraldome thus and pyne,	
Quhat was the caus that he me more comprisit	constrained
Than othir folk to lyve in swich ruyne?	ruin
I suffer allone amang the figuris nyne,	(nine muses/nine numbers?)

13

Ane wofull wrecche that to no wight may spede,   be of service
And yit of every lyvis help hath nede.'   creature's

The long dayes and the nyghtis eke   also
   I wold bewaille my fortune in this wis,
For quhich, agane distress confort to seke,   against
    My custum was on mornis for to rys
    Airly as day; o happy exercis!
By the come I to joye out of turment.   thee (i.e., exercise)
Bot now to purpos of my first entent: intention

Bewailing in my chamber thus allone,
   Despeired of all joye and remedye,
Fortirit of my thoght and wo begone,   tired out
    And to the wyndow gan I walk in hye,   did I; haste
    To se the warld and folk that went forby;   past
As for the tyme, though I of mirthis fude   For the moment
Myght have no more, to luke it did me gude.

Now was there maid fast by the touris wall
   A gardyn fair, and in the corneris set
Ane herber grene with wandis long and small   lawn; palings
    Railit about; and so with treis set
    Was all the place, and hawthorn hegis knet,   hedges joined
That lyf was non walking there forby,   no being walking past
That myght within scars ony wight aspye.   scarcely

So thik the bewis and the leves grene   boughs
   Beschadit all the aleyes that there were,
And myddis every herber myght be sene
    The scharp grene swete jenepere,   juniper
    Growing so fair with branchis here and there,
That, as it semyt to a lyf without,   any being
The bewis spred the herber all about.

And on the small grene twistis sat   twigs
   The lytill swete nyghtingale, and song
So loud and clere the ympnis consecrat   hymns
    Off lufis use, now soft, now lowd among,
    That all the gardyng and the wallis rong
Ryght of thair song, and on the copill next   stanza (couplet)
Off thair swete armony, and lo the text:

Cantus
'Worschippe, ye that loveris bene, this May,   who are lovers
   For of your bliss the kalendis ar begonne,   first days

And sing with us, away, winter, away!
   Cum, somer, cum, the swete sesoun and sonne!
   Awake for schame that have your hevynnis wonne,   *attained*
And amorously lift up your hedis all,
Thank lufe that list you to his merci call.'   *who was pleased*

Quhen thai this song had song a lytill thrawe,   *time*
   Thai stent a quhile, and therewith unaffraid,   *ceased*
As I beheld and kest myn eyne alawe,   *eyes below*
   From beugh to beugh thay hippit and thai plaid,   *hopped*
   And freschly in thair birdis kynd arraid   *manner arranged*
Thair fetheris new, and fret thame in the sonne,   *preened*
And thankit lufe, that had thair makis wonne.   *mates*

This was the plane ditee of thair note,   *ditty*
   And therewithall unto myself I thoght,
'Quhat lyf is this, that makis birdis dote?
   Quhat may this be, how cummyth it of ought?   *from anything*
   Quhat nedith it to be so dere ybought?   *so dearly*
It is nothing, trowe I, bot feynit here,   *I believe; pretence*
And that men list to counterfeten chere.'   *it pleases people to feign cheerfulness*

Eft wald I think; 'O Lord, quhat may this be?   *Afterwards*
   That lufe is of so noble myght and kynde,   *nature*
Lufing his folk, and swich prosperitee
   Is it of him, as we in bukis fynd?   *from*
   May he oure hertes setten and unbynd?   *fix and loosen*
Hath he upon oure hertis swich maistrye?   *control*
Or all this is bot feynyt fantasye!   *false imagining*

For gif he be of so grete excellence,
   That he of every wight hath cure and charge,
Quhat have I gilt to him or doon offens,   *done wrong*
   That I am thrall, and birdis gone at large,   *prisoner; go free*
   Sen him to serve he myght set my corage?   *since to serve him; heart*
And gif he be noght so, than may I seyne,   *say*
Quhat makis folk to jangill of him in veyne?   *babble*

Can I noght elles fynd, bot gif that he   *I can conclude nothing else but*
   Be Lord, and as a God may lyve and regne,
To bynd and lous, and maken thrallis free,
   Than wold I pray his blisfull grace benigne,
   To hable me unto his service digne;   *make (me) fit; worthy*
And evermore for to be one of tho   *those*
Him trewly for to serve in wele and wo.'   *good fortune*

And therwith kest I doun myn eye ageyne,
    Quhare as I sawe, walking under the tour,   *tower*
Full secretly new cummyn hir to pleyne,   *arrived; play*
    The fairest or the freschest yong floure
    That ever I sawe, me thoght, before that houre,
For quhich sodayn abate, anon astert,   *suddenly stopped and at once started*
The blude of all my body to my hert.

And though I stude abaisit tho a lyte   *abashed*
    No wonder was, forquhy my wittis all
Were so ouercom with plesance and delyte,
    Onely throu latting of myn eyen fall,
    That sudaynly my hert become hir thrall
For ever of free wyll; for of manace   *threat*
There was no takyn in hir swete face.   *sign*

And in my hede I drewe ryght hastily,   *drew in my head*
    And eftsones I lent it forth ageyne,   *very soon; leaned*
And sawe hir walk, that verray womanly,   *(creature)*
    With no wight mo bot onely women tweyne.   *person; two*
    Than gan I studye in myself and seyne,   *did*
'A, swete, ar ye a warldly creature,
Or hevinly thing in likeness of nature?

Or ar ye god Cupidis owin princesse,
    And cummyn ar to lous me out of band?   *bonds*
Or ar ye verray Nature the goddess,
    That have depaynted with your hevinly hand
    This gardyn full of flouris, as they stand?
Quhat sall I think, allace! Quhat reverence
Sall I minster to your excellence?

Gif ye a goddess be, and that ye like
    To do me payne, I may it noght astert;   *avoid*
Gif ye be warldly wight, that dooth me sike,   *makes me sigh*
    Quhy lest God mak you so, my derrest hert,
    To do a sely prisoner thus smert,   *poor; pain*
That lufis yow all, and wote of noght bot wo?   *entirely; knows nothing but*
44.308 And therfore, merci, swete, sen it is so.

          *   *   *

187.1302 To rekyn of every thing the circumstance,
    As hapnit me quhen lessen gan my sore   *grief*
Of my rancoure and wofull chance,
    It war to long, I lat it be tharefor.
    And thus this flour, I can seye no more,   *(lady)*

So hertly has unto my help attendit,   *heartily*
That from the deth hir man sche has defendit.

And eke the goddis mercifull wirking,   *also; working*
    For my long pane and trewe service in lufe,
That has me gevin halely myn asking,   *wholly*
    Quhich has my hert for evir sett abufe
    In perfyte joy, that nevir may remufe
Bot onely deth: of quhom, in laud and pris,   *celebration and praise*
With thankfull hert I say richt in this wis: –

'Blissit mot be the goddis all,   *(May the gods be ...)*
    So fair that glateren in the firmament!   *glitter*
And blissit be thare myght celestiall,
    That have convoyit hale, with one assent,   *guided whole*
    My lufe, and to so glade a consequent!
And thankit be fortunys exiltree   *axletree*
And quhile, that thus so wele has quhirlit me.   *wheel; whirled*

Thankit mot be, and fair and lufe befall   *fair (fortune)*
    The nychtingale, that, with so gud entent,
Sang thare of lufe the notis swete and small,
    Quhair my fair hertis lady was present,
    Hir with to glad, or that sche forthir went!   *To gladden her; before; further*
And thou gerafloure mot ithankit be   *gillyflower*
All othir flouris for the lufe of the!

And thankit be the fair castell wall,
    Quhare as I quhilom lukit furth and lent.   *formerly; leaned*
Thankit mot be the sanctis Marciall,   *Saints of March*
    That me first causit hath this accident.
    Thankit mot be the grene bewis bent,   ,   *boughs*
Throu quhom, and under, first fortunyt me   *chanced*
My hertis hele and my confort to be.   *health*

For to the presence swete and delitable,   *delightful*
    Rycht of this floure that full is of plesance,
By process and by menys favorable,   *In due course; means*
    First of the blisfull goddis purveyance,   *providence*
    And syne throu long and trew contynuance   *then*
Of veray faith in lufe and trew service,
I cum am, and forthir in this wis.   *further; way*

Unworthy, lo, bot onely of hir grace,   *except only*
    In lufis yok, that esy is and sure,   *yoke*
In guerdoun of all my lufis space   *reward*

Sche hath me tak, hir humble creature.
And thus befell my blisfull aventure
In youth of lufe, that now, from day to day,
Flourith ay newe, and yit forthir, I say.

Go litill tretis, nakit of eloquence,
   Causing simples and povertee to wit;   simplicity; understand
And pray the reder to have pacience
   Of thy defaute, and to supporten it,   failings
   Of his gudnes thy brukilnes to knytt,   weakness; strengthen
And his tong for to reule and to stere,   rule; guide
That thy defautis helit may ben here.   defects; healed

Allace! And gif thou cumyst in the presence,
   Quhareas of blame faynest thou wald be quite,   most gladly; acquitted
To here thy rude and crukit eloquens,
   Quho sal be thare to pray for thy remyt?   forgiveness
   No wicht, bot giff hir merci will admytt   except
The for gud will, that is thy gyd and stere,   helmsman
To quham for me thou pitously requere.   pray

And thus endith the fotall influence   fatal
   Causit from hevyn, quhare powar is commytt
Of govirnance, by the magnificence
   Of him that hiest in the hevin sitt;
   To quham we think that all oure hath writt,   (destiny)
Quho coutht it red, agone syne mony a yere,   could; read; long ago
'Hich in the hevynnis figure circulere.'   circular heavens' shape

Unto impis of my maisteris dere,   descendants
   Gowere and Chaucere, that on the steppis satt
Of rethorike, quhill thai were lyvand here,
   Superlative as poetis laureate
   In moralitee and eloquence ornate,
I recommend my buk in lynis sevin,
197.1379 And eke thair saulis unto the bliss of hevin. Amen.

Quod Jacobus Primus, Scotorum rex illustrissimus.

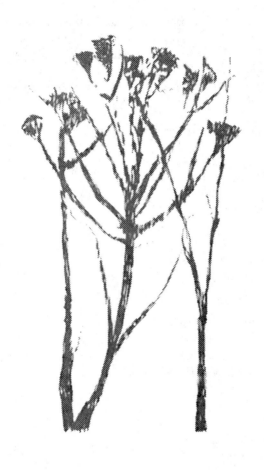

Giolla Críost Brúilingeach (c.1450)

This poem comes from a manuscript of early Gaelic literature started by the Dean of Lismore in 1512 from oral sources in Argyll and Perthshire. The collection – it wasn't published until 1862 – demonstrates how many contacts there were between Irish and Scottish Gaeldom in early times, not least in the exchange of poems and poets. One of the bard's main roles in heroic society was to praise his chief or his host, just

Auctor Huius Giolla Críost Brúilingeach

33 Cruithneacht dearg ar maghaibh míne
fá Thomaltach chosnas Chéis;
bídh ar clár collbhán uí Cholla
lomlán a droma ar gach déis.

Lacht milis ag buaibh i mbuailtibh,
branar fa féaraighe fonn;
fá h-árainn mhín is fá monadh
tír álainn fá toradh trom.

Míolchoin gharga ar iallaibh órdha
ag Tomaltach 's ceann ar cách;
sguir go moch san aonach uallach
44 mán loch bhraonach bhuadhach bhláth.

*   *   *

49 An chúirt as aoibhne ar druim domhain
dún Mheic Dhiarmada as geal gné
i gcaisteal fionn na gcloch mbuadha
ós cionn Locha cuanna Cé.

Cuirn is cuaich is copáin chumhdaigh
i gcúirt líonmhoir Locha Cé;
ibhthear fíon san chonnphort chnuasaigh:
is longphort ríogh uasail é.

Iomdha a theaghlach álainn uasal,
a éideadh 's a eachradh ard;

as the chief's obligation was to be generous with his gifts in return. Giolla Críost Brúilingeach belonged to a family of harpers who served MacDonald of the Isles. These lines are from a long poem addressed to Tomaltach MacDiarmada, the Lord of Moylurg in Connacht, who died in 1458.

The Author of this is Giolla Críost Brúilingeach
(The Poet asks an Irish Patron for a Harp)

Red wheat grows on smooth plains
under the rule of Tomaltach, lord of Céis;
on the white-hazelled domain of Coll's descendant
each ear of corn carries its full burden.

Cows yield sweet milk in milking folds;
he has fallow land most rich in grass;
both in its smooth demesne and its hilly land
it is lovely country bearing a heavy crop.

Tomaltach, lord of all,
has fierce deerhounds on golden leashes;
in early morning there are studs of horses in the proud assembly
round the most warm lough of virtue.

               *   *   *

The most joyous court on the ridge of the world
is Mac Diarmada's fort, with its bright aspect:
the white castle with its precious stones
above the tranquil lough of Cé.

Horns and goblets and fair-wrought cups
are there in the thronging court of Lough Cé;
wine is quaffed in that capital of garnered plenty:
it is the palace of a noble king.

Numerous are the members of his household, comely and noble,
numerous his vestures and tall steeds;

iomdha sleagh is lann is lúireach,
60   agus fear mall glúineach garg.

                    *   *   *

77   Tánaig mise, maith an t-adhbhar,
       dot fhios a hAlbain, ó's cóir,
       mád teist, a Chonnachtaigh chaisghil,
       a Thomaltaigh mhaisigh mhóir.

       Tánag d'iarraidh athchuinge oraibh,
       a hAlbain, a fholt mar ór,
       ar an chuan ghagánach ghailbheach
       uar bhradánach mhaighreach mhór.

       Cláirseach ar leath dom dhán damhsa
       tabhair mar iarraim, a rí;
       ghnúis mar bhláth na h-abhla abaigh,
       ó's ní tharla agaibh í.

       A mheic Chonchobhair chuain Chairrge,
       cubhaidh riotsa díol na ndámh;
       tá cuid do sgéimhe dá sgríobhadh;
       Éire dhuid ar líonadh lámh.

       Inghean Bháiteir a Búrc Breaghdha,
       bean nósmhor neamhghann má ní;
       folt cladhach cúlghlan na gcéibheann:
       rogha úrbhan Éireann í.

       Deárna álainn fhada fháinneach
       ag Caitilín na mbas mbán;
       dearg a h-imle solta saora,
[end] 's ingne corcra laomdha a lámh.

spears and blades and mailcoats,
and sedate, large-kneed, stern men.

*   *   *

I have come – good is my reason –
from Scotland to visit you, as is meet,
drawn by your fame, O white-footed son of Connacht,
O great handsome Tomaltach.

I have come to make a request of you,
from Scotland, O golden-haired one,
over the stormy sea with its clustering wave-tops,
chill and huge, the home of grilse and salmon.

A harp in special, in return for my poem,
grant me at my request, O king,
O countenance like the ripe fruit of the apple-tree,
for this is something that you happen to have.

O Son of Conchobhar of the Rock's haven,
to pay poet-bands befits you well;
the account of your handsomeness is being chronicled;
may Ireland be yours for your filling of hands.

The daughter of Walter de Burgh of Brega
is a famous lady who does not stint store;
her hair is deep-trenched, bright-locked, in tresses:
she is the choice one among Ireland's fair ladies.

Caitilín of the white palms
has a long lovely hand decked with rings;
red her lips, luscious and noble,
gleaming the rosy nails of her hands.

trans. Derick Thomson

Sir Richard Holland (14??–1482?)

The earliest long poem in what has become known as the revival of alliterative verse in the North, *The Buke of the Howlat* was dedicated to Elizabeth Dunbar, wife to Archibald Douglas, the Earl of Moray, for whom Holland worked as private secretary. Most likely written around 1450, this beast fable about the perils of pride (personified by an Owl, the Howlat himself, who wants grander feathers), also sings the praises of the Douglas family, and tells the story of Sir James and his last journey to the Holy Land with Robert the Bruce's heart. Holland may have been born in Orkney, serving as a churchman in Moray for a while, before the failure of the Douglas fortunes led him into exile in England where he died. The following passage describes a courtly banquet, the arrival of a Gaelic bard and some of the wilder entertainments that took place.

from The Buke of the Howlat

5C.755

All thus our lady thai lovit, with lyking and lyst,	delight
Menstralis and musicianis, mo than I mene may.	express
The psaltery, the sytholis, the soft sytharist,	medieval stringed instruments[1]
The croude, and the monycordis, the gittyrnis gay;	clavichord;
The rote, and the recordour, the rivupe, the rist,	harp; rebeck; plectrum(?)
The trumpe, and the talburn, the tympane but tray;	tabor; celtic harp without discord
The lilt pype, and the lute, the fydill in fist,	
The dulset, the dulsacordis, the schalme of assay;	flute; dulcimer; shawm
The amyable organis usit full oft;	
Claryonis lowde knellis,	trumpets'
Portativis, and bellis,	Portable organs
Cymbaclanis in the cellis,	Harpsichords in (their) cases
That soundis so soft.	
Quhen thai had songyn and said, softly a schour,	(of notes)
And playit, as of paradyss it a poynt war,	spot
In com japand the Ja, as a juglour,	Jay
With castis and with cawtelis, a quaynt caryar.	tricks; devices; sharper
He gart thaim se, as it semyt, in the samyn hour,	
Hunting at herdis in holtis so hair;	(of deer) in hoary woods

1. This anthology of plucked, bowed and blown instruments is typical of the period's literary delight in elaborate catalogues. The croude was a Celtic fiddle with six strings, hence the bardic 'blind crowder' of folklore.

Sound saland on the se schippis of towr;	castellated ships
Bernes batalland on burde, brym as a bair;	Warriors; on board; fierce; boar
He couth cary the cowpe of the kingis dess,	cup from; high table
Syne leve in the sted	in (its) place
Bot a blak bunwed;	ragwort
He couth of a hennis hed	
Make a mane mess.	main dish
He gart the Empriour trowe, and trewly behald,	made; believe; behold
That the Corn Crake, the pundar at hand,	pound-keeper
Had pyndit all his pryss horss in a pundfald,	impounded; corral
For causs thai ete of the corne in the kirkland.	
He couth werk wounderis quhat way that he wald:	
Mak of a gray guss a gold garland;	
A lang sper of a betill for a berne bald;	from a mallet; bold warrior
Nobillis of nut schellis, and silver of sand.	gold coins
Thus jowkit with juperdyss the jangland Ja:	tricks; jesting
Fair ladyis in ryngis,	
Knychtis in caralyngis,[1]	
Boith dansis and syngis;	
It semyt as sa.	
Sa come the Ruke with a rerd and a rane roch,	Rook; shout; rough rant
A bard owt of Irland with 'Banachadee!'	'God bless you!'
Said: 'Gluntow guk dynyd dach hala mischy doch;[2]	
Raike hir a rug of the rost, or scho sall ryme the.	Reach (me); chunk; roast; flyte you
Mich macmory ach mach mometir moch loch;	
Set hir doune, gif hir drink; quhat Dele alis the?'	Devil ails
O Deremyne, O Donnall, O Dochardy droch;	droch: evil?
Thir ar his Irland kingis of the Irischerye:	
O Knewlyn, O Conochor, O Gregre Makgrane;	(chiefs or learned families)
The schenachy, the clarschach,	Gaelic genealogist-bard; Scottish harp
The ben schene, the ballach,	playing woman(?); servant
The crekery, the corach,	reciter(?); lamentation(?)
Scho kennis thaim ilkane.	knows; each one
Mony lesingis he maid; wald let for no man	lies; stop
To speik quhill he spokin had, sparit no thingis.	until
The dene rurale, the Ravyn, reprovit him than,	
Bad him his lesingis leif befor thai lordingis.	
The barde worth brane wod, and bitterly couth ban;	became mad; did curse
'How, Corby messinger,' quoth he, 'with sorowe now syngis!	

1. Carols were danced as well as sung.
2. The Rook's outpouring reveals Lowland prejudices about Gaelic – and Irish – speakers. Scholars have proposed that what looks like two lines of phonetic Gaelic gibberish can be decoded, roughly as follows: 'Do you hear? ... when I quaff a drink'; and 'I am MacMuireadhaigh, son of people, son of loch'. Because of the conventions of Gaelic address, Highlanders in Lowland literature are frequently made to refer to themselves as 'she'.

Thow ischit out of Noyes ark, and to the erd wan,   *issued; earth arrived*
Taryit as a tratour, and brocht na tythingis.   *Tarried; news*
I sall ryive the, Ravyne, baith guttis and gall.'   *split*
    The dene rurale worthit reid,   *became red*
    Stawe for schame of the steid;   *Stole away (from); hall*
    The barde held a grete pleid   *palaver*
        In the hie hall.

In come twa flyrand fulis with a fonde fair,   *grinning; foolish demeanour*
The Tuchet and the gukkit Golk, and geid hiddy giddy;   *Lapwing; stupid Cuckoo*
Ruschit baith to the bard, and ruggit his hair;   *tugged*
Callit him thryss 'Thevisnek!', to thrawe in a widdy.   *Thief's neck; twist; noose*
Thai fylit him fra the fortope to the fut thar.   *dirtied; head to foot*
The barde, smaddit lyke a smaik smorit in a smedy,   *stained; sneak smothered; smithy*
Ran fast to the dure, and gaif a gret rair;
Socht wattir to wesche him thar out in ane ydy.   *eddy*
The lordis leuch apon loft, and lyking thai had   *aloud*
    That the barde was so bet.
    The fulis fonde in the flet,   *capered; hall*
    And mony mowis at mete   *grimaces (during the) meal*
        On the flure maid.

Syne for ane figonale of frut thai straif in the steid;   *basket; struggled; place*
The Tuchet gird to the Golk, and gaif him a fall,   *attacked*
Raif his taile fra his rig, with a rath pleid;   *Tore; back; quick cry*
The Golk gat upe agane in the gret hall,
Tit the Tuchet be the tope, ourtirvit his hed,   *Pulled; crest; turned over*
Flang him flat in the fyre, fetheris and all.
He cryid: 'Allace,' with ane rair, 'revyn is my reid!   *split; gizzard*
I am ungraciously gorrit, baith guttis and gall!'
Yit he lap fra the lowe richt in a lyne.   *leapt; blaze*
    Quhen thai had remelis raucht,   *blows dealt*
    Thai forthocht that thai faucht,   *regretted*
    Kissit samyn and saucht;   *together; made peace*
        And sat doune syne.

All thus thir hathillis in hall heirly remanit,   *nobles; grandly*
With all welthis at wiss, and worschipe to wale.   *at command; honour to choose*
The Pape[1] begynnis the grace, as greably ganit,   *rightly proper*
Wosche with thir worthyis, and went to counsall.   *Washed; these*
The pure Howlatis appele completly was planyt,   *explained*
His falt and his foule forme, unfrely but faile.   *defect; ugly without doubt*
For the quhilk thir lordis in leid, nocht to layne it,   *of the people; deny it*
He besocht of sucour, as soverane in saile,   *rulers in the hall*

1. The Pope, in this parliament of fowls, is a Peacock.

That thai wald pray Natur his prent to renewe;   image; improve
     For it was haile his behest,   entirely
     At thar alleris request,   That everyone's
     Mycht dame Natur arrest   detain (persuade)
56.858   Of him for to rewe.   take pity

Anonymous (1480?)
The Taill of Rauf Coilyear

We do not know the name of the author of 'Rauf Coilyear'. The poem has the same 13-line alliterative stanza as *The Buke of the Howlat*, but it uses a more robustly colloquial narrative voice to tell of a common man's encounter with a king in disguise. This theme goes back to romance roots in both England and Europe, but in the Scottish version Rauf is particularly prickly about his rights. The second part of the poem takes him to Court where he discovers the identity of his guest and eventually becomes a knight himself.

Heir Beginnis the Taill of Rauf Coilyear How He Harbreit King Charlis[1]

In the cheif tyme of Charlis, that chosin chiftane,	great days
Thair fell ane ferlyfull flan within thay fellis wyde,	awesome storm; hills
Quhair Empreouris and Erlis, and uther mony ane,	
Turnit fra Sanct Thomas[2] befoir the yule tyde.	returned
Thay past unto Paris, thay proudest in pane,	dress
With mony Prelatis and Princis, that was of mekle pryde;	
All thay went with the King to his worthy wane;	dwelling
Ouir the feildis sa fair thay fure be his syde;	fared
All the worthiest went in the morning,	
Baith Dukis, and Duchepeiris,	
Barrounis, and Bacheleiris,	
Mony stout man steiris	makes his way
Of town with the King.	From

And as that Ryall raid ouir the rude mure,	
Him betyde ane tempest that tyme, hard I tell;	He met with
The wind blew out of the Eist stiflie and sture,	fierce
The drift durandlie draif in mony deip dell;	squall; ceaselessly drove
Sa feirslie fra the Firmament, sa fellounlie it fure,	wickedly
Thair micht na folk hald na fute on the heich fell.	
In point thay war to parische, thay proudest men and pure,	perish; noble
In thay wickit wedderis thair wist nane to dwell.	no one knew (where)
Amang thay myrk Montanis sa madlie thay mer,	wildly; wandered

1. Charlemagne, who ruled Europe in the eighth century.
2. St Thomas day: 21 December.

28

Be it was pryme of the day,   *By the time that*
Sa wonder hard fure thay
That ilk ane tuik ane seir way,   *separate*
    And sperpellit full fer.   *scattered*

Ithand wedderis of the eist draif on sa fast,   *Continual*
It all to-blaisterit and blew that thairin baid.   *(those) that remained*
Be thay disseverit sindrie, midmorne was past;   *By the time they broke up*
Thair wist na Knicht of the Court quhat way the King raid.
He saw thair was na better bot God at the last,   *(than to trust)*
His steid aganis the storme stalwartlie straid;
He cachit fra the Court, sic was his awin cast,   *rode away; lot*
Quhair na body was him about be five mylis braid.
In thay montanis, I-wis, he wox all will,   *became all bewildered*
  In wickit wedderis and wicht,   *fierce*
    Amang thay Montanis on hicht;
    Be that it drew to the nicht,   *By the time that*
      The King lykit ill.   *was unhappy*

Evill lykand was the King it nichtit him sa lait,   *Unhappy; (he was) benighted*
And he na harberie had for his behufe;   *shelter; use*
Sa come thair ane cant carll chachand the gait,   *bold fellow; taking the road*
With ane capill and twa creillis cuplit abufe.   *horse; panniers*
The King carpit to the carll withoutin debait: *said*
'Schir, tell me thy richt name, for the Rude lufe?'   *love of the Cross*
He sayis: 'Men callis me Rauf Coilyear, as I weill wait;   *Collier; know*
I leid my life in this land with mekle unrufe,   *much trouble*
Baith tyde and tyme in all my travale;   *(All seasons); toil*
  Hine ouir sevin mylis I dwell,   *Hence*
  And leidis coilis to sell;   *carry coals*
  Sen thow speiris, I the tell   *Since; ask*
    All the suith hale.'   *whole truth*

'Sa mot I thrife,' said the King,' I speir for nane ill;
Thow semis ane nobill fallow, thy answer is sa fyne.'
'Forsuith,' said the Coilyear, 'traist quhen thow will,   *trust (me) when you like*
For I trow, and it be nocht swa, sum part salbe thyne.'[1]
'Mary, God forbid,' said the King, 'that war bot lytill skill;   *would be pointless*
Baith my self and my hors is reddy for to tyne;   *perish*
I pray the, bring me to sum rest, the wedder is sa schill,   *chill*
For I defend that we fall in ony fechtine;   *That I forbid us to quarrel*
I had mekill mair nait sum freindschip to find: *much more profit*
  And gif thow can better than I,   *know*
  For the name of Sanct July,[2]   *In the name of St Julian*

1. Idiomatically: 'For I reckon, if you're wrong, it's your problem.'
2. St Julian: patron saint of innkeepers.

Thow bring me to sum harbery,   shelter
   And leif me not behind.'

'I wait na worthie harberie heir neir hand,   know of; lodging
For to serve sic ane man as me think the,
Nane bot mine awin hous, maist in this land,
Fer furth in the Forest, amang the fellis hie.
With-thy thow wald be payit of sic as thow fand,   Provided; pleased with
Forsuith thow suld be welcum to pas hame with me,
Or ony uther gude fallow that I heir fand
Walkand will of his way, as me think the;   astray from his path
For the wedderis are sa fell, that fallis on the feild.'   fierce
   The King was blyth, quhair he raid,   cheerful
   Of the grant that he had maid,   (because); undertaking
   Sayand with hart glaid:
      'Schir, God yow foryeild.'   reward

'Na, thank me not ouir airlie, for dreid that we threip,   too soon; in case; quarrel
For I have servit the yit of lytill thing to ruse;   prize
For nouther hes thow had of me fyre, drink, nor meit,
Nor nane uther eismentis for travellouris behuse.   comforts; benefit
Bot, micht we bring this harberie this nicht weill to heip,   (to a good conclusion)
That we micht with ressoun baith thus excuse;   excuse both of us
To-morne on the morning, quhen thow sall on leip,   mount up
Pryse at the parting, how that thow dois;   Appraise
For first to lofe and syne to lak, Peter! it is schame.'   praise; find fault
   The King said: 'In gude fay,
   Schir, it is suith that ye say.'
   Into sic talk fell thay
      Quhill thay war neir hame.   Until

To the Coilyearis hous baith, or thay wald blin,   before; stop
The carll had cunning weill quhair the gait lay;   knowledge; road
'Undo the dure belive! Dame, art thow in?   immediately
Quhy Devill makis thow na dule for this evill day?   complaint
For my gaist and I baith cheveris with the chin,   (have chattering teeth)
Sa fell ane wedder feld I never, be my gude fay.'   felt; faith
The gude wyfe glaid with the gle to begin,   proceeded; entertainment
For durst scho never sit summoundis that scho hard him say: disregard orders
The carll was wantoun of word, and wox wonder wraith.   became; angry
   All abaisit for blame,   abashed
   To the dure went our Dame,
   Scho said: 'Schir, ye ar welcome hame,
      And your gaist baith.'

Dame, I have deir coft all this dayis hyre,   bought; labour
In wickit wedderis and weit walkand full will;   astray

Dame, kyith I am cummin hame, and kendill on ane fire, *show (that)*
I trow our gaist be the gait hes farne als ill. *on the road has fared as badly*
Ane ryall rufe het fyre war my desyre, *royal, strong, hot*
To fair the better for his saik, gif we micht win thair till; *(achieve it)*
Knap doun capounis of the best, but in the byre, *Knock off; capons; out in*
Heir is bot hamelie fair, do belive, Gill.' *do hurry*
Twa cant knaifis of his awin haistelie he bad: *lively servants*
   'The ane of yow my capill ta, *horse take*
   The uther his coursour alswa, *charger*
   To the stabill swyith ye ga.' *swiftly*
     Than was the King glaid.

The Coilyear, gudlie in feir, tuke him be the hand, *with good countenance*
And put him befoir him, as ressoun had bene; *ushered him in; as is right*
Quhen thay come to the dure, the King begouth to stand, *began to halt*
To put the Coilyear in befoir, maid him to mene. *as if he intended*
He said: 'Thow art uncourtes, that sall I warrand.' *(Rauf said)*
He tyt the King be the nek, twa part in tene; *seized; half in anger*
'Thow at bidding suld be boun or obeysand, *ready or obedient*
And gif thow of courtasie couth, thow hes foryet it clene; *knew; clean forgot*
Now is anis,' said the Coilyear, 'kynd aucht to creip,[1] *That's once*
   Sen ellis thow art unknawin, *(since you're ignorant of how else)*
   To mak me Lord of my awin;
   Sa mot I thrive, I am thrawin, *I am upset*
     Begin we to threip.' *We are beginning to quarrel*

Than benwart thay geid, quhair brandis was bricht, *burning logs*
To ane bricht byrnand fyre as the carll bad;
He callit on Gyliane, his wyfe, thair supper to dicht. *prepare*
'Of the best that thair is, help that we had,

     .   .   .   [part of the text seems to be missing here]

'Efter ane evill day to have ane mirrie nicht,
For sa troublit with stormis was I never stad; *beset*
Of ilk airt of the Eist sa laithly it laid, *From each point; foully it blew*
   Yit was I mekle willar than, *more at a loss then*
   Quhen I met with this man.'
   Of sic taillis thay began,
     Quhill the supper was graid. *prepared*

Sone was the Supper dicht, and the fyre bet, *set; mended*
And thay had weschin, I wis the worthiest was thair: *washed; the best was there*
'Tak my wyfe be the hand, in feir, withoutin let, *together; delay*
And gang begin the buird,' said the Coilyear. *go to the head of the table*

---

1. The saying is: 'Nature must creep [before it walks]'; idiomatically: 'Walk before you run', i.e. you can't just do as you like, first things first.

'That war unsemand, forsuith, and thy self unset;'   without your place
The King profferit him to gang, and maid ane strange fair.   strange fuss
'Now is twyse,' said the carll, 'me think thow hes foryet.'   That's twice
He leit gyrd to the King, withoutin ony mair,   let fly at
And hit him under the eir with his richt hand,
    Quhill he stakkerit thair with all
      Half the breid of the hall;   breadth
      He faind never of ane fall,   He never shirked falling
        Quhill he the eird fand.   Till he found the ground

He start up stoutly agane, uneis micht he stand,   scarcely
For anger of that outray that he had thair tane.   outrage
He callit on Gyliane his wyfe: 'Ga, tak him be the hand,
And gang agane to the buird, quhair ye suld air have gane.'   before
'Schir, thow art unskilfull, and that sall I warrand,   clumsy
Thow byrd to have nurtour aneuch, and thow hes nane;   You should; good manners
Thow hes walkit, I wis, in mony wyld land,
The mair vertew thow suld have, to keip the fra blame;   breeding
Thow suld be courtes of kynd, and ane cunnand courteir.   naturally courteous
    Thocht that I simpill be,
    Do as I bid the,
    The hous is myne, pardie,
      And all that is heir.'

The King said to him self: 'This is an evill lyfe,
Yit was I never in my lyfe thusgait leird;   taught in this fashion
And I have oft tymes bene quhair gude hes bene ryfe,   good (men); numerous
That maist couth of courtasie in this Cristin eird.   knew most; earth
Is nane sa gude as leif of, and mak na mair stryfe,   (Best is) to leave off
For I am stonischit at this straik, that hes me thus steird.'   displaced
In feir fairlie he foundis, with the gude wyfe,   (He proceeds fairly together)
Quhair the Coilyear bad, sa braithlie he beird.   so strongly he shouted
Quhen he had done his bidding, as him gude thocht,
    Doun he sat the King neir,
    And maid him glaid and gude cheir,
    And said: 'Ye ar welcum heir,
      Be him that me bocht.'

Quhen thay war servit and set to the suppar,   seated at
Gyll and the gentill King, Charlis of micht,
Syne on the tother syde sat the Coilyear:
Thus war thay marschellit but mair, and matchit that nicht.   without more ado
Thay brocht breid to the buird, and braun of ane bair,   haunch of a boar
And the worthyest wyne went upon hicht;
Thay beirnis, as I wene, thay had aneuch thair,   warriors; think
Within that burelie bigging, byrnand full bricht;   stout building

Syne enteris thair daynteis on deis dicht dayntelie.   *table prepared*
    Within that worthie wane   *dwelling*
    Forsuith wantit thay nane.
    With blyith cheir sayis Gyliane:
        'Schir, dois glaidlie.'   *'eat up'*

The carll carpit to the King cumlie and cleir: *said; comely and fair*
'Schir, the Forestaris, forsuith, of this Forest,
Thay have me all at invy for dreid of the deir;   *a spite at me, fearing for the deer*
Thay threip that I thring doun of the fattest;   *maintain*
Thay say, I sall to Paris, thair to compeir   *appear*
Befoir our cumlie King, in dule to be drest;   *sorrow; dealt with*
Sic manassing thay me mak, forsuith, ilk yeir,   *menacing; each*
And yit aneuch sall I have for me and ane gest;
Thairfoir sic as thow seis, spend on, and not spair.'   *whatever you see, dig in*
    Thus said gentill Charlis the Mane
    To the Coilyear agane:
    'The King him self hes bene fane   *delighted*
        Sum tyme of sic fair.'   *with such fare*

Of capounis and cunningis thay had plentie,   *capons and coneys*
With wyne at thair will, and eik vennysoun;
Byrdis bakin in breid, the best that may be;   *Bird pie*
Thus full freschlie thay fure into fusioun.   *vigorously; stuck into plenty*
The carll with ane cleir voce carpit on he,   *spoke loudly*
Said: 'Gyll, lat the cop raik for my bennysoun;   *pass the cup; blessing*
And gar our gaist begin, and syne drink thow to me;   *make*
Sen he is ane stranger, me think it ressoun.'   *proper*
Thay drank dreichlie about, thay wosche, and thay rais.   *deeply in turn; washed*
    The King with ane blyith cheir
    Thankit the Coilyeir;
    Syne all the thre into feir   *together*
        To the fyre gais.

Quhen thay had maid thame eis, the Coilyear tald   *themselves comfortable*
Mony sindrie taillis efter suppair.   *different*
Ane bricht byrnand fyre was byrnand full bald;
The King held gude countenance and company bair,   *well mannered; companionable*
And ever to his asking ane answer he yald;   *gave*
Quhill at the last he began to frane farther mair: *(Rauf); ask*
'In faith, freind, I wald wit, tell gif ye wald,   *know*
Quhair is thy maist wynning?' said the Coilyear.   *main dwelling*
'Out of weir,' said the King, 'I wayndit never to tell: *Without doubt; never refused*
    With my Lady the Quene
    In office maist have I bene
    All thir yeiris fyftene,
        In the Court for to dwell.'

'Quhat kin office art thow in, quhen thow art at hame,   employment
Gif thow dwellis with the Quene, proudest in pane?'   dress
'Ane chyld of hir chalmer, Schir, be Sanct Jame,   attendant
And thocht my self it say, maist inwart of ane;   intimate of all
For my dwelling to nicht I dreid me for blame.'   delay; I fear blame
'Quhat sal I cal the,' said the Coilyear, 'quhen thow art hyne gane?'   hence
'Wymond of the Wardrop is my richt name,   Wardrobe¹
Quhairever thow findis me befoir the, thi harberie is tane.   lodging is assured
And thow will cum to the Court, this I underta,   (If)
    Thow sall have for thy fewaill,   fuel
    For my saik, the better saill,   sale
    And onwart to thy travaill,   an advance on
245   Worth ane laid or twa.'   load

---

1. 'Wymond' would be in charge of clothes, robes, armour and trappings for the royal household as it moves between castles or palaces.

Blind Harry (1450–1493)

Mentioned in Dunbar's *Lament for the Makars*, 'Blind Hary' appeared at James IV's Court on various festival occasions and received bounty from the King. Describing himself as an 'unlearned' man, he seems to have lived as a professional poet, suffering blindness in later years. Harry's narrative of *The Actes and Deidis of the Illustre and Vallyeant Campioun Schir William Wallace* contains much political and physical detail, enlivened by vivid accounts of physical action and the author's hatred of England and Englishmen in general. Written about 1477, some 170 years after the events it describes, Harry's twelve books in heroic couplets speak for popular Scottish patriotism at the time, immortalising Wallace as guerrilla sword-fighter and martyr for his country.

from The Actes and Deidis of the Illustre and Vallyeant Campioun Schir William Wallace

Book I: the teenage Wallace goes fishing (1296)

So on a tym he desyrit to play.	
In Aperill the thre and twentie day	
Till Erewyn wattir fysche to tak he went,	(River Irvine)
Sic fantasye fell in his entent.	notion
To leide his net a child furth with him geid,	bring
Bot he or nowne was in a felloune dreid.	But; before noon; fearful plight
His swerd he left, so did he nevir agayne;	
It dide him gud suppos he sufferyt payne.	although; distress
Off that labour as than he was nocht sle;	skilled
Happy he was, tuk fysche haboundanle.	
Or of the day ten houris our couth pas,	Before; could
Ridand thar come ner-by quhar Wallace was	
The lorde Persye, was captane than off Ayr.	
Fra thine he turnde and couth to Glaskow fare.	thence
Part of the court had Wallace labour seyne.	
Till him raid five cled in-to ganand greyne.	(men); clad in suitable green
Ane said sone, 'Scot, Martyns fysche we wald have.'[1]	
Wallace meklye agayne answer him gave,	
'It war resone me think ye suld haif part.	would be right
Waith suld be delt in all place with fre hart.'	Game

1. Possibly from a Scottish proverb '"Every man for himself," quod Sir Martin.'

367

35

He bade his child, 'Gyff thaim of our waithyng.'   catch
The Sothroun said, 'As now of thi delyng   distribution
We will nocht tak; thow wald giff us our small.'   too little
He lychtyt doun and fra the child tuk all.
Wallas said than, 'Gentill men gif ye be,
Leiff us sum part, we pray, for cheryte.
Ane agyt knycht servis our lady to-day.
Gud frend, leiff part and tak nocht all away.'
'Thow sall haiff leiff to fysche and tak the ma.   more
All this forsuth sall in our flyttyng ga.   removal
We serff a lord. Thir fysche sall till him gang.'
Wallace answerd, said, 'Thow art in the wrang.'[1]
'Quham "thowis" thow, Scot? In faith thow servis a blaw.'   deserve
Till him he ran and out a swerd can draw.
Willham was wa he had na wapynnis thar   grieved
Bot the poustaff the quhilk in hand he bar.   pole net
Wallas with it fast on the cheik him tuk
Wyth so gud will quhill of his feit he schuk.   off; staggered
The swerd flaw fra him a fur breid on the land.   furrow breadth
Wallas was glaid and hynt it sone in hand,   seized
And with the swerd ane awkwart straik him gave,
Undyr the hat his crage in sondir drawe.   neck
Be that the layff lychtyt about Wallas.   With that the others set
He had no helpe only bot goddis grace.
On athir side full fast on him thai dange.   struck
Gret perell was giff thai had lestyt lang.   continued
Apone the hede in gret ire he strak ane;
The scherand swerd glaid to the colar bane.   glided
Ane othir on the arme he hitt so hardely
Quhill hand and swerd bathe on the feld can ly.   Till
The tothir twa fled to thar hors agayne.
He stekit him was last apon the playne.   stabbed; in the battle
Thre slew he thar, twa fled with all thar mycht
Eftir thar lord, bot he was out off sicht
Takand the mure or he and thai couth twyne.   the moor(road) before they parted
Till him thai raid onon or thai wald blyne   before; stop
And cryit, 'Abide, your men ar martyrit doun   Wait
Rycht cruelly her in this fals regioun.   treacherous
Five of our court her at the wattir baid   retinue; stayed
Fysche for to bryng, thocht it na profyt maid.
We ar chapyt, bot in feyld slayne ar thre.'   escaped
The lord speryt, 'How mony mycht thai be?'   asked
'We saw bot ane that has discumfyst us all.'
Than lewch he lowde and said, 'Foule mot yow fall,   Ill befall you
Sen ane yow all has putt to confusioun.

1. Up to this point Wallace has used the more formal 'ye'.

Quha menys it maist the devyll of hell him droun! · complains most
This day for me in faith he beis nocht socht.' · as far as I'm concerned
Quhen Wallace thus this worthi werk had wrocht,
Thar hors he tuk and ger that levyt was thar, · gear; left
Gaif our that crafft, he geid to fysche no mar; · Abandoned
Went till his eyme¹ and tauld him of this drede, · uncle; situation
And he for wo weil ner worthit to weide, · was like to go mad
And said, 'Sone, thir tithingis syttis me sor, · Son; tidings; trouble
And be it knawin thow may tak scaith tharfor.' · harm
'Uncle,' he said, 'I will no langar bide.
Thir south-land hors latt se gif I can ride.' · This
Than bot a child him service for to mak, · without a page
Hys emys sonnys he wald nocht with him tak.
This gud knycht said, 'Deyr Cusyng, pray I the,
Quhen thow wanttis gud cum fech ynewch fra me.' · lack supplies; fetch enough
Sylvir and gold he gert on-to him geyff.
Wallace inclynis and gudely tuk his leyff. · bows

[End of Book I]

Book XII: the capture of Wallace (1305)

959 Thus Wallace thrys has maid all Scotland fre.
Than he desyryt in lestand pees to be.
For as off wer he was in sumpart yrk, · exhausted
He purpost than to serve god and the kyrk
And for to leiff undyr hys rychtwys king.
That he desyryt atour all erdly thing. · above
The harrold Jop in Ingland sone he send · herald
And wrayt to Bruce rycht hartlie this commend, · greeting
Besekand him to cum and tak his croun;²
Nane suld gaynstand, clerk, burges no barroun. · oppose
The harrald past. Quhen Bruce saw his credans, · went
Tharoff he tuk a perfyt gret plesans,
With hys awn hand agayn wrayt to Wallace
And thankyt him off lawte and kyndnas, · loyalty
Besekand him this mater to conseill, · advise
For he behuffyd out off Ingland to steill; · was obliged
For lang befor was kepyt the ragment · Because; bond
Quhilk Comyn had, to byd the gret parlement · stay (at)
In-to London; and gyff thai him accus, · question
To cum fra thaim he suld mak sum excus.
He prayit Wallace, in Glaskow mur to walk
The fyrst nycht off Juli, for his salk,

---

1. The 16-year-old boy is staying with Sir Richard Wallace of Riccarton in Ayrshire.
2. Wallace had earlier been Guardian of Scotland. Bruce is looking after his own interest in the crown at Edward's court in London.

And bad he suld bot in-to quiet be,
For he with him mycht bryng few chevalre. *could; knights*
Wallace was blyth quhen he this writyng saw. *happy*
His houshauld sone he gert to Glaskow draw. *made to move to*
That moneth thar he ordand thaim to byd. *month; stay*
Kerle he tuk ilk nycht with him to ryd *(Will Kerr); each*
And this yong man that Menteth till him send –
Wyst nane bot thir quhat way at Wallace wend – *None knew but them;*
The quhilk gart warn his Eym the auchtand nycht. *eighth*
Sexte full sone Schyr Jhone Menteth gert dycht *made to prepare*
Off hys awn kyn and off alya born. *allies*
To this tresoun he gert thaim all be sworn.
Fra Dunbertane thai sped thaim haistely. *(Dumbarton)*
Ner Glaskow kyrk thai bownyt thaim prevaly. *prepared secretly*
Wallace past furth quhar at the tryst was set. *meeting*
A spy thai maid and folowed him but let *without hindrance*
Till Robrastoun, was ner be the way syd *(to north-east of Glasgow)*
And bot a hous, quhar Wallace usyt to byd. *only; stay*
He wouk on fut quhill passyt was myd-nycht. *walked*
Kerle and he than for a sleip thaim dycht. *got ready*
Thai bad this cuk that he suld wache his part *rascal; guard his ground*
And walkyn Wallace, com men fra ony art. *direction*
Quhen thai slepyt this traytour tuk graith heid. *prompt heed*
He met his Eym and bad him haiff no dreid: *fear*
'On sleip he is and with him bot a man. *only one*
Ye may him haiff for ony craft he can, *in spite of; skill; knows*
With-out the hous thar wapynnys laid thaim fra.'
For weill thai wyst, gat Wallace ane off tha *knew; if one of them got*
And on his feyt, hys ransoun suld be sauld. *on his feet (alive); sold*
Thus semblyt thai about that febill hauld. *assembled*
This traytour wach fra Wallace than he stall *guard; then stole*
Bathe knyff and swerd, his bow and arowis all.
Eftir mydnycht in handis thai haiff him tane,
Dischevill, on sleipe, wyth him na man bot ane.
Kerle thai tuk and led him off that place,
Dyd him to ded withoutyn langar space.
Thai thocht to bynd Wallace throu strenthis strang.
On fute he gat the feill traytouris amang,
Grippyt about, bot na wapyn he fand.
Apon a syll he saw besyd him stand *Over a beam*
The bak off ane he byrstyt in that thrang *mêlée*
And off ane othir the harnys out he dang. *brains; knocked*
Than als mony as mycht on him handis lay
Be force hym hynt for till haiff him away, *seized*
Bot that power mycht nocht a fute him leid *Without; force*

Out off that hous quhill thai or he war deid.   until
Schir Jhon saw weill be force it coud nocht be,
Or he war tayne he thocht erar to de.   Before; captured; rather
Menteth bad ces and thus spak to Wallace,   ordered stop
Syn schawyt him furth a rycht sutell, fals cace: argument
'Ye haiff so lang her usyt yow allane   (kept so long here on your own)
Quhill witt tharoff is in-till Ingland gane.   That knowledge of it
Tharfor, her me and sobyr your curage.   moderate
The Inglismen with a full gret barnage   baronage (regiment)
Ar semblyt her and set this hous about,
That ye be force on na wayis may wyn out.
Suppos ye had the strenth off gud Ectour,   (Hector of Troy)
Amang this ost ye may nocht lang endour.   host
And thai you tak, in haist your ded is dycht.   And (if) they take you; set
I haiff spokyn with lord Clyffurd that knycht,
Wyth thar chyftanys weill menyt for your lyff.   those; well disposed
Thai ask no mar bot be quyt off your stryff.
To Dunbertane ye sall furth pas with me.
At your awn hous ye may in saifte be.'
Sotheroun sic use with Menteth lang had thai   The English; dealings
That Wallace trowyt sum-part at he wald say.   trusted; a little
Menteth said, 'Schir, lo, wappynnys nane we haiff.
We com in trayst, your lyff gyff we mycht saiff.'
Wallace trowyt weill and he his gossep twys, [1]   godfather twice
That he wald nocht be no maner off wys
Him to betrays, for all Scotland so wyd.
Ane ayth off him he askit in that tid.   oath; time
Thar wantit wit. Quhat suld his aythis mor?   That lacked good sense.
Forsworn till him he was lang tym befor.
The ayth he maid. Wallace com in his will.   submitted
Rycht frawdfully all thus schawyt him till: laid out for him
'Gossep,' he said, 'as presoner thai mon yow se,
Or thai throu force wyll ellis tak yow fra me.'
A courch with slycht apon his handys thai laid   kerchief; stealth
And undyr syn with sevir cordys thai braid,   strong; bound
Bath scharp and tewch, and fast to-gyddyr drew.
Allace, the Bruce mycht sayr that byndyng rew,
Quhilk maid Scotland sone brokyn apon cace,   soon; by chance
For Comyns ded and los off gud Wallace!   On account of; death
Thai led him furth in feyr amang thaim aw.   in company
Kerle he myst. Off na Sotheroun he saw.   missed
Than wyst he weyll that he betraysyt was.
Towart the south with him quhen thai can pas,
Yeit thai him said in trewth he suld nocht de,

---

1. Wallace was godfather to two of Menteith's children.

King Edward wald kep him in gud saufte
For hie honour in wer at he had wrocht.   war; that he had done
The sayr bandys so strowblyt all his thocht,   troubled
Credence tharto forsuth he coud nocht geyff.   Belief
1074   He wyst full weyll thai wald nocht lat him leiff.   knew

Robert Henryson (1425?–1505?)

Henryson was most likely a university man and a schoolmaster. He may have visited Europe, but seems for the most part to have lived quietly in Dunfermline during the eventful reigns of James I to James IV. His poems have a colloquial ease and pace to them that characterises poetry in Scots to this day. The *Morall Fabillis*, from the 1460s, offer a wry and gentle view of the compact between man, God and the animal kingdom. Based on medieval tales of Reynard the Fox and the fables of Aesop, they evoke the daily routines of common folk wittily translated to a familiar Scottish landscape. Henryson's masterpiece, 'The Testament of Cresseid', adds a darker, terser and distinctively Scottish note to *Troilus and Criseyde*, and numerous editions of Chaucer's long poem, from 1532 onwards, contained Henryson's sequel: 'the pyteful and dolorous testament of fayre Creseyde'.

The Two Mice

Esope, myn authour, makis mentioun	
Of twa myis, and thay wer sisteris deir,	
Of quham the eldest dwelt in ane borous toun;	burgh
The uther wynnit uponland weill neir,	dwelt
Richt soliter, quhyle under busk and breir,	sometimes under bush
Quhilis in the corne, in uther mennis skaith,	harm
As owtlawis dois, and levit on hir waith.	wits

This rurall mous in to the wynter tyde	
Had hunger, cauld, and tholit grit distres;	endured
The uther mous, that in the burgh can byde,	
Was gild brother and made ane fre burges,	
Toll-fre also, but custum mair or les,	tax-free also, without charges
And fredome had to ga quhair ever scho list	she liked
Amang the cheis and meill, in ark and kist.	box and chest

Ane tyme quhen scho wes full and unfute-sair,	
Scho tuke in mynd hir sister upon land,	
And langit for to heir of hir weilfair,	
To se quhat lyfe scho led under the wand.	branches
Bairfute allone, with pykestaf in hir hand,	

As pure pylgryme, scho passit owt off town
To seik hir sister, baith oure daill and down.

Throw mony wilsum wayis can scho walk,   wild
Throw mosse and mure, throw bankis, busk, and breir,   bog
Fra fur to fur, cryand fra balk to balk,   furrow; unploughed strip
'Cum furth to me, my awin sweit sister deir!
Cry peip anis!' With that the mous culd heir
And knew hir voce, as kinnisman will do
Be verray kynd, and furth scho come hir to.   by nature itself

The hartlie cheir, Lord God! geve ye had sene   heartfelt; if
Beis kithit quhen thir sisteris twa war met,   that is shown
And gret kyndnes wes schawin thame betwene,
For quhylis thay leuch, and quhylis for joy thay gret,   laughed; cried
Quhyle kissit sweit, quhylis in armis plet,   folded
And thus thay fure quhill soberit wes their mude;   fared
Syne fute for fute unto the chalmer yude.   went

As I hard say, it was ane semple wane,   house
Off fog and farne full misterlyk wes maid,   moss; fern; poorly
Ane sillie scheill under ane erdfast stane,   hovel; earthfast
Off quhilk the entres wes not hie nor braid;
And in the samin thay went, but mair abaid,   without more delay
Withoutin fyre or candill birnand bricht,
For comonly sic pykeris luffis not lycht.   petty thieves

Quhen thay wer lugit thus, thir sely myse,   lodged; simple
The youngest sister into hir butterie hyid,   pantry
And brocht furth nuttis and peis, in steid off spyce;
Giff this wes good fair, I do it on thame besyde.   I leave it to them to decide
This burges mous prunyit forth in pryde,   preened
And said, 'Sister, is this your dayly fude?'
'Quhy not,' quod scho, 'think ye this meit nocht gude?'

'Na, be my saull, I think it bot ane scorne.'
'Madame,' quod scho, 'ye be the mair to blame.
My mother sayd, efter that we wer borne,
That I and ye lay baith within ane wame;   womb/belly
I keip the ryte and custome off my dame,
And off my syre, levand in povertie,
For landis have we nane in propertie.'

'My fair sister,' quod scho, 'have me excusit;
This rude dyat and I can not accord.
To tender meit my stomok is ay usit,

For quhy I fair alsweill as ony lord.   because
Thir wydderit peis and nuttis, or thay be bord,   before they are pierced
Wil brek my teith and mak my wame ful sklender,
Quhilk usit wes before to meitis tender.'

'Weil, weil, sister,' quod the rurall mous,   said
'Geve it yow pleis, sic thing as ye se heir,   If; whatever
Baith meit and dreink, harberie and hous,   lodging
Salbe your awin, will ye remane al yeir.
Ye sall it have wyth blyith and hartlie cheir,   glad; heartfelt
And that suld mak the maissis that ar rude,   dishes; crude
Amang freindis, richt tender, sweit, and gude.

'Quhat plesans is in feistis delicate,
The quhilkis ar gevin with ane glowmand brow?   frowning
Ane gentill hart is better recreate   cheer
With blyith visage, than seith to him ane kow.   being given a cow
Ane modicum is mair for till allow,
Swa that gude will be kerver at the dais,   if good spirits carve at the table
Than thrawin vult and mony spycit mais.'   sour face; spiced dishes

For all this mery exhortatioun
This burges mous had littill will to sing,
Bot hevilie scho kest hir browis doun,
For all the daynteis that scho culd hir bring;
Yit at the last scho said, halff in hething,   scorn
'Sister, this victuall and your royall feist
May weill suffice for sic ane rurall beist.

'Lat be this hole and cum unto my place:
I sall yow schaw, be trewe experience,
My Gude Friday is better nor your Pace,   Easter feast
My dische likingis is worth your haill expence.   lickings
I have housis anew off grit defence;   plenty; security
Off cat, na fall, na trap, I have na dreid.'
'I grant,' quod scho, and on togidder thay yeid.   went

In skugry ay, throw rankest gers and corne,   always in secrecy; grass
Under cowert full prevelie couth thay creip;
The eldest wes the gyde and went beforne,
The younger to hir wayis tuke gude keip.   paid attention
On nicht thay ran and on the day can sleip,
Quhill in the morning, or the laverok sang,   before the lark
Thay fand the town, and in blythlie couth gang.

Not fer fra thyne, unto ane worthie wane,   dwelling
This burges brocht thame sone quhare thay suld be.

Withowt 'God speid' thair herberie wes tane   lodging; taken
In to ane spence with vittell grit plentie: pantry
Baith cheis and butter upon shelfis hie,
Flesche and fische aneuch, baith fresche and salt,
And sekkis full off grotis, meill, and malt.   crushed oats

Efter, quhen thay disposit wer to dyne,
Withowtin grace, thay wesche and went to meit,
With all coursis that cukis culd devyne,   devise
Muttoun and beif, strikin in tailyeis greit.   carved in slices
Ane lordis fair thus couth thay counterfeit
Except ane thing: thay drank the watter cleir
In steid off wyne; bot yit thay maid gude cheir.

With blyith upcast, and merie countenance,
The eldest sister sperit at hir gest   enquired
Giff that scho thocht be ressone difference
Betwix that chalmer and hir sarie nest.   sorry
'Ye, dame,' quod scho, 'bot how lang will this lest?'
'For evermair, I wait, and langer to.'
'Giff it be swa, ye ar at eis,' quod scho.   If; ease

Till eik thair cheir ane subcharge furth scho brocht,   increase; extra dish
Ane plait off grottis and ane disch full off meill;
Thraf caikkis als I trow scho spairit nocht   Unleavened oatcakes
Aboundantlie about hir for to deill,   hand out
And mane full fyne scho brocht in steid off geill,   white bread; jelly
And ane quhyte candill owt off ane coffer stall   stole
In steid off spyce, to gust thair mouth withall.   give relish to

This maid thay merie, quhill thay micht na mair,   until
And 'Haill, Yule, haill!' cryit upon hie.
Yit efter joy oftymes cummis cair,
And troubill efter grit prosperitie.
Thus as thay sat in all thair jolitie,
The spenser come with keyis in his hand,   butler
Oppinnit the dure, and thame at denner fand.

Thay taryit not to wesche, as I suppose,   tarried
Bot on to ga, quha micht formest win.   rushed on, whoever might be first
The burges had ane hole, and in scho gois;
Hir sister had na hole to hyde hir in.
To se that selie mous, it wes grit sin;   pity
So desolate and will off ane gude reid;   without; good plan
For verray dreid scho fell in swoun neir deid.

Bot, as God wald, it fell ane happie cace:
The spenser had na laser for to byde,   *time to stay*
Nowther to seik nor serche, to sker nor chace,   *scare*
Bot on he went, and left the dure up wyde.
The bald burges his passage weill hes spyde;   *bold*
Out off hir hole scho come and cryit on hie,
'How fair ye, sister? Cry peip, quhair ever ye be!'

This rurall mous lay flatling on the ground,
And for the deith scho wes full sair dredand,
For till hir hart straik mony wofull stound;   *struck; pang*
As in ane fever scho trimbillit fute and hand;
And quhan hir sister in sic ply hir fand,   *plight; found*
For verray pietie scho began to greit,   *weep*
Syne confort hir with wordis hunny sweit.   *then comfort*

'Quhy ly ye thus? Ryse up, my sister deir!
Cum to your meit; this perrell is ouerpast.'
The uther answerit with a hevie cheir,
'I may not eit, sa sair I am agast.
I had lever thir fourty dayis fast   *rather*
With watter caill, and to gnaw benis or peis,   *cabbage water*
Than all your feist in this dreid and diseis.'   *unease*

With fair tretie yit scho gart hir upryse,   *entreaty; got her up*
And to the burde thay went and togidder sat.   *table*
And scantlie had thay drunkin anis or twyse,
Quhen in come Gib Hunter, our jolie cat,
And bad 'God speid!' The burges up with that,
And till hir hole scho fled as fyre of flint;   *sparks from flint*
Bawdronis the uther be the bak hes hint.   *Pussy; taken*

Fra fute to fute he kest hir to and fra,
Quhylis up, quhylis doun, als tait as ony kid.   *as lively*
Quhylis wald he lat hir rin under the stra;
Quhylis wald he wink, and play with hir buk heid;   *hide-and-seek*
Thus to the selie mous grit pane he did;   *poor*
Quhill at the last throw fair fortune and hap,
Betwix the dosor and the wall scho crap.   *wall-hanging; crept*

Syne up in haist behind the parraling   *tapestry*
So hie scho clam that Gilbert micht not get hir,
And be the clukis craftelie can hing   *claws*
Till he wes gane; hir cheir wes all the better.
Syne doun scho lap quhen thair wes nane to let hir,   *stop*
Apon the burges mous loud can scho cry,
'Fairweill, sister, thy feist heir I defy!

Thy mangerie is mingit all with cair;   banquet; mixed
Thy guse is gude, thy gansell sour as gall;   garlic sauce
The subcharge off thy service is bot sair;   extra dish
Sa sall thow find heir-efterwart may fall.   whatever befalls hereafter
I thank yone courtyne and yone perpall wall   partition
Off my defence now fra yone crewell beist.
Almichtie God keip me fra sic ane feist.

'Wer I into the kith that I come fra,   If only I were; country
For weill nor wo I suld never cum agane.'   good or ill
With that scho tuke hir leif and furth can ga,
Quhylis throw the corne and quhylis throw the plane.
Quhen scho wes furth and fre scho wes full fane,   very glad
And merilie markit unto the mure;   went
I can not tell how eftirwart scho fure.   fared

Bot I hard say scho passit to hir den,
Als warme as woll, suppose it wes not greit,   wool
Full beinly stuffit, baith but and ben   well supplied
Off peis and nuttis, beinis, ry, and quheit;
Quhen ever scho list scho had aneuch to eit,   wished to
In quyet and eis withoutin ony dreid,
Bot to hir sisteris feist na mair scho geid.

Moralitas
Freindis, heir may ye find, will ye tak heid,
In this fabill ane gude moralitie:
As fitchis myngit ar with nobill seid,   tares are mixed
Swa intermellit is adversitie   intermingled
With eirdlie joy, swa that na state is frie
Without trubill or sum vexatioun,
And namelie thay quhilk clymmis up maist hie,   those who climb
And not content with small possessioun.

Blissed be sempill lyfe withoutin dreid;
Blissed be sober feist in quietie.
Quha hes aneuch, of na mair hes he neid,
Thocht it be littill into quantatie.   although
Grit aboundance and blind prosperitie
Oftymes makis ane evill conclusioun.
The sweitest lyfe, thairfoir, in this cuntrie,
Is sickernes, with small possessioun.   security

O wantoun man that usis for to feid
Thy wambe, and makis it a god to be;   belly
Luke to thy self, I warne the weill on deid.   indeed

The cat cummis and to the mous hes ee;   *has an eye*
Quhat is avale thy feist and royaltie,
With dreidfull hart and tribulatioun?
Thairfoir, best thing in eird, I say for me,   *earth*
Is merry hart with small possessioun.

Thy awin fyre, freind, thocht it be bot ane gleid   *ember*
It warmis weill, and is worth gold to the;
And Solomon sayis, gif that thow will reid,
'Under the hevin I can not better se
Than ay be blyith and leif in honestie.'
Quhairfoir I may conclude be this ressoun: *proposition*
Of eirthly joy it beiris maist degre,   *takes the highest place*
Blyithnes in hart, with small possessioun.

The Cock and the Fox

Thocht brutall beistis be irrationall,
That is to say, wantand discretioun,
Yet ilk ane in thair kyndis naturall   *natures*
Hes mony divers inclinatioun:
The bair busteous, the wolff, the wylde lyoun,   *rough*
The fox fenyeit, craftie and cawtelows,   *cunning*
The dog to bark on nicht and keip the hows.

Sa different thay ar in properteis
Unknawin unto man and infinite
In kynd havand sa fell diversiteis,
My cunning it excedis for to dyte.   *write*
For thy as now, I purpose for to wryte   *therefore*
Ane cais I fand quhilk fell this other yeir   *happened*
Betwix ane foxe and gentill Chantecleir.

Ane wedow dwelt in till ane drop thay dayis   *village*
Quhilk wan hir fude off spinning on hir rok,   *distaff*
And na mair had, forsuth, as the fabill sayis
Except off hennis scho had ane lyttill flok
And thame to keip scho had ane jolie cok,
Richt curageous, that to this wedow ay   *courageous/lustful*
Devydit nicht and crew befoir the day.

Ane lyttill fra this foirsaid wedowis hows,
Ane thornie schaw thair wes off grit defence,   *copse*
Quhairin ane foxe, craftie and cautelous,   *cunning*
Maid his repair and daylie residence,
Quhilk to this wedow did grit violence

In pyking off pultrie baith day and nicht,   *thieving*
And na way be revengit on him scho micht.

This wylie tod, quhen that the lark couth sing,   *fox*
Full sair hungrie unto the toun him drest,   *made his way*
Quhair Chantecleir, in to the gray dawing   *Tired after*
Werie for nicht, wes flowen fra his nest.
Lowrence this saw and in his mynd he kest   *considered*
The jeperdies, the wayis, and the wyle,
Be quhat menis he micht this cok begyle.

Dissimuland in to countenance and cheir,   *Concealing*
On kneis fell and simuland thus he said,   *pretending*
'Gude morne, my maister, gentill Chantecleir!'
With that the cok start bakwart in ane braid.   *jerk*
'Schir, be my saull, ye neid not be effraid,
Nor yit for me to start nor fle abak;
I come bot heir service to yow to mak.

'Wald I not serve to yow, it wer bot blame,
As I have done to yowr progenitouris.
Your father oft fulfillit hes my wame,   *filled my belly*
And send me meit fra midding to the muris: *midden; moors*
And at his end I did my besie curis   *death; services*
To hald his heid and gif him drinkis warme;
Syne at the last, the sweit swelt in my arme.'   *darling died*

'Knew ye my father?' quod the cok, and leuch.
'Yea, my fair sone, forsuth I held his heid
Quhen that he deit under ane birkin beuch;   *birch bough*
Syne said the Dirigie quhen that he wes deid.   *dirge for the dead*
Betwix us twa how suld thair be ane feid?   *feud*
Quhame suld ye traist bot me, your servitour,
That to your father did sa grit honour?

'Quhen I behald your fedderis fair and gent,   *feathers; handsome*
Your beik, your breist, your hekill, and your kame –   *hackle*
Schir, be my saull, and the blissit sacrament,
My hart warmys, me think I am at hame.
Yow for to serve, I wald creip on my wame
In froist and snaw, in wedder wan and weit,
And lay my lyart loikkis under your feit.'   *grey hair*

This fenyeit foxe, fals and dissimulate,   *deceitful*
Maid to this cok ane cavillatioun: *trick*
'Ye ar, me think, changit and degenerate

Fra your father and his conditioun.
Off craftie crawing he micht beir the croun,
For he wald on his tais stand and craw.
This is na le; I stude beside and saw.'   *lie*

With that the cok, upon his tais hie
Kest up his beik, and sang with all his micht.
Quod schir Lowrence, 'Weill said, sa mot I the.   *so may I prosper*
Ye ar your fatheris sone and air upricht,   *rightful heir*
Bot off his cunning yit ye want ane slicht.'   *lack one knack*
'Quhat?' quod the cok. 'He wald, and haif na dout,
Baith wink, and craw, and turne him thryis about.'

The cok, inflate with wind and fals vane gloir,
That mony puttis unto confusioun,
Traisting to win ane grit worschip thairfoir,   *expecting; reputation*
Unwarlie winkand walkit up and doun,   *unwarily*
And syne to chant and craw he maid him boun –   *ready*
And suddandlie, be he had crawin ane note,   *by the time that*
The foxe wes war, and hint him be the throte.   *alert; seized*

Syne to the woid but tarie with him hyit,   *without delay*
Off countermaund haifand bot lytill dout.   *prohibition; fear*
With that Pertok, Sprutok, and Coppok cryit;
The wedow hard, and with ane cry come out.
Seand the cace scho sichit and gaif ane schout,
'How, murther, reylok!' with ane hiddeous beir,   *robbery; clamour*
'Allace, now lost is gentill Chantecleir!'

As scho wer woid, with mony yell and cry,   *mad*
Ryvand hir hair, upon hir breist can beit;   *Tearing*
Syne paill off hew, half in ane extasy,
Fell doun for cair in swoning and in sweit.   *sweat*
With that the selie hennis left thair meit,   *poor/simple/innocent*
And quhill this wyfe wes lyand thus in swoun
Fell of that cace in disputatioun.

'Allace', quod Pertok, makand sair murning,
With teiris grit attour hir cheikis fell,   *over*
'Yone wes our drowrie and our dayis darling,   *sweetheart*
Our nichtingall, and als our orlege bell,   *clock*
Our walkryfe watche, us for to warne and tell   *vigilant*
Quhen that Aurora with hir curcheis gray   *scarves*
Put up hir heid betwix the nicht and day.

'Quha sall our lemman be? Quha sall us leid?   *lover*
Quhen we ar sad quha sall unto us sing?

With his sweit bill he wald brek us the breid;
In all this warld wes thair ane kynder thing?
In paramouris he wald do us plesing,   making love
At his power, as nature list him geif.   pleased; give
Now efter him, allace, how sall we leif?'

Quod Sprutok than, 'Ceis, sister, off your sorrow.
Ye be to mad, for him sic murning mais.
We sall fair weill, I find Sanct Johne to borrow;   St J. be my surety
The proverb sayis, "As gude lufe cummis as gais."
I will put on my haly-dayis clais   holiday
And mak me fresch agane this jolie May,
Syne chant this sang, "Wes never wedow sa gay!"

'He wes angry and held us ay in aw,
And woundit with the speir off jelowsy.
Off chalmerglew, Pertok, full weill ye knaw   bedroom sport
Waistit he wes, off nature cauld and dry.   wasted
Sen he is gone, thairfoir, sister, say I,
Be blyith in baill, for that is best remeid.   happy in sorrow; remedy
Let quik to quik, and deid ga to the deid.'   the living

Than Pertok spak, that feinyeit faith befoir,   faked
In lust but lufe that set all hir delyte,   lust without love
'Sister, ye wait off sic as him ane scoir   know of such
Wald not suffice to slaik our appetyte.
I hecht yow be my hand, sen ye ar quyte,   vow; free
Within ane oulk, for schame and I durst speik,   week
To get ane berne suld better claw oure breik.'   warrior; crotch

Than Coppok lyke ane curate spak full crous: smugly
'Yone wes ane verray vengeance from the hevin.
He wes sa lous and sa lecherous,
Seis coud he nocht with kittokis ma than sevin,   Cease; mistresses
Bot rychteous God, haldand the balandis evin,
Smytis rycht sair, thocht he be patient,
Adulteraris that list thame not repent.   choose not to

'Prydefull he wes, and joyit off his sin,
And comptit not for Goddis favour nor feid,   cared; feud
Bot traistit ay to rax and sa to rin,   grab and run
Quhill at the last his sinnis can him leid
To schamefull end and to yone suddand deid.
Thairfoir it is the verray hand off God
That causit him be werryit with the tod.'   fox

Quhen this wes said, this wedow fra hir swoun
Start up on fute, and on hir kennettis cryde,   hounds
'How, Birkye, Berrie, Bell, Bawsie, Broun,
Rype Schaw, Rin Weil, Curtes, Nuttieclyde!
Togidder all but grunching furth ye glyde!   without grumbling
Reskew my nobill cok or he be slane,   before
Or ellis to me se ye cum never agane!'

With that, but baid, thay braidet ouer the bent;   sans delay; bounded; fields
As fyre off flint thay ouer the feildis flaw;
Full wichtlie thay throw wood and wateris went,   powerfully
And ceissit not, schir Lourence quhill thay saw.
Bot quhen he saw the raches cum on raw,   hunting dogs; in line
Unto the cok in mynd he said, 'God sen   send
That I and thow wer fairlie in my den.'

Then spak the cok, with sum gude spirit inspyrit,
'Do my counsall and I sall warrand the.   guarantee you
Hungrie thow art, and for grit travell tyrit,
Richt faint off force and may not ferther fle:
Swyith turne agane and say that I and ye   swiftly
Freindis ar maid and fellowis for ane yeir.
Than will thay stint, I stand for it, and not steir.'   stop; stir

This tod, thocht he wes fals and frivolus,   though
And had frawdis, his querrell to defend,   tricks; plea
Desavit wes be menis richt mervelous,
For falset failyeis ay at the latter end.   falsehood fails always
He start about, and cryit as he wes kend –   told
With that the cok he braid unto a bewch.   leapt; bough
Now juge ye all quhairat schir Lowrence lewch.   laughed

Begylit thus, the tod under the tre
On kneis fell, and said, 'Gude Chantecleir,
Cum doun agane, and I but meit or fe   without food or wages
Salbe your man and servand for ane yeir.'
'Na, murther, theif, and revar, stand on reir.   robber; stand back
My bludy hekill and my nek sa bla   discoloured blue
Hes partit lowe for ever betwene us twa.   love

'I wes unwyse that winkit at thy will,
Quhairthrow almaist I loissit had my heid.'
'I wes mair fule,' quod he, 'coud nocht be still,   (the fox)
Bot spake to put my pray in to pleid.'   prey up for debate
'Fair on, fals theif, God keip me fra thy feid.'   feud

With that the cok ouer the feildis tuke his flicht;
And in at the wedowis lewer couth he licht.   *louvre*

Moralitas

Now worthie folk, suppose this be ane fabill,
And ouerheillit wyth typis figurall   *covered over*
Yit may ye find ane sentence richt agreabill   *meaning*
Under thir fenyeit termis textuall.   *imagined*
To our purpose this cok weill may we call
Nyse proud men, woid and vaneglorious   *Haughty; reckless*
Of kin and blude, quhilk is presumpteous.   *arrogant*

Fy, puft up pryde, thow is full poysonabill!
Quha favoris the, on force man haif ane fall;   *of necessity must have*
Thy strenth is nocht, thy stule standis unstabill.   *seat*
Tak witnes of the feyndis infernall,
Quhilk houndit doun wes fra that hevinlie hall   *who were*
To hellis hole and to that hiddeous hous,
Because in pryde thay wer presumpteous.

This fenyeit foxe may weill be figurate
To flatteraris with plesand wordis quhyte,   *fair*
With fals mening and mynd maist toxicate,   *thought; poisonous*
To loif and le that settis thair haill delyte.   *flatter and lie*
All worthie folk at sic suld haif despyte,   *contempt*
For quhair is thair mair perrellous pestilence
Nor gif to learis haistelie credence?   *Than to give to liars*

The wickit mynd and adullatioun,
Of sucker sweit haifand similitude,   *sweet-seeming sugar*
Bitter as gall and full of fell poysoun
To taist it is, quha cleirlie understude.
For thy as now schortlie to conclude,
Thir twa sinnis, flatterie and vaneglore,
Ar vennomous: gude folk, fle thame thairfoir!

The Paddock and the Mouse

Upon ane tyme, as Esope culd report,
Ane lytill mous come till ane rever syde:
Scho micht not waid, hir schankis wer sa schort;   *legs*
Scho culd not swym; scho had na hors to ryde;
Off verray force behovit hir to byde;   *sheer necessity forced; stay*
And to and fra besyde that reuir deip
Scho ran, cryand with mony pietuous peip.

'Help ouer! Help ouer!' this silie mous can cry,   poor
'For Goddis lufe, sum bodie, ouer the brym.'   stream
With that ane paddok, in the watter by,   frog
Put up hir heid and on the bank can clym,
Quhilk be nature culd douk and gaylie swym.   dive
With voce full rauk, scho said on this maneir: hoarse
'Gude morne, schir Mous! Quhat is your erand heir?'

'Seis thow', quod scho, 'off corne yone jolie flat,   Do you see; field
Off ryip aitis, off barlie, peis, and quheit?   ripe oats
I am hungrie, and fane wald be thair at,   gladly
Bot I am stoppit be this watter greit;
And on this syde I get na thing till eit
Bot hard nuttis, quhilkis with my teith I bore:
Wer I beyond, my feist wer fer the more.

'I have no boit; heir is no maryner;   boat
And thocht thair war, I have no fraucht to pay.'   even if; ferry fee
Quod scho, 'Sister, lat be your hevie cheir;
Do my counsall, and I sall find the way
Withoutin hors, brig, boit, or yit galay,   bridge; galley
To bring yow ouer saiflie, be not afeird –
And not wetand the campis off your beird.'   whiskers

'I haif mervell', than quod the lytill mous,
'How can thow fleit without fedder or fin?   float
This rever is sa deip and dangerous,
Me think that thow suld droun to wed thairin.   wade
Tell me, thairfoir, quhat facultie or gin   cunning plan
Thow hes to bring the ouer this watter wan.'   gloomy
That to declair the paddok thus began:

'With my twa feit,' quod scho, 'lukkin and braid,   webbed
In steid off airis, I row the streme full styll,   oars
And thocht the brym be perrillous to waid,
Baith to and fra I swyme at my awin will.
I may not droun, for quhy my oppin gill   open gill
Devoidis ay the watter I resaiff: rejects; take in
Thairfoir to droun, forsuith, na dreid I haif.'

The mous beheld unto hir fronsit face,   wrinkled
Hir runkillit cheikis, and hir lippis syde,   wide
Hir hingand browis, and hir voce sa hace,   hoarse
Hir loggerand leggis, and hir harsky hyde.   dangly; rough
Scho ran abak, and on the paddok cryde:
'Giff I can ony skill off phisnomy,
Thow hes sumpart off falset and invy.   some amount; falsehood; malice

For clerkis sayis the inclinatioun
Off mannis thocht proceidis commounly
Efter the corporall complexioun
To gude or evill, as nature will apply:
Ane thrawart will, ane thrawin phisnomy.   perverse; twisted face
The auld proverb is witnes off this *lorum*:   conclusion
Distortum vultum sequitur distortio morum.'   Distorted morals follow a distorted face

'Na,' quod the taid, 'that proverb is not trew,
For fair thingis oftymis ar fundin faikin;   deceiving
The blaberyis, thocht thay be sad off hew,   blaeberries
Ar gadderit up quhen primeros is forsakin;   left untouched
The face may faill to be the hartis takin;   token
Thairfoir I find this scripture in all place:
"Thow suld not juge ane man efter his face."

'Thocht I unhailsum be to luke upon,
I have na wyt; quhy suld I lakkit be?   blame; reproached
Wer I als fair as jolie Absolon,   (a byword for manly beauty)
I am no causer off that grit beutie;
This difference in forme and qualitie
Almychtie God hes causit dame Nature
To prent and set in everilk creature.   imprint

'Off sum the face may be full flurischand,
Off silkin toung and cheir rycht amorous,   lovable
With mynd inconstant, fals, and wariand,   variable
Full off desait and menis cautelous.'   cunning tricks
'Let be thy preiching,' quod the hungrie mous,
'And be quhat craft, thow gar me understand,   by what skill; make me
That thow wald gyde me to yone yonder land.'

'Thow wait,' quod scho, 'ane bodie that hes neid   know
To help thame self suld mony wayis cast.   consider
Thairfoir ga tak ane doubill twynit threid
And bind thy leg to myne with knottis fast:
I sall the leir to swym – be not agast –   teach you
Als weill as I.' 'As thow?' than quod the mous.
'To preif that play, it wer our perrillous!   too

'Suld I be bund and fast, quhar I am fre,
In hoip off help? Na, than I schrew us baith,   curse
For I mycht lois baith lyfe and libertie!
Giff it wer swa, quha suld amend the skaith,   harm
Bot gif thow sweir to me the murthour aith: a deadly oath
But fraud or gyle to bring me ouer this flude,   Without
But hurt or harme?' 'In faith,' quod scho, 'I dude.'

Scho goikit up, and to the hevin can cry: gaped
'How, Juppiter, off nature god and king,
I mak ane aith trewlie to the, that I
This lytill mous sall ouer this watter bring.'
This aith wes maid; the mous, but persaving   without perceiving
The fals Ingyne of this foull crappald pad,   deceit; toady frog
Tuke threid and band hir leg, as scho hir bad.   told

Than fute for fute thay lap baith in the brym,   leapt; stream
Bot in thair myndis thay wer rycht different:
The mous thocht na thing bot to fleit and swym;   thought only to float
The paddok for to droun set hir intent.
Quhen thay in midwart off the streme wer went,
With all hir force the paddok preissit doun,
And thocht the mous without mercie to droun.

Persavand this, the mous on hir can cry:
'Tratour to God, and manesworne unto me!
Thow swore the murthour aith richt now that I
But hurt or harme suld ferryit be and fre.'
And quhen scho saw thair wes bot do or de,
Scho bowtit up and forsit hir to swym,   bolted
And preissit upon the taiddis bak to clym.

The dreid of deith hir strenthis gart incres,   made to
And forcit hir defend with mycht and mane.
The mous upwart, the paddok doun can pres;
Quhyle to, quhyle fra, quhyle doukit up agane.
This selie mous, this plungit in grit pane,
Gan fecht als lang as breith wes in hir breist,
Till at the last scho cryit for ane preist.

Fechtand thusgait, the gled sat on ane twist,   kite; twig
And to this wretchit battell tuke gude heid;
And with ane wisk, or owthir off thame wist,   whoosh; before either; knew
He claucht his cluke betwix thame in the threid;   caught; claw
Syne to the land he flew with thame gude speid,
Fane off that fang, pyipand with mony pew;   Glad of that booty
Syne lowsit thame, and baith but pietie slew.   without

Syne bowellit thame, that boucheour with his bill,   disembowelled
And bellieflaucht full fettislie thame fled,   belly-skinned them neatly
Bot all thair flesche wald scant be half ane fill,
And guttis als, unto that gredie gled.   as well
Off thair debait, thus quhen I hard outred,   heard settled
He tuke his flicht and ouer the feildis flaw.
Giff this be trew, speir ye at thame that saw.

Moralitas
My brother, gif thow will tak advertence,   heed of
Be this fabill thow may persave and se
It passis far all kynd of pestilence   far surpasses
Ane wickit mynd with wordis fair and sle.   cunning
Be war thairfore with quhome thow fallowis the,   associate yourself
For thow wer better beir of stane the barrow,   carry stone in a barrow
Or sweitand dig and delf quhill thow may dre,   delve; endure
Than to be matchit with ane wickit marrow.   companion

Ane fals intent under ane fair pretence
Hes causit mony innocent for to de;
Grit folie is to gif ouer sone credence   too soon
To all that speiks fairlie unto the;
Ane silkin toung, ane hart of crueltie,
Smytis more sore than ony schot of arrow;
Brother, gif thow be wyse, I reid the fle   advise you
To matche the with ane thrawart fenyeit marrow.   twisted, deceitful

I warne the also, it is grit nekligence
To bind the fast quhair thow wes frank and fre:
Fra thow be bund, thow may mak na defence
To saif thy lyfe nor yit thy libertie.
This simpill counsall, brother, tak at me,
And it to cun perqueir se thow not tarrow: know by heart; delay
Better but stryfe to leif allane in le   alone in shelter
Than to be matchit with ane wickit marrow.

This hald in mynd; rycht more I sall the tell
Quhair by thir beistis may be figurate: Which; these; illustrated
The paddok, usand in the flude to duell,
Is mannis bodie, swymand air and late   all the time
In to this warld, with cairis implicate: tangled
Now hie, now law, quhylis plungit up, quhylis doun,
Ay in perrell, and reddie for to droun;

Now dolorus, now blyth as bird on breir;
Now in fredome, now wardit in distres;
Now haill and sound, now deid and brocht on beir;   (funeral) bier
Now pure as Job, now rowand in riches;   poor
Now gounis gay, now brats laid in pres;   rags; cupboard
Now full as fische, now hungrie as ane hound;
Now on the quheill, now wappit to the groun.   wheel (of fortune); hurled

This lytill mous, heir knit thus be the schyn,   tied by the shin
The saull of man betakin may in deid –   signifies in fact

Bundin, and fra the bodie may not twyn,	part
Quhill cruell deith cum brek of lyfe the threid –	
The quhilk to droun suld ever stand in dreid	
Of carnall lust be the suggestioun,	
Quhilk drawis ay the saull and druggis doun.	drags

The watter is the warld, ay welterand	weltering
With mony wall of tribulatioun,	waves
In quhilk the saull and bodye wer steirrand,	moving about
Standand distinyt in thair opinioun:	belief
The spreit upwart, the body precis doun;	
The saull rycht fane wald be brocht ouer, I wis,	gladly
Out of this warld into the hevinnis blis.	

The gled is deith, that cummis suddandlie	
As dois ane theif, and cuttis sone the battall:	soon cuts short; battle
Be vigilant thairfoir and ay reddie,	
For mannis lyfe is brukill and ay mortall.	frail
My freind, thairfoir, mak the ane strang castell	
Of gud deidis, for deith will the assay,	test you
Thow wait not quhen – evin, morrow, or midday.	know

Adew, my freind, and gif that ony speiris	asks
Of this fabill, sa schortlie I conclude,	
Say thow, I left the laif unto the freiris,	rest of it; friars
To mak a sample or similitude.	
Now Christ for us that deit on the rude,	died; cross
Of saull and lyfe as thow art Salviour,	
Grant us till pas in till ane blissit hour.	

The Testament of Cresseid

Ane doolie sessoun to ane cairfull dyte	dreary season; sad tale
Suld correspond and be equivalent:	
Richt sa it wes quhen I began to wryte	
This tragedie; the wedder richt fervent,	severe
Quhen Aries, in middis of the Lent,	(early April)
Schouris of haill gart fra the north discend,	caused
That scantlie fra the cauld I micht defend.	

Yit nevertheles within myne oratur	study/private chapel
I stude, quhen Titan had his bemis bricht	(the sun)
Withdrawin doun and sylit under cure,	closed under cover
And fair Venus, the bewtie of the nicht,	
Uprais and set unto the west full richt	
Hir goldin face, in oppositioun	
Of God Phebus, direct discending doun.	

Throw out the glas hir bemis brast sa fair   *glass; burst*
That I micht se on everie syde me by;
The northin wind had purifyit the air
And sched the mistie cloudis fra the sky;
The froist freisit, the blastis bitterly
Fra Pole Artick come quhisling loud and schill,
And causit me remufe aganis my will.

For I traistit that Venus, luifis quene,
To quhome sum tyme I hecht obedience,   *promised*
My faidit hart of lufe scho wald mak grene,
And therupon with humbill reverence
I thocht to pray hir hie magnificence;
Bot for greit cald as than I lattit was   *prevented*
And in my chalmer to the fyre can pas.   *room*

Thocht lufe be hait, yit in ane man of age   *hot*
It kendillis nocht sa sone as in youtheid,
Of quhome the blude is flowing in ane rage;
And in the auld the curage doif and deid   *desire dull*
Of quhilk the fyre outward is best remeid: *remedy*
To help be phisike quhair that nature faillit   *by medicine*
I am expert, for baith I have assaillit.   *tried*

I mend the fyre and beikit me about,   *stoked and huddled*
Than tuik ane drink, my spreitis to comfort,
And armit me weill fra the cauld thairout.
To cut the winter nicht and mak it schort
I tuik ane quair – and left all uther sport –   *book*
Writtin be worthie Chaucer glorious
Of fair Creisseid and worthie Troylus.

And thair I fand, efter that Diomeid
Ressavit had that lady bricht of hew,   *Had received*
How Troilus neir out of wit abraid   *went out of his mind*
And weipit soir with visage paill of hew;
For quhilk wanhope his teiris can renew,   *despair*
Quhill esperance rejoisit him agane: *hope*
Thus quhyle in joy he levit, quhyle in pane.

Of hir behest he had greit comforting,   *promise*
Traisting to Troy that scho suld mak retour,   *return*
Quhilk he desyrit maist of eirdly thing,
For quhy scho was his only paramour.
Bot quhen he saw passit baith day and hour
Of hir ganecome, than sorrow can oppres   *return*
His wofull hart in cair and hevines.

Of his distres me neidis nocht reheirs,
For worthie Chauceir in the samin buik,
In gudelie termis and in joly veirs,
Compylit hes his cairis, quha will luik.
To brek my sleip ane uther quair I tuik,
In quhilk I fand the fatall destenie
Of fair Cresseid, that endit wretchitlie.

Quha wait gif all that Chauceir wrait was trew?   Who knows
Nor I wait nocht gif this narratioun
Be authoreist, or fenyeit of the new   legitimate or newly invented
Be sum poeit, throw his inventioun
Maid to report the lamentatioun
And wofull end of this lustie Creisseid,   beautiful
And quhat distres scho thoillit, and quhat deid.   endured; death

Quhen Diomeid had all his appetyte,
And mair, fulfillit of this fair ladie,
Upon ane uther he set his haill delyte,
And send to hir ane lybell of repudie   letter of divorce
And hir excludit fra his companie.
Than desolait scho walkit up and doun,
And sum men sayis, into the court, commoun.   (became a prostitute)

O fair Creisseid, the flour and A per se   paragon
Of Troy and Grece, how was thow fortunait   doomed
To change in filth all thy feminitie,
And be with fleschelie lust sa maculait,   stained
And go amang the Greikis air and lait,   all the time
Sa giglotlike takand thy foull plesance!   wantonly; pleasure
I have pietie thow suld fall sic mischance!

Yit nevertheles, quhat ever men deme or say   judge
In scornefull langage of thy brukkilnes,   frailty
I sall excuse als far furth as I may
Thy womanheid, thy wisdome and fairnes,
The quhilk fortoun hes put to sic distres
As hir pleisit, and nathing throw the gilt
Of the – throw wickit langage to be spilt!   slanderous talk; destroyed

This fair lady, in this wyse destitute
Of all comfort and consolatioun,
Richt privelie, but fellowschip or refute,   secretly, without; refuge
Disagysit passit far out of the toun
Ane myle or twa, unto ane mansioun
Beildit full gay, quhair hir father Calchas   Built
Quhilk than amang the Greikis dwelland was.

Quhen he hir saw, the caus he can inquyre
Of hir cumming: scho said, siching full soir,   sighing
'Fra Diomeid had gottin his desyre   From when
He wox werie and wald of me no moir.'   grew
Quod Calchas, 'Douchter, weip thow not thairfoir;
Peraventure all cummis for the best.
Welcum to me; thow art full deir ane gest!'

This auld Calchas, efter the law was tho,   according to the law then
Wes keiper of the tempill as ane preist
In quhilk Venus and hir sone Cupido
War honourit, and his chalmer was neist;
To quhilk Cresseid, with baill aneuch in breist,   sorrow
Usit to pas, hir prayeris for to say
Quhill at the last, upon ane solempne day,   holy

As custome was, the pepill far and neir
Befoir the none unto the tempill went   noon
With sacrifice, devoit in thair maneir;
Bot still Cresseid, hevie in hir intent
Into the kirk wald not hir self present,
For giving of the pepill ony deming   suspicion
Of hir expuls fra Diomeid the king;

Bot past into ane secreit orature,   chapel
Quhair scho micht weip hir wofull desteny.
Behind hir bak scho cloisit fast the dure
And on hir kneis bair fell doun in hy;   haste
Upon Venus and Cupide angerly
Scho cryit out, and said on this same wyse,
'Allace, that ever I maid yow sacrifice!

'Ye gave me anis ane devyne responsaill
That I suld be the flour of luif in Troy;
Now am I maid ane unworthie outwaill,   outcast
And all in cair translatit is my joy.
Quha sall me gyde? Quha sall me now convoy,
Sen I fra Diomeid and nobill Troylus
Am clene excludit, as abject odious?   pariah

'O fals Cupide, is nane to wyte bot thow   blame
And thy mother, of lufe the blind goddes!
Ye causit me alwayis understand and trow   believe
The seid of lufe was sawin in my face,   sown
And ay grew grene throw your supplie and grace.   support
Bot now, allace, that seid with froist is slane,
And I fra luifferis left, and all forlane.'   abandoned

Quhen this was said, doun in ane extasie,
Ravischit in spreit, intill ane dreame scho fell,
And be apperance hard, quhair scho did ly,   *And heard as it seemed*
Cupide the king ringand ane silver bell,
Quhilk men micht heir fra hevin unto hell;
At quhais sound befoir Cupide appeiris
The sevin planetis, discending fra thair spheiris;

Quhilk hes power of all thing generabill,   *over all created things*
To reull and steir be thair greit influence   *rule and move*
Wedder and wind, and coursis variabill:
And first of all Saturne gave his sentence,
Quhilk gave to Cupide litill reverence,
Bot as ane busteous churle on his maneir   *rough bloke*
Come crabitlie with auster luik and cheir.[1]   *ill-naturedly; austere*

His face fronsit, his lyre was lyke the leid,   *wrinkled; skin; lead*
His teith chatterit and cheverit with the chin,
His ene drowpit, how sonkin in his heid,   *eyes drooped*
Out of his nois the meldrop fast can rin,   *snotters*
With lippis bla and cheikis leine and thin;   *bluish*
The ice schoklis that fra his hair doun hang   *icicles*
Was wonder greit, and as ane speir als lang:

Atouir his belt his lyart lokkis lay   *Down over; grey*
Felterit unfair, ouirfret with froistis hoir,   *Tangled; overlaid; hoary*
His garmound and his gyte full gay of gray,   *garb; gown*
His widderit weid fra him the wind out woir   *His withered clothes fluttered*
Ane busteous bow within his hand he boir,   *stout*
Under his girdill ane flasche of felloun flanis   *sheaf of cruel arrows*
Fedderit with ice and heidit with hailstanis.

Than Juppiter, richt fair and amiabill,
God of the starnis in the firmament   *stars*
And nureis to all thing generabill;   *nurse/sustainer*
Fra his father Saturne far different,
With burelie face and browis bricht and brent,   *handsome; smooth*
Upon his heid ane garland wonder gay
Of flouris fair, as it had bene in May.[2]

His voice was cleir, as cristall wer his ene,
As goldin wyre sa glitterand was his hair,

---

1. Henryson draws on astrology and traditional medieval lore for his account of the planets. They are all noted for their inconstancy, which is Cresseid's failing after all. Saturn is the most malign of them, associated with the cold, dry sterility of old age; with pestilence and leprosy (of which he shows symptoms here), and the harshest labours of the poor.
2. Jupiter is portrayed as a ruddy, fair-skinned young man, here dressed in green (like the green man) and associated with growth. As Zeus he overthrew his father Cronos, king of the Titans.

His garmound and his gyte full gay of grene   garb and cloak
With goldin listis gilt on everie gair;   hems; section
Ane burelie brand about his middill bair,   stout sword
In his richt hand he had ane groundin speir,   sharpened
Of his father the wraith fra us to weir.   To guard us from his father's wrath

Nixt efter him come Mars the god of ire,
Of strife, debait, and all dissensioun,
To chide and fecht, als feirs as ony fyre,   as fierce
In hard harnes, hewmound, and habirgeoun,   hard armour and helmet
And on his hanche ane roustie fell falchioun,   hip; cruel curved blade
And in his hand he had ane roustie sword,
Wrything his face with mony angrie word.

Schaikand his sword, befoir Cupide he come,
With reid visage and grislie glowrand ene,
And at his mouth ane bullar stude of fome,   bubble; of froth
Lyke to ane bair quhetting his tuskis kene;   boar
Richt tuilyeour lyke, but temperance in tene,   brawler; without; in anger
Ane horne he blew with mony bosteous brag,   harsh blast

Quhilk all this warld with weir hes maid to wag.   war; shake
Than fair Phebus, lanterne and lamp of licht,
Of man and beist, baith frute and flourisching,
Tender nureis, and banischer of nicht;
And of the warld causing, be his moving
And influence, lyfe in all eirdlie thing,
Without comfort of quhome, of force to nocht   all that is made in this world must go to
Must all ga die that in this warld is wrocht.   /nothing and die

As king royall he raid upon his chair,   chariot
The quhilk Phaeton gydit sum tyme upricht;
The brichtnes of his face quhen it was bair
Nane micht behald for peirsing of his sicht;
This goldin cart with fyrie bemis bricht
Four yokkit steidis full different of hew
But bait or tyring throw the spheiris drew.   Without halting

The first was soyr, with mane als reid as rois,   sorrel
Callit Eoye, into the orient;
The secund steid to name hecht Ethios,   was called
Quhitlie and paill, and sum deill ascendent;   whitish
The thrid Peros, richt hait and richt fervent;   hot; fiery
The feird was blak, and callit Philogie,   fourth
Quhilk rollis Phebus doun into the sey.   sea

Venus was thair present, that goddes gay,
Hir sonnis querrell for to defend, and mak   *son's cause*
Hir awin complaint, cled in ane nyce array,   *wanton*
The ane half grene, the uther half sabill blak,
With hair as gold kemmit and sched abak;   *parted*
But in hir face semit greit variance,
Quhyles perfyte treuth and quhyles inconstance.[1]   *Sometimes*

Under smyling scho was dissimulait,
Provocative with blenkis amorous,   *glances*
And suddanely changit and alterait,
Angrie as ony serpent vennemous,
Richt pungitive with wordis odious;   *stinging*
Thus variant scho was, quha list tak keip: *if one chose to look*
With ane eye lauch, and with the uther weip,

In taikning that all fleschelie paramour   *As a token; love*
Quhilk Venus hes in reull and governance,   *rule*
Is sum tyme sweit, sum tyme bitter and sour,
Richt unstabill and full of variance,
Mingit with cairfull joy and fals plesance,   *Mixed*
Now hait, now cauld, now blyith, now full of wo,
Now grene as leif, now widderit and ago.   *withered and gone*

With buik in hand than come Mercurius,
Richt eloquent and full of rethorie,   *rhetoric*
With polite termis and delicious,   *polished*
With pen and ink to report all reddie,
Setting sangis and singand merilie;
His hude was reid, heklit atouir his croun,   *fringed all round*
Lyke to ane poeit of the auld fassoun.   *style*

Boxis he bair with fyne electuairis,   *pastes and potions*
And sugerit syropis for digestioun,
Spycis belangand to the pothecairis,
With mony hailsum sweit confectioun;
Doctour in phisick, cled in ane skarlot goun,
And furrit weill, as sic ane aucht to be;   *trimmed with fur*
Honest and gude, and not ane word culd lie.[2]

Nixt efter him come lady Cynthia, (the Moon)
The last of all and swiftest in hir spheir;

1. Venus's son (by Mars, or Mercury, or perhaps Jupiter) is Cupid, whom Cresseid has renounced. Her 'variance' associates her with the fickleness of Fortune, symbolised by her contrasting costume, with green for hope and growth (but also inconstancy); and black for despair and death.
2. Associated here with fine speaking and medicine, Mercury's nature is also held to be changeable and many-sided, so this last comment is ironic.

Of colour blak, buskit with hornis twa,   dressed (her hair or a head-dress)
And in the nicht scho listis best appeir;   likes best
Haw as the leid, of colour nathing cleir,   Livid as lead
For all hir licht scho borrowis at hir brother
Titan, for of hir self scho hes nane uther.   (the Sun)

Hir gyte was gray and full of spottis blak,   cloak
And on hir breist ane churle paintit full evin   peasant was painted
Beirand ane bunche of thornis on his bak,   ('the man on the moon')
Quhilk for his thift micht clim na nar the hevin.
Thus quhen thay gadderit war, thir goddes sevin,
Mercurius thay cheisit with ane assent
To be foirspeikar in the parliament.   spokesman

Quha had bene thair and liken for to heir   inclined to listen
His facound toung and termis exquisite,   eloquent
Of rethorick the prettick he micht leir,   practice; learn
In breif sermone ane pregnant sentence wryte.
Befoir Cupide veiling his cap alyte,   taking off; a little
Speiris the caus of that vocatioun,   Asks; summons
And he anone schew his intentioun.   revealed

'Lo', quod Cupide, 'quha will blaspheme the name
Of his awin god, outher in word or deid,
To all goddis he dois baith lak and schame,   insult
And suld have bitter panis to his meid.   pains; reward
I say this by yone wretchit Cresseid,
The quhilk throw me was sum tyme flour of lufe,
Me and my mother starklie can reprufe,   reproach

'Saying of hir greit infelicitie
I was the caus, and my mother Venus,
Ane blind goddes hir cald that micht not se,   called
With sclander and defame injurious.
Thus hir leving unclene and lecherous   life
Scho wald retorte in me and my mother,   blame
To quhome I schew my grace abone all uther.

'And sen ye ar all sevin deificait,   deified
Participant of devyne sapience,   Partaking
This greit injurie done to our hie estait
Me think with pane we suld mak recompence;
Was never to goddes done sic violence:
Asweill for yow as for my self I say,
Thairfoir ga help to revenge, I yow pray!'

Mercurius to Cupide gave answeir
And said, 'Schir King, my counsall is that ye
Refer yow to the hiest planeit heir
And tak to him the lawest of degre,   And attach
The pane of Cresseid for to modifie: determine
As God Saturne, with him tak Cynthia.'
'I am content', quod he, 'to tak thay twa.'

Than thus proceidit Saturne and the Mone
Quhen thay the mater rypelie had degest: maturely; considered
For the dispyte to Cupide scho had done   injury
And to Venus, oppin and manifest,
In all hir lyfe with pane to be opprest,
And torment sair with seiknes incurabill,
And to all lovers be abhominabill.

This duleful sentence Saturne tuik on hand,
And passit doun quhair cairfull Cresseid lay,   sorrowful
And on hir heid he laid ane frostie wand;
Than lawfullie on this wyse can he say,
'Thy greit fairnes and all thy bewtie gay,
Thy wantoun blude, and eik thy goldin hair,
Heir I exclude fra the for evermair.

'I change thy mirth into melancholy,
Quhilk is the mother of all pensivenes;
Thy moisture and thy heit in cald and dry;
Thyne insolence, thy play and wantones,
To greit diseis; thy pomp and thy riches   distress
In mortall neid; and greit penuritie
Thow suffer sall, and as ane beggar die.'

O cruell Saturne, fraward and angrie,   ill-tempered
Hard is thy dome and to malitious!   judgement
On fair Cresseid quhy hes thow na mercie,
Quhilk was sa sweit, gentill and amorous?
Withdraw thy sentence and be gracious –
As thow was never; sa schawis through thy deid,
Ane wraikfull sentence gevin on fair Cresseid.   vengeful

Than Cynthia, quhen Saturne past away,   Then
Out of hir sait discendit doun belyve,   quickly
And red ane bill on Cresseid quhair scho lay,   passed a sentence
Contening this sentence diffinityve:
'Fra heit of bodie here I the depryve,

And to thy seiknes sall be na recure   recovery
Bot in dolour thy dayis to indure.

'Thy cristall ene mingit with blude I mak,
Thy voice sa cleir unplesand hoir and hace,   harsh and hoarse
Thy lustie lyre ouirspred with spottis blak,   beautiful skin
And lumpis haw appeirand in thy face: livid
Quhair thow cummis, ilk man sall fle the place.
This sall thow go begging fra hous to hous
With cop and clapper lyke ane lazarous.'[1]   cup; leper

This doolie dreame, this uglye visioun
Brocht to ane end, Cresseid fra it awoik,
And all that court and convocatioun
Vanischit away: than rais scho up and tuik
Ane poleist glas, and hir schaddow culd luik;
And quhen scho saw hir face sa deformait,
Gif scho in hart was wa aneuch, God wait!   sad; knows

Weiping full sair, 'Lo, quhat it is', quod sche,
'With fraward langage for to mufe and steir   adverse; provoke; stir up
Our craibit goddis; and sa is sene on me!   ill-tempered
My blaspheming now have I bocht full deir;
All eirdlie joy and mirth I set areir.   behind me
Allace, this day; allace, this wofull tyde
Quhen I began with my goddis for to chyde!'

Be this was said, ane chyld come fra the hall   When
To warne Cresseid the supper was reddy;
First knokkit at the dure, and syne culd call,
'Madame, your father biddis yow cum in hy: haste
He hes mervell sa lang on grouf ye ly,   face-down
And sayis your beedes bene to lang sum deill;   prayers; somewhat too long
The goddis wait all your intent full weill.'   know

Quod scho, 'Fair chyld, ga to my father deir
And pray him cum to speik with me anone.'
And sa he did, and said, 'Douchter, quhat cheir?'
'Allace!' quod scho, 'Father, my mirth is gone!'
'How sa?' quod he, and scho can all expone,   explain
As I have tauld, the vengeance and the wraik   revenge
For hir trespas Cupide on hir culd tak.

1. Saturn's curse invokes the symptoms of leprosy, which medieval times associated with sexual promiscuity. Like Saturn, the Moon is also leper-like in her pale and blotched appearance. The clapper is to warn the public when Cresseid walks among them with her begging cup.

He luikit on hir uglye lipper face,
The quhylk befor was quhite as lillie flour;
Wringand his handis, oftymes said allace
That he had levit to se that wofull hour;   *lived*
For he knew weill that thair was na succour
To hir seiknes, and that dowblit his pane;
Thus was thair cair aneuch betwix thame twane.

Quhen thay togidder murnit had full lang,
Quod Cresseid, 'Father, I wald not be kend;   *recognised*
Thairfoir in secreit wyse ye let me gang
To yone hospitall at the tounis end,
And thidder sum meit for cheritie me send
To leif upon, for all mirth in this eird
Is fra me gane; sic is my wickit weird!'   *evil fate*

Than in ane mantill and ane baver hat,
With cop and clapper, wonder prively,   *very secretly*
He opnit ane secreit yet and out thair at
Convoyit hir, that na man suld espy,
Unto ane village half ane myle thairby;
Delyverit hir in at the spittaill hous,   *leper-house*
And daylie sent hir part of his almous.   *alms*

Sum knew hir weill, and sum had na knawledge
Of hir becaus scho was sa deformait,
With bylis blak ouirspred in hir visage,   *boils*
And hir fair colour faidit and alterait.
Yit thay presumit, for hir hie regrait   *distress*
And still murning, scho was of nobill kin;
With better will thairfoir they tuik hir in.

The day passit and Phebus went to rest,
The cloudis blak ouerheled all the sky.   *covered up*
God wait gif Cresseid was ane sorrowfull gest
Seing that uncouth fair and harbery!   *food and lodging*
But meit or drink scho dressit hir to ly   *Without; prepared*
In ane dark corner of the hous allone,
And on this wyse, weiping, scho maid hir mone.

The Complaint of Cresseid
'O sop of sorrow, sonkin into cair,
O cative Creisseid, now and ever mair   *wretched*
Gane is thy joy and all thy mirth in eird;   *earth*
Of all blyithnes now art thou blaiknit bair;   *blanched and bare*
Thair is na salve may saif or sound thy sair!   *heal; wound*

Fell is thy fortoun, wickit is thy weird,   Cruel
Thy blys is baneist, and thy baill on breird!   misery sprouting
Under the eirth, God gif I gravin wer,   buried
Quhair nane of Grece nor yit of Troy micht heird!   hear of it

'Quhair is thy chalmer wantounlie besene,   luxuriously arrayed
With burely bed and bankouris browderit bene;   handsome; covers well embroidered
Spycis and wyne to thy collatioun,
The cowpis all of gold and silver schene,   shining
Thy sweit meitis servit in plaittis clene
With saipheron sals of ane gude sessoun;   saffron sauce; flavour
Thy gay garmentis with mony gudely goun,
Thy plesand lawn pinnit with goldin prene?   linen; pins
All is areir, thy greit royall renoun!   behind you

'Quhair is thy garding with thir greissis gay
And fresche flowris, quhilk the quene Floray
Had paintit plesandly in everie pane,   part
Quhair thou was wont full merilye in May
To walk and tak the dew be it was day,   when
And heir the merle and mavis mony ane,   blackbird; thrush
With ladyis fair in carrolling to gane
And se the royall rinkis in thair array,   soldiers
In garmentis gay garnischit on everie grane?   detail

'Thy greit triumphand fame and hie honour,
Quhair thou was callit of eirdlye wichtis flour,   creatures
All is decayit, thy weird is welterit so;   overturned
Thy hie estait is turnit in darknes dour;
This lipper ludge tak for thy burelie bour,   handsome bower
And for thy bed tak now ane bunche of stro,
For waillit wyne and meitis thou had tho   choice; then
Tak mowlit breid, peirrie and ceder sour;   mouldy; pear juice; cider
Bot cop and clapper now is all ago.

'My cleir voice and courtlie carrolling,
Quhair I was wont with ladyis for to sing,
Is rawk as ruik, full hiddeous, hoir and hace;   raucous; rook
My plesand port, all utheris precelling,   deportment; excelling
Of lustines I was hald maist conding –   beauty; worthy
Now is deformit the figour of my face;
To luik on it na leid now lyking hes.   person
Sowpit in syte, I say with sair siching,   Sunk in sorrow; sighing
Ludgeit amang the lipper leid, "Allace!"

'O ladyis fair of Troy and Grece, attend
My miserie, quhilk nane may comprehend,

My frivoll fortoun, my infelicitie,   *fickle*
My greit mischeif, quhilk na man can amend.
Be war in tyme, approchis neir the end,   *Beware*
And in your mynd ane mirrour mak of me:
As I am now, peradventure that ye
For all your micht may cum to that same end,
Or ellis war, gif ony war may be.   *worse*

'Nocht is your fairnes bot ane faiding flour
Nocht is your famous laud and hie honour   *reputation*
Bot wind inflat in uther mennis eiris,
Your roising reid to rotting sall retour;   *red-rosy (cheeks); return*
Exempill mak of me in your memour
Quhilk of sic thingis wofull witnes beiris.
All welth in eird, away as wind it weiris;
Be war thairfoir, approchis neir your hour;
Fortoun is fikkill quhen scho beginnis and steiris.'   *stirs about*

Thus chydand with hir drerie destenye,
Weiping scho woik the nicht fra end to end;   *stayed awake*
Bot all in vane; hir dule, hir cairfull cry,   *grief*
Micht not remeid, nor yit hir murning mend.
Ane lipper lady rais and till hir wend,   *went*
And said, 'Quhy spurnis thow aganis the wall   *kick*
To sla thy self and mend nathing at all?

'Sen thy weiping dowbillis bot thy wo,   *Since*
I counsall the mak vertew of ane neid;   *necessity*
Go leir to clap thy clapper to and fro,   *learn*
And leif efter the law of lipper leid.'   *live; people*
Thair was na buit, bot furth with thame scho yeid   *help; went*
Fra place to place, quhill cauld and hounger sair
Compellit hir to be ane rank beggair.

That samin tyme, of Troy the garnisoun,   *garrison*
Quhilk had to chiftane worthie Troylus,
Throw jeopardie of weir had strikken doun   *fortunes of war*
Knichtis of Grece in number mervellous;
With greit tryumphe and laude victorious
Agane to Troy richt royallie thay raid
The way quhair Cresseid with the lipper baid.   *stayed*

Seing that companie, all with ane stevin   *one voice*
Thay gaif ane cry, and schuik coppis gude speid,
'Worthie lordis, for Goddis lufe of hevin,
To us lipper part of your almous deid!'

Than to thair cry nobill Troylus tuik heid,
Having pietie, neir by the place can pas
Quhair Cresseid sat, not witting quhat scho was.   knowing who

Than upon him scho kest up baith hir ene,
And with ane blenk it come into his thocht
That he sumtime hir face befoir had sene,
Bot scho was in sic plye he knew hir nocht;   plight
Yit than hir luik into his mynd it brocht
The sweit visage and amorous blenking   glances
Of fair Cresseid, sumtyme his awin darling.

Na wonder was, suppois in mynd that he
Tuik hir figure sa sone, and lo, now quhy: perceived
The idole of ane thing in cace may be   image; by chance
Sa deip imprentit in the fantasy   memory
That it deludis the wittis outwardly,
And sa appeiris in forme and lyke estait
Within the mynd as it was figurait.   imagined

Ane spark of lufe than till his hart culd spring
And kendlit all his bodie in ane fyre;
With hait fevir, ane sweit and trimbling
Him tuik, quhill he was reddie to expyre;
To beir his scheild his breist began to tyre;
Within ane quhyle he changit mony hew;
And nevertheles not ane ane uther knew.

For knichtlie pietie and memoriall   remembrance
Of fair Cresseid, ane gyrdill can he tak,   belt
Ane purs of gold, and mony gay jowall,
And in the skirt of Cresseid doun can swak;   tossed
Than raid away and not ane word he spak,
Pensive in hart, quhill he come to the toun,
And for greit cair oft syis almaist fell doun.   often times

The lipper folk to Cresseid than can draw
To se the equall distributioun
Of the almous, bot quhen the gold thay saw,
Ilk ane to uther prevelie can roun,   secretly whisper
And said, 'Yone lord hes mair affectioun,
How ever it be, unto yone lazarous
Than to us all; we knaw be his almous.'

'Quhat lord is yone,' quod scho, 'have ye na feill,   knowledge
Hes done to us so greit humanitie?'

'Yes,' quod a lipper man, 'I knaw him weill;
Schir Troylus it is, gentill and fre.'
Quhen Cresseid understude that it was he,
Stiffer than steill thair stert ane bitter stound   *stronger; pang*
Throwout hir hart, and fell doun to the ground.

Quhen scho ouircome, with siching sair and sad,   *recovered*
With mony cairfull cry and cald ochane: *cold lamentation*
'Now is my breist with stormie stoundis stad,   *beset*
Wrappit in wo, ane wretch full will of wane!'   *bewildered of hope*
Than fel in swoun full oft or ever scho fane,   *stopped*
And ever in hir swouning cryit scho thus,
'O fals Cresseid and trew knicht Troylus!

'Thy lufe, thy lawtie, and thy gentilnes   *loyalty*
I countit small in my prosperitie,
Sa efflated I was in wantones,   *puffed up*
And clam upon the fickill quheill sa hie.
All faith and lufe I promissit to the
Was in the self fickill and frivolous: *itself*
O fals Cresseid and trew knicht Troilus!

'For lufe of me thow keipt continence,
Honest and chaist in conversatioun;
Of all wemen protectour and defence
Thou was, and helpit thair opinioun;   *reputation*
My mynd in fleschelie foull affectioun
Was inclynit to lustis lecherous:
Fy, fals Cresseid; O trew knicht Troylus!

'Lovers be war and tak gude heid about
Quhome that ye lufe, for quhome ye suffer paine.
I lat yow wit, thair is richt few thairout   *I'll have you know*
Quhome ye may traist to have trew lufe agane;
Preif quhen ye will, your labour is in vaine.   *Prove it*
Thairfoir I reid ye tak thame as ye find,
For thay ar sad as widdercok in wind.   *steady*

'Becaus I knaw the greit unstabilnes,
Brukkill as glas, into my self, I say –
Traisting in uther als greit unfaithfulnes,   *Expecting*
Als unconstant, and als untrew of fay –   *faith*
Thocht sum be trew, I wait richt few ar thay;
Quha findis treuth, lat him his lady ruse;   *praise*
Nane but my self as now I will accuse.'

Quhen this was said, with paper scho sat doun,
And on this maneir maid hir testament:
'Heir I beteiche my corps and carioun   commit
With wormis and with taidis to be rent;   toads
My cop and clapper, and myne ornament,
And all my gold the lipper folk sall have,
Quhen I am deid, to burie me in grave.

'This royall ring, set with this rubie reid,
Quhilk Troylus in drowrie to me send,   love-token
To him agane I leif it quhen I am deid,
To mak my cairfull deid unto him kend.   sorrowful death; known
Thus I conclude schortlie and mak ane end:
My spreit I leif to Diane, quhair scho dwellis,   (Goddess of Chastity)
To walk with hir in waist woddis and wellis.   wild; springs

'O Diomeid, thou hes baith broche and belt
Quhilk Troylus gave me in takning
Of his trew lufe', and with that word scho swelt.   died
And sone ane lipper man tuik of the ring,
Syne buryit hir withouttin tarying;
To Troylus furthwith the ring he bair,
And of Cresseid the deith he can declair.

Quhen he had hard hir greit infirmitie,
Hir legacie and lamentatioun,
And how scho endit in sic povertie,
He swelt for wo and fell doun in ane swoun;   collapsed
For greit sorrow his hart to brist was boun;   burst
Siching full sadlie, said, 'I can no moir;
Scho was untrew and wo is me thairfoir.'

Sum said he maid ane tomb of merbell gray,
And wrait hir name and superscriptioun,
And laid it on hir grave quhair that scho lay,
In goldin letteris, conteining this ressoun: statement
'Lo, fair ladyis! Cresseid of Troyis toun,
Sumtyme countit the flour of womanheid,
Under this stane, lait lipper, lyis deid.'

Now, worthie wemen, in this ballet schort,   poem
Maid for your worschip and instructioun,
Of cheritie, I monische and exhort,   admonish
Ming not your lufe with fals deceptioun: Mix
Beir in your mynd this sore conclusioun
Of fair Cresseid, as I have said befoir.
Sen scho is deid I speik of hir no moir.

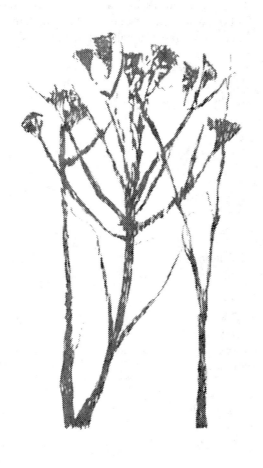

Aithbhreac Inghean Corcadail (c. 1460)

Bards were expected to write elegies as well as eulogies, and they used highly developed poetic conventions of lament and praise to this end. Aithbhreac Inghean Corcadail would not have been a professional bard herself, so she allows a more

A phaidrín do dhúisg mo dhéar

A phaidrín do dhúisg mo dhéar,
ionmhain méar do bhitheadh ort;
ionmhain cridhe fáilteach fial
   'gá raibhe riamh gus a nocht.

Dá éag is tuirseach atáim,
an lámh má mbítheá gach n-uair;
nach cluinim a beith i gclí
agus nach bhfaicim í uaim.

Mo chridhe-se is tinn atá
ó theacht go crích an lá dhúinn;
ba ghoirid do éist ré ghlóir,
ré h-agallaimh an óig úir.

Béal asa ndob aobhdha glór,
dhéantaidhe a ghó is gach tír:
leómhan Muile na múr ngeal,
seabhag Ile na magh mín.

Fear ba ghéar meabhair ar dhán,
ó nach deachaidh dámh gan díol;
taoiseach deigh-einigh suairc séimh,
agá bhfaightí méin mheic ríogh.

Dámh ag teacht ó Dhún an Óir
is dámh ón Bhóinn go a fholt fiar:
minic thánaig iad fá theist,
ní mionca ná leis a riar.

Seabhag seangglan Sléibhe Gaoil,
fear do chuir a chaoin ré cléir ;
dreagan Leódhuis na learg ngeal,
éigne Sanais na sreabh séimh.

personal note to enter this lament for her husband, who was chief of the MacNeill clan on the little island of Gigha. Her song comes to us from the Book of the Dean of Lismore.

O rosary that recalled my tear

O rosary that recalled my tear,
dear was the finger in my sight,
that touched you once, beloved the heart
of him who owned you till tonight.

I grieve the death of him whose hand
you did entwine each hour of prayer;
my grief that it is lifeless now
and I no longer see it there.

My heart is sick, the day has reached
its end for us two, brief the span
that I was given to enjoy
the converse of this goodly man.

Lips whose speech made pleasant sound,
in every land beguiling all,
hawk of Islay of smooth plains,
lion of Mull of the white wall.

His memory for songs was keen,
no poet left him without fee,
nobly generous, courteous, calm,
of princely character was he.

Poets came from Dun an Óir,
and from the Boyne, to him whose hair
was all in curls, drawn by his fame;
to each he gave a generous share.

Slim handsome hawk of Sliabh Gaoil,
who satisfied the clergy's hopes,
salmon of Sanas of quiet stream,
dragon of Lewis of sun-drenched slopes.

A h-éagmhais aon duine a mháin
im aonar atáim dá éis,
gan chluiche, gan chomhrádh caoin,
gan ábhacht, gan aoibh i gcéill.

Gan duine ris dtig mo mhiann
ar sliocht na Niall ó Niall óg;
gan mhuirn gan mheadhair ag mnáibh,
gan aoibhneas an dáin im dhóigh.

Mar thá Giodha an fhuinn mhín,
Dún Suibhne do-chím gan cheól,
faithche longphuirt na bhfear bhfial:
aithmhéala na Niall a n-eól.

Cúis ar lúthgháire má seach,
gusa mbímis ag teacht mall:
's nach fuilngim a nois, mo nuar,
a fhaicinn uam ar gach ard.

Má bhrisis, a Mheic Dhé bhí,
ar bagaide na dtrí gcnó,
fa fíor do ghabhais ar ngiall:
do bhainis an trian ba mhó.

Cnú mhullaigh a mogaill féin
bhaineadh do Chloinn Néill go nua:
is tric roighne na bhfear bhfial
go leabaidh na Niall a nuas.

An rogha fá deireadh díbh
's é thug gan mo bhrígh an sgéal:
do sgar riom mo leathchuing rúin,
a phaidrín do dhúisg mo dhéar.

Is briste mo chridhe im chlí,
agus bídh nó go dtí m'éag,
ar éis an abhradh dhuibh úir,
a phaidrín do dhúisg mo dhéar.

Muire mháthair, muime an Ríogh,
go robh 'gam dhíon ar gach séad,
's a Mac do chruthuigh gach dúil,
a phaidrín do dhúisg mo dhéar.

Bereft of this man, all alone
I live, and take no part in play,
enjoy no kindly talk, nor mirth,
now that his smiles have gone away.

Niall Og is dead; none of his clan
can hold my interest for long;
the ladies droop, their mirth is stilled,
I cannot hope for joy in song.

Gigha of smooth soil is bereft,
no need of music Dun Suibhne feels,   Castle Sween (in Knapdale)
the grass grows green round the heroes' fort;
they know the sorrow of the MacNeills.

The fort that brought us mirth, each time
we made our way there; now the sight
of it is more than I can bear
as I look on it from each height.

If Thou, Son of the living God,
hast breached the cluster on the tree,
Thou hast taken from us our choicest nut,
and plucked the greatest of the three.

The topmost nut of the bunch is plucked,
Clan Neill has newly lost its head:
often the best of the generous men
descends to the MacNeills' last bed.

His death, the finest of them all,
has sapped my strength, and cost me dear,
taking away my darling spouse,
O rosary that recalled my tear.

My heart is broken in my breast,
and will not heal till death, I fear,
now that the dark-eyed one is dead,
O rosary that recalled my tear.

May Mary Mother, the King's nurse,
guard each path I follow here,
and may Her Son watch over me,
O rosary that recalled my tear.

trans. Derick Thomson

William Dunbar (1460–1520?)

Educated at St Andrews' University, Dunbar may have been a Franciscan novice, before visiting Paris and Oxford and serving King James IV as courtier and ambassador during the last ten years of the century. Most of Dunbar's surviving poems date from this period, when Scotland was on the threshold of the Renaissance – a 'golden age' which ended when James IV and so many Scots lords died on Flodden field in 1513. As a professional poet at Court, Dunbar celebrated public events such as the king's marriage or a royal visit to Aberdeen, and he wrote formal poems of great technical brilliance. But there is a wilder humour and also a darker, more personal and melancholic side to his character which gives him a unique and memorable voice.

Quhat is this Lyfe?

Quhat is this lyfe bot ane straucht way to deid,	death
Quhilk hes a tyme to pas and nane to dwell;	(That has) a time to go
A slyding qheill us lent to seik remeid.	moving wheel; salvation
A fre chois gevin to paradice or hell,	
A pray to deid, quhome vane is to repell;	prey to death
A schoirt torment for infineit glaidnes –	
Als schort ane joy for lestand hevynes.	As; lasting sorrow

Ane Ballat of Our Lady

Hale sterne superne; hale, in eterne	glorious star
In Godis sicht to schyne;	
Lucerne in derne for to discerne	Lamp in secret
Be glory and grace devyne;	By way of
Hodiern, modern, sempitern,	Today, now, always
Angelicall regyne:	Queen of the angels
Our tern inferne for to dispern	gloom; dispel
Helpe, rialest rosyne.	rose-bush
Ave Maria, gracia plena:	
Haile, fresche floure femynyne;	
Yerne us guberne, virgin matern	Govern us diligently
Of reuth baith rute and ryne.	compassion; root and bark

Haile, yhyng benyng fresche flurising,	young; blossom
Haile, Alphais habitakle;	God's habitation
Thy dyng ofspring maid us to syng	worthy
Befor his tabernakle;	
All thing maling we doune thring	malign; hurl down
Be sicht of his signakle,	sign (of the Cross)
Quhilk king, us bring unto his ryng	reign
Fro dethis dirk umbrakle.	death's; shade
Ave Maria, gracia plena:	
Haile, moder and maide but makle;	without blemish
Bricht syng, gladyng our languissing	making glad our sorrow
Be micht of thi mirakle.	
Haile, bricht be sicht in hevyn on hicht;	
Haile, day sterne orientale;	
Our licht most richt in clud of nycht	
Our dirknes for to scale:	scatter
Hale, wicht in ficht, puttar to flicht	valiant
Of fendis in battale;	
Haile, plicht but sicht; hale, mekle of mycht;	anchor without display
Haile, glorius virgin, hale;	
Ave Maria, gracia plena:	
Haile, gentill nychttingale;	
Way stricht, cler dicht, to wilsome wicht	straight; prepared for erring folk
That irke bene in travale.	That are weary in travel
Hale, qwene serene; hale, most amene;	
Haile, hevinlie hie emprys;	
Haile, schene unseyne with carnale eyne;	unseen bright one; bodily eyes
Haile, ros of paradys;	
Haile, clene bedene ay till conteyne;	completely pure always to endure
Haile, fair fresche floure delyce;	lily (fleur-de-lis)
Haile, grene daseyne; haile fro the splene	daisy; heart
Of Jhesu genitrice;	mother
Ave Maria, gracia plena:	
Thow baire the prince of prys;	
Our teyne to meyne and ga betweyne	To mediate our affliction
As humile oratrice.	intercessor
Haile, more decore than of before	beautiful
And swetar be sic sevyne,	seven times sweeter
Our glore forlore for to restore	
Sen thow art qwene of hevyn;	
Memore of sore, stern in aurore,	Reminder of affliction; star; dawn
Lovit with angellis stevyne;	loved; voice
Implore, adore, thow indeflore,	undeflowered

To mak our oddis evyne.
   Ave Maria, gracia plena:
With lovingis lowde ellevyn   *eleven loud praises*
Quhill store and hore my youth devore   *struggle and age*
   Thy name I sall ay nevyne.   *declare*

Empryce of prys, imperatrice,
   Bricht polist precious stane;
Victrice of vyce, hie genitrice
   Of Jhesu lord soverayne;
Our wys pavys fro enemys   *shield*
   Agane the Feyndis trayne;   *treachery*
Oratrice, mediatrice, salvatrice,
   To God gret suffragane;   *(holy) deputy*
     Ave Maria, gracia plena:
   Haile, sterne meridiane;   *midday star*
Spyce, flour delice of paradys
   That baire the gloryus grayne.   *seed*

Imperiall wall, place palestrall   *magnificent home*
   Of peirles pulcritud;
Tryumphale hall, hie trone regall   *throne*
   Of Godis celsitud;   *majesty*
Hospitall riall, the lord of all   *Royal lodging*
   Thy closet did include;   *Your (womb) enclosed the Lord of all*
Bricht ball cristall, ros virginall
   Fulfillit of angell fude.   *Replete with*
     Ave Maria, gracia plena:
   Thy birth has with his blude
Fra fall mortall originall
   Us raunsound on the rude.   *Ransomed us on the Cross*

Surrexit Dominus de sepulchro   *The Lord is risen from the tomb*

Done is a battell on the dragon blak;
Our campion Chryst confoundit hes his force:[1]   *champion*
The yettis of hell ar brokin with a crak,   *gates*
The signe triumphall rasit is of the croce,
The divillis trymmillis with hiddous voce,   *devils quake; voice*
The saulis ar borrowit and to the bliss can go,   *redeemed*
Chryst with his blud our ransonis dois indoce: *endorse*
Surrexit Dominus de sepulchro.

---

1. This triumphant vision comes from the tradition that Christ 'harrowed Hell' between the crucifixion and the resurrection.

Dungin is the deidly dragon Lucifer,   Struck down
The crewall serpent with the mortall stang,   sting
The auld kene tegir with his teith on char   fierce; ajar
Quhilk in a wait hes lyne for us so lang
Thinking to grip us in his clowis strang:
The mercifull lord wald nocht that it wer so.
He maid him for to felye of that fang: fall short; capture
Surrexit Dominus de sepulchro.

He for our saik that sufferit to be slane
And lyk a lamb in sacrifice wes dicht
Is lyk a lyone rissin up agane
And as a gyane raxit him on hicht;   giant; stretched
Sprungin is Aurora radius and bricht,   radiant Dawn
On loft is gone the glorius Appollo,   into the air
The blisfull day depairtit fro the nycht:
Surrexit Dominus de sepulchro.

The grit victour agane is rissin on hicht
That for our querrell to the deth wes woundit;   cause
The sone that wox all paill now schynis bricht,   sun/son
And dirknes clerit, our fayth is now refoundit
The knell of mercy fra the hevin is soundit,
The Cristin ar deliverit of thair wo,
The Jowis and thair errour ar confoundit: Jews
Surrexit Dominus de sepulchro.

The fo is chasit, the battell is done ceis,
The presone brokin, the jevellouris fleit and flemit;   jailers
The weir is gon, confermit is the peis   war
The fetteris lowsit and the dungeoun temit,   let loose; emptied
The ransoun maid, the presoneris redemit;
The feild is win, ourcumin is the fo,
Dispulit of the tresur that he yemit: Stripped; guarded
Surrexit Dominus de sepulchro.

In Prays of Wemen

Now of wemen this I say for me,
Off erthly thingis nane may bettir be.
Thay suld haif wirschep and grit honoring
Off men aboif all uthir erthly thing.
Rycht grit dishonour upoun him self he takkis
In word or deid quha evir wemen lakkis,   disparages
Sen that of wemen cumin all ar we;   Since we all come from
Wemen ar wemen and sa will end and de.

Wo wirth the fruct wald put the tre to nocht,   Woe betide the fruit
And wo wirth him rycht so that sayis ocht
Off womanheid that may be ony lak,
Or sic grit schame upone him for to tak.
Thay us consaif with pane, and be thame fed   conceive
Within thair breistis thair we be boun to bed;   ready; childbed
Grit pane and wo and murnyng mervellus
Into thair birth thay suffir sair for us;
Than meit and drynk to feid us get we nane
Bot that we sowk out of thair breistis bane.
Thay ar the confort that we all haif heir –
Thair may no man be till us half so deir;
Thay ar our verry nest of nurissing.
In lak of thame quha can say ony thing,   dispraise
That fowll his nest he fylis, and for thy   bird; defiles; therefore
Exylit he suld be of all gud cumpany;
Thair suld na wyis man gif audience
To sic ane without intelligence.
Chryst to his fader he had nocht ane man;
Se quhat wirschep wemen suld haif than.
That Sone is Lord, that Sone is King of Kingis;
In hevin and erth his majestie ay ringis.
Sen scho hes borne him in hir halines
And he is well and grund of all gudnes,
All wemen of us suld haif honoring,
Service and luve, aboif all uthir thing.

In Secreit Place

In secreit place this hindir nycht   the other night
I hard ane bern say till a bricht: fellow; a fair one
'My hunny, my houp, my hairt, my heill,   hope; health
I haif bene lang your lufar leill   loyal
And can of yow gett confort nane;
How lang will ye with denger deill.   (courtly) reluctance
Ye brek my hart, my bony ane.'   bonny

His bony berd wes kemd and croppit   combed
Bot all with kaill it wes bedroppit   cabbage
And he wes townysche, peirt and gukkit.   bourgeois, forward and foolish
He clappit fast, he kist, he chukkit   stroked; fondled
As with the glaikkis he wer ourgane –   silly lewd frolics
Yit be his feiris he wald haif fukkit: behaviour
'Ye brek my hairt, my bony ane.'

Quod he, 'My hairt, sweit as the hunny,
Sen that I born wes of my mynny   mummy

I wowt nevir ane uder bot yow;   *wooed; other*
My wame is of your lufe so fow
That as ane gaist I glour and grane;   *glower and groan*
I trymmill sa, ye will not trow: *believe*
Ye brek my hairt, my bony ane.'

'Tohie,' quod scho, and gaif ane gawf: *guffaw*
'Be still, my cowffyne and my cawf,   *rascal(?); calf*
My new spaind howphyn fra the sowk   *weaned oaf from suckling*
And all the blythnes of my bowk;   *happiness; body*
My sweit swanky, saif yow allane   *gentle fellow; apart from*
Na leid I luvit all this owk: *No person; week*
Fow leis me that graceles gane.'   *Full dear to me (is); ugly mug*

Quod he, 'My claver, my curledoddy,   *clover; scabious*
My hony soppis, my sweit possoddy,   *honeyed bread; sheep's head broth*
Be nocht our bustious to your billie –   *too rough; companion*
Be warme hartit and nocht illwillie;
Your hals, quhyt as quhalis bane,   *neck; whalebone*
Gars rys on loft my quhillylillie: *Makes; willie*
Ye brek my hairt, my bony ane.'

Quod scho, 'My clip, my unspaynd jyane   *big softie; unweaned giant*
With muderis milk yit in your michane,   *stomach*
My belly huddroun, my sweit hurle bawsy,   *belly-heifer (glutton); skitter-balls*
My honygukkis, my slasy gawsy,   *sweet idiot; handsome slurper(?)*
Your musing wald pers ane hairt of stane;
Sa tak gud confort, my gritheidit gawsy: *big-headed good-looker*
Fow leis me that graceles gane.'

Quod he, 'My kid, my capircalyeane,   *baby goat; capercailzie*
My bony bab with the ruch brilyeane,   *shaggy twat*
My tendir girdill, my wally gowdy,   *delicate belt; fine gold piece*
My tirly mirly, my towdy mowdy;   *rumpy pumpy; pet pussy*
Quhen that our mowthis dois meit at ane
My stang dois storkyn with your towdy: *prick; stiffen; pussy*
Ye brek my hairt, my bony ane.'

Quod scho, 'Tak me by the hand;
Wylcum, my golk of Maryland,   *cuckoo of fairyland*
My chirry and my maikles myngeoun,   *cherry; matchless darling*
My sucker sweit as ony unyeoun,   *baby; onion*
My strummill stirk yit new to spane,   *bony bullock; weaning*
I am applyid to your opinyoun: *inclined*
Fow leis me that graceles gane.'

He gaif till hir ane appill ruby;
'Gramercy,' quod scho, 'My sweit cowhuby.'   booby
Syne tha twa till ane play began
Quhilk that thay call the dirrydan,   hanky-panky
Quhill bayth thair bewis did meit in ane.   limbs
'Fow wo,' quod scho, 'Quhair will ye, man?   Help (very woe); what are you up to
Full leis me that graceles gane.'

Schir, ye have mony servitouris
(To the King)[1]

Schir, ye have mony servitouris   followers/servants
And officiaris of dyvers curis: agents of various tasks
Kirkmen, courtmen and craftismen fyne,
Doctouris in jure and medicyne,   law
Divinouris, rethoris and philosophouris,   Seers; rhetoricians
Astrologis, artistis and oratouris,   envoys
Men of armes and vailyeand knychtis
And mony uther gudlie wichtis;
Musicianis, menstralis and mirrie singaris,
Chevalouris, cawandaris and flingaris,   Poetasters; entertainers; dancers
Cunyouris, carvouris and carpentaris,   Coiners
Beildaris of barkis and ballingaris,   barques; cutters
Masounis lyand upon the land   quartered
And schipwrichtis hewand upone the strand,
Glasing wrichtis, goldsmythis and lapidaris,   Glaziers; jewellers
Pryntouris, payntouris and potingaris –   apothecaries

And all of thair craft cunning
And all at anis lawboring,
Quhilk pleisand ar and honorable
And to your hienes profitable
And richt convenient for to be
With your hie regale majestie,
Deserving of your grace most ding   worthy
Bayth thank, rewarde and cherissing.

And thocht that I amang the laif   others
Unworthy be ane place to have
Or in thair nummer to be tald,   reckoned
Als lang in mynd my work sall hald,   memory; endure
Als haill in everie circumstance,   whole
In forme, in matter and substance,

1. James IV loved all the arts, especially music and dance, encouraging women folk-singers and travelling with an organ on royal visits. He was keen on alchemy, military displays, tournaments and artillery, building the *Great Michael* to lead his fleet, the biggest warship of its day in Europe.

But wering or consumptioun, *Without wasting*
Roust, canker or corruptioun, *Rust*
As ony of thair werkis all –
Suppois that my rewarde be small. *Even if*

Bot ye sa gracious ar and meik *modest*
That on your hienes followis eik *also*
Ane uthir sort, more miserabill
Thocht thai be nocht sa profitable: *Although*
Fenyeouris, fleichouris and flatteraris, *Pretenders; con-men*
Cryaris, craikaris and clatteraris, *Boasters, noisemakers; chatterers*
Soukaris, groukaris, gledaris, gunnaris, *Sooks, crooks, buzzards, gunners*
Monsouris of France (gud clarat cunnaris), *wine-experts*
Inopportoun askaris of Yrland kynd, *Unreasonable petitioners from Ireland*
And meit revaris, lyk out of mynd, *fridge-raiders (beyond number)*
Scaffaris and scamleris in the nuke, *Snackers; pot-lickers in the corner*
And hall huntaris of draik and duik, *drake and duck*
Thrimlaris and thristaris as thai war woid, *Hustlers and thrusters; crazed*
Kokenis, and kennis na man of gude; *Rogues; no decent man respected*
Schulderaris and schovaris that hes no schame,
And to no cunning that can clame, *skill*
And can non uthir craft nor curis *know; office*
Bot to mak thrang, Schir, in your duris, *crowd around*
And rusche in quhair thay counsale heir *discussion*
And will at na man nurtir leyr; *learn good breeding*
In quintiscence eik, ingynouris joly *alchemy also; conceited inventors*
That far can multiplie in folie –
Fantastik fulis bayth fals and gredy,
Off toung untrew and hand evill diedie; *doing*
(Few dar of all this last additioun *Few dare of this last group*
Cum in Tolbuyth without remissioun).[1] *pardon*

And thocht this nobill cunning sort *although; learned*
Quhom of befoir I did report
Rewardit be, it war bot ressoun *only reasonable*
Thairat suld no man mak enchessoun; *objection*
Bot quhen the uther fulis nyce *silly*
That feistit at Cokelbeis gryce[2] *sucking-pig*
Ar all rewardit, and nocht I,
Than on this fals warld I cry, Fy:
My hart neir bristis than for teyne, *vexation*
Quhilk may nocht suffer nor sustene
So grit abusioun for to se
Daylie in court befoir myn e.

1. Tolbooth: where Parliament and the Court of Session met in Edinburgh.
2. 'Cokelbie's Sow': a popular tale in rough alliterative verse with a scene in which a collection of wastrels plan (without success) to roast a piglet.

And yit more panence wald I have   penance
Had I rewarde amang the laif.   others
It wald me sumthing satisfie
And les of my malancolie,
And gar me mony falt ourse   many a fault overlook
That now is brayd befoir myn e.

My mind so fer is set to flyt   scold (satirise)
That of nocht ellis I can endyt,   write
For owther man my hart to breik   either my heart must
Or with my pen I man me wreik;   must; avenge
And sen the tane most nedis be –   since one (of the two) must happen
In to malancolie to de   die
Or lat the vennim ische all out –   gush
Be war anone, for it will spout
Gif that the tryackill cum nocht tyt   If; salve; quickly
To swage the swalme of my dispyt.   relieve; swelling; injury

The Flyting of Dunbar and Kennedie[1]

Schir Johine the Ros, ane thing thair is compild   has composed (a report)
    In generale be Kennedy and Quinting[2]   concerning
Quhilk hes thame self aboif the sternis styld;   honoured above the stars
    Bot had thay maid of mannace ony mynting   attempt at a (particular) threat
    In speciall, sic stryfe sould rys but stynting;   strife should arise without cease
Howbeit with bost thair breistis wer als bendit   Even although; bragging
As Lucifer that fra the hevin discendit,
    Hell sould nocht hyd thair harnis fra harmis hynting.   brains; reach

The erd sould trymbill, the firmament sould schaik,
    And all the air in vennaum suddane stink,   poison
And all the divillis of hell for redour quaik,   terror
    To heir quhat I suld wryt with pen and ynk:
    For and I flyt, sum sege for schame sould sink,   If I; man
The se sould birn, the mone sould thoill ecclippis,   suffer
Rochis sould ryfe, the warld sould hald no grippis,   split; (wouldn't) hold firm
    Sa loud of cair the commoun bell sould clynk.   public; tinkle

Bot wondir laith wer I to be ane baird,   very reluctant
    Flyting to use for gritly I eschame;

1. Walter Kennedy MA, noted for his aureate verse and honoured in Dunbar's own 'Lament for the Makaris', was the
   third son of Lord Kennedy of Dunure in Ayrshire, nephew to the Bishop of Dunkeld and St Andrews and uncle to
   one of James IV's privy councillors. This flyting is the earliest Scots example (c. 1500) of a mock-serious genre
   undoubtedly derived from Gaelic tradition whose bards were said to be able to raise boils on their victims, so scathing
   was the power of their satirical art. Compare the Rook in Holland's *Buke of the Howlat* (c. 1450) who appears as a
   ragged Irish bard threatening to 'ryme' if he isn't fed. Compare Duncan Bàn Macintyre's 'Song to the Tailor' from the
   18th century.
2. One of Kennedy's relatives.

For it is nowthir wynnyng nor rewaird
   Bot tinsale baith of honour and of fame,   *loss*
   Incres of sorrow, sklander and evill name:
Yit mycht thay be sa bald in thair bakbytting
To gar me ryme and rais the Feynd with flytting   *make me*
   And throw all cuntreis and kinrikis thame proclame.   *kingdoms; denounce*
                 Quod Dumbar to Kennedy.[1]   *Said*

Dirtin Dumbar, quhome on blawis thow thy boist,
   Pretendand the to wryte sic skaldit skrowis?   *scabby scrolls*
Ramowd rebald, thow fall doun att the roist   *Raw-mouthed; contest*
   My laureat lettres at the and I lowis: *at you; set loose*
   Mandrag, mymmerkin, maid maister bot in mows,   *Mandrake; dwarflet; joke* MA
Thrys scheild trumpir with ane threid bair goun,   *Thrice-exposed cheat*
Say Deo mercy, or I cry the doun,
   And leif thy ryming, rebald, and thy rowis.   *knave; papers*

Dreid, dirtfast dearch, that thow hes dissobeyit   *Dread; dwarf*
   My cousing Quintene and my commissar;   *representative*
Fantastik fule, trest weill thow salbe fleyit;   *scared off*
   Ignorant elf, aip, owll irregular,   *disorderly*
   Skaldit skaitbird and commoun skamelar,   *Scabby skua; sponger*
Wan fukkit funling that natour maid ane yrle –   *foundling; nature; dwarf*
Baith Johine the Ros and thow sall squeill and skirle   *shriek*
   And evir I heir ocht of your making mair.   *composing*

Heir I put sylence to the in all pairtis;
   Obey and ceis the play that thow pretendis;
Waik walidrag and verlot of the cairtis,   *Weak scruffy runt; knave (of cards)*
   Se sone thow mak my commissar amendis,
   And lat him lay sax leichis on thy lendis   *lashes; buttocks*
Meikly in recompansing of thi scorne,
Or thow sall ban the tyme that thow wes borne;   *curse*
   For Kennedy to the this cedull sendis.   *document*
              Quod Kennedy to Dumbar.
              Juge in the nixt quha gat the war.   *got the worst of it*

Iersche brybour baird, vyle beggar with thy brattis   *Gaelic rascal bard; rags*
   Cuntbittin crawdoun Kennedy, coward of kynd;   *Poxed craven; born coward*
Evill farit and dryit as Denseman on the rattis,[2]   *Ill-favoured; Dane; wheel*
   Lyk as the gleddis had on thy gulesnowt dynd;   *kites; yellowsnout*
   Mismaid monstour, ilk mone owt of thy mynd,   *each month (lunatic notion)*
Renunce, rebald, thy rymyng; thow bot royis;   *rascal; talk rubbish*

---

1. Dunbar and Kennedy take turn about in the contest. Now it is Kennedy who speaks. The two poets' manuscripts may have been circulated in the Court, and the finished work recited in a confrontation between them.
2. Danish criminals were executed and left exposed (dried up and dangling) on a wheel.

Thy trechour tung hes tane ane heland strynd –   strain (character)
   Ane lawland ers wald mak a bettir noyis.   arse (Erse: Gaelic)

Revin, raggit ruke, and full of rebaldrie,   Raven; rook
   Scarth fra scorpione, scaldit in scurrilitie,   hermaphrodite
I se the haltane in thy harlotrie   haughty
   And in to uthir science no thing slie,   knowledge; not expert
   Of every vertew void, as men may sie;
Quytclame clergie and cleik to the ane club,   Give up learning; hang on
   Ane baird blasphemar in brybrie ay to be;   begging
64 For wit and woisdome ane wisp fra the may rub.   a wipe of straw will rub off

            *   *   *

217 Off Edinburch the boyis as beis owt thrawis   throng out like bees
   And cryis owt ay, 'Heir cumis our awin queir clerk!'
Than fleis thow lyk ane howlat chest with crawis,   owl chased by crows
   Quhill all the bichis at thy botingis dois bark.   bitches; boots
   Than carlingis cryis, 'Keip curches in the merk –   crones; hide the headscarfs
Our gallowis gaipis – lo! quhair ane greceles gais!'   the gibbet is hungry
   Ane uthir sayis, 'I se him want ane sark –   lacks a shirt
   I reid yow, cummer, tak in your lynning clais.'   advise you, Mrs; linen

Than rynis thow doun the gait with gild of boyis   run; street; noise
   And all the toun tykis hingand in thy heilis;   mongrels
Of laidis and lownis thair rysis sic ane noyis   From boys and ruffians
   Quhill runsyis rynis away with cairt and quheilis,   horses run
   And caiger aviris castis bayth coillis and creilis,   trader nags; coals; baskets
For rerd of the and rattling of thy butis;   uproar; boots
   Fische wyvis cryis, 'Fy!' and castis doun skillis and skeilis,   baskets; tubs
Sum claschis the, sum cloddis the on the cutis.   slap; pelt; ankles

Loun lyk Mahoun, be boun me till obey,   Ruffian; the devil (Mahomet)
   Theif, or in greif mischeif sall the betyd;
Cry grace, tykis face, or I the chece and fley;   mercy; dogface; chase and scare
   Oule, rare and yowle – I sall defowll thy pryd;   Owl; howl and yell
   Peilit gled, baith fed and bred of bichis syd   Plucked kite
And lyk ane tyk, purspyk – quhat man settis by the!   pickpocket; who trusts you!
   Forflittin, countbittin, beschittin, barkit hyd,   Fully-flyted; thick-skinned
Clym ledder, fyle tedder, foule edder: I defy the!   Climb (gallows) ladder; dirty noose; adder

Mauch muttoun, byt buttoun, peilit gluttoun,   Maggoty; button-biter;
   air to Hilhous,   heir
   Rank beggar, ostir dregar, foule fleggar in the flet,   oyster-dredger; parlour flatterer
Chittirlilling, ruch rilling, lik schilling in the   Pigs-guts; shaggy-shoes; chaff-licker
   milhous,
   Baird rehator, theif of nator, fals tratour, feyindis gett,   vile; offspring

Filling of tauch, rak sauch – cry 'crauch',   Tallow-stuffed, rope-stretcher; 'give-up'
    thow art oursett;
Muttoun dryver, girnall ryver, yadswyvar –   Sheep-rustler, meal-robber, mare-buggerer
    fowll fell the
Herretyk, lunatyk, purspyk, carlingis pet,   old-woman's
Rottin crok, dirtin dok – cry cok, or I sall quell the. Diseased ewe; arse; admit defeat
             Quod Dumbar to Kennedy.

Dathane deivillis sone and dragone dispitous,[1]   pitiless
    Abironis birth and bred with Beliall,   born and bred by
Wod werwoif, worme and scorpion vennemous,   Crazed werewolf
    Lucifers laid, fowll feyindis face infernall,   servant
    Sodomyt, syphareit fra sanctis celestiall: separated
Put I nocht sylence to the, schiphird knaif,
And thow of new begynis to ryme and raif,   once more; rant
    Thow salbe maid blait, bleir eit, bestiall.   afraid; blear-eyed, brutish

How thy forbearis come, I haif a feill,   understanding
    At Cokburnis peth, the writ makis me war,   record; aware
Generit betwix ane scho beir and a deill:
    Sa wes he callit Dewlbeir and nocht Dumbar.   (Devilbear)
This Dewlbeir, generit of a meir of Mar,   mare
Wes Corspatrik erle of Merche, and be illusioun   trickery
The first that evir put Scotland to confusioun
    Wes that fals tratour, hardely say I dar.

Quhen Bruce and Balioll differit for the croun
    Scottis lordis could nocht obey Inglis lawis;
This Corspatrik betrasit Berwik toun   betrayed
    And slew sevin thowsand Scottismen within thay wawis;
    The battall syne of Spottismuir he gart caus,
And come with Edwart Langschankis to the feild
Quhair twelve thowsand trew Scottismen wer keild
    And Wallace chest, as the carnicle schawis.[2]   chased; chronicle

Scottis lordis chiftanis he gart hald and chessone   held and accused
    In firmance fast quhill all the feild wes done   battle
Within Dumbar, that auld spelunk of tressoun;   cave of treason
    Sa Inglis tykis in Scottland wes abone.   were on top
    Than spulyeit thay the haly stane of Scone,   plundered
The croce of Halyrudhous, and uthir jowellis
He birnis in hell, body, banis and bowellis,
    This Corspatrik that Scotland hes undone.

1. Dathan and Abiram rebelled against Moses and were destroyed by God, with all their followers.
2. Patrick the eighth Earl of Dunbar sided with Edward I of England (Longshanks) and opened Berwick's gates to his

Wallace gart cry ane counsale in to Perth
    And callit Corspatrik tratour be his style;   to his name
That dampnit dragone drew him in diserth
    And sayd, he kend bot Wallace, king in Kyle: (did not acknowledge W's authority)
    Out of Dumbar that theif he maid exyle   (he: Wallace)
Unto Edward and Inglis grund agane;
    Tigiris, serpentis and taidis will remane
In Dumbar wallis, todis, wolffis and beistis vyle.   foxes

Na fowlis of effect amangis tha binkis   honest birds; those benches
    Biggis nor abydis for no thing that may be;
Thay stanis of tressone as the bruntstane stinkis,   brimstone
    Dewlbeiris moder, cassin in by the se,   washed up by
    The wariet apill of the forbiddin tre   cursed
That Adame eit quhen he tynt Parradyce   lost
Scho eit, invennomit lyk a cokkatryce,[1]
296   Syne merreit with the Divill for dignite.   married

*   *   *

[Kennedy continues for another 258 lines before the poem ends]

To the Merchantis of Edinburgh

Quhy will ye merchantis of renoun
Lat Edinburgh your nobill toun
For laik of reformatioun
The commone proffeitt tyine, and fame?   benefit lose
    Think ye not schame,
That onie uther regioun
Sall with dishonour hurt your name?

May nane pas throw your principall gaittis
For stink of haddockis and of scaittis,
For cryis of carlingis and debaittis,   old women; arguments
For fowsum flyttingis of defame;   offensive
    Think ye not schame,
Befoir strangeris of all estaittis
That sic dishonour hurt your name?

Your stinkand scull that standis dirk   school; dark
Haldis the lycht fra your parroche kirk;
Your foirstair makis your housis mirk   outside stairs
Lyk na cuntray bot heir at hame;
    Think ye not schame,

1. Mythical serpent with the head, wings and feet of a cock.

Sa litill polesie to wirk   civic planning
In hurt and sklander of your name?

At your hie croce quhar gold and silk   (Mercat cross at St Giles)
Sould be, thair is bot crudis and milk;   curds
And at your trone bot cokill and wilk,   (Tron: public weigh-beam); whelks
Pansches, pudingis of Jok and Jame;   tripes
    Think ye not schame,
Sen as the world sayis that ilk   Considering that; the same
In hurt and sclander of your name?

Your commone menstrallis hes no tone
Bot 'Now the Day dawis', and 'Into Joun';   (popular songs)
Cunningar men man serve Sanct Cloun   (Irish Saint associated with food and drink)
And nevir to uther craftis clame;
    Think ye not schame,
To hald sic mowaris on the moyne   keep; mockers at the moon (loonies)
In hurt and sclander of your name?

Tailyouris, soutteris and craftis vyll   cobblers
The fairest of your streittis dois fyll,   defile
And merchandis at the stinkand styll   (alley near Luckenbooths)
Ar hamperit in ane hony came;   (like bees in a) honeycomb
    Think ye not schame,
That ye have nether witt nor wyll
To win yourselff ane bettir name?

Your burgh of beggeris is ane nest,
To schout thai swentyouris will not rest;   vagabonds; cease
All honest folk they do molest,
Sa piteuslie thai cry and rame;   harangue
    Think ye not schame,
That for the poore hes nothing drest,   prepared
In hurt and sclander of your name?

Your proffeit daylie dois incres,
Your godlie workis les and les;
Through streittis nane may mak progres
For cry of cruikit, blind and lame;
    Think ye not schame,
That ye sic substance dois posses
And will not win ane bettir name?

Sen for the court and the sessioun   (Royal Court and Court of Session)
The great repair of this regioun
Is in your burgh, thairfoir be boun

To mend all faultis that ar to blame,
   And eschew schame;
Gif thai pas to ane uther toun
Ye will decay, and your great name.

Thairfoir strangeris and leigis treit,   *loyal subjects; favour*
Tak not over mekill for thair meit,
And gar your merchandis be discreit;
That na extortiounes be, proclame   *prohibit*
   All fraud and schame;
Keip ordour and poore nighbouris beit,   *assist*
That ye may gett ane bettir name.

Singular proffeit so dois yow blind,   *Private*
The common proffeit gois behind;
I pray that Lord remeid to fynd   *remedy*
That deit into Jerusalem,
   And gar yow schame;   *make you (feel)*
That sumtyme ressoun may yow bind   *good sense*
For to [win bak to] yow guid name.

Ane Dance in the Quenis Chalmer

Sir Jhon Sinclair begowthe to dance   *began*
For he was new cum owt of France;
For ony thing that he do mycht   *Despite*
The ane futt geid ay onrycht –   *wrong*
   And to the tother wald nocht gree.   *agree*
Quod ane, 'Tak up the Quenis knycht!'   *lead out*
   A mirrear dance mycht na man see.

Than cam in Maistir Robert Schaw:
He leuket as he culd lern tham a,   *teach*
Bot ay his ane futt did waver;
He stackeret lyk ane strummall aver   *staggered; knackered cart-horse*
   That hopschackellt war aboin the kne;   *hobbled*
To seik fra Sterling to Stranaver   *(Strathnaver, Sutherland)*
   A mirrear daunce mycht na man see.

Than cam in the maister almaser,   *chief almoner*
Ane hommiltye jommeltye juffler   *hibbeldy-hobbeldy blunderer*
Lyk a stirk stackarand in the ry;
His hippis gaff mony hoddous cry.   *buttocks*
   John Bute the fule said,   *(Court Fool)*
Waes me He is bedirtin; fye, fy!
   A mirrear dance mycht na man see.

Than cam in Dunbar the mackar;   poet
On all the flure thair was nane frackar,   readier
And thair he dancet the dirrye dantoun;   (a lively dance)
He hoppet lyk a pillie wanton   amorous colt
    For luff of Musgraeffe, men tellis me;   (Lady at Court)
He trippet quhill he tint his panton: till he lost; slipper
    A mirrear dance mycht na man see.

Than cam in Maesteres Musgraeffe;   Mistress
Scho mycht heff lernit all the laeffe;   taught; the rest
Quhen I schau hir sa trimlye dance,
Hir guid convoy and contenance,
    Than for hir saek I wissitt to be   wished
The grytast erle or duk in France:
    A mirrear dance mycht na man see.

Than cam in Dame Dounteboir –
God waett gif that schou louket sowr;   knows
Schou maid sic morgeownis with hir hippis,   contortions
For lachtter nain mycht hald thair lippis;
    Quhen schou was danceand bisselye,
Ane blast of wind son fra hir slippis.   soon
    A mirrear dance mycht na man se.

Quhen thair was cum in fyve or sax
The Quenis Dog begowthe to rax,[1]   strain
And of his band he maid a bred   from his collar; leap
And to the danceing soin he him med;   soon
    Quhou mastevlyk abowt geid he!   How mastiff-like
He stinckett lyk a tyk, sum saed:
    A mirrear dance mycht na man see.

The Dance of the Sevin Deidly Synnis

Off Februar the fyiftene nycht[2]
Full lang befoir the dayis lycht
    I lay in till a trance;
    And than I saw baith hevin and hell:
Me thocht amangis the feyndis fell
    Mahoun gart cry ane dance the devil   the devil (Mahomet)
Off schrewis that wer nevir schrevin   scolds; forgiven
Aganis the feist of Fasternis evin

1. An old adversary of Dunbar's, James Dog, keeper of the Queen's wardrobe, is immortalised in another poem for his refusal to give the poet a doublet.
2. Fastern's Eve (Shrove Tuesday) precedes the first day of Lent. At the Scottish Court it was celebrated by mumming and other activities, while different regions of the country had special meals and games associated with it. The poem was most probably written in 1507.

To mak thair observance;
He bad gallandis ga graith a gyis   *gallants; prepare a masque*
And kast up gamountis in the skyis   *draw up gambols*
    That last came out of France.

'Lat se', quod he, 'Now quha begynnis:'
With that the fowll sevin deidly synnis
    Begowth to leip at anis.
And first of all in dance wes Pryd   *PRIDE*
With hair wyld bak and bonet on syd
    Lyk to mak waistie wanis,   *(that would mortgage a house)*
And round abowt him as a quheill
Hang all in rumpillis to the heill   *tails; heel*
    His kethat for the nanis;   *cloak indeed*
Mony prowd trumpour with him trippit –   *pretender*
Throw skaldand fyre ay as thay skippit
    Thay gyrnd with hiddous granis.   *groans*

Heilie harlottis on hawtane wyis   *High-handed; haughty style*
Come in with mony sindrie gyis,   *various fashions*
    Bot yit luche nevir Mahoun   *laughed; the devil*
Quhill preistis come in with bair schevin nekkis –   *Until*
Than all the feyndis lewche and maid gekkis,   *gibes*
    Blak Belly and Bawsy Broun.   *(two fiends?)*

Than Yre come in with sturt and stryfe;   *WRATH; feud*
His hand wes ay upoun his knyfe –
    He brandeist lyk a beir: *swaggered; bear*
Bostaris, braggaris and barganeris
Eftir him passit in to pairis
    All bodin in feir of weir;   *kitted out; warlike style*
In jakkis and stryppis and bonettis of steill   *jerkins; harness*
Thair leggis wer chenyeit to the heill,   *chainmailed to*
    Frawart wes thair affeir;   *Perverse; manner*
Sum upoun uder with brandis beft,   *swords struck*
Sum jaggit uthiris to the heft   *stabbed; haft*
    With knyvis that scherp cowd scheir.   *cut*

Nixt followit in the dance Invy   *ENVY*
Fild full of feid and fellony,   *hostility; cruelty*
    Hid malyce and dispyte;
For pryvie hatrent that tratour trymlit: *secret hatred; trembled*
Him followit mony freik dissymlit   *disguised men*
    With fenyeit wirdis quhyte,   *false soft words*
And flattereris in to menis facis,
And bakbyttaris of sindry racis   *various types*

To ley that had delyte,	*lie*
And rownaris of fals lesingis –	*whisperers; deceits*
Allace, that courtis of noble kingis	
Of thame can nevir be quyte.	*free*
Nixt him in dans come Cuvatyce,	AVARICE
Rute of all evill and grund of vyce,	
That nevir cowd be content:	
Catyvis, wrechis and ockeraris,	*Villains; loan-sharks*
Hud pykis, hurdaris and gadderaris,	*Tightwads; hoarders; acquirers*
All with that warlo went;	*warlock*
Out of thair throttis thay schot on udder	*each other*
Hett moltin gold, me thocht a fudder,	*cartload*
As fyreflawcht maist fervent;	*Like lightning; glowing hot*
Ay as thay tomit thame of schot	*emptied; volley*
Feyndis fild thame new up to the thrott	
With gold of allkin prent.	*all kinds of stamp*
Syne Sweirnes at the secound bidding	SLOTH
Come lyk a sow out of a midding –	*midden*
Full slepy wes his grunyie;	*snout*
Mony sweir bumbard belly huddroun,	*Many an obstinate, lubbard, belly-heifer*
Mony slute daw and slepy duddroun,	*sluttish slattern; sloven*
Him servit ay with sounyie:	*vacillation*
He drew thame furth in till a chenyie,	*chain*
And Belliall with a brydill renyie	*bridle-rein*
Evir lascht thame on the lunyie.	*rump*
In dance thay war so slaw of feit	
Thay gaif thame in the fyre a heit	
And maid thame quicker of counyie.	*on the uptake*
Than Lichery that lathly cors	LECHERY; *loathsome body*
Berand lyk a bagit hors –	*whinnying; well-hung stallion*
And Lythenes did him leid:	*Indolence*
Thair wes with him ane ugly sort	*band*
And mony stynkand fowll tramort	*corpse*
That had in syn bene deid.	*long since been*
Quhen thay wer entrit in the dance	
Thay wer full strenge of countenance	*very strange in appearance*
Lyk turkas birnand reid;	*blacksmith's pincers*
All led thay uthir by the tersis,	*Each; penis*
Suppois thay fycket with thair ersis,	*Even if; squirmed*
It mycht be na remeid.	*relief*
Than the fowll monstir Glutteny	GLUTTONY
Off wame unsasiable and gredy	*belly insatiable*

To dance he did him dres:
Him followit mony fowll drunckart
With can and collep, cop and quart,   (drinking vessels)
    In surffet and exces;
Full mony a waistles wallydrag   fat scruffbag
With wamis unweildable did furth wag   unmanageable
    In creische that did incres: blubber
'Drynk!' ay thay cryit, with mony a gaip –   gawp
The feyndis gaif thame hait leid to laip –   hot lead
    Thair lovery wes na les.   portion

Na menstrallis playit to thame but dowt   for sure
For glemen thair wer haldin owt   entertainers there; barred
    Be day and eik by nycht –
Except a menstrall that slew a man;   Except for any
Swa till his heretage he wan   attained his destiny
And entirt be breif of richt.   legal right

Than cryd Mahoun for a heleand padyane: pageant
Syne ran a feynd to feche Makfadyane   (stereotypical Highlander)
    Far northwart in a nuke.
Be he the correnoch had done schout   By the time; knell
Erschemen so gadderit him abowt   Highlanders
    In hell grit rowme thay tuke.
Thae tarmegantis with tag and tatter   blustering bullies
Full lowd in Ersche begowth to clatter   Gaelic
    And rowp lyk revin and ruke.   croak
The Devill sa devit wes with thair yell   deafened
That in the depest pot of hell
    He smorit thame with smuke.   smothered

This Warld Unstabille

I seik about this warld unstabille
To find ane sentence convenabille,   appropriate judgement
    Bot I can nocht in all my wit
    Sa trew ane sentence fynd off it
As say, it is dessaveabille.   deceitful

For yesterday I did declair
Quhow that the seasoun soft and fair
    Com in als fresche as pako fedder;   lovely; peacock feather
    This day it stangis lyk ane edder,   stings; adder
Concluding all in my contrair.   Bringing all to an end against me

Yisterday fair up sprang the flouris,
This day thai ar all slane with schouris;

And fowllis in forrest that sang cleir
Now walkis with a drery cheir,
Full caild ar baith thair beddis and bouris.   cold

So nixt to summer winter bein;
Nixt eftir confort, cairis kein,
    Nixt dirk mednycht the mirthefull morrow,
    Nixt efter joy aye cumis sorrow
Sa is this warld, and ay hes bein.

In Winter

In to thir dirk and drublie dayis   clouded
Quhone sabill all the hevin arrayis,   black
    With mystie vapouris, cluddis and skyis,
    Nature all curage me denyis   appetite
Off sangis, ballattis and of playis.   For

Quhone that the nycht dois lenthin houris
With wind, with haill and havy schouris,
    My dule spreit dois lurk for schoir;   sad spirit; shrinks under threat
    My hairt for langour dois forloir   with misery; becomes forlorn
For laik of Symmer with his flouris.

I walk, I turne, sleip may I nocht;
I vexit am with havie thocht;
    This warld all ovir I cast about,
    And ay the mair I am in dout
The mair that I remeid have socht.

I am assayit on everie syde;   assailed
Despair sayis, 'Ay in tyme provyde   Always
    And get sum thing quhairon to leif,
    Or with grit trouble and mischeif
Thow sall in to this court abyd.'   dwell

Than Patience sayis, 'Be not agast;
Hald Hoip and Treuthe within the fast
    And lat Fortoun wirk furthe hir rage,   fancy
    Quhome that no rasoun may assuage
Quhill that hir glas be run and past.'   Until her hourglass

And Prudence in my eir sayis ay,
'Quhy wald thow hald that will away?   keep what will pass
    Or craif that thow may have mo space,   beg
    Thow tending to ane uther place   moving
A journay going everie day?'

And than sayis Age, 'My freind, cum neir
And be not strange, I the requeir;   request thee
  Cum brodir, by the hand me tak;
  Remember thow hes compt to mak   on account
Off all thi tyme thow spendit heir.'

Syne Deid castis upe his yettis wyd   Death; throws; gates
Saying, 'Thir oppin sall the abyd;   These open; wait for you
  Albeid that thow wer never sa stout,   Even if; ever so brave
  Undir this lyntall sall thow lowt –   bow
Thair is nane uther way besyde.'

For feir of this all day I drowp:
No gold in kist nor wyne in cowp,   chest
  No ladeis bewtie nor luiffis blys
  May lat me to remember this,   prevent
How glaid that ever I dyne or sowp.   However gladly

Yit quhone the nycht begynnis to schort
It dois my spreit sum pairt confort
  Off thocht oppressit with the schowris;
  Cum lustie Symmer with thi flowris,
That I may leif in sum disport.   diversion

Lament for the Makaris

I that in heill wes and gladnes   health
Am trublit now with gret seiknes
And feblit with infermite:
Timor mortis conturbat me.   The fear of death unsettles me.

Our plesance heir is all vane glory,   joy
This fals warld is bot transitory,
The flesch is brukle, the Fend is sle: fragile; cunning
Timor mortis conturbat me.

The stait of man dois change and vary,
Now sound, now seik, now blith, now sary,   wretched
Now dansand mery, now like to dee:
Timor mortis conturbat me.

No stait in erd heir standis sickir;   earth; secure
As with the wynd wavis the wickir   willow
Wavis this warldis vanite:
Timor mortis conturbat me.

One to the ded gois all estatis,
Princis, prelotis and potestatis,   lords
Baith riche and pur of al degre;
Timor mortis conturbat me.

He takis the knychtis in to feild   battle
Anarmyt undir helme and scheild,   Unarmed
Victour he is at all melle: mêlée
Timor mortis conturbat me.

That strang unmercifull tyrand
Takis on the moderis breist sowkand   mother's
The bab full of benignite: grace
Timor mortis conturbat me.

He takis the campion in the stour,   champion; conflict
The capitane closit in the tour,
The lady in bour full of bewte:
Timor mortis conturbat me.

He sparis no lord for his piscence,   strength
Na clerk for his intelligence;   scholar; knowledge
His awfull strak may no man fle:
Timor mortis conturbat me.

Art magicianis and astrologgis,
Rethoris, logicianis and theologgis –
Thame helpis no conclusionis sle: cunning
Timor mortis conturbat me.

In medicyne the most practicianis,   the most practical men
Lechis, surrigianis and phisicianis,   Blood-letters
Thame self fra ded may not supple: deliver
Timor mortis conturbat me.

I se that makaris amang the laif   poets; rest of us
Playis heir ther pageant, syne gois to graif;
Sparit is nought ther faculte: profession
Timor mortis conturbat me.

He has done petuously devour
The noble Chaucer of makaris flour,
The monk of Bery, and Gower, all thre: (John Lydgate)
Timor mortis conturbat me.

The gud Syr Hew of Eglintoun
And eik Heryot and Wyntoun   also; (Heriot: now unknown)

He has tane out of this cuntre:
Timor mortis conturbat me.

That scorpion fell has done infek
Maister Johne Clerk and James Afflek   (Affleck: now unknown)
Fra balat making and tragide:
Timor mortis conturbat me.

Holland and Barbour he has berevit,
Allace that he nought with us levit   left
Schir Mungo Lokert of the Le: (not now known as a poet)
Timor mortis conturbat me.

Clerk of Tranent eik he has tane
That maid the anteris of Gawane;   adventures
Schir Gilbert Hay endit has he:
Timor mortis conturbat me.

He has Blind Hary and Sandy Traill   (Traill: now unknown)
Slane with his schour of mortall haill
Quhilk Patrik Johnestoun myght nought fle:
Timor mortis conturbat me.

He has reft Merseir his endite   taken away; writing
That did in luf so lifly write,   vividly
So schort, so quyk, of sentence hie: noble substance
Timor mortis conturbat me.

He has tane Roull of Aberdene   (now unknown)
And gentill Roull of Corstorphin –
Two bettir fallowis did no man se:
Timor mortis conturbat me.

In Dunfermelyne he has done roune
With Maister Robert Henrisoun;
Schir Johne the Ros enbrast has he: (in 'Flyting of Dunbar and Kennedy') embraced
Timor mortis conturbat me.

And he has now tane last of aw
Gud gentill Stobo and Quintyne Schaw   (John Reid of Stobo)
Of quham all wichtis has pete: creatures; pity
Timor mortis conturbat me.

Gud Maister Walter Kennedy   (of 'Flyting of Dunbar and Kennedy')
In poynt of dede lyis veraly – [1]

1. Along with the mention of Stobo, this dates the poem to early summer 1505.

Gret reuth it wer that so suld be: pity
Timor mortis conturbat me.

Sen he has all my brether tane
He will naught lat me lif alane;
On forse I man his nyxt pray be;   Inevitably I must
Timor mortis conturbat me.

Sen for the ded remeid is none
Best is that we for dede dispone   prepare
Eftir our deid that lif may we:
Timor mortis conturbat me.

Orisoun

Salvour, suppois my sensualite   although
Subject to syn hes maid my saule of sys,   at times
Sum spark of lycht and spiritualite
Walkynnis my witt, and ressoun biddis me rys;   Wakens my understanding; arise
My corrupt conscience askis, clips and cryis   demands
First grace, syne space for to amend my mys,   sin
Substance with honour doing none surpryis,   Possessions; doing no one harm
Freyndis, prosperite, heir peace, syne hevynis blys.

Anonymous (c. 1513)

The brosnachadh, or 'incitement' poem was a regular part of the bard's armoury, as was his listing of distinguished ancestors. We do not know who composed the following piece (preserved by the Dean of Lismore) to Archibald Campbell, the second Earl of Argyll. Campbell served James IV well by maintaining royal authority

Ar Sliocht Gaodhal

Ar sliocht Gaodhal ó Ghort Gréag
ní fheil port ar a gcoimhéad,
dá dteagmhadh nach b'aordha lat
sliocht Gaodhal do chur tharat.

Is dú éirghe i n-aghaidh Gall,
nocha dóigh éirghe udmhall;
faobhair claidheamh, reanna ga,
cóir a gcaitheamh go h-aobhdha.

Ré Gallaibh adeirim ribh,
sul ghabhadar ar ndúthaigh;
ná léigmid ar ndúthaigh dhínn,
déinmid ardchogadh ainmhín,
ar aithris Gaoidheal mBanbha,
caithris ar ar n-athardha.

Do-chuala mé go roibh sin
uair éigin Inis Incin
fá smacht ag fine Fomhra:
racht le bile Bóromha.

Nó go dtánaig Lugh tar linn,
mór bhfian darab maith dírim,
dár marbhadh Balar ua Néid:
budh samhladh dhúinn a leithéid.

in his Argyll territories, but all was lost on Branxton Hill where he died alongside his King at the disasterous battle of Flodden in 1513. This poem was addressed to him on the eve of that battle.

To the Earl of Argyll

The Gael's race from the Field of Greece[1]
would have no harbour they could keep
if you didn't take it as shame
not to support their ancient name.

To fight the Saxons is right,
no rising followed by flight;
edge of sword, point of spear,
let us ply them with good cheer.

Against Saxons, I say to you,
lest they rule our country too;
fight roughly, like the Irish Gael,
we will have no English Pale.

I heard that once upon a time
the place known as Incin's Isle   (Ireland)
was ruled by the Fomorian race –
to the Prince of Bóromha's disgrace.

Till Lugh came across the sea
with warrior-bands for all to see:
thus Balar úa Néid was slain –
let us try to do the same.[2]

1. Gaelic warrior culture associated itself and indeed had much in common with the heroic world of Homer's Greece.
2. In Celtic Irish legend, the Tuatha Dé Danann (peoples of the goddess Danann) were invaded by the monstrous one-eyed, one-legged Fomorians until saved by the god-like hero Lugh, whose name is commemorated in Carlisle (Luguvalium) and in the Latin roots of Lyons, Laon and Leyden. Lugh slew Balar 'of the baleful eye' with a slingshot.

Seala do Ghallaibh mar sain
ag íoc cíosa as an dúthaigh;
[   ] ar eagal gach cinn,   [original text missing]
mór atá teagamh orainn.

Cia nois ar aithris an fhir
fhóirfeas Gaoidheil ar Ghallaibh,
rér linne, mar do-rinn Lugh
taobhadh a chine ó anghuth?

Ghill-easbuig nach d'eitigh d'fhear,
is tú an Lugh fá dheireadh;
a Iarla Oirir Ghaoidheal,
bí id churaidh ag commaoidheamh.

Cuir th'urfhógra an oir 's an iar
ar Ghaoidhlibh ó Ghort Gáilian;
cuir siar thar ardmhuir na Goill,
nach biadh ar Albain athroinn.

Na fréamha ó bhfuilid ag fás,
díthigh iad, mór a bhforfhás,
nach faighthear Gall beó dot éis,
ná Gaillseach ann ré h-aisnéis.

Loisg a mbantracht nach maith mín,
loisg a gclannmhaicne ainmhín,
is loisg a dtighe dubha,
is coisg dhínn a n-anghutha.

Léig le h-uisge a luaithre sin,
i ndiaidh loisgthe dá dtaisibh;
ná déan teóchroidhe a beó Gall,
a eó bheóghoine anbhfann.

Cuimhnigh féin, a ghruaidh mar shuibh,
go bhfuil orainn ag Gallaibh
annsmacht réd linn agus pléid
'nar chinn gallsmacht [   ].   [original text missing]

Cuimhnigh Cailéin th'athair féin,
cuimhnigh Gill-easbuig ainnséin,
cuimhnigh Donnchadh 'na ndeaghaidh,
an fear conchar cairdeamhail.

There was a time when we paid
the Saxons tribute, I'm afraid:
all this arising out of fear
and deep mistrust that's ever near.

Who in our time will save the Gael
against the Saxons, and not fail
to guard from all reproach our race
as Lugh did in his case?

I know one who'd fight like Lugh:
Archibald, to honour true,
Earl of the Coastland of the Gael
exultant warrior, do not fail!

Send your summons east and west,
let Ireland come at your behest;
drive Saxons back across the sea,
let Scotland not divided be.

Destroy the roots from which they grow –
too great their increase – and lay low
each Saxon, robbing him of life;
give the same treatment to his wife.

Burn their women, coarse, untrue,
burn their uncouth children too,
and burn down their black houses:
rid us of their grouses.

Send their ashes down the flood
when you've burnt their flesh and blood;
show no rue to living Saxon,
death-dealing salmon-hero – tax them!

Remember, cheek of raspberry hue,
that Saxons lord it over you;
keep in memory their spite
as Saxon power has grown in might.

Remember Colin, your own father,
remember Archibald, your grandfather,
remember Duncan after them,
a man who loved both hounds and men.

Cuimhnigh Cailéin eile ann,
cuimhnigh Gill-easbuig Arann;
's Cailéin na gceann, mór a chlí,
lér gabhadh geall an [   ].

Cuimhnigh nach tugsad na fir
umhla ar uamhan do Ghallaibh;
cia mó fá dtugadh tusa
umhla uait an dula-sa?

Ó nach mair acht fuidheall áir
do Ghaoidhlibh ó ghort iomgháidh,
teagair lé chéile na fir,
's cuir th'eagal féine ar náimhdibh.

Saigh ar Ghallaibh 'na dtreibh féin:
bí id dúsgadh, a Mheic Cailéin:
d'fhear cogaidh, a fholt mar ór,
ní maith an codal ramhór.

Remember the other Colin then,
and Archibald of Arran,
and Colin of the Heads, who won
the hero's stakes, ere he was done.

Remember these men did not yield,
for fear of Saxon in the field;
why should you make submission now
and bend before them your proud brow?

Since of the Gael there now remain
but scant survivors of the slain,
together gather all your men;
strike fear into the foe again.

Attack the Saxons in their land,
awake! MacCailein, understand,
O golden-haired one, that a fighter
profits much by sleeping lighter.

trans. Derick Thomson

Gavin Douglas (1475?–1522)

Third son of the powerful fifth Earl of Angus (Archibald Bell-the-Cat), Gavin Douglas was a graduate of St Andrews who travelled abroad before settling in Scotland. His translation of Virgil's *Aeneid*, finished in 1513, was the first complete account of a classical text in Britain. His discussion of the problems of translation, and his defence of the use of Scots in the cause of learning, are milestones of the Northern Renaissance. The descriptions of the natural world in his own Prologues to Virgil's books are justly famous. In later years he gave himself over to political affairs, becoming Bishop of Dunkeld, and ultimately having to seek exile in England.

The Proloug of the First Buke of Eneados

101 Quharfor to hys nobilite and estait, Henry, Lord Sinclair[1]
Quhat so it be, this buke I dedicait, ('it' refers to the Book)
Writtin in the langage of Scottis natioun,
And thus I mak my protestatioun.

Fyrst I protest, beaw schirris, be your leif, good sirs
Beis weill avisit my wark or ye repreif, advised of; before; criticise
Consider it warly, reid oftar than anys; carefully
Weill at a blenk sle poetry nocht tayn is, one glance; skilful
And yit forsuith I set my bissy pane diligent effort
As that I couth to mak it braid and plane,
Kepand na sudron bot our awyn langage, Southern (English)
And spekis as I lernyt quhen I was page.
Nor yit sa cleyn all sudron I refus, wholly
Bot sum word I pronunce as nyghtbouris dois:
Lyke as in Latyn beyn Grew termys sum, Greek
So me behufyt quhilum, or than be dum, at times, rather than be dumb
Sum bastard Latyn, French or Inglys use
Quhar scant was Scottis – I had nane other choys.
Nocht for our tong is in the selvyn skant Not that; in itself
Bot for that I the fowth of langage want, but because I lacked; abundance
Quhar as the cullour of his properte flavour; style
To kepe the sentens tharto constrenyt me, meaning; restricted

---

1. A distant relative of Douglas's who urged him on several occasions to attempt a translation of Virgil.

Or than to mak my sayng schort sum tyme,
Mair compendyus, or to lykly my ryme.   *embellish*
Tharfor, gude frendis, for a gymp or a bourd,   *quibble; joke*
I pray you note me nocht at every word.   *blame*
The worthy clerk hecht Lawrens of the Vaill,   *scholar called*
Amang Latynys a gret patron sans faill,   *certainly*
Grantis quhen twelf yeris he had beyn diligent
To study Virgill, skant knew quhat he ment.
Than thou or I, my frend, quhen we best weyn   *think*
To have Virgile red, understand and seyn,
The rycht sentens perchance is fer to seik.   *meaning*
This wark twelf yeris first was in makyng eyk
And nocht correct quhen the poet gan decess;   *(Virgil) did die*
Thus for small faltis, my wys frend, hald thy pes.
Adherdand to my protestatioun,   *Staying with my justification*
Thocht Wilyame Caxtoun, of Inglis natioun,   *Although*
In prose hes prent ane buke of Inglys gross,   *crude English*
Clepand it Virgill in Eneados,
Quhulk that he says of Franch he dyd translait,   *from French*
It has na thing ado tharwith, God wait,
Ne na mair lyke than the devill and Sanct Austyne.   *St Augustine*
Have he na thank tharfor, bot loys hys pyne;   *Let him have; without praise his effort*
So schamefully that story dyd pervert.
I red his wark with harmys at my hart,   *(with a sore heart)*
That syk a buke but sentens or engyne   *without; skill*
Suldbe intitillit eftir the poet dyvyne;
Hys ornate goldyn versis mair than gilt   *more than gilded (i.e.: real)*
I spittit for dispyte to se swa spilt   *contempt; murdered*
With sych a wyght, quhilk trewly be myne entent   *By; person; to my mind*
Knew never thre wordis at all quhat Virgill ment –
Sa fer he chowpis I am constrenyt to flyte.   *garbles; scold*

The Proloug of the Sevynt Buke

1   As bryght Phebus, scheyn soverane hevynnys e,   *shining; eye*
The opposit held of hys chymmys hie,   *Took the opposite; high mansions*
Cleir schynand bemys, and goldyn symmyris hew,   *summer's hue;*
In laton cullour alteryng haill of new,   *brass; entirely anew*
Kythyng no syng of heyt be hys vissage,   *Showing; by; face*
So neir approchit he his wyntir stage;
Reddy he was to entyr the thrid morn
In clowdy skyis undre Capricorn;   *(morning on Christmas Eve)*
All thocht he be the hart and lamp of hevyn,   *Although*
Forfeblit wolx hys lemand gylty levyn,   *grew; shining golden light*
Throu the declynyng of hys large round speir.   *sphere*
The frosty regioun ryngis of the yer,   *season reigns*

The tyme and sesson bittir, cald and paill,
Tha schort days that clerkis clepe brumaill,   call wintery
Quhen brym blastis of the northyn art   fierce; from; quarter
Ourquhelmyt had Neptunus in his cart,   chariot
And all to schaik the levis of the treis,
The rageand storm ourweltrand wally seys.   rolling over swelling seas

Ryveris ran reid on spait with watir broune,   in flood
And burnys hurlys all thar bankis doune,
And landbrist rumland rudely with sik beir,   surf rumbling; racket
So lowd ne rumyst wild lyoun or ber;   bear; (never roars so loud)
Fludis monstreis, sik as meirswyne or quhalis,   dolphins or whales
Fro the tempest law in the deip devalis.   dive low in the deep
Mars occident, retrograde in his speir,   in the west; moving backwards; sphere
Provocand stryfe, regnyt as lord that yer;
Rany Oryon with his stormy face
Bewavit oft the schipman by hys race;   Blew away; from his course
Frawart Saturn, chill of complexioun,   Perverse
Throu quhais aspect darth and infectioun   dearth
Beyn causyt oft, and mortal pestilens,
Went progressyve the greis of his ascens;   degrees; (of astrological) ascent
And lusty Hebe, Junoys douchtir gay,   (Hebe was the Goddess of Youth)
Stude spulyeit of hir office and array.   despoiled

The soyl ysowpit into watir wak,   soaked; boggy
The firmament ourcast with roukis blak,   clouds
The grond fadyt, and fawch wolx all the feildis,   faded; yellow-brown
Montane toppis slekit with snaw ourheildis;   smoothed; snow-covers
On raggit rolkis of hard harsk quhyn stane   boulder-stone
With frosyn frontis cauld clynty clewis schane.   faces; stony corries shone
Bewte was lost, and barrand schew the landis,   bare showed
With frostis hair ourfret the feldis standis.   hoarfrost; brocaded
Seir bittir bubbis and the schowris snell   Sore; squalls; biting
Semyt on the sward a symylitude of hell,   earth
Reducyng to our mynd, in every sted,   Recalling; place
Gousty schaddois of eild and grisly ded.   Dreary; age; death

Thik drumly skuggis dyrknyt so the hevyn,   clouded shadows
Dym skyis oft furth warpit feirfull levyn,   hurled; lightning
Flaggis of fire, and mony felloun flaw,   Flashes; cruel blast
Scharpe soppys of sleit and of the snypand snaw.   gusts; biting
The dolly dichis war all donk and wait,   dismal; dank; wet
The law valle flodderit all with spait,   spate
The plane stretis and every hie way   level
Full of floschis, dubbis, myre and clay.   marshes; muddy puddles
Laggerit leyis wallowit farnys schew   Bemired pastures; withered ferns

Broune muris kythit thar wysnyt mossy hew,	moors showed; wizened
Bank, bra and boddum blanchit wolx and bar.	low-land; grew blanched and bare
For gurl weddir growit bestis hair.	stormy; shuddered
The wynd maid waif the red wed on the dyke,	weed; wall
Bedovyn in donkis deip was every sike.	Sunk; bogs; brook
Our craggis and the front of rochis seir	Over; separate
Hang gret ische-schouchlis lang as ony speir.	icicles
The grond stud barrant, widderit, dosk or gray,	gloomy
Herbis, flowris and gersis wallowyt away.	withered
Woddis, forrestis, with nakyt bewis blowt,	boughs bare
Stude stripyt of thar weid in every howt.	clothes; copse
So bustuusly Boreas his bugill blew,	violently; the North Wind
The deyr full dern doun in the dalis drew;	deer; secretly
Smale byrdis, flokkand throu thik ronys thrang,	brambles; crowded
In chyrmyng and with cheping changit thar sang,	chirping
Sekand hidlis and hyrnys thame to hyde	nooks and crannies
Fra feirfull thuddis of the tempestuus tyde;	blasts; season
The watir lynnys rowtis, and every lynd	waterfalls resound; tree
Quhislit and brayt of the swouchand wynd.	screeched from; howling
Puyr lauboraris and bissy husband men	farmers
Went wait and wery draglit in the fen.	wet and weary
The silly scheip and thar litil hyrd gromys	simple; shepherd boys
Lurkis undre le of bankis, woddis and bromys;	shelter; broom bushes
And other dantit grettar bestiall,	domestic bigger cattle
Within thar stabillis sesyt into stall,	tethered
Sik as mulis, horssis, oxin and ky,	cows
Fed tuskyt barys and fat swyne in sty,	boars
Sustenyt war by mannys governance	
On hervist and on symmeris purvyance.	provision
Wyde quhar with fors so Eolus schowtis schill	Everywhere (God of the winds) shrill
In this congelit sesson scharp and chill,	
The callour ayr, penetratyve and puyr,	fresh; pure
Dasyng the blude in every creatur,	Numbing
Maid seik warm stovis and beyn fyris hoyt,	seek; pleasant
In dowbill garmont cled and wily coyt,	undercoat
With mychty drink and metis confortyve,	comforting food
Agane the stern wyntir forto stryve.	
Repatyrrit weil, and by the chymnay bekyt,	Replenished; warmed
At evin be tyme doune a bed I me strekyt,	stretched out
Warpit my hed, kest on clathis thrynfald,	Wrapped; bedclothes
Fortil expell the peralus persand cald;	
I crosyt me, syne bownyt forto sleip,	crossed myself; prepared
Quhar, lemand throu the glaiss, I dyd tak kepe	observe
Latonya, the lang irksum nyght,	(the Moon); wearisome

Hir subtell blenkis sched and watry lycht,	glances
Full hie up quhirlyt in hir regioun,	
Till Phebus ryght in oppositioun,	To (the Sun)
Into the Crab, hir proper mansioun, draw,	house (in the Zodiac)
Haldand the hight all thocht the son went law.	although; sun; low
Hornyt Hebowd, quhilk we clepe the nycht owle,	(Fr. *Hibou*); call
Within hir cavern hard I schowt and yowle,	I heard
Laithly of form, with crukyt camscho beke,	twisted
Ugsum to heir was hir wild elrich screke;	Horrible; weird
The wild geiss claking eik by nyghtis tyde	time
Atour the cite fleand hard I glyde.	Out over; heard
On slummyr I slaid full sad, and slepit sound	slumber; slid; deep
Quhil the oryent upwart gan rebound.	Until; East; leap up
Phebus crownyt byrd, the nyghtis orlager,	(the Cock); time-keeper
Clapping his weyngis thryss had crawin cleir;	
Approching neir the greking of the day,	breaking
Within my bed I walkynnyt quhar I lay;	
So fast declynys Synthea the moyn,	
And kays keklis on the ruyf aboyn;	jackdaws; roof above
Palamedes byrdis crowpyng in the sky,[1]	(cranes); cackling
Fleand on randon, schapyn like ane Y,	on course
And as a trumpat rang thar vocis soun,	
Quhois cryis bene pronosticatioun	are a forecast
Of wyndy blastis and ventositeis.	gales
Fast by my chalmyr, in heich wysnyt treis,	Close; wizened
The soir gled quhislis lowd with mony a pew:	red kite
Quhar by the day was dawyn weil I knew,	
Bad beit the fyre and the candill alyght,	(I) ordered the fire stirred
Syne blissyt me, and in my wedis dyght,	blessed myself; dressed
A schot wyndo onschet a litill on char,	opened a hinged window; ajar
Persavyt the mornyng bla, wan and har,	bleak; grey
With clowdy gum and rak ourquhelmyt the ayr,	mist and fog
The sulye stythly, hasart, rouch and hair,	soil stiff, grey, rough; hoary
Branchis bratlyng, and blaknyt schew the brays	rattling; braes
With hirstis harsk of waggand wyndill strays,	harsh ridges; withered grass
The dew droppis congelit on stibbill and rynd,	stubble and rough verges
And scharp hailstanys mortfundeit of kynd	petrified by nature
Hoppand on the thak and on the causay by.	thatch; causeway
The schot I closit, and drew inwart in hy,	window; haste
Chyvirrand for cald, the sesson was so snell,	bitter
Schupe with hayt flambe to fleym the fresyng fell.	Arranged; flame; expel; cruel cold
And, as I bownyt me to the fyre me by,	took myself

1. Palamedes: Greek warrior from the siege of Troy, said to have invented four letters of the alphabet by observing the flight of cranes.

Baith up and down the hows I dyd aspy,
And seand Virgill on a lettron stand,   lectern
To write onone I hynt a pen in hand,   at once; took
Fortil perform the poet grave and sad,   complete
Quham sa fer furth or than begun I had,   so long before then
And wolx ennoyt sum deill in my hart   grew somewhat vexed
Thar restit oncompletit sa gret a part.
And to my self I said: 'In gud effect   earnest
Thou mon draw furth, the yok lyis on thy nek.'   pull ahead; yoke
Within my mynde compasyng thocht I so,   planning
Na thing is done quhil ocht remanys ado;   finished; while anything
For byssynes, quhilk occurrit on cace,   Despite business; by chance
Ourvolvyt I this volume, lay a space;   I turned over; made time
And, thocht I wery was, me list not tyre,   though; I did not wish to tire
Full laith to leif our wark swa in the myre,   loth; so bogged down
Or yit to stynt for bitter storm or rane.   stop
Heir I assayt to yok our pleuch agane,   endeavoured; plough
And, as I couth, with afald diligens,   as far as I could; single-minded
This nixt buke following of profond sentens   substance
Has thus begun in the chil wyntir cald,
162 Quhen frostis doith ourfret baith firth and fald.   brocade; wood and fold

Explicit tristis prologus.

The Proloug of the XII Buke of Eneados

1   Dyonea nycht hyrd and wach of day,   Venus (morning star); shepherd; guard
The starnys chasyt of the hevyn away,
Dame Cynthia doun rollyng in the see,   the Moon
And Venus lost the bewte of hir e,   eye
Fleand eschamyt within Cylenyus cave;   ashamed; the house of Mercury
Mars onbydrew, for all his grundyn glave,   drew away; sharpened sword
Nor frawart Saturn from hys mortall speir   perverse
Durst langar in the firmament appeir,
Bot stall abak yond in hys regioun far
Behynd the circulat warld of Jupiter;
Nycthemyne,[1] affrayt of the lyght,   the night owl
Went ondir covert, for gone was the nycht;
As fresch Aurora, to myghty Tytan spows,   the Dawn
Ischit of hir safron bed and evir hows,   Left; ivory
In crammysyn cled and granyt violat,   crimson; cloth dyed
With sangwyne cape, the selvage purpurat,   blood-red; border
Onschet the wyndois of hir large hall,   Opened up
Spred all with rosys, and full of balm ryall,

---

1. Having slept with her father, the priestess Nyctemene hid in the forests and was changed to an owl by Athene.

And eik the hevynly portis cristallyne   also; gates
Upwarpis braid, the warld till illumyn.   Flung wide
The twynklyng stremowris of the orient
Sched purpour sprangis with gold and asur ment,   bands; blue mixed
Persand the sabill barmkyn nocturnall,   black battlements
Bet doun the skyis clowdy mantill wall;   ramparts
Eous[1] the steid, with ruby harnys red,   collar fittings
Abuf the sey lyftis furth hys hed,
Of cullour soyr, and sumdeill broun as berry,   sorrel
Forto alichtyn and glaid our emyspery,   light up; gladden; hemisphere
The flambe owtbrastyng at his noysthyrlys;
Sa fast Pheton with the quhyp hym quhyrlys,   the charioteer Phaeton; whirls
To roll Appollo hys faderis goldyn char,   chariot
That schrowdith all the hevynnys and the ayr;   covers
Quhill schortly, with the blesand torch of day,
Abilyeit in hys lemand fresch array,   clothed; shining
Furth of hys palyce ryall ischit Phebus,   Phoebus Apollo (the sun)
With goldyn croun and vissage gloryus,
Crysp haris, brycht as chrisolyte or topace,   Curly hair
For quhais hew mycht nane behald hys face,
The fyry sparkis brastyng from hys eyn,
To purge the ayr, and gylt the tendyr greyn,   gild
Defundand from hys sege etheryall   pouring down; seat
Glaid influent aspectis celicall;[2]
Befor hys regale hie magnificens
Mysty vapour upspryngand, sweit as sens,   incense
In smoky soppys of donk dewis wak,   clouds; damp watery dews
Moich hailsum stovys ourheldand the slak;   Moist; vapours blanketing the valley
The aureat fanys of hys trone soverane   golden vanes; throne
With glytrand glans ourspred the occiane,   flashes; ocean
The large fludis lemand all of lycht
Bot with a blenk of hys supernale sycht.   With only a blink

Fortobehald, it was a glor to se
The stablit wyndis and the cawmyt see,   settled
The soft sesson, the firmament sereyn,   spell (time)
The lowne illumynat ayr, and fyrth ameyn;   tranquil; pleasant estuary
The sylver scalyt fyschis on the greit   gravel
Ourthwort cleir stremys sprynkland for the heyt,   all around
With fynnys schynand broun as synopar,   cinnabar
And chyssell talys, stowrand heir and thar;   stirring up
The new cullour alychtnyng all the landis,
Forgane thir stannyris schame the beriall strandis,[3]

1. One of the horses of the sun.
2. 'The glad influence of heavenly (astrological) aspects'.
3. 'Over against the modesty of the gravel shores the beryl (pale green) banks'.

Quhil the reflex of the diurnall bemys	reflection; daily
The beyn bonkis kest ful of variant glemys;	pleasant banks
And lusty Flora[1] dyd hyr blomys spreid	
Under the feit of Phebus sulyart steid;	dazzling
The swardit soyll embrowd with selcouth hewys,	turfed; embroidered; rare
Wod and forest obumbrat with thar bewys,	shadowed; boughs
Quhois blisfull branschis, porturat on the grund,	portrayed
With schaddoys schene schew rochis rubicund;	glittering; reddish rocks
Towris, turettis, kyrnellis, pynnaclys hie	battlements
Of kyrkis, castellis and ilke fair cite,	every
Stude payntit, every fyall, fayn and stage,	round tower, weathervane
Apon the plane grund, by thar awyn umbrage.	own shadows
Of Eolus[2] north blastis havand no dreid,	
The sulye spred hir braid bosum on breid,	soil; abroad (bare)
Zephyrus confortabill inspiratioun	breathing
Fortill ressave law in hyr barm adoun;	low down on her bosom
The cornys croppis and the beris new brerd	new sprouted barley
With glaidsum garmont revestyng the erd;	reclothing; earth
So thik the plantis sprang in every peyce,	
The feildis ferleis of thar fructuus fleyce;	wonder at their fruitful fleece
Byssy Dame Ceres and proud Pryapus[3]	
Rejosyng of the planys plentuus,	
Plenyst sa plesand and mast propyrly,	Stocked
By natur nurysyt wondir nobilly,	nourished
On the fertill skyrt lappys of the grund	skirt folds
Strekyng on breid ondyr the cyrkyll round;	spread out abroad; circle
The variand vestur of the venust vaill	dress; peaceful valley
Schrowdis the scherald fur, and every faill	covers; new-mown furrow; sward
Ourfret with fulyeis of figuris full divers,	embroidered; leaves; various shapes
The spray bysprent with spryngand sprowtis dispers,[4]	
For callour humour on the dewy nyght,	fresh moisture
Rendryng sum place the gerss pilis thar hycht,[5]	
Als far as catal, the lang symmyris day,	As much as cattle
Had in thar pastur eyt and knyp away;	eaten; nibbled
And blisfull blossummys in the blomyt yard	flourished
Submittis thar hedis in the yong sonnys salfgard:	Bend; charge
Ive levys rank ourspred the barmkyn wall,	Ivy; vigorous; rampart
The blomyt hawthorn cled hys pykis all;	dressed all his thorns
Furth of fresch burgionys the wyne grapis yong	Full; buds
Endlang the treilyeis dyd on twystis hyng;	Along; trellis; tendrils
The lowkyt buttonys on the gemmyt treis	closed buds; gemmed
Ourspredand leyvis of naturis tapestreis,	

1. Sensuous goddess of flowers and Spring.
2. Aeolus: god of the winds. Zephyrus is the west wind.
3. Ceres: goddess of the earth and harvest. Priapus: god of fertility and gardens; the son of Bacchus.
4. 'The twig spotted with scattered sprouting shoots'.
5. 'Giving in places the grass-blades back their height'.

Soft gressy verdour eftir balmy schowris
On curland stalkis smylyng to thar flowris;
Behaldand thame sa mony divers hew,   *Beholding*
Sum perss, sum paill, sum burnet, and sum blew,   *dark blue; brown*
Sum greyce, sum gowlys, sum purpour, sum sangwane,   *grey; scarlet; blood-red*
Blanchit or broune, fawch yallow mony ane,   *tawny*
Sum hevynly culloryt in celestiall gre,   *degree*
Sum watry hewit as the haw wally see,   *dull stormy sea*
And sum depart in freklys red and quhite,
Sum brycht as gold with aureat levys lyte.   *little*
The dasy dyd onbreid hir crownell smaill,   *open up; coronet*
And every flour onlappyt in the daill;   *unfolded; dale*
In battill gyrss burgionys the banwart wild,   *thick grass; banewort*
The clavyr, catcluke, and the cammamyld;   *clover, birds foot trefoil, camomile*
The flour delys furthspred hys hevynly hew,   *iris*
Flour dammes, and columby blank and blew;   *primula; columbine; white*
Seir downys smaill on dent-de-lyon sprang   *Many; dandelion*
The yong greyn blomyt straberry levys amang;   *fresh-flourished*
Gymp gerraflouris thar royn levys onschet,   *Graceful gillyflowers; roan; opened*
Fresch prymrois, and the purpour violet;
The roys knoppys, tutand furth thar hed,   *rose-buds; peeping*
Gan chyp, and kyth thar vermel lippys red,   *split; reveal; vermilion*
Crysp scarlet levis sum scheddand, baith atanys   *Curly; at once*
Kest fragrant smell amyd from goldyn granys;
Hevynly lylleis, with lokrand toppys quhyte,   *curling*
Oppynnyt and schew thar creistis redymyte,   *ornate*
The balmy vapour from thar silkyn croppys
Distilland hailsum sugurat hunny droppys,
And sylver schakaris gan fra levys hyng,   *danglers*
With crystal sprayngis on the verdour yong: *streaks*
The plane pulderit with semly settis sound,   *spangled; shoots*
Bedyit full of dewy peirlys round,
So that ilk burgioun, syon, herb and flour   *sprout, branch*
Wolx all enbalmyt of the fresch liquour,   *Grew*
And bathit hait dyd in dulce humouris fleyt,   *bathed heat; sweet moistures; put to flight*
Quharof the beys wrocht thar hunny sweit,
By myghty Phebus operations,
In sappy subtell exalations.
Forgane the cummyn of this prynce potent,
Redolent odour up from rutis sprent,   *leapt*
Hailsum of smell as ony spicery,
Tryakill, droggis, or electuary,   *Medical mixture; syrup*
Seroppys, sewane, sugur, and synamome,   *spice*
Precyus inunctment, salve, or fragrant pome,   *pomander*
Aromatik gummys, or ony fyne potioun,
Must, myr, aloes, or confectioun –   *Musk*

Ane paradyce it semyt to draw neir
Thir galyart gardyngis and ilke greyn herber. *gallant; flowerbed*
Maist amyabill walxis the amerant medis; *emerald river-meadows*
Swannys swouchis throw out the rysp and redis, *rustle; rushes*
Our al thir lowys and the fludis gray *Over; these lochs*
Seirsand by kynd a place quhar thai suld lay. *Searching instinctively*
Phebus red fowle hys corall creist can steir, *(a cock); stir*
Oft strekyng furth hys hekkill, crawand cleir, *hackle*
Amyd the wortis and the rutys gent *plants; delicate*
Pykand hys meyt in alleis quhar he went, *Pecking; food*
Hys wifis, Toppa and Partelot, hym by,
As byrd al tyme that hantis bigamy. *practises*
The pantyt poun, pasand with plomys gym, *painted peacock; neat plumes*
Kest up his taill, a proud plesand quheill rym, *wheelrim*
Yschrowdyt in hys fedrame brycht and scheyn, *feathers; clear*
Schapand the prent of Argus[1] hundreth eyn. *Showing the likeness*
Amang the bronys of the olyve twestis *twigs; branches*
Seir smaill fowlys wirkand crafty nestis, *Many*
Endlang the heggeis thyk and on rank akis, *along; luxuriant oaks*
Ilk byrd rejosyng with thar myrthfull makis. *Each; mates*
In corneris and cleir fenystaris of glass *windows*
Full bissely Aragne[2] wevand was, *(a spider)*
To knyt hir nettis and hir wobbys sle, *cunning webs*
Tharwith to caucht the myghe and litill fle. *midgie*

So dusty pulder upstouris in every streit, *powder stirs up*
Quhil corby gaspyt for the fervent heit. *Until the raven*
Under the bewys beyn in lusty valys, *pleasant boughs; delightful*
Within fermans and parkis cloys of palys, *enclosures; fenced fields*
The bustuus bukkis rakis furth on raw; *bold bucks trot; in a line*
Heyrdis of hertis throw the thyk wod schaw, *harts; appear*
Baith the brokkettis, and with braid burnyst tyndis, *two-year-old stags; tines*
The sprutlyt calvys sowkand the red hyndis, *speckled*
The yong fownys followand the dun days, *fauns; does*
Kyddis skippand throw ronnys efter rays; *thickets; roedeer*
In lyssouris and on leys litill lammys *pastures; leas*
Full tayt and tryg socht bletand to thar dammys, *nimble and neat; sought bleating*
Tydy ky lowys, veilys by thame rynnys; *Plump cattle low; calves*
All snog and slekit worth thir bestis skynnys. *smooth; sleek were becoming these*
On salt stremys wolx Doryda and Thetis,[3] *(sea-goddesses)*
By rynnand strandis Nymphes and Naedes, *streams*
Sik as we clepe wenschis and damysellis, *Such as we call the girls and maidens*

1. Argus had a hundred eyes; Hera punished him for failing in his guard duty by transferring them to the tail of her favourite bird.
2. Arachne, the mistress of weaving, was changed into a spider by Athena.
3. Doris: daughter of Thetis, goddess of the salt sea. The Naiads, on the other hand, are fresh-water nymphs.

In gresy gravys wandrand by spryng wellis,   *grassy groves*
Of blomyt branchis and flowris quhite and red
Plettand thar lusty chaplettis for thar hed;   *Plaiting; delightful garlands*
Sum sang ryng sangis, dansys ledys, and roundis,   *choral rounds; lead dances; ring-dances*
With vocis schill, quhill all the dail resoundis;   *shrill*
Quharso thai walk into thar caralyng,
For amorus lays doith the rochys ryng: *rocks*
Ane sang, 'The schyp salys our the salt faym,
Will bryng thir merchandis and my lemman haym';   *lover home*
Sum other syngis, 'I wilbe blyth and lycht,
Myne hart is lent apon sa gudly wight.'   *given to; person*
And thochtfull luffaris rowmys to and fro,
To lys thar pane, and pleyn thar joly wo,   *lose; bewail*
Eftir thar gys, now syngand, now in sorow,
With hartis pensyve, the lang symmyris morow:
Sum ballettis lyst endyte of hys lady,   *songs seek to write*
Sum levis in hoip, and sum aluterly   *live in hope; utterly*
Disparit is, and sa quyte out of grace,
Hys purgatory he fyndis in every place.
To pleys his lufe sum thocht to flat and feyn,   *flatter; feign*
Sum to hant bawdry and onlesum meyn;   *practise lewdness; forbidden means*
Sum rownys to hys fallow, thame betwene,   *whisper*
Hys myrry stouth and pastans lait yisterevin   *pleasurable stealth; pastimes*
Smyland says ane, 'I couth in previte   *could; private*
Schaw the a bourd.' 'Ha, quhat be that?' quod he,   *jest*
'Quhat thyng?' 'That most be secrete,' said the tother.
'Gud Lord, mysbeleif ye your verray broder?'   *mistrust*
'Na, never a deill, bot harkis quhat I wald;
Thou mon be prevy.' 'Lo, my hand uphald.'   *must be discreet*
'Than sal thou walk at evin.' Quod he, 'Quhidder?'
'In sik a place heir west, we baith togydder,
Quhar scho so freschly sang this hyndyr nycht;   *last*
Do choys the ane, and I sall quynch the lycht.'
'I salbe thar I hope,' quod he and lewch,
'Ga, now I knaw the mater weill eneuch.'
Thus oft dyvulgat is this schamefull play,
Na thyng accordyng to our hailsum May,
Bot rathar contagius and infective,
And repugnant that sesson nutrytyve,   *alien to; nourishing*
Quhen new curage kytlys all gentill hartis,   *feeling rouses; noble*
Seand throu kynd ilk thyng spryngis and revertis.   *naturally; everything (that) springs and sprouts*

Dame Naturis menstralis, on that other part,
Thar blysfull bay entonyng every art,   *birdsong; making tuneful; place*
To beyt thir amorus of thar nychtis baill,   *prepare the amorous for; heartache*
The merl, the mavys and the nychtyngale   *blackbird*

With mery notis myrthfully furth brest, *burst*
Enforcyng thame quha mycht do clynk it best: *Urging; sing*
The cowschet crowdis and pyrkis on the rys, *wood-pigeon; twigs*
The styrlyng changis divers stevynnys nys, *various wanton notes*
The sparrow chyrmys in the wallis clyft, *cleft*
Goldspynk and lyntquhite fordynnand the lyft; *Goldfinch; finch; deafening; sky*
The gukgo galys, and so quytteris the quaill, *cuckoo calls; twitters*
Quhill ryveris rerdit, schawis and every vaill, *echoed, woods*
And tender twystis trymlyt on the treis *branches*
For byrdis sang and bemyng of the beys; *buzzing; bees*
In wrablis dulce of hevynly armonyis *sweet warblings*
The larkis, lowd releschand in the skyis, *carolling*
Lovys thar lege with tonys curyus, *Praise; superior; notes*
Baith to Dame Natur and the fresch Venus,
Rendryng hie lawdis in thar observance; *praises*
Quhais suguryt throtis maid glaid hartis dans,
And al smail fowlys syngis on the spray: *twig*
'Welcum the lord of lycht and lamp of day
Welcum fostyr of tendir herbys grene, *patron*
Welcum quyknar of floryst flowris scheyn, *flourished; bright*
Welcum support of every rute and vayn,
Welcum confort of alkynd fruyt and grayn,
Welcum the byrdis beild apon the brer, *shelter*
Welcum master and rewlar of the yer,
Welcum weilfar of husbandis at the plewys, *welfare; farmers*
Welcum reparar of woddis, treis and bewys, *boughs*
Welcum depayntar of the blomyt medis, *blooming meadows*
Welcum the lyfe of every thyng that spredis,
Welcum storour of alkynd bestiall, *storekeeper; animals*
Welcum be thy brycht bemys, gladyng all,
Welcum celestial myrrour and aspy, *observer*
Attechyng all that hantis sluggardy!' *Reproving; practise laziness*

And with this word, in chalmer quhar I lay,
The nynt morow of fresch temperit May, *(9 May)*
On fut I sprent into my bair sark, *leaped; shirt*
Wilfull fortill compleit my langsum wark *Eager; lengthy*
Twichand the lattyr buke of Dan Virgill, *Concerning; Master*
Quhilk me had tareit al to lang a quhile; *delayed*
And tobehald the cummyng of this kyng, *(the sun)*
That was sa welcum tyll all warldly thyng,
With sic tryumphe and pompos curage glaid *splendid spirit glided*
Than of hys soverane chymmys, as is said, *Then from; mansions*
Newly aryssyn in hys estait ryall, *royal state*
That, by hys hew, but orleger or dyall, *without timekeeper or (sun)dial*
I knew it was past four howris of day,

And thocht I wald na langar ly in May	
Less Phebus suld me losanger attaynt –	Lest; sluggard; accuse
For Procne had or than sung hir complaynt,	(swallow); before then
And eik hir dreidfull systir Philomeyn[1]	also; sad; (nightingale)
Hyr lays endyt, and in woddis greyn	songs compose
Hyd hir selvyn, eschamyt of hir chance;	ashamed; fate
And Esacus[2] completis hys pennance	(cormorant)
In ryveris, fludis, and on every laik;	
And Peristera[3] byddis luffaris awaik:	(dove)
'Do serve my lady Venus heir with me,	
Lern thus to mak your observance,' quod sche,	
'Into myne hartis ladeis sweit presens	
Behaldis how I beynge, and do reverens.'	bow
Hyr nek scho wrynklys, trasyng mony fold,	
With plomys glitterand, asur apon gold,	plumes; blue
Rendryng a cullour betwix greyn and blew,	
In purpour glans of hevynly variant hew;	purple flash; varied
I meyn our awyn natyve byrd, gentill dou,	according to her nature; woo
Syngand in hyr kynd, 'I come hydder to wou,'	
So pryklyng hyr greyn curage forto crowd	spurring; fresh spirit; coo
In amorus voce and wouar soundis lowd,	lover-like
That, for the dynnyng of hir wanton cry,	
I irkyt of my bed, and mycht not ly,	wearied
Bot gan me blys, syne in my wedis dress,	did bless myself; then; clothes
And, for it was ayr morow, or tyme of mess,	early; before; mass
I hynt a scriptour and my pen furth tuke,	seized a pen-case
Syne thus begouth of Virgill the twelt buke.	began
Explicit scitus prologus,	(here ends the skilful prologue)
Quharof the autour says thus:	
The lusty crafty preambill, 'perle of May'	delightful skilful
I the entitil, crownyt quhil domysday,	title you; celebrated until
And al with gold, in syng of stait ryall	sign
Most beyn illumnyt thy letteris capital.	Must be illuminated

from Eneados

Book IV, Canto xii: Heir followys of the famus Queyn Dydo
The fatale dynt of deth and mortale wo

Bot now the hasty, egyr and wild Dydo,
Into hyr cruell purpos enragyt so,

---

1. Philomel was dishonoured by her sister Procne's husband, King Tereus. Taking pity on their pain, the gods changed them into birds.
2. One of Priam's many sons, Esacus drowned himself for love and was changed into a cormorant.
3. Dove sacred to Venus.

The bludy eyn rollyng in hir hed,
Wan and ful paill for feir of the neir ded,   *death*
With chekis freklyt, and al of teris bysprent,   *flecked; tears spattered*
Quakyng throu dreid, ruschit furth, or scho wald stent,   *before; stop*
Onto the innar wardis of hyr place,   *rooms; palace*
As wod woman clam on the byng, allace!   *Like a madwoman, climbs, pyre*
And furth scho drew the Trojane swerd, fute hait,   *hot-foot (immediately)*
A wapyn was never wrocht for syk a nate.   *such a purpose*
And sone as sche beheld Eneas clething,   *Aeneas's clothes*
And eik the bed bekend, a quhile wepyng,   *also the familiar bed*
Stude musyng in hir mynd, and syne, but baid,   *then, without delay*
Fel in the bed, and thir last wordis said: *these*
'O sweit habyte, and lykand bed,' quod sche,   *clothes and pleasing*
'So lang as God lyst suffir and destane,   *pleases to suffer and ordain*
Ressave my blude, and this sawle that on flocht is,   *Accept; in disarray*
And me delyvir from thir hevy thochtis.
Thus lang I levyt have, and now is spent
The term of lyfe that forton heth me lent;
For now my gret gost undir erth mon go.   *weeping spirit; must go*
A richt fair cite have I beild also,   *city (Carthage); built*
Myne awyn wark and wallys behald have I;
My spows,[1] wrokyn of my brothir enemy,   *on whom my enemy brother wreaked vengeance*
Fra hym byreft hys tressour, and quyt hym weill.
Happy, allace! Our happy, and ful of seyll,   *Too happy; joy*
Had I beyn, only gyf that never nane   *if only never at all*
At our cost had arryvit schip Trojane.'   *coast*
And sayand this, hir mouth fast thristis sche   *presses*
Doun in the bed: 'Onwrokyn sal we de?   *unavenged; die*
De us behufis,' scho said, 'and quhou, beheld!'   *We must die; how, behold!*
And gan the scharp sword to hir breist uphald;
'Ya, thus, thus lykis us to starve and depart!'   *perish*
And with that word, rave hir self to the hart.   *cut*
'Now lat yon cruel Trojane swelly and se   *swallow (drink with his eyes)*
This our fyre funerale from the deip see,
And of our deth turs with hym fra Cartage   *carry away*
Thys takyn of myscheif in hys vayage.'   *sign of cruel wrong; voyage*

Quod scho; and tharwith gan hir servandis behald   *did her servants*
Hir fallyn and stekit on the irne cald,   *stabbed; iron*
The blude outbullyrand on the nakyt swerd,   *boiling out*
Hir handis furthsprent. The clamour than and rerd   *outflung; din*
Went to the toppys of the large hallys;
The noys ran wild out our the cite wallis,   *out over*

---

1. Dido's wealthy husband Sichaeus was murdered by her brother Pygmalion. She saved his treasures and fled from Tyre to Africa where she founded Carthage. Virgil's poem makes Dido fall in love with Aeneas as he passes through on his return from the siege of Troy; but in reality Carthage was founded 300 years after Troy fell.

Smate all the town with lamentabil murnyng:
Of greting, gowlyng and wyfly womentyng   *weeping, wailing; female lamentation*
The ruffis dyd resound, bray and rayr,   *bray and roar*
Quhil huge bewalyng al fordynnyt the air –   *resounded through*
Nane other wys than thocht takyn and doun bet   *No less than as if captured and*
War al Cartage, and with enemys ourset;   */battered down*
Or than thar natyve cite the town of Tyre,   *Or as if*
And furyus flambe, kendillit and byrnand schyre,   *bright*
Spredyng fra thak to thak, baith but and ben,   *thatch; outside and in*
Als weill our templis as howsis of othir men.   *As equally over*

Hir systir An, spreitles almaist for dreid,   *fainting*
Herand sa feirful confluens thyddir speid,   *Hearing such a fearful forgathering*
With nalys ryvand reuthfully hir face,   *nails tearing piteously*
And smytand with hir nevis hir breist, allace!   *striking; fists*
Fast ruschis throu the myddis of the rowt,   *rout*
And on there throwand, with mony sprauch and schout,   *twisting; scream*
Callys by name: 'Systir germane,' quod scho,   *(of the same blood)*
'Och! Was this it thou fenyeit the to do?   *this (what) you contrived to do*
Hes thou attempyt me with syk dissait?   *tried me with such deceit*
This byng of treys, thir altaris and fyris hait,   *pyre of trees; these*
Is this the thyng thai have onto me dycht?   *they have prepared for me*
Quhat sall I first compleyn, now dissolate wight?   *deserted wretch*
O deir systir, quhen thou was reddy to de,
Ha! Quhy hes thou sa far dyspysyt me
As to reffus thi systir with the to wend?   *to go with you*
Thou suld have callyt me to the sammyn end,   *same*
That the ilk sorow, the sammyn swerd, bath tway,   *both two (of us)*
And the self hour, mycht have tane hyne away.   *taken (us) hence away*
This funeral fyre with thir handis biggyt I,   *I built with these hands*
And with my voce dyd on our goddis heir cry,
To that effect as, cruel, to be absent,
Thou beand thus sa duylfully heir schent!   *dolefully destroyed here*
Sistir, allace! With my counsell[1] have I
The, and my self, and pepill of Sydony,
The heris all, and eik thi fayr cite,   *All the chiefs; also*
Distroyt and ondeyn for ay,' quod sche.   *undone for ever*
'Fech hiddir sone the well watir lew warm,   *lukewarm*
To wesch hir woundis, and hald hir in myne arm;
Syne with my mouth at I may sowk, and se   *that I may suck*
Gyf spreit of lyve left in hir body be.'
This sayand, the hie byng ascendis onane,   *at once*
And gan enbrays half ded hir systir germane,
Culyeand in hir bosum, and murnand ay,   *Caressing; lamenting still*

---

1. Ann encouraged Dido to prolong Aeneas's stay, seeking his protection for Carthage and ultimately marriage.

And with hir wympil wipyt the blude away.   head band

And scho agane, Dydo, the dedly queyn,
Pressyt fortil uplift hir hevy eyn,   Attempted
Bot tharof falys; for the grysly wound   fails
Deip in hir breist gapis wyde and onsound.   unhealthy
Thrys scho hir self raxit up to rys;   stretched
Thrys on hir elbok lenys; and als feill sys   many times
Scho fallys bakwart in the bed agane.
With eyn rollyng, and twynkland up ful fane,   willingly
Assays scho to spy the hevynnys lyght,   Tries
Syne murmouris, quhen scho tharof gat a sycht.
Almychty Juno havand reuth, by this,   pity
Of hir lang sorow and tarysum ded, I wys,   lingering death
Hir mayd Irys from the hevyn hes send
The throwand sawle to lowys, and mak ane end   writhing soul; release
Of al the juncturis and lethis of hir cors,   joints and hinges
Becaus that nothir of fatis throu the fors   neither by the action of the fates
Nor yit by natural ded peryschit sche,
Bot fey in hasty furour emflambyt hie   unhappy; fury enflamed
Befor hir day had hir self spilt,   her time was up
Or that Proserpyne the yallow haris gilt   golden yellow hair
From hir fortop byreft, or dubbyt hir hed   forehead; consigned
Onto the Stygian hellis flude of ded.   death
Tharfor dewy Iris throu the hevyn
With hir safron weyngis flaw ful evin,   smoothly
Drawand, quhar scho went, forgane the son cleir,   against the sun
A thousand cullouris of divers hewys seir,   various; separate
And abufe Dydos hed arest kan: came to a halt
'I am commandyt,' said scho, 'and I man
Omdo this hayr, to Pluto consecrate,   Undo
And lowis thi sawle out of this mortale stait.'
Thys sayand, with rycht hand hes scho hynt   raised she took
The hair, and cuttis in twa, or that scho stynt;   before she finished
And tharwithall the natural heyt outquent,   ardour
120   And, with a puft of aynd, the lyfe furthwent.   breath

Heyr endys the ferd buke of Eneados
and begynnys the proloug of the fyft.

Book VI: Canto vii: Dido in Hades
55   Amang otheris the Phenyssyane Dido
Within the gret wod walkis to and fro,   wood
The greyn wound gapand in hir breist all new,   green
Quhom as the Trojane barroun nerrer drew,

And throw the dyrk schaddowis first dyd knaw –
Sikwys as quha throw clowdy skyis saw,   Just as
Or, at the leist, wenys he heth do se,   believes
The new moyn quhen first upwalxis sche.   moon
The terys leyt he fall, and tendyrly
With hartly lufe begrat hir thus in hy;   heartfelt; bewailed
'O fey Dido, sen I persave the heir,   fated
A sovir warnyng, now I knaw ful cleir,   certain
Was schawin me, at thou with swerd was slaw,   that you
Byreft thi self the lyfe, and brocht of daw.   deprived of life (daylight)
Allace, I was the causar of thy ded!   death
By al the starnys schynys abone our hed,
And be the goddis abone, to the I swer,
And be the faith and lawte, gif ony heir   fidelity
Trewth may be fund deip undir erd,' quod he,
'Malgre my wyl, Prynces, sa mot I the,   Despite my desires; I assure you
From thy costis depart I was constrenyt.
Bot the commandment of the goddis onfenyt,   unequivocal
Quhais gret mychtis hes me hyddir dryve,   powers; driven
To pas throwout thir dirk schaddowis belyve,   at once
By gowsty placis, welch savorit, must and hair,   dismal; sickly; musty; grey
Quhar profund nycht perpetual doith repar,
Compellit me from the forto dissevir;   from thee to part
Nor in my mynde ymagyn mycht I nevir,
For my departing or absens, I wys,
Thou suldist kaucht sa gret dyseys as this.   hardship
Do stynt thy pays! Abide, thou gentil wight,   stop pacing
Withdraw the not sa sone furth of my sight!
Quham fleist thou? This is the lattir day,   last
By werdis schape, that with the speke I may.'   Arranged by the fates
With sik wordis Eneas, full of wo,
Set him to meys the sprete of Queyn Dido,   calm; spirit
Quhilk, all inflambit, ful of wreth and ire,
With acquart luke glowand hait as fyre,   askance
Maid him to weip and sched furth teris wak.   watery tears
All fremmytly frawart hym, as he spak,   strangely away from
Hir eyn fixit apon the grond held sche,
Moving na mair hir curage, face nor bre,   disposition; brow
Than scho had bene a statu of marbil stane,
Or a ferm rolk of Mont Marpesyane.[1]
Bot finaly, full swyft scho wiskis away,
Aggrevit fled in the darn woddis gray,   dusky
Quhar as Sycheus, hir first spows, ful suyr   husband; surely
Corespondis to hir desyre and cuyr,   responds; care

1. Mountain in Paros where Parian marble is found.

Rendring in lufe amouris equivalent. — Giving equal love for love
And, netheles, fast eftir hir furth sprent — nevertheless; ran
Ene, perplexit of hir sory cace, — Aeneas
And weping gan hir follow a weil lang space, — began to follow her
Regratand in his mynd, and had piete
108 Of the distres that movit hir so to fle.

The Asloan, Bannatyne and Maitland Collections

Many older Scots poems, by well-known and unknown authors alike, have survived because they were copied out by private enthusiasts in the sixteenth century. The leading manuscript collections of the time were made by John Asloan in 1515; by George Bannatyne, a 23-year-old Edinburgh merchant in 1568; and by Sir Richard Maitland, a distinguished judge and Privy Counsellor whose two-volume Folio MS was completed by the end of his life in 1586. The Maitland Quarto MS contains more recent work compiled by his daughter. The Bannatyne and Asloan MSS are held by the National Library of Scotland; Maitland by Magdalene College, Cambridge.

Poems can appear in more than one collection, or once only. There are minor variations between different versions, and disputed or speculative attributions. 'Christ's Kirk on the Green', for example, has been attributed to James I, or to James V, but a now unknown author in the late fifteenth or sixteenth century seems more likely. Its spirit and metre with the 'bob and wheel' effect at the end of each verse are very similar to a contemporary poem 'Peblis to the Play', and both have proved to be enormously influential in the development of vernacular Scots verse, from David Lindsay to the Sempills, Ramsay, Hogg and Burns. 'Christ's Kirk' describes a local fair with dancing, drinking, fighting and some play with bows and arrows. Other anonymous pieces in these collections clearly belong to a lively oral tradition of tall stories, riddles and insults.

Anonymous

Christ's Kirk on the Green

Was never in Scotland hard nor sene
Sic dansing nor deray,   wild revelry
Nother in Falkland on the grene,
Nor Peblis to the play,

As was of wooeris as I wene	suitors; imagine
At Chrystis Kirk on ane day.	
Thair come our Kittie weschen clene	
In hir new kirtill of gray,	dress
Full gay,	
At Chrystis Kirk on the grene.	
To dance the damisallis thame dicht	maidens prepared themselves
And lassis licht of laittis;	manners
Thair gluvis war of the raffell richt	roe-deer skin
Thair schone war of the straitis;	shoes; morocco leather
Thair kirtillis war of the lincum licht	Lincoln green
Weill prest with mony plaitis.	
Thay war so nyce quhen men thame nicht	bashful; approached
Thay squeild lyk ony gaitis,	goats
Ful loud,	
At Chrystis kirk on the grene.	
Off all thir madinis myld as mede	
Was nane sa gymp as Gillie,	slim
As ony rose hir rude was reid	cheek
Hir lyre was lyk the lillie;	skin
Bot yallow yallow was hir heid,	
And sche of luif so sillie,	
Thoch all hir kin suld have bein deid	Though
Sche wald have bot sweit Willie,	
Allane,	
At Chrystis kirk on the grene.	
Sche scornit Jok and scrippit at him	scoffed
And morgeound him with mokkis;	grimaced at; mockery
He wald have luffit hir, sche wald nocht lat him,	
For all his yallow lokkis;	
He cherist hir; scho bad ga chat him,	hang himself
Sche comptit him nocht twa clokkis;	beetles
So schamefullie ane schort goun sat him	
His lymmis was lyk twa rokkis,	spindles
Sche said,	
At Chrystis kirk on the grene.	
Steven come steppand in with stendis	strides
No renk mycht him arrest;	man
Platfut he bobbit up with bendis	Flatfoot; jumps
For Mald he maid request;	
He lap quhill he lay on his lendis,	leaped up; side
Bot risand he was prest	rising

Quhill he hostit at bayth the endis *Until; 'coughed'*
In honour of the feist,
 That day,
At Chrystis kirk on the grene.

Tom Lutar was thair menstrale meet, *suitable*
O Lord, gif he culd lance; *how he could bound*
He playit so schill and sang so sweit *high*
Quhill Towsie tuik ane trance; *Until*
All auld lycht futtis he did forleit *old-fashioned dances; forsake*
And counterfutit France; *imitated*
He him avysit as man discreit *considered himself*
And up the morris dance,
 Scho tuik,
At Chrystis kirk on the grene.

Than Robene Roy begouth to revell *began*
And Dowie to him druggit; *dragged*
'Lat be!' quod Johke, and callit him gavell, *rogue*
And by the taill him tuggit;
He turnit and cleikit to the cavell, *hooked on to; ruffian*
Bot Lord, than gif thai luggit! *how they wrestled!*
Thai partit thair play thane with ane nevell, *battering*
Men wait gif hair wes ruggit, *know; hair; tugged*
 Betwene thame,
At Chrystis kirk on the grene.

Ane bend ane bow, sic sturt couth steir him; *One bent; rage aroused*
Grit scaith war to have scared him; *It were great harm*
He choosit ane flaine as did affeir him, *arrow; suited*
The tother said dirdum dardum; *shouted incoherently*
Throw bayth the cheikis he thocht to cheir him, *pierce*
Or throw the chaftis have charde him; *jaws; spiked*
Bot be ane myle it come nocht neir him,
I can nocht say quhat mard him, *hindered*
 Thair,
At Chrystis kirk on the grene.

With that ane freind of his cryit, fy!
And up ane arow drew,
He forgeit it so fiercely *drew*
The bow in flenders flew; *splinters*
Sa was the will of God, trow I,
For had the tre bene trew *wood*
Men said that kend his archerie
That he had slane anew,
 That day,
At Chrystis kirk on the grene.

Ane haistie hensour callit Harie,	youth
Quhilk wes ane archer heind,	skilful
Tit up ane takill but ony tarye	snatched; weapon; without
That turment so him teind;	turmoil; vexed
I wait nocht quhither his hand cud varie,	
Or gif the man was his freind,	
Bot he chapit throw the michtis of Marie	escaped; power
As man that na evill meind,	intends
That tyme,	
At Chrystis kirk on the grene.	

Than Lowrie as ane lyoun lap,	leaped up
And sone ane flane culd fedder;	arrow; nock
He hecht to pers him at the pape	promised; nipple
Thairon to wed ane wedder;	bet; castrated ram
He hit him on the wambe ane wap	belly; blow
And it bust lyk ane bledder;	bladder
Bot lo! as fortoun was and hap,	chance
His doublat was of ledder,	
And sauft him,	
At Chrystis kirk on the grene.	

The baff so boustuouslie abasit him,	biff; abashed
To the erth he duschit doun;	dashed
The tother for dreid he preissit him	hastened
And fled out of the toun;	
The wyffis come furth and up thay paisit him,	got him on his feet
And fand lyff in the loun,	lad
And with thre routis thay raisit him	shouts
And coverit him of swoune,	recovered
Agane,	
At Chrystis kirk on the grene.	

Ane yaip young man that stude him neist	keen
Lousit off ane schot with ire;	Loosed
He etlit the berne evin in the breist,	aimed at the man
The bout flew owre the byre;	bolt
Ane cryit that he had slane ane preist	
Ane myle beyond ane myre;	bog
Than bow and bag fra him he caist	threw
And fled als fers as fyre,	swift
Off flint,	
At Chrystis kirk on the grene.	

With forkis and flailis thay leit grit flappis	made great
And flang togither with friggis,	clashed with brawny types

With bougaris of barnis thai birst blew cappis,   barn rafters
Quhill thay of bernis maid briggis;   men; bridges
The rerde rais rudlie with the rappis,   din; blows
Quhen rungis was layd on riggis;   cudgels; backbones
The wyffis come furth with cryis and clappis
'Lo quhair my lyking liggis,'   sweetheart lies
   Quod scho,
At Chrystis kirk on the grene.

Thay girnit and leit gird with granis,   moaned; let fly; groans
Ilk gossop uther grevit;   Each neighbour; hurt
Sum straikit stingis sum gadderit stanis,   waved poles;
Sum fled and evill eschevit;   escaped
The menstrale wan within ane wanis,   got inside a house
That day full weill he previt   proved
For he come hame with unbriste banis   unbroken
Quhair fechtaris war mischevit,   injured
   For ever,
At Chrystis kirk on the grene.

Heich Huchoun with ane hissill ryse   hazel branch
To red can throw thame rummill;   sort (them) out; did charge
He mudlit thame doun lyk ony myse   struck
He wes na baty bummill.   feckless bungler
Thocht he wes wicht he wes nocht wys   strong; sensible
With sic jatouris to geummill.   tattlers; meddle
For fra his thoume thay dang ane sklys   thumb; struck; slice
Quhill he cryit 'barlaw fummill,   'Parlay! Truce!'
   Ouris!',
At Chrystis kirk on the grene.

Quhen that he saw his blude so reid,
To fle micht no man lat him;   prevent
He wend it had bene for ald feid,   judged; an ancient feud
The far sairar it sat him;   so much sorer; hurt
He gart his feit defend his heid,   made
He thocht thay cryit 'have at him!'
Quhill he was past out of all pleid,   dispute
He suld be swyft that gat him,   caught
   Throw speid,
At Chrystis kirk on the grene.

The toun soutar in breif was boudin,   shoemaker; rage; swollen
His wyf hang in his waist;   was by his side
His body was in blude all browdin,   stained
He granit lyk ony gaist;   groaned; ghost

Her glitterand hairis that war full goldin
So hard in luif him laist,   held
That for hir saik he wes unyoldin   unsubmitting
Seven myle quhen he wes chaist,
    And mair,
At Chrystis kirk on the grene.

The millar was of manlie mak,   make
To meit him was na mowis;   no joke
Thair durst na ten cum him to tak,   Not even ten dared
So nobbit he thair nowis;   knocked; heads
The buschement haill about him brak   ambush
And bickert him with bowis,   attacked
Syn tratourlie behind his bak
Ane hewit him on the howis,   struck; behind the knees
    Behind,
At Chrystis kirk on the grene.

Twa that was herdismen of the herde   (Shepherds)
Ran upone uther lyk rammis;   each other; rams
Thai forsy freikis richt uneffeird   strong fighting men; unafraid
Bet on with barow trammis;   Laid on; barrow shafts
Bot quhair thair gobbis war bayth ungird   mouths; unguarded
Thai gat upon the gammis,   got it on the gums
Quhill bludie barkit was thair berd   Until; clotted; beards
As thay had worreit lambis,
    Most lyk,
At Chrystis kirk on the grene.

The wyffis cast up ane hiddeous yell
Quhen all the youngkeris yokkit;   set-to
Als fers as ony fyr flauchtis fell   lightning bolts
Freikis to the feild thai flokit;   fighters
Thai cavellis with clubbis culd uther quell,   Those ruffians
Quhill blude at breistis out bokkit;   Until; spurted
So rudlie rang the Commoun bell
Quhill all the steipill rokkit,
    For rerde,   din
At Chrystis kirk on the grene.

Quhen thai had beirit lyk batit bullis   rushed
And brane wode brynt in balis,   brushwood; bonfires
Thai wox als mait as ony mulis   became; worn out
That maggit war with malis;   loaded; packs
For faintnes thay forfochin fulis   exhausted fools
Fell doun lyk flauchter falis;   slices of turf

Fresche men com hame and halit the dulis   rolled up the game
And dang thame doun in dalis,   heaps
    Bedene,   Straight away
At Chrystis kirk on the grene.

Quhen all wes done, Dick with ane ax
Come furth to fell ane futher,   heap
Quod he, 'quhair ar yon hangit smaikis   wretches
Richt now that hurt my brother?'
His wyf bad him gang hame gud glaikis   silly fellow
And sae did Meg his mother;
He turnit and gaif thame bath thair paikis,   deserts
For he durst stryk na uther,
    Men said,
At Chrystis kirk on the grene.

Walter Brown (fl. 15th century)

This poem is all that survives of Walter Brown, one among many makars of the period, both high and low, who played their pageant (in Dunbar's words) and went to the grave.

Letters of gold

Lettres of gold writtin I fand
Intill a buike was fair to reid,
The sentence plane till undirstand
Thairfoir till it I tuik gude heid.
With havy hairt and mekle dreid
I red the scriptour verement,
The quhilk said thus, trew as the creid: the Creed
Ryse deid folk and cum to Jugement.

Ryse deid folk ryse forsuth, it said,
Cum on belyve ye mon compeir   quickly; must present yourself
That law doun on the erth ar laid,   low
Get up gud speid and be nocht sweir,   reluctant
Mak compt how ye haif levit heir,   Give an account; lived
In to this wretchit warld present
Your conscience, tellis yor deidis cleir,
Befoir the Juge in Jugement.

Fra hevin to hell throw erth and air
That hiddous trump sa lowid sall sound   *(last) trumpet*
That throw the blast I yow declair
The stanis sall cleive, erth sall redound.   *split*
Sall no man respect get that stound   *moment*
For gold for riches or for rent,
For all mon cum ouir sea and sound   *must come*
And present thame to Jugement.

In flesche and bane as ye war heir   *just as you are*
Thoch ye wer brint in powder all,   *Even if*
Befoir the Juge ye mon compeir   *must present yourself*
To mak yor compt baith grit and small.
Nane advocat for ocht sall fall,   *lawyer; anyone; shall suit*
Bot yor awin conscience innocent
Sall speik for yow quhen ye ar call
Befoir the Juge in Jugement.

May nocht be hid I yow declair
That evir ye did in deid or thocht;
Sall nocht be cullerit, all beis bair   *will be laid bare*
How prevelly that evir ye wrocht;   *However secretly you worked*
The twynkling of yor ene beis socht   *eyes will be sought out*
Quhen synnaris schamefully ar schent: *disgraced*
Thairfoir be war or ye be brocht   *in case*
Oure soddanly to Jugement.   *Too quickly*

Paip or prelattis precissit of wit   *foremost*
In to this warld that clymis so hie
To win the fowll vane gloir of it
Be war: ye sall accusit be
The folk ye tuke to keip lat se   *undertook to care for*
The faith to teiche as ye wer sent
Hirdis to be, and tuke yor fee,   *Shepherds*
Cum anser now in Jugement.

Ye kingis hie of stait and micht
That warldly conqueist and vanegloir
Desyrit ay baith day and nicht,
And all yor lawbor set thairfoir,
Quhat helpis than yor micht
Yor stoir, quhen warldis welth away is went.   *abundance*
May nane yow hyd in hoill nor boir   *hole or burrow*
For all mon ryse to Jugement.

Gif ye haif keipit just and richt   If
The law allyk to riche and peure,
With blyth hairt in the Jugeis sicht   joyous
Ye may appeir, I yow assure.
Haif ye misgovernit ocht your cure,   Mismanaged your charge in any way
Sair may ye dreid the hard torment
Off hellis fyre that sall indure
Perpetuall eftir Jugement.

O crewall knychtis and men of pryd,
That evir in armes and chevelrye
Hes socht oure all this warld so wyd
Yow till avance with victory
Ay blud to sched sa crewaly;
Gud tyme wer heir for to repent
Or ye be schot doun soddanly,
And brocht on fors to Jugement.   by force

For that day is no grace to gett,   gain
Nor that day sall na mercy be
Fra that the Juge in sait be sett.   From when
Haif thow done weill? Full weill is the
That awfull Juge quhen thow sall se,
Sa full of yre in face fervent
To synneris for iniquitie
That mon upryse to Jugement.   must

Ye men of kirk that cure hes tane   have undertaken
Of sawlis for to watche and keip,
Ye will be tynt and ye tyne ane   lost if you lose one
In your defalt of goddis scheip.
Be walkand ay that ye not sleip;   alert always
Luke that your bow be reddy bent
The wolf abowt yor flok will creip
Ye mon mak compt at Jugement.

Be gude of lyfe and bissie ay
Gud examplis for to schaw
Stark in the faith, and luke allwey   strong
That na man cryme unto yow knaw.   can accuse you of crime
Lat ay yor deid follow yor saw,   actions; sayings
And to this taill ye tak gud tent: pay good heed
Sayweill but doweill is nocht worth a straw   Speaking good without doing good
For yow to schaw in Jugement.

And warldly wemen be ye war
Your wit is waik, leir to be wyse;   *understanding is weak; learn*
Grit caws of syn forsooth ye ar
Throw yor fowll pryd and claithis of pryse,   *fancy clothes*
Ay prowd in busking and garmond nyse,   *get up*
Inflammand lychman of intent
To lichery thame for to tyis;   *to entice them*
Ye mon mak compt in Jugement.

Ye merchantis that the gold sa reid
Upbrace in to yor boxis bad,   *ordered stored away*
Quhat may it help quhen ye ar deid,
The gadderit riches that ye had?
Be all weill win, ye may be glad   *well gained*
Befoir the prince maist prepotent;   *powerful*
Be it not so, ye may be sad
Quhen that ye cum to Jugement.

Leill labouraris that nicht and day   *Loyal*
Dois that thay may for to uphald
This wretchit lyfe: full blyth may thay   *joyously*
Cum to thair compt quhen thay ar cald.   *judgement; called*
Weill may thay byd with hairtis bald;   *remain; confident*
To no man did thay detriment
Bot pure lyfe led heir as God wald   *here; wished*
Yit thay sall cum to Jugement.

Thairfoir me think for to conclude:
Grit rent nor riches proffeitis nocht,
For grit aboundance heir of gude   *here of property*
Dois men grit truble in thair thocht.
Weill sall thay worth that sa hes wrocht   *deserve; have behaved in such a way*
Off sufficence can be content;
Thair can no sickerer way be wrocht   *more secure; worked*
To help thame at Jugement.

All is bot vane and vanitie
Into this warld that we haif heir.
Grit riches and prosperitie
Upfosteris vyce, that is na weir,   *no doubt*
Makis men to fall in synnis seir,   *several*
Misknaw thair God, syne consequent   *then as a result*
To Godis service makis thame maist sweir.   *unwilling*
Ryse deid folk. Cum to Jugement.

ffinis q Wa broun

Anonymous

This warld is all bot fenyeit fair

This warld is all bot fenyeit fair   *falsely*
And als unstable as the wind;
Gud faith is flemit I wat not quhair   *expelled; know*
Trest fallowschip is evill to find;   *Firm*
Gud conscience is all maid blind
And cheritie is nane to gett;
Leill loif and lawte lyis behind,   *Loyal love; fidelity*
And auld kyndnes is quyt forget.

Quhill I had ony thing to spend
And stuffit weill with warldis wrak   *flotsam*
Amang my freindis I wes weill kend;
Quhen I wes prowd and had a pak   *goods/a means of living*
Thay wald me be the oxstar tak   *upper arm*
And at the burd I wes set.   *table*
Bot now thay latt me stand abak
Sen auld kyndnes is quyt forget.

Now I find bot freindis few
Sen I wes prysit to be pure;   *judged; poor*
Thay hald me now bot for a schrew,
To me thay tak bot littill cure,
All that I do is bot injure.
Thoch I am bair I am not bett,   *beaten*
Thay latt me stand bot on the flure
Sen auld kyndnes is quyt forget.

Suppois I mene I am not mendit   *declare; advanced*
Sen I held pairt with poverte,   *met up with*
Away sen that my pak wes spendit: *fortune*
Adew all liberalite.
The proverb now is trew I se –
'Quha may not gife, will littill gett;'
Thairfoir to say the varite   *truth*
Now auld kyndnes is quyt forget.

Thay wald me hals with hude and hatt   *embrace*
Quhill I wes riche and had aneuch,
About me freindis anew I gatt
Ryt blythlie on me thay leuch;   *smiled*
Bot now thay mak it wondir teuch,

And lattis me stand befoir the gett;
Thairfoir this warld is verry freuch   brittle
And auld kyndnes is quyt forget.

Als lang as my cop stud evin   cup; level
I geld bot seindill myn allane,   went; seldom
I squyrit was with sex or seven
Ay quhill I gaif thame twa for ane;
Bot suddanly fra that wes gane   from when
Thay passit by with handis plett,   closed
With purtye fra I wes ourtane   poverty
Than auld kyndnes wes quyt forget.

In to this warld suld na man trow   believe in
Thow may weill se the ressoun quhy;
For evir bot gif thy hand be fou   unless always; full
Thow arte bot littill settin by,   thought of
Thow art not tane in cumpany
Bot thair be sum fisch in thy nett;   Unless
Thairfoir this fals warld I defy
Sen auld kyndnes is quyt forget.

Sen that na kyndnes kepit is
In to this warld that is present,
Gife thow wald cum to hevynnis bliss
Thy self appleiss with sobir rent;   satisfy; income
Leife godly and gife with gud intent   Live
To every man his proper dett.
Quhat evir God send hald thee content,
Sen auld kyndnes is quyt forget.

         ffinis

The Wyf of Auchtermuchty

In Auchtermuchty thair dwelt ane man,
Ane husband, as I hard it tawld,   farmer
Quha weill cowld tippill owt a can   mug
And nathir luvit hungir nor cawld,
Quhill anis it fell upoun a day
He yokkit his pleuch upoun the plane,   yoked; plough
Gif it be trew as I hard say,   If
The day was fowll for wind and rane.

He lowsit the pleuch at the landis end   unyoked
And draif his oxin hame at evin;

Quhen he come in he lukit bend,   into the next room
And saw the wyf baith dry and clene
And sittand at ane fyre beikand bawld   well-stoked
With ane fat sowp, as I hard say.   thick soup
The man being verry weit and cauld,
Betwene thay twa it was na play.

Quoth he, 'Quhair is my horssis corne?
My ox hes nathir hay nor stray!
Dame, ye mon to the pleuch to-morne,   must go
I salbe hussy, gif I may.'   housewife
'Husband,' quo scho, 'content am I
To tak the pleuch my day abowt,
Sae ye will rowll baith calvis and ky   rule; cattle
And all the hous, baith in and owt.

'Bot sen that ye will hussyskep ken,   housekeeping learn
First ye sall sift and syne sall kned;   knead
And ay as ye gang but and ben   around the house
Luk that the bairnis dyrt not the bed;
Yeis lay ane soft wisp to the kill,   dry kindling (straw); kiln
We haif ane deir ferme on our heid;
And ay as ye gang furth and in,
Keip weill the gaslingis fra the gled.'   goslings; kite

The wyf was up richt lait at evin,
I pray God gif hir evill to fair,   lest evil befall her
Scho kirnd the kirne and skymd it clene,   turned the churn
and left the gudman bot the bledoch bair.   husband; buttermilk
Than in the mornyng up scho gatt
And on hir hairt laid hir disjoyne,   stomach; breakfast
Scho put alsmekle in hir lap   as much; belly
As micht haif serd thame baith at noon.

Sayis, 'Jok, will thow be maistir of wark,
And thow sall haud, and I sall kall,   hold; drive
Ise promeis thee ane gud new sark   shirt
Athir of round claith or of small.'   thick or thin cloth
Scho lowsit oxin aucht or nyne,
And hint ane gadstaff in hir hand;   took up a goad
And the gudman raise eftir syne,   next after
And saw the wyf had done command.

And cawd the gaislingis furth to feid,   drove
(Thair was bot sevinsum of thame all)
And by thair cumis the gredy gled   kite

And likkit up fyve, left him bot twa.

Than owt he ran in all his mane   outcry
How sone he hard the gaislingis cry;   As soon as
Bot than or he come in agane   before
The calvis brak lowse and sowkit the ky.

The calvis and ky being met in the lone,   lane
The man ran with ane rung to redd;   stick; rescue
Than by thair cumis ane ill-willy cow   bad-tempered
And brodit his buttok quhill that it bled.   jabbed; so that
Than hame he ran to ane rok of tow   distaff of flax
And he satt doun to assay the spynning.
I trow he lowtit oure neir the lowe: bent down; fire
Quo he, 'This wark hes ill begynning.'

Than to the kirn that he did stour,   swirl
And jumlit at it quhill he swatt.   joggled; sweated
Quhen he had jumlit a full lang houre
The sorow crap of butter he gatt.   (no yield)
Albeit na butter he cowld gett   Although
Yit he wes cummerit with the kirne,   Still; encumbered
And syne he het the milk oure hett,   then; too hot
And sorrow spark of it wald yirne.   not a drop; curdle

Than ben thair come ane gredy sow,
(I trow he cund hir littill thank)   gave
And in scho schot hir mekle mow,   big gob
And ay scho winkit and ay scho drank.
He cleikit up ane crukit club   seized
And thocht to hitt the sow ane rowt: blow
The twa gaislingis the gled had left
That straik dang baith thair harnis owt.   blow; smashed; brains

Than he bure kendling to the kill,   bore; kiln
Bot scho start all up in ane lowe.   blaze
Quhat evir he hard, quhat evir he saw,
That day he had na will to mowe.   joke
Than he geid to tak up the bairnis,   children
Thocht to haif fund thame fair and clene:
The first that he gat in his armis
Was all bedirtin to the ene.   eyes

The first that he gat in his armis
It was all dirt up to the ene.
'The divill cutt of thair handis!' quo he,
'That fild yow all sa fow this strene.   dribble

He trailit the fowll scheitis doun the gait,   *road*
Thocht to haif wechst thame on ane stane;
The burne wes rissin grit of spait   *flood*
Away fra him the scheitis hes tane.

Than up he gat on ane knowe heid,   *hillock top*
On hir to cry, on hir to schowt,
Scho hard him, and scho hard him not,
Bot stowtly steird the stottis abowt.   *guided; oxen*
Scho draif the day unto the nicht;   *drove*
Scho lowisit the pleuch, and syne come hame;   *unyolked*
Scho fand all wrang that sould bene richt:
I trow the man thocht richt grit schame.

Quo he, 'My office I forsaik
For all the dayis of my lyf;
For I wald put ane hows to wraik
Had I been twenty dayis gudewife.'
Quo scho, 'Weill mot ye bruke yer place,   *may; put up with*
For trewlie I will nevir excep it.'   *object to it*
Quo he, 'Feind fall the lyaris face   *Devil take*
Bot yit ye may be blyth to get it.'   *You might yet be happy to get it*

Than up scho gat ane mekle rung   *big stick*
And the gudman maid to the door;
Quo he, 'Deme I sall hald my tung,   *woman*
For and we fecht I'll gett the waur.'   *worse of it*
Quo he, 'Quhen I forsuk my pleuch,
I trow I bot forsuk my seill;   *happiness*
And I will to my pleuch agane,
For I and this hows will nevir do weill.'

       ffinis q Mofat

The Gyre-Carling

Sir David Lindsay recited a version of this grotesque tale to James V when he had the boy king in his care. It most likely dates from the fifteenth century.

In Tiberus tyme, the trew Imperiour,
(Quhen Tynto hillis fra skraiping of toun henis wes keipit)
Thair dwelt ane grit gyre-carling in awld Betokis bour   *witch/ogress*
That levit upoun Christiane menis flesche and rewt heidis unleipit.   *raw; burst open*
Thair wynnit ane hir by on the west syd callit Blasour;   *There came by her one*
For luve of hir lauchand lippis he walit and he weipit,   *laughing*
He gadderit ane menyie of moudiwartis   *tribe of moles;*
       to warp doun the tour.   *cast; tower*

Behind the heill scho hatt him sic ane blaw   heel; hit
Quhill Blasour bled ane quart   So that
Off milk pottage. Inwart   Inwardly
The carling luche and lut fart   laughed
    North Berwick Law.[1]

The King of Fary than come with elffis mony ane
And sett ane sege and ane salt with grit pensallis of pryd;   assault; banners
And all the doggis frae Dumbar wes thair to Dumblane
With all the tykis of Tervey come to thame that tyd,   time
Thay gnew doun with thair gomes mony grit stane.   gnawed; gums
The carling schup hir in ane sow and is hir gaitis gane   shaped herself to; way
Gruntlyng our the Greik sea, and durst na langer byd   Grunting; dare; stay
For brukling of bargane and breking of browis.   breaking; cracking heads
The carling now for dispyte   for revenge
Is mareit with Mahomyte   married; Mohammed/Mahoun (the Devil)
And will the doggis interdyte,   restrain
    For scho is quene of Jowis.   Jews

Sensyne the cokkis of Crawmound crew nevir a day   since then; Crammond
For dule of that devillisch deme wes with Mahoun mareit;   grief
And the hennis of Haddingtoun sensyne wald not lay,
For this wyld wilroun witch thame widlit sa and wareit.   savage; cursed; worried
And the same North Berwick Law, as I heir wyvis say,
This carling with a fals cast wald away carreit,   twist; would have carried
For to luk on quha sa lykis na langer scho tareit.[2]
All this lang or for lufe befoirtymes fell,   long before the Fall
Lang or Betok wes born
Scho bred of ane accorne.   (whom) she bred from an acorn
The laif of the story to morne   rest
    To yow I sall tell.

Explicit

The Sowtar Inveyand aganis the Telyeor   Shoemaker; complaining

Quhen I come by yone telyeoris stall
I saw ane lowss creipand up his wall.   louse
'Snop!' quo the telyeor, 'Snap!' quo the scheiris.   shears
'Cokkis bownis!' quo the lowss,   bones
'I haif lost myne eiris!'   ears

1. A distinctively cone-shaped hill outside North Berwick.
2. 'For she never hesitated to look on whatever pleased her.'

Ane uther

Betwix twa foxis / a crawing cok;
Betwix twa freiris / a maid in hir smok;   friars
Betwix twa cattis / a mowiss;
Betwix twa telyeoris / a lowiss;
Schaw me gud sir, not as a stranger,
Quhilk of thais four is grittest in denger.

Anser

Foxis ar fell / At crawing cokkis;   ruthless
Freiris ar ferss / At maidis in thair smokkis;   fierce
Cattis ar cawtelus / in taking of myiss;   cruel
Telyeoris ar tyrranis in killing of lyiss.

A Complaint

I geid the gait wes nevir gane   went; road
I fand the thing wes nevir fund;   found
I saw under ane tre bowane
A lows man lyand bund;   free; bound
Ane dum man hard I full lowd speik   heard
Ane deid man hard I sing;
Ye may knaw be my talking eik   also
That this is no lesing.   lying

And als ane blindman hard I reid
Upoun a buke allane;
Ane handles man I saw, but dreid,   without doubt
In caichepule fast playane.   hand-tennis
As I come by yone forrest flat
I hard thame baik and brew;   bake
Ane rattoun in a window satt   rat
Sa fair a seme coud schew;   seam; sew
And cumand by Loch Lomond huth   inlet
Ane malwart tred a maw.   mallard; mounted; gull
Gife ye trow not this sang be suth,   believe; true
Speir ye at thame that saw.   Enquire

I saw ane gus virry a fox   goose; worry
Rycht far doun in yone slak;   hollow
I saw ane lavrock slay ane ox   lark
Richt hie up in yone stak;   haystack
I saw a weddir wirry a wouf   castrated ram; wolf
Heich up in a law.   round hill

The killing with hir mekle mowth   *cod; big*
Ane stoir horne cowd scho blaw;   *battle*
The partane with hir mony feit   *crab*
Scho spred the muk on feild.
In frost and snaw wind and weit
The lapstar deip furris teild.   *lobster; furrows; tilled*

I saw baith buck da and ra   *doe and roedeer*
In mercat skarlet sell   *best market clothes*
Twa leisch of grew hundis; I saw alswa   *greyhounds*
The pennyis doun cowd tell.   *coins counted out*
I saw ane wran ane watter waid   *wren wade a stream*
Hir clais wer kiltit hie,   *skirts tucked up*
Upoun hir bak ane milstane braid   *millstone*
Scho bure, this no lie.   *carried*

The air come hirpland to the toun   *circuit judge; limping*
The preistis to leir to spell;   *teach*
The hurchoun to the kirk maid boun   *hedgehog*
To ring the commoun bell;
The mows grat that the cat wes deid   *wept*
That all hir kin mycht rew;   *mourn*
Quhen all thir tailis are trew in deid   *these; indeed*
All wemen will be trew.

    ffinis

How the first heilandman of God was maid of ane horss turd in Argylle, as is said

God and Sanct Petir was gangand be the way   *along the way*
Heiche up in Ardgyle quhair thair gait lay;   *road*
Sanct Petir said to God in a sport word,
'Can ye not mak a heilandman of this horss turd?'
God turnd owre the horss turd with his pykit staff,   *spiked walking stick*
And up start a heilandman blak as ony draff.   *rubbish, dregs*
Quod god to the heilandman, 'Quhair wilt thow now?'
'I will doun in the lawland, Lord, and thair steill a kow.'
'And thow steill a cow, carle, thair thay will hang thee.'   *fellow*
'Quattrack, Lord, of that? For anis mon I die.'   *What matter; (only) once may*
God than he lewch and owre the dyk lap,   *wall jumped*
And owt of his scheith his gully owtgatt.   *pocket knife popped out*
Sanct Petir socht this gully fast up and doun,
Yit cowld not find it in all that braid roun.   *area*
'Now,' quo God, 'Heir a marvell. How can this be,
That I sowld want my gully, and we heir bot three?'   *lack; only*

'Humff!' quo the heilandman, and turnd him abowt,
And at his plaid nuk the gully fell owt.   corner
'Fy!' quo Sanct Petir, 'Thow will nevir do weill,
And thow bot new maid, sa sone gais to steill!'
'Umff!' quo the heilandman, and swere be yon kirk,
'Sa lang as I may geir gett to steill, will I nevir wirk.'   goods

My Hairt is Heich Aboif

My hairt is heich aboif, my body is full of bliss,   high
For I am sett in lufe, als weill as I wald wiss.   wish
I lufe my lady pure, and scho luvis me agane;
I am hir serviture, scho is my soverane;
Scho is my verry harte, I am hir howp and heill;   hope; well-being
Scho is my joy inwart, I am hir luvar leill;   loyal
I am hir bound and thrall, scho is at my command;
I am perpetuall, hir man both fute and hand.   forever

The thing that may hir pleis, my body sall fulfill;   Whatever thing
Quhat evir hir diseis, it dois my body ill.
My bird, my bony ane, my tendir bab venust,   peaceful
My lufe, my lyfe allane, my liking and my lust,
We interchange our hairtis, in utheris armis soft,   (each)
Spreitless we twa depairtis, usand our luvis oft.   Spiritless
We murne quhen licht day dawis, we plene the nycht is schort;   complain
We curss the cok that crawis, that hinderis our disport.

I glowffin up agast, quhen I hir myss on nycht,   glance
And in my oxster fast, I find the bowster richt;   armpit; bolster
Than langor on me lyis, lyk Morpheus the mair,   (God of Sleep)
Quhilk caus me uprys, and to my sweit repair: sweet
And than is all the sorrow furth of remembrance,   out of mind
That evir I had a forrow, in luvis observance.   before
Thus nevir I do rest, so lusty a lyfe I leid
Quhen that I list to test the well of womanheid.   whenever; wish

Luvaris in pane I pray, God send yow sic remeid   comfort
As I haif nycht and day, yow to defend frome deid.   death
Thairfoir be evir trew unto your ladeis fre,
And they will on yow rew, as mine has done on me.   take pity

Quhen Phebus fair

Quhen Phebus fair with bemis bricht
In to the west at mornyng makis repair,   sojourns
Makand his courss in to array full rycht   making his journey
Unto the eist schutand his schaftis schare   sheer

At morn sall ryss out of his courts to care
Norward doun in to the samyn degre:
Than will my reverend lady rew on me.

Quhen lawdiane law for luve hes left the land
And forth is fleitit to France that fair cuntre,
And every woman is also obediand;
Quhen men sall find no wattir in the se,

     .   .   .   [line missing in original]
And falsheid flymit and every man fund trew: banished
Than will my reverend lady on me rew.

Quhen all the grund is groun oure with gold
And every ryver rynnis upward wyne;
In somer quhen thair growis na flour on fold
In wintir quhen thair fallis na frost ryme,
Quhen everilk man will till uthiris inclyne;
In May quhen that the holyne changis hew: holly-tree
Than will my reverend lady on me rew.

Quhen Falkland fair is farit oure the ferry,   gone
And Sulway Sand is brocht attour the se,   all round
And Arthour Sait is brot to Sailisberry,[1]
And everilk man hes conqueist kinrikis thre,   kingdoms
Than mon thay realmes ring in ryelte.   may
Quhen clerkis will na benifice persew:
Than will my reverend lady on me rew.

Quhen that Dumbar is brocht to the Bass[2]
And all the fisch ar fled up in the air;
Quhen that northward no watteris will doun pass;
And men so rich that thay desyr no mair;
And leill luvaris forleitis luvis lair;   forsake; teaching
And walx is wrocht withouttin byk or be: beehive or bee
Than will my reverend lady rew on me.

Quhen schippis off tour and ballingeris of weir   galleons and warships
Be thowsand, sailis rycht swiftly ondir saill,
Thair mastis of gold and all thair uthir geir,
The west wond wappand in thair taill,
Takand thair courss with mony how and haill,   shouts and cries
Pulland doun sailis and landand at Eildoun tre:[3]
Than will my reverend lady rew on me.

---

1. Arthur's Seat, the rocky hill behind Edinburgh, has the Salisbury Crags on the slopes below.
2. The town of Dunbar is on the coast to the east of Edinburgh; the Bass Rock stands in the Firth of Forth.
3. Where Thomas the Rhymer fell asleep in the Eildon Hills, to the south of Melrose and far from the sea.

Sir David Lindsay (1490–1555)

Lindsay was part of the royal household, and after a spell out of favour, he became an ambassador in later years. He recalls entertaining the infant James V, and much of his work comments on life at Court with satires, advice and requests for favour. His most famous work is the play *Ane Satyre of the Thrie Estaitis* (1540; 1552; 1554), which reminded those in power of their duties to the common people and pressed for the reform of Church and State alike. The same straight-speaking democratic energy can be found in his poetry.

from The Dreme of Schir David Lyndesay[1]

Of the Realme of Scotland

806 Quhen that I had oversene this Regioun,
The quhilk, of nature, is boith gude and fair,
I did propone ane lytill questioun,   *propose*
Beseikand hir[2] the sam for to declare.
'Quhat is the cause our boundis bene so bair?'
Quod I: 'or quhate dois mufe our Miserie?
Or quhareof dois proceid our povertie?

For, throw the supporte of your hie prudence,
Off Scotland I persave the properteis,
And, als, considderis, be experience,   *also*
Off this countre the gret commoditeis.
First, the haboundance of fyschis in our seis,
And fructual montanis for our bestiall;   *fertile hills; cattle*
And, for our cornis, mony lusty vaill;   *valleys*

The ryche Ryveris, plesand and proffitabyll;
The lustie loochis, with fysche of sindry kyndis;   *lochs*
Hountyng, halkyng, for nobyllis convenabyll;   *appropriate*
Forrestis full of Da, Ra, Hartis, and Hyndis;   *Does, Roe deer*
The fresche fontanis, quhose holesum cristel strandis   *streams*
Refreschis so the fair fluriste grene medis: *flowering; meads*
So laik we no thyng that to nature nedis.   *lack*

1. The poet reminds us that he used to tutor the young King James V and then recounts a dream in which he is given a guided tour of the cosmos, including heaven and hell, before returning to make some pointed remarks about the condition of Scotland.
2. In his dream Lindsay is speaking to 'Dame Remembrance'.

Off every mettell we have the ryche Mynis,
Baith Gold, Sylver, and stonis precious
Howbeit we want the Spyces and the Wynis,   Even although we lack
Or uther strange fructis delycious,
We have als gude, and more neidfull for us.
Meit, drynk, fyre, clathis, thar mycht be gart abound,   made abundant
Quhilkis als is nocht in al the Mapamound;   Whose like; world

More fairer peple, nor of gretar ingyne,   mental ability
Nor of more strenth gret dedis tyll indure.
Quharefor, I pray yow that ye wald defyne
The principall cause quharefor we ar so pure;
For I marvell gretlie, I yow assure,
Considderand the peple and the ground,
That Ryches suld nocht in this realme redound.'   overflow

'My Sonne', scho said, 'be my discretioun,
I sall mak answeir, as I understand.
I say to the, under confessioun
The falt is nocht, I dar weill tak on hand,   venture
Nother in to the peple nor the land.
As for the land, it lakis na uther thing
Bot laubour and the pepyllis governyng.'

'Than quharein lyis our Inprosperitie?'
Quod I. 'I pray yow hartfullie, Madame,
Ye wald declare to me the veritie   truth
Or quho sall beir of our barrat the blame?   misery
For, be my treuth, to se I thynk gret schame
So plesand peple, and so fair ane land,
And so few verteous dedis tane on hand.'   undertaken

Quod scho: 'I sall, efter my Jugement,
Declare sum causis, in to generall,
And, in to termes schorte, schaw myne intent,
And, syne, transcend more in to speciall.
So, this is myne conclusion fynall:
Wantyng of Justice, polycie, and peace,   The lack of
Ar cause of thir unhappynes, allace,   this

It is deficill Ryches tyll incres,   difficult
Quhare Polycie makith no residence,
And Policey may never have entres,   entrance
Bot quhare that Justice dois delygence   Except
To puneis quhare thare may be found offence.
Justice may nocht have Dominatioun,
Bot quhare Peace makis habitatioun.'

'Quhat is the cause, that wald I understand,
That we sulde want Justice and polycie   lack
More than dois France, Italie, or Ingland?
Madame', quod I, 'schaw me the veritie:
Sen we have Lawis in to this countre,
Quhy want we lawis Exersitioun?
Quho suld put Justice tyll exicutioun?

Quhare in dois stand our principall remeid?   remedy
Or quha may mak mendis of this myschief?'
Quod scho: 'I fund the falt in to the heid;
For thay in quhome dois ly our hole releif,
I fynd thame rute and grund of all our greif,
For, quhen the heddis ar nocht delygent,
The membris man, or neid, be necligent.   limbs must be, of necessity

So I conclude, the causis principall
Off all the trubyll of this Natioun
Ar in to Prencis, in to speciall,   Princes, especially
The quhilkis hes the Gubernatioun,   governing
And of the peple Dominatioun,
Quhose contynewall exersitioun
889 Sulde be in Justice exicutioun.'

                 *   *   *

The Compleynt of the Comoun Weill of Scotland
918 And, thus as we wer walking to and fro,
We saw a boustius berne cum ouir the bent,   rough man; grass
But hors, on fute, als fast as he mycht go,   Without
Quhose rayment wes all raggit, revin, and rent,
With visage leyne, as he had fastit lent: Lent
And fordwart fast his wayis he did advance,
With ane rycht malancolious countynance.

With scrip on hip, and pyikstaff in his hand,   pouch
As he had purposit to passe fra hame.
Quod I: 'gude man, I wald faine understand,
Geve that ye plesit, to wyt quhat wer your name.'   know
Quod he: 'my Sonne, of that I think gret schame;
Bot, sen thow wald of my name have ane feill,
Forsuith, thay call me Jhone the Comoun Weill.'   Common Good

'Schir Commoun Weill, quho hes yow so disgysit?'
Quod I: 'or quhat makis yow so miserabyll?
I have marvell to se yow so supprysit
The quhilk that I have sene so honorabyll.

To all the warld ye have bene proffitabyll,
And weill honorit in everilk Natioun:
How happinnis, now, your tribulatioun?'

'Allace,' quod he, 'thow seis how it dois stand
With me, and quhow I am disherisit   disinherited
Off all my grace, and mon pas of Scotland,   must go from
And go, afore quhare I was cherisit.   where formerly; cherished
Remane I heir, I am bot perysit.
For thare is few that to me takis tent,   take heed
That garris me go so raggit, revin, and rent.   Which makes me

My tender friendis ar all put to the flycht;
For polecey is fled agane in France.
My Syster, Justice, almaist haith tynt hir sycht,   lost
That scho can nocht hald evinly the ballance.
Plane wrang is plane capitane of Ordinance,   Authority
The quhilk debarris Laute and reassoun,   Loyalty
And small remeid is found for oppin treassoun.   little cure

In to the south, allace, I was neir slane[1]
Over all the land I culd fynd no releiff;
Almoist betwix the Mers and Lowmabane
I culde nocht knaw ane leill man be ane theif   loyal; from
To schaw thare reif, thift, murthour, and mischeif,   robbery
And vecious workis, it wald infect the air:
And, als, langsum to me for tyll declair.   tedious; recite

In to the Hieland I could fynd no remeid,
Bot suddantlie I was put to exile.
Tha sweir swyngeoris thay tuke of me non heid,   lazy rogues
Nor amangs thame lat me remane ane quhyle.
Als, in the oute Ylis, and in Argyle,   Isles
Unthrift, sweirnes, falset, povertie, and stryfe
Pat polacey in dainger of hir lyfe.

In the Law land I come to seik refuge,   Lowlands
And purposit thare to mak my residence.
Bot singulare proffect gart me soune disluge,   personal profit; shift house
And did me gret injuris and offence,
And said to me: swyith, harlote, hy the hence;   quick, knave
And in this countre se thow tak no curis,   cares
So lang as my auctoritie induris.

1. James V led two expeditions across the Borders in 1528 and 1529. John has been wandering the border, from the Merse
   territory on the north-east bank of the Tweed, to the borough of Lochmaben near Dumfries in the south-west.

And now I may mak no langer debait;
Nor I wate nocht quhome to I suld me mene;   do I know; complain
For I have socht throw all the Spirituall stait,
Quhilkis tuke na compt for to heir me complene.   count
Thare officiaries, thay held me at disdane;
For Symonie,[1] he rewlis up all that rowte;   rules; crowd
And Covatyce, that Carle, gart bar me oute.   Man; made to expel

Pryde haith chaist far frome thame humilitie;
Devotioun is fled unto the freris;   mendicant friars
Sensuale plesour hes baneist Chaistitie;
Lordis of Religioun, thay go lyke Seculeris,
Taking more compt in tellyng thare deneris   counting their pennies
Nor thay do of thare constitutioun,
Thus ar thay blyndit be ambitioun.

Oure gentyll men ar all degenerate;
Liberalitie and Lawte, boith, ar loste;
And Cowardyce with Lordis is laureate   crowned
And knychtlie curage tumit in brag and boste;   emptied; boasting
The Civele weir misgydis everilk oist.   host (army)
Thare is nocht ellis bot ilk man for hym self,
That garris me go, thus baneist lyke ane elf.

Tharefor, adew; I may no langer taryc.'
'Fair weill,' quod I, 'and with sanct Jhone to borrow.   as St John is my witness
Bot, wyt ye weill, my hart was wounder sarye,
Quhen Comoun Weill so sopit was in sorrow.   plunged
Yit, efter the nycht cumis the glaid morrow;
Quharefor, I pray yow, schaw me, in certane,
Quhen that ye purpose for to cum agane?'

'That questioun, it sall be sone desydit,'
Quod he: 'thare sall na Scot have confortyng
Off me, tyll that I see the countre gydit   From
Be wysedome of ane gude auld prudent kyng,
Quhilk sall delyte hym maist, abone all thyng,
To put Justice tyll exicutioun,
And on strang tratouris mak puneisioun.

Als yit to the I say ane uther thyng:
I se, rycht weill, that proverbe is full trew,
Wo to the realme that hes ouir young ane king.'   too young
With that, he turnit his bak, and said adew.

1. Simony: the buying and selling of Church benefices or preferments.

Ouer firth and fell rycht fast fra me he flew,   forest and moor
Quhose departyng to me was displesand.
With that, Remembrance tuk me be the hand,

And sone, me thocht, scho brocht me to the roche,
And to the cove quhare I began to sleip.
With that, ane schip did spedalye approche,
Full plesandlie saling apone the deip,
And syne did slake hir salis, and gan to creip
Towart the land, anent quhare that I lay:
Bot, wyt ye weill, I gat ane fellown fraye.   terrible fright

All hir Cannounis sche leit craik of at onis:
Down schuke the stremaris frome the topcastell;   pennants; fighting top
Thay sparit nocht the poulder, nor the stonis;   gunpowder; cannonballs
Thay schot thare boltis, and doun thar ankeris fell;
The Marenaris, thay did so youte and yell,   shout
That haistalie I stert out of my dreme,
Half in ane fray, and spedalie past hame,   fright

And lychtlie dynit, with lyste and appityte,   happily; heartily
Syne efter, past in tyll ane Oritore,   private study
And tuke my pen, and thare began to wryte
All the visioun that I have schawin afore.
Schir, of my dreme as now thou gettis no more,
Bot I beseik God for to send the grace
To rewle thy realme in unitie and peace.

    Heir Endis the Dreme

from The Historie of Squyer Meldrum[1]

849 Out throw the land than sprang the fame,
That Squyer Meldrum wes cum hame
Quhen thay hard tell how he debaitit   fought
With everie man he was sa treitit
That, quhen he travellit throw the land
Thay bankettit him fra hand to hand   banqueted
With greit solace: till, at the last,
Out throw Straitherne the Squyer past.
And, as it did approch the nicht
Of ane Castell he gat ane sicht,

1. Lindsay's racy narrative poem purports to recount the adventures of William Meldrum, the laird of Cleish and Binns who died in 1550. The conventions of chivalric romance are given fresh energy and a cheerfully colloquial force in the telling. Meldrum is returning from his heroic exploits in the Scottish naval expedition to France in 1513, when he falls in with Marjorie Lawson, Lady Gleneagles, a widow at her castle in Strathearn.

Beside ane Montane, in ane vaill:
And than, efter his greit travaill,   hardships
He purpoisit him to repois,
Quhair ilk man did of him rejois.
Of this triumphant plesand place
Ane lustie Ladie wes Maistres,
Quhais Lord was deid schort tyme befoir,[1]
Quhairthrow hir dolour wes the moir.   grief
Bot yit scho tuke sum comforting,
To heir the plesant dulce talking   sweet
Of this young Squyer, of his chance,   luck
And how it fortunit him in France.
This Squyer and the Ladie gent   elegant
Did wesche, and then to supper went.
During that nicht thair was nocht ellis
Bot for to heir of his Novellis.   news
Eneas, quhen he fled from Troy,
Did not Quene Dido greiter Joy,
Quhen he in Carthage did arryve,
And did the seige of Troy discryve.
The wonderis that he did reheirs
Wer langsum for to put in vers,   tedious
Of quhilk this Ladie did rejois.
Thay drank, and syne went to repois.
He fand his Chalmer weill arrayit
With dornik work on buird displayit.   fine Flemish cloth; table
Of Venisoun he had his waill,   pick
Gude Aquavite, Wyne, and Aill,   Brandy
With nobill Confeittis, Bran, and Geill;   sweetmeats, brawn and jelly
And swa the Squyer fuir richt weill.   fared
Sa, to heir mair of his narratioun,
This Ladie come to his Collatioun,
Sayand he was richt welcum hame.
'Grandmercie than' (quod he) 'Madame.'
Thay past the time with Ches and Tabill;   Backgammon
For he to everie game was abill.
Than unto bed drew everie wicht:
To Chalmer went this Ladie bricht,
The quhilk this Squyer did convoy.   whom; escort
Syne, till his bed he went, with Joy.
That nicht he sleipit never ane wink,
Bot still did on the Ladie think;
Cupido, with his fyrie dart,
Did peirs him so out throw the hart.
Sa all that nicht he did bot murnit,

1. Sir John Haldane of Gleneagles was killed at Flodden in 1513.

Sum tyme sat up, and sumtyme turnit,
Sichand with monie gant and grane,   complaint
To fair Venus makand his mane,
Sayand, 'Ladie, quhat may this mene?
I was ane fre man lait yistrene,
And now ane cative bound and thrall
For ane that I think Flour of all.

I pray God sen scho knew my mynd,   send
How, for hir saik, I am sa pynd.   distressed
Wald God I had bene yit in France,
Or I had hapnit sic mischance,   Ere; happened
To be subject or serviture
Till ane quhilk takis of me na cure.'   heed
This Ladie ludgit neirhand by,
And hard the Squyer prively,   heard; secretly
With dreidful hart, makand his mone,   fearful
With monie cairfull gant and grone.   yawn
Hir hart fulfillit with pietie,   filled up
Thocht scho wald haif of him mercie,
And said, 'howbeit I suld be slane,   even if
He sall have lufe for lufe agane.
Wald God I micht, with my honour,
Have him to be my Paramour.'   lover
This wes the mirrie tyme of May,
Quhen this fair Ladie, freshe and gay,
Start up, to take the hailsum Air,
With pantonis on hir feit ane pair,   slippers
Airlie into ane cleir morning,
Befoir fair Phoebus uprysing,
Kirtill alone, withouttin Clok,   Gown
And saw the Squyeris dure unlok.
Scho slippit in, or ever he wist,   knew
And fenyeitlie past till ane kist,   pretended to go; chest
And with hir keyis oppinnit the Lokkis,
And maid hir to take furth ane Boxe:
Bot that was not hir erand thair.
With that, this lustie young Squyar
Saw this Ladie so plesantlie
Cum to his Chalmer quyetlie,
In Kyrtill of fyne Damais broun,   Damask
Hir goldin traissis hingand doun.
Hir Pappis wer hard, round, and quhyte,   breasts
Quhome to behald wes greit delyte.
Lyke the quhyte lyllie wes hir lyre;   skin
Hir hair was like the reid gold wyre;

Hir schankis quhyte withouttin hois,   legs; stockings
Quhairat the Squyer did rejois.
And said than, 'now, vailye quod vailye,   come what may
Upon the Ladie thow mak ane sailye.'   sally
Hir Courtlyke Kirtill was unlaist,   courtly
And sone into his armis hir braist,   he embraced her
And said to hir; 'Madame, gude-morne;
Help me, your man that is forlorne.
Without ye mak me sum remeid,   help
Withouttin dout I am bot deid;
Quhairfoir, ye mon releif my harmes.'   relieve; troubles
With that, he hint hir in his armes,   held
And talkit with hir on the flure;
Syne, quyetlie did bar the dure.
'Squyer' (quod scho) 'quhat is your will?
Think ye my womanheid to spill?   deflower
Na, God forbid, it wer greit syn;
My Lord and ye wes neir of Kyn.
Quhairfoir, I mak yow supplicatioun,
Pas, and seik ane dispensatioun;[1]
Than sall I wed yow with ane Ring;
Than may ye leif at your lyking.
For ye ar young, lustie, and fair,
And als ye ar your Fatheris Air.   also
Thair is na Ladie, in all this land,
May yow refuse to hir Husband;
And gif ye lufe me as ye say,
Haist to dispens the best ye may;   Hurry to get the dispensation
And thair to yow I geve my hand,
I sall yow take to my Husband.'
(Quod he) 'Quhill that I may indure,   for as long as I live
I vow to be your serviture;
Bot I think greit vexatioun
To tarie upon dispensatioun.'   wait until a dispensation
Than in his armis he did hir thrist,   thrust
And aither uther sweitlie kist,   each the other
And wame for wame thay uther braissit;   embraced
With that, hir Kirtill wes unlaissit.
Than Cupido, with his fyrie dartis,
Inflammit sa thir Luiferis hartis,
Thay micht na maner of way dissever,
Nor ane micht not part fra ane uther;
Bot, like wodbind, thay wer baith wrappit.   woodbine
Thair tenderlie he hes hir happit,   covered
Full softlie up, intill his Bed.

1. Distant cousins required Church permission to marry.

Judge ye gif he hir schankis shed.   legs parted
'Allace' (quod scho) 'quhat may this mene?'
And with hir hair scho dicht hir Ene.   covered; eyes

I can not tell how they did play;
Bot I beleve scho said not nay.
He pleisit hir sa, as I hard sane,
That he was welcum ay agane.
Scho rais, and tenderlie him kist,
And on his hand ane Ring scho thrist;   thrust
And he gaif hir ane lufe drowrie,   dowry
Ane Ring set with ane riche Rubie,
In takin that thair Lufe for ever   token
Suld never frome thir twa dissever.
And than scho passit unto hir Chalmer,
And fand hir madinnis, sweit as Lammer,   amber
Sleipand full sound; and nothing wist   knew
How that thair Ladie past to the Kist.   had gone to the chest
(Quod thay) 'Madame, quhair have ye bene?'
(Quod scho) 'into my Gardine grene,
To heir thir mirrie birdis sang.
I lat yow wit, I thocht not lang,   let you know
Thocht I had taryit thair quhill None.   Though; until noon
(Quod thai) 'quhair wes your hois and schone?   stockings and shoes
Quhy yeid ye with your bellie bair?'   did you go
(Quod scho) 'the morning wes sa fair:
For, be him that deir Jesus sauld,   sold (Judas)
I felt na wayis ony maner of cauld.'
(Quod thay) 'Madame, me think ye sweit.'   sweat
(Quod scho) 'ye see I sufferit heit;
The dew did sa on flouris fleit,   float
That baith my Lymmis ar maid weit:
Thairfoir ane quhyle I will heir ly,
Till this dulce dew be fra me dry.   sweet
Ryse, and gar mak our denner reddie.'
'That salbe done' (quod thay) 'my Ladie.'
Efter that scho had tane hir rest,
Scho rais, and in hir Chalmer hir drest,
And, efter Mes, to denner went.   morning Mass
Than wes the Squyer diligent
To declair monie sindrie storie
Worthie to put in Memorie.
Quhat sall we of thir Luiferis say,   these
Bot, all this tyme of lustie May,
They past the tyme with Joy and blis,
1038   Full quyetlie, with monie ane kis.

Richard Maitland of Lethingtoun
(1496–1586)

As a judge and distinguished counsellor at Court, Maitland saw long service with James V, Mary and James VI. The Maitland folio is a vital record of many old Scots poems, collected by him over the years. A certain melancholy in his work may be explained by the fact that he went blind in middle age and didn't start writing poetry until he was in his 60s.

Sum tyme to court I did repair

Sum tyme to court I did repair,	set out
Thairin sum eirrandis for to dres,	address
Thinkand I had sum freindis thair	
To help fordwarte my beseynes;	
Bot not the les	
I fand no thing bot doubilnes:	duplicity
Auld kyndnes helpis not ane hair.	
To ane grit courtman I did speir,	ask
That I trowit my freind had bene;	believed
Becaus we war of kyn sa neir	(related)
To him my mater I did mene;	business; explain
Bot withe disdene	
He fled as I had done him tene,	made him angry
And wald not byd my teill to heir.	stay
I wend that he in word and deid	think
For me, his kynnisman sould have wrocht,	applied himself
Bot to my speiche he tuke na heid;	
Neirnes of blude he sett at nocht.	
Than weill I thocht,	
Quhone I for sibnes to him socht	kinship
It wes the wrang way that I geid.	
My hand I putt in to my sleif	
And furthe of it ane purs I drew,	

And said I brocht it him to geif;
Bayth gold and silver I him schew.
   Than he did rew   regret
That he unkyndlie me misknew,   unnaturally refused to know
And hint the purs fast in his neif.   seized; fist

Fra tyme he gat the purs in hand
He kyndlie cousing callit me,
And baid me gar him understand   make
My beseynes all haillalie,   completely
   And sweir that he
My trew and faythfull freind sould be
In courte, as I pleis him command.

For quhilk bettir it is, I trow,
In to the courte to get supple,   help
To have ane purse of fyne gold fow   full
Nor to the hiast of degre   Than
   Off kyn to be:
Sa alteris oure nobilite,
Grit kynrent helpis lytill now.   Powerful relations

Thairfore, my freindis, gif ye will mak
All courte men youris as ye wald,
Gude gold and sylver with yow tak;
Than to get help – ye may be bald.
   For it is tald,
Kyndnes of courte is coft and sald;   bought
Neirnes of kyn na thing thai rak.   heed

The Gude and Godlie Ballatis

Collected and composed by Robert Wedderburn (1510?–57), a priest of Dundee and his two older brothers, *Ane Compendious Buik of Godlie Psalms and Spirituall Sangs* contained a 12-year almanac, psalms and the catechism, but is best known for its popular airs and songs with the words turned to pious purposes. Often from German originals with a Lutheran spirit, the vernacular energy of these pieces, and the book's popularity, argue for a livelier kirk in the early days of the Reformation than is often supposed to be the case.

Anonymous

My lufe murnis for me
My lufe murnis for me, for me,
My lufe that murnis for me,
I am not kynde, hes not in mynde
My lufe that murnis for me.

Quha is my lufe, bot God abufe,
Quhilk all this world hes wrocht;
The King of blis, my lufe he is,
Full deir he hes me bocht.

His precious blude he sched on rude,   Cross
That was to mak us fre;
This sall I preve, be Goddis leve,   prove; leave
That sair my lufe murnis for me.

This my lufe come fra abufe,
And borne was of ane maid:
For till fulfill, his Fatheris will,
Till filfurth that he said.   carry out

Man haif in mynde, and thow be kynde,
Thy lufe that murnis for thee,
How he on Rude did sched his blude,
From Sathan to mak thee fre.

Downe Be Yone River I Ran

Downe be yone river I ran,
Downe be yone river I ran,
Thinkand on Christ sa fre,
That brocht me to libertie,
And I ane sinful man.

Quha suld be my lufe bot he,
That hes onlie savit me,
And be his deith me wan:
On the Croce sa cruellie,
He sched his blude aboundantlie,
And all for the lufe of man.

How suld we thank that Lord,
That was sa misericord,   pitiful
Be quhome all grace began!
With cruell paine and smart,
He was peirsit throw the hart,
And all for the lufe of man.

That gaif him in the Jewis handis,
To brek bailfull Baliallis bandis,   Belial's
First quhen he began:
Thair gaif him self to die,
To mak us catives fre,   wretches
Remember, sinfull man.

Thay spittit in his face,
All for our lufe, allace!
That Lord he sufferit than,
The cruel panis of deid,
Quhilk was our haill remeid,
Remember, sinfull man.

Love we that Lord allone,
Quhilk deit on the throne,
Our sinnis to refraine: restrain
Pryse him with all our mycht,   Praise
Sing till him day and nycht,
The gloir of God and man.

Do all that thow art abill,
Yit thow art unproffitabill,   Still
Do all that thow can:
Except thow weschin be,
With Christis blude allanerlie,   alone
Thow art condampnit Man.

And sa I mak ane end,
Christ grant us all to kend,   know
And steidfast to remaine:
Into Christis Passioun,
Our onlie Salvatioun,
And in nane uther man.

With Huntis Up

With huntis up, with huntis up,
It is now perfite day,
Jesus, our King, is gaine in hunting,
Quha lykis to speid thay may.

Ane cursit Fox lay hid in rox,   rocks
This lang and mony ane day,
Devoring scheip, quhill he mycht creip,
Nane mycht him schaip away.   scare

It did him gude to laip the blude
Of yung and tender lambis,
Nane culd he mis, for all was his,
The yung anis with thair dammis.   dams

The hunter is Christ, that huntis in haist,
The hundis ar Peter and Paull,
The Paip is the Fox, Rome is the Rox,
That rubbis us on the gall.

That creull beist, he never ceist,
Be his usurpit power,
Under dispens, to get our penneis,   pence
Our saulis to devoir.

Quha culd devise sic merchandis,
As he had thair to sell,
Onles it war proude Lucifer,
The greit maister of Hell.

He had to sell the Tantonie bell,   St Anthony's bell
And Pardonis thairin was,
Remissioun of sinnis, in auld scheip skinnis,
Our saulis to bring from grace.

With bullis of leid, quhyte wax and reid,   papal Bulls
And uther quhylis with grene,
Closit in ane box, this usit the Fox,
Sic peltrie was never sene.   trash

With dispensationis and obligationis,
According to his Law,
He wald dispence, for money from hence,
With thame he never saw.

To curs and ban the sempill pure man,
That had nocht to fle the paine,
Bot quhen he had payit all to ane myit,   to the last mite
He mon be absolvit than.   must

To sum, God wot, he gaif tot quot,   to the number specified
And uther sum pluralitie,[1]
Bot first with penneis, he mon dispens,
Or ellis it will nocht be.

Kingis to marie and sum to tarie,   marry
Sic is his power and mycht,
Quha that hes gold, with him will he hold,
Thoch it be contrair all rycht.   against

O blissit Peter, the Fox is ane lier,
Thow knawis weill it is nocht sa,
Quhill at the last, he salbe downe cast,
His peltrie, Pardonis and all.   trash

Psalm 23

The Lord God is my Pastor gude,
Aboundantlie me for to feid:
Than how can I be destitute
Of ony gude thing in my neid?
He feidis me in feildis fair,
To Reveris sweit, pure, and preclair,   excellent
He dryvis me but ony dreid.   herds; without

---

1. Dispensations are being offered to a quoted number, or an open plurality.

My Saull and lyfe he dois refresche,
And me convoyis in the way
Of his Justice and rychteousnes.
And me defendis from decay,
Nocht for my warkis verteousnes,
Bot for his name sa glorious,
Preservis me baith nycht and day.

And thocht I waver, or ga wyll,   astray
Or am in danger for to die,
Na dreid of deide sall cum me till,
Nor feir of cruell Tyrannie.
Because that thow art me besyde,
To governe me and be my gyde,
From all mischeif and miserie.

Thy staffe, quhair of I stand greit awe,
And thy scheip huke me for to fang,   seize
Thay nurtour me, my faultis to knaw,
Quhen fra the hie way I ga wrang.
Thairfoir my spreit is blyith and glaid,   cheerful
Quhen on my flesche thy scurge is laid,
In the rycht way to gar me gang.   make me go

And thow ane Tabill dois provyde
Befoir me, full of all delyte,
Contrair to my persewaris pryde,   pursuers'
To thair displesour and dispyte.
Thow hes annoyntit weill my heide,
And full my coupe thow hes maid,
With mony dischis of delyte.

Thy gudnes and beningnitie
Lat ever be with me thairfoir;
And quhill I leve untill I die,
Thow lay thame up with me in stoir,
That I may haif my dwelling place,
Into thy hous befoir thy face,
To ring with the for ever moir.

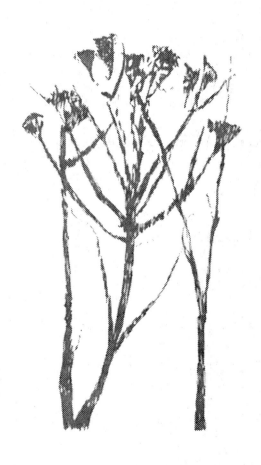

Mrs MacGregor of Glenstrae

(c. 1570)

The MacGregor lands were flanked by Campbell territory in Argyll and Breadalbane. While the chiefs of MacGregor tried to stay independent, Clan Campbell did better for itself by siding with central authority and the King. As part of this struggle, MacGregor of Glenstrae was beheaded at the Earl of Breadalbane's Balloch Castle at

Cumha Ghriogair MhicGhriogair Ghlinn Sreith

Moch madainn air latha Lùnasd'
Bha mi sùgradh mar ri m'ghràdh,
Ach mun tàinig meadhon latha
Bha mo chridhe air a chràdh.

Ochain, ochain, ochain uiridh
   Is goirt mo chridhe, laoigh,
Ochain, ochain, ochain uiridh
    Cha chluinn t'athair ar caoidh.

Mallachd aig maithibh is aig càirdean
Rinn mo chràdh air an-dòigh,
Thàinig gun fhios air mo ghràdh-sa
Is a thug fo smachd e le foill.

Nam biodh dà fhear dheug d'a chinneadh
Is mo Ghriogair air an ceann,
Cha bhiodh mo shùil a' sileadh dheur,
No mo leanabh féin gun dàimh.

Chuir iad a cheann air ploc daraich,
Is dhòirt iad fhuil mu làr:
Na'm biodh agamsa an sin cupan,
Dh'òlainn dìth mo shàth.

Is truagh nach robh m'athair an galar,
Agus Cailean Liath am plàigh,
Ged bhiodh nighean an Ruadhanaich
Suathadh bas is làmh.

Taymouth in 1570. We do not know his young widow's name, but she seems to have been a Campbell by birth. This lament, ascribed to her, links classic bardic syllabic elements to the freer qualities of folk-song. By 1604, Glenstrae was forfeited and the entire MacGregor Clan was outlawed.

Lament for MacGregor of Glenstrae

One morning of August
I was dallying with my love,
but before the moon was shining
my heart had learned to grieve.

Ochone, ochone my little one   Alas
   my heart is deathly sore.
Ochone, ochone my little one
   your father cannot hear.

A curse on my family and friends
who brought me to this plight,
who stole upon my love by stealth
and killed him by deceit.

If there were twelve of his people
and Gregor at their head,
my eyes would not be tearful,
nor my child's father dead.

They placed his head on an oak stump
and let his blood fall:
if I had had a cup there
I'd have drunk it all.

May sickness kill my father
and Colin die of the plague,   Colin Campbell of Glenorchy
and the daughter of the Red-haired one   His wife (daughter of Lord Ruthven)
suffer grief's fatigue.

Chuirinn Cailean Liath fo ghlasaibh,
Is Donnchadh Dubh an làimh;
Is gach Caimbeulach th' ann am Bealach
Gu giùlan nan glas-làmh.

Ràinig mise réidhlean Bhealaich,
Is cha d'fhuair mi ann tàmh:
Cha d'fhàg mi ròin de m'fhalt gun tarraing
No craiceann air mo làimh.

Is truagh nach robh mi an riochd na h-uiseig,
Spionnadh Ghriogair ann mo làimh:
Is i a' chlach a b'àirde anns a' chaisteal
A' chlach a b'fhaisge do'n bhlàr.

Is ged tha mi gun ùbhlan agam
Is ùbhlan uile aig càch,
Is ann tha m' ubhal cùbhraidh grinn
Is cùl a chinn ri làr.

Ged tha mnàthan chàich aig baile
'Nan laighe is 'nan cadal sàmh,
Is ann bhios mise aig bruaich mo leapa
A' bualadh mo dhà làimh.

Is mór a b'annsa bhith aig Griogair
Air feadh coille is fraoich,
Na bhith aig Baran crìon na Dalach
An taigh cloiche is aoil.

Is mór a b'annsa bhith aig Griogair
Cur a' chruidh do'n ghleann,
Na bhith aig Baran crìon na Dalach
Ag òl air fìon is air leann.

Is mór a b'annsa bhith aig Griogair
Fo bhrata ruibeach ròin,
Na bhith aig Baran crìon na Dalach
A' giùlan sìoda is sròil.

Ged a bhiodh ann cur is cathadh
Is latha nan seachd sìon,
Gheibheadh Griogair dhòmh-sa cragan
'S an caidlimid fo dhìon.

White Colin I would lock in jail,
Black Duncan I'd arrest;   (Eldest son of Colin Campbell)
and every Campbell now in Balloch
I'd padlock by the wrist.

When I reached the fields of Balloch,
there was no peace to be found:
I tore each hair from my head
and the skin from my hand.

If only I were in the lark's shape,
with Gregor's strength in my hand:
the highest stone in the castle
would be nearest to the ground.

And though I have no apples left
when other apples are entire,
my fragrant complete apple
has his head on the bare floor.

When other wives are sleeping soft
by husbands without wounds,
I'll be at my bed's edge   (his grave)
beating my two hands.

Better to be with Gregor
in the wood of wild rain,
than with the withered Baron[1]
in his house of lime and stone.

Better to be with Gregor
driving cattle to the glen,
than with the withered Baron
drunk on beer and wine.

Better to be with Gregor
beneath the warm seal's skin,
than with the withered Baron
wearing silk and satin.

Though there would be hail and snow
day of the seven showers,
Gregor would find me shelter
to sleep from the storm's force.

1. The Baron of Dall, on the south of Loch Tay, whom her parents wished her to marry.

Ba hu, ba hu, àsrain bhig,
    Cha'n 'eil thu fhathast ach tlàth:
Is eagal leam nach tig an latha
    Gun dìol thu t'athair gu bràth.

O lullaby my little child
   you are yet but small:
I fear the day will never come
   when you'll destroy them all.

trans. Iain Crichton Smith

Alexander Scott (1525?–1584?)

Employed as a musician for the Chapel Royal at Court, Scott later became a landowner. He writes in the familiar gentlemanly tradition of courtly love complaint, and although he can celebrate joy, he tends to favour the trials and betrayals of love or open attacks on the inconstancy of women, the result, perhaps, of personal experience.

To Luve Unluvit

To luve unluvit it is ane pane;
For scho that is my soverane,
Sum wantoun man so he hes set hir,   so high (haughty)
That I can get no lufe agane,
Bot brekis my hairt, and nocht the bettir.

Quhen that I went with that sweit may,   maid
To dance, to sing, to sport and pley,
And oft tymes in my armis plet hir;   encircled
I do now murne both nycht and day,
And brekis my hart, and nocht the bettir.

Quhair I wes wont to se hir go
Rycht trymly passand to and fro,   smartly
With cumly smylis quhen that I met hir;
And now I leif in pane and wo,   live
And brekis my hairt, and nocht the bettir.

Quhattane ane glaikit fule am I   senseless
To slay myself with malancoly,
Sen weill I ken I may nocht get hir!
Or quhat suld be the caus, and quhy,
To brek my hairt, and nocht the bettir?

My hairt, sen thou may nocht hir pleiss,
Adew, as gude lufe cumis as gaiss,
Go chuss ane udir and forget hir;
God gif him dolour and diseiss,   sorrow and trouble
That brekis thair hairt and nocht the bettir.

q. Scott, Quhen His Wyfe Left Him.

Luve preysis but comparesone

Luve preysis but comparesone,	*values without distinction*
Both gentill, sempill, generall,	*well bred; humble; common*
And of fre will gevis waresone,	*by; reward*
As Fortoun chansis to befall;	
For luve makis nobill ladeis thrall	*slave*
To bassir men of birth and blud;	
So luve garris sober wemen small	*makes; low-born*
Get maistrice our grit men of gud.	*mastery over; of substance*
Ferme luve, for favour, feir or feid,	*Constant; friendship or enmity*
Of riche nor pur to speik suld spair,	*forbear*
For luve to hienes hes no heid,	*heed*
Nor lychtleis lawlines ane air;	*slights; a jot*
Bot puttis all personis in compair,	*on equal footing*
This proverb planely for till preve:	*prove*
That men and wemen, less and mair,	*high and low*
Ar cumd of Adame and of Eve.	
So, thocht my lyking wer a leddy	*although*
And I no lord, yit nocht the less	
Scho suld my servyce find als reddy	
As duke to duches docht him dress;	*could manage*
For, as prowd princely luve express	*especially*
Is to haif soverenitie,	
So service cumis of sympilnes,	*homage; humility*
And leilest lufe of law degre.	
So luvaris lair no neid suld lak,	*learning*
A lord to lufe a silly lass;	
A leddy als, for luf to tak	*as well*
Ane propir page, hir tyme to pass.	
For quhy, as bricht bene birneist brass	*burnished brass is as bright*
As silver wrocht at all devyss,	*most skilfully*
And als gud drinking out of glass	
As gold, thocht gold gif grittar pryss.	
Suld I presome this sedull schaw,	*manuscript*
Or lat me langouris be lamentit?	*To allow*
Na I effrey, for feir and aw	*Nay I fear*
Hir comlie heid be miscontenttit;	
I dar nocht preiss hir to present it,	
For be scho wreth I will not wow it;	*angry; avow*
Bot, pleiss hir proudens to imprent it,	*(if it) please; good sense; study*
Scho may persave sum Inglis throw it.	*sense*

A Rondel of Luve

Lo! quhat it is to lufe,
Lerne ye, that list to prufe,   like
Be me, I say, that no wayis may
The grund of greif remufe,
Bot still decay, both nycht and day:
Lo! quhat it is to lufe.

Lufe is ane fervent fyre,
Kendillit without desyre:
Schort plesour, lang displesour;
Repentence is the hyre;   price
Ane pure tressour without mesour: poor; beneath counting
Lufe is ane fervent fyre.

To lufe and to be wyiss,   prudent
To rege with gud advyiss,   be mad with deliberation
Now thus, now than, so gois the game,
Incertane is the dyiss: dice
Thair is no man, I say, that can
Both lufe and to be wyiss.

Fle alwayis frome the snair;
Lerne at me to be ware;
It is ane pane and dowbill trane   lure
Of endless wo and cair;
For to refrane that denger plane,   avoid
Fle alwayis frome the snair.

Alexander Montgomerie
(1545?–1610?)

Montgomerie was the best of James VI's 'Castalian band' of court poets and a personal favourite of the King. With their bright imagery and effective meters, many of his lyrics were set to music. Unlike Alexander Scott, he remained in the Roman Catholic faith and was eventually banished, accused of treason and sent to die in exile. *The Cherrie and the Slae* is a long visionary poem which shifts from a love complaint to a strange allegory about having to choose between the Reformed and the Catholic Church.

The Night is Neir Gone[1]

Hay! now the day dawis;	
The jolie Cok crawis;	
Now shroudis the shawis,	groves
Throw Natur anone.	
The thissell-cok cryis	male mistle-thrush
On lovers wha lyis.	
Now skaillis the skyis:	empty
The nicht is neir gone.	
The feildis owerflowis	
With gowans that growis	daisies
Quhair lilies lyk low is,	a blaze
Als rid as the rone.	rowan berry
The turtill that trew is,	dove
With nots that renewis,	
Hir pairtie persewis:	partner
The night is neir gone.	
Now Hairtis with Hyndis,	
Conforme to thair kyndis,	natures
Hie tursis thair tyndis,	Toss high; antlers
On grund whair they grone.	groan
Now Hurchonis, with Hairis,	hedgehogs; hares

1. This is a new setting to an old song mentioned in *The Complaynt of Scotland.*

Ay passis in pairis;
Quhilk deuly declaris
The night is neir gone.

The sesone excellis
Thrugh sweetnes that smellis;
Now Cupid compellis
Our hairtis echone,
On Venus wha waikis,
To muse on our maikis,   *partners*
Syn sing, for thair saikis;
The night is neir gone.

All curageous knichtis
Aganis the day dichtis   *get ready*
The breist plate that bright is,
To feght with thair fone.   *foes*
The stoned steed stampis   *stallion*
Throw curage and crampis,   *prances*
Syn on the land lampis: *strides*
The night is neir gone.

The freikis on feildis   *troops*
That wight wapins weildis   *stout weapons*
With shyning bright shieldis
As Titan in trone: *throne*
Stiff speiris in reistis,   *rests*
Ower cursoris cristis,   *chargers' crests*
Ar brok on thair breistis:
The night is neir gone.

So hard ar thair hittis,
Some sweyis, some sittis,
And some perforce flittis
On grund whill they grone.
Syn groomis that gay is,
On blonkis that brayis,   *horses*
With swordis assayis: *set-to*
The night is neir gone.

from The Cherrie and the Slae[1]

155   I sprang up on Cupidoes wingis,
Quha bow and quavir baith resingis,   *relinquishes*
    To lend me for ane day:

1. On a perfect May morning, Cupid appears to Montgomerie and lends him his wings and arrows, but the poet has scarcely soared before he wounds himself and suffers the pains of love.

As Icarus with borrowit flicht,
I mountit hichar nor I micht,
   Ouir perrelous ane play: Too
Than furth I drew that deadlie dairt,
   Quhilk sumtyme schot his mother:
Quhairwith I hurt my wanton heart,
   In hope to hurt ane uther:
      It hurt me, it burt me,   burned
        The ofter I it handill:
      Cum se now, in me now,
        The butter-flie and candill.   (like a moth to a flame)

As scho delytis into the low,   blaze
Sa was I browdin in my bow,   enamoured of
   Als ignorant as scho:
And as scho flies quhill sche be fyrit,
Sa with the dart that I desyrit,
   My hand hes hurt me to:
As fulisch Phaeton be sute,   by entreaty
   His fatheris Cart obteind: chariot
I langt in Luiffis bow to shute,
   Bot weist not what it meind: knew; meant
      Mair wilfull, than skilfull,
        To flie I was so fond:
      Desyring, Impyring,   aspiring
        And sa was sene upond.   upon it

To late I knaw quha hewis to hie,   he who cuts too high
The spail sall fall into his eie,   chips
   To late I went to Scuillis:
To late I heard the swallow preiche,[1]
To late Experience dois teiche,
   The Skuil-maister of fuillis:
To late to fynde the nest I seik,
   Quhen all the birdis are flowin:
To late the stabill dore I steik,   bar
   Quhen all the steids are stowin: stolen
      To lait ay, their stait ay,   always
        All fulische folke espye:
      Behynd so, they fynd so,
        Remeid and so do I.   remedy

Gif I had rypelie bene advysit,   in time
I had not rashlie enterprysit,
   To soir with borrowit pennis: wings

1. See Henryson's fable 'The Preiching of the Swallow' which recommends prudence and foresight.

Nor yit had saied the archer craft,   tried
Nor schot myself with sik a schaft
   As resoun quyte miskennis:
Fra wilfulnes gave me my wound,
   I had na force to flie: necessity
Then came I granand to the ground,   groaning
   Freind welcome hame quod he:
      Quhair flew ye, quhome slew ye,
        Or quha bringis hame the buiting: booty
      I sie now, quod he now,
        Ye haif bene at the schuting.

As skorne cummis commonlie with skaith,   harm
Sa I behuifit to byde them baith,   thole
   O quhat an stakkering stait!
For under cure I gat sik chek,   cover; check
Quhilk I micht nocht remuif nor nek   move or parry
   Bot eyther stail or mait.   Without; stalemate or checkmate
My agonie was sa extreme,
   I swelt and soundt for feir: fainted and swooned
Bot or I walkynnit of my dreme,
   He spulyied me of my geir: despoiled
      With flicht than, on hicht than,
        Sprang Cupid in the skyis:
      Foryetting, and setting,
        At nocht my cairfull cryis.

Sa lang with sicht I followit him,
Quhill baith my feiblit eyis grew dim,
   With staring on the starnis,   stars
Quhilk flew sa thick befoir my ein,
Sum reid, sum yellow, blew and grein,
   Sa trublit all my harnis: brains
Quhill every thing apperit two,
   To my barbuilyeit braine: disordered
Bot lang micht I lye luiking so,
   Or Cupid come againe: Before
      Quhais thundring, with wondring,
        I hard up throw the air:
      Throw cluddis so, he thuddis so,
        And flew I wist not quhair.   knew

Fra that I saw that God was gane,
And I in langour left allane,
   And sair tormentit to:
Sum tyme I sicht quhill I was sad,   sighed

Sum tyme I musit and maist gane mad,
    I wist not quhat to do:
Sum tyme I ravit halfe in a rage,
    As ane into dispaire:
To be opprest with sic ane page
    Lord gif my heart was saire:
        Like Dido, Cupido
            I widill and I warye: *fret and curse*
            Quha reft me, and left me,   *bereft*

252   In sik a feirie-farye.   *kerfuffle*

The Perversitie of his Inclinationes throu Love

My fansie feeds upon the sugred gall;
    Against my will my weill does work my wo;   *happiness*
My cairfull chose does chuse to keep me thrall;   *choice*
    My frantik folie fannis upon my fo: *fawns*
        My lust alluirs my licorous lippis to taist   *eager*
        The bait wharin the suttle hook is plaic't.

My hungry hope doth heap my hevy hap;   *luck*
    My sundrie sutes procuris the mair disdane;   *entreaties*
My stedfast steppis yit slydis into the trap;
    My trued treuth intanglis me in trane: *trap*
        I spy the snair, and will not bakwards go
        My resone yeelds, and yit sayis na thairto.

In plesand path I tred upon the snaik;
    My flamming thrist I quench with venemous wyne;
In daintie dish I do the poyson tak;
    My langour bids me rather eit nor pyne:
        I sau, I sett; no flour nor fruit I find;   *sow; plant*
        I prik my hand, yit leavis the rose behind.

To Robert Hudsone[1]

My best belovit brother of the band,
I grein to sie the sillie smiddy smeik: *long to sift; smithy smoke*
This is no lyfe that I live upaland   *in the country*
On raw rid herring reistit in the reik,   *cured; smoke*
Syn I am subject somtyme to be seik,   *sick*
And daylie deing of my auld diseis.[2]   *dying*
Eit breid, ill aill, and all things are ane eik;   *Oatmeal bread; poor ale; as bad*

1. A poet and musician at the Court of King James VI; originally from the North of England, he shared favour with his brother Thomas.
2. He suffered from urinary gravel.

This barme and blaidry buists up all my bees.   *froth; flummery; clots; imagination*
Ye knaw ill guyding genders mony gees,   *poor fare; fits of sulkiness*
And specially in poets: for example,
Ye can pen out tua cuple and ye pleis.   *couplets whenever you like*
Yourself and I, old Scot and Robert Semple: *(Alexander Scott)*
   Quhen we ar dead, that all our dayis bot daffis,   *fool about*
   Let Christian Lyndesay wryt our epitaphis.

With mightie maters mynd I not to mell,   *I must remember; mix*
As copping courts, or comonwelthis, or kings: *high*
Quhais craig yoiks fastest, let tham sey thame sell;   *neck itches most (for the gallows)*
My thoght culd nevir think upon sik things.
I wantonly wryt under Venus wings;
In Cupids court ye knaw I haif bene kend,
Quhair Muses yit som of my sonets sings,
And shall do alwayis to the worlds end.
Men hes no caus my cunning to commend,   *skill*
That it suld merit sik a memorie;
Yit ye have sene his Grace oft for me send
Quhen he took plesure into poesie.
   Quhill tyme may serve, perforce I must refrane,
   That pleis his Grace, I come to court agane.

I feid affectione when I sie his Grace,
To look on that whairin I most delyte;
I am a lizard,[1] fainest of his face;   *fondest*
And not a snaik, with poyson him to byte;
Quhais shapes alyk, thoght fashions differ quyt: *though manners*
The one doth love, the other hateth still.   *one (person)*
Whare some taks plesur, others tak despyte;
One shap, one subject, wishis weill and ill:
Even so will men (bot no man judge I will)
Baith love and loth, and only bot ane thing.   *hate*
I can not skan these things above my skill:
Love Whom they lyk, for me, I love the King,
   Whose Highnes laughed som tym for to look
   Hou I chaist Polwart from the chimney nook.[2]

Remembers thou in Esope of a taill?
A loving dog wes of his maister fane;   *fond*
To faun on him wes all his pastym haill.
His courteous maister clappit him agane.   *patted*
By stood ane asse, a beist of blunter brane:
Perceiving this, bot looking to no freet,   *omen*

1. The lizard was traditionally a friend to man.
2. Sir Patrick Hume of Polwarth, a court poet whom the author blasted in the 'Flyting betwixt Montgomerie and Polwart'.

To pleis hir maister with the counterpane,   equivalent
Sho clambe on him with hir foull clubbit feet.
To play the messan thoght sho wes not meit,   pet dog; suited
Sho meinit weill, I grant; hir mynd wes guid,
Bot whair sho troude hir maister suld hir treit,   believed; reward
They battound hir whill that they saw hir bluid.   thrashed; until
    So stands with me, who loves with all my hairt
    My maister best: some taks it in ill pairt.

Bot sen I sie this proverbe to be true,
'Far better hap to court, nor service good',   luck at; than
Fairweill, my brother Hudsone nou to you,
Who first fand out of Pegase fut the flood,   found; Pegasus' foot
And sacred hight of Parnase mytred hood,[1]
From Whence som tyme the son of Venus sent   (Cupid)
Twa severall shaftis wher he of Delphos stood,
With Penneus dochter hoping to acquent.
Thy Homers style, thy Petrarks high invent   (Petrarch)
Sall vanquish death, and live eternally;
Quhais boasting bow, thoght it be alwayis bent,
Sall never hurt the sone of Memorie.
    Thou onlie brother of the Sisters Nyne,   (Muses)
    Shaw to the King this poor complaint of myne.

High architectur, wondrous vautit rounds

High architectur, wondrous vautit rounds;   vaulted
Huge host of Hevin in restles rolling spheers;
Firme fixit polis whilk all the axtrie beirs;   poles; axletree
Concordant discords, swete harmonious sounds;
Bowd Zodiac, belting Phebus bounds;   Bowed; containing (the sun's)
Celestiall signis, of moneths making yeers;
Bright Titan, to the tropiks that reteirs,   (the sun)
Quhais fyrie flammis all Chaos face confounds;
Just balanced ball, amidst the hevins that hings;
All creaturs that Natur creat can
To serve the use of most unthankfull man –
Admire your Maker, only King of Kings.
    Praise Him, O man, His mervels that remarks,
    Quhais mercyis far exceidis His wondrous warks.

1. The fountain Hippocrene, sacred to the muses, sprang up from where Pegasus struck the ground with his hoof.
Mt Parnassus is also sacred to the muses, and its cleft summits might be described as a bishop's mitre. The river god
Peneus's daughter was Daphne, pursued by amorous Apollo who has an oracle at Delphi on the slopes of Parnassus.

Hugh Barclay (1560?–1597)

Like his friend Montgomerie, to whom he addressed this poem, Hew Barclay of Ladyland was involved with Catholic intrigues, and they led to his death in the end.

To Alexander Montgomerie

My best belovit brother of the craft,
God if ye knew the stait that I am in!
Thocht ye be deif, I know ye ar not daft
Bot kynd aneugh to any of your kin.
If ye bot saw me in this winter win   *wind*
With old bogogers hotching on a sped,   *leggings; jumping; spade*
Draiglit in dirt, whylis wat evin to the skin   *draggled; wet*
I trow thair suld be tears or we twa shed.
Bot maist of all, that hes my bailis bred   *woes*
To heir how ye on that syde of the mure   *moor*
Birlis at the wyne, and blythlie gois to bed,   *Carouses*
Forgetting me, pure pleuman, I am sure.
So, sillie I, opprest with barmie juggis,   *(the thought of) foaming jugs*
Invyis your state that's pouing Bacchus luggis.   *pulling; ears*

Mark Alexander Boyd (1563–1601)

Boyd's best-known sonnet in Scots (he wrote mostly in Latin) gains a special force from his turbulent nature and a career which took him to France and Italy as a legal scholar and a fighting soldier caught up in the French civil war. He returned to Scotland at the end of his life.

Sonet

Fra banc to banc, fra wod to wod, I rin	wood
Ourhailit with my feble fantasie,	Overcome
Lyc til a leif that fallis from a trie	
Or til a reid ourblawin with the wind.	
Twa gods gyds me: the ane of tham is blind,[1]	
Ye, and a bairn brocht up in vanitie;	child
The nixt a wyf ingenrit of the se,	born; (Venus)
And lichter nor a dauphin with hir fin.	dolphin
Unhappie is the man for evirmaire	
That teils the sand and sawis in the aire;	tills; sows
Bot twyse unhappier is he, I lairn,	
That feidis in his hairt a mad desyre,	
And follows on a woman throw the fyre,	
Led be a blind and teichit be a bairn.	

1. Cupid, whose mother Venus was born from the waves, is sometimes shown blindfolded.

The Ballad Tradition

The oral tradition has always been very strong in Scotland, not least in the way that its succinct vigour has influenced more formal poetry at regular intervals in literary history. The great tradition of what Scott called 'the Border ballads' flourished in the sixteenth and seventeenth centuries, although they may derive from earlier versions, or refer to much earlier events. Anonymously or collectively composed, these tragic tales of war, feud, love and the supernatural were transmitted orally and sung in differing versions throughout the country, and indeed similar motifs can be found in folk-songs and tales throughout Europe. Women were most often the tradition bearers in this respect, from Anna Brown of Falkland in the eighteenth century to Jeannie Robertson and her daughter Lizzie Higgins in present-day Aberdeenshire.

After the Union of the Parliaments in 1707, this storehouse of tunes and tales seized the attention of a succession of collectors and scholars, who set about transcribing and publishing them as a particular expression of what they feared was a fading Scottish identity. Contributions were made by Allan Ramsay, Bishop Percy, David Herd, John Pinkerton, Joseph Ritson, Walter Scott, James Hogg, Andrew Crawfurd and Gavin Greig. In the late nineteenth century, the American scholar Francis J. Child made a life's work of collecting and classifying all the variations he could assemble. The popular tradition is by no means over, however, for 'bothy ballads' in the nineteenth century and the Scottish folk-song revival in the 1960s have been followed by an outpouring of more contemporary music on tape and disc. With their mixture of sudden leaps and a lingering repetitive narrative progress, the old Border ballads rank among the finest songs and tales of their kind anywhere in the world.

Anonymous

Sir Patrick Spence[1]

The king sits in Dumferling toune,   Dunfermline
   Drinking the blude-reid wine:
'O whar will I get guid sailor,
   To sail this schip of mine?'

1. A local mariner lost off Aberdour in the late seventeenth century. Some versions of the ballad conflate his name with a much earlier expedition to marry the King's daughter to Eric of Norway in 1281.

Up and spak an eldern knicht,
   Sat at the kings richt kne:
'Sir Patrick Spence is the best sailor
   That sails upon the se.'

The king has written a braid letter,
   And signd it wi his hand,
And sent it to Sir Patrick Spence,
   Was walking on the sand.

The first line that Sir Patrick red,
   A loud lauch lauched he;
The next line that Sir Patrick red,
   The teir blinded his ee.

'O wha is this has don this deid,
   This ill deid don to me,
To send me out this time o' the yeir,
   To sail upon the se!

'Mak haste, mak haste, my mirry men all,
   Our guid schip sails the morne:'
'O say na sae, my master deir,
   For I feir a deadlie storme.

'Late late yestreen I saw the new moone,
   Wi the auld moone in hir arme,
And I feir, I feir, my deir master,
   That we will cum to harme.'

O our Scots nobles wer richt laith   loath
   To weet their cork-heild schoone –   shoes
Bot lang owre a' the play wer playd,
   Thair hats they swam aboone.

O lang, lang may their ladies sit,
   Wi thair fans into their hand,
Or eir they se Sir Patrick Spence
   Cum sailing to the land.

O lang, lang may the ladies stand
   Wi thair gold kems in their hair
Waiting for thair ain deir lords,
   For they'll se thame na mair.

Haf owre, haf owre to Aberdour,
   It's fiftie fadom deip
And thair lies guid Sir Patrick Spence,
   Wi the Scots lords at his feit.

Child, 58A

The Cruel Brother

There was three ladies playd at the ba,
   With a hey ho and a lillie gay;
There came a knight and played oer them a',
   As the primrose spreads so sweetly.

The eldest was baith tall and fair,
But the youngest was beyond compare.

The midmost had a graceful mien,
But the youngest lookd like beautie's queen.

The knight bowd low to a' the three,
But to the youngest he bent his knee.

The ladie turned her head aside,
The knight he woo'd her to be his bride.

The ladie blushd a rosy red,
And sayd, 'Sir knight, I'm too young to wed.'

'O ladie fair, give me your hand,
And I'll make you ladie of a' my land.'

'Sir knight, ere ye my favor win,
Ye maun get consent frae a' my kin.'

He's got consent frae her parents dear,
And likewise frae her sisters fair.

He's got consent frae her kin each one,
But forgot to spiek to her brother John.

Now, when the wedding day was come,
The knight would take his bonny bride home.

And many a lord and many a knight
Came to behold that ladie bright.

And there was nae man that did her see,
But wishd himself bridegroom to be.

Her father dear led her down the stair
And her sisters twain they kissd her there.

Her mother dear led her thro the closs,   courtyard
And her brother John set her on her horse.

She leand her oer the saddle-bow,
To give him a kiss ere she did go.

He has taen a knife, baith lang and sharp,
And stabbd that bonny bride to the heart.

She hadno ridden half thro the town,
Until her heart's blude staind her gown.

'Ride softly on,' says the best young man,
'For I think our bonny bride looks pale and wan.'

'O lead me gently up yon hill,
And I'll there sit down, and make my will.'

'O what will you leave to your father dear?'
'The silver-shode steed that brought me here.'

'What will you leave to your mother dear?'
'My velvet pall and my silken gear.'   mantle; clothes

'What will you leave to your sister Anne?'
'My silken scarf and my gowden fan.'

'What will you leave to your sister Grace?'
'My bloody cloaths to wash and dress.'

'What will you leave to your brother John?'
'The gallows-tree to hang him on.'

'What will you leave to your brother John's wife?'
'The wilderness to end her life.'

This ladie fair in her grave was laid,
And many a mass was oer her said.

But it would have made your heart right sair,
　　With a hey ho and a lillie gay;
To see the bridegroom rive his haire,　　　　　　　　　　　tear
　　As the primrose spreads so sweetly.

Child, 11A

The Bonny Earl of Murray[1]

Ye Highlands, and ye Lawlands,
　　Oh where have you been?
They have slain the Earl of Murray,
　　And they layd him on the green.

'Now wae be to thee, Huntly!
　　And wherefore did you sae?
I bade you bring him wi you,
　　But forbade you him to slay.'

He was a braw gallant,
　　And he rid at the ring　　　　　　　　　　　　　　　　　rode
And the bonny Earl of Murray,
　　Oh he might have been a king!

He was a braw gallant,
　　And he playd at the ba;
And the bonny Earl of Murray
　　Was the flower amang them a'.

He was a braw gallant,
　　And he playd at the glove;
And the bonny Earl of Murray,
　　Oh he was the Queen's love!

Oh lang will his lady
　　Look oer the castle Down,
Eer she see the Earl of Murray
　　Come sounding thro the town!
Eer she see the Earl of Murray
　　Come sounding thro the town!

Child, 181A

---

1. James Stewart of Doune (near Stirling) was killed in 1592 by his old enemy the Earl of Huntly, who had been instructed to take him safely to the King's presence.

Mary Hamilton[1]

Word's gane to the kitchen,
    And word's gane to the ha,
That Marie Hamilton gangs wi bairn
    To the hichest Stewart of a'.[2]

He's courted her in the kitchen,
    He's courted her in the ha,
He's courted her in the laigh cellar,   bottom
    And that was warst of a'.

She's tyed it in her apron
    And she's thrown it in the sea –
Says, 'Sink ye, swim ye, bonny wee babe!
    You'll neer get mair o me.'

Down then cam the auld queen
    Goud tassels tying her hair:
'O Marie, where's the bonny wee babe
    That I heard greet sae sair?'

'There was never a babe intill my room,
    As little designs to be;
It was but a touch o my sair side,
    Come oer my fair bodie.'

'O Marie, put on your robes o black,
    Or else your robes o brown
For ye maun gang wi me the night,
    To see fair Edinbro town.'

'I winna put on my robes o black,
    Nor yet my robes o brown;
But I'll put on my robes o white,
    To shine through Edinbro town.'

When she gaed up the Cannogate,
    She laughd loud laughters three;
But whan she cam down the Cannogate
    The tear blinded her ee.

When she gaed up the Parliament stair,
    The heel cam aff her shee;   shoe

1. When she was six years old, Mary Stuart did have four companions of her own age called Mary, although the fourth one was a Mary Livingstone. There was a scandal at Court in 1563 concerning the Queen's apothecary and a French lady in waiting; but the particular tale of Mary Hamilton comes from an incident at the Russian Court of Peter the Great at the end of the seventeenth century. The dates may not fit, but the theme remains timeless.
2. This would be Lord Darnley, husband to Mary Queen of Scots.

And lang or she cam down again
    She was condemnd to dee.

When she cam down the Cannogate,
    The Cannogate sae free,
Many a ladie lookd oer her window,
    Weeping for this ladie.

'Ye need nae weep for me,' she says,
    'Ye need nae weep for me;
For had I not slain mine own sweet babe,
    This death I wadna dee.

'Bring me a bottle of wine,' she says,
    'The best that eer ye hae,
That I may drink to my weil-wishers,
    And they may drink to me.

'Here's a health to the jolly sailors,
    That sail upon the main –
Let them never let on to my father and mother
    But what I'm coming hame.

'Here's a health to the jolly sailors,
    That sail upon the sea;
Let them never let on to my father and mother
    That I cam here to dee.

'Oh little did my mother think,
    The day she cradled me,
What lands I was to travel through,
    What death I was to dee.

'Oh little did my father think,
    The day he held up me,
What lands I was to travel through,
    What death I was to dee.

'Last night I washd the queen's feet,
    And gently laid her down;
And a' the thanks I've gotten the nicht
    To be hangd in Edinbro town!

'Last nicht there was four Maries
    The nicht there'll be but three –
There was Marie Seton, and Marie Beton,
    And Marie Carmichael, and me.'

Child, 173A

The Dowy Houms o Yarrow
sad low-lying riverside land

Late at een, drinkin the wine,
   Or early in a mornin,
They set a combat them between,
   To fight it in the dawnin.
evening

'O stay at hame, my noble lord!
   O stay at hame, my marrow!
My cruel brother will you betray,
   On the dowy houms o Yarrow.'
mate/companion

'O fare ye weel, my lady gaye!
   O fare ye weel, my Sarah!
For I maun gae, tho I neer return
   Frae the dowy banks o Yarrow.'[1]

She kissd his cheek, she kaimd his hair,
   As she had done before, O;
She belted on his noble brand,
   An he's awa to Yarrow.
sword

O he's gane up yon high, high hill –
   I wat he gaed wi sorrow –
An in a den spied nine armd men,
   I the dowy houms o Yarrow.

'O ir ye come to drink the wine,
   As ye hae doon before, O?
Or ir ye come to wield the brand
   On the bonny banks o Yarrow?'

'I im no come to drink the wine,
   As I hae doon before, O,
But I im come to wield the brand,
   On the dowy houms o Yarrow.'

Four he hurt, an five he slew,
   On the dowy houms o Yarrow,
Till that stubborn knight came him behind,
   An ran his body thorrow.

'Gae hame, gae hame, good-brother John,
   An tell your sister Sarah
To come an lift her noble lord,
   Who's sleepin sound on Yarrow.'

---

1. The Yarrow Water in Ettrick Forest at the Borders near Selkirk.

'Yestreen I dreamd a dolefu dream;
   I kend there wad be sorrow;
I dreamd I pu'd the heather green,
   On the dowy banks o Yarrow.'

She gaed up yon high, high hill –
   I wat she gaed wi sorrow –
An in a den spy'd nine dead men,
   On the dowy houms o Yarrow.

She kissd his cheek, she kaimd his hair,
   As oft she did before, O;
She drank the red blood frae him ran,
   On the dowy houms o Yarrow.

'O haud your tongue, my douchter dear,
   For what needs a' this sorrow?
I'll wed you on a better lord
   Than him you lost on Yarrow.'

'O haud your tongue, my father dear,
   An dinna grieve your Sarah;
A better lord was never born
   Than him I lost on Yarrow.

'Tak hame your ousen, tak hame your kye,   oxen; cattle
   For they hae bred our sorrow;
I wiss that they had a' gane mad
   Whan they cam first to Yarrow.'

Child, 214E

Edward

'Why dois your brand sae drap wi bluid   sword
      Edward, Edward,
Why dois your brand sae drap wi bluid,
   And why sae sad gang yee O?'
'O I hae killed my hauke sae guid,
      Mither, mither
O I hae killed my hauke sae guid,
   And I had nae mair bot hee O.'

'Your haukis bluid was nevir sae reid,
      Edward, Edward,
Your haukis bluid was nevir sae reid,

My deir son I tell thee O.'
'O I hae killed my reid-roan steid,
  Mither, mither,
O I hae killed my reid-roan steid,
  That erst was sae fair and frie O.'

'Your steid was auld, and ye hae gat mair
  Edward, Edward,
Your steid was auld, and ye hae gat mair,
  Sum other dule ye drie O.'   sorrow; endure
'O I hae killed my fadir deir
  Mither, mither,
O I hae killed my fadir deir,
  Alas, and wae is mee O!'

'And whatten penance wul ye drie for that,   suffer
  Edward, Edward?
And whatten penance will ye drie for that?
  My deir son, now tell me O.'
'Ile set my feit in yonder boat,
  Mither, mither,
Ile set my feit in yonder boat,
  And Ile fare ovir the sea O.'

'And what wul ye doe wi your towirs and your ha,
  Edward, Edward?
And what wul ye doe wi your towirs and your ha,
  That were sae fair to see O?'
'Ile let thame stand tul they doun fa,
  Mither, mither,
Ile let thame stand tul they doun fa,
  For here nevir mair maun I bee O.'   may

'And what wul ye leive to your bairns and your wife,
  Edward, Edward?
And what wul ye leive to your bairns and your wife,
  Whan ye gang ovir the sea O?'
'The warldis room, late them beg thrae life,
  Mither, mither,
The warldis room, late them beg thrae life,
  For thame nevir mair wul I see O.'

'And what wul ye leive to your ain mither deir,
  Edward, Edward?
And what wul ye leive to your ain mither deir?
  My deir son, now tell me O.'

'The curse of hell frae me sall ye beir,
    Mither, mither,
The curse of hell frae me sall ye beir,
    Sic counseils ye gave to me O.'

Child, 13B

The Twa Corbies
ravens/carrion crows

As I was walking all alane,
I heard twa corbies making a mane;
The tane unto the t'other say,
'Where sall we gang and dine to-day?'

grumbling

'In behint yon auld fail dyke,
I wot there lies a new slain knight
And naebody kens that he lies there,
But his hawk, his hound, and lady fair.

turf wall

'His hound is to the hunting gane
His hawk to fetch the wild-fowl hame,
His lady's ta'en another mate
So we maun mak our dinner sweet.

may

'Ye'll sit on his white hause-baue
And I'll pike out his bonny blue een;
Wi ae lock o his gowden hair
We'll theek our nest when it grows bare.

collarbone
pick/peck/steal
thatch

'Mony a one for him makes mane
But nane sall ken where he is gane
Oer his white banes, when they are bare,
The wind sall blaw for evermair.'

mourns

Child, 26

The Three Ravens[1]

There were three ravens sat on a tree
   Downe a downe, hay down, hay downe;
There were three ravens sat on a tree,
   With a downe;
There were three ravens sat on a tree,
They were as blacke as they might be.
   With a downe derrie, derrie, derrie, downe, downe.

---

1. This English ballad is a much more optimistic counterpart to 'The Twa Corbies'.

The one of them said to his mate,
'Where shall we our breakefast take?'

'Downe in yonder greene field,
There lies a knight slain under his shield.

'His hounds they lie downe at his feete,
So well they can their master keepe.

'His haukes they flie so eagerly,
There's no fowle dare him come nie.'

Downe there comes a fallow doe,
As great with yong as she might goe.

She lift up his bloudy hed,
And kist his wounds that were so red.

She got him up upon her backe,
And carried him to earthen lake.

She buried him before the prime,
She was dead herselfe ere even-song time.

God send every gentleman,
Such haukes, such hounds, and such a leman.   beloved

Child, 26

Thomas the Rhymer[1]

True Thomas lay oer yond grassy bank
    And he beheld a ladie gay,
A ladie that was brisk and bold,
    Come riding oer the fernie brae.

Her skirt was of the grass-green silk,
    Her mantel of the velvet fine,
At ilka tett of her horse's mane   each tuft
    Hung fifty silver bells and nine.

True Thomas he took off his hat,
    And bowed him low down till his knee:

---

1. A poet and a seer in the late thirteenth century, Thomas of Ercildoune is remembered for his prophecies. A medieval version of the ballad survives from the 1450s and 'True Thomas' has entered folklore. He is supposed to have met the Elf Queen while sleeping on Huntly Bank in the Eildon Hills to the south of Melrose in the Borders.

'All hail, thou mighty Queen of Heaven!
   For your peer on earth I never did see.'

'O no, O no, True Thomas,' she says,
   'That name does not belong to me;
I am but the queen of fair Elfland,
   And I'm come here for to visit thee.

'But ye maun go wi me now, Thomas,   must
   True Thomas, ye maun go wi me,
For ye maun serve me seven years,
   Thro weel or wae as may chance to be.'   good or ill

She turned about her milk-white steed,
   And took True Thomas up behind,
And aye wheneer her bridle rang,
   The steed flew swifter than the wind.

For forty days and forty nights
   He wade thro red blude to the knee,
And he saw neither sun nor moon,
   But heard the roaring of the sea.

O they rade on, and further on,
   Until they came to a garden green:
'Light down, light down, ye ladie free,
   Some of that fruit let me pull to thee .'

'O no, O no, True Thomas,' she says,
   'That fruit maun not be touched by thee
For a' the plagues that are in hell
   Light on the fruit of this countrie.

'But I have a loaf here in my lap,
   Likewise a bottle of claret wine,
And now ere we go farther on,
   We'll rest a while, and ye may dine.'

When he had eaten and drunk his fill,
   'Lay down your head upon my knee,'
The lady sayd, 'ere we climb yon hill,
   And I will show you fairlies three.

'O see not ye yon narrow road
   So thick beset wi thorns and briers?
That is the path of righteousness
   Tho after it but few enquires.

'And see not ye that braid braid road,
    That lies across yon lillie leven?
That is the path of wickedness,
    Tho some call it the road to heaven.

'And see not ye that bonny road,
    Which winds about the fernie brae?
That is the road to fair Elfland
    Where you and I this night maun gae.

'But Thomas, ye maun hold your tongue
    Whatever you may hear or see,
For gin ae word you should chance to speak,
    You will neer get back to your ain countrie.'

He has gotten a coat of the even cloth
    And a pair of shoes of velvet green,
And till seven years were past and gone
    True Thomas on earth was never seen.

Child, 37A

Tam Lin[1]

O I forbid you, maidens a
    That wear gowd on your hair,
To come or gae by Carterhaugh,[2]
    For young Tam Lin is there.

There's nane that gaes by Carterhaugh
    But they leave him a wad,   *pledge*
Either their rings, or green mantles,
    Or else their maidenhead.

Janet has kilted her green kirtle   *gown*
    A little aboon her knee,
And she has broded her yellow hair   *braided*
    A little aboon her bree,   *brow*
And she's awa to Carterhaugh,
    As fast as she can hie.

When she came to Carterhaugh
    Tam Lin was at the well,
And there she fand his steed standing,
    But away was himsel.

1. Tam Lin's tale is mentioned among many others in *The Complaynt of Scotland* from 1549, and Child traces the roots of the story to a Cretan legend nearly 2,500 years old. Compare Liz Lochhead's version, 'Tam Lin's Lady'.
2. A wooded stretch between the meeting of Ettrick and Yarrow Waters outside Selkirk.

She had na pu'd a double rose
    A rose but only twa,
Till up then started young Tam Lin,
    Says, 'Lady, thou's pu nae mae.

'Why pu's thou the rose, Janet,
    And why breaks thou the wand?   stem
Or why comes thou to Carterhaugh
    Withoutten my command?'

'Carterhaugh, it is my ain,
    My daddie gave it me;
I'll come and gang by Carterhaugh,
    And ask nae leave at thee.'

Janet has kilted her green kirtle
    A little aboon her knee,
And she has snooded her yellow hair   bound up
    A little aboon her bree,
And she is to her father's ha,
    As fast as she can hie.

Four and twenty ladies fair
    Were playing at the ba,
And out then cam the fair Janet,
    Ance the flower amang them a'.

Four and twenty ladies fair
    Were playing at the chess,
And out then cam the fair Janet,
    As green as onie glass.

Out then spak an auld grey knight,
    Lay oer the castle wa,
And says, 'Alas, fair Janet, for thee
    But we'll be blamed a'.'

'Haud your tongue, ye auld knight,
    Some ill death may ye die!
Father my bairn on whom I will,
    I'll father nane on thee.'

Out then spak her father dear,
    And he spak meek and mild
'And ever alas, sweet Janet,' he says
    'I think thou gaes wi child.'

'If that I gae wi child, father,
  Mysel maun bear the blame –
There's neer a laird about your ha
  Shall get the bairn's name.

'If my love were an earthly knight,
  As he's an elfin grey,
I wad na gie my ain true-love
  For nae lord that ye hae.

'The steed that my true-love rides on
  Is lighter than the wind;
Wi siller he is shod before   silver
  Wi burning gowd behind.'

Janet has kilted her green kirtle
  A little aboon her knee,
And she has snooded her yellow hair
  A little aboon her bree,
Aud she's awa to Carterhaugh,
  As fast as she can hie.

When she cam to Carterhaugh,
  Tam Lin was at the well.
And there she fand his steed standing,
  But away was himsel.

She had na pu'd a double rose,
  A rose but only twa,
Till up then started young Tam Lin,
  Says, 'Lady, thou pu's nae mae.

'Why pu's thou the rose, Janet,
  Amang the groves sae green,
And a' to kill the bonie babe
  That we gat us between?'

'O tell me, tell me, Tam Lin,' she says,
  'For's sake that died on tree,   (the Cross)
If eer ye was in holy chapel,
  Or christendom did see?'

'Roxbrugh he was my grandfather,
  Took me with him to bide,   dwell
And ance it fell upon a day
  That wae did me betide.

'And ance it fell upon a day,
　A cauld day and a snell,
When we were frae the hunting come,
　That frae my horse I fell;
The Queen o Fairies she caught me,
　In yon green hill to dwell.

'And pleasant is the fairy land,
　But, an eerie tale to tell,
Ay at the end of seven years   Always
　We pay a tiend to hell;   tithe/levy
I am sae fair and fu o flesh,
　I'm feard it be mysel.   afraid

'But the night is Halloween,¹ lady,
　The morn is Hallowday;
Then win me, win me, an ye will,
　For weel I wat ye may.

'Just at the mirk and midnight hour
　The fairy folk will ride,
And they that wad their true-love win,
　At Miles Cross they maun bide.'   wait

'But how shall I thee ken, Tam Lin,
　Or how my true-love know,
Amang sae mony unco knights   strange
　The like I never saw?'

'O first let pass the black, lady,
　And syne let pass the brown,
But quickly run to the milk-white steed.
　Pu ye his rider down.

'For I'll ride on the milk-white steed.
　And ay nearest the town;
Because I was an earthly knight
　They gie me that renown.

'My right hand will be glovd, lady,
　My left hand will be bare,
Cockt up shall my bonnet be,
　And kaimd down shall my hair,
And thae's the takens I gie thee,   tokens
　Nae doubt I will be there.

---

1. All Hallows eve, 31 October, derived from the Celtic Samhuinn, a festival of the dead which heralds the start of winter. The supernatural world is particularly close at this time.

'They'll turn me in your arms. lady,
   Into an esk and adder;   newt
But hold me fast, and fear me not,
   I am your bairn's father.

'They'll turn me to a bear sae grim,
   And then a lion bold;
But hold me fast, and fear me not,
   As ye shall love your child.

'Again they'll turn me in your arms
   To a red het gaud of airn;   bar; iron
But hold me fast, and fear me not,
   I'll do to you nae harm.

'And last they'll turn me in your arms
   Into the burning gleed;   coal
Then throw me into well water,
   O throw me in wi speed.

'And then I'll be your ain true-love,
   I'll turn a naked knight;
Then cover me wi your green mantle,
   And cover me out o sight.'

Gloomy, gloomy was the night,
   And eerie was the way,
As fair Jenny in her green mantle
   To Miles Cross she did gae.

About the middle o the night
   She heard the bridles ring;
This lady was as glad at that
   As any earthly thing.

First she let the black pass by,
   And syne she let the brown;
But quickly she ran to the milk-white steed,
   And pu'd the rider down.

Sae weel she minded what he did say,
   And young Tam Lin did win;
Syne coverd him wi her green mantle,   Then
   As blythe's a bird in spring.   happy

Out then spak the Queen o Fairies,
   Out of a bush o broom:
'Them that has gotten young Tam Lin
   Has gotten a stately groom.'

Out then spak the Queen o Fairies,
   And an angry woman was she:
'Shame betide her ill-far'd face,   *ill-favoured*
   And an ill death may she die,
For she's taen awa the boniest knight
   In a' my companie.

'But had I kend, Tam Lin,' she says,
   'What now this night I see,
I wad hae taen out thy twa grey een,
   And put in twa een o tree.'   *wood*

Child, 39A

The Wife of Usher's Well

There lived a wife at Usher's Well,
   And a wealthy wife was she;
She had three stout and stalwart sons,
   And sent them oer the sea.

They hadna been a week from her,
   A week but barely ane,
Whan word came to the carline wife   *old woman*
   That her three sons were gane.

They hadna been a week from her
   A week but barely three,
Whan word came to the carlin wife
   That her sons she'd never see.

'I wish the wind may never cease,
   Nor fashes in the flood,   *disturbances*
Till my three sons come hame to me,
   In earthly flesh and blood.'

It fell about the Martinmass,[1]
   When nights are lang and mirk,
The carlin wife's three sons came hame,
   And their hats were o the birk.   *birch*

---

1. 11 November, dedicated to St Martin of Tours of the fourth century, patron of Scotland's own St Ninian, but the festival goes back to the celebration of Samhuinn, and in the ballads it is frequently associated with uncanny and melancholy events.

It neither grew in syke nor ditch,   marshy rivulet
    Nor yet in ony sheugh;   drainage ditch
But at the gates o Paradise,
    That birk grew fair eneugh.

'Blow up the fire, my maidens,
    Bring water from the well;
For a' my house shall feast this night,
    Since my three sons are well.'

And she has made to them a bed
    She's made it large and wide,
And she's taen her mantle her about
    Sat down at the bed-side.

Up then crew the red, red cock
    And up and crew the gray;
The eldest to the youngest said,
    ''Tis time we were away.'

The cock he hadna crawd but once
    And clappd his wings at a',
When the youngest to the eldest said,
    'Brother, we must awa.

'The cock doth craw, the day doth daw,
    The channerin worm doth chide;   whining
Gin we be mist out o our place,
    A sair pain we maun bide.   must endure

'Fare ye weel, my mother dear!
    Fareweel to barn and byre!   cowshed
And fare ye weel, the bonny lass
    That kindles my mother's fire!'

                                                                      Child, 79A

The Great Silkie of Sule Skerry[1]

An earthly nourris sits and sings,   nurse
    And aye she sings, 'Ba, lily wean!
Little ken I my bairnis father
    Far less the land that he staps in.'   stays

---

1. Silkies, or selkies, are the seal-folk who can take human shape, often to woo a human lover before returning to the sea. Sule Skerry is a group of sea-washed rocks off the Shetland Isles.

Then ane arose at her bed-fit,
    An a grumly guest I'm sure was he: sullen
'Here am I, thy bairnis father
    Although that I be not comelie.

'I am a man, upo the lan,
    An I am a silkie in the sea;
And when I'm far and far frae lan
    My dwelling is in Sule Skerrie.'

'It was na weel,' quo the maiden fair
    'It was na weel, indeed,' quo she,
'That the Great Silkie of Sule Skerrie
    Suld hae come and aught a bairn to me.'   charged

Now he has taen a purse of goud,
    And he has pat it upo her knee,
Sayin, 'Gie to me my little young son,
    An tak thee up thy nourris-fee.

'An it sall come to pass on a simmer's day,
    When the sin shines het on evera stane,
That I will tak my little young son,
    An teach him for to swim the faem.

'An thu sall marry a proud gunner
    An a proud gunner I'm sure he'll be,
An the very first schot that ere he schoots
    He'll schoot baith my young son and me.'

Child, 113

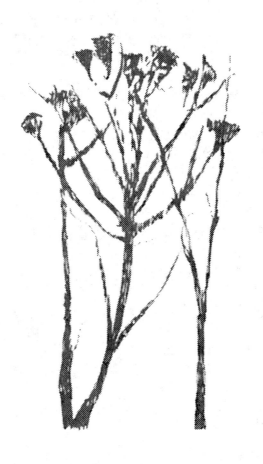

Anonymous (c. 1650?)

This fine poem by a rejected lover speaks for the central contribution which many women have made to Gaelic song, even if some of their names have been lost in the process of oral transmission. The following piece comes from John Mackenzie's

Thig trì nithean gun iarraidh

Thig trì nithean gun iarraidh
An t-eagal, an t-iadach 's an gaol,
'S bu bheag a' chùis mhaslaidh
Ged 'ghlacadh leo mis air a h-aon,
'S a liuthad bean uasal
A fhuaras 'sa' chiont ud robh mi,
A thug an gaol fuadain
Air ro bheagan duaise ga chionn.

Fhir a dhìreas am bealach
Beir mo shoraidh d' an ghleannan o thuath
Is innis do m' leannan,
Gur maireann mo gaol 's gur buan
Fear eile cha ghabh mi
'S chan fhuiling mi idir a luaidh;
Gus an dèan thu ghaoil m' àicheadh,
Cha chreid mi o chàch gur fuath.

Fhir nan gorm shùilean meallach
O 'n ghleannan am bitheadh an smùid,
Gam beil a' chaoin mhala
Mar chanach an t-slèibh fo dhriùchd;
Nuair rachadh tu air t' uilinn
Bhiodh fuil air fear dhìreadh nan stùc,
'S nam biodh tu ghaoil mar rium
Cha b' anaid an cèile leam thu.

Nam faicinn thu tighinn
Is fios domh gur tusa bhiodh ann,

Sàr Obair, first published in 1841. An earlier version was published in a collection made by Eòin Gillies in Perth in 1786.

Three things come without seeking[1]

Three things come without seeking,
jealousy, terror and love.
Nor is it shame to be counted
among those whom such agonies grieve,
since so many great ladies
have suffered the crime that I have,
being exiled by passion.
They gave but they did not receive.

You who are climbing the defile
bear my love to the glen of the north:
take this vow to my sweetheart:
'I am his while I live on the earth.
I will marry no other
nor allow such news to go forth.
Till, my dear, you've denied me,
I'll distrust the words of their mouth.'

You, of the blue eyes beguiling,
(from the glen where the mist would arise)
your eyebrows showed courteous mildness
like the moor-cotton dewed from the skies:
when you aimed as you lay on your elbow
the stag would be caught by surprise:
my love, if you lived in my dwelling,
no one could mock or despise.

My dear, if I saw you arriving
and knew that it really was you,

---

1. Triads are common in Gaelic folklore and proverbs, e.g.: 'Trì nithean brèagha: long fo sheòl, craobh fo blàth, is duine naomh air leabaidh-bàis. / Three beautiful things: a ship under sail, a tree in bloom and a godly man on his deathbed.'

Gun èireadh mo chridhe
Mar aiteal na grèin' thar nam beann;
'S gun tugainn mo bhriathar
Gach gaoisdean tha liath 'na mo cheann
Gum fàsadh iad buidhe
Mar dhìthein am bruthaich nan allt.

Cha b' ann air son beairteis
No idir ro-phailteas na sprèidh,
Cha b' fhear do shìol bhodach
Bha m' osna cho trom ad dhèidh,
Ach mhac an duin' uasail
Fhuair buaidh air an dùthaich gu lèir;
Ge do bhitheamaid falamh
'S ioma caraid a chitheadh oirnn feum.

Mur tig thus fèin tuilleadh
Gur aithne dhomh mhalairt a th'ann,
Nach eil mi cho beairteach
Ri cailinn an achaidh ud thall.
Cha tugainn mo mheisneach,
Mo ghliocas is grinneas mo làimh
Air buaile chrodh ballach
Is cailinn gun lùil 'nan ceann.

Ma chaidh thu orm seachad
Gur taitneach, neo-thuisleach mo chliù:
Cha d' rinn mi riut comann
'S cha d' laigh mi leat riamh ann an cùil.
Chan àraichinn arachd
Do dhuine chuir ad air a chrùn
On bha mi cho beachdail
'S gun smachdaich mi gaol nach fiù.

Bu laoghaid mo thàmailt
Nam b' airidh ni b' fheàrr a bhiodh ann,
Ach dubh chail' a' bhuachair
'Nuair ghlacas i buarach 'na làimh;
'Nuair a thig an droch earrach
'S a chaillear an nì anns a' ghleann,
Bitheas is' air an t-siulaid
Gun tuille dhe bunailteas ann.

my heart's blood ascending
would break like the sun into view:
and I'll give you my promise
each hair that was grey would renew
its greyness to yellow
like the flowers that the waters pursue.

It was not for your riches
and not for your numerous herd:
it was not for a weakling
that my heart was troubled and stirred:
but the son of a noble
who conquered a land with his sword:
we'd suffer no hunger
for many would furnish our board.

If you're never returning,
I'll know an exchange has been made,
that being more wealthy
another has suited your trade.
I'd not give my courage,
my wisdom, the love you betrayed,
for a field of bright cattle,
and a girl without sense at their head.

And though you've disowned me
I've no dark dishonour to hide:
my fame is unsullied;
I've never lain down at your side.
For a man who'd crowned monarchs
I suffer more pangs from my pride
than to rear him young bastards.
I'd strangle my love till it died.

Yet gentler the insult
if her love were higher than mine:
but a slatternly scullion
whom even the cows would disdain:
when the spring comes with tempest
and the cattle are lost in the glen
she'll be lying in child-bed,
the house without rudder or rein.

trans. Iain Crichton Smith

Robert Sempill of Beltrees
(1590?–1660?)

The son of a courtier and theologian, Sempill went to Glasgow University and fought on behalf of Charles I in the English civil war. He recalled a local piper in an artless serio-comic elegy which produced countless poems in the same vein, while its distinctive verse form, soon known as 'standard Habbie', practically took over Scottish vernacular verse for the next 100 years.

The Life and Death of Habbie Simson, the Piper of Kilbarchan

Kilbarchan now may say alas!	
For she hath lost her game and grace,	
Both *Trixie* and *The Maiden Trace*;	(tunes)
But what remead?	help
For no man can supply his place:	
Hab Simson's dead.	
Now who shall play *The Day it Dawis*,	
Or *Hunt's Up*, when the cock he craws?	
Or who can for our kirk-town cause	
Stand us in stead?	
On bagpipes now nobody blaws	
Sen Habbie's dead.	
Or wha will cause our shearers shear?	
Wha will bend up the brags of weir,	play the vaunting war-tunes
Bring in the bells, or good play-meir	celebrate New Year; play more
In time of need?	
Hab Simson cou'd, what needs you speir?	ask
But now he's dead.	
So kindly to his neighbours neast	nearest
At Beltan and St. Barchan's feast	
He blew, and then held up his breast,	
As he were weid:	feverish
But now we need not him arrest,	stop
For Habbie's dead.	

At fairs he play'd before the spear-men
All gaily graithed in their gear men: *kitted-out*
Steel bonnets, jacks, and swords so clear then
       Like any bead: *ring of folk*
Now wha shall play before such weir-men   *warriors*
       Sen Habbie's dead?

At clark-plays[1] when he wont to come
His Pipe play'd trimly to the drum;
Like bikes of bees he gart it bum,   *hives; made it drone*
       And tun'd his reed:
Now all our pipers may sing dumb,
       Sen Habbie's dead.

And at horse races many a day,
Before the black, the brown, the gray,
He gart his pipe, when he did play,
       Baith skirl and skreed: *shriek and screech*
Now all such pastime's quite away
       Sen Habbie's dead.

He counted was a weil'd wight-man,   *was reckoned a chosen brave man*
And fiercely at football he ran:
At every game the gree he wan   *prize*
       For pith and speed.
The like of Habbie was na than,
       But now he's dead.

And than, besides his valiant acts,
At bridals he won many placks;   *coins*
He bobbed ay behind fo'k's backs
       And shook his head.
Now we want many merry cracks   *lack; jokes*
       Sen Habbie's dead.

He was convoyer of the bride,
With Kittock hinging at his side;   *Katie*
About the kirk he thought a pride
       The ring to lead:
But now we may gae but a guide,   *without*
       For Habbie's dead.

So well's he keeped his decorum
And all the stots of *Whip-meg-morum*;   *hops of (a dance tune)*

---

1. A play composed or acted by clerics or school-men.

He slew a man, and wae's me for him,
       And bure the fead!   *put up with the feud*
But yet the man wan hame before him,   *got*
       And was not dead.

And whan he play'd, the lasses leugh
To see him teethless, auld, and teugh,
He wan his pipes besides Barcleugh,   *earned*
       Withouten dread!
Which after wan him gear eneugh;   *won; plenty wealth*
       But now he's dead.

Ay when he play'd the gaitlings gedder'd,   *urchins gathered*
And when he spake, the carl bledder'd,   *old man boasted*
On Sabbath days his cap was fedder'd,
       A seemly weid;   *proper outfit*
In the kirk-yeard his mare stood tedder'd
       Where he lies dead.

Alas! for him my heart is saur,
For of his spring I gat a skair,   *dancetune; share*
At every play, race, feast, and fair,
       But guile or greed;   *Without*
We need not look for pyping mair,
       Sen Habbie's dead.

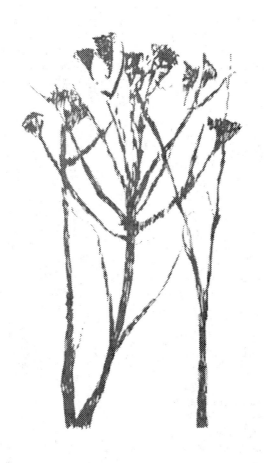

Donnchadh MacRaoiridh/ Duncan MacRyrie (c. 1630)

As bard to the MacDonalds of Sleat, on Skye, Duncan MacRyrie also owed clan loyalties to the Mackenzies of Wester Ross around Inverness whom he praises in 'Too long I live after these'. Here the formal qualities of bardic verse have started

Fada ata mise an deidh chaich

Fada atà mise an déidh chàich
   'S an saoghal gu bràth d' am dhragh;
Saoghal bha againn gus an diugh
   Nach 'eil fios an diugh cia a fheadh.

An saoghal a bha againn uair
   Gun ghoideadh e bhuainn gun fhios;
Agus an saoghal atà
   Ciod è a phlàigh nì sinne ris?

Dìth Chailin is tuirseach leam
   Fear bho faighinn mùirn gu bràth,
Agus a bheireadh orm mios:
   Fada atà mise an déidh chàich.

'N déidh Ruairidh is Choinnich fa thrì,
   A dh'fhuasgladh mì as gach càs,
Dh'fhàg mi fuireach ri mo sgrid:
   Fada atà mise an déidh chàich.

Gun mhian, gun aighear, gun cheòl,
   Ach laighe fo bhròn gu bràth;
Ach gu faighim bàs gun fhios,
   Fada atà mise aII déidh chàich.

to use a more colloquial vocabulary and personal utterance, although the tone of resignation from the world comes from a long-familiar Christian tradition.

Too long I live after these

Long I live and the others away
   while the world is a trial to me yet;
and the fashion we had till today
   none remains who can tell us of that.

The life that was there until now
   it has stolen away like a thief;
the little that's left, tell me how
   the devil we'll spend it in peace.

The losing of Colin I mourn[1]
   the man that made joyful my day,
who gave to me honour in turn:
   long I live and the others away.

Now that Rory and Kenny have gone,[2]
   that baled me out from each scrape,
I'm left to the struggle alone:
   long I live and the others asleep.

Without wish, without joy, without song,
   I hope, here alone in my grief,
that death will soon take me along:
   here I wake while my friends are asleep.

1. Chief of the Seaforth Mackenzies (d. 1594).
2. Roderick Mackenzie of Coigach (d. 1626); Kenneth, first Lord of Kintail (d. 1611).

Tà fear am Manchainn nan Lios
   Nach léigeadh mise as mu nì:
Do bhì an Cananaich nan Clag
   Triùir a dh'fhàg gu lag mì.

Mairg atà beò 'nan déidh
   'S atà gun spéis fo bheil cion:
Thug an anshocair mo leòn
   Bho nach maireann beò na fir.

A MhicChoinnich, Chailin Oig,
   Mhic an t-seòid nach robh gu lag,
A nis bho is goirid mo théirm
   Bidh mise agad féin gu fad.
               Fada atà mise.

In the Garden of Beauly one lies   (Beauly Priory)
   who will not let me live at my rest:
where the steeples of Chanonry rise   (Fortrose Cathedral)
   three that leave my sad spirit oppressed.

What a plague they have gone while I stay
   to live without honour or gear:
I am weak with a wounding each day
   while my comrades lie cold in the lair.   tomb

Colin Og, Earl of Seaforth's great line,[1]
   hardy heroes, sons of the brave,
may my years soon fall to the time
   when I join you all there in the grave.
          Too long I live.

trans. William Neill

---

1. First Earl of Seaforth, chief from 1611–33.

Murchadh MacCoinnich/ Murdo MacKenzie (c. 1650)

Allied – like Duncan MacRyrie – to the Seaforth Mackenzies, Murdo, like his father before him, was head of his family sept in Strathpeffer, near Dingwall, and a poet in his own right. Here, too, the bardic tradition is changing under the influence of

Diomhanas nan Diomhanas

Dìomhain bhur dlùthchiabh air tuiteam chon làir,
Dìomhain bhur pìosa, bhur cupanna clàir,
Dìomhain bhur n-uchdshnaidhm, bhur n-usgair gun stàth,
Dìomhain gach aon nì, an uair thigeas am bàs.

Dìomhain bhur caisteil fo bhaideal 's fo bhlàth,
Dìomhain bhur n-aitribh d'an cailceadh gach là,
Dìomhain, giodh ait libh, bhur macnas ri mnà,
Dìomhain gach aon nì an uair thigeas am bàs.

Dìomhain bhur saidhbhreas, bhur n-aoibhneas ri bàrr,
Dìomhain bhur n-uailse, giodh uallach am blàth,
Dìomhain bhur bantrachd làn annsachd is gràidh,
Dìomhain gach aon nì an uair thigeas am bàs.

Dìomhain bhur codla, bhur socair gun sàst,
Dìomhain bhur cosnadh fa osnadh gach là,
Dìomhain bhur gràinnsich, bhur tàinte air blàr,
Dìomhain gach aon nì an uair thigeas am bàs.

Dìomhain bhur léigheann, bhur léirsinn a bhàn,
Dìomhain bhur geurchuis 'sna speuraibh gu h-àrd,
Dìomhain bhur tuigse tha tuisleach a ghnàth,
Dìomhain gach aon nì an uair thigeas am bàs.

Dìomhain na daoine nach smaoinich am bàs,
Dìomhain an saoghal, a thaobhadh is bàth,
Bho thà e d'am chlaoidheadh 's mi daonnan an spàirn,
Sguirim d'a shìor-ruith bho is dìomhanas à.

non-professional poets, familiar with the Bible and using a more colloquial Gaelic. This poem is said to be a veiled attack on those who betrayed Charles II.

Vanity of Vanities

Vain are your ringlets that fall to the floor,
vain is your silver, your cups on the board,
vain is your breast-knot, your jewelry store,
vain are all things when death comes to your door.

Vain is your castle of tower and dune,
vain is your dwelling that's limed in each room,
vain is your lust for a woman in bloom,
vain are all these for death comes to you soon.

Vain is your money, your joy in the pile,
vain is your blood-line, though noble its style,
vain your fair women though beauty beguile,
vain are all these things that death shall defile.

Vain is your sleeping, your comforts that please,
vain are your wages, you toil without ease,
vain are your crops and the cattle you seize,
vain are your things when death smothers all these.

Vain is your learning, your clearness of mind,
vain the high stars by your wisdom defined,
vain is your thought that is stumbling and blind,
vain are all these when death follows behind.

Vain is the man with no thought for the end,
vain is this life with its making and mend,
since all things defeat me for all I defend,
I'll cease the vain striving on which I depend.

trans. William Neill

217

Iain Lom/John MacDonald
(1620?–1707?)

'Bare' or 'lean' Iain was the grandson of a deposed chief of the MacDonalds of Keppoch, who held land around Spean Bridge to the north-east of Fort William. Tradition has it that he was intended for the Catholic priesthood and trained in Spain, before returning to secular life. As a young poet and a fierce Royalist, he was noted and feared for his sharp tongue and his whole-hearted engagement with political affairs, as in his invective against the Campbells, defeated by Montrose at the Battle of Inverlochy in 1645. His verse has a vivid, concentrated, oblique and

Cumha Aonghais Mhic Raghnaill Oig na Ceapaich

Rìgh gur mór mo chuid mulaid,
Ged as fheudar dhomh fhulang,
Ge bè dh'éisdeadh ri m'uireasbhaidh àireamh.

On a chaill mi na gadhair,
Is an t-eug 'gan sior thadhal,
'S beag mo thoirt gar an tadhail mi 'm Bràighe.

Is eun bochd mi gun daoine
Air mo lot air gach taobh dhiom:
Is tric rosad an aoig air mo chàirdean.

Gur mi an gèadh air a spìonadh,
Gun iteach gun lìnnidh,
'S mi mar Oisean fo bhinn an taigh Phàdraig.

Gur mi a' chraobh air a rùsgadh,
Gun chnothan gun ùbhlan,
'S a snodhach 's a rùsg air a fàgail.

'N ruaig sin cheann Locha Tatha,
'S i chuir mis' ann am ghaibhtheach:
Dh'fhàg mi Aonghas 'na laighe 'san àraich.

imagistic quality, whose colloquial force is backed up by strong metric stresses. In this respect he marks the end of the classic bardic style, and the start of the colloquial flowering that was to come in the eighteenth century. 'Lament for Angus, son of young Ranald of Keppoch' is a poem of personal feeling rather than a formal eulogy, while the late 'Song Against the Union' (the poet was in his 80s), is no less than a scatological public attack in the flyting tradition. Iain Lom is said to have died in poverty and is buried in a small churchyard at the Braes of Lochaber.

Lament for Angus son of Young Ranald of Keppoch[1]

Lord, low is my spirit,
though courage must bear it,
whoever will hear of my losses.

Since death, that brisk caller,
kills my friends of high valour,
what pleasure to me in Lochaber?

Lonely, unfriended
on each side I am wounded:
Death's arrows descend on my comrades.

I'm a goose that is plucked,
without feather or brood,
or like Ossian condemned by Saint Patrick.

Or a tree that is stripped,
without apple or nut,
the sap and the bark having left it.

That raid to Loch Tay
has darkened my way:
Angus lay dead by its waters.

1. The young poet was present at this skirmish for the Royalist cause near Killin in Perthshire in 1646 at which his father was also killed. Angus was a young chief of the Keppoch MacDonalds.

Mun do dhìrich sibh 'm bruthach
'S ann 'nur deaghaidh bha 'n ulaidh:
Bha gìomanach gunn' air dhroch càramh.

Ged a dh'fhàg mi ann m'athair,
Chan ann air tha mi labhairt,
Ach an drùdhadh rinn an claidheamh mu t'àirnean.

Gur e dhrùidh air mo leacainn
'M buille mór a bha 'd leathtaobh
'S tu ad laighe 'n taigh beag Choire Charmaig.

B'i mo ghràdh do ghnùis aobhach
Dhèanadh dath le t'fhuil chraobhaich,
'S nach robh seachnach air aodann do nàmhaid.

La Inbhir Lochaidh

    Hì rim hó ro, hó ro leatha,
    Hì rim hó ro, hó ro leatha,
    Hì rim hó ro, hó ro leatha,
    Chaidh an latha le Clann Dòmhnaill.

'N cuala sibhse 'n tionndadh duineil
Thug an camp bha 'n Cille Chuimein?
'S fada chaidh ainm air an iomairt,
Thug iad as an naimhdean iomain.

Dhìrich mi moch madainn Dòmhnaich
Gu bràigh caisteil Inbhir Lòchaidh;
Chunnaic mi 'n t-arm dol an òrdugh,
'S bha buaidh a' bhlàir le Clann Dòmhnaill.

Dìreadh a mach glùn Chùil Eachaidh,
Dh'aithnich mi oirbh sùrd bhur tapaidh;
Ged bha mo dhùthaich 'na lasair,
'S éirig air a' chùis mar thachair.

Ged bhitheadh iarlachd a' Bhràghad
An seachd bliadhna so mar tha e,
Gun chur gun chliathadh gun àiteach,
'S math an riadh o bheil sinn pàighte.

When we climbed the high hill
we left many a skull
of these masterly marksmen we slaughtered.

Though my father was slain,
it's not he whom I mourn,
but you, sworded deep in the kidneys.

What wrung tears from my eyes
was the gap in your side
as you lay in the house of Cor Charmaig.

For I loved your gay face
branched with blood and with race,
both ruthless and graceful in warfare.

trans. Iain Crichton Smith

The Battle of Inverlochy[1]

Hì rim hó ro, hó ro with her,
Hì rim hó ro, hó ro with her,
Hì rim hó ro, hó ro with her,
The day went to Clan Donald.

Have you heard of the stalwart countermarch
that the armed band at Cill Chuimein made?
Their foray was famed far and wide,
they drove their enemies away.

I climbed early on Sunday morning
to the brae above Inverlochy Castle;
I saw the army taking up position,
and victory lay with Clan Donald.

As you climbed the spur of Cùl Eachaidh,
I recognised your high mettle;
though my country had been left ablaze
what has happened now repays the score.

Though the earldom of Brae Lochaber
were for seven years now as it is,
unsown, unharrowed and fallow,
we are repaid with good interest.

1. Squeezed between the Seaforth Mackenzies at Loch Ness and Clan Campbell at Fort William, Montrose's out-
   numbered Royalist troops made a spectacular climb over the hills, in the worst snow for years, to outflank and defeat
   the Covenanting forces at Inverlochy. Over 1,500 died in this battle on Sunday, 2 February 1645.

Air do làimh-sa, Thighearna Labhair,
Ge mór do bhòsd as do chlaidheamh,
'S iomadh òglach chinne t'athar
Tha 'n Inbhir Lòchaidh 'na laighe.

'S iomadh fear gòrsaid is pillein
Cho math 's a bha beò de d' chinneach
Nach d'fhaod a bhòtainn thoirt tioram,
Ach fòghlam snàmh air Bun Nibheis.

'S iomadh fear aid agus pìce
Agus cuilbheire chaoil dhìrich
Bha 'n Inbhir Lòchaidh 'na shìneadh,
'S bha luaidh nam ban à Cinn-tìr' ann.

Sgeul a b'aite 'n uair a thigeadh
Air Caimbeulaich nam beul sligneach:
H-uile dream dhiubh mar a thigeadh
Le bualadh lann 'n ceann 'gam bristeadh.

'N là a shaoil iad a dhol leotha
'S ann bha laoich 'gan ruith air reodhadh:
'S iomadh slaodanach mór odhar
A bh'air aodann Ach' an Todhair.

Ge bè dhìreadh Tom na h-Aire,
'S iomadh spòg ùr bh'air dhroch shailleadh,
Neul marbh air an sùil gun anam,
225   An déidh an sgiùrsadh le lannan.

                    *   *   *

258   Alasdair nan geurlann guineach,
       Nam biodh agad àrmainn Mhuile,
       Thug thu air na dh'fhalbh dhiubh fuireach,
       'S retreut air pràbar an duilisg.

       Alasdair mhic Cholla ghasda,
       Làmh dheas a sgoltadh nan caisteal,
       Chuir thu 'n ruaig air Ghallaibh glasa,
       'S ma dh'òl iad càl chuir thu asd' e.

       'M b'aithne dhuibh-se 'n Goirtean Odhar?
       'S math a bha e air a thodhar;
       Chan innear chaorach no ghobhar,
       Ach fuil Dhuibhneach an déidh reodhadh.

Laird of Lawers, I do declare,
though you boast greatly of your sword,
that many young warriors of your clan
lie dead in Inverlochy.

Many a well-saddled, armoured man,
as good as the Campbells have alive,
could not escape with his boots dry,
but learned to swim at Nevis Foot.

Many a man carrying a helmet and bow,
and musket straight and slender,
lay stretched on Inverlochy field,
and the Kintyre women's love was among them.

The news was welcome when it came,
of the Campbells with their shell-curved lips:
each of their companies as they came
had their heads broken with blows from blades.

On the day they thought all would go well
the heroes chased them over frozen ground:
many a great sallow-skinned sloucher
lay on the surface of Ach an Todhair.

Those who climbed the Mound of the Watch
could see newly-lopped paws ill-salted,
the film of death on their lifeless eyes,
after the slashing they had from sword-blades.

                    *   *   *

Alasdair of sharp, biting blades,
if you had the heroes of Mull with you,
you would have stopped those who got away,
as the dulse-eating rabble took to their heels.   (edible) seaweed

Alasdair, son of handsome Colla,
skilled hand at cleaving castles,
you put to flight the Lowland pale-face:
what kale they had taken came out again.

You remember the place called the Tawny Field?
It got a fine dose of manure;
not the dung of sheep or goats,
but Campbell blood well congealed.

Sgrios oirbh mas truagh leam bhur càramh,
'G éisdeachd anshocair bhur pàisdean,
Caoidh a' phannail bh'anns an àraich,
Donnalaich bhan Earra-Ghaidheal.

Oran an Aghaidh an Aonaidh

Ge bè dh'éireadh 'san lasair
    An am fadadh na smùide,
Théid an cuibhreach mu'n chapall
    Mar bhiodh fada fo glùinibh;
Ach fhir a dh'éirich le gradachd
    Chur fastadh nan taod rith',
Spàrr thu 'n gòisnein mu ladhar
    Mar eun chladhach an rùcain.

Bhris thu lairg anns a' chrann sin
    'S chaidh an seanndamh am mearachd,
Le beuc nan damh òga
    Chaidh an Dròbhair am mearal;
Fhir a b'àbhaist an ceannsach'
    'S an tionndadh le h-ainiochd,
'S e Diùc Atholl le dùrachd
    A bhris do lùban a dh'aindeoin.

Ge bè leanadh gu dìreach
    Diùc fìrinneach Atholl,
'S raghainn chruthaicht' thar sluagh e
    Bhuidhneadh buaidh mar rinn athair;
Bha thu 'n aghaidh luchd cìse
    Ghabh na mìltean mar raghainn,
Ach fàgaidh mis' iad gu h-ìseal
    'Nan laighe shìos anns na spleadhan.

'S mór tha ghliocas na rìoghachd
    Deagh sgrìobht' ann ad mheamhail,
Bha thu foghlam as t'òige
    Chur na còrach air adhart

To Hell with you if I care for your plight,
as I listen to your children's distress,
lamenting the band that went to battle,
the howling of the women of Argyll.

trans. Derick Thomson

Song Against the Union[1]

In the reek of the kindling
   will arise from the flames,
what will hobble the mare
   round her fetlocks for sure;
but you who rushed forward
   to fasten her binding,
looped a rope on her hooves
   like a snare for a buzzard.

You broke the plough-stilt there,
   the old ox went straying;
at the roar of young bullocks
   the drover went witless;
the man who once drove them
   and turned at the head-rig,
't was the goodwill of Atholl
   broke your fetters despite you.

Who would follow the Duke
   the true lineage of Atholl
finest leader of armies
   wins the day like his father;
how you hated the tax-men
   who skimmed off the thousands,
but I'll leave them humbled
   laid low in their writhing.

Great the wisdom of ruling
   in your mind written strongly,
you were taught from your boyhood
   advancement of justice

---

1. The poet was not alone in his opposition to the Union of the Parliaments, which was finally carried out in January 1707. There had been unrest, large gatherings and riots throughout the country for months before. Edinburgh was full of armed Highlanders. Part of the agreement included financial reparations for the exchange of currencies and for the failure of the Darien scheme; undoubtedly bribes and other inducements were also exchanged. (See Robert Burns, 'Such a parcel of rogues in a nation'.) The Duke of Queensberry and the Earl of Seafield were among the chief Commissioners appointed to arrange the Union. They were sympathetic to the English Court, and Queensberry in particular pursued his own advantage shamelessly. The Duke of Hamilton and the Marquis of Tweeddale, Lord Dupplin, were supporters of the Presbyterian faction. The Duke of Atholl, once associated with the 'Country' party and Jacobite sympathies, changed allegiances (like most of the Scots Peers) to suit his own advantage.

'N aghaidh Banndairean misgeach
   Bha ri bristeadh an lagha,
Nam biodh iad uile gu m'òrdugh
   Gheibheadh iad còrd agus teadhair.

Na biodh ort-sa bonn airtneil –
   Tha fir Atholl 'nan seasamh,
Luchd nan gormlanna geura
   Dhèanadh feum dhuit 'gad fhreasdal;
Mar sud 's do dheagh bhràithre,
   Luchd nan sàrbhuillean sgaiteach,
Fir a chaitheadh nan saighead
   'S a ro-ghleidheadh na cartach.

Na biodh ort-sa bonn mìghean –
   Tha fir do thìre glé ullamh,
Còrr mór is deich mile
   Ged a libhinn a thuille;
Mheud 's a bhuinnig e phrìs duit
   Chaidh e sgrìobhte do Lunnainn
Na chuireadh dragh air an Alba
   Gu robh 'nan armaibh glé ullamh.

Là randabù 'n t-sléibhe
   Bha mi fhéin ann is chunnaic,
Bha na trupanna sréin' ann,
   Bha na ceudan ag cruinneach';
Ge bè ghabhadh air anam
   Gu robh mnathan mar dhuin' ann,
Gu rachadh saighead 'nan àrnaibh
   Gus an teàrrail i 'n fhuil asd'.

Mhorair *Duplin* gun fhuireach
   Dh'fhosgail uinneag do sgòrnain,
Dh'éirich rosgal ad chridhe
   'N uair chual' thu tighinn an t-òr ud;
Shluig thu 'n aileag de'n gheanach,
   Dh'at do sgamhan is bhòc e,
Dh'fhosgail teannsgal do ghoile
   'S lasaich greallag do thòna.

Cha b'iongnadh sud duit a thachairt,
   Ogha baigeire Liunnsaidh,
'S a liuthad dorus mór caisteil
   Ris 'n do stailc e chnàimh tiompain;
Cha d'fhàg e baile gun siubhal
   O Chill-a-rubha gu Grainse,

against mad Covenanters
    the breakers of laws, they'd
get tethers and tying
    were they under my orders.

Let no cloud come upon you –
    Men of Atholl hold firmly
folk of sharpened blue blades
    who shall rescue and serve you;
at their side your true bretheren
    of the sharp-smiting buffets
who will shower their arrows
    that find a true target.

Let no gloom come upon you –
    for your comrades are ready,
ten thousand and more
    should I leave out some others;
there's respect for your name
    in dispatches to London
that the Scots are in arms
    that will give them some trouble.

At yon moorland rally
    I was present and saw it,
troops of cavalry there
    in their hundreds assembled;
who swear there were women
    in disguise there as men,
may a shaft in the kidneys
    drain all their blood from them.

Lord *Duplin*, there straightly
    your maw opened widely,
and your heart wildly beat
    when you heard gold was coming;
but you stifled greed's breath
    till your lungs swelled and hiccuped,
till you could not contain it
    and set light to your arsehole.

Small wonder that mishap
    to the Lundy tramp's grandson,
many a door of a castle
    he braced with his backside;
not a mansion he passed by
    from Grange to Kilarrow,

Mar ghabhas sin 's an t-Ord Gallach
   Gu ruige baile Iarl Aondrom.

Ogha baigeir na lùirich,
   Ciod e do chùis an Taigh-Phàrla?
Mur deach thu dh'fhoghlam a' gheanaich
   Mar bha an seanair on d'fhàs thu;
Cha d'fhàg e ursainn gun locradh
   Eadar Ros is Cinn t-Sàile;
Bhiodh a dhiosg-san glé ullamh
   An am cromadh fo'n àrd'rus.

Tha *Queensberry* 'n tràth-sa
   Mar fhear-stràice cur thairis,
Eis' a' tarraing gu dìreach
   Mar ghearran dian ann an greallaig;
Is luchd nam putagan anairt
   Làn smear agus geire,
'S nam bu mhise an ceannair'
   Bhiodh 'n ceann d'an amall air deireadh.

Tha Diùc Atholl 's Diùc Gòrdon
   Glé chlòiste 's iad dùinte,
Air an sgrìobhadh gu daingeann,
   Ach tha *Hamilton* dùbailt;
Iarla Bhrathainn bhiodh mar ris,
   Cha bhiodh mealladh 'sa' chùis ac',
Toirt a' chrùin uainn le ceannach
   An ceart fhradharc ar sùilean.

Tha Mèinnearach Uaimh ann
   Glé luaineach 'na bhreathal,
'S e mar dhuine gun sùilean
   'G iarraidh iùil air feadh ceathaich;
Ach thig e fathasd le h-ùmhlachd
   Chum an Diùc mas i bheatha,
'S bidh a shannt 's a mhì-dhùrachd
   Anns an smùr gun aon rath air.

Iarla Bhrathainn a Sìoford,
   Cha bhi sìothshaimh ri d' bheò dhuit,
Gum bi ort-sa cruaidh fhaghaid
   Thall a staigh de'n Roinn Eòrpa;
Ach nam faighinn mo raghainn
   Is dearbh gu leaghainn an t-òr dhuit,
A staigh air faochaig do chlaiginn
   Gus an cas e do bhòtainn.

the whole lot from Caithness
   to the Earl's place in Antrim.

What, ragged tramp's grandson,
   is your case in the Council?
Unless to learn greed
   like the grandad who bred you;
no threshold left scraped
   between Ross and Kintail;
set the floorboards to creaking
   as he bowed at the lintel.

And *Queensberry* there
   taking fistful from bagful,
as he draws tight the string
   as a gelding pulls traces;
they who like clootie dumplings
   well marrowed and larded,
if I harnessed that team
   I'd yoke last in the traces.

Dukes of Atholl and Gordon
   make agreement in secret,
though their names firm in writing,
   but *Hamilton's* two-faced;
but with Brathan his crony,
   their minds were united,
to trade in full view
   crown and sovereign rights.

And Menzies of Weem there
   his brains in a swither,
like a man of poor sight
   seeking guidance through mist;
but he'll come up there creeping
   to the Duke if he's welcome,
though his malice and greed
   get an answer in dust.

No peace, Seaforth of Brahan,
   you'll get in your lifetime,
hot pursuit you will find
   on your tail throughout Europe;
but if I had my way
   I would melt your gold payment,
pour it into your skull
   till it reached to your boots.

trans. William Neill

Màiri Nighean Alasdair Ruaidh/ Mary MacLeod (1615?–1706?)

Born in Rodel in Harris, Mary was employed as a nurse to the MacLeods of Skye. Over a lifetime's service she claimed to have brought up no fewer than five lairds (sons and brothers) in the family line. She began to compose poetry in her later years but, having offended one of the chiefs, she had to leave the castle of Dunvegan for a while, travelling first to the tiny island of Scarba where she wrote of her 'banishment', and then to Mull. With Iain Lom she stands at the beginning of Gaelic's

Tuireadh

(A rinn Màiri nighean Alasdair Ruaidh
goirid an déis a fàgail an Sgarbaidh.)

> Hóireann ó ho bhì ó
> Hóireann ó ho bhì ó
> Hóireann ó ho bhì ó
> Ri hóireann ó o hao o!

Is muladach mì, hì ó
  Hóireann ó ho bhì o
O cheann seachdain, hì ó
  Ro hóireann ó o hao o,

Is mi an eilean gun
Fhiar gun fhasgadh.

Ma dh'fhaodas mi
Théid mi dhachaidh;

Nì mi an t-iomramh
Mar as fhasa,

Do Uilbhinnis
A' chruidh chaisfhinn,

Far an d'fhuair mi
Gu h-òg m'altrum,

most fruitful period when non-bardic poets began to use stressed versification and a freer, more colloquial language. She was one among several remarkable women poets at this time of change, including Sìleas na Ceapaich. Mary ended her days back in Dunvegan, known for her pride of birth and a liking for whisky and snuff. She is buried at Rodel.

Lamentation

(Made by Mary daughter of Alasdair the Red
soon after she was left in Scarba.)

> Hóireann ó ho bhì ó
> Hóireann ó ho bhì ó
> Hóireann ó ho bhì ó
> Ri hóireann ó o hao o!

It's me that's gloomy
   Hóireann ó ho bhì ó
At the week's end,
   Ro hóireann ó o hao o,

On an isle sans
grass or shelter.

If I could
it's home I'd journey;

Making travel
homeward easy,

To Uillinish
of white hoofed cattle,

Where I got my
young upbringing,

Air bainne chìoch
Nam ban basgheal,

Thall aig Fionnghail
Dhuinn nighean Lachainn,

Is ì 'na banchaig
Ris na martaibh

Aig Ruairidh mór Mac
Leoid nam bratach.

'S ann 'na thigh mór
A fhuair mi am macnas,

Danns' le sunnd air
Urlar farsaing,

An fhìdhleireachd 'gam
Chur a chadal,

A' phìobaireachd
Mo dhùsgadh maidne.

Thoir mo shoraidh, hò ó
    Hóireann ó ho bhi o,
Gu Dùn Bheagain, hi ó
    Ro hóireann ó o hao o.

An T-Eudach

(Duanag a rinn Màiri nighean Alasdair Ruaidh
mar gum biodh i ag eudach ri ban-Ilich a
mheall a leannan oirre, nam b'fhìor i.)

    Hìrirì ohù robhó,
    Roho ì ohì o.

Gur a mise tha iar mo chlisgeadh,
Tha loch uisge fo m' chluasaig.

Ged a théid mi do m' leabaidh
Chan e an cadal as dual domh,

Milk from breasts
of soft-palmed women,

With brown-haired Flora
Lachlan's daughter,

She the milker
of the milch-cows

Of Great Rory
MacLeod of banners.

In whose great house
I got sporting,

Happy dancing
on broad flooring,

Violins my
bedtime music,

Piper's tune
my morning waking.

Give my greeetings,
   Hóireann ó ho bhi o,
to Dunvegan,
   Ro hóireann ó o hao o.

trans. William Neill

Jealousy

(A little poem made by Mary as it were in jealousy
of an Islay woman who, according to Mary, enticed
her sweetheart from her.)

   Hìrirì ohù robhó,
   Roho ì ohì o.

It is I got my wounding,
pool of tears on my pillow.

Off to bed I betake me
with no hope of sleeping,

Is a' bhean tha an Ile
Sìor mhiadachadh m'euda;

Bhean thug uamsa mo roghainn,
Is gun taghainn thar cheud e.

Ach nam bithinn 'na fianuis,
Gum biodh spìonadh air bhréidean.

Chì mi an Fhionnairigh thall ud
Is ì gun earras fo'n ghréin oirr'.

Gum faca mise uair a
Bha daoine-uaisle mu d'réidhlean.

Rachadh cuid do'n bheinn-sheilg dhiubh,
Cuid a mharbhadh an éisg dhiubh,

Air Linne na Ciste
Am bi na bric anns an leumraich.

Tha mo chean air an lasgair,
Saighdear sgairteil fo sgéith thu.

An uair a thig thu do'n chaisteal
Bheir thu dhachaidh do cheud ghràdh.

Ged a tha mi air m'aineol
O'n bhaile fo éislean,

Chan ion do'n bhan-Ilich
Bhith strìth rium mu d'dhéidhinn.

And that woman in Islay
sets my envy to swelling;

She who's stolen my darling
that I'd choose from a hundred.

Were I in her presence
there'd be tearing of headgear.

I see Fiunary yonder
with no speck there of riches.

But I mind on the time
of lawns crowded with gentry.

Off to mountains a-hunting
or to catching of fish there,

On the Pool of the Coffin
where the trout will be leaping.

How I fancy the gallant
warrior brisk behind buckler.

When you come to the castle
you'll take home your first darling.

Though I'm in strange surroundings
far from home and dejected,

For your love no fit rival
yon woman of Islay.

trans. William Neill

Roderick Morison (1656?–1714?)

Born of an educated family in Lewis, Morison is said to have lost his eyesight when he went to Inverness to study for the ministry and caught smallpox. He was sent to Ireland to take up the harp and a new trade as an itinerant poet and singer. Iain Breac MacLeod of Dunvegan met Morison in Edinburgh and took him back to Skye where he kept a large household in the style of the old chiefs, with an official bard, a piper (the famous Patrick Og MacCrimmon), a fiddler, a fool and now a harper. (Mary Macleod was under the chief's protection, too, but it's not clear whether she and

Oran do Mhacleòid Dhùn Bheagain

Miad a' mhulaid tha 'm thadhal
dh'fhàg treaghaid am chliabh co goirt,
   on a rinneas air m'adhart
ad dheaghaidh an triall gun toirt;
   tha mis' ort an tòir,
is mi mios gu robh còir agam ort,
   a mhic athar mo ghraidh,
is tu m'aighear, 's tu m'àdh, 's tu m'olc.

Chaidh a' chuibhle mun cuairt,
ghrad thionndaidh gu fuachd am blàths:
   gum faca mi uair
Dùn ratha nan cuach 'n seo thràigh,
   far 'm biodh tathaich nan duan,
iomadh mathas gun chruas, gun chàs:
   dh'fhalbh an latha sin uainn,
's tha na taighean gu fuarraidh fàs.

Tha Mac-alla fo ghruaim
anns an talla 'm biodh fuaim a' cheòil
   'n ionad tathaich nan cliar,
gun aighear, gun mhiadh, gun phòit,
   gun mhire, gun mhuirn,
gun iomartas dlùth nan corn,

Morison were there at the same time.) 'An clàrsair dàll', the blind harper, left Dunvegan in 1688, but tradition has it that he returned to the castle in his old age and is buried there. His 'Song to MacLeod', composed when Iain Breac died in 1693, paints a vivid picture of the old way of life, and gives a bitter account too, of how his son Roderick threw it all away with gambling and spending in the South – an all-too-familiar pattern for absentee Highland chiefs in the years to come.

Song to MacLeod of Dunvegan

It is the great sorrow oppressing me
that has left such a sharp pain in my breast,
   ever since I made to go forward
after you on a journey that was of no avail.
   I am a client of yours, considering,
as I do, that I had a claim to your patronage,
   son of the father beloved by me –
you are my joy, and my inspiration, and my disquiet.

The wheel has come full circle,   (of fortune)
warmth has suddenly turned cold.
   But I once saw here a bountiful castle,
well stocked with drinking-cups that have now gone dry,
   a song-haunted place abounding in good things,
given without stint or question.
   That day has gone from us,
and the buildings are chill and desolate.

Echo is dejected in the hall
where music was wont to sound,
   in the place resorted to by poet-bands,
now without mirth, or pleasure, or drinking,
   without merriment or entertainment,
without the passing round of drinking-horns in close succession,

gun chuirm, gun phailteas ri dàimh,
24　gun mhacnas, gun mhanran beòil.

*　　　*　　　*

113　　Ach tillidh mise gu d' chainnt,
on a b'fhiosrach mi anns gach sìon:
　　gur tric a chunncas gill' òg
bhith gun uireasbhuidh stòir no nì;
　　's gum biodh a bheachd aige fhéin
'n uair a cheann'cheadh e feudail saor,
　　a dh'aindeoin caithinnich dhà,
nach b'eagal da làmh nam maor.

Ach cha b'ionann a bhà
do na fir sin 's a thà Mhac Leòid:
　　ann an sonas 's an sìth,
gun uireasbhuidh nì no lòin;
　　ann an daor chùirt nan Gall,
ged tha thoil fuireach ann ri bheò –
　　tighearn Eilg is Chlàr Sgìth,
cha b'eagal da dìobhail stòir.

Ach 's ionann sin 's mar a bha,
's soilleir chithear a bhlàth air bhuil:
　　bho nach léir dhaibh an call,
miad an déidh air cùirt Ghall cha sguir,
　　gus an togar do'n Fhraing,
a dhol ann an geall na chuir;
　　siod an niosgaid a' fàs
air an iosgaid 's a cràdh 'na bun.

Théid seachd trusail air dhàil
air each crudhach as gàirmhor srann;
　　diallaid làsdail fo'n tòin;
's mór gum b'fheairrd' e srian òir 'na cheann.
　　Fichead ginidh, 's beag fhiach,
gun téid siod a chur sìos an geall;
　　cha téid peighinn dha 'm feum,
's bonn cha ghleidhear dha 'n déis a chall.

An uair a thig e bho'n réis
théid e dh'iomairt ri béist air glac,
　　's mur tig làmh 'sam bi feum,
gun caill e an leum gu grad;

without feasting, without liberality to men of learning,
without dalliance, or voice raised in tuneful song.[1]

        *   *   *

But I shall revert to what you have said,
since I was privy to every detail:
    often has a young lad been seen
without lack of provision or goods,
    and he would think to himself,
when he bought cattle cheaply,
    that, despite his spending, he had no cause
to fear the (grasping) hands of the bailiffs.

But the case did not stand
for those men as it does for MacLeod:
    in happiness and peace,
without lack of goods or victuals,
    leading an expensive life at court among southron strangers –
what though his inclination is to remain there all his life,
    when he is the lord of Glenelg and Skye,
and could never have cause to fear lack of means.

But that is just how the case stands,
and the proof may be clearly seen in the outcome:
    since they cannot visualise their losses,
their fondness for court life among southron strangers is unabated,
    until they hie them to France,
(there) to give a bond for their outlay.
    Then does the boil fester
on the thigh with its pain at the root.

Seven collections are borrowed   (worth of rent)
for a shod, loud-snorting horse;
    a lordly saddle under the bottom;
and he would of course be much the better of a golden bridle on his head.
    Twenty guineas – it is considered a mere trifle –
that is put down in payment;
    not a penny of it is put to good use,
and, once lost, not a single coin can be salvaged for him.

When he returns from the races,
he goes to play catch-the-ten with a sharper,
    and if a useful hand is not forthcoming
he soon misses the call.

1. The poet talks to Echo, which describes how merry and full the household used to be, with music, gaming and dancing. It says that it never saw the castle 'without tutor or lord', but Morison disagrees, and points out that times have changed.

mas iad dìsnean a mhiann,
bheir e thairis h-aon-diag mu seach,
    's ged a chailleadh cóig ciad,
fire faire, 's beag fhiach am mairt.

    Cóig ginidhean òir –
gun téid siod ann an cord d'an aid;
    urad eil' oirre féin –
faire, faire, 's math feum gu spaid;
    's a' ghrabhata nach saor –
gur punnd Sasannach ì gun stad,
    air a chunntadh air clàr
dh'an ionntas gun dàil am fad.

    Théid luach mairt no nas mò
'm paidhear stocainn de'n t-seòrsa 's fearr,
    is cha chunntar an corr,
ducatùn air dà bhròig bhuinn ard;
    clachan criostail 's math snuadh
ann am bucaill mun cuairt gun smàl;
    siod na gartain a suas
air dà thastan 's an luach 'nam barr.

    Thig e mach as a' bhùth
leis an fhasan as ùr bho'n Fhraing,
    's an t-aodach gasda bha 'n dé
m'a phearsa le spéis nach gann
    théid a shadadh an cùil –
'Is dona 'm fasan, chan fhiù e plang.
    Air màl baile no dhà
glac am peana 's cuir làmh ri bann.'

    Cha bhi 'm péids' ann am meas
mur bi eudach am fasan chàich;
    ged chosd e ginidh an t-slat –
gheibhear siod air son mart 'sa' mhàl;
    urad eile ri chois,
gun téid siod ann an casag dhà,
    's briogais bheilibheid mhìn
gu bhith gabhail mu ghaoith a mhàis.

    Cha bhi 'm péids' ann am prìs
's e gun snàithe dh'a dhìth ach cleòc;
    giort a' chlaidheimh cha b'fhiach,
's bu chùis athais ceann iarainn dò:
    crios dealbhach o'n bhùth,

If it is dice he hankers after,
he hands over eleven in turn,
   and though the loss should be five hundred,
well-a-day, the equivalent is small reckoned in marts.

   Five golden guineas –
that is spent on a cord for the hat,
   and as much more again for the hat itself.
Lackaday, it is well bought in the cause of elegance!
   And the cravat, by no means cheap,
costs a pound sterling out of the funds straight away,
   counted out in full on the table,
and no credit allowed.

   The price of a mart or more
is paid for a pair of stockings of the best kind,
   and the change is not counted;
also a ducatoon for two high-soled shoes.
   Crystal stones of finest lustre
are set in flawless buckles;
   and for two shillings on go the garters,
whose value is in their tips.

   He comes out of the shop
with the latest fashion from France
   and the fine clothes worn on his person
yesterday with no little satisfaction
   are tossed into a corner –
'The style is unmodish, not worth a plack.
   On the security of a townland or two,
take the pen and sign a bond.'

   The page will not be regarded
unless his clothes are in the current fashion;
   though it should cost a guinea a yard,
that can be got for a mart given in lieu of rent.
   As much again in addition
will go to the purchase of a doublet for him,
   and breeches of soft velvet
to wrap up gusts at his rear.

   The page will not be esteemed though,
but for a cloak, he does not lack a stitch.
   The sword-belt was no good,
and it was shameful that it should have an iron hilt.
   A finely fashioned belt from the shop,

bogh' chinn airgid is biùgail òir –
   's fheudar faighinn sin dà:
's thig air m'fhearann-sa màl nas mò.

   An uair a thilleas e rìs
a dh'amharc a thìre féin,
   'n déis na mìltean chur suas,
gun tig sgrìob air an tuath mu spréidh,
   gus an togar na mairt
'n déidh an ciùradh 's an reic air féill:
   siod na fiachan ag at,
gus am fiarach ri mhac 'na dhéidh.

   Théid Uilleam Màrtainn a mach
glé stràiceil air each 's e triall –
   is co ard e 'na bheachd
ris an àrmann a chleachd bhith fial;
   cha ghlacar leis crann,
cas-chaibe 'na làimh cha b'fhiach,
   's e cho spaideil ri diùc,
ged bha athair ri bùrach riamh.

   Thoir teachdaireachd uam
le deatam gu Ruaidhri òg,
   agus innis da féin
cuid d'a chunnart giodh e Mac Leòid;
   biodh e 'g amharc 'na dhéidh
air an Iain a dh'eug 's nach beò:
   gum bu shaidhbhir a chliù,
is chan fhàgadh e 'n Dùn gun cheòl.

   A Mhic-alla 'n seo bhà
anns a' bhaile 'n robh gràdh nan cliar,
   an triath tighearnail theann,
is an cridhe gun fheall 'na chliabh –
   ghabh e tlachd dh'a thir féin,
's cha do chleachd e Dùn-éideann riamh;
   dh'fhàg e 'm bannach gun bhearn,
's b'fhearr gun aithriseadh càch a chiall.

a silver-tipped bow and a golden bugle –
   that must be got for him:
and a higher rent will be charged for my land.

   When he returns again
to view his own country,
   though thousands (of pounds) have already been sent away,
a cattle levy is imposed on the tenantry,
   and so the marts are exported,
after being cured and sold at the market.
   Thus do the debts increase,
to be demanded from his son after him.

   William Martin goes out, very much the grand gentleman
as he sets off on horseback,
   of as high degree to his own mind
as the chief who made a practice of liberality.
   He will not touch a plough,
while a spade in his hand would be beneath his dignity.
   The man is as elegant as a duke,
though his father laboured the soil all his days.

   Take a message from me,
as a matter of urgency, to young Roderick,
   and make known to him some of the dangers
that threaten him even though he is chief of MacLeod.
   Let him constantly look back to the John
who died and is no more:
   renown in rich measure was his,
and he would never leave Dunvegan without music.

   You, Echo, were here
in the homestead where dwelt one beloved of poet-bands,
   the chief lordly in authority,
and the heart in his breast without guile –
   he took pleasure in his own country,
and never cultivated Edinburgh society.
   He left the bannock ungapped,
and it were well if others copied his good sense.

trans. William Matheson

Sìleas na Ceapaich/ Cicely MacDonald (1660?–1729?)

Daughter of Gilliesbuig MacDonald, fifteenth chief of the Keppoch MacDonalds, Cicely MacDonald was an ardent Jacobite who shared her countryman Iain Lom's concern with politics and clan affairs, though her later work was to take a strong religious note. The elegy to Alasdair Dubh of Glengarry is a formal lament typical of

Alasdair á Gleanna Garadh

Alasdair a Gleanna Garadh,
Thug thu 'n diugh gal air mo shùilibh;
'S beag ionghnadh mi bhith fo chreuchdaibh
'S gur tric 'gan reubadh as ùr iad;
'S beag ionghnadh mi bhith trom-osnach,
'S meud an dosgaidh th' air mo chàirdibh;
Gur tric an t-eug uainn a' gearradh
Rogha nan darag as àirde.

Chaill sinn ionann agus còmhla
Sir Dòmhnall 's a mhac 's a bhràthair;
Ciod e 'n stà dhuinn bhith 'gan gearan?
Thuit Mac Mhic Ailein 's a' bhlàr uainn;
Chaill sinn darag làidir liath-ghlas
A chumadh dìon air ar càirdean,
Capull-coille bhàrr na giùthsaich,
Seobhag sùil-ghorm lùthmhor làidir.

Bu tu ceann air céill 's air comhairl'
Anns gach gnothach am biodh cùram,
Aghaidh shoilleir sholta thlachdmhor,
Cridhe fial farsaing mu 'n chùinneadh;
Bu tu roghainn nan sàr-ghaisgeach,
Ar guala thaice 's tu b' fhiùghail;

many that were written to clan chieftains, yet it is also informed by Sìleas' own grief at the loss of her husband Alexander Gordon, and her daughter Anna who died within weeks of each other in 1720, a year or so before Glengarry himself.

Alasdair of Glengarry

Alasdair of Glengarry
you brought tears to my eyes today;
no wonder that I am wounded,
and that my wounds open up again;
no wonder that my sighs are heavy,
misfortune falls heavy on my kin;
Death often cuts and takes from us
the choicest and the tallest oaks.

We lost, just about together,
Sir Donald, his son and his brother;[1]
what good will it do us to complain?
We lost Clanranald in the battle;[2]
we lost a strong grey oak
that would keep our friends protected,
a capercailzie in the pine-wood,
a strong, supple, blue-eyed hawk.

For everything we were concerned with
you were our source of advice and wisdom,
your face was bright, modest, attractive,
your heart generous, liberal with money;
you were the choice of the great heroes,
our supporting shoulder, a worthy one;

1. Sir Donald Macdonald of Sleat died in 1718; his son died two years later as did his uncle who succeeded him.
2. Allan of Clanranald, mortally wounded at the battle of Sheriffmuir in 1715.

Leómhann smiorail fearail feumail,
Ceann feachda chaill Seumas Stiùbhart.

Nam b' ionann duit-se 's do Dhòmhnall,
An uair a chuir e 'n long air muir,
Cha tigeadh tu dhachaidh gu bràth
Gun fhios dé 'm fàth as 'n do chuir;
'Nuair a chunncas air an tràigh sibh
A bhith 'gur fàgail air faondradh,
Thuit ar cridheachan fo mhulad:
'S léir a bhuil – cha robh sibh saogh'lach.

Bu tu 'n lasair dhearg 'gan losgadh,
Bu tu sgoltadh iad gu 'n sàiltibh,
Bu tu curaidh cur a' chatha,
Bu tu 'n laoch gun athadh làimhe;
Bu tu 'm bradan anns an fhìor-uisg,
Fìreun air an eunlaith 's àirde,
Bu tu 'n leómhann thar gach beathach,
Bu tu damh leathan na cràice.

Bu tu 'n loch nach fhaoidte thaomadh,
Bu tu tobar faoilidh na slàinte,
Bu tu Beinn Nibheis thar gach aonach,
Bu tu chreag nach fhaoidte theàrnadh;
Bu tu clach uachdair a' chaisteil,
Bu tu leac leathan na sràide,
Bu tu leug lòghmhor nam buadhan,
Bu tu clach uasal an fhàinne.

Bu tu 'n t-iubhar thar gach coillidh,
Bu tu 'n darach daingean làidir,
Bu tu 'n cuileann 's bu tu 'n draigheann,
Bu tu 'n t-abhall molach blàthmhor;
Cha robh do dhàimh ris a' chritheann
Na do dhligheadh ris an fheàrna;
Cha robh bheag ionnad de 'n leamhan;
Bu tu leannan nam ban àlainn.

Bu tu céile na mnà priseil,
'S oil leam fhéin d' a dith an dràsd thu;
Ged nach ionann domh-sa 's dhi-se,

a helpful, valiant, spirited lion,
James Stuart has lost a battle leader.

Had you fared as well as Donald
when he put his ship to sea,
you would never have come home
without knowing why he launched it.[1]
When we saw you on the shore,
leaving us here abandoned,
our hearts fell, stricken by grief:
we see the result – your life was short.

You were the red torch to burn them,
you would cleave them to the heels,
you were a hero in the battle,
a champion who never flinched;
a fresh-run salmon in the water,
an eagle in the highest flock,
lion excelling every creature,
broad-chested, strong-antlered stag.

A loch that could not be emptied,
a well liberal in health,
Ben Nevis towering over mountains,
a rock that could not be scaled;
topmost stone of the castle,
broad pave-stone of the street,
precious jewel of virtues
noble stone of the ring.

The yew above every wood,
the oak, steadfast and strong,
you were the holly, the blackthorn,
the apple rough-barked in bloom;
you were not akin to the aspen,
the alder made no claim on you,
there was none of the lime-tree in you,[2]
you were the darling of lovely dames.

You were the spouse of a precious wife,
I'm sad that she has lost you now;
though I must not compare myself with her

1. This is probably a reference to the abortive Jacobite attempt of 1719 in which troops were landed at the mouth of
   Loch Duich and their ships sent back to Spain.
2. Oak, yew, holly, blackthorn and apple are sacred trees. Aspen, alder and lime are associated with ill. Tradition has it,
   for example, that the aspen trembles for shame because its wood was used to make Christ's cross.

'S goirt a fhuair mise mo chàradh;
H-uile bean a bhios gun chéile,
Guidheadh i Mac Dé 'n a àite,
O 's E 's urra bhith 'ga còmhnadh
Anns gach bròn a chuireas càs oirr'.

Guidheam t' anam a bhith sàbhailt
Ona chàradh anns an ùir thu;
Guidheam sonas air na dh'fhàg thu
Ann ad àros 's ann ad dhùthaich:
Gum faic mi do mhac ad àite
Ann an sàibhreas 's ann an cùram:
Alasdair a Gleanna Garadh,
Thug thu 'n diugh gal air mo shùilibh.

I too have borne a bitter fate;
let every wife who lacks a spouse
pray that God's Son take his place,
since He is able to give her help
in the grief and distress that come on her.

I pray that your soul may be saved,
now that your resting is in the clay;
I pray joy for those behind you
in your home and in your lands:
may I see your son in your place,
in wealth and responsibility:
Alasdair of Glengarry,
you brought tears to my eyes today.[1]

trans. Derick Thomson

1. See Sorley MacLean's poem 'Curaidhean'/'Heroes', which echoes this line.

Allan Ramsay (1685–1758)

A burgess of Edinburgh and a wig-maker to trade, Ramsay opened a bookshop in the city and set about making his reputation as a poet, publisher, librarian and theatre owner. His own poems celebrate the city's street life and local characters in a lively Scots vernacular (for which he provided his own glossary), while his pastoral comedy *The Gentle Shepherd* took a somewhat higher tone and proved very popular for many years. He also published collections of songs, *The Tea-Table Miscellany*, and of older Scottish poetry, *The Ever Green*, which helped to initiate a wide revival of interest in Scots literature, paving the way for Fergusson and Burns.

To the Phiz an Ode

Vides ut alta stet nive candidum Soracte …[1]
             Horace

Look up to Pentland's towring taps,   Pentland Hills (behind Edinburgh)
Buried beneath great wreaths of snaw,
O'er ilka cleugh, ilk scar and slap,   each hollow; bare slope and gap
As high as ony Roman wa'.

Driving their baws frae whins or tee,   gorse bushes
There's no ae gowfer to be seen,   golfer
Nor dousser fowk wysing a jee   graver; bending to one side
The byas bouls on Tamson's green.   bias bowls

Then fling on coals, and ripe the ribs,   rake the grate
And beek the house baith butt and ben,   warm; in all rooms
That mutchken stoup it hads but dribs,   English pint mug; holds
Then let's get in the tappit hen.   Scots quart tankard

Good claret best keeps out the cauld,
And drives away the winter soon,
It makes a man baith gash and bauld,   shrewd
And heaves his saul beyond the moon.

---

1. 'See how high the snow stands on gleaming Soracte': Horace, *Odes* 1, ix. Ramsay's free version of this poem is dedicated to one of Edinburgh's drinking and social societies, the 'Phiz Club'.

Leave to the gods your ilka care,   every
If that they think us worth their while,
They can a rowth of blessings spare,   plenty
Which will our fashious fears beguile.   troublesome

For what they have a mind to do,
That will they do, should we gang wood,   mad
If they command the storms to blaw,
Then upo' sight the hailstains thud.

But soon as e'er they cry, 'Be quiet',
The blatt'ring winds dare nae mair move,
But cour into their caves, and wait   cower
The high command of supreme love.

Let neist day come as it thinks fit,
The present minute's only ours,
On pleasure let's imploy our wit,
And laugh at fortune's feckless power.   ineffective

Be sure ye dinna quat the grip   give up
Of ilka joy when ye are young,   each
Before auld age your vitals nip,
And lay ye twafald o'er a rung.   doubled (up) over a stick

Sweet youth's a blyth and heartsome time,
Then lads and lasses while it's May,
Gae pou the gowan in its prime,   daisy
Before it wither and decay.

Watch the saft minutes of delyte,
When Jenny speaks beneath her breath,
And kisses, laying a the wyte   blame
On you if she kepp ony skaith.   comes to any harm

'Haith ye're ill bred', she'll smiling say,   Faith
'Ye'll worry me ye greedy rook;'
Syne frae your arms she'll rin away,   Then
And hide her sell in some dark nook:

Her laugh will lead you to the place
Where lies the happiness ye want,
And plainly tells you to your face,
Nineteen nay-says are haff a grant.   half a 'yes'

Now to her heaving bosom cling,
And sweetly toolie for a kiss,   struggle

Frae her fair finger whop a ring,
As taiken of a future bliss.   token

These bennisons, I'm very sure,
Are of the gods indulgent grant;
Then surly carles, whisht, forbear   old men
To plague us with your whining cant.

from Epistle to Mr. H. S. at London, November 1738

37   Ye want to know, ye say, what passes
     Amongst the Edinburgh Lads & Lasses,
     'Mongst Statesmen, and Kirk moderators,
     'Mongst Gamsters, Bawds, & fornicators,
     Then be it known, in this same place
     folk seem as little crampt with grace,
     as the unhallowd crouds who dwell
     from Wapping west to the Pall-Mall.
     The Scarlet Whore, indeed, they snarl at   (Church of Rome)
     but like right well a whore in scarlet,
     and here, in plenty, ev'ry Lad
     may have them in all collours clad,
     from the silk Damask doun to Tartane
     that's manufactur'd at Dunbartane,
     a choice of goods, & mighty cheap,
     for one a pox or clap may reap,
     if with but little pains he'll try,
     for sixpence wet & sixpence dry,   (sexual favours)
     and, if he's not a simple Stirk,   bullock
     may bite the Treasurer of the Kirk,
     for now, none heeds that dismall Dunner,   harper-on
     unless it be some sighing Sinner.
         Thus whore, & Bawd, Doctor & pox,
     the Tavern & a large white Ox,
     are the whole sum for Lord or clown
     of the Diversions of our Town,
     since by a late sour-snouted law[1]
     which makes great Heroes stand in awe
     the morall Teachers of broad Truths
     have gotten padlocks on their mouths,
     fierce Bajezet, and bold Macbeth
     Othello, Cato, & Macheath,
     now dumb, and of their Buskins stript,   (tragic art)
     Our stage is in its blossom nipt,

1. Ramsay had opened a playhouse in Carruber's Close in 1736 only to have it attacked by the Church as a threat to
   public morality and closed under an inapposite Licensing Act.

which spreads ane universall frown
to see a Theater pull'd down,
which for seven years, at small expence,
had pleasd, without the least offence,
advanced a great way to remove
that Scarcrow of all social Love,
Enthousiastick vile delusion
which glorys in stift-rumpt confusion,
gives sanction to Rebellious plots,
and finds out grace in cutting Throats,
which, in the reigns of James & Charles,
prompted these Covenanted Quarles   *quarrels*
and heezd the Leaguers[1] up the Ladders   *(of gallows)*
to swing aloft in hempen Tedders.   *tethers*
Now since the softener of this rage,
the mannerly reforming Stage,
is tane away, 'tis justly dreaded,
'twill be by Biggotry succeeded,
Divisions from Divisions spring,
and partys spiteful dart the sting.
   My friend be blyth, nor fash your Head   *merry; bother*
with nick-nack of each different creed
that various molds the Golden Calf
from stile of Rome to that of Ralf;
yet never from these virtues start
which spring up in an honest Heart
quite strangers to the party Squable
which mads the great & little Rable,
enjoy your Laugh, your friend, & Glass,
and, with chast Love, a chosen Lass,
sleep sound & never break your brains,
whither the Turk, or Russian gains.   *(i.e.: a choice of evils)*
   Farewell, & let me be your debtor
for what would over-cram a letter,
till we meet fairly nose to nose,
then balance shall be payd in prose.

Lucky Spence's Last Advice[2]   *(Goodwife)*

Three times the carline grain'd and rifted,   *old woman; groaned; belched*
Then frae the cod her pow she lifted,   *pillow; head*
In bawdy policy well gifted,
      When she now faun,   *found*

1. Supporters of the Solemn League and Covenant, executed in the 17th century for defying the State on matters of religious principle.
2. Lucky Spence was one of Edinburgh's best-known brothel keepers.

That Death na langer wad be shifted,
    She thus began:

'My loving lasses, I maun leave ye,
But dinna wi' ye'r greeting grieve me,   weeping
Nor wi' your draunts and droning deave me,   moans; pester
    But bring's a gill;   (a small measure of drink)
For faith, my bairns, ye may believe me,
    'Tis 'gainst my will.

O black-ey'd Bess and mim-mou'd Meg,   demure-mouthed
O'er good to work or yet to beg;   Too
Lay sunkots up for a sair leg,   something
    For whan ye fail
Ye'r face will not be worth a feg,   fig
    Nor yet ye'r tail.

When e'er ye meet a fool that's fow,   drunk
That ye're a maiden gar him trow,   make him believe
Seem nice, but stick to him like glew;
    And whan set down,
Drive at the jango till he spew,   press liquor on him
    Syne he'll sleep soun.

Whan he's asleep, then dive and catch
His ready cash, his rings or watch;
And gin he likes to light his match   if
    At your spunk-box,   tinder-box
Ne'er stand to let the fumbling wretch   don't allow
    E'en take the pox.

Cleek a' ye can be hook or crook,   Catch
Ryp ilky poutch frae nook to nook;   Plunder every pocket
Be sure to truff his pocket-book,   steal
    Saxty pounds Scots
Is nae deaf nits: In little bouk   empty nuts; bulk
    Lie great bank-notes.[1]

To get a mends of whinging fools,   be revenged on
That's frighted for repenting-stools.   frightened of public disgrace
Wha often, whan their metal cools,
    Turn sweer to pay,   reluctant
Gar the kirk-boxie hale the dools   Make the Church fine-box win the game
    Anither day.

1. This puns on a proverb: 'Guid gear in sma bouk' ('size isn't everything').

But dawt Red Coats, and let them scoup,   make much of (soldiers); move freely
Free for the fou of cutty stoup;   fill; little (brandy) pot
To gee them up, ye need na hope   stir
      E'er to do well:
They'll rive ye'r brats and kick your doup,   rip; togs; arse
      And play the Deel.

There's ae sair cross attends the craft,
That curst Correction-house, where aft   often
Vild Hangy's taz ye'r riggings saft   Vile hangman's whip; (back)
      Makes black and blae,
Enough to pit a body daft;
      But what'll ye say.

Nane gathers gear withouten care,
Ilk pleasure has of pain a skare;   Each; share
Suppose then they should tirl ye bare,   strip
      And gar ye fike,   make; twitch
E'en learn to thole; 'tis very fair   endure
      Ye're nibour like.

Forby, my looves, count upo' losses,   Besides
Ye'r milk-white teeth and cheeks like roses,
Whan jet-black hair and brigs of noses,
      Faw down wi' dads   fall; in lumps
To keep your hearts up 'neath sic crosses,
      Set up for bawds.

Wi' well-crish'd loofs I hae been canty,   greased palms; merry
Whan e'er the lads wad fain ha'e faun t'ye;   like to have fallen
To try the auld game Taunty Raunty,   Rumpy Pumpy
      Like coofers keen,   fools
They took advice of me your aunty,
      If ye were clean.

Then up I took my siller ca'   silver caller
And whistl'd benn whiles ane, whiles twa;   into the room
Roun'd in his lug, that there was a   Whispered; ear
      Poor country Kate,
As halesom as the well of Spaw,
      But unka blate.   very shy

Sae whan e'er company came in,
And were upo' a merry pin,   mood
I slade away wi' little din   smoothed along
      And muckle mense,   great discretion

Left conscience judge, it was a' ane   (their own conscience)
          To Lucky Spence.

My bennison come on good doers,   blessing
Who spend their cash on bawds and whores
May they ne'er want the wale of cures   best
          For a sair snout:[1]
Foul fa' the quacks wha that fire smoors,   smothers (cover up)
          And puts nae out.   (don't cure)

My malison light ilka day   curse fall
On them that drink, and dinna pay,
But tak a snack and rin away;   bite
          May't be their hap
Never to want a gonorrhoea,   lack
          Or rotten clap.

Lass gi'e us in anither gill,
A mutchken, Jo, let's tak our fill;   pint
Let Death syne registrate his bill   send in
          Whan I want sense,   lack
I'll slip away with better will,'
          Quo' Lucky Spence.

1. Syphilis can destroy the nose.

James Thomson (1700–1748)

After taking divinity at Edinburgh University, Thomson gave up his ministry and moved to London in 1726 where he worked as a tutor and pursued his literary career. He made his reputation with 'The Seasons', a sequence of four poems completed in 1730, but extensively revised and expanded in later editions. This work is often cited as a forerunner to the Romantic movement's interest in landscape, weather and humankind's place in the cosmos. 'Winter' was first published on its own in 1726, and the following extracts come from this version, undoubtedly influenced by the Northern scene, and part of a long Scottish literary tradition in snell weather.

from Winter: a Poem

80   Now, when the western sun withdraws the day,
And humid Evening, gliding o'er the sky.
In her chill progress, checks the straggling beams.
And robs them of their gather'd, vapoury, prey.
Where marshes stagnate, and where rivers wind,
Cluster the rolling fogs, and swim along
The dusky-mantled lawn then slow descend.
Once more to mingle with their watry friends.
The vivid stars shine out, in radiant files;
And boundless Ether glows, till the fair moon
Shows her broad visage, in the crimson'd east;
Now, stooping, seems to kiss the passing cloud:
Now, o'er the pure cerulean, rides sublime.
Wide the pale deluge floats with silver waves,
O'er the sky'd mountain, to the low-laid vale;
From the white rocks, with dim reflexion, gleams,
And faintly glitters thro' the waving shades.

All night, abundant dews, unnoted, fall,
And, at return of morning, silver o'er
The face of Mother-Earth; from every branch
Depending, tremble the translucent gems,
And, quivering, seem to fall away, yet cling
And sparkle in the sun, whose rising eye,
With fogs bedim'd, portends a beauteous day.

Now, giddy youth, whom headlong passions fire,
Rouse the wild game, and stain the guiltless grove,
With violence, and death; yet call it sport,
To scatter ruin thro' the realms of Love,
And Peace, that thinks no ill: but these, the Muse;
Whose charity, unlimited, extends
As wide as Nature works, disdains to sing,
Returning to her nobler theme in view –

For, see! where Winter comes, himself, confest,
Striding the gloomy blast. First rains obscure
Drive thro' the mingling skies, with tempest foul;
Beat on the mountain's brow, and shake the woods,
That, sounding, wave below. The dreary plain
Lies overwhelm'd, and lost. The bellying clouds
Combine, and deepening into night, shut up
The day's fair face. The wanderers of heaven,
Each to his home, retire; save those that love
To take their pastime in the troubled air,
And, skimming, flutter round the dimply flood.
The cattle, from th' untasted fields, return,
And ask, with meaning low, their wonted stalls;
Or ruminate in the contiguous shade:
Thither, the household, feathery, people croud,
The crested cock, with all his female train,
Pensive and wet. Mean while, the cottage-swain,
Hangs o'er th' enlivening blaze, and, taleful, there,
Recounts his simple frolic: much he talks,
And much he laughs, nor recks the storm that blows
Without, and rattles on his humble roof.

At last, the muddy deluge pours along,
Resistless, roaring; dreadful down it comes
From the chapt mountain, and the mossy wild,
Tumbling thro' rocks abrupt, and sounding far:
Then o'er the sanded valley, floating, spreads,
Calm, sluggish, silent; till again constrain'd,
Betwixt two meeting hills, it bursts a way,
Where rocks, and woods o'erhang the turbid stream.
There gathering triple force, rapid, and deep,
It boils, and wheels, and foams, and thunders thro'.

Nature! great parent! whose directing hand
Rolls round the seasons of the changeful year,
How mighty! how majestick are thy works!
With what a pleasing dread they swell the soul,

That sees, astonish'd! and, astonish'd sings!
You too, ye Winds! that now begin to blow,
With boisterous sweep, I raise my voice to you.
Where are your stores, ye viewless Beings! say?
Where your aerial magazines reserv'd,
Against the day of tempest perilous?
In what untravel'd country of the air,
154   Hush'd in still silence, sleep you, when 'tis calm?

        *   *   *

301   Clear frost succeeds, and thro' the blew serene,
For sight too fine, th' aetherial nitre[1] flies,
To bake the glebe, and bind the slip'ry flood.
This of the wintry season is the prime;
Pure are the days, and lustrous are the nights,
Brighten'd with starry worlds, till then unseen.
Mean while, the orient, darkly red, breathes forth
An icy gale, that, in its mid career,
Arrests the bickering stream. The nightly sky,
And all her glowing constellations pour
Their rigid influence down: it freezes on   (astrological)
Till morn, late-rising, o'er the drooping world,
Lifts her pale eye, unjoyous: then appears
The various labour of the silent night,
The pendant icicle, the frost-work fair,
Where thousand figures rise, the crusted snow,
Tho' white, made whiter, by the fining north.
On blithsome frolics bent, the youthful swains,
While every work of man is laid at rest,
Rush o'er the watry plains, and, shuddering, view
The fearful deeps below: or with the gun,
And faithful spaniel, range the ravag'd fields,
And, adding to the ruins of the year,
Distress the feathery, or the footed game.

But hark! the nightly winds, with hollow voice,
Blow, blustering, from the south – the frost subdu'd,
Gradual, resolves into a weeping thaw.
Spotted, the mountains shine: loose sleet descends,
And floods the country round: the rivers swell,
Impatient for the day. – Those sullen seas,
That wash th' ungenial pole, will rest no more,
Beneath the shackles of the mighty north;
But, rousing all their waves, resistless heave, –

1. It was thought that a nitrous element in the air caused freezing.

And hark! – the length'ning roar, continuous, runs
Athwart the rifted main; at once, it bursts,
And piles a thousand mountains to the clouds!
Ill fares the bark, the wretches' last resort,
That, lost amid the floating fragments, moors
Beneath the shelter of an icy isle;
While night o'erwhelms the sea, and horror looks
More horrible. Can human hearts endure
Th' assembled mischiefs, that besiege them round:
Unlist'ning hunger, fainting weariness,
The roar of winds, and waves, the crush of ice,
Now, ceasing, now, renew'd, with louder rage,
And bellowing round the main: nations remote,
Shook from their midnight-slumbers, deem they hear
Portentous thunder, in the troubled sky.
More to embroil the deep, Leviathan,
And his unwieldy train, in horrid sport,
Tempest the loosen'd brine; while, thro' the gloom,
Far, from the dire, unhospitable shore,
The lyon's rage, the wolf's sad howl is heard,
And all the fell society of night.
Yet, Providence, that ever-waking eye
Looks down, with pity, on the fruitless toil
Of mortals, lost to hope, and lights them safe,
Thro' all this dreary labyrinth of fate.

'Tis done! – Dread Winter has subdu'd the year,
And reigns, tremenduous, o'er the desart plains!
How dead the vegetable kingdom lies!
How dumb the tuneful! Horror wide extends
His solitary empire. – Now, fond Man!
Behold thy pictur'd life: pass some few years,
Thy flow'ring Spring, thy short-liv'd Summer's strength,
Thy sober Autumn, fading into age,
And pale, concluding, Winter shuts thy scene,
368   And shrouds thee in the grave ...

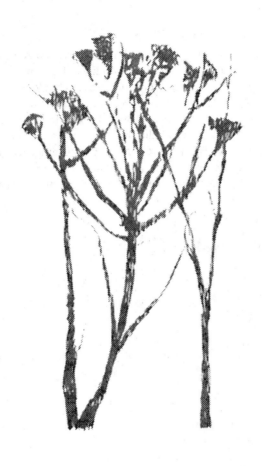

Alasdair MacMhaighstir Alasdair/ Alexander MacDonald (1695?–1770?)

Born in Moidart as a son of an Episcopalian minister, Alasdair MacMhaighstir Alasdair married early and had to give up his studies at Glasgow University. In later years he joined the Presbyterian kirk and worked as a schoolteacher for the Society for Propagating Christian Knowledge, for whom he published a Gaelic vocabulary. Although the SPCK's aims included the spread of literacy in English, MacMhaighstir Alasdair was deeply committed to bardic tradition and the Jacobite cause, fighting for Clanranald in the '45, writing poems on the Prince, and eventually converting to Catholicism. He wrote scurrilous local satires and witty and raunchy love poems, but hoped, too, to bring something of the high achievement of the bardic voice back

Oran an t-Samhraidh

Moch 's mi 'g éiridh 's a' mhaduinn,
   'S an dealt air a' choill,
Ann a' maduinn ro shoilleir,
   Ann an lagan beag doilleir,
Gu 'n cualas am feadan
   Gu leadarra seinn;
'S mac-talla nan creagan
   'Ga fhreagairt gu binn.

Bi am beithe, deagh bholtrach
   'Urail, dosrach nan carn,
Ri maoth-bhlàs driùchd céitein,
   Mar ri caoin-dheàrrsadh gréine,
Brùchdadh barraich troimh gheugan,
   Am mìos ceutach a' Mhàigh:
Am mìos breac-laoghach, buailteach,
   Bainneach, buadhach gu dàir.

Bi gach doire dlùth, uaignidh
   'S trusgan uain' uim' a' fàs;
Bi an snodhach a' dìreadh
   As gach freumhaich is ìsle,

to life. Alasdair published the first printed collection of contemporary Gaelic verse in Edinburgh in 1751, calling it 'The Resurrection of the Ancient Scottish Language', and indeed he remains the first, the most influential, and perhaps the greatest of the poets of the eighteenth-century Gaelic revival. 'Song of Summer' started a vogue for extended natural description, and although it was most probably influenced by James Thomson's 'Seasons', it refuses to philosophise or go beyond its own delighted engagement with the immediate physical world. The same drive can be found in 'Claranald's Galley', a heroically extended *tour de force* of descriptive and poetic intricacy.

Song of Summer

On waking this morning,
   with the dew on the woods,
on this very bright morning,
   in a shady wee hollow
I heard then the chanter
   with elegance played,
and the rocks' Echo sounded
   their sweet-sad reply,

The fine-scented birch-tree,
   new-branched over the cairn,
wet with tender warm May-dew
   warm with sun's kindly shining,
exudes foliage from twiglets
   in this lovely month, May:
month of dappled calves folded,
   month for mating and milk.

Each grove, close and secret,
   has its mantle of green,
the wood-sap is rising
   from the roots at the bottom,

Troimh na cuisleanan sniòmhain
  Gu meudachadh blàth;
Cuach is smeòrach 's an fheasgar
  Seinn an leadain 'nam bàrr.

Am mìos breac-ubhach, braonach,
  Creamhach, maoth-ròsach àigh!
Chuireas sgeadas neo-thruaillidh
  Air gach àite da dhuaichneachd;
A dh' fhògras sneachd le chuid fuachd
  Mach air bruaich nam beann àrd;
'S aig meud eagail roimh *Phoebus*
  Théid 's na speuran 'na smàl.

Am mìos lusanach, mealach,
  Feurach, failleanach, tlàth;
'S e gu gucagach, duilleach,
  Luachrach, dìtheineach, lurach,
Beachach, seilleineach, dearcach,
  Ciùrach, dealtach, trom, blàth;
'S i mar chùirneanan daoimein,
  Bhratach bhoillsgeil air làr.

'S moch bhios Phoebus ag òradh
  Air bàrr nam mór chruach 's nam beann,
'S bi 's an uair sin le sòlas
  Gach eun binn-fhaclach, bòidheach,
Ceumadh mhearbhuillean ceòlmhor,
  Feadh phreas, ògan is ghleann,
A' chorruil chùirteach gun sgreadan
48   Aig pòr is beadarraich' cainnt.

                *   *   *

81   Bidh bradan seang-mhear an fhìor-uisg',
       Gu brisg, slinn-leumnach, luath;
     Na bhuidhnean tàrr-ghealach, lannach;
       Gu h-iteach, dearg-bhallach, earrach;
     Le soillsean airgid d'a earradh
       'S mion bhreac, lainnireach tuar;
     'S e féin gu crom-ghobach ullamh,
       Ceapadh chuileag le cluain.

     A' Bhealltainn bhog-bhailceach, ghrianach,
       Lònach, lianach, mo ghràidh,
     Bhainneach, fhionn-mheògach, uachdrach
       Omhnach, loinideach, chuachach,

through arteries twisting
    to swell out the growth;
thrush and cuckoo at evening
    sing their litany above.

Month of speckled eggs, dewy,
    fine month for garlic and rose,
that with elegance decks out
    places formerly gloomy,
expels snow with its coldness
    from high mountains' harsh gloom;
so great its fear is of *Phoebus*
    it dissolves in the sky.

Month of plants and of honey,
    warm, with grasses and shoots,
month of buds and of leafage,
    rushes, flowers that are lovely,
wasps, bees and berries,
    mellow mists, heavy dews,
like spangles of diamonds,
    a sparkling cover for earth.

Phoebus early turns yellow
    the cap of mountain and peak;
lovely birds full of joy then
    shape their notes with precision
swift melodious rhythm
    in bush, sapling and glen,
a courtly chorale, no screeching
    from that frolicksome crew.

               *   *   *

Lithe brisk fresh-water salmon,
    lively, leaping the stones;
bunched, white-bellied, scaly,
    fin-tail-flashing, red spot;
speckled skin's brilliant hue
    lit with flashes of silver;
with curved gob at the ready
    catching insects with guile.

May, with soft showers and sunshine,
    meadows, grass-fields I love,
milky, whey-white and creamy,
    frothing, whisked up in pails,

Ghruthach, shlamanach, mhiosrach,
  Mhiodrach, mhiosganach làn,
Uanach mheannanach, mhaoiseach,
96 Bhocach mhaoineach lan àil.

*   *   *

129 Nis tréigidh 'n coileach a' ghucag,
  'S caitean brùchdach nan craobh;
'S théid gu mullach nan sliabh-chnoc,
  Le chirc ghearr-ghobaich riabhaich,
B' e sud an suiridhche cùirteil,
  Am pillean cùlghorma fraoich;
'S ise freagradh le tùchan,
  Pi-hu-hù, tha thu faoin.

A choilich chraobhaich nan gearr-sgiath,
  'S na falluinne duibh;
Tha dubh is geal air am measgadh
  Gu ro òirdheirc ad itich,
Muineal loinnireach, sgibidh,
  Uaine slios-mhìn, 's tric crom;
Gob nam ponganan milis,
  Nach faicte sileadh nan ronn.

Sud an turraraich ghlan loinneil,
  Is binne coilleag air tom;
'S iad ri burruras sèamh ceutach,
  Ann am feasgar ciùin céitein:
Am bannal mogant, uchd-ruadh,
  Mala ruiteach, chaol, chrom;
'S iad gu h-uchd-ardach, earr-gheal,
  Grian-dhearrsgnaidh, druim-dhonn.

from **Birlinn Chlann Raghnaill**

xvi [1]

Grian a' faosgnadh gu h-òrbhuidh
  As a mogul;
Chinn an speur gu dubhaidh, dòite,
  Làn de ogl'achd;

---

1. Everything in the boat has been prepared for the voyage, and described at length in the poem's previous sections. It is the Feast of St Bride. In this final passage, the boat sets sail from Loch Eynort in South Uist and encounters a storm before it reaches safety at Carrickfergus to the north of Belfast.

time for crowdie and milk-curds,
   time for firkins and kits,
lambs, goat-kids and roe-deer,
   bucks, a rich time for flocks.

       *   *   *

Now the cock leaves the budding
   thick blossom of trees,
for the heights of the heath-hills,
   with hen short-beaked and brindled;
he's a right courtly wooer
   on purple cushions of heather,
and she answers him hoarsely:
   'Pi-hu-hù, you vain thing!'

Short-winged cock of the woodlands
   with your dark sable cloak,
black and white are commingled
   in your feathers most finely;
throat well groomed and shining,
   green and sleek, often bending,
beak that never drips slaver
   but melodious notes.

A clean, elegant twittering
   with sweetest notes on a knoll
warbling seemly and gentle
   on a pleasant May evening:
a group white-skirted, red-breasted,
   with strong but finely arched brows,
white-tailed and high-chested,
   sun-burnished, brown-backed.

trans. Derick Thomson

Clanranald's Galley

xvi
Sun unhusking to gold-yellow
   from its shell,
the sky growing seared and lurid,
   amber bell.

Dh' fhàs i tonnghorm, tiugh, tàrrlachdunn
    Odhar, iargalt;
Chinn gach dath bhiodh ann am breacan,
    Air an iarmailt;

Fadadh-cruaidh 's an àird 'n iar oirr' –
    Stoirm 'n a coltas,
Neòil shiùbhlach aig gaoith 'g an riasladh –
    Fuaradh-frois' oirr.

Thog iad na siùil bhreaca,
    Bhaidealach, dhìonach;
Shìn iad na calpannan raga,
    Teanna rìghne,
Ri fiodhannan àrda, fada,
    Nan colg bìdhearg;

Cheangladh iad gu gramail, snaopach,
    Gu neo-chearbach,
Troimh shùilean nan cromag iarainn,
    'S nan cruinn fhailbheag.

Cheartaich iad gach ball de 'n acfhuinn,
    Ealamh, dòigheil,
'S shuidh gach fear gu freasdal tapaidh,
    Bhuill bu chòir dha.

An sin dh' fhosgail uinneagan an athair,
    Ballach, liath-ghorm,
Gu séideadh na gaoithe greannaich',
    Spannail, iargalt.

Tharruing an cuan a bhrat dùbhghlas
    Air gu h-uile,
Mhantul garbh, caiteineach, ciar-dhubh,
    'S sgreataidh buinne;

Dh' at e 'n a bheannaibh 's 'n a ghleannaibh
    Molach, robach;
Gu 'n do bhòc an fhairge cheigeach
    Suas 'n a cnocaibh.

Dh' fhosgail a' mhuir ghorm 'n a craosan
    Farsaing, cràcach;
An glaicibh a chéile ri taosgadh,
    'S caonnag bhàsmhor.

Thick and gloomy and dun-bellied,
    surly curtain,
vibrating with every colour
    in a tartan.

Rainbow in the west appearing
    tempest-born,
speeding clouds by growing breezes
    chewed and torn.

So they raised the speckled sails
    wind-tight, towering.
They stretched the stiff ropes against
    her sudden flowering,
timbers of the resin red
    tapering proudly.

They were knotted with fierce vigour,
    neatly, firmly,
through the eyes of iron hooks
    and round the ring bolts.

Every rope of their equipment
    was adjusted.
Coolly each took his position
    as accustomed.

Windows of the heavens opened
    blue-grey, spotted,
with the banging of the tempest
    fierce and haughty.

The sea gathered round about it
    a black cloak,
a rough, ruffled, swarthy mantle
    of ill look.

It swelled to mountains and to valleys
    shaggy-billowed,
the matted lumpy waters rearing
    up to hillocks.

The blue waves were mouthing chasms,
    horned and brutish,
fighting each other in a pouring
    deathly tumult.

Gu 'm b' fhear-ghnìomh bhi 'g amharc an aodann
   Nam maom teinntidh:
Lasraichean sradanach sionnachain
   Air gach beinn diubh.

Na beulanaich àrda liathcheann,
   Ri searbh bheucail;
Na cùlanaich 's an cladh dùdaidh
   Ri fuaim gheumraich.

An uair dh' éireamaid gu h-allail
   Am bàrr nan tonn sin,
B' éiginn an t-abhsadh a bhearradh
   Gu grad-phongail.

'S 'n uair a thuiteamaid le ion-slugaidh
   Sìos 's na gleanntaibh,
Bheirteadh gach seòl a bhiodh aice
   Am bàrr nan crann dith.

Na ceòsanaich àrda, chroma,
   Teachd 's a' bhàirich;
Mu 'n tigeadh iad idir 'n ar caraibh,
   Chluinnteadh 'n gàirich;

Iad a' sguabadh nan tonn beaga
   Lom 'g an sgiùrsadh.
Chinneadh i 'na h-aon mhuir bhàsmhor:
   'S càs a stiùradh.

'N uair thuiteamaid fo bhàrr
   Nan àrdthonn giobach,
Cur beag nach dochainneadh a sàil
   An t-aigeal sligneach.

An fhairge 'g a maistreadh 's 'g a sluistreadh
   Troimh a chéile,
Gu 'n robh ròin is mialan mòra
   Am barrachd éiginn':

Onfhadh is confhadh na mara,
   'S falbh na luinge,
Sradadh an eanchainnean geala,
   Feadh gach tuinne;

Iad ri nuallanaich àrd-uamhannaich,
   Shearbh, thùrsaich,

It needed courage to be facing
    such tall towerings
phosphorescent flashes sparking
    from each mountain

Grey-headed wave-leaders towering
    with sour roarings,
their followers with smoking trumpets
    blaring, pouring.

When the ship was poised on wave crest
    in proud fashion
it was needful to strike sail
    with quick precision.

When the valleys nearly swallowed us
    by suction
we fed her cloth to take her up to
    resurrection.

The wide-skirted curving waters,
    bellowing, lowing,
before they even had approached you,
    you'd hear roaring,

sweeping before them the small billows,
    onward sheering.
There'd be a massive deathly water
    hard for steering.

When she would plunge from towering summits
    down pell-mell
almost the ship's heel would be bruised
    by the sea-floor's shells,

the ocean churning, mixing, stirring
    its abyss,
seals and huge sea creatures howling
    in distress.

Impetuous tumult of the waters,
    the ship's going,
sparking their white brains about
    an eerie snowing!

And they howling in their horror
    with sad features

Ag éigheach, 'Is iochdarain sinne,
   Dragh chum bùird sinn.'

Gach mion-iasg bha 's an fhairge
   Tàrrgheal tionndaidht',
Le gluasad confadh na gailbhinn',
   Marbh gun chunntas.

Clachan is maorach an aigeil
   Teachd an uachdar:
Air am buain a nuas le slachdraich
   A' chuain uaibhrich.

An fhairge uile 's i 'na brochan,
   Srioplach, ruaimleach;
Le fuil 's le gaorr nam biast lorcach,
   Droch dhath ruadh orr'.

Na biastan adharcach, iongach,
   Pliutach, lorcach,
Làn cheann, sian am beòil gu 'n gialan,
   'S an craos fosgailt'.

An aibheis uile làn bhòcan,
   Air cràgradh;
Le spògan 's le earbaill mhorbhiast
   Air màgradh.

Bu sgreamhail an ròmhan sgreuchach –
   Bhi 'g a éisdeachd,
Thogadh iad air caogad mìlidh
   Aotruim' céille.

Chaill an sgioba càil an claisteachd,
   Ri bhi 'g éisdeachd
Ceilearadh sgreadach nan deamhan,
   'S mothair bhéistean.

Foghar na fairge, 's a slachdraich
   'Gleachd ri darach;
Fosghair a toisich a' sloistreadh
   Mhuca-mara;

Ghaoth ag ùrachadh a fuaraidh
   As an iar àird':
Bha sinn leis gach seòrsa buairidh,
   Air ar pianadh;

pleading by us to be rescued,
   'Save your creatures.'

Every small fish in the ocean
   belly-white
by the rocking violent motion
   killed outright.

Stones and shell fish of the bottom
   on the surface
mown by the relentless threshing
   of the current.

The whole ocean in a porridge
   foul and muddied,
with filth and gore of the sea-monsters
   red and bloodied,

the horned splay-footed vast sea-creatures
   clawed, misshapen,
their many heads in ghastly screaming,
   mouths jammed open,

the deeps teeming with hobgoblins,
   ghostly pawing,
monstrous crawling, phantom seething,
   vague out-clawing.

Loathsome their abhorrent groaning
   and their raving:
they'd have driven fifty soldiers
   wholly crazy.

The crew entirely lost their hearing
   in the maelstrom,
the screaming discord of the demons,
   beastly wailing.

Crashing of water and its smashing
   smiting planking,
the prow's rushing as it dashed
   the ghastly monsters.

Breezes freshening from windward
   from the west,
torment everywhere from ocean
   and from beast.

Sinn dallte le cathadh-fairge
   Sìor dhol tharainn;
Tàirneineach aibheiseach ré oidhche,
   'S teine-dealain.

Peileirean beathrach a' losgadh
   Ar cuid acfhuinn.
Fàileadh is deathach na riofa
   'G ar glan-thachdadh.

Na dùilean uachdrach is ìochdrach,
   Ruinn a' cogadh:
Talamh, teine, uisge, 's sian-ghaoth
   Ruinn air togail.

Ach 'n uair dh' fhairtlich air an fhairge
   Toirt oirnn strìochdadh,
Ghabh i truas le faite gàire,
   'S rinn i sìth ruinn.

Ged rinn, cha robh crann gun lùbadh,
   Seòl gun reubadh,
Slat gun sgaradh, rachd gun fhàillinn,
   Ràmh gun éislein.

Cha robh stadh gun stuadh-leumnadh,
   Beairt gun ghaise,
Tarrang no cupladh gun bhristeadh –
   Fise, faise! –

Cha robh tobhta no beul-mór ann
   Nach tug aideach;
Bha h-uile crannaghail is goireas
   Air an lagadh.

Cha robh achlasan no aisne dhith
   Gun fhuasgladh;
A slat-bheòil 's a sguitichean-asgail
   Air an tuairgneadh.

Cha robh falmadair gun sgoltadh,
   Stiùir gun chreuchdadh, –
Cnead is dìosgan aig gach maide,
   'S iad air déasgadh.

Cha robh cranntarrang gun tarruing,
   Bòrd gun obadh, –

Blinded by the pouring spindrift
    sky unbrightening,
incredible thunder during nighttime
    flash of lightning.

Fire balls burning up our tackle
    and our gear
acrid smell and smoke of brimstone
    everywhere.

The elements above below us
    seeking slaughter,
water, earth and fire and air,
    a hostile quartet.

But when the ocean could not beat us
    make us yield
she became a smiling meadow,
    summer field.

Though there was no bolt unbending,
    sail intact,
yard unwrenched or ring unweakened,
    oar uncracked.

There was no stay that had not sprung
    or gear undamaged
no shroud or halyard without ripping.
    Snapping, cracking!

Each bench and gunwale all gave witness
    to the storm.
Every timber, every fitting
    suffered harm.

There was no angle-piece or rib
    which wasn't loosened.
The wale and stern sheets all were damaged,
    smashed, unfastened.

There was no rudder without splitting,
    helm unwounded,
sob and groan from every timber
    sea had pounded.

There was no tree-nail left unpulled,
    or board in use,

H-uile lann a bh' air am barradh,
   Ghabh iad togail.

Cha robh tarrang gun tràladh,
   Cha robh calp' ann gun lùbadh, –
Cha robh aon bhall a bhuineadh dhise
   Nach robh na 's miosa na thùbhradh.

Ghairm an fhairge sìochaint ruinne
   Air còrs' Chaol-Ile;
'S fhuair a' gharbh-ghaoth, shearbh-ghlòireach
   Ordugh sìnidh.

Thog i bhuainn do ionadan uachdrach
   An athair;
'S chìnn i dhuinn 'n a clàr réidh, mìn-gheal,
   An déidh a tabhainn.

'S thug sinn buidheachas do 'n Airdrigh
   Chum na dùilean,
Deadh Chlannràghnuill a bhi sàbhailt'
   Bho bhàs brùideil.

'S an sin bheum sinn na siùil thana,
   Bhallach, de thùilinn,
'S leag sinn a croinn mhìndhearg, ghasda,
   Air fad a h-ùrlair.

'S chuir sinn a mach ràimh chaola, bhaisgeant',
   Dhaite, mhìne,
De 'n ghiuthas a bhuain Mac Bharrais
   An Eilean-Fhìonain.

'S rinn sinn an t-iomramh réidh tulganach,
   Gun dearmad;
'S ghabh sinn deagh longphort aig barraibh
   Charraig Fhearghuis.

Thilg sinn acraichean gu socair
   Anns an ròd sin;
Ghabh sinn biadh is deoch gun airceas,
   'S rinn sinn còmhnuidh.

every single well-clinched washer
    had been loosed.

There was no nail that was untwisted,
    there was no rivet without bending,
there was no part that still existed
    that wasn't worse at the storm's ending.

The tranquil sea benignly saw us
    in Islay Sound,
the bitter-voiced breezes were appeased
    by God's command.

They left us for the upper regions
    of the heavens
and made for us a noiseless even
    level plain.

We gave thanks to the great Father
    and Creator
that Clanranald came unharmed
    from brutal water.

But we furled then our thin sails
    of linen woven
and we lowered her red masts
    across her floor boards.

We put out melodious oar blades
    finely tinted
of red pine that had been cut
    on Isle of Finnan.

We rowed with smooth and springy motion
    not neglectful
entering harbour at the heights
    of Carrickfergus.

We anchored easily and calmly
    in that roadstead
and we ate and drank, unstinted,
    and abode there.

                                        trans. Iain Crichton Smith

Iain Mhic Fhearchair/ John MacCodrum (1693?–1779)

MacCodrum lived quietly on North Uist for most of his life and only started to compose in his elder years. He wrote formal praise poems when he was made bard to Sir James MacDonald of Sleat, but he is best remembered for the wit and humour of his poems on local events, greedy landlords, lazy tailors, a bad piper, or his uncaring third wife. Like so many unlettered poets in the oral tradition, MacCodrum's memory gave him access to a wealth of literature from the past, along with the capacity to learn or imitate other works from no more than a single hearing. He was visited

Oran Mu 'n Eideadh Ghaidhealach

Tha mi cràiteach tinn
'S tha mi sgìth làn dochair,
Ceangal air mo bhuill,
Cha dean mì ceum coiseachd;
Mallachd air an rìgh
Thug am breacan dhìnn,
Guidheam air beul sìos
O 'n a shìn e 'n t-osan.
Ged tha 'n stocaidh fada
'S i 'n a cochull farsaing,
B'annsa 'n t-osan geàrr
Nach biodh réis o 'n t-sàil an gartan.

Luthaig thu ar còta
'N a sgeòl fharsaing,
'S luthaig thu ar brògan
Na 's leòr phailte;
Mheudaich thu ar cìs
'S lughdaich thu ar nì,
'S dh'fhàg thu sinn gun phrìs:
Chan 'eil dìreadh againn.
Thug thu dhuinn a' bhriogais,
Theannaich thu ar n-iosgaid:
B'annsa 'm breacan sgaoilte,
An t-aodach aotrom sgiobalt.

by James Macpherson, looking for Ossianic poems in 1760, and by Alasdair
MacMhaighstir Alasdair more than once. 'Song to the Highland Dress' attacks the
laws against wearing the kilt which were part of the Disarming Act of 1748 – this
complaint was to be a familiar one for many years in the North, for the prohibition
was not lifted until 1782. Highland life was affected again in the 1770s when
thousands emigrated, willingly or by force of circumstances, to seek a new life in
America, most especially South Carolina.

Song to the Highland Dress

Sick and sore I am, worn and weary
walking no more since my limbs are bound.
Cursed be the king who stretched our stockings
down in the dust may his face be found.
The length of our legs in these lubber wrinkles
scarce does such gear become a man:
better we loved our graceful short-hose
from heel to garter but a span.

Coats he'll allow us with tails a-flapping
shoes he'll leave us by the score,
but treat us with no trace of honour,
grabbing our gear to make us poor;
worse than all this he forces backsides
into these niggard peasant breeches,
knowing the spreading comely tartan
meant more to us than all our riches.

'S olc a' chulaidh oidhche
Bhith 'n lùib na casaig;
Chan fhaigh mi cas a shìneadh,
Chan fhaigh mì cadal;
B'fheàrr an sòlas inntinn
Na deich slatan singillte
Phaisginn anns an fhéile
'N am éirigh 's mhaduinn.
Siod an t-aodach dreachmhor
Chumadh gaoth is fras uam:
Mallachd an dà shaoghail
Air an aon fhear chuir as da.

Chan 'eil culaidh shamhraidh
As feàrr na 'm breacan;
Tha e aotrom fonnmhor
An am an t-sneachda;
Bha e cleachdt' r' an cùmhdach
Aig na gaisgich lùthmhor:
'S acaid air an giùlan
Nach 'eil e aca.
Chulaidh bha cur fasgaidh
Air na Gàidheil ghasda,
Rìgh, gur mór am beud
Le pléid a chur a fasan.

Chan fhaca tu mac màthar
Air sràid no faithche
'S deise na mac Gàidheil
Le shàr phearsain:
Breacan air am féile
'S a chlaidheamh air cùl sgéithe,
Le dhagachan cho gleusda
Nach éisd iad sradag;
Sgiath air gual' a' ghaisgich
Cuilbheir caol 'n a achlais:
Chan 'eil Gall 's an t-saoghal
Nach aognaich roimh fhaicinn.

'S math thig boineid ghorm
Air chùl borb an cocadh,
Còta geàrr is féile
Air sléisdean nochdte,

In this clumsy cassock I'm tangled nightly
can't stretch my legs, no wink of sleeping.
Better the ease of the ten yards single
that in the morning I'd be pleating –[1]
a lightsome dress, kept wind an rain off
every gallant lad who had it:
the curse of the two worlds upon
the mean usurper who forbade it.   (King George II)

No summer dress that can beat the tartan,
lightsome and cheerful when it's snowing
the favoured garb of hardy warriors
pain for its lack impedes their going;
the sheltering cloth of splendid Gaels,
Lord! it's a blow that pains us quite
that they should ban the belted plaid
to kill our fashion out of spite.

You would seldom see a mother's son
that strolled the street or on parade
more handsomely in his native dress
than those of Gaeldom's son's arrayed,
with tartan gathered at waist and pleated,
broadsword and musket behind shield,
pistols that never would misfire
what foeman would face him on the field?

How trimly the blue bonnet sits
on locks that tumble from his head,
short coat and kilt around bare thighs
marching to meet the foeman's blade

---

1. The poet is describing the traditional féile-mór, the Highland plaid that wraps over the shoulder as well as being
   pleated around the middle, held in with a belt.

Dhol an láthair cruadail
Gu fuilteach nimheil buailteach,
A liodairt nam fear ruadha –
Bhiodh smuais 'g a fhosgladh:
Le neart ball nan curaidh,
Cur nan lann gu 'm fulang,
Bhiodh luchd nan casag millte
'S an cinn a dhìth am muineal.

'N uair chruinnicheas na Gàidheil
An làthair troda
Le 'n geur lannan Spàinneach
'S an deàrrsadh chlogad,
Pàighidh iad gu daor
Ann am fuil 's an gaorr,
'S cha bhi bonn gun dìoladh
De bhlàr Chùil-lodair.
Chan 'eil urra chaidh a chreachadh
No urra chaidh a ghlacadh
Nach fhaigh iad luchd am mìoruin
Gu 'n rogha dìol thoirt asda.

'N uair chluinneas fir na h-Alba
Do dhearbh chaismeachd,
Théid iad gu neo-chearbach
Fo d' dhealbh-bhrataich;
Domhnallaich bu dual,
'S dàine théid 's an ruaig,
Tàilleirean clò ruaidh,
Gar nach fuaigh ach sracadh;
Le 'n cruaidh lannan sgaiteach
Snaidheadh chluas is chlaignean,
'S gum bi àireamh cheann
Air a h-uile ball 's a' bhreacan.

Nach doimheach dhuinn ar n-aodach
Bhith air chaochladh cumadh,
Chluinn sinn bhith 'g a dhìoladh
Math dh'fhaoidt' an Lunnuinn,
Leis na fleasgaich bhòidheach
Chluicheas mar na leómhainn,
Chuireas geilt air Deòrsa
'S nach faod e fuireach.
Théid Rìgh Deòrsa dhachaidh
'S am prionns' òg a ghlacadh,
Bidh Teàrlach 'n a rìgh,
'S gur fheàirrde prìs a' bhreacain.

in bloody furious battle-mood,
to crush those uniformed in red
strong men that swing their lusty blades
to leave each neck without a head.

When the Gael gathers on the field
with gleaming helmet, Spanish blade
how dearly then their blood will flow
and all Culloden's debts be paid,
no man of honour, plundered there
or led away in captive chains,
but he shall learn how well redeemed
by alien gore are all his pains.

When Scottish men shall hear your tread
they'll swiftly join the figured banner
Clan Donald marching as is their wont,
to trim red-coats in the tailor's manner,
not sewing up but cutting cloth,
with blades whose aim is sure and certain
to claim a debt of ears and skulls,
for every check within the tartan.

What grief our dress has changed its shaping,
well may our vengeance fall on London,
fighting like lions in that place
so Geordie shall his throne abandon,
go off to find his native dwelling,
and his young prince be swiftly fettered.   (Frederick Louis, Prince of Wales)
When Charlie's safely throned as monarch   (Charles Edward Stuart)
the tartan's value will be bettered.

'S ionann 's a bhith 'm prìosan
Bhith dhìth a' bhreacain;
Nì sinn ùrnuigh dhìcheallach
'S gheibh sinn taice:
'N uair thig iad a nall oirnn,
Cóig ceud mìle Frangach,
Bidh Teàrlach air an ceann,
Bidh am ball fo 'n casan.
Siod an sluagh beachdail
Chuireas an gleò reachdmhor,
Armailteach gu leòr,
A luaidheas an clò Catach;
'S 'n uair théid a' mhuc a dhaghadh,
'S a cuid uircean fhaileadh,
Air claidheamh no air breacan
Cha bhi tuilleadh bacaidh.

Oran do na Fogarraich

Togaibh misneach is sòlas,
Bithibh inntinneach ceòlmhor,
Agus cuiribh ur dòchas
Ann an comhnadh an Airdrigh;
O 'n as fheudar dhuibh seòladh,
Is nach ann do ur deoin e,
Do rìoghachd nach eòl duibh,
Mar a thòisich ur càirdean;
O nach fuiling iad beò sibh
Ann an crìochaibh ur n-eòlais,
'S feàrr dhuibh falbh do ur deoin
Na bhith fòdha mar thràillean;
'S iad na h-uachdarain ghòrach
A chuir fuaradh fo 'r srònaibh,
A bhris muineal Rìgh Deòrsa
'N uair a dh'fhògradh na Gàidheil.

Ma thig cogadh is creachan,
Mar as minig a thachair,
'S ann a bhios sibh 'n ur starsaich
Fo chasaibh ur nàmhaid;
Tha sibh soirbh ri bhur casgairt,
'S gun neach ann gu 'm bacadh,

Life is a prison when plaids are lacking
we'll send a prayer up to restore 'em.
When half a million Frenchmen come,
with general Charlie there before them
the Sutherland tweed they'll soon be waulking[1]
engage in battle, wise and sudden,
when the sow's singed and boiled her litter,[2]
broadsword and tartan no more forbidden.

trans. William Neill

Song to the Fugitives

Be courageous and joyful
of cheerful high spirit,
and place all your hope in
the heavenly King.
Since sailing is forced,
and is not your desiring,
to a kingdom unknown
though your comrades have learned.
Now they won't let you live
in the land you're acquaint with
let your choice be to leave
and not yield as their slaves.
'Twas the idiot lairds
put cold wind on your nose
broke the neck of King George
with the exile of Gael.

If war comes and looting
as often has happened
you will be but a step
to the feet of your foe:[3]
you'll be easily slaughtered
with none to oppose them

1. The Northern clans were Whigs who supported King George. New cloth is waulked, drubbed, by a process of soaking and beating.
2. i.e.: the Hanovarian dynasty.
3. The poem addresses both the departing tacksmen and, as here, their landlord and chief Sir Alexander MacDonald, soon to be made ninth Baronet of Sleat.

Tha bhur guaillean gun tacsa,
'S na gaisgich 'g ur fàgail.
Rìgh! gur sgiolta ri 'm faicinn
'N an seasamh air faithche
Le 'n aodaichean gasda
De bhreacanan càrnaid
Na tha falbh uaibh an ceartuair
De dh'òganaich dhreachmhor,
Gun truailleadh gun ghaiseadh,
Gun taise gun tàire.

Thug siod sgrìob air Mac Dhomhnaill,
Thug e spùilleadh air Mórar,
Thug e lomadh air Cnòideart,
Thug e leòn air Clann Raghnaill:
Falbh nam fear òga,
Falbh nam fear móra,
Falbh nam fear cròdha
'N am na tòrachd a phàigheadh;
Bidh cinn-chinnidh 'n an ònar,
'S an slinnean gun chomhdach,
Gun treise gun chomhnadh
'N uair thig fòirneart an làthair:
Ur nàimhdean gu spòrsail
'G ur stampadh fo 'm brògan;
Luchd fòirneart gu treòrach
Gun neach beò gus an àicheadh.

'S truagh an gnothuch ri smaoineach',
Tha 'm fearann 'g a dhaoradh;
Ghrad dh'fhalbh ar cuid daoine,
'S thàinig caoirich 'n an àite:
'S lag an sluagh iad 's is faoin iad
Dol an carraid no 'n caonnaig,
Làn bracsaidh is caoile,
'S iad fo dhraoidh ghille-màrtuinn;
Cha dèan smiùradh ur saoradh
'N làthair batail air raonaidh,
No fead cìbeir an aonaich
Gnè chaochladh dhe 'r n-ànradh;
'S ged a chruinnicheadh sibh caogad
Mholt is reitheachan maola,
'S beag a thogadh a h-aon diubh
Claidheamh faobharach stàilinn.

Ciod am fàth dhomh bhith 'g innse
Gun d'fhàs sibh cho mìodhar

no guard at your shoulder
now warriors leave.
Ah! how tidy they seem
as they stand on the green there
most fitly arrayed
in their tartans of red.
Those hardy young gallants
who are set now to leave you
unstained and unblemished,
nor weak without rule.

There's a scar on MacDonald,
and Morar is ravaged,
Knoydart is laid bare
and Clan Ranald sore hurt.
Gone are the young ones
gone are the great ones
gone are the brave ones
whose worth's in defence.
The chiefs are alone now,
their backs without cover,
no power and no succour
when tyranny comes:
the sport of your foes
as their boots stamp you under;
for tyrants grow strong
when there's none to defy.

Sad business to brood on,
the land-rent grow dearer;
our people leave promptly,
sheep come in their stead:
they're a silly weak race
in a skirmish or battle,
all braxy and wasting   diseased
the prey to the fox.
Their smearing won't save you
in forefront of battle
nor moor-shepherd's whistle
change ill-fortune's drift;
though you muster up fifty
bald rams and bell-wethers   hornless; castrated
scarce one there could raise up
a keen-edged steel sword.

What good now is telling
you've grown to a miser

'S gun spothadh sibh frìghde
Far an dìreadh i fàrdan?
Dh'fhalbh na ceannardan mìleant'
Dh'an robh sannt air an fhìrinn,
Dh'an robh geall air an dìlsean
Agus cuing air an nàmhaid;
Air an tuath bha iad cuimhneach,
Cha b'ann gus an sgrìobadh;
Bhiodh bantraichean 's dìlleachdain
Dìolta gu saidhbhir;
Gach truaghan gun dìth air
Mun cuairt air na suinn sin
Nach sealladh gu h-ìseal –
Bha 'n inntinn ro stàtail.

Dia a stiùireadh ur gnothuich
Air gach taobh agus romhaibh
A null air chuan domhain
As coimhiche gàire;
Thugadh Eolus earail
Do 'n ghaoith a bhith tairis
Gun giùlain i thairis
Ur mnathan 's ur pàisdean;
Biodh an fhairge le mothar
Toirt an spìd as an robhairt;
Biodh Neptiun 'g a clothadh
Gun tomhas ro àrd oirr':
Gus an ruig sibh am fearann
Gun eagal a ghabhail,
Dol air tìr mar as math leibh
Ann an calaichean sàbhailt.

Triallaibh nis fhearaibh
Gu dùthaich gun ghainne –
Cuiribh cùl ris an fhearann
Chaidh thairis am màl oirbh –
Gu dùthaich a' bhainne,
Gu dùthaich na meala,
Gu dùthaich an ceannaich sibh
Fearann gu 'r n-àilgheas,
Gu dùthaich gun aineis,
Gun chrìonadh gun stanard,
Far an cnuasaich sibh barrachd
'S a mhaireas ri 'r làithean:
'S e 'n saighdeir glic fearail,
'N uair chitheadh e barrachd,

who'd geld a crablouse
for a farthing of gain:
brave captains are gone
who were keen for the truth
who could raise loyal men
and put fetters on foes.
They cared for their tenants
but not to rack-rent them;
the widow and orphan
were richly endowed;
no pauper would starve
in the bounds of these heroes
whose minds were too noble
to turn from the poor.

May God guide your lot   (the emigrants)
on each side and before you
across the deep sea
of most terrible roar;
let Aeolus order   (the god, or king of the winds)
the winds in your favour
to voyage across
with your children and wives;
may the sea with a murmur
take speed from the spring-tide;
let Neptune subdue it
from reaching too high,
till you come to the land
without reason for terror
to beach at your will
in a haven of peace.

Now off with you, lads
to a land without famine –
turn your backs to the country
that racked you for rent –
to the country of milk,
to the country of honey,
to the country where land
can be bought at your will,
to a country of friendship
without stint or skimping,
to gather a store
that will last you for life.
'Tis a manly wise soldier
when odds overwhelm him

A theicheadh le anam
'S nach fanadh air làraich.

Seallaibh mun cuairt duibh
Is faicibh na h-uaislean
Gun iochd annt' ri truaghain,
Gun suairceas ri dàimhich;
'S ann a tha iad am barail
Nach buin sibh do 'n talamh,
'S ged dh'fhàg iad sibh falamh
Chan fhaic iad mar chall e;
Chaill iad an sealladh
Air gach reachd agus gealladh
Bha eadar na fearaibh
Thug am fearann-s' o 'n nàmhaid:
Ach innseadh iad dhomhsa,
'N uair théid sibh air fògradh,
Mur caill iad an còir air
Gun dòigh air a theàrnadh.

who flees with his life
and abandons the field.

Look all around you
And see the great nobles:
no pity to hardship
or kindness to clan;
they hold the opinion
the land's not your business,
that leaving you paupered
is not to their loss;
they have lost every vision
of just obligation
that united the men
who took land from the foe:
but let them inform me
when you go to exile,
how long their right lasts
without rescue at hand?

                                        trans. William Neill

Rob Donn MacAoidh/
Robert Mackay (1714–1778)

Born in Sutherland, Rob Donn ('Brown Robert') Mackay spent most of his years in his home county, working as a cattle herdsman, although he served in the Sutherland Highlanders for a spell during the 1760s. Like John MacCodrum he could neither read nor write, but his oral skills and a prodigious memory made him anything but 'illiterate'. Familiar with the works of Pope, he liked to comment – often satirically

Is Trom Leam an Airigh

Is trom leam an àirigh 's a' ghàir seo a th'innt',
Gun a' phàirtinn a dh'fhàg mi bhith 'n dràsd air mo chinn:
Anna chaol-mhalach chìoch-chorrach shlìob-cheannach chruinn,
Is Iseabail a' bheòil mhilis, mhànranach bhinn.
Heich! mar a bhà, air mo chinn,
A dh'fhàg mi cho cràiteach 's nach stàth dhomh bhith 'g inns'.

Shiubhail mis' a' bhuaile 's a suas feadh nan craobh,
'S gach àit' anns am b'àbhaist bhith pàgadh mo ghaoil;
Nuair chunnaic mi 'm fear bàn ud 's e mànran r'a mhnaoi,
B'fheàrr leam nach tiginn idir làimh riu, no 'n gaoith.
'Se mar a bhà, air mo chinn,
A dh'fhàg mi cho cràiteach 's nach stàth dhomh bhith 'g inns'.

'Ach Anna bhuidh' Ni'n Dòmhnaill, nam b'eòl duit mo nì,
'Se do ghràdh gun bhith pàight' leag a-bhàn uam mo chlì;
Tha e dhomh á t'fhianais cho gnìomhach 's nuair chì,
Diogalladh, 's a' smùsach, gur ciùrrtach mo chrìdh.
Air gach tràth, 's mi ann an strì,
A' feuchainn r'a àicheadh 's e fàs rium mar chraoibh.'

Ach labhair i gu fàiteagach, àilgheasach rium:
'Chan fhàir thu bhith làimh rium do chàradh mo chinn;
Tha sianar gam iarraidh o bhliadhna do thìm,

– on the community around him. Although he was a Protestant in the employ of the Hanovarian Lord Reay, his sympathies with the Jacobite cause and his hatred for the exploitation of his fellow Highlanders come across strongly in a poem such as 'The Black Coats'.

The Shieling Song[1]

The shieling is a sad place for me, when the present company in it
– rather than the company who used to be there – are near to me
– Anna of the passionate breast, finely arched brows, shining hair, style;
and honey-mouthed Isabel, melodious, sweet.
Alas for things as they were at the back of my croft –
I have grown so bereft, there is no point in talking about it.

I wandered across the fold and up into the woods
and everywhere I used to caress my love.
When I saw that fair fellow courting his wife
I wish I had not come near them or beside them.
That's how it was behind my croft
to make me so dispirited – though it's shameful to sing about it.

'Fair Anna, Donald's daughter, if you knew my condition,
it is unrequited love for you that deprived me of my reason.
It remains as lively with me as in your presence,
teasing and provoking, wounding me to the heart.
All through the day I am in turmoil,
trying to quench it, while it grows in me like a tree.'

But she spoke very disdainfully, superciliously to me,
'You don't deserve to be beside me, stroking my head.
Six men have been seeking me since the year of your courtship

1. The shieling is a hut on high pasture. Village boys and girls would take the cattle there for summer grazing and their own first experience of the joys and pains of love.

'S cha b'àraidh le càch thu, thoirt bàrr os an cinn.
Ha, ha, hà! an d'fhàs thu gu tinn?
'N e 'n gaol a bheir bàs ort, gum pàigh thu d'a chinn!'

Ach cionnas bheir mi fuath dhuit, ged dh'fhuaraich thu rium?
Nuair 's feargaich mo sheanchas mu t'ainm air do chùl,
Thig t'ìomhaigh le h-annsachd 'na shamhladh 'nam ùidh,
Saoilidh mi an sin gun dèan an gaol sin an tùrn,
'S theid air a ràth gu h-às-ùr,
Is fàsaidh e 'n tràth sin cho àrda ri tùr.

On chualas gun gluaiseadh tu uam leis an t-Saor
Tha mo shuain air a buaireadh le bruadraichean gaoil;
De 'n chàirdeas a bhà siud chan fhàir mi bhith saor,
Gun bhàrnaigeadh làimh riut tha 'n gràdh dhomh 'na mhaor.
Nis, ma tha mi ga do dhìth
Gum b'fheàirrde mi pàg uait mus fàgainn an tìr.

Briogais MhicRuaridh

An d'fhidir no 'n d'fhairich no 'n cuala sibh
Cò idir thug briogais Mhic Ruairidh leis?
Bha 'bhriogais ud againn an àm dol a chadal
'S nuair thàinig a' mhadainn cha d'fhuaireadh i.

Chaidh 'bhriogais a stàmpadh am meadhon na connlaich,
'S chaidh Hùistein a dhanns leis na gruagaichibh,
'S nuair dh'fhàg a chuid misg e gun tug e 'n sin briosgadh
A dh'iarraidh na briogais, 's cha d'fhuair e i.

Nam bitheadh tu làimh ris gun deanadh tu gàire,
Ged a bhiodh siataig sa' chruachan agad.
Na faiceadh tu dhronnag nuair dh'ionndrain e 'pheallag,
'S e coimhead 's gach callaid 's a' suaithteachan.

Iain Mhic Eachainn, mas tusa thug leat i,
Chur grabadh air peacadh 's air buaireadh leath',
Mas tù a thug leat i cha ruigeadh tu leas e,
Chaidh t'uair-sa seachad mun d'fhuair thu i.

Chaitrìona Ni'n Uilleim, dean briogais do'n ghille,
'S na cumadh siud sgillinn a thuarasdal;
Ciod am fios nach e t'athair thug leis i g'a caitheamh –
Bha feum air a leithid 's bha uair dhe sin.

and the others would hardly expect you to surpass them.
Ha! Ha! Ha! Are you deranged?
If it's love that will cause your death, you are going to pay for it.'

But how can I hate you, even though you have grown so cold to me?
Whenever I disparage your name behind your back
your image floats with its fascination as an embodiment of my dreams
so that I will conceive love to be that which will never alter,
and this is proved as it wells up again
and it grows then as high as a tower.

Since it was rumoured that you would forsake me for the carpenter
my sleep is disturbed with dreams of love.
Of the affection that was between us I cannot break free:
When I am not beside you, love is like a bailiff to me.
But if I am to be without you
it would do me good to get a kiss from you before you leave the district.

trans. Ian Grimble

MacRory's Trousers[1]

Did you hear any rumour at all
who took MacRory's breeks away?
The breeks were there when he went to bed
but in the morning he couldn't find them.

The breeks were trampled amongst the straw
and Hugh went dancing with the lassies.
When his intoxication left him he took a bound
in search of his trousers and couldn't find them.

If you had been near him, you would have laughed
even if you had rheumatism in your hip-joints,
to have seen his loins when he missed his covering,
and he searching in every corner and shrugging his shoulders.

Iain Mac Eachainn, if you carried them off   (the bride's father)
to prevent sin and remove temptation,
if you took them you had no need to.
You had had your day before you found them.

Catherine, William's daughter, make some trousers for the lad   (the bride's mother)
and don't take a penny in payment for them.
Who knows but it was your father who took them to wear?
He needed as much and time was when he would have done it.

1. The poet was snubbed by not being invited to the wedding of his neighbour Iseabail Nic Aoidh to John Sutherland
   in 1747. But he turned up anyway with this satirical poem. The kilt was proscribed at this time, and trousers the butt
   of many jokes and complaints.

Briogais a' chonais chaidh chall air a' bhanais,
Bu liutha fear fanaid na fuaigheil oirr';
Mur do ghlèidh Iain Mac Dhòmhnaill gu pocan do'n òr i
Cha robh an Us-mhòine na luaidheadh i.

Mur do ghlèidh Iain Mac Dhòmhnaill gu pocan do'n or i
Cha robh an Us-mhòine na ghluaiseadh i.
Mu Uilleam Mac Phàdraig, cha deanadh i stàth dha,
Cha ruigeadh i 'n àird air a' chruachan dha.

Tha duine 'n Us-mhòine d'an ainm Iain Mac Sheòrais,
'S gur iongantas dhòmhsa ma ghluais e i;
Bha i cho cumhang, mur cuir e i 'm mudhadh,
Nach dean i nas mutha na buarach dha.

Na leigibh ri bràigh e 'm feadh 's a bhios e mar thà e
Air eagal gun sàraich an luachair e;
Na leigibh o bhail' e do mhòinteach nan coileach
Mun tig an labhallan 's gum buail i e.

Chan eil fitheach no feannag no iolair no clamhan,
No nathair a' ghlinne 'na cuachanan
No smàgach an luisean, ged 's gràineil an cuspair,
Nach b'fheàrr leo na musaidh do shuaitheadh riu.

Nam faiceadh sibh 'leithid, bha bann oirr' do leathar,
Bha toll air a speathar 's bha tuathag air,
'S bha feum aic' air cobhair mu bhrèidean a gobhail
Far am biodh am ball odhar a' suathadh rith'.

Ach Iain Mhic Choinnich 'sann ort a bha 'n sonas,
Ged 's mòr a bha dhonadas sluaigh an seo,
Nuair bha thu cho sgiobalt 's nach do chaill thu dad idir
'S gur tapaidh a' bhriogais a bhuannaich thu!

Na Casagan Dubha

Làmh Dhé leinne, dhaoine,
C' uime chaochail sibh fasan:
'S nach 'eil agaibh de shaorsa

The trousers whose loss caused friction at the wedding –
there were more mockers than there were patches on them.
Unless John son of Donald kept them to make pouches for the gold,[1]
there weren't in West Moine enough people to waulk them.

Unless John son of Donald made pouches for the gold of them,
there weren't in West Moine enough people to waulk them.
As for William son of Patrick, they would be no use to him –
they wouldn't reach up to his hips.

There's a man in West Moine called John son of George
and I wouldn't be surprised if he walked off with them.
They were so tight that unless he alters them
they will be more like cow-fetters on him.

Don't let him out on the braes in his present condition,
for fear he will be vexed by the bulrushes.
Don't let him leave home for the moors or the woods
lest the water-shrew come and nip him.

There's not a raven or crow or eagle or buzzard
or serpent of the glen in its coils,
nor creeping things in the plants – though the subject's disgusting –
that they wouldn't prefer to the nasty fellow rubbing against them.

If you saw any like them, they had a leather belt.
There was a hole on the fly and a patch on it,
and it needed repairs to the cloth of the breech
where the dun member used to rub against it.

John, son of Kenneth you're the one who was lucky –   (the groom)
though there were a lot of bad people here –
when you were so adroit that you never lost a thing
and so smart over the trousers you won.

                                                                    trans. Ian Grimble

The Black Coats[2]

God's hand with us, friends
what's the change in your fashion
are we not free to wear still

---

1. A local man who boasted of having got gold from the Jacobite sloop 'Prince Charles', abandoned after fleeing from a Royal naval warship, but the laird got to hear of it and made him return the loot.
2. Mackay's chief, as well as his employer Lord Reay, supported the Hanoverian side during the '45. After Culloden, however, 'loyal' and 'disloyal' were treated alike. Landlords lost their jurisdiction in local courts, and Highlanders were forbidden to own a gun, wear the kilt or play the pipes. Rob Donn's Jacobite sympathies were dangerous and he had to add the last two stanzas to get him out of trouble when called to account at a hearing in Tongue.

Fiù an aodaich a chleachd sibh;
'S i mo bharail mu 'n éibhe
Tha 'n aghaidh fhéileadh is osan,
Gu bheil caraid aig Teàrlach,
Ann am Pàrlamaid Shasuinn.

Faire, faire! Righ Deòrsa,
'N ann a' spòrs air do dhìlsean,
'Deanamh achdachan ùra
Gu bhi dùblachadh 'n daorsa;
Ach o 's balaich gun uails' iad,
'S feàrr am bualadh no 'n caomhnadh,
'S bidh na 's lugha 'g ad fheitheamh
'N uair thig a leithid a rìs oirnn.

Ma gheobh do nàmhaid 's do charaid
An aon pheanas an Albainn,
'S iad a dh' éirich 'n ad aghaidh
'Rinn an roghainn a b' fhearra dhiubh;
Oir tha caraid math cùil ac'
A rinn taobh ris na dh' earb ris,
'S a' chuid nach d' imich do 'n Fhrainc leis,
Fhuair iad *pension* 'n uair dh' fhalbh e.

Cha robh oifigeach Gàidhealach,
Eadar seàirdsean is còirneil,
Nach do chaill a *chomission*
'N uair chaidh 'm briseadh le fòirneart;
A' mheud 's a fhuair sibh an uiridh,
Ged bu diombuan r' a òl e,
Bheir sibh 'm bliadhn' air ath-philleadh
Air son uinneagan leòsain.

Cha robh bhliadhna na taic so
Neach a sheasadh mar sgoilear,
Gun *chomission* Righ Breatainn,
Gu bhi 'n a chaiptein air onoir;
Chaidh na ficheadan as diubh
Nach do leasaich sud dolar,
Ach an sgiùrsaigeadh dhachaidh
Mar chù a dh' easbhuidh a choilear.

Ach ma dh' aontaich sibh rìreadh
Ri bhur sìor dhol am mugha,
Ged a bha sibh cho rìoghail,
Chaidh bhur cìsean am mughad;

our own native clothing?
It's my thought on the ban
against short-hose and tartan
there's a friend of Prince Charles
in the Councils of England.

Have a care now, King George!
Making sport of your faithful
do you bring out new acts
to redouble their bindings?
Since they're lads of no birth
better crush them than save them:
they'll be fewer to serve you
in another such rising.

If both friends and foes
get the same fate in Scotland,
those who rose in revolt
took the better of choices:
for a good friend's been left here
that sides with supporters:
for those not in France
got a dole on his leaving.   (Prince Charles)

Not one Highland rating
from sergeant to colonel
but lost his commission
with unjust dismissal.
And what you got last year,
that vanished in drinking,
you shall gather next year
with the taxing of windows.

But just a year back
one who claimed to be scholar
sans the British King's warrant
was no captain of honour;
whole scores were disbanded
without a brass farthing
and whipped to their dwellings
like dogs lacking collars.

If you truly persist
who was formerly royal
in your present declining,
while your taxes grow greater:

S math an airidh gu 'm faicteadh
Dream cho tais ribh a' cumha
Bhi tilgeadh dhibh bhur cuid bhreacan
'S a' gabhail chasagan dubha.

Och, mo thruaighe sin Albainn!
'S tur a dhearbh sibh bhur reuson;
Gur i 'n rainn bh' ann bhur n-inntinn
'N rud a mhill air gach gleus sibh;
Leugh an gòbharmad sannt
Anns gach neach a theanndaidh ris féin dhibh,
'S thug iad baoight do bhur gionaich,
Gu 'r cur fo mhionach a chéile.

Ghlac na Sasunnaich fàth oirbh
Gus bhur fàgail na 's laige,
Chum 's nach bithteadh 'g ur cunntadh
'N ur luchd-còmh-strì na b' fhaide;
Ach 'n uair a bhios sibh a dh' easbhuidh
Bhur n-airm, 's bhur n-acfhuinnean sraide,
Gheobh sibh sèarsaigeadh mionaich,
Is bidh bhur peanas na 's graide.

Tha mi 'faicinn bhur truaighe,
Mar ni nach cualas a shamhuil;
A' chuid a 's feàrr de bhur seabh'gan,
Bhi air slabhruidh aig clamhan;
Ach ma tha sibh 'n ar leòmhann,
Pillibh 'n dòghruinn-s' 'n a teamhair,
'S deanaibh 'n deudach a thrusadh,
Mu's téid ur busan a cheangal.

'N uair thig bagradh an nàmhaid
Gus an àit anns do phill e,
'S ann bu mhath leam, a chàirdean,
Sibh bhi 'n àireamh na buidhne
D' am biodh spiorad cho Gàidhealach
'S gu 'm biodh an sàr ud 'n an cuimhne,
Gus bhur pilleadh 's an amhainn,
Oir tha i raimhibh na 's doimhne.

Nis, a Thèarlaich òig Stiubhaird,
Riut tha dùil aig gach fine,
Chaidh a chothachadh crùin dhuit,

rightly they should be seen
who cry meekly before you
abandoning plaids
to take black coats upon them.

O alas for you, Scotland
how your reason is proven
that the choice of your thinking
on each count has destroyed you:
For the Government saw
greed in all their supporters
and dangled a bait
to set you to brawling.

Now the English have grabbed
means to leave you in weakness,
so no longer they'll count you
a cause of contention;
And when you are lacking
marching order and weapons
you'll be thoroughly searched
for more sudden reprisal.

I watch your affliction
a thing beyond bearing,
the best of your hawks[1]
are now fettered to buzzards;
but act now as lions
that strain at the tether,
and bare your teeth now
before muzzles conceal them.

When the threat of your foes
comes back where it turned from
then my friends I would like
you to join with that band
in a spirit so Highland
they'll never forget it,
till you turn at the river
that runs deep before you.

Now young Charlie Stuart
you give hope to each clan
that battled to crown you

1. The Gaelic for hawk, 'seabhag', is also used as a synonym for a chieftain.

'S a leig an dùthaich 'n a teine;
Tha mar nathraichean falaicht',
A chaill an earradh an uiridh,
Ach tha 'g ath-ghleusadh an gathan
Gu éirigh latha do thighinn.

'S iomadh neach a tha guidheadh
Ri do thighinn, a Thèarlaich,
Gus an éireadh na cuinghean
Dhe na bhuidheann tha 'n éiginn;
A tha 'cantuinn 'n an cridhe,
Ged robh an teanga 'g a bhreugadh,
'Làn do bheatha gu t' fhaicinn,
A dh' ionnsuidh Bhreatainn is Eirinn.'

'S iomadh òganach aimsicht'
Tha 's an àm so 'n a chadal,
Eadar bràighe Srath-Chluanaidh
Agus bruachan Loch-Abair
Rachadh 'n cùisibh mhic t' athar,
'S a chrùn, 's a chaithir r' an tagradh,
'S a dh' ath-philleadh na ceathairn
A dhìoladh latha Chul-odair.

Ach a chàirdean na cùirte,
Nach 'eil a' chùis a' cur feirg oirbh;
No 'n do dh' fhosgail bhur sùilean
Gus a' chùis a bhi searbh dhuibh;
Bidh bhur duais mar a' ghobhair
A théid a bhleoghainn gu tarbhach,
'S a bhith'r a' fuadach 's an fhoghair,
Is ruaig nan gadhar r' a h-earball.

Ma 's e 'm peacach a 's mugha
'S còir a chumhachd a chlaoidheadh:
Nach e Seumas an seachdamh
Dhearbh bhi seasmhach 'n a inntinn?
C' uim' an dìteadh sibh 'n onoir,
Na bhiodh sibh moladh na daoidheachd?
'S gur h-e dhlùitheachd d' a chreidimh
A thug do choigrich an rìoghachd.

set flame in the land;
who lost weapons last year
are like adders from hiding
but their venom gets stronger
to rise at your coming

There's many that pray now,
Prince Charles for your coming
that the yoke may be raised
from the clans in their hardship;
who will say in their hearts
though their tongues may be lying,
'How welcome you are
back to Britain and Ireland.'

Now there's many a young blade
that meantime lies sleeping,
between Strath-Cluny's braes
and the banks of Lochaber
who would take up your cause
for the crown and the throne,
would remuster the ranks
in revenge for Culloden.

But, you friends of the court
does it not stir your anger?
Do you open your eyes
to the gall you've been given?
Recompense like the goat
that was milked while it lasted
and chased in the autumn
with hounds at her backside.

If the sinner that's worse
deserves toppling from power
was it not James the Seventh
who proved steadfast in mind?
Would you now condemn honour
give praise to perversity?
When faith to his creed
gave his crown to the strangers?[1]

---

1. James VII, Charles II's brother, was the last of the Stuart kings, followed by William and Mary who had no children, and then the German-speaking George I of Hanover. Rob Donn's point is to claim loyalty to the original royal line.

Fhuair sinn Rìgh à Hanòbhar:
Sparradh oirnne le h-achd e;
Tha againn Prionnsa 'n a aghaidh,
Is neart an lagha 'g a bhacadh:
O Bhith tha h-urad 'n ad bhritheamh,
Gun chron 's an dithis nach fac thu, –
Mur h-e a th' ann, cuir air adhairt
An t-aon a 's lugha 'm bi 'pheacadh.

A King out of Hanover
forced by an Act on us:
set against him our Prince
by the power of law banned.
Divine judge set above us,
you have found neither blameless –
since it's so, give preferment
to him who's less sinning.

trans. William Neill

Donnchadh Bàn Mac an t-Saoir/ Duncan Ban Macintyre (1724–1812)

Born and raised in Glen Orchy, Duncan Bàn's clan allegience to the Campbells put him on the government side during the '45. After Culloden (he wasn't at the battle), the poet worked for some twenty years as a gamekeeper for the Earl of Breadalbane, and then the Duke of Argyll. His professional, loving knowledge of the Highland landscape and his expertise in deer-hunting inform every detail of poems such as 'Song to Misty Corrie' and the famous 'Praise of Ben Dorain', whose elaborate form echoes the structure of pibroch. Macintyre's work is colloquial and overtly musical – often set to tunes to be sung. A later poem, 'Song to the Foxes', praises them for

Oran do 'n Tàillear

(an éirig òrain a rinn esan an adhbhar a charaid.)

A Dhòmhnaill Bhain Mhic O Neachdain
Tha 'n droch nàdur ad phearsain;
Cha ghnàthaich thu 'n ceartas
Gus am bàsaich thu 'n pheacadh;
'S mairg àit anns 'n a thachair
Am ball-sampaill gun chneasdachd,
    A rinn gràineil an sgaiteachd ud òirnn,
    A rinn gràineil an sgaiteachd ud òirnn.

Fhir a thòisich ri ealaidh,
Bha thu gòrach ad bharail,
'Ga seòladh am charaibh,
'S gun mi t' fheòraich no t' fharraid;
Chuir thu sgleò dhìot is fanaid:
Co dhiùbh 's deòin leat no 's aindeoin,
    Tha mi 'n dòchas gum faigh thu do leòr,
    Tha mi 'n dòchas gum faigh thu do leòr.

killing the sheep whose arrival cost him his job and indeed precipitated the Clearances. The poet spent the latter part of his long life in Edinburgh where he joined the City Guard, Fergusson's 'black banditti', and kept a whisky shop with his wife Màiri. Although he was unlettered, he could recite his own and large amounts of other Gaelic verse as well. A subscription volume of his poems was published in 1768 and two more followed. He went on poetry tours in his old age and served for a while with the Breadalbane Fencibles. He is buried in Greyfriar's Kirkyard, Edinburgh.

Song to the Tailor[1]

(in return for a song he made in the interests of his friend.)

Fair haired Donald MacNaughton
ill-nature's your fashion;
no habit of justice
till you die in your sins;
there's no luck where he goes
that graceless example,
   that made yon ugly flyting upon us,
   that made yon ugly flyting upon us.

You who started on satire,
how daft your ambition,
to point it towards me,
neither asked for nor seeking;
you spewed falsehood and mocking:
and like it or lump it,
   I'm in hopes that you'll swallow your share,
   I'm in hopes that you'll swallow your share.

---

1 The subject of this relentless flyting was a tailor called Donald MacNaughton who paid a high price for mocking the bard in a lampoon of his own (compare 'the Flyting of Dunbar and Kennedie' from the 1500s).

Dhomh-sa b' aithne do bheusan:
Tha thu aineolach beumnach,
Is do theanga mar reusar
Le tainead 's le géiread;
Thug thu deannal domh fhéin dith;
O 's ann agad tha 'n eucoir,
    Cuim' nach pàighinn thu 'n éirig do sgeòil?
    Cuim' nach pàighinn thu 'n éirig do sgeòil?

'S tu chraobh ghrodlaich air crìonadh,
Làn mosgain is fhìneag,
A dh' fhàs croganach ìosal
Goirid crotach neo-dhìreach;
Stoc thu togairt do 'n ghrìosaich,
A thoill do losgadh mar ìobairt,
    Leig thu 'n soisgeul air diochuimhn gu mór,
    Leig thu 'n soisgeul air diochuimhn gu mór.

Bu bheag an diùbhail e thachairt
An latha thùr thu na facail,
Dà phunnd agus cairteal
A dh' fhùdar cruaidh sgairteil
A bhith ad bhroinn air a chalcadh,
'S bhith 'gad sgàineadh le maitse,
    Gus am fàsadh tu 'd ablach gun deò,
    Gus am fàsadh tu 'd ablach gun deò.

'S blianach righinn gun fheum thu;
Ged a bhitheadh tu 'm féithe,
Coin is fithich ad theumadh,
Cha bhiodh an dìol béidh ac'.
'S tric thu teann air na h-éibhlean,
Bhreac do shuimeir gu t' éislich,
    Blàth an tein' air do shléisdibh gu mór,
    Blàth an tein' air do shléisdibh gu mór.

O nach tàillear as fhiù thu,
Chuir càch as a' chùirt thu;
Bidh tu ghnàth anns na cùiltean
A' càradh nan lùireach;
Bu tu àsainn nan clùdan,
'S tric a shuidh thu 'san smùraich
    'N uair a bhithinn-s' air cùl fir nan cròc,
    'N uair a bhithinn-s' air cùl fir nan cròc.

Well I know of your manners:
you're an ignorant griper,
tongue sharp as a razor
both narrow and mean;
and I got a full dose of your
unjust accusing,
 you deserve to be paid for your tales,
 you deserve to be paid for your tales.

Withered dry-rotten trunk,
mouldy, ridden with bugs,
all stunted and gnarled
scrunty, humpy and small;
a mere stob for the ashes,   stump
to be burned for an offering,
 since the gospel's long gone from your ken,
 since the gospel's long gone from your ken.

Small loss it would be
on that day you set words,
two pound and a quarter
of gunpowder hard
to be rammed in your guts,
with a fuse for your splitting,
 till you shrunk to a carrion corpse,
 till you shrunk to a carrion corpse.

You tough useless gristle you;
stuck in a boghole, you,
curs and crows tearing you,
wouldn't get a meal from you.
Stuck close to the embers,
to the crupper red-mottled,
 thighs all speckled with fireside-tartan,
 thighs all speckled with fireside-tartan.

Just a jag-the-flea tailor,
the rest wouldn't own you;
always skulking in corners
at your stitching of rags;
a mere cobbler of patches,
with feet in the ashes
 and me stalking the high-antlered stag,
 and me stalking the high-antlered stag.

'S e do choltas r' a ìnnseadh,
Fear sopcheannach grìmeach,
Gun bhonaid gun phìorbhuic,
Gun bhad-mullaich gun chìrean,
Lom uil' air a spìonadh;
Càrr gu t' uilinn a sìos ort,
    Stràc na dunach de 'n sgrìobaich mu d' cheòs,
    Stràc na dunach de 'n sgrìobaich mu d' cheòs.

'S iomadh àit anns 'n a thachair
An tàillear Mac Neachdain
Eadar Albainn is Sasainn,
Bailtean margaidh is machair;
'S tric a shealg thu air praisich:
O nach d' fhalbh thu le clapa,
    Chaoidh cha mharbh e duin' aca de 'n t-slògh,
    Chaoidh cha mharbh e duin' aca de 'n t-slògh.

'S duine dona gun mhios thu
Dh' fhàs gun onoir gun ghliocas;
Fear gun chomas gun bhriosgadh,
Chaill do spionnadh 's do mhisneach
Leis na rinn thu de 'n bhidseachd;
Bu tu 'n slaidhtire misgeach,
    'S cian on thoill thu do chuipeadh mu 'n òl,
    'S cian on thoill thu do chuipeadh mu 'n òl.

'S iomadh ceapaire ròmais
Rinn thu ghlacadh ad chrògan,
Is bhith 'ga stailceadh le t' òrdaig
Ann ad chabdheudach sgòrach;
'S reamhar farsaing do sgòrnan,
Brù mar chuilean an òtraich;
    Fhuair thu urram nan geòcach ri d' bheò,
    Fhuair thu urram nan geòcach ri d' bheò.

Bidh na mnathan ag ràite,
'N uair a rachadh tu 'n àirigh,
Gun tolladh tu 'n t-àros
Anns am bitheadh an càise;
'N uair a dh' itheadh tu pàirt deth,
'S a bhiodh tu air tràsgadh,
    Anns a' mhuidhe gun spàrr thu do chròg,
    Anns a' mhuidhe gun spàrr thu do chròg.

Here's your likeness again,
a wisp-headed scowler,
without hat or wig,
without topknot or crest,
you're bare-plucked and baldy;
with mange at your elbows,
    and the scratch-marks of itch round your arse,
    and the scratch-marks of itch round your arse.

There is many a place
found you, tailor MacNaughton
In Scotland and England,
on market and moor;
always hunting of whores;
and since clap hasn't killed you,
    it can never kill anyone else,
    it can never kill anyone else.

You're a low-rated fellow
lacking honour and wisdom;
neither able nor lively;
gone your force and your guts
with continual whoring;
and villainous boozing,
    well you merit a flogging for drink,
    well you merit a flogging for drink.

Many blue-moulded chunks
you have clasped in your claws,
and pushed down with a thumb
through your snaggled buck teeth;
with a belly and maw,
like a pup on a midden;
    you're the prince of all gluttons alive,
    you're the prince of all gluttons alive.

The women report,
when you go to the shieling
you make for the cupboard
in search of the cheese;
when you'd eaten your share,
and the drouth came upon you,   thirst
    you'd stick a paw into the crock,
    you'd stick a paw into the crock.

'S tu 'n tollaran cnàimhteach:
Ge bu ghionach do mhàileid,
Tha do mhionach air t' fhàgail
Gun chrioman deth làthair;
Cochull glogach mu t' àrainn,
Tha do sgamhan is t' àinean
    Làn galair is fàslaich is chòs,
    Làn galair is fàslaich is chòs.

Beul do chléibh air a thachdadh,
Air séideadh 's air brachadh,
'S e gu h-éidigh air malcadh,
'S mór fheum air a chartadh;
Gach aon eucail ad phearsain,
Caitheamh, éitich is casdaich,
    Gus an d' éirich do chraiceann o t' fheòil,
    Gus an d' éirich do chraiceann o t' fheòil.

Tha do chreuchdan 's do chuislean
Làn eucail is trusdair,
'S thu feumach air furtachd;
Tha 'n déideadh ad phluicean,
'S tu 'd éigin le clupaid;
T' anail bhreun gu trom murtaidh,
    'S mairg a dh' fheuchadh dhìot mochthrath do thòchd,
    'S mairg a dh' fheuchadh dhìot mochthrath do thòchd.

Do dheud sgròbbhearnach cabach
A bheil na sgòirfhiaclan glasa,
Mosgain còsacha sgealpach,
Lùbte grannda cam feacta,
A null 's a nall air an tarsainn,
Cuid diubh caillt' air dol asad,
    'S na bheil ann diubh air spagadh do bheòil,
    'S na bheil ann diubh air spagadh do bheòil.

Bidh na ronnan gu silteach
'Nan tonnaibh gorm ruithteach,
A' gabhail toinneamh o d' liopan
Thar cromadh do smige;
'S dorcha doilleir do chlisneach,
Cho dubh ris a' phice;
    Uchd na curra, ceann circ' ort, gob geòidh,
    Uchd na curra, ceann circ' ort, gob geòidh.

You're a crack gormandiser:
though greedy your wallet,
your guts hasn't left you
a crumb to put in it;
fat encases your kidneys,
your lungs and your liver
　　full of horrors and hollows and holes,
　　full of horrors and hollows and holes.

There's a wheeze in your chest,
always puffing and bubbling,
that's like putrefaction,
in great need of cleansing;
every ill's in your frame,
waste, consumption and cough,
　　so your hide drops away from your meat,
　　so your hide drops away from your meat.

All your sores and your veins
full of matter and filth,
you're in need of a cure;
there's an ache in your jaws,
and your throat gives you hell;
your foul breath is sheer murder,
　　God help those who sniff you at morning,
　　God help those who sniff you at morning.

Notch and gap in your teeth
and green buck teeth in front,
Holed, rotten and split,
bent, ugly and crooked,
some crossed here and there,
some so bad they dropped out,
　　those left there have twisted your mouth,
　　those left there have twisted your mouth.

The slavers are flowing
in running green wavelets,
lacing down from your lips
past the curve of your chin;
grimly dark is your frame,
and all blackened like pitch;
　　pigeon-chested, hen-headed, goose beaked,
　　pigeon-chested, hen-headed, goose beaked.

Do mhaol chnuacach air faileadh,
Gun chluasan gun fhaillean;
Tha thu uainealach tana,
Cho cruaidh ris an darach,
'S tu gun suanach gun anart;
'S adhbhar truais thu ri d' ghearan,
    'S gur fuair' thu na gailleann an reòt',
    'S gur fuair' thu na gailleann an reòt'.

Tha ceann binneach 'na stùic ort,
Geocach lethcheannach giùgach;
Aodann brucanach gnùgach,
Sròn phlucach na mùire;
Tha cruit air do chùlaibh,
'S móran lurcaich ad ghlùinibh;
    Dà chois chama chaol chrùbach, gun treòir,
    Dà chois chama chaol chrùbach, gun treòir.

Chan 'eil uiread nan sàiltean
Aig a' phliutaire spàgach,
Nach 'eil cuspach is gàgach,
Tha thu 'd chrioplach 's ad chràigeach:
'S lìonmhor tubaist an tàilleir,
Dh' fhàg an saoghal 'na thràill e,
    'S mairg a shaothraich air t' àrach 's tu òg,
    'S mairg a shaothraich air t' àrach 's tu òg.

Mas ann de shliochd Adhamh thu,
Cha choslach ri càch thu
Aig olcas 's a dh' fhàs thu,
O thoiseach do làithean;
Cha tig cobhair gu bràth ort,
Gus am foghainn am bàs duit,
    'S do chorp odhar a chàradh fo 'n fhòid,
    'S do chorp odhar a chàradh fo 'n fhòid.

from **Moladh Beinn Dóbhrain**
Air fonn Pìobaireachd[1]

1. Urlar

An t-urram thar gach beinn
Aig Beinn Dóbhrain;
De na chunnaic mi fo 'n ghréin,
'S i bu bhòidhche leam:

1. The poem follows the developmental pattern of pibroch, by establishing a basic theme, the *urlar* or 'ground', and then
reworking it with variations, until the tune comes to a climax with the grand finale of the *crunluath* – the most elaborate
variation yet. Sections 1, 2, 4 and 8 (the conclusion) are offered here.

Your bumpy head moulting,
ears gone with no roots;
you are peaky and skinny,
and stiff as an oak,
without topcoat or shirt;
cause of pity your plaint,
    and you're colder than frost in a gale,
    and you're colder than frost in a gale.

Head that peaks to a point,
wrynecked, lolling and fawning;
face spotted and surly,
nose pimply with scurvy;
a hump on your back,
and a lameness of knee-joints;
    and two weak bandy legs with a limp,
    and two weak bandy legs with a limp.

Not the space of his heels
has this tottering flunkey,
free from chilblains and chaps
you're a splay-footed cripple:
many ills has the tailor,
that the world made its lackey,
    what a trial to the people who raised you,
    what a trial to the people who raised you.

If Adam's clan bred you,
you're not like the others
in ill form you grew up
from your earliest days;
but you'll never get help,
till death shall subdue you,
    and your dun corpse is laid below turf,
    and your dun corpse is laid below turf.

trans. William Neill

Praise of Ben Dorain
To the tune of Pibroch

1.   *Theme*
Honour past all bens
to Ben Dorain.
Of all beneath the sun
I adore her.

Munadh fada réidh,
Cuilidh 'm faighte féidh,
Soilleireachd an t-sléibh
Bha mi sònrachadh;

Doireachan nan geug,
Coill' anns am bi feur,
'S foinneasach an spréidh
Bhios a chòmhnaidh ann;

Greadhain bu gheal céir,
Faghaid air an déidh,
'S laghach leam an sreud
A bha sròineiseach.

'S aigeannach fear eutrom
Gun mhórchuis,
Theid fasanda 'na éideadh
Neo-spòrsail:

Tha mhanntal uime féin,
Caithtiche nach tréig,
Bratach dhearg mar chéir
Bhios mar chòmhdach air.

'S culaidh g' a chur eug –
Duine dhèanadh teuchd,
Gunna bu mhath gleus
An glaic òganaich;

Spor anns am biodh bearn,
Tarrann air a ceann,
Snap a bhuaileadh teann
Ris na h-òrdaibh i;

Ochdshlisneach gun fheall,
Stoc de 'n fhiodh gun mheang,
Lotadh an damh seang
Is a leònadh e;
'S fear a bhiodh mar cheàird
Riutha sònraichte,
Dh' fhóghnadh dhaibh gun taing
Le chuid seòlainean;

Gheibhte siud ri am,
Pàdraig anns a' ghleann,

Mountain ranges clear,
storehouse of the deer,
the radiance of the moor
I've observed there.

Leafy branchy groves,
woods where the grass grows,
inquisitive the does
that are roaming there.

Herds with white rumps race –
hunters in the chase.
O I love the grace
of these noble ones.

Spirited and delicate
and shy,
in fashionable coat
he goes by

in mantle well arrayed,
suit that will not fade,
dress of waxen-red
that he's wearing now.

Weapon that brings death,
bullet that stops breath,
expert studied youth
with his rifle there.

Flint that's notched and true,
on its head a screw,
a cock that would strike to
the hammers, it.

Eight sided, without flaw,
gun-stock would lay low
the great stag in the flow
of his own blood there.
One whose craft was dear –
Mozart of them –
would kill them with a pure
trick and stratagem.

One would find such men –
Patrick in the glen –

Gillean is coin sheang,
'S e toirt òrdugh dhaibh;

Peileirean 'nan deann,
Teine 'gan cur ann;
Eilid nam beann ard'
Théid a leònadh leo.

2.   *Siubhal*
'S i 'n eilid bheag bhinneach
Bu ghuiniche sraonadh,
Le cuinnean geur biorach
A' sireadh na gaoithe:
Gasganach speireach,
Feadh chreachainn na beinne,

Le eagal roimh theine
Cha teirinn i h-aonach;
Ged théid i 'na cabhaig,
Cha ghearain i maothan:

Bha sìnnsireachd fallain;
'N uair shìneadh i h-anail,
'S toil-inntinn leam tannasg
Dh' a langan a chluinntinn,
'S i 'g iarraidh a leannain
'N am daraidh le coibhneas.

'S e damh a' chinn allaidh
Bu ghealcheireach feaman,
Gu cabarach ceannard,
A b' fharamach raoiceadh;
'S e chòmhnaidh 'm Beinn Dóbhrain,
'S e eòlach m' a fraoinibh.

'S ann am Beinn Dóbhrain,
Bu mhór dhomh r' a innseadh
A liuthad damh ceannard
Tha fantainn 'san fhrìth ud;

Eilid chaol-eangach,
'S a laoighean 'ga leantainn,
Le 'n gasgana geala,
Ri bealach a' dìreadh,
Ri fraigh Choire Chruiteir,
A' chuideachda phìceach.

boys and dogs at one,
and he'd order them.

Bullets left and right,
fires creating light,
the hind on mountain height
gets its wound from them.

2.   *Variation*
The hind that's sharp-headed
is fierce in its speeding:
how delicate, rapid,
its nostrils, wind-reading!
Light-hooved and quick limbèd,
she runs on the summit,

from that uppermost limit
no gun will remove her.
You'll not see her winded,
that elegant mover.

Her forebears were healthy.
When she stopped to take breath then,
how I loved the pure wraith-like
sound of her calling,
she seeking her sweetheart
in the lust of the morning.

It's the stag, the proud roarer,
white-rumped and ferocious,
branch-antlered and noble,
would walk in the shaded
retreats of Ben Dorain,
so haughtily-headed.

O they are in Ben Dorain,
so numerous, various,
the stags that go roaring
so tall and imperious.

Hind, nimble and slender,
with her calves strung behind her
lightly ascending
the cool mountain passes
through Harper's Dell winding
on their elegant courses.

'N uair a shìneas i h-eangan
'S a théid i 'na deannaibh,
Cha saltradh air thalamh
Ach barra nan ìngnean:
Có b' urrainn g' a leantainn
A dh' fhearaibh na rìoghachd?

'S arraideach faramach
Carach air grìne,
A' chòisridh nach fhanadh
Gnè smal air an inntinn;

Ach caochlaideach curaideach
Caolchasach ullamh,
An aois cha chuir truim' orra,
Mulad no mìghean.

'S e shlànaich an culaidh,
Feòil mhàis agus mhuineil,
Bhith tàmhachd am bunailt
An cuilidh na frìthe;

Le àilgheas a' fuireach
Air fàsach 'nan grunnaibh;
'S i 'n àsainn a' mhuime
Tha cumail na cìche

Ris na laoigh bhreaca bhallach
Nach meathlaich na sianta,
Le 'n cridheacha meara
Le bainne na cìoba;

Gnoiseanach eangach,
Le 'n girteaga geala,
Le 'n corpanna glana
Le fallaineachd fìoruisg;
Le faram gun ghearan
Feadh ghleannan na mìltich.

Ged thigeadh an sneachda
Chan iarradh iad aitreabh,
'S e lag a' Choir' Altram
Bhios aca g' an dìdean;

Feadh stacan is bhacan
Is ghlacaga dìomhair,
Le 'n leapaichean fasgach
An taic Ais an t-Sìthein.

Accelerant, speedy,
when she moves her slim body
earth knows nought of this lady
but the tips of her nails.
Even light would be tardy
to the flash of her pulse.

Dynamic, erratic,
by greenery spinning,
this troupe never static,
their minds free from sinning.

Coquettes of the body,
slim-leggèd and ready,
no age makes them tardy,
no grief nor disease.

Their coats get their shimmer –
fat flesh of their glamour –
from their local rich summer
in the store of the moor.

With pleasure abiding
in the pasture providing
 – like milk for our children –
fresh grass from the heath.

Calves speckled and spotted,
unchilled by the showers,
are nursed by the rooted
gay, various grass.

Brindled, bright-hoovèd,
white-belted and vivid
as cinders quick-moving,
with the health of spring waters,
uncomplaining, belovèd –
these elegant daughters!

Though the snow should bewilder
they'll be seeking no shelter
except in the Corrie
other dwelling disdaining.

Among banks and steep columns
and hollows mysterious
they'd bed by the solemn
Haunt of the Fairies.

4.   *Siubhal*
A' bheinn luiseanach fhailleanach
Mheallanach lìontach,
Gun choimeas dh' a fallaing
Air thalamh na Crìosdachd:

'S ro-neònach tha mise,
Le bòidhchead a sliosa,
Nach 'eil còir aic' an ciste
Air tiotal na rìoghachd;

'S i air dùbladh le gibhtibh,
'S air lùisreadh le miosaibh
Nach 'eil bitheant' a' bristeadh
Air phriseanaibh tìre.

Làn-trusgan gun deireas,
Le usgraichean coille,
Bàrr-guc air gach doire,
Gun choir' ort r' a ìnnseadh;

Far an uchdardach coileach,
Le shriutaichibh loinneil,
'S eoin bhuchallach bheag' eile
Le 'n ceileiribh lìonmhor.

'S am buicean beag sgiolta
Bu sgiobalt' air grìne,
Gun sgiorradh gun tubaist
Gun tuisleadh gun dìobradh;

Crodhanach biorach,
Feadh coire 'ga shireadh,
Feadh fraoich agus firich,
Air mhireadh 'ga dhìreadh;
Feadh rainich is barraich
Gum b' arraideach inntinn;

Ann an ìosal gach feadain,
'S air àirde gach creagain,
Gu mireanach beiceasach
Easgannach sìnteach.

'N uair a théid e 'na bhoile
Le clisge 'sa' choille,
'S e ruith feadh gach doire,

4.   *Theme*

Luxuriant mountain
sprouting and knolled
more healthy and cloudless
than all hills in the world.

How long my obsession!
My song and my passion!
She's the first in the nation
for grace and for beauty.

Her gifts are so many,
her fruits are so bonny,
and rarer than any
her bushes and leafage

in flawless green raiment
as bright as the diamond
your blooms in agreement
like elegant music.

The cock with his vital
and rapid recital,
colourful, brutal,
among the small birds.

The buck small and nimble
quick on the green
neat as a thimble –
a clever machine!

Bright-hooved in the weather,
as light as a feather,
among moorland and heather
exploring the corrie
he saunters forever
through bracken and story

along by each river
on the height of each hillock
playful and vivid
eel-like, elusive.

When he's startled to motion
he's as swift as your vision
with speed and precision

Air dheireadh cha bhì e;
Leis an eangaig bu chaoile
'S e b' aotruime sìnteag,

Mu chnocanaibh donna,
Le ruith dara-tomain,
'S e togairt an coinneamh
Bean-chomuinn os n-ìosal.

Tha mhaoisleach bheag bhrangach
'Sa' ghleannan a chòmhnaidh
'S i fuireach 'san fhireach
Le minneanan òga:
Cluas bhiorach gu claisteachd,
Sùil chorrach gu faicinn,
'S i earbsach 'na casaibh
Chur seachad na mòintich.

Ged thig Caoilte 's Cù Chulainn,
'S gach duine de 'n t-seòrs' ud,
Na tha dhaoine 's a dh' eachaibh
Air fasdadh Rìgh Deòrsa,

Nan tèarnadh a craiceann
O luaidhe 's o lasair
Cha chual' is chan fhac' i
Na ghlacadh r' a beò i;
'S i gradcharach fadchasach
Aigeannach neònach

Gealcheireach gasganach,
Gealtach roimh mhadadh,
Air chaisead na leacainn
Cha saltradh i còmhnard;
'S i noigeanach gnoigeasach
Gogcheannach sòrnach,

Biorshuileach sgurshuileach
Frionasach furachair,
A' fuireach 'sa' mhunadh
An do thuinich a seòrsa.

8.   *An Crunluath*
Tha 'n eilid anns a' ghleannan seo,
'S chan amadan gun eòlas
A leanadh i mur b' aithne dha
Tighinn farasda 'na còmhdhail:

he speeds through each forest
without seeming exertion
he's nearest, then furthest!

In the autumn-hued landscape
he skips in his gallop
each second brown hillock
as he's greeting his sweetheart.

His small doe is dwelling
with the fawns in a corrie:
sullen and snarling
she guards them with fury:
sharp ear cocked for hearing,
quick eye ever peering,
she relies on the veering
quick tricks of her motion.

Though Caoilt and Cuchulain
are expert and nimble
and every battalion
King George can assemble

if the flash and the bullet
would leave her unsullied
no man on this planet
would catch her or find her:
just like the minute
and brilliant cinder.

White-tailed and lightning-like
though hunting dogs can frighten her –
steep though the height to her
you'll not see her blunder.
Haughty and spritely she's
a head-tossing wonder!

Sharp-eyed, disdainful,
restless and wary,
her home is the corrie
along with her neighbours.

8.   *Finale*
When the hind is in this solitude
O ignorant the stalker
who (untrained, unpractised) would
seek to find or take her.

Gu faiteach bhith 'na h-earalas,
Tighinn am faigse dhi mun caraich i,
Gu faicilleach, glé earraigeach,
Mum fairich i 'ga còir e.

Feadh shloc is ghlac is chamhanan,
Is chlach a dhèanadh falach air,
Bhith beachdail air an talamh
'S air a' char a thig na neòil air;

'S an t-astar bhith 'ga tharraing air
Cho macanta 's a b' aithne dha,
Gun glacadh e dh' a h-aindeoin i
Le h-anabharra seòltachd;

Le tùr, gun ghainne baralach,
An t-sùil a chur gu danarra,
A' stiùradh na dubh-bannaiche,
'S a h-aire ri fear cròice.

Bhiodh rùdan air an tarraing
Leis an lùbt' an t-iarann-earra,
Bheireadh ionnsaigh nach biodh mearachdach
Do 'n fhear a bhiodh 'ga seòladh;

Spor ùr an déis a teannachadh,
Buill' ùird a' sgailceadh daingean ris,
Cha diùlt an t-srad 'n uair bheanas i
Do 'n deannaig a bha neònach.

'S e 'm fùdar tioram teannabaich
Air chùl an asgairt ghreannaich,
Chuireadh smùid ri acainn mheallanaich
A baraille Nic Còiseim.

'S i 'n teachdaire bha dealasach,
Nach mealladh e 'na dhòchas,
'N uair lasadh e mar dhealanach
Gu feareigin a leònadh;

Gu silteach leis na peileirean
Bhiodh luchd nan luirgnean speireacha,
'S nam bus bu tirme bheileanaich,
Gun mheilliche, gun tòicean.

'S e camp na Craige Seiliche
Bha ceannsalach 'nan ceithreamhnaibh;
Le aingealtas cha teirinn iad
Gu eirthir as an eòlas,

Cautiously and stealthily
prudently and perfectly
wisely, with such delicacy –
else she will evade him!

Every pit and shallow he
must deploy to follow her
every stone and hollow and
cloud-shade to aid him.

Gently he will creep and edge
using every subterfuge
till he traps her in her lodge
by excelling cunning

with judgement and carefulness
he'll bring his gun to bear on her
she's fixed in that gold radiance
in her aloof hauteur.

His finger on the trigger
he watches her fixed figure –
exactitude and rigour
are what his training's taught him.

A gun flint – and he's tightened it –
hammers that would strike to it –
the powder always will ignite
for the experienced stalker.

The powder dry and virulent
behind the rags of tow or lint
would soon create a violent
hailstone of small fire.

O what more zealous messenger?
What Mercury more fatal?
How lightning-like this passenger
that pierces to the vital!

Bleeding from that armament
the deer of finest lineament
whose bodies are an ornament
to the health-giving moorland.

The army of the Willow Crag
(so arrogant in monologue)
will not for man or gun or dog
be driven from their homeland.

Mur ceannsaichear iad deireasach
Ri am an crìche deireannaich,
An tabhannaich le deifir
A bhith deileann air an tòrach;

Gun channtaireachd, gun cheilearachd,
Ach dranndail chon a' deileis rith',
A ceann a chur gu peirealais,
Aig eilid Beinne Dóbhrain.

'S O! b' ionmhainn le fir cheanalta
Nach b' aineolach mu spòrsa,
Bhith timcheall air na bealaichibh
Le fearalachd na h-òige;

Far am bi na féidh gu faramach,
'S na fir 'nan déidh gu caithriseach,
Le gunna bu mhath barantas
Thoirt aingil 'n uair bu chòir dhi;

Le cuilean foirmeil togarrach,
'G am biodh a stiùir air bhogadan,
'S e miolairtich gu sodanach,
'S nach ob e dol 'nan còmhdhail.

'Na fhuirbidh làidir cosgarrach,
Ro-inntinneach neo-fhoisinneach,
Gu guineach sgiamhach gobeasgaidh
'San obair bh' aig a sheòrsa;

'S a fhrioghan cuilg a' togail air,
Gu mailgheach gruamach doicheallach,
'S a gheanachan cnuasaicht' fosgailte
Comh-bhogartaich r' an sgòrnan.

Gum b' arraideach a' charachd ud
'S bu chabhagach i 'n còmhnaidh,
'N uair shìneadh iad na h-eanganan
Le h-athghoirid na mòintich;

Na beanntaichean 's na bealaichean,
Gum freagradh iad mac-talla dhuit,
Le fuaim na gairme galanaich
Aig faram a' choin ròmaich,

'Gan tèarnadh as na mullaichibh
Gu linnichean nach grunnaich iad,
'S ann bhitheas iad feadh na tuinne
Anns an luinneinich 's iad leòinte;

Unless subdued and mastered there
by dogs that fill the pasture there
with the barks that bring disaster and
grief and death in chorus.

The music then diminishing
as the dogs close to finish her
– she frenzied 'mong these sinister
assassins of the morning.

A pleasure for professionals
ingenious in stalking
to be about the passes when
sport was for the taking.

When the deer were bellowing
and the men were following
and the light was yellow and
red in its explosion.

With dog that's quick, discriminate
– his tail alert and animate
tonguing, whining, dynamite
vigorous and joyful.

Assassin, fierce and serious,
courageous and imperious
single (and not various)
in the art that is his own.

His hackles rising, bristling,
sandy, shag-browed, vicious,
he quivers like a species
of animated Murder.

Erratic was the veering then
and rapid in its motion
when they would go sheering on
short cuts with exertion.

Tumultuous the baying and
echo of the crying as
the hairy-coated violent
dogs would show their paces.

Driving them from summits to
lakes that are unplumbable
bleeding dying swimming and
floundering in water.

'S na cuileanan gu fulasgach
'Gan cumail air na muinealaibh,
'S nach urrainn iad dol tuilleadh as,
Ach fuireach 's bhith gun deò annt'.

Is ged a thuirt mi beagan riu,
Mun ìnnsinn uil' an dleasdnas orr',
Chuireadh iad am bhreislich mi
Le deisimireachd chòmhraidh.

Oran nam Balgairean

Ho hù o hó na balgairean,
*   O 's ainmig iad r' am faotainn!*
Ho hù o hó na balgairean.

Mo bheannachd aig na balgairean,
    A chionn bhith sealg nan caorach.
    Ho hù o hó na balgairean, &c.

An iad na caoraich cheannriabhach
    Rinn aimhreit feadh an t-saoghail

Am fearann a chur fàs oirnn,
    'S am màl a chur an daoiread?

Chan 'eil àit aig tuathanach,
    Tha bhuannachd-san air claonadh;

Is éigin dhà bhith fàgail
    An àit anns an robh dhaoine.

Na bailtean is na h-àirighean
    Am faighte blàths is faoileachd,

Gun taighean ach na làraichean,
    Gun àiteach air na raointean.

Tha h-uile seòl a b' àbhaist
    Anns a' Ghàidhealtachd air caochladh,

Air cinntinn cho mì-nàdurra
    'Sna h-àitean a bha aoigheil.

Hounds hanging to their quarries while
they sway and toss and rock and kill –
their jaws will never let them feel
their haughty style again.

The little that I've sung of them
is not enough to tell of them
O you'd need a tongue for them
of a most complex kind.

trans. Iain Crichton Smith

Song to the Foxes[1]

Ho hù o hó the cunning dogs,
   Not often that we find them!
Ho hù o hó the cunning dogs.

My blessing on the foxes,
   for their hunting of the sheep.
   Ho hù o hó the cunning dogs, &c.

How could these sheep of brindled head
   set on the world's contention;

to make our land a wilderness
   and yet its rent increasing?

No farmer has a place here,
   the profit's ever shrinking;

No other course but exile
   from the homeland of his people.

The townships and the shielings
   where once dwelt warmth and kindness –

no houses but the tumbled stones,
   no ploughing of the meadows.

The customs that were followed,
   they have perished now in Gaeldom,

have come to be unnatural
   in hospitable places.

1. 'Balgairean/foxes' can mean 'cunning ones', as in 'cunning dogs' in English.

Chan 'eil loth no làir
  Bhiodh searrach làimh r' a taobh ann.

Chan 'eil aighean dàra
  Bhios ag àrach an cuid laogh ann.

Chan 'eil feum air gruagaichean,
  Tha h-uile buail' air sgaoileadh.

Chan fhaigh gille tuarasdal
  Ach buachaille nan caorach.

Dh' fhalbh na gobhair phrìseil;
  Bu rìgh a dh' òrdaich saor iad.

Earba bheag na dùslainn,
  Cha dùisgear i le blaodhan.

Chan 'eil fiadh air fuaran
  On chaill na h-uaislean gaol daibh.

Tha gach frìthfhear fuasgailte,
  Gun duais a chionn a shaoithreach.

Is diombach air an duine mi
  A nì na sionnaich aoireadh;

A chuireas cù g' an ruagadh
  No thilgeas luaidhe chaol orr'.

Guma slàn na cuileanan
  Tha fuireach ann an saobhaidh.

Nam faigheadh iad mo dhùrachd,
  Cha chùram dhaibh cion saoghail.

Bhiodh piseach air an òigridh,
  Is bhiodh beò gus am marbh' aois iad.

No filly's found or brood mare
   with foal at heel beside her.

There are no two-year heifers
   who will suckle their own calves now.

There is no need for milkmaids,
   when all milking-folds are scattered.

No lad can earn his keep there
   but the minder of the sheep-flocks.

The treasured goats are gone now;
   though a king gave them their freedom.[1]

The small doe of the greenwood
   will not be waked with calling.

No deer comes to the spring there
   now the gentry have lost liking.

They have turned off every stalker,
   without reward of labour.

I'm angered by the fellow
   who speaks ill of the foxes.

Who sets a hound to hunt them
   or scatters them with lead-shot.

May all the foxcubs prosper
   that live within an earth there.

Could they get my earnest wishes,
   they'd thrive there never fearing.

Young foxes would breed youngsters,
   and they'd live till old age killed them.

trans. William Neil

---

1. Legend has it that Robert the Bruce granted free pasture to goats in Strath Fillan, in gratitude for having found shelter there in a goat herd's hut.

James Macpherson (1736–1796)

Macpherson's own verse was overshadowed by his 'translations' of third-century Gaelic epic poetry, most notably the heroic tales about Fingal, as recounted by his bardic son Ossian. Macpherson did consult Gaelic scholars in the Highlands, but his version proposes Scotland rather than Ireland for the original, and owes as much to neo-classical English epic as to anything from the native canon. Nevertheless, 'Ossian' and his translator became famous throughout Europe as sophisticated readers responded to the romance of primitive nobility from 'l'Homère du Nord'. *Fingal: An Ancient Epic Poem* was published in 1761, and the controversy lasted until the next century.

from Fingal

Book I[1]

As rushes a stream of foam from the dark shady deep of Cromla; when the thunder is travelling above, and dark-brown night sits on half the hill. Through the breaches of the tempest look forth the dim faces of ghosts. So fierce, so vast, so terrible rushed on the sons of Erin. The chief like a whale of ocean, whom all his billows pursue, poured valour forth, as a stream, rolling his might along the shore. The sons of Lochlin heard the noise, as the sound of a winter-storm. Swaran struck his bossy shield: he called the son of Arno, 'What murmur rolls along the hill, like the gathering flies of the eve? The sons of Erin descend, or rustling winds roar in the distant wood! Such is the noise of Gormal, before the white tops of my waves arise. O son of Arno ascend the hill; view the dark face of the heath!'

He went. He, trembling, swift returned. His eyes rolled wildly round. His heart beat high against his side. His words were faltering, broken, slow. 'Arise, Son of ocean, arise, chief of the dark-brown shields! I see the dark, the mountain stream of battle! The deep-moving strength of the sons of Erin! The car, the car of war comes on, like the flame of death! the rapid car of Cuthullin, the noble son of Semo! It bends behind like a wave near a rock; like the sun-streaked mist of the heath. Its sides are embossed with stones, and sparkle like the sea round the boat of night. Of polished yew is its beam; its seat of the smoothest bone. The sides are replenished with spears; the bottom is the footstool of heroes! Before the right side of the car is seen the snorting

---

1. The action opens in Ireland. Swaran, king of Lochlin, has invaded Ulster where Cuthullin (Cú Chulainn) is general of the Irish tribes. Some chiefs are away on a hunting trip, and Fingal and his Caledonians have not yet arrived, but Cuthullin decides to go to battle anyway.

horse! The high-maned, broad breasted, proud, wide-leaping, strong steed of the hill. Loud and resounding is his hoof; the spreading of his mane above is like a stream of smoke on a ridge of rocks. Bright are the sides of the steed! his name is Sulin-Sifadda.

'Before the left side of the car is seen the snorting horse! The thin-maned, high-headed, strong-hoofed feet, bounding son of the hill: his name is Dusronnal among the stormy sons of the sword! A thousand thongs bind the car on high. Hard polished bits shine in a wreath of foam. Thin thongs, bright studded with gems, bend on the stately necks of the steeds. The steeds that like wreaths of mists fly over the streamy vales! The wildness of deer is in their course, the strength of eagles descending on their prey. Their noise is like the blast of winter, on the sides of the snowheaded Gormal.

'Within the car is seen the chief; the strong-armed son of the sword. The hero's name is Cuthullin, son of Semo, king of shells. His red cheek is like my polished yew. The look of his blue rolling eye is wide, beneath the dark arch of his brow. His hair flies from his head like a flame, as bending forward he wields the spear. Fly, king of ocean, fly! He comes, like a storm, along the streamy vale!'

'When did I fly?' replied the king. 'When fled Swaran from the battle of spears? When did I shrink from danger, chief of the little soul? I met the storm of Gormal, when the foam of my waves beat high. I met the storm of the clouds; shall Swaran fly from a hero? Were Fingal himself before me, my soul should not darken with fear. Arise to battle, my thousands! pour round me like the echoing main. Gather round the bright steel of your king; strong as the rocks of my land; that meet the storm with joy, and stretch their dark pines to the wind!'

Like autumn's dark storms, pouring from two echoing hills, towards each other approached the heroes. Like two deep streams from high rocks meeting, mixing, roaring on the plain; loud, rough and dark in battle meet Lochlin and Innis-fail. Chief mixes his strokes with chief, and man with man; steel, clanging, sounds on steel. Helmets are cleft on high. Blood bursts and smokes around. Strings murmur on the polished yews. Darts rush along the sky. Spears fall like the circles of light, which gild the face of night. As the noise of the troubled ocean, when roll the waves on high. As the last peal of thunder in heaven, such is the din of war! Though Cormac's hundred bards were there to give the fight to song; feeble was the voice of a hundred bards to send the deaths to future times! For many were the deaths of heroes; wide poured the blood of the brave!

Mourn, ye sons of song, mourn the death of the noble Sithallin. Let the sighs of Fiŏna rise, on the lone plains of her lovely Ardan. They fell, like two hinds of the desert, by the hands of the mighty Swaran: when, in the midst of thousands, he roared; like the shrill spirit of a storm. He sits dim, on the clouds of the north, and enjoys the death of the mariner. Nor slept thy hand by thy side, chief of the isle of mist![1] many

---

1 The Isle of Skye.

were the deaths of thine arm, Cuthullin, thou son of Semo! His sword was like the beam of heaven when it pierces the sons of the vale; when the people are blasted and fall, and all the hills are burning around. Dusronnal snorted over the bodies of heroes. Sifadda bathed his hoof in blood. The battle lay behind them, as groves overturned on the desert of Cromla; when the blast has passed the heath, laden with the spirits of night!

Weep on the rocks of roaring winds, O maid of Inistore! Bend thy fair head over the waves, thou lovelier than the ghost of the hills; when it moves, in a sunbeam, at noon, over the silence of Morven! He is fallen! thy youth is low! pale beneath the sword of Cuthullin! No more shall valour raise thy love to match the blood of kings. Trenar, graceful Trenar died, O maid of Inistore! His grey dogs are howling at home! they see his passing ghost. His bow is in the hall unstrung. No sound is in the hill of his hinds!

Robert Fergusson (1750–1774)

Born and educated in Edinburgh, and later at the University of St Andrews, Fergusson's degree was cut short when his father died and he had to return to the capital to take a job as a copying clerk. He started publishing poems in Ruddiman's *Weekly Magazine* in 1771 and although, like Ramsay, he wrote many poems in English, his best work uses Scots to celebrate daily life in the streets of the city around him. He had two years of extraordinary creativity before his health, never strong, began to fail and he became prone to bouts of religious melancholia. An accidental injury to his head plunged him into delirium and virtual insanity and he died at the age of barely 25 in a cell of the Edinburgh Bedlam. The vigour of Fergusson's language, like his comic and racy spirit, was to prove hugely influential for the future direction of Scots poetry. Robert Burns acknowledged a debt to his 'elder brother in misfortune, by far my elder brother in the muse', and erected a headstone over Fergusson's unmarked grave in Canongate Churchyard, Edinburgh.

from Auld Reikie: a Poem[1]

1 Auld Reikie, wale o ilka Town   *best*
    That Scotland kens beneath the Moon;
    Where couthy Chiels at E'ening meet   *sociable fellows*
    Their bizzing Craigs and Mous to weet;   *dry throats*
    And blythly gar auld Care gae bye   *cheerfully make*
    Wi' blinkit and wi' bleering Eye:
    O'er lang frae thee the Muse has been   *Too long*
    Sae frisky on the Simmer's Green,
    Whan Flowers and Gowans wont to glent   *daisies; gleam*
    In bonny Blinks upo' the Bent;   *sunny spots; field*
    But now the Leaves a Yellow die
    Peel'd frae the Branches, quickly fly;
    And now frae nouther Bush nor Brier
    The spreckl'd Mavis greets your ear;   *thrush*
    Nor bonny Blackbird Skims and Roves
    To seek his Love in yonder Groves.

    Then, Reikie, welcome! Thou canst charm

---

1. 'Old Smoky': the traditional name for Edinburgh whose smoky skyline could be seen for miles across the Firth.

Unfleggit by the year's Alarm;   unfrightened
Not Boreas that sae snelly blows,   keenly
Dare here pap in his angry Nose:
Thanks to our Dads, whase biggin stands   fathers; construction (castle walls)
A Shelter to surrounding Lands.[1]   tenements

Now Morn, with bonny Purpie-smiles,
Kisses the Air-cock o' St Giles;   weathervane
Rakin their Ein, the Servant Lasses   rubbing their eyes
Early begin their Lies and Clashes;   gossip
Ilk tells her Friend of saddest Distress,   Each
That still she brooks frae scouling Mistress;   bears
And wi' her Joe in Turnpike Stair   sweetheart; spiral stair in tenement
She'd rather snuff the stinking Air,
As be subjected to her Tongue,
When justly censur'd in the Wrong.

On Stair wi' Tub, or Pat in hand,   (chamber) pot
That antrin Fock may ken how Snell   occasional; sharp
Auld Reikie will at Morning Smell:
Then, with an Inundation Big as
The Burn that neath the Nore Loch Brig is,
They kindly shower Edina's Roses,[2]
To Quicken and Regale our Noses.
Now some for this, wi' Satyr's Leesh,   satire's whip
Ha'e gi'en auld Edinburgh a Creesh: lash
But without Souring nocht is sweet;
The Morning smells that hail our Street,
Prepare, and gently lead the Way
To Simmer canty, braw and gay: cheerful, brave
Edina's Sons mair eithly share,   easily
Her Spices and her Dainties rare,
Than he that's never yet been call'd
Aff frae his Plaidie or his Fauld.   (shepherd's) plaid; (sheep)fold

Now Stairhead Critics,[3] senseless Fools,
Censure their Aim, and Pride their Rules,
In Luckenbooths, wi' glouring Eye,   (lockable shops opposite St Giles)
Their Neighbours sma'est Faults descry:
If ony Loun should dander there,   fellow
Of aukward Gate, and foreign Air,

1. Streets in the old town were noted for their high tenement buildings, which imparted a considerable degree of
   communal living on people of all classes. Most dining, visiting and entertaining had to take place in taverns and
   howffs, and this also helped to mould the city's particularly free and open social life.
2. Chamberpots and slops, 'the flowers of Edinburgh', were simply emptied into the street, often from upstairs windows.
   (The Nor' Loch was drained to make the present Princes Street gardens.)
3. The head (top) of the common stairway was a natural vantage point for observation and gossip.

They trace his Steps, till they can tell
His Pedigree as weel's himsell.

Whan Phoebus blinks wi' warmer Ray   (the sun)
And Schools at Noonday get the play,   playtime break
Then Bus'ness, weighty Bus'ness comes;
The Trader glours; he doubts, he hums: looks darkly
The Lawyers eke to Cross[1] repair,   also
Their Wigs to shaw, and toss an Air;
While busy Agent closely plies,
And a' his kittle Cases tries.   tricky

Now Night, that's cunzied chief for Fun,   recognised
Is wi' her usual Rites begun;
Thro' ilka Gate the Torches blaze,   each street
And Globes send out their blinking Rays.
The usefu' Cadie[2] plies in Street,
To bide the Profits o' his Feet;
For by thir Lads Auld Reikie's Fock   Because of these; folk
Ken but a Sample, o the Stock   experience only
O' Thieves, that nightly wad oppress,
And make baith Goods and Gear the less.
Near him the lazy Chairman stands,   sedan chair porter
And wats na how to turn his Hands,
Till some daft Birky, ranting fu',   conceited fellow; drunk
Has Matters somewhere else to do;
The Chairman willing, gi'es his Light
To Deeds o' darkness and o' Night:
Its never Sax Pence for a Lift
That gars thir Lads wi' fu'ness rift;   belch
For they wi' better Gear are paid,
And Whores and Culls support their Trade.   dupes

Near some Lamp-post, wi' dowy Face,   mournful
Wi' heavy Ein, and sour Grimace,
Stands she that Beauty lang had kend,
Whoredom her Trade, and Vice her End.
But see wharenow she wuns her Bread
By that which Nature ne'er decreed;
And sings sad Music to the Lugs,   ears
'Mang Burachs o' damn'd Whores and Rogues.   rowdy groups
Whane'er we Reputation loss

1. The Market Cross. Stalls, shops, tenements, St Giles Cathedral, the Tolbooth and the Court of Session all share the
   same narrow stretch of the old High Street.
2. Cadies (Fr. *cadet*): street messengers, guides or servants for hire.

Fair Chastity's transparent gloss!
Redemption seenil kens the Name,   seldom
But a's black Misery and Shame.

Frae joyous Tavern, reeling drunk
Wi' fiery Phizz, and Ein half sunk,   face
Behad the Bruiser, Fae to a'   behold the prize-fighter; foe
That in the reek o' Gardies fa':   commotion of fists
Close by his Side, a feckless Race   ineffectual
O' Macaronies shew their Face,   dandies
And think they're free frae Skaith or Harm,   hurt
While Pith befriends their Leaders Arm: power
Yet fearfu' aften o' their Maught,   strength
They quatt the Glory o' the Faught   leave; fight
To this same Warrior wha led
Thae Heroes to bright Honour's Bed;
And aft the hack o' Honour shines   scar
In Bruiser's Face wi' broken Lines:
Of them sad Tales he tells anon,
Whan Ramble and whan Fighting's done;
And, like Hectorian, ne'er impairs   Hector (Greek hero)/one who hectors
The Brag and Glory o' his Sairs.

Whan Feet in dirty Gutters plash,
And Fock to wale their Fitstaps fash;   choose; footsteps; bother
At night the Macaroni drunk,   dandy
In Pools or Gutters aftimes sunk:
Hegh! what a Fright he now appears,
Whan he his Corpse dejected rears!
Look at that Head, and think if there
The Pomet slaister'd up his Hair!   pomade; greased
The Cheeks observe, where now cou'd shine
The scancing Glories o' Carmine?   shining; rouge
Ah, Legs! in vain the Silk-worm there
Display'd to View her eidant Care;   diligent
For Stink, instead of Perfumes, grow,
And clarty Odours fragrant flow.   filthy

Now some to Porter, some to Punch,
Some to their Wife, and some their Wench,
Retire, while noisy Ten-hours Drum[1]
Gars a' your Trades gae dandring Home.   compels; wandering
Now mony a Club, jocose and free,   jocular
Gie a' to Merriment and Glee,

1. A drum sounded through the streets at 10 p.m. to mark the end of tavern serving hours. (The city's many drinking and social clubs were not so constrained.)

Wi' Sang and Glass, they fley the Pow'r
O' Care that wad harrass the Hour:
For Wine and Bacchus still bear down
Our thrawart Fortunes wildest Frown: contrary
It maks you stark, and bauld and brave,   stout
141   Ev'n whan descending to the Grave.

Braid Claith

Ye wha are fain to hae your name   eager
Wrote in the bonny book of fame,
Let merit nae pretension claim
         To laurel'd wreath,
But hap ye weel, baith back and wame,   wrap up; belly
         In gude Braid Claith.[1]

He that some ells o' this may fa,   yards; come to possess
An' slae-black hat on pow like snaw,   sloe; head (of hair)
Bids bauld to bear the gree awa'   prize
         Wi' a' this graith,   outfit
Whan bienly clad wi' shell fu' braw   prosperously; brave/fine
         O' gude Braid Claith.

Waesuck for him wha has na fek o't!   amount
For he's a gowk they're sure to geck at,   fool; scoff
A chield that ne'er will be respekit   fellow
         While he draws breath,
Till his four quarters are bedeckit
         Wi' gude Braid Claith.

On Sabbath-days the barber spark,
Whan he has done wi' scrapin wark,
Wi' siller broachie in his sark,   silver broach; shirt
         Gangs trigly, faith!   neatly
Or to the Meadow, or the Park,[2]
         In gude Braid Claith.

Weel might ye trow, to see them there,   believe
That they to shave your haffits bare,   sidewhiskers
Or curl an' sleek a pickle hair,   little bit of
         Wou'd be right laith,   loath
Whan pacing wi' a gawsy air   imposing
         In gude Braid Claith.

1. Quality double-width woven cloth, usually black, for men's suiting.
2. The Kings Park beneath Arthur's Seat to the south, and the Meadows beyond George Square to the east were favourite places for the respectable to promenade.

If ony mettl'd stirrah green   spirited fellow longs
For favour frae a lady's ein,
He maunna care for being seen   must not
        Before he sheath
His body in a scabbard clean
        O' gude Braid Claith.

For, gin he come wi' coat thread-bare
A feg for him she winna care,   fig
But crook her bony mou' fu' sair,   twist; pretty; grievously
        An' scald him baith.   scold
Wooers shou'd ay their travel spare   avoid
        Without Braid Claith.

Braid Claith lends fock an unco heese,   folk; remarkable lift
Makes mony kail-worms butter-flies,   caterpillars (lit.: cabbage-worms)
Gies mony a doctor his degrees
        For little skaith: expense
In short, you may be what you please
        Wi' gude Braid Claith.

For thof ye had as wise a snout on
As Shakespeare or Sir Isaac Newton,
Your judgment fouk wou'd hae a doubt on,   folk
        I'll tak my aith,   oath
Till they cou'd see ye wi' a suit on
        O' gude Braid Claith.

Hallow-Fair[1]

At Hallowmas, whan nights grow lang,
    And starnies shine fu' clear,
Whan fock, the nippin cald to bang,   overcome
    Their winter hap-warms wear,   warm clothes
Near Edinbrough a fair there hads,
    I wat there's nane whase name is,
For strappin dames and sturdy lads,
    And cap and stoup, mair famous   cup and flagon
        Than it that day.

Upo' the tap o' ilka lum   each chimney
    The sun began to keek,   peep
And bad the trig made maidens come   trimly formed
    A sightly joe to seek   sweetheart

1. An ancient fair in the first week of November, held about half a mile from the Grassmarket in Fergusson's time.

At Hallow-fair, where browsters rare   ale-wives
   Keep gude ale on the gantries,
And dinna scrimp ye o' a skair   share
   O' kebbucks frae their pantries,   cheeses
      Fu' saut that day.   salty

Here country John in bonnet blue,
   An' eke his Sunday's claise on,   also; clothes
Rins after Meg wi' rokelay new,   cloak
   An' sappy kisses lays on;
She'll tauntin say, 'Ye silly coof!   fool
   Be o' your gab mair spairin';   mouth
He'll tak the hint and criesh her loof   grease her palm
   Wi' what will buy her fairin,   a present from the fair
      To chow that day.   chew

Here chapmen billies tak their stand,   pedlar fellows
   An' shaw their bonny wallies;   gewgaws
Wow, but they lie fu' gleg affhand   very glibly
   To trick the silly fallows:
Heh, sirs! what cairds and tinklers come,   beggars; tinkers
   An' ne'er-do-weel horse-coupers,   dealers
An' spae-wives fenying to be dumb,   fortune tellers; pretending
   Wi' a' siclike landloupers,   vagabonds
      To thrive that day.

Here Sawny cries, frae Aberdeen;
   'Come ye to me fa need:[1]   who
The brawest shanks that e'er were seen   stockings
   I'll sell ye cheap an' guid.
I wyt they are as protty hose   know; pretty
   As come frae weyr or leem: wire (knitting needles); loom
Here tak a rug and shaw's your pose: tug; stock of money
   Forseeth, my ain's but teem   empty
      An' light this day.'

Ye wives, as ye gang thro' tho fair,
   O mak your bargains hooly!   carefully
Of a' thir wylie lowns beware,   these; lads
   Or fegs they will ye spulzie,   truly; rob
For fairn-year Meg Thamson got,   last year
Frae thir mischievous villains,
A scaw'd bit o' a penny note,   worthless
   That lost a score o' shillins
      To her that day.

1. Aberdeen had a thriving hosiery industry. The poet's family came from the North-East and here he imitates its distinctive dialect, with forms such as *fa* for *wha*; *leem* for *loom*, etc.

The dinlin drums alarm our ears,   rattling
   The serjeant screechs fu' loud,   recruiting sergeant
'A' gentlemen and volunteers   All
   That wish your country gude,
Come here to me, and I sall gie
   Twa guineas and a crown,
A bowl o' punch, that like the sea
   Will soum a lang dragoon   float; (cavalry) carbine
       Wi' ease this day.'

Without, the cuissers prance and nicker,   Outside; stallions
   An' owr the ley-rig scud;   grass field; dash
In tents the carles bend the bicker,   men drink up the mug
   An' rant an' roar like wud.   mad
Then there's sic yellowchin and din,   yelling
   Wi' wives and wee-anes gablin,
That ane might true they were akin   believe
   To a' the tongues at Babylon,
       Confus'd that day.

Whan Phoebus ligs in Thetis[1] lap,   lies; (at sunset)
   Auld Reikie gies them shelter,
Whare cadgily they kiss the cap,   gaily; cup
   An' ca't round helter-skelter.   send it
Jock Bell gaed furth to play his freaks,   tricks
   Great cause he had to rue it,
For frae a stark Lochaber aix[2]   stout; axe
   He got a clamihewit,   drubbing
       Fu' sair that night.

'Ohon!' quo' he, 'I'd rather be   Alas (Gaelic)
   By sword or bagnet stickit,   bayonet
Than hae my crown or body wi'
   Sic deadly weapons nicket.'
Wi' that he gat anither straik,
   Mair weighty than before,
That gar'd his feckless body aik,   made; feeble
An' spew the reikin gore,
       Fu' red that night.

He peching on the cawsey lay,   panting; street
   O' kicks and cuffs weel sair'd;
A Highland aith the serjeant gae,   oath
   'She maun pe see our guard.'   'He must be seen by ...'

1. A goddess of the sea.
2. A Highland axe with a blade and a hook on a long shaft: carried by the City Guard, Fergusson's 'black banditti', who
   were often Highlanders themselves. He mocks their accent in a following stanza.

Out spak the weirlike corporal,   warlike
  'Pring in ta drunken sot.'
They trail'd him ben, an' by my saul,
  He paid his drunken groat   (Scots coin: a fine)
      For that neist day.

Good fock, as ye come frae the fair,
  Bide yont frae this black squad;   Stay away
There's nae sic savages elsewhere
  Allow'd to wear cockade.
Than the strong lion's hungry maw,
  Or tusk o' Russian bear,
Frae their wanruly fellin paw   cruel
  Mair cause ye hae to fear
      Your death that day.

A wee soup drink dis unco weel   little drop does very well
  To had the heart aboon;   hold (keep up)
It's gude as lang's a canny chiel   prudent fellow
  Can stand steeve in his shoon.   firm; shoes
But gin a birkie's owr weel sair'd,   if; vain lad; too well served
  It gars him aften stammer   stumble
To pleys that bring him to the guard,   into ploys
  An' eke the Council-chawmir,   also; (magistrate's) chamber
      Wi' shame that day.

Caller Oysters   cold/fresh

Happy the man who, free from care and strife,
In silken or in leathern purse retains
A splendid shilling. He nor hears with pain
New oysters cry'd, nor sighs for chearful ale.

Philips[1]

Of a' the waters that can hobble   move
A fishin yole or salmon coble,   yawl; flat-bottomed boat
And can reward the fishers trouble,
      Or south or north,
There's nane sae spacious and sae noble
      As Firth o' Forth.

In her the skate and codlin sail,
The eil fou souple wags her tail,

1. From *The Splendid Shilling*, by John Philips.

Wi' herrin, fleuk, and mackarel,	flounder
And whitens dainty:	young sea-trout
Their spindle-shanks the labsters trail,	bony legs; lobsters
Wi' partans plenty.	crabs

Auld Reikie's sons blyth faces wear;	happy
September's merry month is near,	
That brings in Neptune's caller chere,	cold cheer
New oysters fresh;	
The halesomest and nicest gear	
Of fish or flesh.	

O! then we needna gie a plack	small coin
For dand'ring mountebank or quack,	strolling
Wha o' their drogs sae bauldly crack,	drugs; boldly boast
And spred sic notions,	
As gar their feckless patient tak	make
Their stinkin potions.	

Come prie, frail man! for gin thou art sick,	try; if
The oyster is a rare cathartic,	
As ever doctor patient gart lick	made to
To cure his ails;	
Whether you hae the head or heart-ake,	
It ay prevails.	

Ye tiplers, open a' your poses,	stores of money
Ye wha are faush'd wi' plouky noses,	troubled; pimply
Fling owr your craig sufficient doses,	throat
You'll thole a hunder,	tolerate a hundred
To fleg awa' your simmer roses,	scare; (drinker's rash)
And naething under.	(less)

Whan big as burns the gutters rin,	
Gin ye hae catcht a droukit skin,	
To Luckie Middlemist's[1] loup in,	jump
And sit fu snug	
O'er oysters and a dram o' gin,	
Or haddock lug.	fillet

When auld Saunt Giles, at aught o'clock,	(bells)
Gars merchant lowns their chopies lock,	makes; lads; shops
There we adjourn wi' hearty fock	folk
To birle our bodles,	spend; coins
And get wharewi' to crack our joke	
And clear our noddles.	heads

1. Lucky (Goodwife) Middlemass kept an oyster-cellar in the Cowgate; oysters were not then a luxury item, and the cellars offered humbler fare than full-fledged taverns.

Whan Phoebus did his windocks steek,   (sun); shut
How aften at that ingle cheek   fireside
Did I my frosty fingers beek,   warm
      And taste gude fare?
I trow there was nae hame to seek
      Whan steghin there.   gorging

While glakit fools, o'er rife o' cash,   silly; (with too much)
Pamper their weyms wi' fousom trash,   bellies; disgusting
I think a chiel may gayly pass;   fellow
      He's no ill boden   furnished
That gusts his gabb wi' oyster sauce,   pleases
      And hen weel soden   boiled

At Musselbrough, and eke Newhaven,
The fisher wives will get top livin,
When lads gang out on Sunday's even
      To treat their joes,   sweethearts
And tak of fat pandours a prieven,   (large oysters from Prestonpans); taste
      Or mussel brose: soup

Than sometimes 'ere they flit their doup,   shift their bum
They'll ablins a' their siller coup   perhaps; spend all their money
For liquor clear frae cutty stoup,   small jug
      To weet their wizen,   throat
And swallow o'er a dainty soup,   sup
      For fear they gizzen.   dry up

A' ye wha canna stand sae sicker,   securely
Whan twice you've toom'd the big ars'd bicker,   emptied; big-bottomed beaker
Mix caller oysters wi' your liquor,
      And I'm your debtor,   (ie: I'll be surprised)
If greedy priest or drouthy vicar[1]   thirsty
      Will thole it better.   stand up to (drink)

To the Principal and Professors of the University of St. Andrews, on their superb treat to Dr. Samuel Johnson[2]

St. Andrews town may look right gawsy,   stately
Nae Grass will grow upon her cawsey,   street
Nor wa'-flow'rs of a yellow dye,
Glour dowy o'er her Ruins high,   frown sadly
Sin Samy's head weel pang'd wi' lear   crammed; learning
Has seen the Alma mater there:

1. Oysters were thought to offset drunkenness; the poet suggests that men of the cloth are experts of that condition.
2. 'The professors entertained us with a very good dinner', Boswell, *Tour to the Hebrides*, 19 August 1773.

Regents, my winsome billy boys! — *Professors; likely lads*
'Bout him you've made an unco noise;
Nae doubt for him your bells wad clink,
To find him upon Eden's[1] brink,
An' a' things nicely set in order,
Wad kep him on the Fifan border: — *(of Fife)*
I'se warrant now frae France an' Spain, — *I bet*
Baith Cooks and Scullions mony ane
Wad gar the pats an' kettles tingle — *make; pots*
Around the college kitchen ingle, — *fireside*
To fleg frae a' your craigs the roup, — *chase; throats; hoarseness*
Wi' reeking het and crieshy soup; — *steaming; fatty*
And snails and puddocks mony hunder — *frogs*
Wad beeking lie the hearth-stane under, — *warming*
Wi' roast and boild, an' a' kin kind, — *(such like)*
To heat the body, cool the mind.
    But hear me lads! gin I'd been there, — *if*
How I wad trimm'd the bill o' fare! — *altered*
For ne'er sic surly wight as he — *creature*
Had met wi' sic respect frae me,
Mind ye what Sam, the lying loun! — *Don't you remember; rascal*
Has in his Dictionar laid down?
That Aits in England are a feast
To cow an' horse, an' sican beast, — *suchlike*
While in Scots ground this growth was common
To gust the gab o' Man an' Woman.[2] — *please the mouth*
Tak tent, ye Regents! then, an' hear — *Pay heed*
My list o' gudely hamel gear, — *home-bred stuff*
Sic as ha'e often rax'd the wyme — *stretched the stomach*
O' blyther fallows mony time;
Mair hardy, souple, steive an' swank, — *firm; active*
Than ever stood on Samy's shank. — *leg (place)*
Imprimis, then, a haggis fat, — *In the first place*
Weel tottl'd in a seything pat, — *boiled; seething pot*
Wi' spice and ingans weel ca'd thro', — *onions; stirred in*
Had help'd to gust the stirrah's mow, — *please; bloke's*
And plac'd itsel in truncher clean — *wooden platter*
Before the gilpy's glowrin een. — *big lump's scowling eyes*
Secundo, then a gude sheep's head
Whase hide was singit,[3] never flead, — *singed; flayed*
And four black trotters cled wi' girsle, — *gristle*
Bedown his throat had learn'd to hirsle. — *slide*

1. The river Eden enters the sea at St Andrews Bay.
2. 'Oats: A grain which, in England, is generally given to horses, but in Scotland supports the people.' – Johnson's *Dictionary*.
3. Sheep's head broth is made with the whole head, only the nose is scraped out and the wool singed off.

What think ye neist, o' gude fat brose[1]
To clag his ribs? a dainty dose!   *stick to*
And white and bloody puddins[2] routh,   *plenty*
To gar the Doctor skirl, O Drouth!   *make; cry out; thirst*
Whan he cou'd never houp to merit
A cordial o' reaming claret,   *foaming*
But thraw his nose, and brize and pegh   *strain; push and pant*
O'er the contents o' sma' ale quegh: *quaich (two-handled cup)*
Then let his wisdom girn an' snarl   *whine*
O'er a weel-tostit girdle farl,   *girdle oatcake*
An' learn, that maugre o' his wame,   *despite; stomach*
Ill bairns are ay best heard at hame.   *troublesome children (proverb)*
    Drummond, lang syne, o' Hawthornden,
The wyliest an' best o' men,   *wisest*
Has gi'en you dishes ane or mae,[3]   *more*
That wad ha' gard his grinders play,   *made; teeth work*
Not to roast beef, old England's life,
But to the auld east nook of Fife,
Whare Creilian crafts cou'd weel ha'e gi'en   *(village of) Crail*
Scate-rumples to ha'e clear'd his een;   *skate tails*
Then neist, when Samy's heart was faintin,
He'd lang'd for scate to mak him wanton.
    Ah! willawins, for Scotland now,   *alack*
Whan she maun stap ilk birky's mow   *stuff; each conceited fellow's*
Wi' eistacks, grown as 'tware in pet   *dainties; ill-humour*
In foreign land, or green-house het,
When cog o' brose an' cutty spoon   *(wooden) bowl; short*
Is a' our cottar childer's boon,
Wha thro' the week, till Sunday's speal,   *holiday*
Toil for pease-clods an' gude lang kail.   *coarse meal rolls; unchopped cabbage*
Devall then, Sirs, and never send   *Desist*
For daintiths to regale a friend,
Or, like a torch at baith ends burning,
Your house'll soon grow mirk and mourning.
    What's this I hear some cynic say?
'Robin, ye loun! it's nae fair play;   *Robert; rascal*
Is there nae ither subject rife   *plentiful*
To clap your thumb upon but Fife?
Gi'e o'er, young man, you'll meet your corning,   *get your deserts*
Than caption war, or charge o' horning;[4]   *Worse than*
Some canker'd surly sour-mow'd carline   *bad-tempered; old woman*
Bred near the abbey o' Dumfarline,

1. Oatmeal and boiling water or milk, mixed with salt and butter.
2. Oatmeal and blood sausages usually boiled in their skins and cut open.
3. His poem *Polemo-Middinia* begins with a celebration of the fish to be caught off the Fife coast.
4. 'Caption' and 'horning': procedures to arrest a debtor until the debt is paid.

Your shoulders yet may gi'e a lounder,   wallop
An' be of verse the mal-confounder.'
Come on ye blades! but 'ere ye tulyie,   tussle
Or hack our flesh wi' sword or gulyie,   knife
Ne'er shaw your teeth, nor look like stink,
Nor o'er an empty bicker blink: beaker
What weets the wizen an' the wyme,   throat and stomach
Will mend your prose and heal my rhyme.

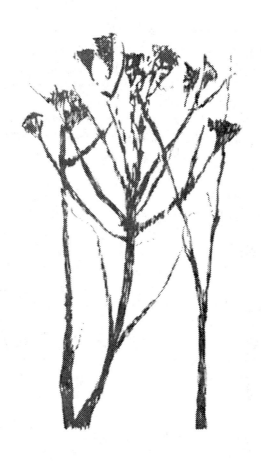

Uilleam Ros/William Ross
(1762–1790)

Born on Skye and educated in the classics at a grammar school in Forres on the mainland, Ross helped his father as a travelling packman before settling down as a schoolmaster in Gairloch. Legend has it that he died of unrequited love for Marion Ross, and certainly the affair left its mark, but it was tuberculosis that killed him at the early age of 28. He wrote conventional enough praise poems to whisky and to summer, as well as satires against randy priests and the toothache, but he is chiefly

Oran air Cupid

Hò ro ladie duibh, hò ro eile,
Hò ro ladie duibh, hò ro eile,
Hò ro ladie duibh, hò ro eile,
Gu'm b' éibhinn le m' aigne
An ladie na'm feudadh.

Nach mireagach *Cupid*,
'S e sùgradh ri mhàthair?
Dia brionnach gun sùilean,
An dùil gur ceol-gàir' e,
A' tilgeadh air thuaiream
Mu'n cuairt anns gach àite
A shaigdean beag, guineach,
Mar's urrainn e 'n sàthadh.

Bha sagart 's na crìochan,
'S bu diadhaidh 'm fear leughaidh
Air dùnadh le creideamh,
'S le eagnachd cho eudmhor;
'S b' ann a cheann-eagair,
A theagasg bhi beusach,
Gun ofrail a nasgadh
Aig altairean *Bhenuis*.

remembered for the more directly personal lyric note of his love poems – a new direction in Gaelic verse, and one that has led him to be compared with Robert Burns. (Compare his first sight of Marion in 'Monday Evening' with Burns's 'Mary Morison'; or compare the starker personal pain of 'Another Song on the Same Theme' with Sorley Maclean's *Songs to Eimhir*.)

Song to Cupid [1]

> Horo my dark laddie, horo eile
> Horo my dark laddie, horo eile
> Horo my dark laddie, horo eile
> What joy to my spirit
> that laddie could be.

Is not Cupid naughty
to joke with his mother?
The pretty blind god
hopes his sorties amuse,
to shoot off at random
all round in all places,
his small stinging arrows
that none may refuse.

A priest of the rough-bounds
well-read in theology,
cloistered in creed
and with wisdom his aim;
his ultimate purpose
a lesson most proper;
to the altars of Venus
no offerings came.

1. Here blind Cupid has smitten a priest, the 'dark laddie'.

'Nuair a chunnaic a' bhaindia
Fear-teampuil cho dùire,
Gun urram dha màildeachd,
Gun mhiadh air a sùgradh;
Chuir i 'n dia dalldach,
Beag, feallsach, gun sùilean,
Dh' fheuchainn am feudadh e
A ghleusadh gu h-ùrlaim.

'N uair dhiùchd an dia baothar,
Beag, faoilteach, mu'n cuairt da,
Gu'n thilg e air saighead
O chailin na buaile;
Chaidh 'n sagart 'na lasair,
'S cha chuirt' as gu là-luain e,
Mur bhiodh gu'n ghéill e
Do *Bhenus* 'san uair sin.

'S b' e aidmheil an Lebhit,
'N uair a b' éiginn da ùmhlachd,
Gu'm b' fheàirrde gach buachaille
Gruagach a phùsadh;
'S bha cailin na buaile
Cho buan ann a shùilean,
'S gu'n robh i 'na aigne
'Na chadal 's 'na dhùsgadh.

'S e fàth ghabh an sagart
Air caidrimh na h-òighe,
Air dha bhi air madainn
'Ga h-aidmheil 'na sheòmar,
A glacadh 's a leagadh
Air leabaidh bhig chòmhnaird,
'S mus maitheadh e peacadh,
Bhi tacan 'ga pògadh.

Achmhasan an Deideidh
(a deudach Dhomhnuill Fhriseal)

Mìle marbhaisg ort, a dhéideidh,
    Thar gach galair,
'S duilich leam mar dh'fhàg thu m' eudail
    Dhe na fearaibh;
Bheir gach tinneas eile dhuinne
    Fànadh 's fàth furtachd,

When the goddess took note
of this cleric most stubborn,
not counting her kindness
or weighing affairs;
she sent the blind godling
small, cunning and eyeless,
to strike up if possible
livelier airs.

When the silly god flew,
small and happily round him
he loosed off a shaft
at the lass in the fank;   fold
lit such flames in the cleric,
they'd burn till the Judgement,
but vassal to Venus
he instantly sank.

When the priest then confessed
how he'd mightily fallen,
thought best that each shepherd
a milkmaid should take;
the lass of the cow-fank
stuck fast in his thinking,
and troubled his spirit
asleep or awake.

The ploy of this priest
with the lass not refusing:
at morn to confess
in his room he'd beguile;
where he led her and laid her
on a little smooth cot and
before he would shrive her
he kissed her a while.

trans. William Neill

Toothache Reprimanded
(from Donald Fraser's toothache)

A thousand curses on you, Toothache
    of all ailments,
you left the comrade of my choosing
    sore afflicted;
every other ill gives promise
    of relieving,

Ach 's e bheir thus', a bhruidear mhilltich,
    Ionnsaidh mhort oirnn:
Chan àill leat gu'n téid deoch, no drama,
    Steach fo'r carbad,
Ach gabhail dhuinn as ar claigeann
    'S ar grad mharbhadh.
Cha luaithe dh'éirich Domhnull Friseil
    As a' chuartaich,
Na chuir thusa do nimh an ìre
    Gus a thruailleadh;
Chan fhòghnadh leat na rinn an teasach
    Air an truaghan,
Ach thu féin, a dhroch bhuill deis
    A dhol da thuairgneadh!
Bha cnàimhean a chinn, a's eudann
    'S a dheud uile,
Mar gu'm biodh muillear 'ga riasladh
    Fo chloich mhuilinn:
No mar gu'm biodh gobha Gallda
    'Ga theann-spàrradh
An glàmaire teannta, cruaghach
    Do chruaidh stàilinn.
Ach thig do dhriug mur 'eil mi meallt'
    Ma chluinn Mac-Shimidh
An diol a rinn thu, a thrudair bhrùideal,
    Air fhear-cinnidh,
'S esan a loisgeas an dù'-thuill ort,
    'S cha sinn uile!
Bheir e 'n t-arm dearg a Sasgunn
    Gu do sgiùrsadh,
Le peileirean dearga, lasrach,
    A's neart fùdair.
Gràin ort nach do ghabh thu trudar
    No fear doicheil,
Ach an duine fiughantach, fialaidh,
    Chur o chosnadh,
'S a liuthad cailleach sgaiteach, bheur,
    A's rèabhair caile
Tha feum an carbad 's an deudach
    A léir sgaradh,
Eadar Irt, a's Peairt, a's Ìle
    'S tìr Mhic-Ailein,
No geda thogradh tu sìneadh,
    Aig a' bhaile.

but one gift you give us, monster
   pains of dying.
Drink or dram you'll not let travel
   between jawbones,
but brains within our skulls unravel
   like death's smiting.
From an ague Donald Fraser
   lately rising,
you brought pains as sharp's a razor
   to tormenting;
not content with heat of fever,
   in poor fellows,
but yourself the Torture-giver
   come to twist him!
All his face and all his skull-bones
   all his molars,
like a crunching under millstones
   without ceasing:
as within some Lowland smithy
   fixing tightly
a Vulcan punded on his stithy
   hardest metal.
Revenge comes soon, I can aver it,
   from MacShimidh,   Lord Lovat (Clan chief)
the fate, foul demon, that you merit
   from his chieftain,
he'll fire at you a double-barrel
   and that's certain!
Or call the redcoats to the quarrel
   up from England,
with a flying blazing bullet
   and strong powder.
Curse you, why not grip some callet   tart
   of evil living?
But this most brave and noble fellow
   take from business,
while screeching witches, wrinkled, yellow
   and roaming strumpets,
ought to have their teeth and jawbones
   quickly parted,
where Macallan's rule of law runs
   Perth to Islay,
Hirt to Moidart, would you rather   St Kilda
   reach your arm out,
or somewhere nearer home foregather,
   to dish your harm out?

trans. William Neill

Oran Gaoil/Feasgar Luain

Feasgar luain, a's mi air chuairt,
Gu'n cualas fuaim nach b'fhuathach leam,
Ceòl nan teud gu h-òrdail, réidh,
A's còisir da réir os a chionn;
Thuit mi'n caochladh leis an ioghnadh,
A dh'aisig mo smaointean a null;
'S chuir mi 'n céill gu'n imichinn céin
Le m'aigne féin, 's e co'-streap rium.

Chaidh mi steach an ceann na còisridh,
An robh òl, a's ceòl, a's dàmhs',
Rìbhinnean, a's fleasgaich òga,
'S iad an òrdugh grinn gun mheang;
Dhearcas fa leath air na h-òighean,
Le rosg fòil a null 's a nall;
'S ghlacadh mo chridhe, 's mo shùil cò'ladh,
'S rinn an gaol mo leòn air ball.

Dhiùchd mar aingeal, ma mo choinneamh,
'N ainnir òg, bu ghrinne snuadh;
Seang shlios fallain air bhlà canaich,
No mar an eal' air a' chuan;
Sùil ghorm, mheallach, fo chaoil mhala
'S caoin' a sheallas 'g amharc uath',
Beul tlà, tairis, gun ghnè smalain,
Dha'n gnà carthannachd gun uaill.

Mar ghath gréin' am madainn Chéitein,
Gu'n mheath i mo léirsinn shùl,
'S i ceumadh ùrlair, gu réidh iompaidh,
Do réir pungannan a' chiùil;
Rìbhinn mhodhail, 's fìor-ghlan fòghlum,
Dh'fhìon-fhuil mhòrdhalach mo rùin;
Reul nan òighean, grian gach còisridh,
'S i 'n chiall chòmhraidh, cheòl-bhinn, chiùin.

'S tearc an sgeula sunnailt t' eugaisg
Bhi ri fheatainn 'san Roinn-Eòrp,
Tha mais' a's féile, tlachd a's ceutaidh
Nach facas leam féin fa m'chòir,
Gach cliù a'fàs riut am mùirn, 's an àillteachd,
An sùgradh, 's am màran beòil;

Love Song/Monday Evening[1]

On Monday night I walked the street,
I heard a tune upon the air,
music on well-tuned strings and sweet,
that rose above the chatter there;
the melody quite changed my mood,
turning my thoughts another road;
so I resolved to seek the place
from where my spirit's pleasure flowed.

I mingled with the tuneful crowd,
who danced and drank within the hall,
lasses and men by age unbowed,
dressed in their splendour for the ball;
I looked upon the maidens there,
each one, with slow admiring eye;
love's sudden onset held my stare,
and I was wounded instantly.

An angel stood before my sight,
a fair young lass, of lovely face;
light as the moorland cotton-down,
and like the ocean swan in grace;
slender her brows, blue laughing eye
that shone there in a gentle dance,
shapely her lips without a flaw,
not haughty, warm and kind her glance.

Like a May morning's sunny rays,
she melted boldness from my glance,
as stepping to the music's pace,
she glided round within the dance;
a maid of manners, nobly bred,
of that proud race that I admire;
like sun and star her grace was shed,
of lovely speech the queen entire.

Seldom is heard such fine report
of loveliness in Europe's bound,
her gentle mien in such a sort
in my life's ways I'd never found,
all fame that goes to beauty, love,
to gaiety and humoured speech;

1. This poem, with its elaborate classical references and stately air, is supposed to have been composed in recollection
of seeing Marion Ross at a ball in her native Stornoway.

'S gach buaidh a b'àilli, bh' air *Diàna*,
Gu léir mar fhàgail, tha aig Mòir.

'S bachlach, dualach, cas-bhuidh', cuachach,
Càradh suaineas gruaig do chinn,
Gu h-àluinn, bòidheach, fàinneach, òr-bhuidh',
An caraibh seòighn 's an òrdugh grinn,
Gun chron a'fàs riut, a dh'fheudt' àireamh,
O do bhàrr gu sàil do bhuinn;
Dhiùchd na buaidhean, òigh, mu'n cuairt dut,
Gu meudachdain t' uaill 's gach puing.

Bu leigheas eugail, slàn o'n eug,
Do dh'fhear a dh' fheudadh bhi ma d' chòir
B' fheàrr na 'n cadal bhi 'nad fhagaisg,
'G éisdeachd agallaidh do bheòil;
Cha robh *Bhenus* am measg leugaibh
Dh' aindeoin feucantachd cho bòidh'ch,
Ri Mòr nigh'n mhìn, a leòn mo chridh',
Le buaidhean, 's mi 'ga dìth ri m' bheò.

'S glan an fhìon-fhuil as na fhriamhaich
Thu, gun fhiaradh, mhiar, no mheang;
Cinneadh mòrdhalach, bu chròdha,
Tional cò'ladh chò'-stri lann,
Bhuinneadh cùis a bhàrr nan Dùbh-Ghall,
Sgiùrsadh iad gu'n dùthchas thall,
Leanadh ruaig air Cataich fhuara,
'S a' toirt buaidh orr' anns gach ball.

Tha 'n cabar-fèigh an dlùth's do réir dhut,
Nach biodh éisleineach 'san t-strìth,
Fir nach obadh leis 'gan togail
Dol a chogadh 'n aghaidh Rìgh;
Bu cholgail, faiceant' an stoirm feachdaidh,
Armach, breacanach, air tì
Dol 'san iomairt gun bhonn gioraig,
'S iad nach tilleadh chaoidh fo chìs.

'S trom leam m'osnadh, 's cruaidh leam m' fhortan
Gun ghleus socair, 's mi gun sunnd,
'S mi ri smaointean air an aon rùn,
A bhuin mo ghaol gun ghaol da chionn.
Throm na Dùilean peanas dùbailt,
Gu mis' ùmhlachadh air ball,
Thàlaidh *Cupid* mi 'san dùsal,
As na dhùisg mi brùite, fann!

such gifts as round Diana move,
a share has Marion of each.

The curling, flowing, well-bound tress,
like golden banner frames your head,
the ringlets, handsome, bonny, dress
your hair like pearls in order laid,
no fault is found to number there,
from that fair crowning to your heel –
are all forms that proclaim the fair,
and gracefulness to set the seal.

A cure for ill, from death a stay,
to such as knew your presence near,
better than sleep, to hear your play
of converse, witty and sincere;
Venus herself in jewelled art
and girdled in her queen's array,
sweet Marion, who stole my heart,
as fair to me, and far away.

Clean noble blood from purest springs,
runs in your veins, no fault or flaw,
from kin most fine in bravest things,
nor loth the sword of right to draw,
to save the day from Viking foe,
and scourge them to their dens once more,
to Sutherland their rout would go,
our final victory clinch the score.

The 'deer's head' slogan in your heart
that rises high in battle's hour,
it does not shun the warlike art
when even the royal standards lour;
hardy and wild in storm of strife,
well armed, and clad in belted plaid,
they charge with no regard for life,
for thraldom's fetters never made.

Heavy my sigh, for cruel fate,
no glint of joy or happiness,
my thoughts are aye on that sad state,
that made me love without redress.
The Fates decree my double pain,
and all my pride is humbled low,
I wake from out my dream again,
pained by the wound from Cupid's bow!

Beir soraidh uam do'n rìbhinn shuairc,
De'n chinneadh mhòr a's uaisle gnàs,
Thoir mo dhùrachd-sa g'a h-ionnsaidh,
'S mi'n deagh rùn da cùl-bhuidh bàn.
'S nach bruadar cadail a ghluais m'aigne,
'S truagh nach aidich e dhomh tàmh,
'S ge b' ann air chuairt, no thall an cuan,
Gu'm bi mi smuainteach' ort gu bràth.

Oran Eile, air an Aobhar Cheudna

Tha mise fo mhulad 'san àm,
   Cha n-òlar leam dram le sunnd,
Tha durrag air ghur ann mo chàil
   A dh'fhiosraich do chàch mo rùn;
Chan fhaic mi dol seachad air sràid
   An cailin bu tlàithe sùil,
'S e sin a leag m'aigne gu làr
   Mar dhuilleach o bhàrr nan craobh.

A ghruagach as bachlaiche cùl
   Tha mise ga t' iunndruinn mòr,
Ma thagh thu deagh àite dhut féin
   Mo bheannachd gach ré dha d' chòir:
Tha mise ri osnaich 'nad dhéidh,
   Mar ghaisgeach an déis a leòn,
'Na laighe 'san àraich gun fheum,
   'S nach téid anns an t-streup ni's mò!

'S e dh' fhàg mi mar iudmhail air treud,
   Mar fhear nach toir spéis do mhnaoi,
Do thuras thar chuan fo bhréid,
   Thug bras shileadh dheur o m'shùil —
B'fheàrr nach mothaichinn féin
   Do mhaise, do chéill, 's do chliù;
No suairceas milis do bhéil
   'S binne no séis gach ciùil.

Gach anduin' a chluinneas mo chàs
   A' cur air mo nàdur fiamh,
A' cantainn nach 'eil mi ach bàrd
   'S nach cinnich leam dàn is fiach —
Mo sheanair ri pàigheadh a mhàil,
   'S m' athair ri màlaid riabh;

Take from me then my fond farewell,
to yon fine lass so nobly bred,
let all my heartfelt wishes tell,
my passion to that golden head.
No sleeping vision stirred my soul,
a living dream that robs my rest,
no voyage to the farthest pole,
would calm the longing in my breast.

trans. William Neill

Another Song on the Same Theme

I am lonely here and depressed.
   No more can I drink and be gay.
The worm that feeds on my breast
   is giving my secret away.
Nor do I see, walking past,
   the girl of the tenderest gaze.
It is this which has brought me to waste
   like the leaf in the autumn days.

O girl of the ringleted hair,
   how much I deplore you, and miss.
In spite of the riches you wear
   I shall never curse you, but bless.
What can I do but despair
   like the wounded soldier whose pain
cries out from the field of the war
   he'll never join battle again?

I'm a stray who is far from the herd
   or a man to whom love is dead.
The voyage you took as a bride
   wrung the hot tears from my head.
Better not to have stored
   your beauty and fame in my mind
or the affable grace of your word,
   a language to music refined.

Ill-wishers who hear of my plight
   call me a coward and worse.
They say that I'm only a poet
   whose fate is as dead as my verse.
(His father's a packman. You know it.
   His father, in turn, couldn't boast.)

Chuireadh iad gearrain an crann
   A's ghearainn-sa rann ro' chiad.

'S fad a tha m' aigne fo ghruaim,
   Cha mhosgail mo chluain ri ceòl,
'M breislich mar ànrach a' chuain
   Air bhàrraibh nan stuagh ri ceò.
'S e iunndaran t' àbhachd bhuam
   A chaochail air snuadh mo neòil,
Gun sùgradh, gun mhire, gun uaill,
   Gun chaithream, gun bhuaidh, gun treòir.

Cha dùisgear leam ealaidh air àill',
   Cha chuirear leam dàn air dòigh,
Cha togar leam fonn air clàr,
   Cha chluinnear leam gàir nan òg:
Cha dìrich mi bealach nan àrd
   Le suigeart mar bha mi'n tòs,
Ach triallam a chadal gu bràth
   Do thalla nam bàrd nach beò!

They'd take a good field and plough it.
    I cut better poems than most.

My spirit is dulled by your loss,
    the song of my mouth is dumb.
I moan with the sea's distress
    when the mist lies over the foam.
It's the lack of your talk and your grace
    which has clouded the sun from my eyes
and has sunk it deep in the place
    from which light will never arise.

I shall never praise beauty again.
    I shall never design a song.
I shall never take pleasure in tune,
    nor hear the clear laugh of the young.
I shall never climb hill with the vain
    youthful arrogant joy that I had.
But I'll sleep in a hall of stone
    with the great bards who are dead.

                                        trans. Iain Crichton Smith

Robert Burns (1759–1796)

The eldest son of a farmer, Burns was born and educated in Ayrshire. Much of the political and social spirit of his work stems from the values of his father and other independent-minded farmers like him, not to mention the folk tradition carried by his mother and female relatives. After their father's death, Burns and his brother Gilbert took responsibility for the rest of the family. In his early 20s, the poet was under considerable pressure – his farmland was poor, he had literary ambitions and his hectic love life had fueled local scandal. *Poems, Chiefly in the Scottish Dialect* was produced by subscription in Kilmarnock in 1786, and Burns became famous over-night. He finally married his lover Jean Armour in 1788, and started editing a collection of Scots songs, improving many old airs and writing a number of his own. In later years he gained a post with the Customs and Excise in Dumfries but hard labour had weakened his health and he died of a rheumatic heart condition at the age of 37. 'Tam o' Shanter' and 'Love and Liberty' go beyond the democratic energies of his best work to challenge *all* social and conceptual boundaries with a gloriously wild and subversive world of their own.

The Twa Dogs: A Tale[1]

'Twas in that place o' Scotland's isle,
That bears the name o' auld king Coil,   (Kyle)
Upon a bonie day in June,
When wearing thro' the afternoon,
Twa Dogs, that were na thrang at hame,   busy
Forgather'd ance upon a time.

    The first I'll name, they ca'd him Ceasar,
Was keepet for his Honor's pleasure;
His hair, his size, his mouth, his lugs,   ears
Show'd he was nane o' Scotland's dogs;
But whalpet some place far abroad,
Whare sailors gang to fish for Cod.   (Newfoundland)

    His locked, letter'd, braw brass-collar,
Show'd him the gentleman an' scholar;

---

1. Compare Fergusson's dialogue 'Mutual Complaint of Plainstanes and Causey'.

But tho' he was o' high degree,
The fient a pride na pride had he,   devil a pride (none at all)
But wad hae spent an hour caressan,
Ev'n wi' a Tinkler-gipsey's messan: pet dog
At Kirk or Market, Mill or Smiddie,   Smithy
Nae tawtied tyke, tho' e'er sae duddie,   matted; ragged
But he wad stan't, as glad to see him,   stand
An' stroan't on stanes an' hillocks wi' him.   pissed

    The tither was a ploughman's collie,
A rhyming, ranting, raving billie,
Wha for his friend an' comrade had him,
And in his freaks had Luath ca'd him;   fancy
After some dog in Highlan Sang,[1]
Wi' never-ceasing toil;
Was made lang syne, lord knows how lang.

    He was a gash an' faithfu' tyke,   shrewd
As ever lap a sheugh, or dyke!   leaped; ditch; wall
His honest sonsie, baws'nt face,   amiable; with a white blaze
Ay gat him friends in ilka place;
His breast was white, his towzie back,   shaggy
Weel clad wi' coat o' glossy black;
His gawsie tail, wi' upward curl,   full
Hung owre his hurdies wi' a swirl.   backside

    Nae doubt but they were fain o' ither,   fond
An' unco pack an' thick the gither;   intimate
Wi' social nose whyles snuff'd an' snowcket;   sometimes; prodded
Whyles mice an' modewurks they howcket;   moles; dug up
Whyles scour'd awa in lang excursion,
An' worry'd ither in diversion;   further
Untill wi' daffin weary grown,   dallying
Upon a knowe they sat them down,
An' there began a lang digression
About the lords o' the creation.

      CEASAR
    I've aften wonder'd, honest Luath,
What sort o' life poor dogs like you have;
An' when the gentry's life I saw,
What way poor bodies liv'd ava.   folk; at all

---

1. Luath was Cuchullin's dog in Ossian's *Fingal*, and the name of Burns's own dog, inspired no doubt by Macpherson's version of the Gaelic epic.

Our Laird gets in his racked rents,
His coals, his kane, an' a' his stents;   payment in kind; levies
He rises when he likes himsel;
His flunkies answer at the bell;
He ca's his coach; he ca's his horse;   rides
He draws a bonie, silken purse
As lang's my tail, whare thro' the steeks,   fastening
The yellow, letter'd Geordie keeks.   (gold sovereign)

    Frae morn to een it's nought but toiling,
At baking, roasting, frying, boiling:
An' tho' the gentry first are steghan,   stuffing themselves
Yet ev'n the ha' folk fill their peghan   (servants); belly
Wi' sauce, ragouts, an' sic like trashtrie,
That's little short o' downright wastrie.
Our Whipper-in, wee, blastiet wonner,   huntsman dog handler; withered
Poor, worthless elf, it eats a dinner,   dwarf
Better than ony Tenant-man
His Honor has in a' the lan':
An' what poor Cot-folk pit their painch in,   cottagers; belly
I own it's past my comprehension. –

LUATH
    Trowth, Ceasar, whyles they're fash'd eneugh;   harassed
A Cotter howckan in a sheugh,   ditch
Wi' dirty stanes biggan a dyke,
Bairan a quarry, an' sic like,   clearing
Himsel, a wife, he thus sustains,
A smytrie o' wee, duddie weans,   ragged
An' nought but his han'-daurk, to keep   hand-work
Them right an' tight in thaek an' raep.   thatch and rope (safe and sound)

    An' when they meet wi' sair disasters,
Like loss o' health, or want o' masters,   lack
Ye maist wad think, a wee touch langer,   almost
An' they maun starve o' cauld an' hunger: must
But how it comes, I never kent yet,
They're maistly wonderfu' contented;
An' buirdly chiels, an' clever hizzies,   stalwart fellows; wenches
Are bred in sic a way as this is.

CEASAR
    But then, to see how ye're negleket,
How huff'd, an' cuff'd, an' disrespeket!
Lord man, our gentry care as little
For delvers, ditchers, an' sic cattle;

They gang as saucy by poor folk   snooty
As I wad by a stinkan brock.   badger

    I've notic'd, on our Laird's court-day,   rent-day
An' mony a time my heart's been wae,
Poor tenant-bodies, scant o' cash,
How they maun thole a factor's snash;   put up with a steward's abuse
He'll stamp an' threaten, curse an' swear,
He'll apprehend them, poind their gear,   seize; goods
While they maun stand, wi' aspect humble,
An' hear it a', an' fear an' tremble!

    I see how folk live that hae riches,
But surely poor-folk maun be wretches!

LUATH
    They're no sae wretched's ane wad think;
Tho' constantly on poortith's brink,
They're sae accustom'd wi' the sight,
The view o't gies them little fright.

    Then chance an' fortune are sae guided,
They're ay in less or mair provided;
An' tho' fatigu'd wi' close employment,
A blink o' rest's a sweet enjoyment.

    The dearest comfort o' their lives,
Their grushie weans, an' faithfu' wives;   thriving children
The prattling things are just their pride,
That sweetens a' their fire-side.

    An' whyles, twalpennie-worth o' nappy   at times; ale
Can mak the bodies unco happy;
They lay aside their private cares,
To mind the Kirk an' State affairs;   think of

They'll talk o' patronage[1] an' priests,
Wi' kindling fury i' their breasts,
Or tell what new taxation's comin,
An' ferlie at the folk in Lon'on.   marvel

    As bleak-fac'd Hallowmass returns,   (1 November: All Saints' Day)
They get the jovial, rantan Kirns,   end of harvest celebration
When rural life, of ev'ry station,

---

1. The right for landowners to appoint parish ministers, as opposed to the congregation itself.

Unite in common recreation;
Love blinks, Wit slaps, an' social Mirth
Forgets there's care upo' the earth.

That merry day the year begins,
They bar the door on frosty win's;
The nappy reeks wi' mantling ream,   ale; creaming froth
An' sheds a heart-inspiring steam;
The luntan pipe, an' sneeshin mill,   glowing; snuff-box
Are handed round wi' right guid will;
The cantie, auld folks, crackan crouse,   lively; gossiping merry
The young anes rantan thro' the house
My heart has been sae fain to see them,   glad
That I for joy hae barket wi' them.   barked

Still it's owre true that ye hae said,
Sic game is now owre aften play'd;
There's monie a creditable stock
O' decent, honest, fawsont folk,   respectable
Are riven out baith root an' branch,
Some rascal's pridefu' greed to quench,
Wha thinks to knit himsel the faster
In favor wi' some gentle Master,
Wha, aiblins, thrang a parliamentin,   perhaps; busy with
For Britain's guid his saul indentin –   pledging

CEASAR
Haith lad, ye little ken about it;
For Britain's guid! guid faith! I doubt it.
Say rather, gaun as Premiers lead him,
An' saying aye or no's they bid him:
At Operas an' Plays parading,
Mortgaging, gambling, masquerading:
Or maybe, in a frolic daft,
To Hague or Calais takes a waft,   sail
To make a tour an' take a whirl,
To learn *bon ton* an' see the worl'.

There, at Vienna or Versailles,
He rives his father's auld entails;[1]   breaks up;
Or by Madrid he takes the rout,
To thrum guittarres an' fecht wi' nowt;   cattle
Or down Italian Vista startles,
Whore-hunting amang groves o' myrtles

---

1. An entail specifies the future inheritance of property.

Then browses drumlie German-water   boozes cloudy (Spa-water)
To make himsel look fair an' fatter,
An' clear the consequential sorrows,
Love-gifts of Carnival Signioras.   (venereal disease)
For Britain's guid! for her destruction!
Wi' dissipation, feud an' faction!

LUATH
Hech man! dear sirs! is that the gate,   the way
They waste sae mony a braw estate!
Are we sae foughten an' harass'd
For gear to gang that gate at last!   goods/property

O would they stay aback frae courts,
An' please themsels wi' countra sports,
It wad for ev'ry ane be better,
The Laird, the Tenant, an' the Cotter!
For thae frank, rantan, ramblan billies,
Fient haet o' them's illhearted fellows;   Devil a jot
Except for breakin o' their timmer,   cutting down their trees
Or speakin lightly o' their Limmer;   mistress
Or shootin of a hare or moorcock,
The ne'er-a-bit they're ill to poor folk.   hardly at all

But will ye tell me, master Cesar,
Sure greatfolk's life's a life o' pleasure?
Nae cauld nor hunger e'er can steer them,
The vera thought o't need na fear them.   frighten

CEASAR
Lord man, were ye but whyles where I am,   sometimes
The gentles ye wad ne'er envy them!

It's true, they needna starve or sweat,
Thro' Winter's cauld, or Summer's heat;
They've nae sair-wark to craze their banes,
An' fill auld-age wi' grips an' granes:
But human-bodies are sic fools,
For a' their Colledges an' Schools,   Despite
That when nae real ills perplex them,
They mak enow themsels to vex them;
An' ay the less they hae to sturt them,   trouble
In like proportion, less will hurt them.

A countra fallow at the pleugh,
His acre's till'd, he's right eneugh;

A countra lassie at her wheel,
Her dizzen's done, she's unco weel;   day's work (a dozen hanks of yarn)
But Gentlemen, an' Ladies warst,   worst of all
Wi' ev'n down want o' wark they're curst.   downright lack
They loiter, lounging, lank an lazy;
Tho' deil-haet ails them, yet uneasy;
Their days, insipid, dull an' tasteless,
Their nights, unquiet, lang an' restless.

   An' ev'n their sports, their balls an' races,
Their galloping thro' public places,
There's sic parade, sic pomp an' art,
The joy can scarcely reach the heart.

   The Men cast out in party-matches,   fall out in card sessions
Then sowther a' in deep debauches.   patch up
Ae night, they're mad wi' drink an' whoring,
Niest day their life is past enduring.

   The Ladies arm-in-arm in clusters,
As great an' gracious a' as sisters;
But hear their absent thoughts o' ither,   another
They're a' run-deils an' jads the gither   thorough devils and hussies
Whyles, owre the wee bit cup an' platie,
They sip the scandal-potion pretty;
Or lee-lang nights, wi' crabbet leuks,
Pore owre the devil's pictur'd beuks;   (playing cards)
Stake on a chance a farmer's stackyard,   gamble
An' cheat like ony unhang'd blackguard.

   There's some exceptions, man an' woman;
But this is Gentry's life in common.

By this, the sun was out o' sight,
An' darker gloamin brought the night: twilight
The bum-clock humm'd wi' lazy drone,   flying beetle
The kye stood rowtan i' the loan;   cattle; lowing; grassy lane
When up they gat, an' shook their lugs,
Rejoic'd they were na men but dogs;
An' each took off his several way,
Resolv'd to meet some ither day.

To a Mouse, On turning her up in her Nest, with the Plough, November, 1785

Wee, sleeket, cowran, tim'rous beastie,
O, what a panic's in thy breastie!

Thou need na start awa sae hasty,
      Wi' bickering brattle!   *scurrying hurry*
I wad be laith to ruin an' chase thee,
      Wi' murd'ring pattle!   *trowel*

I'm truly sorry Man's dominion
Has broken Nature's social union,
An' justifies that ill opinion,
      Which makes thee startle,
At me, thy poor, earth-born companion,
      An' fellow-mortal!

I doubt na, whyles, but thou may thieve;
What then? poor beastie, thou maun live!
A daimen-icker in a thrave   *An ear or two of corn in 2 dozen sheaves*
      'S a sma' request:
I'll get a blessin wi' the lave,   *remainder*
      An' never miss 't!

Thy wee-bit housie, too, in ruin!
It's silly wa's the win's are strewin!
An' naething, now, to big a new ane,
      O' foggage green!   *rough grass*
An' bleak December's winds ensuin,
      Baith snell an' keen!   *sharp*

Thou saw the fields laid bare an' wast,
An' weary Winter comin fast,
An' cozie here, beneath the blast,
      Thou thought to dwell,
Till crash! the cruel coulter past   *(nose of the ploughshare)*
      Out thro' thy cell.

That wee-bit heap o' leaves an' stibble,
Has cost thee monie a weary nibble!
Now thou's turn'd out, for a' thy trouble,
      But house or hald,   *Without*
To thole the Winter's sleety dribble,
      An cranreuch cauld!   *hoar-frost*

But Mousie, thou art no thy-lane,
In proving foresight may be vain:
The best laid schemes o' Mice an' Men,
      Gang aft agley,   *awry*
An' lea'e us nought but grief an' pain,
      For promis'd joy!

Still, thou art blest, compar'd wi' me!
The present only toucheth thee:
But Och! I backward cast my e'e,
    On prospects drear!
An' forward, tho' I canna see,
    I guess an' fear!

To a Louse, On Seeing one on a Lady's Bonnet at Church

Ha! whare ye gaun, ye crowlan ferlie!   curiosity
Your impudence protects you sairly:
I canna say but ye strunt rarely,   strut
    Owre gawze and lace;
Tho' faith, I fear ye dine but sparely,
    On sic a place.

Ye ugly, creepan, blastet wonner,
Detested, shunn'd, by saunt an' sinner,
How daur ye set your fit upon her,
    Sae fine a Lady!
Gae somewhere else and seek your dinner,
    On some poor body.   person

Swith, in some beggar's haffet squattle;   Shoo; sideburn
There ye may creep, and sprawl, and sprattle,
Wi' ither kindred, jumping cattle,
    In shoals and nations;
Whare horn nor bane ne'er daur unsettle,   (combs)
    Your thick plantations.

Now haud you there, ye're out o' sight,
Below the fatt'rels, snug and tight,   falderals
Na faith ye yet! ye'll no be right,
    Till ye've got on it,
The vera tapmost, towrin height
    O' Miss's bonnet.

My sooth! right bauld ye set your nose out,
As plump an' gray as onie grozet: gooseberry
O for some rank, mercurial rozet,   resin
    Or fell, red smeddum,   fierce; powder
I'd gie you sic a hearty dose o't,
    Wad dress your droddum!   spank; backside

I wad na been surpriz'd to spy
You on an auld wife's flainen toy;   tight flannel cap with flaps

Or aiblins some bit duddie boy,   ragged
          On's wylecoat;   underjerkin
But Miss's fine Lunardi,¹ fye!   balloon-shaped bonnet
          How daur ye do 't?

O Jenny dinna toss your head,
An' set your beauties a' abread!
Ye little ken what cursed speed
          The blastie's makin!   wretched creature
Thae winks and finger-ends, I dread,
          Are notice takin!

O wad some Pow'r the giftie gie us
To see oursels as others see us!
It wad frae monie a blunder free us
          An' foolish notion:
What airs in dress an' gait wad lea'e us,
          And ev'n Devotion!

Holy Willie's Prayer

          And send the Godly in a pet to pray –
                         POPE.
                    Argument.

Holy Willie was a rather oldish batchelor Elder in the parish of Mauchline,² and
much and justly famed for that polemical chattering which ends in tippling
Orthodoxy, and for that Spiritualized Bawdry which refines to Liquorish Devotion.
– In a Sessional process with a gentleman in Mauchline, a Mr Gavin Hamilton, Holy
Willie, and his priest, father Auld, after full hearing in the Presbytry of Ayr, came
off but second best; owing partly to the oratorical powers of Mr Robt Aiken,
Mr Hamilton's Counsel; but chiefly to Mr Hamilton's being one of the most
irreproachable and truly respectable characters in the country. – On losing his
Process, the Muse overheard him at his devotions as follows –

O thou that in the heavens does dwell!
Wha, as it pleases best thysel,
Sends ane to heaven and ten to hell,
          A' for thy glory!
And no for ony gude or ill
          They've done before thee.³

---

1. Lunardi was a pioneering balloonist who made several flights in Scotland in the 1780s.
2. His name was William Fisher (1739–1809), and he was 48 when the poem was written.
3. Extreme 'Auld Licht' Calvinist doctrine held that only the 'elect' are saved and all others are damned (even new-born babies), regardless of whether they do good deeds on earth or not. This stems from God's inevitable omniscience and guards against people 'earning' their way into Heaven in unseemly fashion.

I bless and praise thy matchless might,
When thousands thou has left in night,
That I am here before thy sight,
   For gifts and grace,
A burning and a shining light
   To a' this place. –

What was I, or my generation,
That I should get such exaltation?
I, wha deserv'd most just damnation,
   For broken laws
Sax thousand years ere my creation,
   Thro' Adam's cause!   (at the Fall of Man)

When from my mother's womb I fell,
Thou might hae plunged me deep in hell,
To gnash my gooms, and weep, and wail,
   In burning lakes,
Where damned devils roar and yell
   Chain'd to their stakes. –

Yet I am here, a chosen sample,
To shew thy grace is great and ample:
I'm here, a pillar o' thy temple
   Strong as a rock,
A guide, a ruler and example
   To a' thy flock. –

O Lord thou kens what zeal I bear,
When drinkers drink, and swearers swear,
And singin' there, and dancin' here,
   Wi' great an' sma';
For I am keepet by thy fear,
   Free frae them a'. –

But yet – O Lord – confess I must –
At times I'm fash'd wi' fleshly lust;   bothered
And sometimes too, in warldly trust
   Vile Self gets in;
But thou remembers we are dust,
   Defil'd wi' sin. –

O Lord – yestreen – thou kens – wi' Meg –
Thy pardon I sincerely beg!
O may't ne'er be a living plague,
   To my dishonor!

And I'll ne'er lift a lawless leg
      Again upon her. –

Besides, I farther maun avow,
Wi' Leezie's lass, three times – I trow –
But Lord, that friday I was fou   drunk
      When I cam near her;
Or else, thou kens, thy servant true
      Wad never steer her. –   molest

Maybe thou lets this fleshly thorn[1]
Buffet thy servant e'en and morn,
Lest he o'er proud and high should turn,
      That he's sae gifted;
If sae, thy hand maun e'en be borne
      Untill thou lift it. –

Lord bless thy Chosen in this place,
For here thou has a chosen race:
But God, confound their stubborn face,
      And blast their name,
Wha bring thy rulers to disgrace
      And open shame. –

Lord mind Gaun Hamilton's deserts!
He drinks, and swears, and plays at cartes,
Yet has sae mony taking arts   fetching ways
      Wi' Great and Sma',
Frae God's ain priest the people's hearts
      He steals awa. –

And when we chasten'd him therefore,
Thou kens how he bred sic a splore,   uproar
And set the warld in a roar
      O' laughin at us:
Curse thou his basket and his store,
      – Kail and potatoes. –   Cabbage

Lord hear my earnest cry and prayer
Against that Presbytry of Ayr!
Thy strong right hand, Lord, make it bare
      Upon their heads!
Lord visit them, and dinna spare,
      For their misdeeds!

1. Sexual desire. See Paul's second epistle to the Corinthians, 12:7.

O Lord my God, that glib-tongu'd Aiken!
My very heart and flesh are quaking
To think how I sat, sweating, shaking,
         And piss'd wi' dread,
While Auld wi' hingin lip gaed sneaking
         And hid his head!

Lord, in thy day o' vengeance try him!
Lord visit him that did employ him!
And pass not in thy mercy by them,
         Nor hear their prayer;
But for thy people's sake destroy them,
         And dinna spare!

But Lord, remember me and mine
Wi' mercies temporal and divine!
That I for grace and gear may shine,   goods
         Excell'd by nane!
And a' the glory shall be thine!
         AMEN! AMEN!

Address to the Unco Guid, or the Rigidly Righteous

    My Son, these maxims make a rule,
      And lump them ay thegither;
    The Rigid Righteous is a fool,
      The Rigid Wise anither:
    The cleanest corn that e'er was dight
      May hae some pyles o' caff in;   chaff
    So ne'er a fellow-creature slight
      For random fits o' daffin.   dalliance
           SOLOMON. – Eccles. ch. vii. vers. 16.

O ye wha are sae guid yoursel,
    Sae pious and sae holy,
Ye've nought to do but mark and tell
    Your Neebours' fauts and folly!
Whase life is like a weel-gaun mill,
    Supply'd wi' store o' water,
The heaped happer's ebbing still,   hopper
    And still the clap¹ plays clatter.   clapper

Hear me, ye venerable Core,
    As counsel for poor mortals,

---

1. The clapper distributes grain from the hopper to the turning millstones.

That frequent pass douce Wisdom's door | sober
   For glaikit Folly's portals; | daft
I, for their thoughtless, careless sakes
   Would here propone defences,
Their donsie tricks, their black mistakes, | hapless
   Their failings and mischances.

Ye see your state wi' theirs compar'd,
   And shudder at the niffer, | comparison
But cast a moment's fair regard
   What maks the mighty differ;
Discount what scant occasion gave,
   That purity ye pride in,
And (what's aft mair than a' the lave) | often; all the rest
   Your better art o' hiding.

Think, when your castigated pulse
   Gies now and then a wallop,
What ragings must his veins convulse,
   That still eternal gallop:
Wi' wind and tide fair i' your tail,
   Right on ye scud your sea-way;
But, in the teeth o' baith to sail,
   It maks an unco leeway.

See Social-life and Glee sit down,
   All joyous and unthinking,
Till, quite transmugrify'd, they're grown
   Debauchery and Drinking:
O would they stay to calculate | pause
   Th' eternal consequences;
Or your more dreaded hell to state,
   Damnation of expences!

Ye high, exalted, virtuous Dames,
   Ty'd up in godly laces,
Before ye gie poor Frailty names,
   Suppose a change o' cases;
A dear-lov'd lad, convenience snug,
   A treacherous inclination –
But, let me whisper i' your lug, | ear
   Ye're aiblins nae temptation. | perhaps

Then gently scan your brother Man,
   Still gentler sister Woman;
Tho' they may gang a kennin wrang, | little

To step aside is human:
One point must still be greatly dark,
    The moving Why they do it;
And just as lamely can ye mark,
    How far perhaps they rue it.   regret

Who made the heart, 'tis He alone
    Decidedly can try us,
He knows each chord its various tone,
    Each spring its various bias:
Then at the balance let's be mute,
    We never can adjust it;
What's done we partly may compute,
    But know not what's resisted.

Second Epistle to Davie[1]

AULD NIBOR,
I'm three times, doubly, o'er your debtor,
For your auld-farrent, frien'ly letter;   good old-fashioned
Tho' I maun say 't, I doubt ye flatter,   must
        Ye speak sae fair;
For my puir, silly, rhymin' clatter
        Some less maun sair.   Something less (flattering) must serve

Hale be your heart, hale be your fiddle;
Lang may your elbuck jink an' diddle,   elbow
Tae cheer you thro' the weary widdle   trouble
        O' war'ly cares,
Till bairns' bairns kindly cuddle   (grandchildren)
        Your auld, gray hairs.

But Davie, lad, I'm red ye're glaikit;   advised; daft
I'm tauld the Muse ye hae negleckit;
An' gif it's sae, ye sud be licket   smacked
        Until ye fyke;   fidget
Sic hauns as you sud ne'er be faikit,   excused
        Be hain't wha like.   Whoever (else) is spared

For me, I'm on Parnassus brink,
Rivan the words tae gar them clink;   pulling; make them ring
Whyles daez't wi' love, whyles daez't wi' drink,
        Wi' jads or masons;[2]   wenches

1. David Sillar (1760–1830) played the fiddle and published his own poems in 1789.
2. Burns joined the Freemasons in Tarbolton in 1784.

An' whyles, but ay owre late, I think
    Braw sober lessons

Of a' the thoughtless sons o' man,
Commen' me to the Bardie clan;   *Commend; poetic*
Except it be some idle plan   *Unless*
    O' rhymin clink,   *jingle*
The devil-haet, that I sud ban,   *curse*
    They never think.

Nae thought, nae view, nae scheme o' livin',
Nae cares tae gie us joy or grievin':
But just the pouchie put the nieve in,   *pocket; fist*
    An' while ought's there,
Then, hiltie, skiltie, we gae scrivin',   *pell-mell; writing*
    An' fash nae mair.   *bother*

Leeze me on rhyme! it's ay a treasure,   *My blessings*
My chief, amaist my only pleasure,
At hame, a-fiel, at wark or leisure,   *in the field*
    The Muse, poor hizzie!   *wench*
Tho' rough an' raploch be her measure, *coarse-woven*
    She's seldom lazy.

Haud tae the Muse, my dainty Davie: *Stick with*
The warl' may play you monie a shavie;   *trick*
But for the Muse, she'll never leave ye,
    Tho' e'er sae puir,
Na, even tho' limpan wi' the spavie   *rheumatism*
    Frae door tae door.

Address to the Deil

O Prince, O chief of many throned pow'rs,
That led th' embattl'd Seraphim to war –
    MILTON.

O thou, whatever title suit thee!
Auld Hornie, Satan, Nick, or Clootie,   *Hoofy*
Wha in yon cavern grim an' sooty
    Clos'd under hatches,
Spairges about the brunstane cootie, *Splurges; brimstone bowl*
    To scaud poor wretches!

Hear me, auld Hangie, for a wee,   *Hangman*
An' let poor, damned bodies bee;
I'm sure sma' pleasure it can gie,

       Ev'n to a deil,
To skelp an' scaud poor dogs like me,   slap; scald
       An' hear us squeel!

Great is thy pow'r, an' great thy fame;
Far ken'd, an' noted is thy name;
An' tho' yon lowan heugh's thy hame,   blazing ravine
       Thou travels far;
An' faith! thou's neither lag nor lame,   laggard
       Nor blate nor scaur.   bashful; skittish

Whyles, ranging like a roaring lion,[1]
For prey, a' holes an' corners tryin;
Whyles, on the strong-wing'd Tempest flyin,
       Tirlan the kirks;   rattling; churches
Whyles, in the human bosom pryin,
       Unseen thou lurks.

I've heard my rev'rend Graunie say,
In lanely glens ye like to stray;
Or where auld-ruin'd castles, gray,
       Nod to the moon,
Ye fright the nightly wand'rer's way,
       Wi' eldritch croon.   unearthly

When twilight did my Graunie summon,
To say her pray'rs, douse, honest woman,   sober
Aft 'yont the dyke she's heard you bumman,
       Wi' eerie drone;
Or, rustling, thro' the boortries[2] coman,   elder trees
       Wi' heavy groan.

Ae dreary, windy, winter night,
The stars shot down wi' sklentan light,   slanting
Wi' you, mysel, I gat a fright
       Ayont the lough;   loch
Ye, like a rash-buss, stood in sight,   clump of rushes
       Wi' waving sugh: sigh

The cudgel in my nieve did shake,   fist
Each bristl'd hair stood like a stake,
When wi' an eldritch stoor, quaick, quaick,   commotion
       Amang the springs,
Awa ye squatter'd like a drake,
       On whistling wings.

1. See Peter's first epistle, 5:8.
2. The elder, like the rowan, was thought to protect against evil spirits.

Let Warlocks grim, an' wither'd Hags,
Tell, how wi' you, on ragweed nags,   ragwort steeds
They skim the muirs an' dizzy crags,
        Wi' wicked speed;
And in kirk-yards renew their leagues,
        Owre howcket dead.   dug-up

Thence, countra wives, wi' toil an' pain,
May plunge an' plunge the kirn in vain;   butter-churn
For Oh! the yellow treasure's taen,   stolen
        By witching skill;
An' dawtit, twal-pint Hawkie's gane   petted; (trad. name for a cow)
        As yell's the Bill.   dry as the bull

Thence, mystic knots mak great abuse,   strange spells
On Young-Guidmen, fond, keen an' croose;   husbands; merry
When the best warklum i' the house,   tool (loom/penis)
        By cantraip wit,   magic
Is instant made no worth a louse,
        Just at the bit.   key moment

When thowes dissolve the snawy hoord,   thaws
An' float the jinglan icy-boord,
Then, Water-kelpies¹ haunt the foord,
        By your direction,
An' nighted Trav'llers are allur'd
        To their destruction.

An' aft your moss-traversing Spunkies   will of the wisps
Decoy the wight that late an' drunk is;
The bleezan, curst, mischievous monkies
        Delude his eyes,
Till in some miry slough he sunk is,
        Ne'er mair to rise.

When Masons' mystic word an' grip,
In storms an' tempests raise you up,
Some cock, or cat, your rage maun stop,
        Or, strange to tell!
The youngest Brother ye wad whip   (Mason)
        Aff straught to Hell.

Lang syne in Eden's bonie yard,   Long ago
When youthfu' lovers first were pair'd,

1. Celtic water spirit who appears in the form of a horse and carries people off.

An' all the Soul of Love they shar'd,
            The raptur'd hour,
Sweet on the fragrant, flow'ry swaird,
            In shady bow'r:

Then you, ye auld, snick-drawing dog!   latch-lifting
Ye cam to Paradise incog,
An' play'd on a man a cursed brogue,   trick
            (Black be your fa'!)
An' gied the infant warld a shog,   jolt
            'Maist ruin'd a'.   Almost

D'ye mind that day, when in a bizz,
Wi' reeket duds, an' reestet gizz,   smoky clothes; cured wig
Ye did present your smoutie phiz   smutty face
            'Mang better folk,
An' sklented on the man of Uz[1]   picked on (Job)
            Your spitefu' joke?

An' how ye gat him i' your thrall,
An' brak him out o' house an' hal',   hold (dwelling place)
While scabs an' botches did him gall,
            Wi' bitter claw,
An' lows'd his ill-tongu'd, wicked Scawl   scolding woman
            Was warst ava?

But a' your doings to rehearse,
Your wily snares an' fechtin fierce,
Sin' that day Michael[2] did you pierce,
            Down to this time,
Wad ding a' Lallan tongue, or Erse,   defeat; Scots; Gaelic
            In Prose or Rhyme.

An' now, auld Cloots, I ken ye're thinkan,
A certain Bardie's rantin, drinkin,
Some luckless hour will send him linkan,   skipping
            To your black pit;
But faith! he'll turn a corner jinkan,   dodging
            An' cheat you yet.

But fare you weel, auld Nickie-ben!
O wad ye tak a thought an' men'!   mend
Ye aiblins might – I dinna ken –   perhaps
            Still hae a stake –   have enough

1. See Job 1:1. Satan afflicted Job with boils to test his faith in God.
2. The Archangel Michael expelled Satan from Heaven and confronted him again in Eden.

I'm wae to think upo' yon den,   sorry
      Ev'n for your sake.

To a Haggis

Fair fa' your honest, sonsie face,   Good luck to; friendly
Great Chieftan o' the Puddin-race!
Aboon them a' ye tak your place,
      Painch, tripe, or thairm: paunch; guts
Weel are ye wordy of a grace   worthy
      As lang's my arm.

The groaning trencher there ye fill,
Your hurdies like a distant hill,   buttocks
Your pin wad help to mend a mill[1]
      In time o' need,
While thro' your pores the dews distil
      Like amber bead.

His knife see Rustic-labour dight,   wipe
An' cut you up wi' ready slight,   skill
Trenching your gushing entrails bright
      Like onie ditch;
And then, O what a glorious sight,
      Warm-reekin, rich!

Then, horn for horn they stretch an' strive,   (horn) spoon
Deil tak the hindmost, on they drive,   'Devil take the last one'
Till a' their weel-swall'd kytes belyve   bellies soon
      Are bent like drums;
Then auld Guidman, maist like to rive,   burst
      Bethankit hums.

Is there that owre his French ragout,
Or olio that wad staw a sow,   olive oil; glut
Or fricassee wad mak her spew
      Wi' perfect sconner,   disgust
Looks down wi' sneering, scornfu' view
      On sic a dinner?

Poor devil! see him owre his trash,
As feckless as a wither'd rash,   rush
His spindle shank a guid whip-lash,   skinny legs
      His nieve a nit;   fist; nut
Thro' bluidy flood or field to dash,
      O how unfit!

1. 'A pin (peg or latch) fit to mend a mill' is anything small which is yet capable of great things.

But mark the Rustic, haggis-fed,
The trembling earth resounds his tread,
Clap in his walie nieve a blade,   ample hand
       He'll mak it whissle;
An' legs, an' arms, an' heads will sned,   lop off
       Like taps o' thrissle.

Ye Pow'rs wha mak mankind your care,
And dish them out their bill o' fare,
Auld Scotland wants nae skinking ware   soupy stuff
       That jaups in luggies;   sloshes in (wooden) bowls
But, if ye wish her gratefu' pray'r,
       Gie her a Haggis!

Tam o' Shanter: a Tale[1]

Of Brownyis and of Bogillis full is this buke.
    GAWIN DOUGLAS   (*Eneados*, Book VI, Prologue)

When chapman billies leave the street,   pedlar lads
And drouthy neebors, neebors meet,   thirsty
As market-days are wearing late,
An' folk begin to tak the gate;   road
While we sit bousing at the nappy,   ale
And getting fou and unco happy,   drunk; very happy
We think na on the lang Scots miles,
The mosses, waters, slaps, and styles,   gaps in walls
That lie between us and our hame,
Whare sits our sulky sullen dame,
Gathering her brows like gathering storm,
Nursing her wrath to keep it warm.

   This truth fand honest Tam o' Shanter,
As he frae Ayr ae night did canter,
(Auld Ayr, wham ne'er a town surpasses,
For honest men and bonny lasses.)

   O Tam! hadst thou but been sae wise,
As ta'en thy ain wife Kate's advice!
She tauld thee weel thou was a skellum,   scoundrel
A blethering, blustering, drunken blellum;   chattering; babbler
That frae November till October,
Ae market-day thou was nae sober;
That ilka melder, wi' the miller,   each day's grinding of corn

1. Tam is said to be based on Douglas Graham of Shanter farm. 'Kirkton Jean' and 'Soutar Johnnie' can also be identified with local folk.

Thou sat as lang as thou had siller;   *money*
That every naig was ca'd a shoe on,   *nag that was shod*
The smith and thee gat roaring fou on;
That at the Leddie's house,[1] even on Sunday,
Thou drank wi' Kirkton Jean till Monday.

   She prophesied that late or soon,
Thou would be found deep drown'd in Doon;
Or catch'd wi' warlocks in the mirk,   *wizards; night*
By Alloway's auld haunted kirk.

   Ah, gentle dames! it gars me greet,   *makes me cry*
To think how mony counsels sweet,
How mony lengthen'd sage advices,
The husband frae the wife despises!

   But to our tale: Ae market-night,
Tam had got planted unco right;
Fast by an ingle, bleezing finely,   *fireplace; blazing (also 'drunk')*
Wi' reaming swats, that drank divinely;   *foaming new ale*
And at his elbow, Souter Johnny,   *(Cobbler)*
His ancient, trusty, drouthy crony;   *thirsty*
Tam lo'ed him like a vera brither;
They had been fou for weeks thegither.   *drunk*
The night drave on wi' sangs and clatter;
And ay the ale was growing better:
The landlady and Tam grew gracious,
Wi' favours, secret, sweet, and precious:
The Souter tauld his queerest stories;
The landlord's laugh was ready chorus:
The storm without might rair and rustle,   *roar*
Tam did na mind the storm a whistle.

   Care, mad to see a man sae happy,
E'en drown'd himsel amang the nappy:
As bees flee hame wi' lades o' treasure,
The minutes wing'd their way wi' pleasure:
Kings may be blest, but Tam was glorious,
O'er a' the ills o' life victorious!

   But pleasures are like poppies spread,
You seize the flower, its bloom is shed;
Or like the snow falls in the river,
A moment white – then melts for ever;

1. A pub in Kirkoswald run by Jean Kennedy.

Or like the borealis race,   (Northern Lights)
That flit ere you can point their place;
Or like the rainbow's lovely form
Evanishing amid the storm.
Nae man can tether time or tide;
The hour approaches Tam maun ride;   must
That hour, o' night's black arch the key-stane,
That dreary hour he mounts his beast in;
And sic a night he taks the road in,
As ne'er poor sinner was abroad in.

   The wind blew as 'twad blawn its last;
The rattling showers rose on the blast;
The speedy gleams the darkness swallow'd;
Loud, deep, and lang, the thunder bellow'd:
That night, a child might understand,
The Deil had business on his hand.

   Weel mounted on his gray mare, Meg,
A better never lifted leg,
Tam skelpit on thro' dub and mire,   slapped; puddles
Despising wind, and rain, and fire;
Whiles holding fast his gude blue bonnet;
Whiles crooning o'er some auld Scots sonnet;
Whiles glowring round wi' prudent cares,   glaring
Lest bogles catch him unawares: hobgoblins
Kirk-Alloway was drawing nigh,
Whare ghaists and houlets nightly cry. –   owls

   By this time he was cross the ford,
Whare, in the snaw, the chapman smoor'd;   peddler smothered
And past the birks and meikle stane,   birches; big stone
Whare drunken Charlie brak's neck-bane;
And thro' the whins, and by the cairn,   gorse
Whare hunters fand the murder'd bairn;
And near the thorn, aboon the well,   above
Whare Mungo's mither hang'd hersel.
Before him Doon pours all his floods;
The doubling storm roars thro' the woods;
The lightnings flash from pole to pole;
Near and more near the thunders roll:

   When, glimmering thro' the groaning trees,
Kirk-Alloway seem'd in a bleeze;
Thro' ilka bore the beams were glancing;   gap
And loud resounded mirth and dancing. –

Inspiring bold John Barleycorn!   whisky (distilled from grain)
What dangers thou canst make us scorn!
Wi' tippeny, we fear nae evil;   two-penny ale
Wi' usquabae, we'll face the devil!   whisky (Gaelic)
The swats sae ream'd in Tammie's noddle,   new beer; head
Fair play, he car'd na deils a boddle.   a farthing (very small coin)
But Maggie stood right sair astonish'd,
Till, by the heel and hand admonish'd,
She ventured forward on the light;
And, vow! Tam saw an unco sight!   strange
Warlocks and witches in a dance;
Nae cotillion brent new frae France,   (a stately dance); brand-new
But hornpipes, jigs, strathspeys, and reels,
Put life and mettle in their heels.
A winnock-bunker in the east,   window-seat
There sat auld Nick, in shape o' beast;
A towzie tyke, black, grim, and large,   shaggy dog
To gie them music was his charge:
He screw'd the pipes and gart them skirl,   made them screech
Till roof and rafters a' did dirl.   ring
Coffins stood round, like open presses,   cupboards
That shaw'd the dead in their last dresses;
And by some devilish cantraip slight   magic trick
Each in its cauld hand held a light.
By which heroic Tam was able
To note upon the haly table,
A murderer's banes in gibbet airns;   gallows irons
Twa span-lang, wee, unchristen'd bairns;   (hand-span)
A thief, new-cutted frae a rape,   rope
Wi' his last gasp his gab did gape;   mouth
Five tomahawks, wi' blude red-rusted;
Five scymitars, wi' murder crusted;
A garter, which a babe had strangled;
A knife, a father's throat had mangled,
Whom his ain son o' life bereft,
The grey hairs yet stack to the heft;
Wi' mair o' horrible and awefu',
Which even to name wad be unlawfu'.
Three Lawyers' tongues, turn'd inside out,
Wi' lies seam'd like a beggar's clout;   rag
And Priests' hearts, rotten, black as muck,
Lay stinking, vile, in every neuk. –¹

As Tammie glow'rd, amaz'd, and curious,
The mirth and fun grew fast and furious:

1. Burns omitted these last four lines from later editions on the advice of Alexander Fraser Tytler, a man of the law himself.

The piper loud and louder blew;
The dancers quick and quicker flew;
They reel'd, they set, they cross'd, they cleekit,   *linked arms*
Till ilka carlin swat and reekit,   *each old woman*
And coost her duddies to the wark,   *cast off her clothes*
And linket at it in her sark!   *tripped; shift*

    Now, Tam, O Tam! had thae been queans,   *girls*
A' plump and strapping in their teens,
Their sarks, instead o' creeshie flannen,   *greasy flannel*
Been snaw-white seventeen hunder linnen!   *(finely woven)*
Thir breeks o' mine, my only pair,   *trousers*
That ance were plush, o' gude blue hair,
I wad hae gi'en them off my hurdies,   *backside*
For ae blink o' the bonie burdies!   *pretty chicks*

    But wither'd beldams, auld and droll,   *grannies*
Rigwoodie hags wad spean a foal,   *bony horse-backed; wean (put off milk)*
Lowping and flinging on a crummock,   *jumping; crook*
I wonder didna turn thy stomach.

    But Tam kend what was what fu' brawlie,   *knew*
There was ae winsome wench and wawlie,   *strapping*
That night enlisted in the core,   *corps*
(Lang after kend on Carrick shore;
For mony a beast to dead she shot,
And perish'd mony a bony boat,
And shook baith meikle corn and bear,   *a lot of; barley*
And kept the country-side in fear)
Her cutty sark, o' Paisley harn,   *short shift; yarn*
That while a lassie she had worn,
In longitude tho' sorely scanty,
It was her best, and she was vauntie.   *proud*
Ah! little kend thy reverend grannie,
That sark she coft for her wee Nannie,   *bought*
Wi' twa pund Scots, ('twas a' her riches),
Wad ever grac'd a dance of witches!

    But here my Muse her wing maun cour;   *fold*
Sic flights are far beyond her pow'r;
To sing how Nannie lap and flang,
(A souple jade she was, and strang),
And how Tam stood, like ane bewitch'd,
And thought his very een enrich'd;
Even Satan glowr'd, and fidg'd fu' fain,   *twitched with pleasure*
And hotch'd and blew wi' might and main: *jerked*

Till first ae caper, syne anither,   then
Tam tint his reason a' thegither,   lost
And roars out, 'Weel done, Cutty-sark!'
And in an instant all was dark:
And scarcely had he Maggie rallied,
When out the hellish legion sallied.

As bees bizz out wi' angry fyke,   fuss
When plundering herds assail their byke;   herdsmen; hive
As open pussie's mortal foes,   As (start to bark); the hare's
When, pop! she starts before their nose;
As eager runs the market-crowd,
When 'Catch the thief!' resounds aloud;
So Maggie runs, the witches follow,
Wi' mony an eldritch skreech and hollow.   unearthly

Ah, Tam! Ah, Tam! thou'll get thy fairin!   deserts
In hell they'll roast thee like a herrin!
In vain thy Kate awaits thy comin!
Kate soon will be a woefu' woman!
Now, do thy speedy utmost, Meg,
And win the key-stane of the brig;   gain; bridge
There at them thou thy tail may toss,
A running stream they dare na cross.
But ere the key-stane she could make,
The fient a tail she had to shake!   devil a tail (none at all)
For Nannie, far before the rest,
Hard upon noble Maggie prest,
And flew at Tam wi' furious ettle;   intent
But little wist she Maggie's mettle   knew
Ae spring brought off her master hale,   whole
But left behind her ain gray tail:
The carlin claught her by the rump,   clutched
And left poor Maggie scarce a stump.

Now, wha this tale o' truth shall read,
Ilk man and mother's son, take heed: Each
Whene'er to drink you are inclin'd,
Or cutty-sarks run in your mind,
Think, ye may buy the joys o'er dear,
Remember Tam o' Shanter's mare.

Love and Liberty – A Cantata[1]

RECITATIVO –[2]

When lyart leaves bestrow the yird,   *grizzled; earth*
Or wavering like the Bauckie-bird,   *bat*
　　Bedim cauld Boreas' blast;   *(the wind)*
When hailstanes drive wi' bitter skyte,   *rebound*
And infant Frosts begin to bite,
　　In hoary cranreuch drest;   *hoar-frost*
Ae night at e'en a merry core   *evening; corps*
　　O' randie, gangrel bodies,   *riotous vagrant folk*
In Poosie-Nansie's[3] held the splore,   *spree*
　　To drink their orra dudies: *spare clothes (pawned for drink)*
　　　　Wi' quaffing, and laughing,
　　　　　　They ranted an' they sang;
　　　　Wi' jumping, an' thumping,
　　　　　　The vera girdle rang.   *griddle for baking scones*

First, niest the fire, in auld, red rags,   *next*
Ane sat; weel brac'd wi' mealy bags,   *flour-sacks*
　　And knapsack a' in order;
His doxy lay within his arm;   *wench/doll*
Wi' Usqebae an' blankets warm,   *whisky (Gaelic: 'water of life')*
　　She blinket on her Sodger: *soldier*
An' ay he gies the tozie drab   *rumpled*
　　The tither skelpan kiss,   *smacking*
While she held up her greedy gab,
　　Just like an aumous dish: *alms*
　　　　Ilk smack still, did crack still,
　　　　　　Just like a cadger's whip;   *carter's*
　　　　Then staggering, an' swaggering,
　　　　　　He roar'd this ditty up –

Tune, Soldier's Joy
I am a Son of Mars who have been in many wars,
　　And show my cuts and scars wherever I come;
This here was for a wench, and that other in a trench,
　　When welcoming the French at the sound of the drum.
　　　　　　　　Lal de daudle &c.

1. Also known as 'The Jolly Beggars', Hugh Blair advised Burns to leave this piece out of the 1787 Edinburgh edition on the grounds of taste and it was never published in the poet's lifetime. It belongs to a long-standing Goliardic anti-pastoral tradition, but transcends even that in its wild, subversive and carnivalesque energy.
2. These stanzas adapt the ryhme scheme of Montgomerie's *Cherry and the Slae*.
3. The hostess of *Poosie Nansie's Tavern* in Mauchline.

My Prenticeship I past where my Leader breath'd his last,
   When the bloody die was cast on the heights of Abram;[1]
And I served out my Trade when the gallant game was play'd,
   And the Moro low was laid at the sound of the drum.

I lastly was with Curtis among the floating batt'ries
   And there I left for witness, an arm and a limb;
Yet let my Country need me, with Elliot to head me,
   I'd clatter on my stumps at the sound of a drum.

And now tho' I must beg, with a wooden arm and leg,
   And many a tatter'd rag hanging over my bum,
I'm as happy with my wallet, my bottle and my Callet,   tart (girl)
   As when I us'd in scarlet to follow a drum.

What tho', with hoary locks, I must stand the winter shocks,
   Beneath the woods and rocks oftentimes for a home,
When the tother bag I sell and the tother bottle tell,
   I could meet a troop of HELL at the sound of a drum.

          RECITATIVO –
He ended; and the kebars sheuk,   roof-beams
   Aboon the chorus roar;
While frighted rattons backward leuk,   rats
   An' seek the benmost bore: furthest hole
A fairy Fiddler frae the neuk,   corner
   He skirl'd out, Encore.
But up arose the martial Chuck,   sweetheart
   An' laid the loud uproar –

Tune, Sodger Laddie
I once was a Maid, tho' I cannot tell when,
And still my delight is in proper young men:
Some one of a troop of Dragoons was my dadie,   father
No wonder I'm fond of a Sodger Laddie.
                    Sing lal de dal &c.

The first of my Loves was a swaggering blade,
To rattle the thundering drum was his trade;
His leg was so tight and his cheek was so ruddy,
Transported I was with my Sodger Laddie.

1. General Wolfe died in battle with the French on the Heights of Abraham in Quebec in 1759. The old soldier goes
   on to recall the Moro fortress at the capture of Cuba in 1762, and action with Admiral Curtis and General Elliot in
   defence of Gibralter in 1782; all before the peace treaty of Versailles the following year.

But the godly old Chaplain left him in the lurch,
The sword I forsook for the sake of the church;
He ventur'd the Soul, and I risked the Body,
'Twas then I prov'd false to my Sodger Laddie.

Full soon I grew sick of my sanctified Sot,
The Regiment at large for a Husband I got;
From the gilded Spontoon to the Fife I was ready;[1]   infantry officer's pike
I asked no more but a Sodger Laddie.

But the Peace it reduc'd me to beg in despair,
Till I met my old boy in a Cunningham fair;   (in Ayrshire)
His Rags Regimental they flutter'd so gaudy,
My heart it rejoic'd at a Sodger Laddie.

And now I have lived – I know not how long,
And still I can join in a cup and a song;
But whilst with both hands I can hold the glass steady,
Here's to thee, my Hero, my Sodger Laddie.

         RECITATIVO –
Poor Merry-andrew, in the neuk,   corner
    Sat guzzling wi' a Tinkler-hizzie;[2]   tinker hussy
They mind't na wha the chorus teuk,   didn't care
    Between themsels they were sae busy:
At length wi' drink an' courting dizzy,
    He stoiter'd up an' made a face;   staggered
Then turn'd an' laid a smack on Grizzie,
    Syne tun'd his pipes wi' grave grimace.

Tune, Auld Sir Symon
Sir Wisdom's a fool when he's fou;   drunk
    Sir Knave is a fool in a Session,[3]
He's there but a prentice, I trow,
    But I am a fool by profession.

My Grannie she bought me a beuk,
    An' I held awa to the school;   set off for
I fear I my talent misteuk,
    But what will ye hae of a fool.

For drink I would venture my neck;
    A hizzie's the half of my Craft: wench

1. 'From the infantry officer to the flute-boy': also a sexual joke about size.
2. The tinker families of Scotland are travelling pot menders and seasonal labourers.
3. Court of Session, the highest civil court in Scotland.

But what could ye other expect
   Of ane that's avowedly daft.

I, ance, was ty'd up like a stirk,[1]   bullock
   For civilly swearing and quaffing;
I, ance, was abus'd i' the kirk,
   For towsing a lass i' my daffin.   dishevelling; flirtation

Poor Andrew that tumbles for sport,
   Let nae body name wi' a jeer;
There's even, I'm tauld, i' the Court
   A Tumbler ca'd the Premier.

Observ'd ye yon reverend lad   (Church minister)
   Mak faces to tickle the Mob;
He rails at our mountebank squad,
   Its rivalship just i' the job.

And now my conclusion I'll tell,
   For faith I'm confoundedly dry:
The chiel that's a fool for himsel,   fellow
   Guid Lord, he's far dafter than I.

RECITATIVO –
Then niest outspak a raucle Carlin,   raw-boned old woman
Wha ken't fu' weel to cleek the Sterlin;   hook; (money)
For mony a pursie she had hooked,
An' had in mony a well been douked: ducked (for theft)
Her Love had been a Highland Laddie,
But weary fa' the waefu' woodie!   curse; hangman's rope
Wi' sighs an' sobs she thus began
To wail her braw John Highlandman –   lament

Tune, O an' ye were dead Gudeman
A Highland lad my Love was born,
The lalland laws he held in scorn;   Lowland
But he still was faithfu' to his clan,
My gallant, braw John Highlandman.   brave/fine

CHORUS –
   Sing hey my braw John Highlandman!
   Sing ho my braw John Highlandman!
   There's not a lad in a' the lan'
   Was match for my John Highlandman.

1. In the public stocks.

With his Philibeg, an' tartan Plaid,   kilt
An' guid Claymore down by his side,   Highland sword
The ladies' hearts he did trepan,   beguile
My gallant, braw John Highlandman.[1]
       Sing hey &c.

We ranged a' from Tweed to Spey,
An' liv'd like lords an' ladies gay:
For a lalland face he feared none,
My gallant, braw John Highlandman.
       Sing hey &c.

They banish'd him beyond the sea,
But ere the bud was on the tree,
Adown my cheeks the pearls ran,
Embracing my John Highlandman.
       Sing hey &c.

But Och! they catch'd him at the last,
And bound him in a dungeon fast,
My curse upon them every one,
They've hang'd my braw John Highlandman.
       Sing hey &c.

And now a Widow I must mourn
The Pleasures that will ne'er return;
No comfort but a hearty can,   mug (of ale)
When I think on John Highlandman.
       Sing hey &c.

RECITATIVO –
A pigmy Scraper wi' his Fiddle,
Wha us'd to trystes an' fairs to driddle,   cattle-markets; dawdle
Her strappan limb an' gausy middle,   ample
    (He reach'd nae higher)
Had hol'd his Heartie like a riddle,   made holes in
    An' blawn't on fire.

Wi' hand on hainch, and upward e'e,   hip
He croon'd his gamut, One, Two, Three,
Then in an Arioso key,   (declamatory singing, like an aria)
    The wee Apollo
Set off wi Allegretto glee   (Italian: moderately quick)
    His Giga Solo –   (Italian *giga*: a lively dance)

1. As well as being her lover, 'John Highlandman' symbolises all Jacobite rebels, wearing the tartan and carrying a sword (both prohibited in 1746), banished 'beyond the sea' and ultimately hanged.

Tune, Whistle owre the lave o't
Let me ryke up to dight that tear,   reach; wipe
An' go wi' me an' be my Dear;
An' then your every Care an' Fear
 May whistle owre the lave o't.   for the rest of it

   CHORUS –
 I am a Fiddler to my trade,
 An' a' the tunes that e'er I play'd,
 The sweetest still to Wife or Maid,
 Was whistle owre the lave o't.

At Kirns an Weddins we'se be there,   harvest festivals
An' O sae nicely's we will fare!
We'll bowse about till Dadie Care   drink in turns
 Sing whistle owre the lave o't.
   I am &c.

Sae merrily's the banes we'll pyke,   pick over
An' sun oursells about the dyke;   wall
An' at our leisure when ye like
 We'll whistle owre the lave o't.
   I am &c.

But bless me wi' your heav'n o' charms,
An' while I kittle hair on thairms[1]   tickle hair on guts
Hunger, Cauld, an a' sic harms
 May whistle owre the lave o't.
   I am &c.

   RECITATIVO –
 Her charms had struck a sturdy Caird,   tinker
  As weel as poor Gutscraper;
 He taks the Fiddler by the beard,
  An' draws a roosty rapier –
 He swoor by a' was swearing worth
  To speet him like a Pliver,[2]   plover
 Unless he would from that time forth
  Relinquish her for ever:

 Wi ghastly e'e poor Tweedledee
  Upon his hunkers bended,
 An' pray'd for grace wi' ruefu' face,
  An' so the quarrel ended;

1. 'Play the fiddle', also a sexual pun.
2. This line imitates a Highland accent.

But tho' his little heart did grieve,
   When round the Tinkler prest her
He feign'd to snirtle in his sleeve   snigger
   When thus the Caird address'd her –

Tune, Clout the Caudron
My bonie lass I work in brass,
   A Tinkler is my station;
I've travell'd round all Christian ground
   In this my occupation;
I've ta'en the gold an' been enroll'd   (enlisted)
   In many a noble squadron;
But vain they search'd when off I march'd
   To go an clout the Caudron.   patch; cauldron
           I've ta'en the gold &c.

Despise that Shrimp, that withered Imp,
   With a' his noise an' cap'rin;
An' take a share, with those that bear
   The budget and the apron!   leather bag
And by that Stowp! my faith an' houpe,   tankard
   And by that dear Kilbaigie,   (whisky distilled in Clackmannan)
If e'er ye want, or meet with scant,   dearth
   May I ne'er weet my Craigie!   throat
           And by that Stowp, &c.

          RECITATIVO –
The Caird prevail'd – th' unblushing fair
   In his embraces sunk;
Partly wi' Love o'ercome sae sair,
   An' partly she was drunk:
Sir Violino with an air,
   That show'd a man o' spunk,   spirit
Wish'd Unison between the Pair,
   An' made the bottle clunk
        To their health that night.

But hurchin Cupid shot a shaft,   urchin
   That play'd a Dame a shavie –   trick
The Fiddler Rak'd her, Fore and Aft,
   Behint the Chicken cavie: coop
Her lord, a wight of Homer's craft,   creature
   Tho' limpan wi' the Spavie,   rheumatism
He hirpl'd up an' lap like daft,   hobbled; leaped
   An' shor'd them Dainty Davie[1]   urged
        O' boot that night.   Into the bargain

1. 'Handsome David' Williamson was a 17th-century minister noted for his sexual prowess.

He was a care-defying blade,
   As ever Bacchus listed!
Tho' Fortune sair upon him laid,   assailed
   His heart she ever miss'd it.
He had no Wish but – to be glad,
   Nor Want but – when he thristed;
He hated nought but – to be sad,
   An' thus the Muse suggested
         His sang that night.

Tune, For a' that an' a' that
I am a Bard of no regard,
   Wi' gentle folks an' a' that;
But Homer-like the glowran byke,   staring crowd
   Frae town to town I draw that.

      CHORUS –
   For a' that an' a' that,
     An' twice as muckle's a' that,
   I've lost but Ane, I've Twa behin',
    I ve Wife Eneugh for a that.

I never drank the Muses' Stank,   pond
   Castalia's[1] burn an' a' that,   stream
But there it streams an' richly reams,   froths (ale)
   My Helicon I ca that.
      For a' that &c.

Great love I bear to all the Fair,
   Their humble slave an' a' that;
But lordly Will, I hold it still
   A mortal sin to thraw that.   force/extort
      For a' that &c.

In raptures sweet this hour we meet,
   Wi' mutual love an' a' that;
But for how lang the Flie may Stang,   fly (desire); goad
   Let Inclination law that.   decide
      For a' that &c.

Their tricks an' craft hae put me daft,
   They've ta'en me in, an' a' that,
But clear your decks an' here's the sex!
   I like the jads for a' that.   jades

1. A fountain of the muses on Mt Parnassus. Further to the south, Mt Helicon also has sacred fountains and has come
to represent a source of inspiration.

For a' that an' a' that
   An' twice as muckle's a' that,
My Dearest Bluid to do them guid,
   They're welcome till't for a' that.   *to it*

     RECITATIVO –
So sung the Bard – and Nansie's waws
Shook with a thunder of applause
   Re-echo'd from each mouth!
They toom'd their pocks, they pawn'd their duds,   *emptied; bags*
They scarcely left to coor their fuds   *cover; scuts*
   To quench their lowan drouth: *burning thirst*
Then owre again the jovial thrang   *once more; crowd*
   The Poet did request
To lowse his Pack an' wale a sang,   *open; choose*
   A Ballad o the best.
     He, rising, rejoicing,
       Between his Twa Deborahs,
     Looks round him an' found them
       Impatient for the Chorus.

Tune, Jolly Mortals fill your glasses
See the smoking bowl before us,
   Mark our jovial, ragged ring!
Round and round take up the Chorus,
   And in raptures let us sing –

     CHORUS –
   A fig for those by law protected!
     Liberty's a glorious feast!
   Courts for Cowards were erected,
     Churches built to please the Priest.

What is Title, what is Treasure,
   What is Reputation's care?
If we lead a life of pleasure,
   'Tis no matter How or Where.
       A fig, &c.

With the ready trick and fable
   Round we wander all the day;
And at night, in barn or stable,
   Hug our doxies on the hay.
       A fig for &c.

Does the train-attended Carriage
   Thro' the country lighter rove?

Does the sober bed of Marriage
   Witness brighter scenes of love?
      A fig for &c.

Life is all a Variorum,   constant change
   We regard not how it goes;
Let them cant about Decorum,   proper behaviour
   Who have character to lose.
      A fig for &c.

Here's to Budgets, Bags and Wallets!
   Here's to all the wandering train!
Here's our ragged Brats and Callets!   garments and caps
   One and all cry out, AMEN!

A fig for those by Law protected,
   Liberty's a glorious feast!
Courts for Cowards were erected,
   Churches built to please the Priest.

For a' that and a' that

Is there, for honest Poverty
   That hings his head, and a' that;
The coward-slave, we pass him by,
    We dare be poor for a' that!
   For a' that, and a' that,
     Our toils obscure, and a' that,
   The rank is but the guinea's stamp,   (gold coin)
     The Man's the gowd for a' that.

What though on hamely fare we dine,
    Wear hoddin grey, and a' that.   homespun
Gie fools their silks, and knaves their wine,
    A Man's a Man for a' that.
   For a' that, and a' that,
     Their tinsel show, and a' that;
   The honest man, though e'er sae poor,
     Is king o' men for a' that.

Ye see yon birkie ca'd, a lord,   conceited fellow
    Wha struts, and stares, and a' that,
Though hundreds worship at his word,
    He's but a coof for a' that.   fool
   For a' that, and a' that,
     His ribband, star and a' that,

The man of independant mind,
   He looks and laughs at a' that.

A prince can mak a belted knight,   make/appoint
   A marquis, duke, and a' that;
But an honest man's aboon his might,   above; power
   Gude faith he mauna fa' that!   must not claim that
   For a' that, and a' that,
      Their dignities, and a' that,
   The pith o' Sense, and pride o' Worth,
      Are higher rank than a' that.

Then let us pray that come it may,
   As come it will for a' that,
That Sense and Worth, o'er a' the earth
   Shall bear the gree, and a' that.   win the day
   For a' that, and a' that,
      Its comin yet for a' that,
   That Man to Man the warld o'er,
      Shall brothers be for a' that.

Such a parcel of rogues in a nation[1]

Fareweel to a' our Scotish fame,
   Fareweel our ancient glory;
Fareweel even to the Scotish name,
   Sae fam'd in martial story!
Now Sark rins o'er the Solway sands,
   And Tweed rins to the ocean,
To mark whare England's province stands,
   Such a parcel of rogues in a nation!

What force or guile could not subdue,
   Thro' many warlike ages,
Is wrought now by a coward few,
   For hireling traitors' wages.
The English steel we could disdain,
   Secure in valor's station;
But English gold has been our bane,
   Such a parcel of rogues in a nation!

O would, or I had seen the day   before
   That treason thus could sell us,
My auld grey head had lien in clay,
   Wi Bruce and loyal Wallace!

1. Burns improves on a popular refrain lamenting the Union of 1707, widely seen (not without justice) as a betrayal of
   Scottish sovereignty for the personal gain of a few lords.

But pith and power, till my last hour,
    I'll mak this declaration;
We're bought and sold for English gold,
    Such a parcel of rogues in a nation!

It was a' for our rightfu' king[1]

It was a' for our rightfu' king
    We left fair Scotland's strand;
It was a' for our rightfu' king,
    We e'er saw Irish land, my dear,
    We e'er saw Irish land.

Now a' is done that men can do,
    And a' is done in vain:
My Love and Native Land fareweel,
    For I maun cross the main, my dear,   must
    For I maun cross the main.

He turn'd him right and round about,
    Upon the Irish shore,
And gae his bridle-reins a shake,
    With, Adieu for evermore, my dear,
    And adieu for evermore.

The soger frae the wars returns,
    The sailor frae the main,
But I hae parted frae my Love,
    Never to meet again, my dear,
    Never to meet again.

When day is gane, and night is come,
    And a' folk bound to sleep;
I think on him that's far awa,
    The lee-lang night and weep, my dear,
    The lee-lang night and weep.

Does haughty Gaul invasion threat?[2]

Does haughty Gaul invasion threat?
    Then let the loons beware, Sir,

1. A chapbook ballad from around 1746 reworked by Burns. Jacobite songs frequently conflate Prince Charlie with a loved one in the romantic genre, but the reference here may be to his deposed grandfather's unsuccessful campaign against William of Orange in Ireland in 1689–90.
2. Written when Burns joined a company of Volunteers at Dumfries, when invasion was feared in 1795. Two years earlier, the poet's declared support for the French Revolution had led to his loyalty being questioned. The last line of this song makes a quietly democratic coda to its overt patriotism.

There's wooden walls upon our seas,   (naval warships)
    And volunteers on shore, Sir.
The Nith shall run to Corsincon,[2]
    And Criffel sink in Solway,
Ere we permit a foreign foe
    On British ground to rally!

O let us not like snarling tykes
    In wrangling be divided,
Till, slap! come in an unco loon   strange rascal
    And wi' a rung decide it.   cudgel
Be Britain still to Britain true,
    Amang oursels united;
For never but by British hands
    Maun British wrangs be righted!   Must

The kettle o' the kirk and state,
    Perhaps a clout may fail in't;   patch
But deil a foreign tinkler loon
    Shall ever ca' a nail in't.   put a nail (mend)
Our father's blude the kettle bought,
    An' wha wad dare to spoil it?
By heavens! the sacrilegious dog
    Shall fuel be to boil it!

The wretch that would a tyrant own,
    And the wretch, his true-born brother,
Who'd set the mob aboon the throne, –
    May they be damned together!
Who will not sing *God save the King!*
    Shall hang as high's the steeple;
But while we sing *God save the King!*
    We'll not forget the people!

The De'il 's awa' wi' the Exciseman[2]

The De'il cam fiddling thro' the town,
    And danced awa wi' the Exciseman;
And ilka wife cried 'Auld Mahoun,   every woman; Satan (Mahomet)
    We wish you luck o' your prize, man.'

We'll mak our maut, and brew our drink,   malt (whisky)
    We'll dance, and sing, and rejoice, man;
And mony thanks to the muckle black De'il   big
    That danced awa wi' the Exciseman.

1. Corsincon is a hill at the source of the River Nith. Criffel is a hill where the Nith meets the Solway Firth.
2. Burns himself worked as an excise officer in Dumfries during the last six years of his life.

There's threesome reels, and foursome reels,
    There's hornpipes and strathspeys, man;
But the ae best dance e'er cam to our lan',
    Was – the De'il 's awa wi' the Exciseman.

Now Westlin Winds

Now westlin winds and slaughtering guns
    Bring autumn's pleasant weather;
The moorcock springs, on whirring wings,
    Amang the blooming heather:
Now waving grain, wide o'er the plain,
    Delights the weary farmer;
And the moon shines bright, when I rove at night
    To muse upon my charmer.

The partridge loves the fruitful fells;
    The plover loves the mountains;
The woodcock haunts the lonely dells;
    The soaring hern the fountains: heron
Thro' lofty groves the cushat roves,   dove
    The path of man to shun it;
The hazel bush o'erhangs the thrush,
    The spreading thorn the linnet.

Thus ev'ry kind their pleasure find,
    The savage and the tender;
Some social join, and leagues combine;
    Some solitary wander;
Avaunt, away! the cruel sway,
    Tyrannic man's dominion;
The sportsman's joy, the murdering cry,
    The fluttering, gory pinion!

But, Peggy dear, the ev'ning's clear,
    Thick flies the skimming swallow;
The sky is blue, the fields in view,
    All fading-green and yellow:
Come let us stray our gladsome way,
    And view the charms of nature;
The rustling corn, the fruited thorn,
    And every happy creature.

We'll gently walk, and sweetly talk,
    Till the silent moon shine clearly;

I'll grasp thy waist, and, fondly prest,
    Swear how I love thee dearly:
Not vernal show'rs to budding flow'rs,
    Not autumn to the farmer;
So dear can be as thou to me,
    My fair, my lovely charmer!

Mary Morison[1]

Tune, Duncan Davison
O Mary, at thy window be,
    It is the wish'd, the trysted hour;   appointed
Those smiles and glances let me see,
    That make the miser's treasure poor:
How blythely wad I bide the stoure,   put up with the fight
    A weary slave frae sun to sun;
Could I the rich reward secure,
    The lovely Mary Morison!

Yestreen when to the trembling string
    The dance gaed through the lighted ha',
To thee my fancy took its wing,
    I sat, but neither heard, nor saw:
Though this was fair, and that was braw,
    And yon the toast of a' the town,
I sigh'd, and said amang them a',
    'Ye are na Mary Morison.'

O Mary, canst thou wreck his peace,
    Wha for thy sake wad gladly die!
Or canst thou break that heart of his,
    Whase only faute is loving thee!
If love for love thou wilt na gie,
    At least be pity to me shown;
A thought ungentle canna be
    The thought o' Mary Morison.

A red red Rose[2]

O my Luve's like a red, red rose,
    That's newly sprung in June;
O my Luve's like the melodie
    That's sweetly play'd in tune. –

1. Mary Morison died of TB in 1791, but the song may have been inspired by another girl.
2. Largely based on folk sources, or perhaps a little reworked by Burns, the stock epithets of love lyrics are simplified and purified in this song to an extraordinary degree.

As fair art thou, my bonie lass,
  So deep in luve am l;
And I will love thee still, my Dear,
  Till a' the seas gang dry. –

Till a' the seas gang dry, my Dear,
  And the rocks melt wi' the sun:
I will love thee still, my Dear,
  While the sands o' life shall run. –

And fare thee weel, my only Luve!
  And fare thee weel, a while!
And I will come again, my Luve,
  Tho' it were ten thousand mile!

Ae fond kiss[1]

Ae fond kiss, and then we sever;
Ae fareweel, and then for ever!
Deep in heart-wrung tears I'll pledge thee,
Warring sighs and groans I'll wage thee.

Who shall say that Fortune grieves him,
While the star of hope she leaves him:
Me, nae chearful twinkle lights me;
Dark despair around benights me.

I'll ne'er blame my partial fancy,
Naething could resist my Nancy:
But to see her, was to love her;
Love but her, and love for ever.

Had we never lov'd sae kindly,
Had we never lov'd sae blindly!
Never met – or never parted,
We had ne'er been broken-hearted.

Fare-thee-weel, thou first and fairest!
Fare-thee-weel, thou best and dearest!
Thine be ilka joy and treasure,
Peace, Enjoyment, Love and Pleasure!

Ae fond kiss, and then we sever!
Ae fareweel, Alas, for ever:

1. Written on parting from Mrs McLehose ('Clarinda') – whom he had met in Edinburgh – who was leaving to rejoin
   her husband in Jamaica.

Deep in heart-wrung tears I'll pledge thee,
Warring sighs and groans I'll wage thee.

Oh wert thou in the cauld blast[1]

Oh wert thou in the cauld blast,
   On yonder lea, on yonder lea;   *fallow hillside*
My plaidie to the angry airt,   *plaid; (wind) direction*
   I'd shelter thee, I'd shelter thee:
Or did misfortune's bitter storms
   Around thee blaw, around thee blaw,
Thy bield should be my bosom,   *shelter*
   To share it a', to share it a'.

Or were I in the wildest waste,
   Sae black and bare, sae black and bare,
The desart were a paradise,
   If thou wert there, if thou wert there.
Or were I monarch o' the globe,
   Wi' thee to reign, wi' thee to reign;
The brightest jewel in my crown,
   Wad be my queen, wad be my queen.

---

1. Written by Burns during his final illness, and dedicated to 18-year-old Jessy Lewars who was nursing him.

Scots Songs in the 18th and 19th Centuries

The success of four volumes of Ramsay's *Tea Table Miscellany* (1724–32) and of William Thomson's *Orpheus Caledonius* (1725) heralded a revival of popular interest in old Scots songs, along with an upsurge in the quality of new ones, with further input from dance and fiddle music, the folk tradition and broadside ballads. The trend was to continue well into the nineteenth century as vigorous airs and sad songs gradually gave way to more self-consciously 'characterful' utterances, genteel melancholy or parlour Jacobitism. Nevertheless, many of these lyrics, with their often beautiful tunes, are still sung today. After all, Burns had done some of his best work in the versions and revisions he contributed to *The Scots Musical Museum*, while Scott and Hogg were equally influential in collecting and in embellishing old ballads. David Herd (1732–1810) took a more scholarly approach in his *Ancient and Modern Scots Songs* (1769; 1776); while *The Scottish Minstrel* edited in Paisley by R. A. Smith (1780–1829), had a wide following, publishing much of Lady Nairne's work among others.

Anonymous

Waly, Waly

O waly, waly, up the bank,	alas (welaway)
And waly, waly, doun the brae,	
And waly, waly, yon burn-side,	that
Where I and my Love wont to gae!	
I lean'd my back unto an aik,	oak
I thocht it was a trustie tree;	
But first it bow'd and syne it brak –	then
Sae my true love did lichtlie me.	slight
O waly, waly, gin love be bonnie	if
A little time while it is new!	

But when 'tis auld it waxeth cauld,
    And fades awa' like morning dew.
O wherefore should I busk my heid,   adorn
    Or wherefore should I kame my hair?
For my true Love has me forsook,
    And says he'll never lo'e me mair.

Now Arthur's Seat[1] sall be my bed,
    The sheets sall ne'er be 'filed by me;   defiled
Saint Anton's well sall be my drink;
    Since my true Love has forsaken me.
Marti'mas wind when wilt thou blaw,   (Martinmas: 11 November)
    And shake the green leaves aff the tree?
O gentle Death, when wilt thou come?
    For of my life I am wearie.

'Tis not the frost, that freezes fell,   cruel
    Nor blawing snaw's inclemencie,
'Tis not sic cauld that makes me cry;   such
    But my Love's heart grown cauld to me.
When we cam in by Glasgow toun,
    We were a comely sicht to see;
My Love was clad in the black velvèt,
    And I mysel in cramasie.   crimson

But had I wist, before I kist,   known
    That love had been sae ill to win,   bad to gain
I had lock'd my heart in a case o' gowd,
    And pinn'd it wi' a siller pin.
And O! if my young babe were born,
    And set upon the nurse's knee;
And I mysel were dead and gane,
    And the green grass growing over me!

Jenny Nettles[2]

Saw ye Jenny Nettles,
Jenny Nettles, Jenny Nettles,
Saw ye Jenny Nettles
Coming frae the Market;
Bag and Baggage on her Back,

---

1. Precipitous hill in the King's Park, overlooking Holyrood Palace in Edinburgh. St Anthony's Well and a ruined chapel are there too.
2. A traditional song collected in Ramsay's *Tea Table Miscellany*. See Hugh MacDiarmid's lyric 'Empty Vessel'.

Her Fee and Bountith in her Lap;   (servant's) wages; bonus
Bag and Baggage on her Back,
And a Babie in her Oxter.   armpit (under her arm)

I met ayont the Kairny,[1]   beyond
Jenny Nettles, Jenny Nettles,
Singing till her Bairny,
Robin Rattles' Bastard;
To flee the Dool upo' the Stool,   punishment
And ilka ane that mocks her,
She round about seeks Robin out,
To stap it in his Oxter.   stick

Fy, fy! Robin Rattle,
Robin Rattle, Robin Rattle;
Fy, fy! Robin Rattle,
Use Jenny Nettles kindly:
Score out the Blame, and shun the Shame,
And without mair Debate o't,
Take hame your Wain, make Jenny fain,   baby; glad
The leal and leesome Gate o't.   loyal and loving way of it.

Adam Skirving (1719–1803)

Skirving owned a farm in East Lothian, between Prestonpans and Dunbar. He may well have witnessed Cope's defeat.

Johnnie Cope[2]

Hey, Johnnie Cope, are ye wauking yet?   waking
Or are your drums a-beating yet?
If ye were wauking I wad wait
    To gang to the coals i' the morning.

Cope sent a challenge frae Dunbar:
'Charlie, meet me an ye daur,

1. A cairn (little pile of stones) marks a high point, or a path or boundary in open country.
2. General Sir John Cope, commander of the Hanoverian forces in Scotland, marched north to confront the Jacobite army in 1745. Roundly out-manœuvred, he failed to engage them until they reached as far south as Dunbar, where he lost the battle of Prestonpans in only 15 minutes, surprised by a dawn raid.

And I'll learn you the art o' war   teach
   If you'll meet me i' the morning.'

When Charlie looked the letter upon
He drew his sword the scabbard from:
'Come, follow me, my merry, merry men,
   And we'll meet Johnnie Cope i' the morning!

'Now, Johnnie, be as good's your word;
Come, let us try both fire and sword;
And dinna rin like a frighted bird,
   That's chased frae its nest i' the morning.'

When Johnnie Cope he heard of this,
He thought it wadna be amiss
To hae a horse in readiness
   To flee awa' i' the morning.

Fy now, Johnnie, get up and rin;
The Highland bagpipes mak a din;
It's best to sleep in a hale skin,
   For 'twill be a bluidy morning.

When Johnnie Cope to Dunbar came,
They speered at him, 'Where's a' your men?'   asked
'The deil confound me gin I ken,
   For I left them a' i' the morning.'

'Now Johnnie, troth, ye are na blate   shy
To come wi' the news o' your ain defeat,
And leave your men in sic a strait
   Sae early in the morning.'

'I' faith,' quo' Johnnie, 'I got a fleg   fright
Wi' their claymores and philabegs;   kilts
If I face them again, deil break my legs!
   So I wish you a gude morning.'

John Skinner (1721–1807)

An Episcopal minister in Aberdeenshire, Skinner wrote an Ecclesiastical History of Scotland and a number of lively songs including 'Tullochgorum' to an old tune of the same name, which Burns called 'the best Scotch song Scotland ever saw'.

Tullochgorum

Come gie's a sang, Montgomery cry'd,
And lay your disputes all aside,
What signifies't for folks to chide
    For what was done before them:
Let Whig and Tory all agree,
  Whig and Tory, Whig and Tory,[1]
  Whig and Tory all agree,
    To drop their Whig-mig-morum;   (political haggling)
Let Whig and Tory all agree
To spend the night wi' mirth and glee,
And cheerful sing alang wi' me
    The Reel o' Tullochgorum.

O Tullochgorum's my delight,
It gars us a' in ane unite,   makes
And ony sumph that keeps a spite,
    In conscience I abhor him:
For blythe and cheerie we's be a',
  Blythe and cheerie, blythe and cheerie,
  Blythe and cheerie we's be a',
    And make a happy quorum,
For blythe and cheerie we's be a'
As lang as we hae breath to draw,
And dance till we be like to fa'
    The Reel o' Tullochgorum.

What needs there be sae great a fraise   fulsome gush
Wi' dringing dull Italian lays,   droning
I wadna gie our ain Strathspeys
    For half a hunder score o' them;
They're dowf and dowie at the best,   dull and sad
  Dowf and dowie, dowf and dowie,
  Dowf and dowie at the best,
    Wi' a' their variorum;
They're dowf and dowie at the best,
Their *allegros* and a' the rest,
They canna' please a Scottish taste
    Compar'd wi' Tullochgorum.

Let warldly worms their minds oppress
Wi' fears o' want and double cess   tax
And sullen sots themsells distress
    Wi' keeping up decorum:

1. In effect, Liberal and Conservative political parties.

Shall we sae sour and sulky sit
   Sour and sulky, sour and sulky,
   Sour and sulky shall we sit
      Like old philosophorum!
Shall we sae sour and sulky sit,
Wi' neither sense, nor mirth, nor wit,
Nor ever try to shake a fit   *foot*
      To th' Reel o' Tullochgorum?

May choicest blessings ay attend
Each honest, open-hearted friend,
And calm and quiet be his end,
      And a' that's good watch o'er him;
May peace and plenty be his lot,
   Peace and plenty, peace and plenty,
   Peace and plenty be his lot,
      And dainties a great store o' them;
May peace and plenty be his lot,
Unstain'd by any vicious spot,
And may he never want a groat,   *(small) Scots coin*
      That's fond o' Tullochgorum!

But for the sullen frumpish fool,
That loves to be oppression's tool,
May envy gnaw his rotten soul,
      And discontent devour him –
May dool and sorrow be his chance,   *grief*
   Dool and sorrow, dool and sorrow,
   Dool and sorrow be his chance,
      And nane say, wae's me for him!
May dool and sorrow be his chance,
Wi' a' the ills that come frae France,
Wha e'er he be that winna dance   *Whoever*
      The Reel o' Tullochgorum.

Jean Elliot (1727–1805)

Daughter to Sir Gilbert Elliott of Minto, an Edinburgh judge and music lover, Jean (Jane) published her most famous song anonymously around 1755. It seems to have been adapted from a now lost original, for another reworking was published ten years later by Mrs Cockburn, a relative of Walter Scott's.

The Flowers of the Forest

I've heard the lilting at our yowe-milking,   *ewe*
     Lasses a-lilting before the dawn o' day;
But now they are moaning on ilka green loaning: *common pasture ground*
     'The Flowers of the Forest are a' wede away.'   *withered*

At buchts, in the morning, nae blythe lads are scorning;   *sheep pens*
     The lasses are lonely, and dowie, and wae;   *sad; woeful*
Nae daffin', nae gabbin', but sighing and sabbing: *dallying*
     Ilk ane lifts her leglen, and hies her away.   *wooden milk pail*

In hairst, at the shearing, nae youths now are jeering,   *harvest*
     The bandsters are lyart, and runkled and grey;   *binders; grizzled*
At fair or at preaching, nae wooing, nae fleeching: *flattering*
     The Flowers of the Forest are a' wede away.

At e'en, in the gloaming, nae swankies are roaming   *young bucks*
     'Bout stacks wi' the lasses at bogle to play,   *haystacks; hide and seek*
But ilk ane sits drearie, lamenting her dearie:
     The Flowers of the Forest are a' wede away.

Dule and wae for the order sent our lads to the Border;   *Grief*
     The English, for ance, by guile wan the day;
The Flowers of the Forest, that foucht aye the foremost,
     The prime o' our land, are cauld in the clay.

We'll hear nae mair lilting at our yowe-milking,
     Women and bairns are heartless and wae;
Sighing and moaning on ilka green loaning:
     'The Flowers of the Forest are a' wede away.'

Lady Anne Lindsay (1750–1826)

Daughter of the Earl of Balcarres, later married to Andrew Barnard. Her best-known song was a sentimental hit for many years, but it is grounded in economic and domestic truths which were familiar enough to many women.

Auld Robin Gray

When the sheep are in the fauld, and the kye a' at hame,   *cattle*
When a' the weary warld to sleep are gane,

The waes o' my heart fa' in showers frae my e'e,
While my gudeman lies sound by me.

Young Jamie lo'ed me weel, and sought me for his bride;
But saving a croun he had naething else beside.   apart from
To mak the croun a pound, my Jamie gaed to sea,
And the croun and the pound, they were baith for me.

He hadna been awa' a week but only twa,
When my mither she fell sick and the cow was stown awa';   stolen
My father brak his arm – my Jamie at the sea;
And auld Robin Gray cam a-courtin' me.

My father couldna wark, my mither couldna spin;
I toil'd day and nicht, but their bread I couldna win:
Auld Rob maintain'd them baith, and wi' tears in his e'e,
Said, 'Jeanie, for their sakes, will ye marry me?'

My heart it said na – I look'd for Jamie back;
But the wind it blew hie, and the ship it was a wrack;
His ship it was a wrack – why didna Jamie dee?
And why do I live to cry, Wae's me?

My father urged me sair; my mither didna speak,   forcefully
But she looked in my face till my heart was like to break.
They gied him my hand – my heart was at the sea;
Sae auld Robin Gray, he was gudeman to me.   husband

I hadna been a wife a week but only four,
When, mournfu' as I sat on the stane at the door,
I saw my Jamie's wraith – I couldna think it he,
Till he said, 'I'm come hame, my love, to marry thee.'

O sair did we greet, and meikle did we say: sorely; weep; much
We took but ae kiss, and I bade him gang away.   one
I wish that I were dead, but I'm no like to dee;   likely
And why was I born to say, Wae's me?

I gang like a ghaist, and I carena to spin;
I daurna think o' Jamie, for that wad be a sin.
But I'll do my best a gude wife to be,
For auld Robin Gray, he is kind to me.

John Hamilton (1761–1814)

A music-seller and tutor in Edinburgh, Hamilton married one of his well-born pupils, much to the consternation of her family.

Up in the Mornin' Early

Cauld blaws the wind frae north to south,
    The drift is drifting sairly;
The sheep are cowerin' in the heugh;   *gully*
    Oh, sirs, it's winter fairly!
Now, up in the mornin's no for me,
    Up in the mornin' early;
I'd rather gae supperless to my bed
    Than rise in the mornin' early.

Loud roars the blast amang the woods,
    And tirls the branches barely;   *rattles*
On hill and house hear how it thuds!
    The frost is nippin' sairly.
Now, up in the mornin's no for me,
    Up in the mornin' early;
To sit a' nicht wad better agree
    Than rise in the mornin' early.

The sun peeps owre yon southland hills,
    Like ony timorous carlie;   *wee fellow*
Just blinks a wee, then sinks again;   *a little bit*
    And that we find severely.
Now, up in the mornin's no for me,
    Up in the mornin' early;
When snaw blaws in at the chimley cheek
    Wha'd rise in the mornin' early?

Nae linties lilt on hedge or bush: *linnets*
    Poor things, they suffer sairly;
In cauldrife quarters a' the nicht,   *freezing*
    A' day they feed but sparely.
Now, up in the mornin's no for me,
    Up in the mornin' early;
A penniless purse I wad rather dree   *suffer*
    Than rise in the mornin' early.

A cosie house and a canty wife   *cheerful*
    Aye keep a body cheerly;

And pantries stowed wi' meat and drink,   larders stuffed
   They answer unco rarely.   very well
But up in the mornin' – na, na, na!
   Up in the mornin' early!
The gowans maun glint on bank and brae   (summer) daisies; must
   When I rise in the mornin early.

Carolina Oliphant, Lady Nairne
(1766–1845)

Daughter of a Perthshire Jacobite, Carolina Oliphant married William Nairne and called herself 'Mrs Bogan of Bogan' to write her songs, many of which are still widely popular today, including 'Caller Herrin', 'Will ye no come back again?' and 'The Auld Hoose'.

The Laird o' Cockpen

The laird o' Cockpen, he's proud an' he's great,
His mind is ta'en up wi' things o' the State;
He wanted a wife his braw house to keep,
But favour wi' wooin' was fashous to seek.   troublesome

Down by the dyke-side a lady did dwell,   beside the wall
At his table head he thought she'd look well,
McClish's ae daughter o' Claverse-ha' Lee,
A penniless lass wi' a lang pedigree.

His wig was weel pouther'd, and as gude as new;   powdered
His waistcoat was white, his coat it was blue;
He put on a ring, a sword and cock'd hat,
And wha could refuse the laird wi' a' that?

He took the grey mare, and rade cannily,
An' rapped at the yett o' Claverse-ha' Lee;   gate
'Gae tell Mistress Jean to come speedily ben,   into the room
She's wanted to speak to the laird o' Cockpen.'

Mistress Jean was makin' the elder-flower wine.
'An' what brings the laird at sic a like time?'
She put aff her apron, and on her silk gown,
Her mutch wi' red ribbons, and gaed awa' down.   close-fitting cap

An' when she cam ben she bowed fu' low,
An' what was his errand he soon let her know;
Amazed was the laird when the lady said 'Na,'
And wi' a laigh curtsie she turned awa'.   low

Dumfounder'd he was, nae sigh did he gie,   Flabbergasted
He mounted his mare – he rade cannily;   carefully
And aften he thought, as he gaed thro' the glen,
She's daft to refuse the laird o' Cockpen.

The Land o' the Leal   (The Afterworld)

I'm wearin' awa', John,
Like snaw-wreaths in thaw, John,
I'm wearin' awa'
    To the land o' the leal.   loyal
There's nae sorrow there, John,
There's neither cauld nor care, John,
The day is aye fair
    In the land o' the leal.

Our bonnie bairn's there, John,
She was baith gude and fair, John,
And, oh! we grudged her sair
    To the land o' the leal.
But sorrow's sel' wears past, John,
And joy is comin' fast, John,
The joy that's aye to last
    In the land o' the leal.

Sae dear's that joy was bought, John,
Sae free the battle fought, John,
That sinfu' man e'er brought
    To the land o' the leal.
Oh! dry your glist'nin' e'e, John,
My saul langs to be free, John,
And angels beckon me
    To the land o' the leal.

Oh! haud ye leal an' true, John,
Your day it's wearin' thro', John,
And I'll welcome you
    To the land o' the leal.
Now fare ye weel, my ain John,
This warld's cares are vain, John,
We'll meet, and we'll be fain,   loving
    In the land o' the leal.

Anonymous

Canadian Boat Song

Fair these broad meads – these hoary woods are grand;
But we are exiles from our fathers' land.

Listen to me, as when ye heard our father
   Sing long ago the song of other shores –
Listen to me, and then in chorus gather
   All your deep voices, as ye pull your oars.

From the lone shieling of the misty island   summer hut on high pasture
   Mountains divide us, and the waste of seas –
Yet still the blood is strong, the heart is Highland,
   And we in dreams behold the Hebrides.

We ne'er shall tread the fancy-haunted valley,
   Where 'tween the dark hills creeps the small clear stream,
In arms around the patriarch banner rally,
   Nor see the moon on royal tombstones gleam.

When the bold kindred, in the time long vanish'd,
   Conquer'd the soil and fortified the keep –
No seer foretold the children would be banish'd,
   That a degenerate lord might boast his sheep.

Come foreign rage – let Discord burst in slaughter!
O then for clansman true, and stern claymore –
The hearts that would have given their blood like water,
   Beat heavily beyond the Atlantic roar.

Allan Cunningham (1784–1842)

Inspired by Burns at the age of six, Cunningham worked as a stonemason, collected ballads and met with Scott and Hogg before going to London to make a literary reputation with poems of exile such as 'Hame, Hame, Hame' and the popular nautical poem 'A Wet Sheet and a Flowing Sea'.

The Wee, Wee German Lairdie[1]

Wha the deil hae we got for a King,
    But a wee, wee German lairdie!   *petty landowner*
An' whan we gaed to bring him hame,
    He was delving in his kail-yardie.   *digging; kitchen garden*
Sheughing kail an' laying leeks,   *planting curly cabbage*
    But the hose and but the breeks,   *Without stockings; trousers*
Up his beggar duds he cleeks,   *hitches*
    The wee, wee German lairdie.

An' he's clapt down in our gudeman's chair,   *(the throne)*
    The wee, wee German lairdie;
An' he's brought fouth o' foreign leeks,   *plenty*
    An' dibblet them in his yardie.   *planted*
He's pu'd the rose o' English louns,   *rascals*
    An' brak the harp o' Irish clowns,
But our thistle will jag his thumbs,
    The wee, wee German lairdie.

Come up amang the Highland hills,
    Thou wee, wee German lairdie;
An' see how Charlie's lang-kail thrive,   *Scottish brassica*
    He dibblet in his yardie.
An' if a stock ye daur to pu',
    Or haud the yoking of a pleugh,   *manage a day's ploughing*
We'll break yere sceptre o'er yere mou',
    Thou wee bit German lairdie.

Our hills are steep, our glens are deep,
    Nae fitting for a yardie;   *garden*
An' our norlan' thistles winna pu',
    Thou wee, wee German lairdie.
An' we've the trenching blades o' weir,   *war*
    Wad twine ye o' yere German gear;   *separate; clothes*
An' pass ye 'neath the claymore's shear,   *Should you*
    Thou feckless German lairdie.   *ineffectual*

1. The accession of the House of Hanover (George I in 1714 and George II in 1727) was felt to be a foreign intrusion by many Englishmen, as well as by Catholic Jacobite supporters in the North.

James Hogg (1770–1835)

The son of a sheepfarmer and brought up as shepherd himself, Hogg had little formal education after the age of seven, but one of his employers gave him the chance and encouraged his writing. The song 'Donald MacDonald' became widely popular, and a collection of poems, *Scottish Pastorals*, was published in 1801. Within ten years Hogg had moved to Edinburgh to seek a literary career. With the success of *The Queen's Wake* (1813), he gained the patronage of the Duke of Buccleuch and the friendship of Walter Scott. Although he contributed regularly to *Blackwood's* magazine, his strong roots in the folk tradition meant that he was never fully at one with Edinburgh's more privileged circles. He produced many short stories and novels, most notably *The Three Perils of Man* (1822) and his masterpiece, *The Private Memoirs and Confessions of a Justified Sinner* (1824).

Donald MacDonald[1]

My name it is Donald M'Donald,
   I leeve in the Heelands sae grand;
I hae follow'd our banner, and will do,
   Wherever my Maker has land.
When rankit amang the blue bonnets,
   Nae danger can fear me ava;   *at all*
I ken that my brethren around me
   Are either to conquer or fa'.
      Brogues[2] an' brochin an' a',   *(Highland) shoes and plaid*
      Brochin an' brogues an' a';
      An' is nae her[3] very weel aff
      Wi' her brogues an' brochin an' a'?

What though we befriendit young Charlie? –
   To tell it I dinna think shame;
Poor lad, he cam to us but barely,
   An' reckon'd our mountains his hame.
'Twas true that our reason forbade us;

1. Written around 1799 when it was feared that Napoleon might invade Britain. Compare Burns, 'Does haughty Gaul invasion threat?' from 1795.
2. The original Highland brogue was an untanned hide moccasin, secured on the leg by thongs.
3. Hogg continues a traditional Lowland locution by which Gaels speaking English are made to refer to themselves as 'she' or 'her'. See the bardic rook in *The Buke of the Howlat*.

But tenderness carried the day; –
Had Geordie come friendless amang us,   (King George III)
   Wi' him we had a' gane away.
     Sword an' buckler an' a',
     Buckler an' sword an' a';
     Now for George we'll encounter the devil,
     Wi' sword an' buckler an' a'!

An' O, I wad eagerly press him
   The keys o' the East to retain;
For should he gie up the possession,
   We'll soon hae to force them again.
Than yield up an inch wi' dishonour,
   Though it were my finishing blow,
He ay may depend on M'Donald,
   Wi' his Heelanders a' in a row:
     Knees an' elbows an' a',
     Elbows an' knees an a';
     Depend upon Donald M'Donald,
     His knees an' elbows an' a'!

Wad Bonaparte land at Fort-William,
   Auld Europe nae langer should grane;   groan
I laugh when I think how we'd gall him,
   Wi' bullet, wi' steel, an' wi' stane;
Wi' rocks o' the Nevis and Gairy
   We'd rattle him off frae our shore,
Or lull him asleep in a cairny,
   An' sing him – Lochaber no more!
     Stanes an' bullets an' a',
     Bullets an' stanes an' a';
     We'll finish the Corsican callan   lad
     Wi' stanes an' bullets an' a'!

For the Gordon is good in a hurry,
   An' Campbell is steel to the bane,
An' Grant, an' M'Kenzie, an' Murray,
   An' Cameron will hurkle to nane;   submit
The Stuart is sturdy an' loyal,
   An' sae is M'Leod an' M'Kay;
An' I, their gudebrither, M'Donald,   brother-in-law
   Shall ne'er be the last in the fray!
     Brogues an' brochin an' a',
     Brochin an' brogues an' a';
     An' up wi' the bonny blue bonnet,
     The kilt an' the feather an' a'!

Kilmeny
(the thirteenth bard's song *from* **The Queen's Wake**[1])

    Bonny Kilmeny gaed up the glen;
But it wasna to meet Duneira's men,[2]
Nor the rosy monk of the isle to see,
For Kilmeny was pure as pure could be.
It was only to hear the Yorlin sing,   *yellowhammer*
And pu' the cress-flower round the spring;
The scarlet hypp and the hindberrye,   *wild raspberry*
And the nut that hang frae the hazel tree;
For Kilmeny was pure as pure could be.
But lang may her minny look o'er the wa',   *mother*
And lang may she seek i' the green-wood shaw;   *thicket*
Lang the laird of Duneira blame,
And lang, lang greet or Kilmeny come hame!   *weep; before*

    When many a day had come and fled,
When grief grew calm, and hope was dead,
When mess for Kilmeny's soul had been sung,
When the bedes-man had prayed, and the deadbell rung,
Late, late in a gloamin when all was still,   *twilight*
When the fringe was red on the westlin hill,
The wood was sere, the moon i' the wane,
The reek o' the cot hung over the plain,   *smoke; cottage*
Like a little wee cloud in the world its lane;   *on its own*
When the ingle lowed with an eiry leme,   *hearth blazed; gleam*
Late, late in the gloamin Kilmeny came hame!

    'Kilmeny, Kilmeny, where have you been?
Lang hae we sought baith holt and den;   *wooded hill; ravine*
By linn, by ford, and green-wood tree,   *waterfall pool*
Yet you are halesome and fair to see.
Where gat you that joup o' the lilly scheen?   *skirt*
That bonny snood of the birk sae green? *girl's hairband; birch*
And these roses, the fairest that ever were seen?[3]
Kilmeny, Kilmeny, where have you been?'

    Kilmeny looked up with a lovely grace,
But nae smile was seen on Kilmeny's face;
As still was her look, and as still was her ee,
As the stillness that lay on the emerant lea,   *emerald pasture*

1. The first (1813) edition of 'Kilmeny' was published in 'medieval' Scots; this revised version dates from the following year.
2. Dunira, belonging to the Dundas family, is two miles from the eastern end of Loch Earn.
3. The snood frequently symbolises virginity. White and red have their own associations with purity and passion, while the colour green and the birch tree are associated with the fairy folk.

Or the mist that sleeps on a waveless sea.
For Kilmeny had been she knew not where,
And Kilmeny had seen what she could not declare;
Kilmeny had been where the cock never crew,
Where the rain never fell, and the wind never blew,
But it seemed as the harp of the sky had rung,
And the airs of heaven played round her tongue,
When she spake of the lovely forms she had seen,
And a land where sin had never been;
A land of love, and a land of light,
Withouten sun, or moon, or night:
Where the river swa'd a living stream,   swelled
And the light a pure celestial beam:
The land of vision it would seem,
A still, an everlasting dream.

   In yon green-wood there is a waik,   walk
And in that waik there is a wene,[1]   dwelling
   And in that wene there is a maike,   mate/companion
That neither has flesh, blood, nor bane;
   And down in yon green-wood he walks his lane.

   In that green wene Kilmeny lay,
Her bosom happed wi' the flowerits gay;   covered
But the air was soft and the silence deep,
And bonny Kilmeny fell sound asleep.
She kend nae mair, nor opened her ee,
Till waked by the hymns of a far countrye.

   She 'wakened on couch of the silk sae slim,
All striped wi' the bars of the rainbow's rim;
And lovely beings round were rife,
Who erst had travelled mortal life;   once
And aye they smiled, and 'gan to speer,   began to ask
'What spirit has brought this mortal here?' –

   'Lang have I journeyed the world wide,'
A meek and reverend fere replied;   comrade/companion
'Baith night and day I have watched the fair,
Eident a thousand years and mair.   Diligent
Yes, I have watched o'er ilk degree,   each
Wherever blooms femenitye;
But sinless virgin, free of stain

---

1. These lines echo a stanza from the traditional ballad 'Erlinton'. Other aspects are reminiscent of 'Thomas the Rhymer', 'Tam Lin' and 'The Wife of Usher's Well', but Hogg's poem has an added element of visionary, even Christian, Platonism.

In mind and body, fand I nane.
Never, since the banquet of time,
Found I a virgin in her prime,
Till late this bonny maiden I saw
As spotless as the morning snaw:
Full twenty years she has lived as free
As the spirits that sojourn this countrye.
I have brought her away frae the snares of men,
That sin or death she never may ken.' –

    They clasped her waiste and her hands sae fair,
They kissed her cheek, and they kemed her hair,   *combed*
And round came many a blooming fere,   *companion*
Saying, 'Bonny Kilmeny, ye're welcome here!
Women are freed of the littand scorn: *blush-making*
O, blessed be the day Kilmeny was born!
Now shall the land of the spirits see,
Now shall it ken what a woman may be!
Many a lang year in sorrow and pain,
Many a lang year through the world we've gane,
Commissioned to watch fair womankind,
For its they who nurice th'immortal mind.
We have watched their steps as the dawning shone,
And deep in the green-wood walks alone;
By lilly bower and silken bed,
The viewless tears have o'er them shed;   *invisible*
Have soothed their ardent minds to sleep,
Or left the couch of love to weep.
We have seen! we have seen! but the time must come,
And the angels will weep at the day of doom!

    'O, would the fairest of mortal kind
Aye keep the holy truths in mind,
That kindred spirits their motions see,
Who watch their ways with anxious ee,
And grieve for the guilt of humanitye!
O, sweet to Heaven the maiden's prayer,
And the sigh that heaves a bosom sae fair!
And dear to Heaven the words of truth,
And the praise of virtue frae beauty's mouth!
And dear to the viewless forms of air,
The minds that kyth as the body fair!   *appear*

'O, bonny Kilmeny! free frae stain,
If ever you seek the world again,
That world of sin, of sorrow and fear,

O, tell of the joys that are waiting here;
And tell of the signs you shall shortly see;
Of the times that are now, and the times that shall be.' –

They lifted Kilmeny, they led her away,
And she walked in the light of a sunless day:
The sky was a dome of crystal bright,
The fountain of vision, and fountain of light:
The emerald fields were of dazzling glow,
And the flowers of everlasting blow.
Then deep in the stream her body they laid,
That her youth and beauty never might fade;
And they smiled on heaven, when they saw her lie
In the stream of life that wandered bye.
And she heard a song, she heard it sung,
She kend not where; but sae sweetly it rung,   knew
It fell on her ear like a dream of the morn:
'O! blest be the day Kilmeny was born!
Now shall the land of the spirits see,
Now shall it ken what a woman may be!
The sun that shines on the world sae bright,
A borrowed gleid frae the fountain of light;   spark
And the moon that sleeks the sky sae dun,   dusky
Like a gouden bow, or a beamless sun,
Shall wear away, and be seen nae mair,
And the angels shall miss them travelling the air.
But lang, lang after baith night and day,
When the sun and the world have elyed away;   slipped slowly
When the sinner has gane to his waesome doom,
Kilmeny shall smile in eternal bloom!' –

They bore her away she wist not how,   knew
For she felt not arm nor rest below;
But so swift they wained her through the light,   carried
'Twas like the motion of sound or sight;
They seemed to split the gales of air,
And yet nor gale nor breeze was there.
Unnumbered groves below them grew,
They came, they past, and backward flew,
Like floods of blossoms gliding on,
In moment seen, in moment gone.
O, never vales to mortal view
Appeared like those o'er which they flew!
That land to human spirits given,
The lowermost vales of the storied heaven;
From thence they can view the world below,

And heaven's blue gates with sapphires glow,
More glory yet unmeet to know.   *unfitting*

    They bore her far to a mountain green,
To see what mortal never had seen;
And they seated her high on a purple sward,
And bade her heed what she saw and heard,
And note the changes the spirits wrought,
For now she lived in the land of thought.
She looked, and she saw nor sun nor skies,
But a crystal dome of a thousand dies.
She looked, and she saw nae land aright,
But an endless whirl of glory and light.
And radiant beings went and came
Far swifter than wind, or the linked flame.
She hid her een frae the dazzling view;
She looked again and the scene was new.

    She saw a sun on a summer sky,
And clouds of amber sailing bye;
A lovely land beneath her lay,   *(Scotland)*
And that land had glens and mountains gray;
And that land had vallies and hoary piles,
And marled seas, and a thousand isles;
Its fields were speckled, its forests green,
And its lakes were all of the dazzling sheen,
Like magic mirrors, where slumbering lay
The sun and the sky and the cloudlet gray;
Which heaved and trembled and gently swung,
On every shore they seemed to be hung;
For there they were seen on their downward plain
A thousand times and a thousand again;
In winding lake and placid firth,
Little peaceful heavens in the bosom of earth.

    Kilmeny sighed and seemed to grieve,
For she found her heart to that land did cleave;
She saw the corn wave on the vale,
She saw the deer run down the dale;
She saw the plaid and the broad claymore,
And the brows that the badge of freedom bore;
And she thought she had seen the land before.

    She saw a lady sit on a throne,
The fairest that ever the sun shone on!
A lion licked her hand of milk,

And she held him in a leish of silk;
And a leifu' maiden stood at her knee,
With a silver wand and melting ee;
Her sovereign shield till love stole in,
And poisoned all the fount within.[1]

Then a gruff untoward bedeman came,   *man of prayer*
And hundit the lion on his dame:
And the guardian maid wi' the dauntless ee,
She dropped a tear, and left her knee;
And she saw till the queen frae the lion fled,
Till the bonniest flower of the world lay dead.
A coffin was set on a distant plain,
And she saw the red blood fall like rain:
Then bonny Kilmeny's heart grew sair,
And she turned away, and could look nae mair.

Then the gruff grim carle girned amain,   *fellow snarled/complained*
And they trampled him down, but he rose again;
And he baited the lion to deeds of weir,   *war*
Till he lapped the blood to the kingdom dear;
And weening his head was danger-preef,   *imagining*
When crowned with the rose and clover leaf,[2]
He gowled at the carle, and chased him away   *bellowed*
To feed wi' the deer on the mountain gray.
He gowled at the carle, and he gecked at heaven,   *mocked/gawped*
But his mark was set, and his arles given.[3]   *deserts*
Kilmeny a while her een withdrew;
She looked again, and the scene was new.

She saw below her fair unfurled
One half of all the glowing world,
Where oceans rolled, and rivers ran,
To bound the aims of sinful man.
She saw a people, fierce and fell,   *cruel*
Burst frae their bounds like fiends of hell;
There lilies grew, and the eagle flew,
And she herked on her ravening crew,   *whispered*
Till the cities and towers were wrapt in a blaze,
And the thunder it roared o'er the lands and the seas.[4]

1. An allegory of Mary Queen of Scots, with the heraldic Lion of Scotland, the Catholic faith and an unhappy love-life. The 'bedeman' represents Knox and the Reformed Church, with religious strife on the horizon. In the context of 'The Queen's Wake' this is a vision of the future.
2. At the Union of the Crowns.
3. If 'he' is the lion (King James VII), then these lines refer to the Protestant revolution of 1688 and the accession of William of Orange.
4. An allegory of the French Revolution, followed by Britain's war with Napoleon and the Imperial Eagle of France.

The widows they wailed, and the red blood ran,
And she threatened an end to the race of man:
She never lened, nor stood in awe,   rested
Till claught by the lion's deadly paw.
Oh! then the eagle swinked for life,   struggled
And brainzelled up a mortal strife;   erupted
But flew she north, or flew she south,
She met wi' the gowl of the lion's mouth.

　　With a mooted wing and waefu' maen,   moulted; demeanour
The eagle sought her eiry again;
But lang may she cour in her bloody nest,
And lang, lang sleek her wounded breast,
Before she sey another flight,   try
To play wi' the norland lion's might.

　　But to sing the sights Kilmeny saw,
So far surpassing nature's law,
The singer's voice wad sink away,
And the string of his harp wad cease to play.
But she saw till the sorrows of man were bye,
And all was love and harmony;
Till the stars of heaven fell calmly away,
Like the flakes of snaw on a winter day.

　　Then Kilmeny begged again to see
The friends she had left in her own country,
To tell of the place where she had been,
And the glories that lay in the land unseen;
To warn the living maidens fair,
The loved of Heaven, the spirits' care,
That all whose minds unmeled remain   innocent
Shall bloom in beauty when time is gane.

　　With distant music, soft and deep,
They lulled Kilmeny sound asleep;
And when she awakened, she lay her lane,
All happed with flowers in the green-wood wene.   covered; dwelling
When seven lang years had come and fled;
When grief was calm, and hope was dead;
When scarce was remembered Kilmeny's name,
Late, late in a gloamin Kilmeny came hame!
And O, her beauty was fair to see,
But still and stedfast was her ee!
Such beauty bard may never declare,
For there was no pride nor passion there;

And the soft desire of maidens een
In that mild face could never be seen.
Her seymar was the lilly flower,   *loose upper garment (shawl)*
And her cheek the moss-rose in the shower;
And her voice like the distant melodye,
That floats along the twilight sea.
But she loved to raike the lanely glen,   *roam*
And keeped afar frae the haunts of men;
Her holy hymns unheard to sing,
To suck the flowers, and drink the spring.
But wherever her peaceful form appeared,
The wild beasts of the hill were cheered;
The wolf played blythly round the field,
The lordly byson lowed and kneeled;
The dun deer wooed with manner bland,
And cowered aneath her lilly hand.
And when at even the woodlands rung,
When hymns of other worlds she sung,
In ecstacy of sweet devotion,
O, then the glen was all in motion.
The wild beasts of the forest came,
Broke from their bughts and faulds the tame,   *enclosures*
And goved around, charmed and amazed;   *gazed*
Even the dull cattle crooned and gazed,
And murmured and looked with anxious pain
For something the mystery to explain.
The buzzard came with the throstle-cock;
The corby left her houf in the rock;   *raven; haunt*
The blackbird alang wi' the eagle flew;
The hind came tripping o'er the dew;
The wolf and the kid their raike began,   *journey*
And the tod, and the lamb, and the leveret ran;   *fox; hare*
The hawk and the hern attour them hung,   *heron; around*
And the merl and the mavis forhooyed their young;   *blackbird; thrush; abandoned*
And all in a peaceful ring were hurled:
It was like an eve in a sinless world!

When a month and a day had come and gane,
Kilmeny sought the greenwood wene;   *dwelling*
There laid her down on the leaves sae green,
And Kilmeny on earth was never mair seen.
But O, the words that fell from her mouth,
Were words of wonder, and words of truth!
But all the land were in fear and dread,
For they kendna whether she was living or dead.   *knew not*
It wasna her hame, and she couldna remain;

She left this world of sorrow and pain,
And returned to the land of thought again.

from **The Flying Tailor**[1]

If ever chance or choice thy footsteps lead
Into that green and flowery burial-ground
That compasseth with sweet and mournful smiles
The church of Grassmere, – by the eastern gate
Enter – and underneath a stunted yew,
Some three yards distant from the gravel-walk,
On the left-hand side, thou wilt espy a grave,
With unelaborate head-stone beautified,
Conspicuous 'mid the other stoneless heaps
'Neath which the children of the valley lie.
There pause – and with no common feelings read
This short inscription – 'Here lies buried
The Flying Tailor, aged twenty-nine!'

　　Him from his birth unto his death I knew,
And many years before he had attain'd
The fulness of his fame, I prophesied
The triumphs of that youth's agility,
And crown'd him with that name which afterwards
He nobly justified – and dying left
To fame's eternal blazon – read it here –
'The Flying Tailor!'
　　　　　　　　　　It is somewhat strange
That his mother was a cripple, and his father
Long way declined into the vale of years
When their son Hugh was born. At first the babe
Was sickly, and a smile was seen to pass
Across the midwife's cheek, when, holding up
The sickly wretch, she to the father said,
'A fine man-child!' What else could they expect.
The mother being, as I said before,
A cripple, and the father of the child
Long way declined into the vale of years.

　　But mark the wondrous change – ere he was put
By his mother into breeches, Nature strung
The muscular part of his economy
To an unusual strength, and he could leap,
All unimpeded by his petticoats,
Over the stool on which his mother sat

---

1. Hogg adopted the style of several writers in *The Poetic Mirror*. This extract from 'The Flying Taylor' is an outright parody of Wordsworth's mature voice.

When carding wool, or cleansing vegetables,
Or meek performing other household tasks.
Cunning he watch'd his opportunity,
And oft, as house-affairs did call her thence,
Overleapt Hugh, a perfect whirligig,
More than six inches o'er th' astonished stool.
What boots it to narrate, how at leap-frog
Over the breech'd and unbreech'd villagers
He shone conspicuous? Leap-frog do I say?
Vainly so named. What though in attitude
The Flying Tailor aped the croaking race
When issuing from the weed-entangled pool,
Tadpoles no more, they seek the new-mown fields,
A jocund people, bouncing to and fro'
Amid the odorous clover – while amazed
The grasshopper sits idle on the stalk
With folded pinions and forgets to sing.
Frog-like, no doubt, in attitude he was;
But sure his bounds across the village green
Seem'd to my soul – (my soul for ever bright
With purest beams of sacred poesy)
Like bounds of red-deer on the Highland-hill,
When, close-environed by the tinchel's chain,   ring of hunters
He lifts his branchy forehead to the sky,
Then o'er the many-headed multitude
Springs belling half in terror, half in rage,
And fleeter than the sunbeam or the wind
Speeds to his cloud-lair on the mountain-top.

    No more of this – suffice it to narrate,
In his tenth year he was apprenticed
Unto a Master Tailor by a strong
And regular indenture of seven years,
Commencing from the date the parchment bore,
And ending on a certain day, that made
The term complete of seven solar years.
Oft have I heard him say, that at this time
Of life he was most wretched, for, constrain'd
To sit all day cross-legg'd upon a board,
The natural circulation of the blood
Thereby was oft impeded, and he felt
So numb'd at times, that when he strove to rise
Up from his work he could not, but fell back
80 Among the shreds and patches ...

Doctor Monro[1]

'Dear Doctor, be clever, and fling off your beaver;   (hat)
  Come bleed me, and blister me, do not be slow:
I'm sick, I'm exhausted, my schemes they are blasted,
  And all driven heels-o'er-head, Doctor Monro.'
'Be patient, dear fellow, you foster your fever;
  Pray, what's the misfortune that troubles you so?'
'O, Doctor! I'm ruin'd! I'm ruin'd for ever!
  My lass has forsaken me, Doctor Monro.

'I meant to have married, and tasted the pleasures,
  The sweets, the enjoyments in wedlock that flow;
But she's ta'en another, and broken my measures,
  And fairly confounded me, Doctor Monro.'
'I'll bleed and I'll blister you, over and over;
  I'll master your malady ere that I go:
But raise up your head from below the bed cover,
  And give some attention to Doctor Monro.

If Christy had wed you, she would have misled you,
  And laugh'd at your love with some handsome young beau.
Her conduct will prove it; but how would you love it?'
  'I soon would have lam'd her, dear Doctor Monro.'
'Each year brings a pretty young son, or a daughter;
  Perhaps you're the father; but how shall you know?
You hugg them – her gallant is bursting with laughter – '
  'That thought's like to murder me, Doctor Munro.'

'The boys cost you many a penny and shilling;
  You breed them with pleasure, with trouble, and woe:
But one turns a rake, and another a villain.' –
  'My heart could not bear it, dear Doctor Munro.'
'The lasses are comely, and dear to your bosom;
  But virtue and beauty has many a foe!
O think what may happen; just nipt in their blossom!' –
  'Ah! merciful Heaven! cease, Doctor Munro.

'Dear Doctor, I'll thank you to hand me my breeches;
  I'm better; I'll drink with you ere that you go;
I'll never more sicken for women or riches,
  But love my relations and Doctor Munro.
I plainly perceive, were I wedded to Christy,
  My peace and my pleasures I needs must forego.'
He still lives a bachelor; drinks when he's thirsty;
  And sings like a lark, and loves Doctor Monro.

---

1. Rewritten in 1831, this is the first (1810) version of the song.

The Lament of Flora Macdonald[1]

Far over yon hills of the heather so green,
    And down by the Correi that sings to the sea,   corrie (wide hillside gulley)
The bonny young Flora sat sighing her lane,   alone
    The dew on her plaid and the tear in her ee.
She look'd at a boat with the breezes that swung
    Away on the wave, like a bird of the main,
And aye as it lessen'd she sigh'd and she sung,
    Fareweel to the lad I shall ne'er see again;
Fareweel to my hero, the gallant and young,
    Fareweel to the lad I shall ne'er see again.

The Moorcock that craws on the brows o' Ben-Connal,
    He kens o' his bed in a sweet mossy hame;   knows
The Eagle that soars o'er the cliffs of Clan-Ronald
    Unawed and unhunted his eiry can claim,
The Solan can sleep on his shelve of the shore,   (goose)
    The Cormorant roost on his rock of the sea;
But Oh! there is ane whose hard fate I deplore,
    Nor house, ha', nor hame in his country has he;
The conflict is past, and our name is no more,
    There's nought left but sorrow for Scotland and me!

The target is torn from the arms of the just,   round shield
    The helmet is cleft on the brow of the brave,
The claymore for ever in darkness must rust;   Highland sword
    But red is the sword of the stranger and slave;
The hoof of the horse, and the foot of the proud
    Have trode o'er the plumes on the bonnet of blue.
Why slept the red bolt in the breast of the cloud
    When tyranny revelled in blood of the true?
Fareweel my young hero, the gallant and good!
    The crown of thy Fathers is torn from thy brow.

1. Who took a small boat to help Charles Edward Stuart escape to Skye after the defeat at Culloden.

Sir Walter Scott (1771–1832)

After the success of *The Minstrelsy of the Scottish Border*, a collection of old ballads some of which he had restored or written himself, Scott's literary reputation was founded on his long narrative poems, starting with *The Lay of the Last Minstrel* in 1805. This was followed by *Marmion* (1808) and his best and most popular romance *The Lady of the Lake* (1810), which sold over 20,000 copies in its first year and started a lively tourist industry around its setting on Loch Katrine. When public taste began to favour the verse romances of Byron, the Edinburgh lawyer turned to prose with *Waverley* (1814), the first of many books which more or less invented the genre of the historical novel and made Scott the best-known author in Europe. Verses, songs and ballads continued to feature in these novels to almost Shakespearean effect.

Jock of Hazeldean[1]

'Why weep ye by the tide, ladie?
   Why weep ye by the tide?
I'll wed ye to my youngest son,
   And ye sall be his bride:
And ye sall be his bride, ladie,
   Sae comely to be seen' –
But aye she loot the tears down fa'
   For Jock of Hazeldean.

'Now let this wilfu' grief be done,
   And dry that cheek so pale;
Young Frank is chief of Errington,
   And lord of Langley-dale;
His step is first in peaceful ha',
   His sword in battle keen' –
But aye she loot the tears down fa'
   For Jock of Hazeldean.

'A chain of gold ye sall not lack,
   Nor braid to bind your hair;
Nor mettled hound, nor managed hawk,
   Nor palfrey fresh and fair;

1. The first stanza is based on an old ballad.

And you, the foremost o' them a',
    Shall ride our forest queen' –
But aye she loot the tears down fa'
    For Jock of Hazeldean.

The kirk was decked at morning-tide,
    The tapers glimmered fair;
The priest and bridegroom wait the bride,
    And dame and knight are there.
They sought her baith by bower and ha';
    The ladie was not seen!
She's o'er the Border, and awa'
    Wi' Jock of Hazeldean.

from The Lady of the Lake

Canto ii[1]

xvi

331 Far up the lengthened lake were spied
Four darkening specks upon the tide,
That, slow enlarging on the view,
Four manned and masted barges grew,
And, bearing downwards from Glengyle,
Steered full upon the lonely isle;
The point of Brianchoil they passed,
And, to the windward as they cast,
Against the sun they gave to shine
The bold Sir Roderick's bannered Pine.   (clan emblem)
Nearer and nearer as they bear,
Spears, pikes, and axes flash in air.
Now might you see the tartans brave,
And plaids and plumage dance and wave:
Now see the bonnets sink and rise,
As his tough oar the rower plies;
See, flashing at each sturdy stroke,
The wave ascending into smoke;
See the proud pipers on the bow,
And mark the gaudy streamers flow
From their loud chanters down, and sweep
The furrowed bosom of the deep,
As, rushing through the lake amain,
They plied the ancient Highland strain.

1. Exiled Ellen Douglas (the lady of the lake) witnesses the arrival of Roderick MacAlpine and his men on the shore of Loch Katrine, between Loch Lomond and Callander in the west highlands of Perthshire. 'Black Roderick' is Ellen's cousin and an unwanted suitor. He, too, is banished from King James V's court, but rules the fastness of the Trossachs like some dark Satanic prince.

xvii
Ever, as on they bore, more loud
And louder rung the pibroch[1] proud.
At first the sound, by distance tame,
Mellowed along the waters came,
And, lingering long by cape and bay,
Wailed every harsher note away;
Then bursting bolder on the ear,
The clan's shrill Gathering they could hear;
Those thrilling sounds, that call the might
Of old Clan-Alpine to the fight.
Thick beat the rapid notes, as when
The mustering hundreds shake the glen,
And, hurrying at the signal dread,
The battered earth returns their tread.
Then prelude light, of livelier tone,
Expressed their merry marching on,
Ere peal of closing battle rose,
With mingled outcry, shrieks, and blows;
And mimic din of stroke and ward,
As broadsword upon target jarred;   (small round shield)
And groaning pause, ere yet again,
Condensed, the battle yelled amain;
The rapid charge, the rallying shout,
Retreat borne headlong into rout,
And bursts of triumph, to declare
Clan-Alpine's conquest – all were there.
Nor ended thus the strain; but slow
Sunk in a moan prolonged and low,
And changed the conquering clarion swell
For wild lament o'er those that fell.

xviii
The war-pipes ceased; but lake and hill
Were busy with their echoes still;
And, when they slept, a vocal strain
Bade their hoarse chorus wake again,
While loud a hundred clansmen raise
Their voices in their Chieftain's praise.
Each boatman, bending to his oar,
With measured sweep the burden bore,
In such wild cadence, as the breeze
Makes through December's leafless trees.
The chorus first could Allan know,

1. The 'classical music' of the solo Highland bagpipe, often a lament or a war-song. Gaelic *pìobaireachd*: lit. 'piping'.

'Roderick Vich Alpine, ho! iro!'   (Vich: *mhic*, Eng.: Mac)
And near, and nearer as they rowed,
Distinct the martial ditty flowed.

xix: Boat Song
'Hail to the Chief who in triumph advances!
  Honoured and blessed be the evergreen Pine!
Long may the tree, in his banner that glances,
  Flourish, the shelter and grace of our line!
    Heaven send it happy dew,
    Earth lend it sap anew,
Gaily to burgeon, and broadly to grow,
    While every Highland glen
    Sends our shout back again,
Roderigh Vich Alpine dhu, ho! ieroe!   (*dhu*, Gaelic: black)

Ours is no sapling, chance-sown by the fountain,
  Blooming at Beltane,[1] in winter to fade;
When the whirlwind has stripped every leaf on the mountain,
  The more shall Clan-Alpine exult in her shade.
    Moored in the rifted rock,
    Proof to the tempest's shock,
Firmer he roots him the ruder it blow;
    Menteith and Breadalbane, then,
    Echo his praise again,
Roderigh Vich Alpine dhu, ho! ieroe!

xx
'Proudly our pibroch has thrilled in Glen Fruin,
  And Bannochar's groans to our slogan replied;   (Gaelic, lit.: war cry)
Glen Luss and Ross-dhu, they are smoking in ruin,
  And the best of Loch Lomond lie dead on her side.
    Widow and Saxon maid
    Long shall lament our raid,
Think of Clan-Alpine with fear and with woe;
    Lennox and Leven-glen
    Shake when they hear again,
Roderigh Vich Alpine dhu, ho! ieroe!

Row vassals, row, for the pride of the Highlands!
  Stretch to your oars, for the evergreen Pine!
O! that the rose-bud that graces yon islands
  Were wreathed in a garland around him to twine!
    O that some seedling gem,
    Worthy such noble stem,

1. Celtic fire festival at start of summer: 1 May.

    Honoured and blessed in their shadow might grow!
       Loud should Clan-Alpine then
       Ring from her deepmost glen,
438 Roderigh Vich Alpine dhu, ho! ieroe!'

*   *   *

Canto v[1]

iii

36 At length they came where, stern and steep,
    The hill sinks down upon the deep.
    Here Vennachar in silver flows,
    There, ridge on ridge, Benledi rose;
    Ever the hollow path twined on,
    Beneath steep bank and threatening stone
    An hundred men might hold the post
    With hardihood against a host.
    The rugged mountain's scanty cloak
    Was dwarfish shrubs of birch and oak,
    With shingles bare, and cliffs between,
    And patches bright of bracken green,
    And heather black, that waved so high,
    It held the copse in rivalry.
    But where the lake slept deep and still,
    Dank osiers fringed the swamp and hill;
    And oft both path and hill were torn,
    Where wintry torrents down had borne,
    And heaped upon the cumbered land
    Its wreck of gravel, rocks, and sand.
    So toilsome was the road to trace,
    The guide, abating of his pace,
    Led slowly through the pass's jaws,
    And asked Fitz-James, by what strange cause
    He sought these wilds, traversed by few,
    Without a pass from Roderick Dhu.

iv

    'Brave Gael, my pass in danger tried,
    Hangs in my belt, and by my side;   (his sword)
    Yet, sooth to tell,' the Saxon said,
    'I dreamed not now to claim its aid.
    When here, but three days since, I came,
    Bewildered in pursuit of game,

---

1. King James V has been hunting incognito, calling himself 'James Fitz-James'. In returning to Loch Katrine he loses his way, but falls in with a Highland stranger who offers to be his guide but is not who he seems to be.

All seemed as peaceful and as still
As the mist slumbering on yon hill;
Thy dangerous Chief was then afar,
Nor soon expected back from war.
Thus said, at least, my mountain-guide,
Though deep, perchance, the villain lied.' –
'Yet why a second venture try?' –
'A warrior thou, and ask me why?
Moves our free course by such fixed cause
As gives the poor mechanic laws?
Enough, I sought to drive away
The lazy hours of peaceful day;
Slight cause will then suffice to guide
A Knight's free footsteps far and wide –
A falcon flown, a greyhound strayed,
The merry glance of mountain maid:
Or, if a path be dangerous known,
The danger's self is lure alone.' –

v
'Thy secret keep, I urge thee not;
Yet, ere again ye sought this spot,
Say, heard ye nought of Lowland war,
Against Clan-Alpine, raised by Mar?' –
'No, by my word; – of bands prepared
To guard King James's sports I heard;
Nor doubt I aught, but, when they hear
This muster of the mountaineer,
Their pennons will abroad be flung,
Which else in Doune had peaceful hung.' –
'Free be they flung! – for we were loth
Their silken folds should feast the moth.
Free be they flung! – as free shall wave
Clan-Alpine's pine in banner brave.
But, Stranger, peaceful since you came,
Bewildered in the mountain game,
Whence the bold boast by which you show
Vich-Alpine's vowed and mortal foe?' –
'Warrior, but yester-morn, I knew
Nought of thy Chieftain, Roderick Dhu,
Save as an outlawed desperate man,
The chief of a rebellious clan,
Who, in the Regent's court and sight,
With ruffian dagger stabbed a knight:
Yet this alone might from his part
Sever each true and loyal heart.'

vi

Wrathful at such arraignment foul,
Dark lowered the clansman's sable scowl.
A space he paused, then sternly said,
'And heard'st thou why he drew his blade?
Heard'st thou that shameful word and blow
Brought Roderick's vengeance on his foe?
What recked the Chieftain if he stood   cared
On Highland heath, or Holy-Rood?[1]
He rights such wrong where it is given,
If it were in the court of Heaven.' –
'Still was it outrage; – yet, 'tis true,
Not then claimed sovereignty his due;
While Albany,[2] with feeble hand,
Held borrowed truncheon of command,
The young King, mewed in Stirling tower,
Was stranger to respect and power.
But then, thy Chieftain's robber life! –
Winning mean prey by causeless strife,
Wrenching from ruined Lowland swain
His herds and harvest reared in vain –
Methinks a soul like thine should scorn
The spoils from such foul foray borne.'

vii

The Gael beheld him grim the while,
And answered with disdainful smile,
'Saxon, from yonder mountain high,
I marked thee send delighted eye,
Far to the south and east, where lay,
Extended in succession gay,
Deep waving fields and pastures green,
With gentle slopes and groves between:
These fertile plains, that softened vale,
Were once the birthright of the Gael;
The stranger came with iron hand,
And from our fathers reft the land.
Where dwell we now? See, rudely swell
Crag over crag, and fell o'er fell.
Ask we this savage hill we tread,
For fattened steer or household bread;
Ask we for flocks these shingles dry,   rocky scree
And well the mountain might reply –

1. Church of the Holy Rude (Cross), in Stirling.
2. John Stewart, Duke of Albany, governor in the name of the young prince, after James IV's death at Flodden.

"To you, as to your sires of yore,
Belong the target and claymore!   (shield and sword)
I give you shelter in my breast,
Your own good blades must win the rest."
Pent in this fortress of the North,
Think'st thou we will not sally forth
To spoil the spoiler as we may,
And from the robber rend the prey?
Ay, by my soul! While on yon plain
The Saxon rears one shock of grain,
While of ten thousand herds there strays
But one along yon river's maze,
The Gael, of plain and river heir,
Shall with strong hand redeem his share.
Where live the mountain Chiefs who hold
That plundering Lowland field and fold
Is aught but retribution true?
Seek other cause 'gainst Roderick Dhu.'

viii
Answered Fitz-James, 'And, if I sought,
Think'st thou no other could be brought?
What deem ye of my path waylaid?
My life given o'er to ambuscade?' –
'As of a meed to rashness due:
Hadst thou sent warning fair and true –
I seek my hound, or falcon strayed,
I seek, good faith, a Highland maid –
Free hadst thou been to come and go,
But secret path marks secret foe.
Nor yet, for this, even as a spy,
Hadst thou unheard been doomed to die,
Save to fulfil an augury.' –
'Well, let it pass; nor will I now
Fresh cause of enmity avow,
To chafe thy mood and cloud thy brow.
Enough, I am by promise tied
To match me with this man of pride:
Twice have I sought Clan-Alpine's glen
In peace; but when I come again,
I come with banner, brand, and bow,
As leader seeks his mortal foe.
For love-lorn swain, in lady's bower,
Ne'er panted for the appointed hour,
As I, until before me stand
This rebel Chieftain and his band!'

ix

'Have, then, thy wish!' He whistled shrill,
And he was answered from the hill;
Wild as the scream of the curlew,
From crag to crag the signal flew.
Instant, through copse and heath, arose
Bonnets and spears and bended bows;
On right, on left, above, below,
Sprung up at once the lurking foe;
From shingles grey their lances start,
The bracken bush sends forth the dart,
The rushes and the willow-wand
Are bristling into axe and brand,
And every tuft of broom gives life
To plaided warrior armed for strife.
That whistle garrisoned the glen
At once with full five hundred men,
As if the yawning hill to heaven
A subterranean host had given.
Watching their leader's beck and will,
All silent there they stood, and still.
Like the loose crags, whose threatening mass
Lay tottering o'er the hollow pass,
As if an infant's touch could urge
Their headlong passage down the verge,
With step and weapon forward flung,
Upon the mountain-side they hung.
The Mountaineer cast glance of pride
Along Benledi's living side,
Then fixed his eye and sable brow
Full on Fitz-James – 'How say'st thou now?
These are Clan-Alpine's warriors true;
227   And, Saxon, – I am Roderick Dhu!'

Young Men will love thee[1]

Young men will love thee more fair and more fast;
   Heard ye so merry the little bird sing?
Old men's love the longest will last,
   And the throstle-cock's head is under his wing.

The young man's wrath is like light straw on fire;
   Heard ye so merry the little bird sing?
But like red-hot steel is the old man's ire,
   And the throstle-cock's head is under his wing.

1. Sung by Davie Gellatley, a wise fool in *Waverley*.

The young man will brawl at the evening board;
   Heard ye so merry the little bird sing?
But the old man will draw at the dawning the sword,
   And the throstle-cock's head is under his wing.

Proud Maisie[1]

… And it was remarkable, that there should always be traced in her songs something appropriate, though perhaps only obliquely or collaterally so, to her present situation. Her next seemed the fragment of some old ballad:

Cauld is my bed, Lord Archibald,
   And sad my sleep of sorrow;
But thine sall be as sad and cauld,
   My fause true-love! tomorrow.

And weep ye not, my maidens free,
   Though death your mistress borrow;
For he for whom I die to-day,
   Shall die for me tomorrow.

Again she changed the tune to one wilder, less monotonous, and less regular. But of the words, only a fragment or two could be collected by those who listened to this singular scene:

Proud Maisie is in the wood,
   Walking so early;
Sweet Robin sits on the bush,
   Singing so rarely.

'Tell me, thou bonny bird,
   When shall I marry me?' –
'When six braw gentlemen
   Kirkward shall carry ye.' –

'Who makes the bridal bed,
   Birdie, say truly?' –
'The grey-headed sexton
   That delves the grave duly.

The glow-worm o'er grave and stone
   Shall light thee steady.
The owl from the steeple sing,
   "Welcome, proud lady."'

Her voice died away with the last notes, and she fell into a slumber …

1. Sung on her deathbed by the madwoman Madge Wildfire, as printed in *The Heart of Midlothian*.

Joanna Baillie (1762–1851)

Joanna Baillie's father, a minister in Lanarkshire, died when she was 16 years old. Six years later, the family moved to London where Joanna became known as a dramatist with a number of plays to her name, much admired by her friend Walter Scott. Baillie's songs became well known and widely published in various magazines and collections, although many of them are reworked versions of older originals.

Tam o' the Lin[1]

Tam o' the Lin was fu' o' pride,
And his weapon he girt to his valorous side,
A scabbard o' leather wi' de'il-haiit within.   lit.: devil have it (nothing at all)
'Attack me wha daur!' quo' Tam o' the Lin.

Tam o' the Lin he bought a mear;   mare
She cost him five shillings, she wasna dear.
Her back stuck up, and her sides fell in.
'A fiery yaud,' quo' Tam o' the Lin.   jade

Tam o' the Lin he courted a May;
She stared at him sourly, and said him nay;
But he stroked down his jerkin and cocked up his chin.
'She aims at a laird, then,' quo' Tam o' the Lin.

Tam o' the Lin he gaed to the fair,
Yet he looked wi' disdain on the chapman's ware;   pedlar's
Then chucked out a sixpence; the sixpence was tin.
'There's coin for the fiddlers,' quo' Tam o' the Lin.

Tam o' the Lin wad show his lear,   learning
And he scann'd o'er the book wi' wise-like stare.
He muttered confusedly, but didna begin.
'This is dominie's business,'quo' Tam o' the Lin.   school-master's

Tam o' the Lin had a cow wi' ae horn,
That likit to feed on his neighbour's corn.

---

1. Based on a children's rhyme, rather than the elf-struck lover of the ballad.

The stanes he threw at her fell short o' the skin:
'She's a lucky auld reiver,' quo' Tam o' the Lin.   robber

Tam o' the Lin he married a wife,
And she was the torment, the plague o' his life;
She lays sae about her, and maks sic a din,   such a noise
'She frightens the baby,' quo' Tam o' the Lin.

Tam o' the Lin grew dowie and douce,   dispirited; quiet
And he sat on a stane at the end o' his house.
'What ails, auld chield?' He looked haggard and thin.   fellow
'I'm no very cheery,' quo' Tam o' the Lin.

Tam o' the Lin lay down to die,
And his friends whispered softly and woefully –
'We'll buy you some masses to scour away sin.'
'And drink at my lyke-wake,' quo' Tam o' the Lin.   (vigil over the body)

Woo'd and Married and a'[1]

The bride she is winsome and bonny,
Her hair it is snooded sae sleek,   tied up in a ribbon
And faithfu' and kind is her Johnny
Yet fast fa' the tears on her cheek,
New pearlins are cause of her sorrow,   lace trimmings
New pearlins and plenishing too;   furnishings
The bride that has a' to borrow
Has e'en right mickle ado.   a lot to do
Woo'd and married and a'!
Woo'd and married and a'!
Isna she very weel aff
To be woo'd and married and a'?

Her mither then hastily spak:
'The lassie is glaikit wi' pride;   foolish
In my pouch I had never a plack   pocket; coin
The day that I was a bride.
E'en tak' to your wheel and be clever,
And draw out your thread in the sun;
The gear that is gifted, it never   goods
Will last like the gear that is won.   earned
Woo'd and married and a'!'
Wi' havins and tocher sae sma'!   clothing; dowry
I think ye are very weel aff
To be woo'd and married and a'!'

1. Derived from a vigorous song of the same name by Alexander Ross (1699–1784), Baillie's version takes a more ironic stance from the woman's point of view.

'Toot! toot!' quo' her grey-headed faither,
'She's less o' a bride than a bairn;
She's ta'en like a cowt frae the heather,   raw youth
Wi' sense and discretion to learn.
Half husband, I trow, and half daddy,
As humour inconstantly leans,
The chiel maun be patient and steady   chap must
That yokes wi' a mate in her teens.   (marries)
A kerchief sae douce and sae neat,   seemly
O'er her locks that the wind used to blaw!
I'm baith like to laugh and to greet   weep
When I think o' her married at a'!'

Then out spak the wily bridegroom;
Weel waled were his wordies I ween: chosen; judge
'I'm rich, though my coffer be toom,   empty
Wi' the blink o' your bonny blue e'en.
I'm prouder o' thee by my side,
Though thy ruffles and ribbons be few,
Than if Kate o' the Craft were my bride,
Wi' purples and pearlins enou'.
Dear and dearest of ony!
Ye're woo'd and buiket and a'!   registered (in parish bans)
And do ye think scorn o' your Johnny,
And grieve to be married at a'?'

She turn'd, and she blush'd, and she smiled,
And she lookit sae bashfully down;
The pride o' her heart was beguiled,
And she play'd wi' the sleeve o' her gown,
She twirled the tag o' her lace,
And she nippit her boddice sae blue,
Syne blinkit sae sweet in his face,
And aff like a mawkin she flew.   hare
Woo'd and married and a'!
Wi' Johnny to roose her and a'!   excite
She thinks hersel' very weel aff
To be woo'd and married and a'!

Robert Tannahill (1774–1810)

A frail and modest man, Tannahill had numerous poems and songs published while working as a weaver in Paisley. He met James Hogg there, and many of his most popular pieces were set to music by R. A. Smith, editor of *The Scottish Minstrel*. An edition of his poems appeared in 1807 and he became well known, but high hopes for his play *The Soldier's Return* were not shared by the critics. His health failed, and after a minor publishing set-back he took his own life.

Eild

Old age

The rough hail rattles thro the trees,
  The sullen lift low'rs gloomy gray,   *sky*
The trav'ller sees the swelling storm,
  And seeks the alehouse by the way.

But, waes me! for yon widowed wretch,
  Borne doun wi years an heavy care;
Her sapless fingers scarce can nip
  The wither'd twigs tae beet her fire.   *kindle*

Thus youth and vigour fends itsel;
  Its help, reciprocal, is sure,
While dowless Eild, in poortith cauld,   *feeble; poverty*
  Is lanely left tae stan the stoure.   *endure the storm*

The Tap-Room

This warl's a tap-room owre and owre,
  Whaur ilk ane tak's his caper,
Some taste the sweet, some drink the sour,
  As waiter Fate sees proper;
Let mankind live, ae social core,
  An drap a' selfish quar'ling,
An whan the Landlord ca's his score,
  May ilk ane's clink be sterling.   *money; (good)*

Jessie, the Flower o' Dunblane

The sun has gane down o'er the lofty Benlomond,
   And left the red clouds to preside o'er the scene,
While lanely I stray, in the calm simmer gloamin',   twilight
   To muse on sweet Jessie, the flower o' Dunblane.

How sweet is the brier wi' its saft faulding blossom,
   And sweet is the birk, wi' its mantle o' green;   birch
Yet sweeter, and fairer, and dear to this bosom,
   Is lovely young Jessie, the flower o' Dunblane.

She's modest as ony, and blythe as she's bonnie,   cheerful
   For guileless simplicity marks her its ain;
And far be the villain, divested o' feelin',
   Wha'd blight in its bloom thee sweet flower o' Dunblane.

Sing on, thou sweet mavis, thy hymn to the e'ening,   thrush
   Thou'rt dear to the echoes o' Calderwood glen;
Sae dear to this bosom, sae artless and winning,
   Is charming young Jessie, the flower o' Dunblane.

How lost were my days till I met wi my Jessie,
   The sports o the city seemed foolish and vain;
I ne'er saw a nymph I would ca' my dear lassie,
   Till charmed wi sweet Jessie, the flower o Dunblane.

Tho mine were the station o loftiest grandeur,
   Amidst its profusion I'd languish in pain,
And reckon as naething the heicht o its splendour,
   If wanting sweet Jessie, the flower o Dunblane.   lacking

Barochan Jean

'Tis haena ye heard man, o Barochan Jean?   (Jean from Barochan)
   An haena ye heard, man, o Barochan Jean
How death an starvation cam o'er the haill nation,
   She wrocht sic mischief wi her twa pawkie een.   worked; sly eyes
The lads an the lasses were deein in dizzens,
   The tane killed wi luve, an the tither wi spleen;
The ploughin, the sawin, the shearin, the mawin –   mowing
   A wark was forgotten for Barochan Jean.   All

Frae the south an the north, o'er the Tweed an the Forth,
   Sic comin an gangin there never was seen;
The comers were cheerie, the gangers were blearie,
   Despairin or hopin for Barochan Jean.

The carlins at hame were a girnin and granin,   old women; grumbling; groaning
　　The bairns were a greetin frae mornin till e'en;   crying
They gat naethin for crowdie but runts boiled tae sowdie,   (food); cabbage-stalks; broth
　　For naethin gat growin for Barochan Jean.

The doctors declared it was past their descrivin,
　　The ministers said 'twas a judgment for sin;
But they lookit sae blae, an their hearts were sae wae,   grey; sorrowful
　　I was sure they were deein for Barochan Jean.
The burns on roadsides were a dry wi their drinkin,
　　Yet a wadna sloken the drouth in their skin;   slake; thirst
A roun the peatstacks, an alangst the dyke backs,
　　E'en the win's were a sighin, 'Sweet Barochan Jean.'

The timmer ran dune wi the makin o coffins,   timber
　　Kirkyairds o thar swaird were a howkit fu clean;   turf; dug up
Deid lovers were packit like herrin in barrels,
　　Sic thousan's were deein for Barochan Jean.
But mony braw thanks tae the Laird o Glenbrodie,
　　The grass owre their graffs is now bonnie an green:
He staw the proud heart o our wanton young leddie,   stole
　　An spoilt a the charms o her twa pawkie een.

William Tennant (1784–1848)

Born lame, Tennant (largely self-educated) found employment as a clerk and a schoolteacher, and ultimately became Professor of Oriental Languages at the University of St Andrews. He wrote blank verse dramas, but gained most success with his mock epic poem 'Anster Fair' (1812) which inflated 'Rob the Ranter's' wooing of 'Maggie Lauder' into a lengthy extravaganza of rival suitors in active competition. This used a stanza modified from Ariosto's *ottavo rima*, which Byron also used to effect in his later verse. Choosing Scots for his next mock-epic, 'Papistry Stormed' (1827), Tennant cited David Lindsay as his mentor in a remarkable attempt to invest the Reformers' destruction of St Andrews Cathedral with all the burlesque and furious glee of 'Christis Kirk on the Green'. The result, with comic interventions from the Gods, is not unlike the wilder verses of Sydney Goodsir Smith over a hundred years later.

from **Anster Fair**   Anstruther (in Fife)

Canto iv

l

401 Nor ceas'd the business of the day meanwhile;
       For as the monarch chew'd his sav'ry cake,   (James v)
     The man, whose lungs sustain the trumpet's toil,
       Made haste again his noisy tube to take,
     And with a cry, which, heard full many a mile,
       Caus'd the young crows on Airdrie's trees to quake,
     He bade the suitor-pipers to draw nigh,
     That they might, round the knoll, their powers of piping try.

li

     Which when the rabble heard, with sudden sound
       They broke their circle's huge circumference,
     And, crushing forward to the southern mound,
       They push'd their many-headed shoal immense,
     Diffusing to an equal depth around
       Their mass of bodies wedg'd compact and dense,
     That, standing nigher, they might better hear
     The pipers squeaking loud to charm Miss MAGGIE'S ear.

452

lii

And soon the pipers, shouldering along
    Through the close mob their squeez'd uneasy way,
Stood at the hillock's foot, an eager throng,
    Each asking license from the king to play;
For with a tempest, turbulent and strong,
    Labour'd their bags impatient of delay,
Heaving their bloated globes outrageously,
As if in pangs to give their contents to the sky.

liii

And every bag, thus full and tempest-ripe,
    Beneath its arm lay ready to be prest,
And, on the holes of each fair-polish'd pipe,
    Each piper's fingers long and white were plac'd;
Fiercely they burn'd in jealous rivalship;
    Each madding piper scoff'd at all the rest,
And fleer'd and toss'd contemptuously his head,
As if his skill alone deserv'd fair MAGGIE'S bed.

liv

Nor could they wait, so piping-mad they were,
    Till James gave each man orders to begin,
But in a moment they displode their air
    In one tumultuous and unlicens'd din;
Out-flies, in storm of simultaneous blare,
    The whizzing wind comprest their bags within,
And, whiffling through the wooden tubes so small,
Growls gladness to be freed from such confining thrall.

lv

Then rose, in burst of hideous symphony,
    Of pibrochs and of tunes one mingled roar;   (Highland piping)
Discordantly the pipes squeal'd sharp and high,
    The drones alone in solemn concord snore;
Five hundred fingers, twinkling funnily,
    Play twiddling up and down on hole and bore
Now passage to the shrilly wind denying,
And now a little rais'd to let it out a-sighing.

lvi

Then rung the rocks and caves of Billyness,
    Reverberating back that concert's sound,
And half the lurking Echoes that possess
    The glens and hollows of the Fifan ground,
Their shadowy voices strain'd into excess

Of out-cry, loud huzzaing round and round
To all the Dryads of Pitkirie wood,
That now they round their trees should dance in frisky mood.

lvii

As when the sportsman with report of gun
    Alarms the sea-fowl of the Isle of May,
Ten thousand mews and gulls that shade the sun
    Come flapping down in terrible dismay,
And with a wild and barb'rous concert stun
    His ears, and scream, and shriek, and wheel away;
Scarce can the boatman hear his plashing oar;
Yell caves and eyries all, and rings each Maian shore.   (i.e.: of the Isle of May)

lviii

Just so around the knoll did pipe and drone
    Whistle and hum a discord strange to hear,
Tort'ring with violence of shriek and groan
    Kingly, and courtly, and plebeian ear;
And still the men had humm'd and whistled on,
    Ev'n till each bag had burst its bloated sphere,
Had not the king, uprising, wav'd his hand,
And check'd the boist'rous din of such unmanner'd band.

lix

On one side of his face a laugh was seen,
    On t'other side a half-form'd frown lay hid;
He frown'd, because they petulantly keen,
    Set up their piping forward and unbid;
He laugh'd, for who could have controul'd his mien,
    Hearing such crash of pibrochs as he did?
He bade them orderly the strife begin,
And play each man the tune wherewith the fair he'd win.

lx

Whereat the pipers ceas'd their idle toil
    Of windy music wild and deafening,
And made too late (what they forgot e'erwhile)
    A general bow to MAGGIE and their king;
But, as they vail'd their bare heads tow'rd the soil,
    O then there happ'd a strange portentous thing,
Which had not good my Muse confirm'd for true,
Myself had not believ'd, far less have told to you.

lxi

For lo! whilst all their bodies yet were bent,
    Breaks from the spotless blue of eastern sky

A globe of fire, (miraculous ostent!)
   Bursten from some celestial cleft on high;
And thrice in circle round the firmament
   Trail'd its long light the gleamy prodigy,
Till on the ring of pipers down it came,
And set their pipes and drones and chanters in a flame.

lxii

'Twas quick and sudden as th' electrick shock;
   One moment lighted and consum'd them all;
As is the green hair of the tufted oak
   Scath'd into blackness by the fulmin'd ball,
Or, as spark-kindled, into fire and smoke,
   Flashes and fumes the nitrous grain so small,
So were their bagpipes, in a twink, like tinder
Fir'd underneath their arms and burn'd into a cinder.

lxiii

Yet so innocuous was the sky-fall'n flame
   That, save their twangling instruments alone,
Unsing'd their other gear remain'd the same,
   Ev'n to the nap that stuck their coats upon;
Nor did they feel it's heat when down it came
   On errand to destroy pipe, bag and drone,
But stood in blank surprise, when to the ground
Dropt down in ashes black their furniture of sound.

lxiv

Crest-fall'n they stood, confounded and distrest,
   And fix'd upon the turf their stupid look,
Conscious that Heav'n forbade them to contest
   By such a burning token of rebuke:
The rabble, too, it's great alarm confest,
   For every face the ruddy blood forsook,
As with their white, uprolling, ghastly eyes
They spy'd the streaky light wheel whizzing from the skies.

lxv

And still they to that spot of orient heav'n,
   Whence burst the shining globe, look up aghast,
Expecting when th' empyreal pavement riven
   A second splendour to the earth should cast;
But when they saw no repetition given,
   Chang'd from alarm to noisy joy at last,
They set up such a mix'd tremendous shout,
As made the girdling heav'ns to bellow round about.

lxvi

And such a crack and peal of laughter rose,
    When the poor pipers bagpipe-less they saw,
As when a flock of inky-feather'd crows,
    On winter morning when the skies are raw,
Come from their woods in long and sooty rows,
    And over ANSTER through their hoarse throats caw;
The sleepy old-wives, on their warm chaff-beds,
Up from their bolsters rear, afear'd, their flannel'd heads.

lxvii

Then did th' affronted pipers slink away,
    With faces fix'd on earth for very shame,
For not one remnant of those pipes had they
    Wherewith they late so arrogantly came,
But in a black and ashy ruin lay
    Their glory moulder'd by the scathing flame;
Yet in their hearts they curs'd (and what the wonder?)
That fire to which their pipes so quick were giv'n a plunder.

lxviii

And scarce they off had slunk, when with a bound
    Great ROBERT SCOT sprung forth before the king,
For he alone, when all the pipers round
    Stood rang'd into their fire-devoted ring,
Had kept snug distance from the fated ground,
    As if forewarn'd of that portentous thing;
He stood and laugh'd, as underneath his arm
552 He held his bagpipe safe, unscath'd with fiery harm.

from Papistry Storm'd

Sang First

               Argument
        The Muse, invokit for this wark,
            Screeds aff her dainty dittie;
        How folk begoud to gowl and bark   howl
            Contrair the Roman city;   (Catholic St Andrews)
        And how Dan Momus stirr'd a clark   (the God of Mirth)
            Of stalwart saul and witty;
        And how wi' dreams a chieftain stark
            Was fir'd withouten pity.

1   I sing the steir, strabush, and strife,   disturbance; uproar
     Whan, bickerin' frae the towns o' Fife,   rushing

Great bangs of bodies, thick and rife,   people; crowded
   Gaed to Sanct Androis town,
And, wi' John Calvin i' their heads,
And hammers i' their hands and spades,
Enrag'd at idols, mass, and beads,
   Dang the Cathedral down:[1]
I wat the bruilzie then was dour,   battle; hard
Wi' sticks, and stanes, and bluidy clour,   blow
Ere Papists unto Calvin's power
   Gaif up their strangest places;
And fearfu' the stramash and stour,   commotion; dust
Whan pinnacle cam doun and tow'r,
And Virgin Maries in a shower
   Fell flat and smash't their faces;
The capper roofs, that dazzlit heaven,   copper
Were frae their rafters rent and riven;
The marble altars dash't and driven;
   The cods wi' velvet laces,   cushions
The siller ewers and candlesticks,
The purple stole and gowden pyx,   (vessel for the sacred host)
And tunakyls and dalmatyks,   tunics; bishop's garments
   Cam tumblin' frae their cases;
The Devil stood bumbaz'd to see   stupified
The bonny cosy byke, whair he   bees-nest
Had cuddlit monie a centurie,
   Ripp't up wi' sic disgraces!

O Muse, that frae Parnassus' crown
Cam in thy multi-spanglet shoon,   shoes
Lampin' alang in joyeus glee   loping
Frae jaw to jaw athort the sea,   wave; across
To meet the Chian king o' sang,   (Homer)
That in his cave the lee day lang,
Sat culyieing thee beside the shore   fondling
Whairon th' Aegean's jappers roar;   breakers
There sat he, on lone bink reclin'd,   bench
Deep musin' in his mightie mind,
Some famous argument to find;
Thou at his elbuck stood unseen,
And wi' thy glamour glaik'd his een,
   Bewitchin' them to joy;
Than, than, by him was brightlie seen
The bitter collieshangie keen   uproar (dogfight)

---

1. Crowds rioted in St Andrews after an anti-Catholic sermon by John Knox on 11 June 1559, but the cathedral was
not in fact demolished at that time.

That wrocht the Greeks annoy;[1]
Ilk bluidy brulziement and battle   embroilment
Wi' swords, and stanes, and chariots' brattle,
That never blindit nor did sattle
Till erthlins wi' a dunderin' rattle   earthwards
    Tummlet the tow'rs o' Troy;
O come down frae thy cloud on hie,
Whair thou art singin' merrilie,
And wi' thy wings owrshadow me,
    And fan my spreit to joy;
And up thy magic lantern hold,
That in its lookin'-glass o' gold,
My glaikit ee may well behold   foolish
    The Papists and their faes comminglit
In monie a fecht and tulzie-mulzie   noisy wrangle
Herryin' o' kirks, and image-spulzie,   harrying; plunder
    Whairwi' nae ear as yet hath tinglet;
Thou kenn'st it a'; for thou wert there
Pitch't on the steeple's tap in air,
Markin' the faces, everilk one,   each and every
O' them by wham the wark was done
And notin; down within thy book
Ilk motion, gesture, speik, and look,   Each
Aiblins to use on future time   Perhaps
And blazon them abraid in rhime:
Till, underneath thy feet, I trow,
Dinnelin' *Deaf Meg* and *Crookit Mou*[2]   thundering
Begoud wi' ane terrifick blatter   Began; percussion
At the great steeple's found to batter,   foundation
    Garrin' the stanes to dance;   Causing
The steeple rock't at ilka swack;   stroke
Thou saw'st the comin' crash and wrack;
And flaff't thy wings, and in a crack
    Flew frae th' unsicker stance!   insecure

Say, first, what set the folks a-fire,
And made them wraithly to conspire,   angrily
Contrair Cathedral, monk, and spire?   Against
The Cardinal's bluid (now rest his saul!)[3]
Lay clotter't on the castill-wall,
And bauld Johne Knox, now grown the baulder,
That Beaton lay in's kist the caulder,
Past like a lion round the land,

1. Tennant imagines that the muse which inspired Homer to write the *Iliad* was also present at St Andrews.
2. Names given to two cannons.
3. Cardinal Beaton was assassinated there in 1547.

And wi' the wangyle in his hand,   evangel (the Bible)
And wechtie Calvin in his wallet,
Was as it were an iron mallet
To break the Man o' Sin to flinders,   (the Pope); shreds
And hurl the *mass* amang the cinders;
He preachit east, he preachit wast;
His voice was as the whirlwind's blast,
   That aftentimes, in days o' simmer,
Comes swirlin' sudden frae the sea,
And swoops the hay-cocks aff the lea,   haystacks; pasture
   And tirls the kirks, and strips the timmer;   rattles; trees
The vera steeples round about
Rebellow'd to his nobill shout,
And rang wi' texts baith in and out;
The dows and daws that there aboundit,   pigeons and jackdaws
As if affrichtit and confoundit,   terrified
Out-whirr'd and whitter't at the sound o't;
The bells and bartisans reboundit;   parapets
Strang pupits flew about in blads,[1]   Strong pulpits; splinters
Breakin' the hearers' pows wi' dads;   bits
Men, women, kirtled girls, and lads,
Were fir'd and furiated in squads;
Sae wud and wicket was their wraith   mad
Gainst Papish trash and idol-graith,   gear
   The patter'd prayers and beads,
They scarce could sattle on the benches,
But cock't their fists in fearfu' clenches,
And slappit furiouslie their henches,   thighs
   And shook their angrie heads.
Ae man bang't upwarts frae his place,
And toss'd his nieve, withouten grace,   fist
Richt i' the Virgin Mary's face.
Anither wicht was mair uncivil: creature
He brak St Ayle owr by the neevil,   fist
And bann'd baith pieces to the deevil.   consigned
Some say, – maybe 'twas but a clatter, –   gossip
That the town's piper, wi' a blatter,
Whummlet and skail't the halie water;   swooshed and emptied out
Be't true, be't fause, it's little matter:
Had Bellarmine[2] been sittin' cockin
In Anster kirk, he'd gat a yokin'   rough ride
Yon day, that wou'd hae cow'd his croakin',
And garr'd his head hing like a doken: made; dock-leaf

1. Knox is said to have preached so fiercely that he was in danger of smashing the pulpit.
2. Cardinal Bellarmine (1542–1621), dedicated anti-Protestant.

The vera dead men's mooler't banes,   mouldered
   That i' the kirk-ayle lay at rest,
Amaist caught life aneath their stanes,
And bowtit up amang the rest   leapt
To smash the stany saints, whilk they   which
Had worship't on a former day
Whan tabernaclin' i' their clay!   embodied

But hoolie, Muse! reprime your haste;   gently
   Descrybe mair gently a' the matter;
Ye needna rin as ye were chas'd,   as if
140   And blast and blaw wi' sic a blatter!

       *   *   *

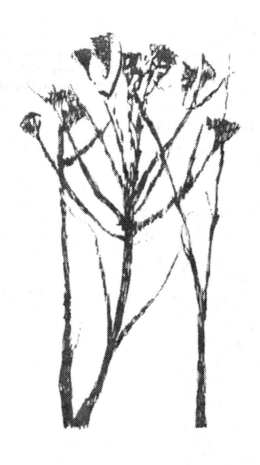

Ann Campbell, Scalpay, Harris
(c. 1773)

Work songs, and love songs – frequently composed and almost always sung by women
– provide a store of more personal and colloquial utterance in the Gaelic tradition.
This is also found in songs of lament associated with the tradition of keening, as in

Ailein Duinn, shiùbhlainn leat

Gura mise th' air mo sgaradh!
Chan e sùgradh nochd th' air m' aire.

SEISD: Ailein duinn ò-hì, shiùbhlainn leat,
           Hi ri ri ri ibh ò hio hùg oirinn ò,
           Ailein duinn ò-hì, shiùbhlainn leat.

Ach stoirm nan sianta 's meud na gaillinn,
Dh'fhuadaicheadh na fir o'n chala.
Ailein duinn, a luaidh nan leannan.
Chuala mi gun deach thu thairis.
Air a' bhàta chaol, dhubh, dharaich.
'S gun deach thu air tìr am Manainn.
Cha b'e sud mo rogha cala
Ach caolas Stiadair anns na Hearadh,
No Loch Mhiabhag anns na beannaibh.

Ailein duinn, a laoidh mo chéille,
Gur-a h-òg a thug mi spéis dhuit.
'S ann an nochd is bochd mo sgeula
Chan e bàs a' chruidh san fhéisidh
Ach a fhliuichead 's tha do léine.
'S muca-mara bhith gad reubadh.
Ged bu leamsa buaile spréidhe.
'S ann an nochd bu bheag mo spéis di.
'S mi nach iarradh caochladh céile,
B' anns' bhith leat air mullach sléibhe.

the following verses to the poet's fiancé Allan Morison, who was drowned – according to tradition – on his way to marry her. As originally sung, every other line of the lament would be linked with the keening lines of the chorus.

Brown-haired Allan, I would go with you

I am devastated tonight!
I have no thought of love-making,

CHORUS: Brown-haired Allan, ò-hì, I would go with you,
                Hi ri ri ri ibh ò hio hùg oirinn ò,
                Brown-haired Allan, ò-hì, I would go with you.

Thinking only of the storms and the strength of the tempest
that would drive the men from harbour.
Brown-haired Allan, darling sweetheart,
I heard that you had made the crossing
in the slim black boat built with oak,
and that you had landed in Man:
that would not be my choice of harbour
but rather Stiadair Sound in Harris
or Miavaig Loch among the hills.

Brown-haired Allan, my own darling,
I gave you my love as a youngster:
it is a sad tale I have tonight,
not of the death of the cattle in want,
but of the wetness of your shirt,
and of the porpoises tearing at you.
Though I had a foldful of cattle
I would care little for it now,
I would not wish a change of spouse,
better to be with you on the mountain-top.

Ailein duinn, a chill 's a nàire!
Chuala mi gun deach' do bhàthadh.
Gura truagh nach mi bha làmh riut.
Ge b'e sgeir no bogh' an tràigh thu.
Ge b'e tiùrr am fàg an làn thu.
Dh' òlainn deoch ge b'oil le m' chàirdibh.
Cha b' ann a dh' fhìon dearg na Spàinne.
Ach a dh' fhuil do chuim, 's i b'fheàrr leam.

O gum pàigheadh Dia do d' anam,
Na fhuair mi dhe d' chòmhradh falaich.
Na fhuair mi dhe d' chuid gun cheannach.
Pìosan dhe an t-sìoda bhallach,
Ged nach téid e 'm feum ri m' mhaireann.
M' achanaich-sa, Rìgh na Cathrach.
Gun mi dhol an ùir no 'n anart.
'N talamh-toll no 'n àite falaich.
Ach sa' bhall an deach' thu, Ailein.

Gura mise th' air mo sgaradh!

Brown-haired Allan,
I heard that you had been drowned,
would that I were beside you,
on whatever rock or bank you come ashore,
in whatever heap of seaweed the high tide leaves you.
I would drink a drink, whatever my kin say,
not of the red wine of Spain
but of your breast's blood, I would prefer that.

May God give payment to your soul
for what I had of your private talk,
for what I had of your goods without purchase,
lengths of speckled silk,
though I shall never live to use them.
My prayer to God on His throne
that I should not go in earth or shroud,
in a hole in the ground or a secret place,
but in the place you went, Allan.

I am devastated tonight!

trans. Derick Thomson

Iain MacGhillEathain/ John MacLean (1787–1848)

Born on Tiree, MacLean wrote praise poems under the patronage of MacLean of Coll, before emigrating to Nova Scotia in 1819, like so many Gaels before and after him. He continued to write in Canada, adding religious themes to his topics, but the

Am Bàrd an Canada

Gu bheil mi am ònrachd 'sa' choille ghruamaich,
   Mo smaointinn luaineach, cha tog mi fonn:
Fhuair mi an t-àit so an aghaidh nàduir,
   Gu'n thréig gach tàlant a bha 'nam cheann.
Cha dèan mi òran a chur air dòigh ann,
   An uair nì mi tòiseachadh bidh mi trom:
Chaill mi a' Ghàidhlig seach mar a b'àbhaist dhomh
   An uair a bhà mi 'san dùthaich thall.

Cha'n fhaigh mi m' inntinn leam ann an òrdugh,
   Ged bha mi eòlach air dèanamh rann;
Is e mheudaich bròn dhomh 's a lùghdaich sòlas
   Gun duine còmhla rium a nì rium cainnt.
Gach là is oidhche is gach car a nì mi
   Gu'm bi mi cuimhneachadh anns gach am
An tìr a dh' fhàg mi tha an taic an t-sàile,
   Ged tha mi an dràsd ann am bràighe ghleann.

Cha'n iongnadh dhòmh-sa ged tha mi brònach,
   Is ann tha mo chòmhnuidh air cùl nam beann,
Am meadhon fàsaich air Abhainn Bhàrnaidh[1]
   Gun dad as fheàrr na buntàta lom.
Mu'n dèan mi àiteach 's mu'n tog mi bàrr ann,
   Is a' choille ghàbhaidh chur as a bonn
Le neart mo ghàirdein gu'm bi mi sàraichte
   Is treas air fàillinn mu'm fàs a' chlann.

1. Barney's River, in Pictou County, Nova Scotia.

following poem gives a particularly telling glimpse of the disillusionment that awaited so many Highland emigrants when they found conditions in the New World to be much harder than the emigration agents had led them to believe.

The Poet in Canada

I'm all alone in this gloomy woodland,
    my mind is troubled, I sing no song:
against all nature I took this place here
    and native wit from my mind has gone.
I have no spirit to polish poems,
    my will to start them is dulled by care;
I lose the Gaelic that was my custom
    in yon far country over there.

I cannot muster my thoughts in order
    though making songs was my great delight;
there's little joy comes to smoor my sadness
    with no companion to ease my plight;
each night and day, in each task I turn
    to the ache of memory grows more and more;
I left my dear land beside the ocean
    and now no sea laps my dwelling's shore.

It is no wonder I should be grieving
    behind these hills in a desert bare,
in this hard country of Barney's River[1]
    a few potatoes my only fare;
I must keep digging to win bare living
    to hold these wild threatening woods at bay;
my strength alone serves till sons reach manhood
    and I may fail long before that day.

1. In Pictou County, Nova Scotia.

Is i so an dùthaich 's a bheil an cruadal
   Gun fhios do'n t-sluagh a tha tighinn a nall;
Gur h-olc a fhuaras oirnn luchd a' bhuairidh
   A rinn le an tuairisgeul ar toirt ann.
Ma nì iad buannachd cha mhair i buan dhaibh;
   Cha dèan i suas iad 's cha'n iongnadh leam,
Is gach mallachd truaghain a bhios 'gan ruagadh
   Bho'n chaidh am fuadach a chur fo'n ceann.

Bidh gealladh làidir 'ga thoirt an tràth sìn,
   Bidh cliù an àite 'ga chur am meud;
Bidh iad ag ràitinn gu bheil bhur càirdean
   Gun sona sàidhbhir gun dad a dh' éis.
Gach naidheachd mheallta 'ga toirt g' ur n-ionnsaigh-se
   Feuch an sanntaich sibh dol 'nan déidh;
Ma thig sibh sàbhailt 'n uair chì sibh àdsan,
   Cha'n fheàrr na stàtachan na sibh féin.

An uair théid na dròbhairean sin g' ur n-iarraidh
   Is ann leis na briagan a nì iad feum,
Gun fhacal fìrinne bhi 'ga innse,
   Is an cridhe a' dìteadh na their am beul.
Ri cur am fiachaibh gu bhell 'san tìr so
   Gach nì as prìseile tha fo'n ghréin:
An uair thig sibh innte gur beag a chì sibh
   Ach coille dhìreach toirt dhibh an speur.

An uair thig an geamhradh is am na dùbhlachd
   Bidh sneachd a' dlùthadh ri cùl nan geug,
Is gu domhain dùmhail dol thar na glùine,
   Is ge maith an triùbhsair cha dean i feum,
Gun stocain dhùbailt 'sa' mhocais chlùdaich
   Bhios air a dùnadh gu dlùth le éill:
B'e am fasan ùr dhuinn a cosg le fionntach
   Mar chaidh a rùsgadh de'n bhrùid an dé.

Mar bi mi eòlach air son mo chòmhdaich
   Gum faigh mi reòta mo shròn 's mo bheul,
Le gaoith a tuath a bhios neimheil fuaraidh
   Gum bi mo chluasan an cunnart geur.
Tha an reothadh fuathasach, cha seas an tuagh ris,
   Gum mill e a' chruaidh ged a bha i geur;
Mur toir mi blàs di, gum brist an stàilinn,
   Is gun dol do'n cheàrdaich cha gheàrr i beum.

This is a country that's hard and cruel,
   they do not know it who journey still;
evil the yarns of the smooth-tongued coaxers
   who brought us hither against our will;
yet if they profit it won't advance them,
   may they not prosper despite their loot,
the cursed wretches who drive out people
   since first this Clearance was set afoot.

Strong is the promise that they will make you
   this place's virtues they'll loudly boast;
your friends, they'll say, now grow rich and prosper
   nor lack for those things that men want most.
They'll fill your ears with each lying rumour
   to make you follow them where they will;
where they appear, few escape them safely,
   fortunate they who evade them still.

Drovers of men who come to seek you
   will seal their bargain with a lie,
no single word of the truth they're telling
   for what their tongues say, their hearts deny;
loud is their boasting of what this land holds
   each thing that's rarest, waits to be won,
but when you come here, little you'll see then
   but great tall forests that steal the sun.

When comes the winter, a bitter season
   the forest branches are clothed in snow,
and no plain cloth is defence against it,
   thigh deep and thick on the ground below;
but clouted moccasins and double stockings
   and leather thongs are our forest boots;
rawhide and fur are our latest fashions
   ripped from the backs of the forest brutes.

Without true learning and skill in dressing
   I would be frozen from brow to chin,
the stinging winds of the freezing northland
   kill feet and hands did I let them in;
a frightful cold takes the edge from axes,
   the bite of frost blunts the hardest blade;
no smith or forge here to heal spoiled metal
   so fire must melt ere one notch be made.

An uair thig an samhradh 's am mìosa céitein
    Bidh teas na gréine 'gam fhàgail fann;
Gu'n cuir i spéirid 's a h-uile creutair
    A bhios fo éislean air feadh nan toll.
Na mathain bhéisteil gun dèan iad éirigh
    Dhol feadh an treud, is gur mór an call:
Is a' chuileag ìneach gu socach puinseanta
    'Gam lot gu lìonmhor le rinn a lainn.

Gun dèan i m'aodann gu h-olc a chaobadh,
    Chan fhaic mi an saoghal, 's ann bhios mi dall;
Gun at mo shùilean le neart a cungaidh,
    Ro-ghuineach drùidheach tha sùgh a teang'.
Chan fhaigh mi àireamh dhuibh ann an dànachd
    Gach beathach gràineil a thogas ceann;
Is cho liutha plàigh ann 's a bha air rìgh Phàro
    Air son nan tràillean 'n uair bhàth e an camp.

Gur h-iomadh caochladh tighinn air an t-saoghal,
    Is ro-bheag a shaoil mi an uair bha mi thall;
Bu bheachd dhomh 'n uair sin mun d'rinn mi gluasad
    Gum fàsainn uasal 'n uair thiginn ann.
An car a fhuair mi cha b'ann gu m' bhuannachd,
    Tighinn thar a' chuain air a' chuairt bha meallt',
Gu tìr nan craobh anns nach 'eil an t-saorsainn
    Gun mhart gun chaora is mi dh' aodach gann.

Gur h-iomadh ceum anns am bi mi an déislàimh
    Mu'n dèan mi saidhbhir mo theachd-an-tìr;
Bidh m' obair éigneach mun toir mi feum aisd',
    Is mun dèan mi réiteach air son a' chroinn:
Cur sgonn nan teinntean air muin a chéile
    Gun do lasaich féithean a bha 'nam dhruim,
Is a h-uile ball dhiom cho dubh a' sealltainn,
    Bidh mi 'gam shamhlachadh ris an t-sùip.

Ge mór an seanchas a bh'aca an Albainn,
    Tha a' chùis a' dearbhadh nach robh e fìor;
Na dolair ghorma chan fhaic mi falbh iad,
    Ged bha iad ainmeil a bhith 'san tìr.
Ma nìtear bargain chan fhaighear airgead,
    Ged 's éiginn ainmeachadh anns a' phrìs;
Ma gheibhear cùnnradh air feadh nam bùthan
    Gu'm pàighear null e le flùr no ìm.

The month of May and the first of summer,
   my strength is drained by the blazing sun,
that wakes from winter the forest creatures
   where they lay weakly in den and run;
the prowling bears rise from winter slumbers,
   a roaming band that's a sore mischance;
the snouted fly with his store of poison
   deals wounds unceasing from his sharpened lance.

He stabs my face with an eager malice
   till with his venom my eyelids swell;
there's no escaping his burning juices
   that gall my eye like a flame of hell;
I have not space to relate the boldness
   of each foul crawler that seeks its prey;
like to the plagues that the Pharoah suffered,
   my mean condition from day to day.

In this wide world there come many changes;
   I little knew in that other land,
how fond my dreams at the time of leaving
   that in due time I'd be rich and grand;
a turn I took that was not for profit,
   a lying hope made me cross the sea.
This land of trees is no land of freedom,
   no herd gives milk nor flock their wool for me.

There's many a shift I must turn my hand to
   before I'm sure of my daily fare;
rough is the task till I win its profit
   and make arrangement for needful gear:
stacking the tree-trunks to set them burning
   lights fire in sinews across my back,
and like a man who's been sweeping chimneys,
   my body changes to sooty black.

Great were the tales that they told in Scotland
   their falsehood proved by our sorry lot;
I've never handled a silver dollar
   although I'm told that they can be got.
A deal is made, but there's no coin passes,
   though you have bargained that cash be paid,
they'll take your gear but they'll pay no money,
   for flour and butter is all their trade.

Cha'n fhaic mi margadh no latha féille
    No iomain feudalach ann an dròbh,
No nì nì feum dhuinn a measg a chéile:
    Tha an sluagh 'nan éiginn 's a h-uile dòigh.
Cha chulaidh fharmaid iad leis an ainbhfhiach,
    A' reic na shealbhaicheas iad an còir;
Bidh fear nam fiachan is cromadh cinn air
    'Ga chur do'n phrìosan mur diol e an stòr.

Mun tig na cùisean a tigh na cùirte
    Gun téid an dùblachadh aig a' mhòd;
Tha an lagh a' giùlan o làimh na *jury*
    Gu'n téid a spùinneadh 's nach fiù e an còrr.
Bidh earraid siùbhlach air feadh na dùthcha
    'Gan ruith le cùnntasaibh air an tòir;
Gur mór mo chùram gun tig e am ionnsaigh:
    Cha ghabh e diùltadh 's bidh diùbhail òirnn.

Cha'n fhaigh mi innseadh dhuibh anns an dàn so,
    Cha dèan mo nàdur a chur air dòigh
Gach fios a b' àill leam thoirt do mo chàirdean
    'San tìr a dh'fhàg mi, rinn m' àrach òg.
Gach aon a leughas e, tuigibh reusan,
    Is na tugaibh éisdeachd do luchd a' bhòsd,
Na fàidhean bréige a bhios 'gur teumadh,
    Gun aca spéis dhibh ach déidh bhur n-òir.

Ged bhithinn dìcheallach ann an sgrìobhadh
    Gun gabhainn mìosa ris agus còrr,
Mun cuirinn crìoch air na bheil air m' inntinn
    Is mun tugainn dhuibh e le cainnt mo bheòil.
Tha mulad dìomhair an déidh mo lìonadh
    On is éiginn strìocadh an so ri m' bheò,
Air bheag thoil-inntinn 'sa' choille chruinn so.
    Gun duine faighneachd an seinn mi ceòl.

Cha b'e sin m' àbhaist an tùs mo làithean,
    Is ann bhithinn ràbhartach aig gach bòrd,
Gu cridheil sùnndach an comunn cùirteil
    A' ruith ar n-ùine gun chùram òirnn.
An uair thug mi cùl ribh bha mi 'gar n-ionndrainn
    Gun shil mo shùilean gu dlùth le deòir,
Air moch Diar-daoin a' dol seach an caolas
    Is an long fo h-aodach 's a' ghaoth o'n chòrs'.

I see no market, I see no fair day,
   no wealthy drovers of cattle here,
nought in our townland but want and shortage
   that can't be bettered for lack of gear.
No cause of envy, our sorry debtors
   whose trifling treasures don't match the score,
head hung in shame and a debtors' prison
   when they have rouped all the meagre store.

Before the case ever reaches courtroom
   be sure the roup will increase the debt;   *selling-up auction*
the law they get from the jury's handling
   makes sure the reiving's not over yet;
through our poor country the sheriff travels,
   by the court's warrant he hounds the poor;
I live in fear that I'll see him bringing
   his debtor's summons towards my door.

I cannot say in these simple verses,
   no skill have I in such words as tell
to distant friends all the thoughts that fill me
   of yon dear land where I used to dwell.
But let who read this heed well its meaning
   and give no ear to the liars there
who boast this land only but to hook you
   and trim their profits from your passage fare.

Though I've been diligent in the writing
   it's taken me a full month or more
to set to rights all the things I'm thinking,
   to shape in words all that grieves me sore;
in my soul's depth such a sadness fills me,
   each weary day adds its hours of strife,
no joyful song fills this forest prison
   that holds me fast for what's left of life.

How changed my custom from my youth's gladness,
   the sounding days round each merry board;
joyful my heart in each happy meeting
   our days a-flying while our spirits soared;
now since I left you my heart beats sadly:
   the hot salt tears on my cheeks were shed,
on Thursday last as I saw the packet,   *mail-boat*
   her head turned eastward and her canvas spread.

trans. William Neill

George Gordon, Lord Byron
(1788–1824)

Born in London to warring parents, Byron was taken to Scotland by his mother when he was two, spending the next nine years of his life there. She was Elizabeth Gordon of Gight, a wilful and difficult woman, who could trace her family back to James I. 'Half a Scot by birth, and bred a whole one', as he claimed in *Don Juan*, Byron was educated at a day school in Aberdeen and then at Aberdeen Grammar School, spending his summers in Deeside where he conceived a lasting love of the hills and rivers of the North-East. He inherited the barony on his father's side in 1798 and returned to England to take up residence at Newstead Abbey. Surrounded by rumours and scandals, he travelled abroad and seemed to live the part of the satanically fascinating 'Byronic hero' who figured in his own verse romances – works such as *The Giaour* (1813) and *Lara* (1814), which were enormously popular throughout Europe. His reputation as a major poet of his times was made when the third canto of *Childe Harold's Pilgrimage* appeared in 1816. More mature libertarian sentiments began to appear in the later verse epics and in *The Vision of Judgment* (1823) which mounted a satirical attack on the dead King George III. Arguably Byron's greatest work is *Don Juan*, a comic epic verse masterpiece which he worked on from 1818 until he sailed for Greece in 1823. The poet died at Missolonghi where he had gone to support the Greeks in their fight for independence from Turkish rule.

When I Roved a Young Highlander

When I roved a young Highlander o'er the dark heath,
And climb'd thy steep summit, oh Morven[1] of snow!
To gaze on the torrent that thunder'd beneath,
Or the mist of the tempest that gather'd below,
Untutor'd by science, a stranger to fear,
And rude as the rocks where my infancy grew,
No feeling, save one, to my bosom was dear;
Need I say my sweet Mary,[2] 'twas centred in you?

---

1. A hill in Aberdeenshire, north of Ballater. Byron was much reminded of it when he saw the hills of Greece.
2. Mary Duff, whom the poet met in Aberdeen when he was no more than eight years old, and long before he knew any sexual attraction – 'yet my misery, my love for that girl were so violent, that I sometimes doubt if I have ever been really attached since'.

Yet it could not be love, for I knew not the name, –
What passion can dwell in the heart of a child?
But still I perceive an emotion the same
As I felt, when a boy, on the crag-cover'd wild:
One image alone on my bosom impress'd,
I loved my bleak regions, nor panted for new;
And few were my wants, for my wishes were bless'd;
And pure were my thoughts, for my soul was with you.

I arose with the dawn; with my dog as my guide,
From mountain to mountain I bounded along;
I breasted the billows of Dee's rushing tide
And heard at a distance the Highlander's song:
At eve, on my heath-cover'd couch of repose,
No dreams, save of Mary, were spread to my view;
And warm to the skies my devotions arose,
For the first of my prayers was a blessing on you.

I left my bleak home, and my visions are gone;
The mountains are vanish'd, my youth is no more;
As the last of my race, I must wither alone,
And delight but in days I have witness'd before:
Ah! splendour has raised, but embitter'd my lot;
More dear were the scenes which my infancy knew:
Though my hopes may have fail'd, yet they are not forgot;
Though cold is my heart, still it lingers with you.

When I see some dark hill point its crest to the sky,
I think of the rocks that o'ershadow Colbleen;[1]
When I see the soft blue of a love-speaking eye,
I think of those eyes that endear'd the rude scene;
When, haply, some light-waving locks I behold
That faintly resemble my Mary's in hue,
I think on the long flowing ringlets of gold,
The locks that were sacred to beauty, and you.

Yet the day may arrive when the mountains once more
Shall rise to my sight in their mantles of snow:
But while these soar above me, unchanged as before,
Will Mary be there to receive me? – ah, no!
Adieu, then, ye hills, where my childhood was bred!
Thou sweet flowing Dee, to thy waters adieu!
No home in the forest shall shelter my head, –
Ah! Mary, what home could be mine but with you?

1. Culblean Hill, below Morven.

from The Vision of Judgment

i

Saint Peter sat by the celestial gate:
   His keys were rusty, and the lock was dull,
So little trouble had been given of late;
   Not that the place by any means was full,
But since the Gallic era 'eighty-eight'[1]
   The devils had ta'en a longer, stronger pull,
And 'a pull altogether,' as they say
At sea – which drew most souls another way.

ii

The angels all were singing out of tune,
   And hoarse with having little else to do,
Excepting to wind up the sun and moon,
   Or curb a runaway young star or two,
Or wild colt of a comet, which too soon
   Broke out of bounds o'er the ethereal blue,
Splitting some planet with its playful tail,
As boats are sometimes by a wanton whale.

iii

The guardian seraphs had retired on high,
   Finding their charges past all care below;
Terrestrial business fill'd nought in the sky
   Save the recording angel's black bureau;
Who found, indeed, the facts to multiply
   With such rapidity of vice and woe,
That he had stripp'd off both his wings in quills,
And yet was in arrear of human ills.

iv

His business so augmented of late years,
   That he was forced, against his will, no doubt,
(Just like those cherubs, earthly ministers,)
   For some resource to turn himself about
And claim the help of his celestial peers,
   To aid him ere he should be quite worn out
By the increased demand for his remarks;
Six angels and twelve saints were named his clerks.

v

This was a handsome board – at least for heaven;
   And yet they had even then enough to do,

1. The time of the French Revolution, signalled by the storming of the Bastille in 1789.

So many conquerors' cars were daily driven,
  So many kingdoms fitted up anew;
Each day too slew its thousands six or seven
  Till at the crowning carnage, Waterloo,
They threw their pens down in divine disgust –
The page was so besmear'd with blood and dust.

vi

This by the way; 'tis not mine to record
  What angels shrink from: even the very devil
On this occasion his own work abhorr'd,
  So surfeited with the infernal revel:
Though he himself had sharpen'd every sword
  It almost quench'd his innate thirst of evil.
(Here Satan's sole good work deserves insertion –
'Tis, that he has both generals in reversion.)

vii

Let's skip a few short years of hollow peace,
  Which peopled earth no better, hell as wont,
And heaven none – they form the tyrant's lease,
  With nothing but new names subscribed upon 't:
'Twill one day finish: meantime they increase,
  'With seven heads and ten horns,' and all in front,
Like Saint John's foretold beast,[1] but ours are born
Less formidable in the head than horn.

viii

In the first year of freedom's second dawn[2]
  Died George the Third; although no tyrant, one
Who shielded tyrants, till each sense withdrawn
  Left him nor mental nor external sun:
A better farmer ne'er brushed dew from lawn,
  A worse king never left a realm undone!
He died – but left his subjects still behind,
One half as mad – and t'other no less blind.   (George IV)

ix

He died! – his death made no great stir on earth:
  His burial made some pomp; there was profusion
Of velvet, gilding, brass, and no great dearth
  Of aught but tears – save those shed by collusion,
For these things may be bought at their true worth;
  Of elegy there was the due infusion –

1. In the Book of Revelations.
2. 1820, when revolutions broke out again in southern Europe.

Bought also,[1] and the torches, cloaks, and banners,
Heralds, and relics of old Gothic manners,

x

Form'd a sepulchral melodrame. Of all
    The fools who flock'd to swell or see the show,
Who cared about the corpse? The funeral
    Made the attraction, and the black the woe.
There throbb'd not there a thought which pierced the pall;
    And when the gorgeous coffin was laid low,
It seem'd the mockery of hell to fold
80   The rottenness of eighty years in gold.

           *   *   *

xlii

329 'Look to the earth, I said,[2] and say again:
    – When this old, blind, mad, helpless, weak, poor worm
Began in youth's first bloom and flush to reign,
    The world and he both wore a different form,
And much of earth and all the watery plain
    Of ocean call'd him king, through many a storm
His isles had floated on the abyss of time;
For the rough virtues chose them for their clime.

xliii

'He came to his sceptre young; he leaves it old:
    Look to the state in which he found his realm,
And left it; and his annals too behold,
    How to a minion first he gave the helm;
How grew upon his heart a thirst for gold,
    The beggar's vice, which can but overwhelm
The meanest hearts; and for the rest, but glance
Thine eye along America and France.

xliv

''Tis true, he was a tool from first to last
    (I have the workmen safe), but as a tool
So let him be consumed. From out the past
    Of ages, since mankind have known the rule
Of monarchs – from the bloody rolls amass'd
    Of sin and slaughter – from the Caesars' school,
Take the worst pupil; and produce a reign
More drench'd with gore, more cumber'd with the slain.

1. Byron's great satirical poem was inspired by his contempt for an inflated official elegy written by Robert Southey, the poet laureate, called 'A Vision of Judgement'.
2. Satan is speaking before the gate of Heaven, claiming George III as his own. A huge quarrel will soon break out, and the King will sneak into Paradise unnoticed.

xlv

'He ever warr'd with freedom and the free:
   Nations as men, home subjects, foreign foes,
So that they utter'd the word "Liberty!"   (For as long as)
   Found George the Third their first opponent. Whose
History was ever stain'd as his will be
   With national and individual woes?
I grant his household abstinence; I grant
His neutral virtues, which most monarchs want;   lack

xlvi

'I know he was a constant consort; own   husband
   He was a decent sire, and middling lord.
All this is much, and most upon a throne;
   As temperance, if at Apicius'[1] board,
Is more than at an anchorite's supper shown.
   I grant him all the kindest can accord;
And this was well for him, but not for those
Millions who found him what oppression chose.

xlvii

'The New World shook him off; the Old yet groans
   Beneath what he and his prepared, if not
Completed: he leaves heirs on many thrones
   To all his vices, without what begot
Compassion for him – his tame virtues; drones
   Who sleep, or despots who have now forgot
A lesson which shall be re-taught them, wake
376 Upon the thrones of earth; but let them quake!

           *   *   *

---

1. A notorious glutton in the time of the Roman emperor Tiberius. Anchorite monks withdraw from the world and live sparsely.

Uilleam MacDhunléibhe/
William Livingston (1808–1870)

Livingston was apprenticed as an itinerant tailor on his native Islay, before moving
to the mainland in South-West and Central Scotland where he set about educating
himself. He wrote long poems based on ancient history and old clan battles in the
Highlands, and was noted as a difficult and melancholy man, with a strong prejudice

Fios thun a' Bhàird

Tha mhadainn soilleir grianach,
    'S a' ghaoth 'n iar a' ruith gu réidh;
Tha 'n linne sleamhuinn, sìochail,
    O'n a chiùinich strì nan speur;
Tha 'n long 'na h-éideadh sgiamhach,
    'S cha chuir sgìos i dh' iarraidh tàimh,
Mar a fhuair 's a chunnaic mise.
    Thoir am fios so chun a' Bhàird.

        *   *   *

17   Tha miltean spréidh air faichean;
    'S caoraich gheal air creachainn fhraoich;
'S na féidh air stùcan fàsail
    Far nach truaillear làr na gaoith;
An sìolach fiadhaich, neartmhor,
    Fliuch le dealt na h-oiteig thlàth;
Mar a fhuair 's a chunnaic mise:
    Thoir am fios so chun a' Bhàird.

        *   *   *

41   Tha Bogha-mòr an t-sàile
    Mar a bha le reachd bith-bhuan;
Am mòrachd maise nàduir
    'S a cheann-àrd ri tuinn a' chuain;
A riombal geal seachd mìle,
    Gainmhean sìobt' o bheul an làin,

against the English. Nevertheless, the Clearances and his pain at the depopulation of his beloved Islay gave him plenty cause for the anger which energises 'A Message to the Bard', after its opening stanzas have described the beauty he once found there.

A Message to the Bard

The morning's bright and sunny,
    and the west wind softly blows;
the loch is smooth and peaceful
    with the strife of sky at rest.
Under its lovely canvas
    the ship's lively – does not tire,
as it carries this clear message,
    as I see it, to the Bard.

        *   *   *

There are cattle in their thousands,
on the plains, white sheep on slopes,
and the deer in the wild mountains
undisturbed by foreign scent,
their offspring, wild and powerful,
wet with dew from mildest breeze;
will you carry this clear message,
as I see it, to the Bard.

        *   *   *

The great sea-bay lies murmuring
    in its everlasting power,
majestic in its beauty,
    head-high to waves that roll,
with its seven-mile white halo
    of sand swept from edge of tide;

Mar a fhuair 's a chunnaic mise:
   Thoir am fios so chun a' Bhàird.

      *   *   *

57 'Ged a roinneas gathan gréine,
     Tlus nan speur ri blàth nan lòn,
  'S ged a chithear spréidh air àirigh,
     Is buailtean làn de dh' àlach bhó,
  Tha Ile'n diugh gun daoine,
     Chuir a' chaor a bailtean fàs,
  Mar a fhuar 's a chunnaic mise:
     Thoir am fios so chun a' Bhàird.

  Ged thig ànrach aineoil
     Gus a' chala, 's e 'sa cheò,
  Cha 'n fhaic e soills o'n chagailt
     Air a' chladach so na's mò;
  Chuir gamhlas Ghall air fuadach
     Na tha bh' uainn 's nach till gu bràth,
  Mar a fhuair 's a chunnaic mise:
     Thoir am fios so chun a' Bhàird.

      *   *   *

97 Cha'n fhaigh an déirceach fasgadh;
     No 'm fear astair fois o sgìos;
  No soisgeulach luchd-éisdeachd;
     Bhuadhaich eucoir, Gaill is cis,
  Tha'n nathair bhreac 'na lùban
     Air na h-ùrlair far an d' fhàs
  Na fir mhòra chunnaic mise:
     Thoir am fios so chun a' Bhàird.

will you carry this clear message,
   as I see it, to the Bard.

      *   *   *

Though the rays of sun may ration
   heaven's warmth to meadow's bloom,
though the shielings have their cattle,
   with folds full of lowing calves,
Islay has lost her people,
   the sheep have emptied homes;
will you carry this clear message,
   as I see it, to the Bard.

Though a stranger, in his wanderings
   comes to harbour in the mist,
the hearth has no light shining
   any more upon this coast;
for Lowland spite has scattered
   those who will not come again;
will you carry this clear message,
   as I see it, to the Bard.

      *   *   *

The poor will find no shelter,
   nor the traveller his rest;
nor will preacher find an audience;
   strangers, wrong and tax have won.
The spotted adder's coiling
   on the floors whereon there grew
the great men that I saw here:
   take this message to the Bard.

trans. Derick Thomson

Màiri Nic a' Phearsain/ Mary Macpherson (1821–1898)

Màiri Mhór nan Oran/Big Mary of the Songs was born on Skye, and although in later years she lived in Inverness and Glasgow, she is forever associated with the local scene in Skye, and with the land reform in which cause many of her most popular songs were composed. 'Brosnachadh nan Gaidheal' enlivened the elections of 1885, and

Brosnachadh nan Gaidheal

Cuiribh Teàrlach suas le aighear,
 'S deagh MhacPhàrlain suas le caithreim,
Cuiribh Aonghas suas le buaidh,
 Air ceann an t-sluaigh far 'n d'fhuair e aran.

Chuidich sud le neart nan Gàidheal,
 Air taobh Theàrlaich Bhàin gun mhearachd,
Na sgeith an *Courier* de chlàbar,
 'S ann am fàbhor ri Sir Coinneach.

Cuiribh Teàrlach suas le cliù,
 Oir dhearbh e dhuibh a dhùrachd cheana,
Is gheibh sibh cead air féidh nan stùc,
 Is còir ás ùr air bhur cuid fearainn.

'Sa' cheàrn 's na dh'àithneadh dhuinn le Dia,
 Chan fhaod sinn triall air sliabh no gaineimh,
A h-ùile nì 'n robh smear no luach,
 Gun spùinn iad uainn le lagh an fhearainn.

Chan eil bileag ghorm no uaine,
 Far 'n robh dualachas mo sheanar,
Leis na bric tha snàmh fo'n chuan,
 Nach tug iad uainn, a dheòin no dh'aindeoin.

many other songs were equally prepared to criticise the authorities, landlords and even churchmen in the boldest terms. The more personal 'Soraidh leis an Nollaig ùir'/'Farewell to the new Christmas' and 'Nuair bha mi òg'/'When I was young' evoke the changes and the depopulation which overcame so many Highland communities.

Incitement of the Gaels

Raise up Charles in joyful style,
    and good MacFarlane with a chorus,
Angus with a victory shout,
    to lead the folk who nurtured him.[1]

Aid the cause with strength of Gaels,
    as fair-haired honest Charlie's help,
the filth the *Courier* vomits out,
    done as favour to Sir Kenneth.[2]

Lift our famous Charles on high,
    he's shown you all his wish already,
your freedom on the mountain deer,
    new title to your piece of land.

The place commanded us by God,
    where we can't travel moor or strand,
and every bit of fat or value,
    they have grabbed with Land Law from us.

Neither stalk or blade of green,
    that was our fathers' heritage,
nor the trout that swim the sea,
    they have not claimed in our despite.

1. Charles MacIntosh, Donald MacFarlane and Angus Sutherland were Land Law Reform candidates for Inverness-shire, Argyll and Sutherland at the elections of December 1885. Only the first two were successful.
2. Sir Kenneth Mackenzie, supported by the *Inverness Courier*.

Ma thog neach eisir ann an cliabh,
   No maorach ann an meadhon mara,
Théid an cur fo ghlais 's fo dhìon,
   Le laghan diongmhalt' dìon an fhearainn.

Faodaidh gu bheil a' chainnt so garbh,
   Ach 's tric tha 'n fhìrinn searbh ri labhairt,
Chaidh luingeas-chogaidh 's sluagh fo airm,
   A dhìon 's a theàrmunn lagh an fhearainn.

Nuair a bha na h-uachdarain cruinn,
   Ann am baile-cinn na siorrachd,
Cuimhnichear ri iomadh linn,
   An guim a rinn iad gus ar mealladh.

Sgrìobh iad àithne dhaingeann dhian,
   Do'n ionad air nach dèan sinn labhairt,
Na h-aingle is am fear nach b'fhiach
   A thighinn a riaghladh lagh an fhearainn.

Nuair leugh Ivory an àithne,
   Chùnnt e chuid a b'fheàrr d'a aingil,
Ach dh'fhàg e chuid thàinig an Bhràighe,
   Oir bha'n cnàmhan air am prannadh.

'Togaidh sinn òirnn do na glinn,
   Leis na tha de Ghoill fainear dhuinn,
'S ma bhios sibhse fo m'chomannd,
   Théid an ceannsachadh dha'n aindeoin.'

Nuair a ràinig iad na glinn,
   'S ann bha na suinn nach dèanadh mearachd
Air an crioslachadh le fìrinn,
   'S cha robh innleachd air am prannadh.

Ghlaoidh Ivory an sin le gruaim,
   Ris na truaghain, a chuid aingeal –
'Chan fhaigh sinn am feasd a' bhuaidh,
   'S e seo an sluagh a fhuair a' bheannachd.

'Cha till mise gun mo dhiùmbadh,
   Nì mi cùirt am measg nan aingeal,

Let one get oysters in a creel,
   or shellfish from the flowing sea,
they'll be locked securely up,
   with strong law to guard the land.

If the language here is blunt,
   truth is often sore to speak,
they send warships and armed men[1]
   to guard and save their law of land.

When the landlords gathered round
   assembled in the county town,
'twill be recalled in every age,
   the tricks they practised to deceive us.

Commandment strong and tight they wrote,
   to a place we'll put no name on,
inviting Satan and his angels[2]
   as masters over their Land Law.

When Ivory read this command,
   he counted up his angel band
but some were left upon the Braes,[3]
   where their bones were sorely pounded.

'Let's go off now to the glens,
   with such Lowlanders as listen,
and with myself in charge of things,
   spite of all they'll come to order.'

But when they had reached the glens,
   they found the lads who make no errors
girt with justice in their cause,
   who by no means would take a pounding.

Said Ivory with surly face,
   to his wretched troop of angels –
'We'll never get a victory here,
   these must be a blessed people.'

'But I'll not return unthankful,
   I'll hold court among my angels,

1. A boatload of soldiers and policemen had sailed into Uig to put down unrest the previous year. They were led by Sheriff Ivory. This led a local minister to cite Kings 10:22 which refers to a famous cargo of 'ivory, and apes, and peacocks'.
2. Ivory's description of himself and his troops.
3. A community in Skye which lost its traditional grazing rights and protested by withholding their rent. Ivory and his policemen sought to arrest the ringleaders but were routed, largely by the women of the community. 'The Battle of the Braes' happened in April 1882.

Bheir mi bheathachadh bho Dhùghall,
    'S cuiridh mi an crùn air Calum.'

Dh'ainmichinn iad air an cinn,
    Bha seinn air ainneart luchd an fhearainn,
A thionndaidh 'n còta air an druim,
    'S a dh'ith na rainn dhe'n d'rinn iad ealain.

Falbh le leabhraichean 's 'gan seinn
    Dha na suinn a bh'aig a' bhaile –
'Gheibh sibh mil air bhàrr an fheòir
    Am Manitòba, is na fanaibh.'

Phàidh na h-uachdarain dhaibh duais
    Mas do ghluais iad o'n a' bhaile,
Ach 's e 'n gad air an robh 'n t-iasg
    A fhuair na sìochairean, 's iad falamh.

Soraidh leis an Nollaig ùir

Soraidh leis an Nollaig ùir,
Thogadh gean air comunn ciùin,
'S air nach cuireadh reodhadh giùig,
    Ged a bhiodh an Dùbhlachd fuar.

Dh'fhàg mi Eilean gaoil nan Sgiath,
Bho chionn còrr 's dà fhichead bliadhn':
'S mar a chaochail iad an rian,
    'S cianail leam a dhol g'a luaidh.

'S iomadh Gàidheal tha fo bhròn,
A thogadh ann an Tìr a' Cheò,
'Ga thacadh anns a' bhaile-mhór,
    Le stùr agus le ceò a' ghuail.

Agus mìltean air dol fàs,
Dh'fhearann torach bheireadh bàrr.
Far na dh'àraicheadh na sàir,
    Anns na blàir a chuireadh ruaig.

Ach thàinig caochladh air na neòil,
Air na cnuic is air na lòin,

I'll get a livelihood from Dougal,
  then I'll put the crown on Calum.'

I'll nominate to take the lead,
  those who sang of violent crofters,
turned the coats upon their backs,
  betrayed the tongue that made their verses.

Going with songbooks there to sing[1]
  to the champions of the township –
'You'll get honey on the grass-tops
  In Manitoba, so don't wait.'

The landlords offering a bounty
  if they'd only leave the township,
got a bare hook and no fish.
  Left those miscreants with nothing.

trans. William Neill

Farewell to the new Christmas

Farewell to the new Noël,
brought goodwill to the quiet band,
who would not cower in the frost,
  for all December season's cold.

I left the lovely Isle of Skye,
more than two score years ago;
and now the custom's altered there,
  and sad for me to tell the tale.

Bowed with sadness many a Gael,
bred up in the Land of Mists,
smothers now in urban streets,
  from city dust and reek of coal.

The miles are growing barren now,
of fertile earth that fosters crops,
where once brave warriors were bred,
  who put their enemies to rout.

But change has come upon the clouds,
and on the hills and pasture-lands,

1. Landowners and their agents tried to persuade their tenants to emigrate by various means, often by painting a rosy picture of life abroad. See William Livingston, 'A Message to the Bard'.

Far an robh na daoine còir',
   'S e th'ann caoraich-mhór' is uain.

Nuair a nochd mi ris an àit',
Far an robh mo shluagh a' tàmh,
Coin a' comhartaich ri m'shàil,
   Cur na fàilt' orm cho fuar.

Nuair a ràinig mi na dùin,
Tigh mo sheanmhar sìos 'na smùir,
Toman rainich fàs 'sa' chùil
   Far an robh mi mùirneach uair.

'S ràinig mi Tobar-a'-Mhàil,
Far an tric a dh'òl mi sàth,
Sligean eisirean 'na mhàs,
   'S tha e 'n diugh cho làn de dhruaip.

Ràinig mi tobar Iain Bhàin,
Dh'ainmichinn athair mo ghràidh,
'S na clachan mar a chuir a làmh,
   Air am fàgail dhomh mar dhuais.

Nuair a sheas mi os an cionn,
Shil na frasan bho mo shùil,
Cuimhneachadh air luchd mo rùin,
   A tha 'n diugh 'san ùir 'nan suain.

Chaill mo bhuadhan uile 'n lùth,
'S thàinig neul a' bhàis am ghnùis;
Dh'òl mi làn mo bhois de'n bhùrn,
   'S rinn e m'ùrachadh 'san uair.

Ràinig mi 'n tobhta bha làn,
Uair le cuid, is sluagh, is gràn,
Far an tric an d'rinneadh bàigh,
   Ris na h-anraich a bh'air chuairt.

Dh'fheuch mi 'm faithnichinn an t-àit',
Far an robh mo mhàthair ghràidh,
Suidhe maille rium mu'n chlàr,
   'S i 'gar sàsachadh le uaill.

Ach cha robh ùrnaigh 'ga cur suas,
Anns an fhàrdaich nach robh fuar,
'G iarraidh bheannachdan a-nuas
   Air an t-sluagh a bhiodh 'na broinn.

where once the honest people lived,
  only the great sheep and their lambs.

When I arrived beside the place,
wherein my race was wont to rest,
the dogs were barking at my heels,
  to give me a chill welcome there.

When I walked over to the knolls,
my grandsire's dwelling lay in dust,
behind it grew the bracken clumps
  where once in happiness I played.

When I came to the Tribute Well,
where I was wont to drink my fill,
the bottom's filled with oyster shells,
  and holds today a filthy scum.

I reached the well of Iain Bàn,   Fair Iain
that my beloved father named,
the stones whereon he laid his hands,
  are left a legacy to me.

I stood a while above it there,
the tears came raining from my eyes,
as I recalled the dear-loved folk,
  earthed now in their eternal sleep.

Then all my senses ebbed away,
death's pallor came upon my cheek;
but there I cupped my hand and drank,
  and felt my being made anew.

I reached the walls that once were full,
with gear and grain, and people there,
where often a kind welcome met,
  the wanderer upon his way.

I wondered if I'd know the place,
where once my darling mother sat,
beside me at the table there,
  and nurtured us with quiet pride.

But not a grace was being said,
in that home that was never cold,
to seek a blessing from above
  upon the folk within its walls.

Cha robh mi fada 'san àit'
Nuair a chaidh an sgeul os àird –
'Thàinig Màiri, Nighean Iain Bhàin,
  'S tha i tàmh 'sa' ghleann ud shuas.'

Chruinnich an sin luchd mo ghràidh,
A' cur furan orm le fàilt,
'S thuirt gach aon thug dhomh a làmh,
  'Bidh cuimhne air Iain Bàn gun fhuath.'

Thiormaich mi 'n sin suas mo dheòir,
'S thòisich mi air seinn mo cheòil,
Chumail m'aigne air a dòigh –
  Tha cunnart anns a' bhròn air uair.

'S chaidh mi sìos ri taobh an lòin,
Far an tric an robh mi òg,
Dh'iasgach chaimheineach le snòd,
  'S iad 'nan greòdan ris a' bhruaich.

Chaidh mi sìos thun a' bheul-àth,
Far am bithinn tric a' snàmh,
'S thug mi cuigealach nam màg
  Leam mar chuimhn' air gràdh an t-sluaigh.

Ach cha robh maighdean no bean òg
A' snìomh an t-snàth gu dèanamh clò,
'N duine 's maid' aige 'na dhòrn,
  Falbh air tòir na mnatha-luaidh.

Nuair a chruinnicheadh gach òigh,
'S ann an sud a bhiodh an ròic,
Measair chabhruich air a' bhòrd,
  'S na fleasgaich anns an t-seòmar shuas.

Cha robh seiche 'ga cur suas,
Air an spàrr gu'm biodh i cruaidh,
Oidhche Challainn tighinn a-nuas,
  'S chluinnteadh fuaim oirre le 'n cloinn.

Nuair a chruinnicheadh an greòd,
'S ann an sud a bhiodh an ròl,
'G éigheach 'Challainn, Challainn O!'
  'S fear a' tòiseachadh ri dhuan.

I was not long about the place
until the gossip went around –
'Mary's here, Fair Iain's daughter,
    staying up there in the glen.'

Round my dearest people gathered,
made for me warm welcome then,
saying as they took my hand,
    'Iain Bàn's remembered well.'

Tears ebbed away as I began,
to sing the melodies I knew,
that bring my spirit to its peace –
    for danger sometimes lies in grief.

And I went down beside the field,
wherein I often wandered young,
or fished for troutlets with a line,
    and they in shoals beneath the bank.

Down to the margin of the ford,
where in time past I'd often swim,
and pluck the orchis flowers, to me
    a memory of my people's love.

I found no maiden or young wife
spinning thread for making tweed,
nor husband going with stick in hand,
    to bring the waulking-women home.

When the lasses gathered round,
that's when the banter would begin,
a dish of sowens on the board,   a creamy sour-meal dip
    the young blades in the other room.

Never was a cowhide stored,[1]
upon the beams but hardened there,
until brought down at Hogmanay,
    when noisy bairns would follow sure.

When the crowd assembled then,
that's when a fine din began,
with shouting 'Ne'erday, Ne'erday O!'
    till one would start upon a song.

1. A hide was carried round the house and chased and beaten with shinty sticks as part of the New Year rituals in the
   Highlands.

H-uile fear 's a chasan rùisgt',
'S caman aig' air chaol d'a dhùirn,
Sracadh dhroineagan le sùrd,
   Cur bhannagan 'nan smùr 's 'nam bruan.

Nuair thàinig crìoch air an duain,
Bhiodh an caisean-Callainn suas,
Bean an tighe 's i gun ghruaim,
   Tighinn a-nuas dhaibh leis an dram.

Cha b'e glaine bheag gun tuar
Gheibheadh gille glas an duain,
Ach slige-chreachainn cur m'a bruaich,
   Chuireadh tuainealaich 'na cheann.

Ach chuala mi guth air mo chùl,
Mar gun éireadh neach o'n ùir –
'Nach eil Lachlann Og an Uird
   'Na cheann-iùil air ceann an t-sluaigh?'

Gum faithnich sinn air na cluain,
Air na daisean 's iodhlann chruach,
Gun robh cridheachan an t-sluaigh
   'Gan cur suas cho math ri'n làimh.

Nuair bha mi òg

Moch 's mi 'g éirigh air bheagan éislein,
   Air madainn Chéitein 's mi ann an Os,
Bha spréidh a' geumnaich an ceann a chéile,
   'S a' ghrian ag éirigh air Leac-an-Stòrr;
Bha gath a' boillsgeadh air slios nam beanntan,
   Cur tuar na h-oidhche 'na dheann fo sgòd,
Is os mo chionn sheinn an uiseag ghreannmhor,
   Toirt 'na mo chuimhne nuair bha mi òg.

Toirt 'na mo chuimhne le bròn is aoibhneas,
   Nach fhaigh mi cainnt gus a chur air dòigh,
Gach car is tionndadh an corp 's an inntinn,
   Bho'n dh'fhàg mi 'n gleann 'n robh sinn gun ghò;
Bha sruth na h-aibhne dol sìos cho tàimhidh,
   Is toirm nan allt freagairt cainnt mo bheòil,
'S an smeòrach bhinn suidhe seinn air meanglan,
   Toirt 'na mo chuimhne nuair bha mi òg.

Every man barefooted now,
a shinty stick held in his fist,
to batter at the mealy bag,   poke of meal used as a ball
    and bash the bannocks into crumbs.

When all the singers made an end,
the New-Year-candles set alight,
the smiling woman of the house,
    came in to serve a dram around.

No little shallow tasteless tot
a sallow lad might get for verse
a bumper lipping to the brim,
    that put a thunder in the head.

I heard a voice behind me say,
as one just risen from the grave –
'Is not Lachlan Og in Ord[1]
    as leader at his people's head?'

We would know again the fields,
the cornstacks standing in the yard,
if but the spirit of the folk
    could rise again in hand and heart.

                                                        trans. William Neill

When I was young

Easement of sadness in early rising,
    on a May morning and I in Os,
one to another the cattle calling,
    the dawn arising above the Storr;
a spear of sunlight upon the mountains
    saw the last shadow of darkness gone,
the blithesome lark high above me singing
    brought back to mind days when I was young.

A memory mingled with joy and sadness,
    I lack the words that can tell them true,
each case and change of my mind and body,
    far from the glen whose bright peace I knew;
the river rippling so gently seawards,
    my own speech echoed in the streamlet's flow,
sweet sang the mavis in budding branches,
    to wake the memories of long ago.

1. Lachlann MacDonald of Skeabost, one of the better landlords.

Nuair bha mi gòrach a' siubhal mòintich,
    'S am fraoch a' sròiceadh mo chòta bàn,
Feadh thoman còinnich gun snàthainn a bhrògan,
    'S an eigh 'na còsan air lochan tàimh;
A' falbh an aonaich ag iarraidh chaorach,
    'S mi cheart cho aotrom ri naosg air lòn,
Gach bot is poll agus talamh toll …
    Toirt 'na mo chuimhne nuair bha mi òg.

Toirt 'na mo chuimhn' iomadh nì a rinn mi,
    Nach faigh mi 'm bann gu ceann thall mo sgeòil,
A' falbh 'sa' gheamhradh gu luaidh is bainnsean
    Gun solus lainnteir ach ceann an fhòid;
Bhiodh òigridh ghreannmhor ri ceòl is dannsa …
    Ach dh'fhalbh an t-ám sin 's tha 'n gleann fo bhròn;
Bha 'n tobht aig Anndra 's e làn de fheanntaig,
    Toirt 'na mo chuimhne nuair bha mi òg.

Nuair chuir mi cuairt air gach gleann is cruachan,
    Far 'n robh mi suaimhneach a' cuallach bhó,
Le òigridh ghuanach tha nis air fuadach,
    De shliochd na tuath bha gun uaill gun ghò;
Na raoin 's na cluaintean fo fhraoch is luachair,
    Far 'n tric na bhuaineadh leam sguab is dlò,
'S nam faicinn sluagh agus tighean suas annt',
    Gum fàsainn suaimhneach mar bha mi òg.

An uair a dhìrich mi gual an t-Sìthein,
    Gun leig mi sgìos dhiom air bruaich an lòin;
Bha buadhan m'inntinn a' triall le sìnteig,
    Is sùil mo chinn faicinn loinn gach pòir:
Bha 'n t-sóbhrach mhìn-bhuidh' 's am beàrnan-brìghde,
    An cluaran rìoghail, is lus an òir,
'S gach bileag aoibhneach fo bhraon na h-oidhche,
    Toirt 'na mo chuimhne nuair bha mi òg.

Nuair chuir mi cùl ris an eilean chùbhraidh,
    'S a ghabh mi iùbhrach na smùid gun seòl,
Nuair shéid i 'n dùdach 's a shìn an ùspairt,
    'S a thog i cùrsa o Thìr a' Cheò;
Mo chridhe brùite 's na deòir le m'shùilean,
    A' falbh gu dùthaich gun sùrd, gun cheòl,
Far nach faic mi cluaran no neòinean guanach,
    No fraoch no luachair air bruaich no lòn.

In careless joy I would roam the moorland,
   the heather tips brushing on my dress,
through mossy knowes without help of footgear,
   when ice was forming on the lochan's face;
seeking the sheep on the mountain ridges,
   light as the snipe over meadow grass,
each mound and lochan and rolling hollow ...
   these are the memories of time that's past.

I bring to mind all the things I did there
   that will not fade till my story's end,
walking in winter to prayer or wedding,
   my only lantern a peat in hand;
the splendid youngsters, with song and dancing ...
   gone are their days now and sad the glen;
now Andrew's croft under shrouding nettles
   brings back to mind how our days were then.

How I would travel each glen and hill-top,
   herding the cattle with tranquil mind,
with lively youngsters now long in exile,
   a sturdy breed without foolish pride.
Pasture and ploughland now heath and rushes,
   where sickle swept and the sheaf was tied;
could I see dwellings again and people
   as once in youth, there I'd gladly bide.

There I would climb on the mountain shoulder,
   to take my ease on the grassy height;
my thought would leap in a blaze of wonder,
   such beauty lying below my sight:
the royal thistle and the yellow primrose,
   the golden blossom of sweet Saint Bride,
each joyous leaf under dew at evening
   brings back a memory of youth's delight.

I turned my back on that fragrant homeland,
   to take the vessel that needs no breeze,
but sounds a horn to put power in motion
   and set her course from the island seas;
My heart was crushed and the tears were flowing,
   going to a place lacking song or peace,
where there's no thistle or nodding gowan,   daisy
   rush bank or heather or grassy lease.

trans. William Neill

Alexander Smith (1830–1867)

Educated in Kilmarnock, Smith followed his father's trade as a pattern designer, until his poems and essays gained him a literary career and a modest post as secretary to the University of Edinburgh. His lengthy poem *A Life-Drama* was well received in its day but later parodied as grandiloquent and 'spasmodical' verse. His best prose work includes *A Summer in Skye* and the essays in *Dreamthorp*. 'Glasgow', from *City Poems* (1857), makes a notable attempt to deal with new visions of an industrial age.

Glasgow

Sing, Poet, 'tis a merry world;
That cottage smoke is rolled and curled
    In sport; that every moss
Is happy, every inch of soil: –
Before me runs a road of toil
    With my grave cut across.
Sing trailing showers and breezy downs –
I know the tragic heart of towns.

City! I am true son of thine:
Ne'er dwelt I where great mornings shine
    Around the bleating pens:
Ne'er by the rivulets I strayed,
And ne'er upon my childhood weighed
    The silence of the glens.
Instead of shores where ocean beats
I hear the ebb and flow of streets.

Black Labour draws his weary waves
Into their secret-moaning caves;
    But with the morning light
That sea again will overflow
With a long, weary sound of woe,
    Again to faint in night.
Wave am I in that sea of woes,
Which night and morning ebbs and flows.

I dwelt within a gloomy court
Wherein did never sunbeam sport;
    Yet there my heart was stirred –
My very blood did dance and thrill
When on my narrow window sill
    Spring lighted like a bird.
Poor flowers! I watched them pine for weeks
With leaves as pale as human cheeks.

Afar, one summer, I was borne;
Through golden vapours of the morn
    I heard the hills of sheep:
I trod with a wild ecstasy
The bright fringe of the living sea,
    And on a ruined keep
I sat and watched an endless plain
Blacken beneath the gloom of rain.

O fair the lightly sprinkled waste
O'er which a laughing shower has raced
    O fair the April shoots!
O fair the woods on summer days,
While a blue hyacinthine haze
    Is dreaming round the roots!
In thee, O City, I discern
Another beauty sad and stern.

Draw thy fierce streams of blinding ore,
Smite on a thousand anvils, roar
    Down to the harbour bars;
Smoulder in smoky sunsets, flare
On rainy nights, with street and square
    Lie empty to the stars.
From terrace proud to alley base
I know thee as my mother's face.

When sunset bathes thee in his gold
In wreaths of bronze thy sides are rolled,
    Thy smoke is dusky fire;
And, from the glory round thee poured,
A sunbeam, like an angel's sword,
    Shivers upon a spire.
Thus have I watched thee, Terror! Dream!
While the blue Night crept up the stream.

The wild train plunges in the hills,
He shrieks across the midnight rills;

Streams through the shifting glare
The roar and flap of foundry fires,
That shake with light the sleeping shires
    And on the moorlands bare
He sees afar a crown of light
Hung o'er thee in the hollow night.

At midnight, when thy suburbs lie
As silent as a noonday sky,
    When larks with heat are mute,
I love to linger on thy bridge,
All lonely as a mountain ridge,
    Disturbed but by my foot;
While the black, lazy stream beneath
Steals from its far-off wilds of heath.

And through thy heart, as through a dream,
Flows on that black, disdainful stream;
    All scornfully it flows,
Between the huddled gloom of masts,
Silent as pines unvexed by blasts –
    'Tween lamps in streaming rows.
O wondrous sight! O stream of dread!
O long, dark river of the dead!

Afar, the banner of the year
Unfurls; but dimly prisoned here,
    'Tis only when I greet
A dropt rose lying in my way,
A butterfly that flutters gay
    Athwart the noisy street,
I know the happy summer smiles
Around thy suburbs, miles on miles.

'Twere neither paean now, nor dirge,
The flash and thunder of the surge
    On flat sands wide and bare;
No haunting joy or anguish dwells
In the green light of sunny dells
    Or in the starry air.
Alike to me the desert flower,
The rainbow laughing o'er the shower.

While o'er thy walls the darkness sails,
I lean against the churchyard rails;
    Up in the midnight towers

The belfried spire; the street is dead;
I hear in silence overhead
    The clang of iron hours.
It moves me not – I know her tomb
Is yonder in the shapeless gloom.

All raptures of this mortal breath,
Solemnities of life and death,
    Dwell in thy noise alone;
Of me thou hast become a part –
Some kindred with my human heart
    Lives in thy streets of stone;
For we have been familiar more
Than galley-slave and weary oar.

The beech is dipped in wine; the shower
Is burnished; on the swinging flower
    The latest bee doth sit.
The low sun stares through dust of gold,
And o'er the darkening heath and wold
    The large ghost-moth doth flit.
In every orchard autumn stands
With apples in his golden hands.

But all these sights and sounds are strange,
Then wherefore from thee should I range?
    Thou hast my kith and kin,
My childhood, youth, and manhood brave –
Thou hast that unforgotten grave
    Within thy central din.
A sacredness of love and death
Dwells in thy noise and smoky breath.

James Thomson (1834–1882)

When Thomson's father suffered a stroke (he was a merchant ship's officer from Port Glasgow), the family fell upon hard times and had to move to London. When his mother died, the boy found himself in a children's home. Working first as an army schoolmaster and then as a critic and journalist, Thomson published poetry under the pen name 'BV', along with numerous free-thinking articles for the *National Reformer*, learning French, German and Italian (he translated Leopardi), and keeping in touch with modern European literature in general. Thomson's vision shows an increasing pessimism in what had started as a kind of spiritual evolutionism. The death of his wife after only two years of marriage exacerbated the despair and the alcoholism which eventually killed him by internal haemorrhage. Not all his work is dark, but the long poem in 21 sections, 'The City of Dreadful Night', written between 1870 and 1874, marks a turning point when late Romanticism begins to look ahead to more modern visions of the city, and human existence, as a waste land.

from Sunday at Hampstead

(An idle idyll by a very humble member of
the great and noble London mob.)

i

1   This is the Heath of Hampstead,
    There is the dome of Saint Paul's;
    Beneath, on the serried house-tops,
    A chequered lustre falls:

    And the mighty city of London,
    Under the clouds and the light,
    Seems a low wet beach, half shingle,
    With a few sharp rocks upright.

    Here will we sit, my darling,
    And dream an hour away:
    The donkeys are hurried and worried,
    But we are not donkeys to-day:

Through all the weary week, dear,
We toil in the murk down there,
Tied to a desk and a counter,
A patient stupid pair!

But on Sunday we slip our tether,
And away from the smoke and the smirch;
Too grateful to God for His Sabbath
To shut its hours in a church.

Away to the green, green country,
Under the open sky;
Where the earth's sweet breath is incense
And the lark sings psalms on high.

On Sunday we're Lord and Lady,
With ten times the love and glee
Of those pale and languid rich ones
Who are always and never free.

They drawl and stare and simper,
So fine and cold and staid,
Like exquisite waxwork figures
That must be kept in the shade:

We can laugh out loud when merry,
We can romp at kiss-in-the-ring,
We can take our beer at a public,
We can loll on the grass and sing ...

Would you grieve very much, my darling,
If all yon low wet shore
Were drowned by a mighty flood-tide,
And we never toiled there more?

Wicked? – there is no sin, dear,
In an idle dreamer's head;
He turns the world topsy-turvy
To prove that his soul's not dead.

I am sinking, sinking, sinking;
It is hard to sit upright!
Your lap is the softest pillow
48   Good-night, my Love, good night!

from The City of Dreadful Night

i

1   The City is of Night; perchance of Death,
    But certainly of Night; for never there
Can come the lucid morning's fragrant breath
    After the dewy dawning's cold grey air;
The moon and stars may shine with scorn or pity;
The sun has never visited that city,
    For it dissolveth in the daylight fair.

Dissolveth like a dream of night away;
    Though present in distempered gloom of thought
And deadly weariness of heart all day.
    But when a dream night after night is brought
Throughout a week, and such weeks few or many
Recur each year for several years, can any
    Discern that dream from real life in aught?

For life is but a dream whose shapes return,
    Some frequently, some seldom, some by night
And some by day, some night and day: we learn,
    The while all change and many vanish quite,
In their recurrence with recurrent changes
A certain seeming order; where this ranges
    We count things real; such is memory's might.

A river girds the city west and south,
    The main north channel of a broad lagoon,
Regurging with the salt tides from the mouth;
    Waste marshes shine and glister to the moon
For leagues, then moorland black, then stony ridges;
Great piers and causeways, many noble bridges,
    Connect the town and islet suburbs strewn.

Upon an easy slope it lies at large,
    And scarcely overlaps the long curved crest
Which swells out two leagues from the river marge.
    A trackless wilderness rolls north and west,
Savannahs, savage woods, enormous mountains,
Bleak uplands, black ravines with torrent fountains
    And eastward rolls the shipless sea's unrest.

The city is not ruinous, although
    Great ruins of an unremembered past,

With others of a few short years ago
  More sad, are found within its precincts vast.
The street-lamps always burn; but scarce a casement
In house or palace front from roof to basement
  Doth glow or gleam athwart the mirk air cast.

The street-lamps burn amidst the baleful glooms,
  Amidst the soundless solitudes immense
Of ranged mansions dark and still as tombs.
  The silence which benumbs or strains the sense
Fulfils with awe the soul's despair unweeping:
Myriads of habitants are ever sleeping,
  Or dead, or fled from nameless pestilence!

Yet as in some necropolis you find
  Perchance one mourner to a thousand dead,
So there; worn faces that look deaf and blind
  Like tragic masks of stone. With weary tread,
Each wrapt in his own doom, they wander, wander,
Or sit foredone and desolately ponder
  Through sleepless hours with heavy drooping head.

Mature men chiefly, few in age or youth,
  A woman rarely, now and then a child:
A child! If here the heart turns sick with ruth
  To see a little one from birth defiled,
Or lame or blind, as preordained to languish
Through youthless life, think how it bleeds with anguish
  To meet one erring in that homeless wild.

They often murmur to themselves, they speak
  To one another seldom, for their woe
Broods maddening inwardly and scorns to wreak
  Itself abroad; and if at whiles it grow
To frenzy which must rave, none heeds the clamour,
Unless there waits some victim of like glamour,
  To rave in turn, who lends attentive show.

The City is of Night, but not of Sleep;
  There sweet sleep is not for the weary brain;
The pitiless hours like years and ages creep,
  A night seems termless hell. This dreadful strain
Of thought and consciousness which never ceases,
Or which some moments' stupor but increases,
  This, worse than woe, makes wretches there insane.

They leave all hope behind who enter there:[1]
  One certitude while sane they cannot leave,
One anodyne for torture and despair;
  The certitude of Death, which no reprieve
Can put off long; and which, divinely tender,
But waits the outstretched hand to promptly render
84   That draught whose slumber nothing can bereave.

XX

1 I sat me weary on a pillar's base,
  And leaned against the shaft; for broad moonlight
O'erflowed the peacefulness of cloistered space,
  A shore of shadow slanting from the right:
The great cathedral's western front stood there,
A wave-worn rock in that calm sea of air.

Before it, opposite my place of rest,
  Two figures faced each other, large, austere;
A couchant sphinx in shadow to the breast,
  An angel standing in the moonlight clear;
So mighty by magnificence of form,
They were not dwarfed beneath that mass enorm.

Upon the cross-hilt of a naked sword
  The angel's hands, as prompt to smite, were held;
His vigilant intense regard was poured
  Upon the creature placidly unquelled,
Whose front was set at level gaze which took
No heed of aught, a solemn trance-like look.

And as I pondered these opposed shapes
  My eyelids sank in stupor, that dull swoon
Which drugs and with a leaden mantle drapes
  The outworn to worse weariness. But soon
A sharp and clashing noise the stillness broke,
And from the evil lethargy I woke.

The angel's wings had fallen, stone on stone,
  And lay there shattered; hence the sudden sound:
A warrior leaning on his sword alone
  Now watched the sphinx with that regard profound;
The sphinx unchanged looked forthright, as aware
Of nothing in the vast abyss of air.

1. *Lasciate ogni speranza voi ch'entrate!*/'Abandon all hope, you who enter here': lines written above the gate to Hell in Dante's *Inferno*.

Again I sank in that repose unsweet,
    Again a clashing noise my slumber rent;
The warrior's sword lay broken at his feet:
    An unarmed man with raised hands impotent
Now stood before the sphinx, which ever kept
Such mien as if with open eyes it slept.

My eyelids sank in spite of wonder grown;
    A louder crash upstartled me in dread:
The man had fallen forward, stone on stone,
    And lay there shattered, with his trunkless head
Between the monster's large quiescent paws,
Beneath its grand front changeless as life's laws.

The moon had circled westward full and bright,
    And made the temple-front a mystic dream,
And bathed the whole enclosure with its light,
    The sworded angel's wrecks, the sphinx supreme:
I pondered long that cold majestic face
48 Whose vision seemed of infinite void space.

Ellen Johnston   (?1835–?1874)

Ellen Johnston was born in Hamilton. Her father left the family when she was 18 months old, and she was mostly brought up by her grandparents and a stepfather. By the time she was 11 years old, she was working as a powerloom weaver. Writing and publishing in later years as 'the Factory Girl', she did not hesitate to bring her verses to bear on the industrial, social and political injustices of her time. She died in a Glasgow poorhouse.

The Last Sark

Gude guide me, are ye hame again, and hae ye got nae wark?
We've naething noo tae pit awa, unless your auld blue sark.
My heid is rinnin roond aboot, far lichter nor a flee:
What care some gentry if they're weel though a' the puir wad dee?

Our merchants and mill-masters they wad never want a meal   lack
Though a' the banks in Scotland wad for a twalmonth fail;
For some o them hae far mair gowd than ony ane can see.
What care some gentry if they're weel though a' the puir wad dee?

Oor hoose aince bien and cosy, John, oor beds aince snug and warm,   well-stocked
Feels unco cauld and dismal noo, and empty as a barn;
The weans sit greetin in our face, and we hae nocht tae gie.   crying
What care some gentry if they're weel though a' the puir wad dee?

It is the puir man's hard-won cash that fills the rich man's purse;
I'm sure his gowden coffers they are het wi mony a curse.
Were it no for the workin man what wad the rich man be?
What care some gentry if they're weel though a' the puir wad dee?

My head is licht, my heart is weak, my een are growing blin';
The bairn is faen' aff my knee – oh! John, catch haud o' him,
You ken I hinna tasted meat for days far mair than three;
Were it no for my helpless bairns I wadna care to dee.

Robert Louis Stevenson (1850–1894)

Born and educated in Edinburgh, and afflicted with poor lungs and ill health for most of his life, Stevenson showed a surprising physical and spiritual toughness in his many travels – from the Cevennes in France to Switzerland, Canada, California, Australia and eventually to the South Seas where he was to die of a cerebral stroke. Best known for his many brilliant novels, Stevenson was content to write occasional verses and poems for young readers. His best lyrics have a simplicity which can be deceptive, not unlike Blake's 'Songs of Innocence'. When he wrote in Scots, it was usually to evoke a sense of exile and longing.

The Maker to Posterity
(Makar: poet)

Far 'yont amang the years to be	
When a' we think, an' a' we see,	
An' a' we luve, 's been dung ajee	knocked aside
By time's rouch shouther,	rough shoulder
An' what was richt and wrang for me	
Lies mangled throu'ther,	higgledy-piggledy
It's possible – it's hardly mair –	
That some ane, ripin' after lear –	rummaging; knowledge
Some auld professor or young heir,	
If still there's either –	
May find an' read me, an' be sair	sorely
Perplexed, puir brither!	
'What tongue does your auld bookie speak?'	little old book
He'll spier; an' I, his mou to steik:	ask; shut
'No bein' fit to write in Greek,	
I wrote in Lallan,	Lowland Scots
Dear to my heart as the peat reek,	smoke
Auld as Tantallon.[1]	
'Few spak it than, an' noo there's nane.	then
My puir auld sangs lie a' their lane,	all alone

1. Tantallon Castle, featured in Scott's *Marmion*, is a picturesque ruin on sea-washed rocks to the east of North Berwick, a coast featured in Stevenson's *Catriona*.

Their sense, that aince was braw an' plain,
    Tint a'thegether,   lost altogether
Like runes upon a standin' stane
    Amang the heather.

'But think not you the brae to speel;   hill; climb (summit to attain)
You, tae, maun chow the bitter peel;   too; must eat
For a' your lear, for a' your skeel,   learning; skill
    Ye're nane sae lucky;   not so fortunate
An' things are mebbe waur than weel   worse than well
    For you, my buckie.   bold lad

'The hale concern (baith hens an' eggs,
Baith books an' writers, stars an' clegs)   horse-flies
Noo stachers upon lowsent legs   staggers; loosened
    An' wears awa';   wastes away
The tack o' mankind, near the dregs,   lease
    Rins unco' law.   very low

'Your book, that in some braw new tongue,
Ye wrote or prentit, preached or sung,   printed
Will still be just a bairn, an' young
    In fame an' years,
Whan the hale planet's guts are dung   whole; knocked down
    About your ears;

'An' you, sair gruppin' to a spar   fiercely gripping
Or whammled wi' some bleezin' star,   tossed about
Cryin' to ken whaur deil ye are,   where the devil
Hame, France, or Flanders –
Whang sindry like a railway car   jerk apart
    An' flie in danders.'   clinkers (spent coals)

Escape at Bedtime

The lights from the parlour and kitchen shone out
    Through the blinds and the windows and bars;
And high overhead and all moving about,
    There were thousands of millions of stars.

There ne'er were such thousands of leaves on a tree,
    Nor of people in church or the Park,
As the crowds of the stars that looked down upon me,
    And that glittered and winked in the dark.

The Dog, and the Plough, and the Hunter, and all,
    And the star of the sailor, and Mars,

These shone in the sky, and the pail by the wall
   Would be half full of water and stars.
They saw me at last, and they chased me with cries,
   And they soon had me packed into bed;
But the glory kept shining and bright in my eyes,
   And the stars going round in my head.

Armies in the Fire

The lamps now glitter down the street;
Faintly sound the falling feet;
And the blue even slowly falls
About the garden trees and walls.

Now in the falling of the gloom
The red fire paints the empty room:
And warmly on the roof it looks,
And flickers on the backs of books.

Armies march by tower and spire
Of cities blazing, in the fire;
Till as I gaze with staring eyes,
The armies fade, the lustre dies.

Then once again the glow returns;
Again the phantom city burns;
And down the red-hot valley, lo!
The phantom armies marching go!

Blinking embers, tell me true
Where are those armies marching to,
And what the burning city is
That crumbles in your furnaces!

To Any Reader

As from the house your mother sees
You playing round the garden trees,
So you may see, if you will look
Through the windows of this book,
Another child, far, far away,
And in another garden, play.
But do not think you can at all,
By knocking on the window, call
That child to hear you. He intent
Is all on his play-business bent.

He does not hear; he will not look,
Nor yet be lured out of this book.
For, long ago, the truth to say,
He has grown up and gone away,
And it is but a child of air
That lingers in the garden there.

John Davidson (1857–1909)

Born and brought up in Glasgow and Greenock, Davidson had to leave school early, pursuing a rather unsettled career as a laboratory assistant, a clerk and latterly a schoolteacher. During this period he produced verse dramas, prose and poetry without much recognition or success. Determined to be a full-time writer, he moved to London and worked as a journalist, meeting writers of the 1890s such as Max Beerbohm, Edmund Gosse, Yeats and Beardsley. His *Fleet Street Eclogues* (1893) and *Ballads and Songs* (1894) were well-received, but he had less luck with subsequent poems which were too long and too abstruse for popular taste. Ill-health, disappointment, depression and finally cancer led to suicide in the end. In their attempt to combine metaphysical intensity and the mystery of identity with hard scientific knowledge, Davidson's poems are a milestone in early modernism and an acknowledged influence on Hugh MacDiarmid's later verse. T. S. Eliot also admired aspects of his work, from the bitter passion of 'Thirty Bob a Week' to his visions of beauty and squalor in the streets of the modern city.

Thirty Bob a Week

I couldn't touch a stop and turn a screw,
   And set the blooming world a-work for me,
Like such as cut their teeth – I hope, like you –
   On the handle of a skeleton gold key;
I cut mine on a leek, which I eat it every week:
   I'm a clerk at thirty bob as you can see.[1]

But I don't allow it's luck and all a toss;
   There's no such thing as being starred and crossed;
It's just the power of some to be a boss,
   And the bally power of others to be bossed:
I face the music, sir; you bet I ain't a cur;
   Strike me lucky if I don't believe I'm lost!

For like a mole I journey in the dark,
   A-travelling along the underground
From my Pillar'd Halls and broad Suburbean Park,

---

1. 30 shillings: £1.50. 'Ten bob': 50p.

To come the daily dull official round;
And home again at night with my pipe all alight,
   A-scheming how to count ten bob a pound.

And it's often very cold and very wet,
   And my missis stitches towels for a hunks;
And the Pillar'd Halls is half of it to let –
   Three rooms about the size of travelling trunks.
And we cough, my wife and I, to dislocate a sigh,
   When the noisy little kids are in their bunks.

But you never hear her do a growl or whine,
   For she's made of flint and roses, very odd;
And I've got to cut my meaning rather fine,
   Or I'd blubber, for I'm made of greens and sod:
So p'r'aps we are in Hell for all that I can tell,
   And lost and damn'd and served up hot to God.

I ain't blaspheming, Mr. Silver-tongue;
   I'm saying things a bit beyond your art:
Of all the rummy starts you ever sprung,
   Thirty bob a week's the rummiest start!
With your science and your books and your the'ries about spooks,
   Did you ever hear of looking in your heart?

I didn't mean your pocket, Mr., no:
   I mean that having children and a wife,
With thirty bob on which to come and go,
   Isn't dancing to the tabor and the fife:
When it doesn't make you drink, by Heaven! it makes you think,
   And notice curious items about life.

I step into my heart and there I meet
   A god-almighty devil singing small,
Who would like to shout and whistle in the street,
   And squelch the passers flat against the wall;
If the whole world was a cake he had the power to take
   He would take it, ask for more, and eat them all.

And I meet a sort of simpleton beside,
   The kind that life is always giving beans;
With thirty bob a week to keep a bride
   He fell in love and married in his teens:
At thirty bob he stuck; but he knows it isn't luck:
   He knows the seas are deeper than tureens.

And the god-almighty devil and the fool
   That meet me in the High Street on the strike,
When I walk about my heart a-gathering wool,
   Are my good and evil angels if you like.
And both of them together in every kind of weather
   Ride me like a double-seated bike.

That's rough a bit and needs its meaning curled.
   But I have a high old hot un in my mind –
A most engrugious notion of the world,
   That leaves your lightning 'rithmetic behind:
I give it at a glance when I say 'There ain't no chance
   Nor nothing of the lucky-lottery kind.'

And it's this way that I make it out to be:
   No fathers, mothers, countries, climates – none;
No Adam was responsible for me,
   Nor society, nor systems, nary one:
A little sleeping seed, I woke – I did, indeed –
   A million years before the blooming sun.

I woke because I thought the time had come;
   Beyond my will there was no other cause;
And everywhere I found myself at home,
   Because I chose to be the thing I was;
And in whatever shape of mollusc or of ape
   I always went according to the laws.

I was the love that chose my mother out;
   I joined two lives and from the union burst;
My weakness and my strength without a doubt
   Are mine alone for ever from the first:
It's just the very same with a difference in the name
   As 'Thy will be done.' You say it if you durst!

They say it daily up and down the land
   As easy as you take a drink, it's true;
But the difficultest go to understand,
   And the difficultest job a man can do,
Is to come it brave and meek with thirty bob a week,
   And feel that that's the proper thing for you.

It's a naked child against a hungry wolf;
   It's playing bowls upon a splitting wreck;
It's walking on a string across a gulf
   With millstones fore-and-aft about your neck;

But the thing is daily done by many and many a one;
    And we fall, face forward, fighting, on the deck.

Yuletide

Now wheel and hoof and horn
In every street
Stunned to its chimney-tops,
In every murky street –
Each lamp-lit gorge by traffic rent
Asunder,
Ravines of serried shops
By business tempests torn –
In every echoing street,
From early morn
Till jaded night falls dead,
Wheel, hoof, and horn
Tumultuous thunder
Beat
Under
A noteless firmament
Of lead.

When the winds list
A fallen cloud
Where yellow dregs of light
Befouled remain,
The woven gloom
Of smoke and mist,
The soot-entangled rain
That jumbles day and night
In city and town,
An umber-emerald shroud
Rehearsing doom,
The London fog comes down.

But sometimes silken beams,
As bright
As adamant on fire,
Of the uplifted sun's august attire,
With frosty fibrous light
Magnetic shine
On happier dreams
That abrogate despair,
When all the sparkling air
Of smoke and sulphur shriven,

Like an iced wine
Fills the high cup
Of heaven;
For urban park and lawn,
The city's scenery,
Heaths, commons, dells
That compass London rich
In greenery,
With diamond-dust of rime
Empowdered, flash
At dawn;
And tossing bells
Of stealthy hansome chime
With silvery crash
In radiant ways
Attuned and frozen up
To concert pitch –
In resonant ways,
Where wheels and hoofs inwrought,
Cars, omnibuses, wains,
Beat, boom, and clash
Discordant fugal strains
Of cymbals, trumpets, drums;
While careless to arrive,
The nerved pedestrian comes
Exulting in the splendour overhead,
And in the live
Elastic ground,
The pavement, tense and taut,
That yields a twangling sound
At every tread.

Snow

i

'Who affirms that crystals are alive?'
    I affirm it, let who will deny: –
Crystals are engendered, wax and thrive,
    Wane and wither; I have seen them die.

Trust me, masters, crystals have their day
    Eager to attain the perfect norm,
Lit with purpose, potent to display
    Facet, angle, colour, beauty, form.

ii

Water-crystals need for flower and root
   Sixty clear degrees, no less, no more;
Snow, so fickle, still in this acute
   Angle thinks, and learns no other lore:

Such its life, and such its pleasure is,
   Such its art and traffic, such its gain,
Evermore in new conjunctions this
   Admirable angle to maintain.

Crystalcraft in every flower and flake
   Snow exhibits, of the welkin free:
Crystalline are crystals for the sake
   All and singular, of crystalry.

Yet does every crystal of the snow
   Individualize, a seedling sown
Broadcast, but instinct with power to grow
   Beautiful in beauty of its own.

Every flake with all its prongs and dints
   Burns ecstatic as a new-lit star:
Men are not more diverse, finger-prints
   More dissimilar than snow-flakes are.

Worlds of men and snow endure, increase,
   Woven of power and passion to defy
Time and travail: only races cease,
   Individual men and crystals die.

iii

Jewelled shapes of snow whose feathery showers,
   Fallen or falling wither at a breath,
All afraid are they, and loth as flowers
   Beasts and men to tread the way to death.

Once I saw upon an object-glass,
   Martyred underneath a microscope,
One elaborate snow-flake slowly pass,
   Dying hard, beyond the reach of hope.

Still from shape to shape the crystal changed,
   Writhing in its agony; and still,
Less and less elaborate, arranged
   Potently the angle of its will.

Tortured to a simple final form,
    Angles six and six divergent beams,
Lo, in death it touched the perfect norm
    Verifying all its crystal dreams!

iv
Such the noble tragedy of one
    Martyred snow-flake. Who can tell the fate
Heinous and uncouth of showers undone,
    Fallen in cities! – showers that expiate

Errant lives from polar worlds adrift
    Where the great millennial snows abide;
Castaways from mountain-chains that lift
    Snowy summits in perennial pride;

Nomad snows, or snows in evil day
    Born to urban ruin, to be tossed,
Trampled, shovelled, ploughed and swept away
    Down the seething sewers: all the frost

Flowers of heaven melted up with lees,
    Offal, excrement, but every flake
Showing to the last in fixed degrees
    Perfect crystals for the crystal's sake.

v
Usefulness of snow is but a chance
    Here in temperate climes with winter sent,
Sheltering earth's prolonged hibernal trance:
    All utility is accident.

Sixty clear degrees the joyful snow,
    Practising economy of means,
Fashions endless beauty in, and so
    Glorifies the universe with scenes

Arctic and antarctic: stainless shrouds,
    Ermine woven in silvery frost, attire
Peaks in every land among the clouds
    Crowned with snows to catch the morning's fire.

Fleet Street[1]

Wisps and rags of cloud in a withered sky,
A strip of pallid azure, at either end,

1. A famous street in central London, once the home of many newspapers and the heart of the news industry.

Above the Ludgate obelisk, above
The Temple griffin, widening with the width
Below, and parallel with the street that counts
Seven hundred paces of tesselated road
From Ludgate Circus west to Chancery Lane:
By concrete pavement flanked and precipice
Of windowed fronts on this side and on that,
A thoroughfare of everything that hastes
The sullen tavern-loafers notwithstanding
And hawkers in the channel hunger-bit.
Interfluent night and day the tides of trade,
Labour and pleasure, law and crime, are sucked
From every urban quarter: through this strait
All business London pours. Amidst the boom
And thud of wheel and hoof the myriad feet
Are silent save to him who stands a while
And hearkens till his passive ear, attuned
To new discernment like an erudite
Musician's, which can follow note by note
The part of any player even in the din
And thrashing fury of the noisiest close
Orchestral, hears chromatic footsteps throb,
And tense susurrant speech of multitudes
That stride in pairs discussing ways and means,
Or reason with themselves, in single file
Advancing hardily on ruinous
Events; and should he listen long there comes
A second-hearing like the second-sight
Diviners knew, or as the runner gains
His second-breath; then phantom footsteps fall,
And muffled voices travel out of time:
Alsatians pass and Templars; stareabouts
For the new motion of Nineveh, morose
Or jolly tipplers at the Bolt-in-Tun,
The Devil Tavern; Johnson's heavy tread
And rolling laughter; Drayton trampling out
The thunder of Agincourt as up and down
He paces by St. Dunstan's; Chaucer, wroth,
Beating the friar that traduced the state;[1]
And more remote, from centuries unknown,
Rumour of battle, noises of the swamp
The gride of glacial rock, the rush of wings,   grating sound
The roar of beasts that breathed a fiery air
Where fog envelops now electric light,

1. Dr Samuel Johnson (1709–84), poet and noted lexicographer. Michael Drayton (1563–1631), poet and author of 'The Ballad of Agincourt'. Geoffrey Chaucer (1340?–1400), poet and man of affairs.

The music of the spheres, the humming speed
Centrifugal of molten planets loosed
From pregnant suns to find their orbits out,
The whirling spindles of the nebulae,
The rapture of ethereal darkness strung
Illimitable in eternal space.
Fleet Street was once a silence in the ether.
The carbon, iron, copper, silicon,
Zinc, aluminium vapours, metalloids,
Constituents of the skeleton and shell
Of Fleet Street – of the woodwork, metalwork,
Brickwork, electric apparatus, drains
And printing-presses, conduits, pavement, road –
Were at the first unelemented space,
Imponderable tension in the dark
Consummate matter of eternity.
And so the flesh and blood of Fleet Street, nerve
And brain infusing life and soul, the men,
The women, woven, built and kneaded up
Of hydrogen, of azote, oxygen,
Of carbon, phosphorus, chlorine, sulphur, iron,
Of calcium, kalium, natrium, manganese,   sodium (obs.)
The warm humanities that day and night
Inhabit and employ it and inspire,
Were in the ether mingled with it, there
Distinguished nothing from the road, the shops,
The drainpipes, sewage, sweepings of the street:
Matter of infinite beauty and delight
Atoning offal, filth and all offence
With soul and intellect, with love and thought;
Matter whereof the furthest stars consist,
And every interstellar wilderness
From galaxy to galaxy, the thin
Imponderable ether, matter's ghost,
But matter still, substance demonstrable
Being the icy vehicle of light.

Flung off in teardrops spirally, or cast
In annular fission forth like Saturn's hoops,
Earth and the planets girdled solar space,
The offspring and the suburbs of the sun.
In rings or drops – the learned are unresolved
How planets and their satellites arrive;
But vision, vouching both, is more obsessed
By Saturn's way of circles here at hand.
Saturn has uttered many moons; his rings

May be the last abortive birth of powers
Luniparous unmatched in heaven, or else   Moon-producing
These still-born undeveloped satellites
Denote an overweening confidence
Determined, risking all, on something new.
Having outstreated spirally and well
A brilliant series of customary moons,
The hazardous and genial orb began
A segregation annular instead,
Attempting boldly the impossible,
Thus to become the wonder of the skies
For ever hampered with the rings we see.
Stupendous error still eclipses net
Achievement; as in art the Sistine roof
Sublimely figured, or hardihood in war
That wastes a troop for glory, or as earth
In sheer terrestrial wantonness flung up
The Mariposan Vale,[1] so in the skies
The most enchanting vision of the night,
Our belted Saturn shines, extravagance
Celestial jewelled with its dazzling fault.
Now, in the ether with all the universe,
And in the nebula of our solar scheme,
Fleet Street and Saturn's rings were interfused
One mass of molecules being set apart
For the high theme of wonder and the butt
Of speculation, and the other doomed,
Although the most renowned throughout the world,
To be a little noisy London street.
How think we then? The metal, stone and lime,
Brick, asphalt, wood, the matter that renews
The shell of Fleet Street, does it still begrudge
The luminous zones with which it once was blent
Their lofty glory? Or must the carapace
Of Fleet Street, welded of the selfsame stuff
As man, be utterly oblivious? Thought
And passion, envy, joy – are these unfelt
By carbon, iron, azote, oxygen,
And other liberal substances that know
Rejoice and suffer in mankind, when power
Selective turns them into street? Things wrought
By us, are they, too, psychophysical?
Do these piled storeys and purlieus quaint of square
And alley envy Saturn's belts – a brief

1. The gorge of the Yosemite Valley in California.

Not outwardly distinguished urban street
Upon a planet only remarkable
Among the spheres for insignificance,
And they so lovely and unparagoned
A thousand million of mundane miles away?
Are able editors, leader-writers, apt
Telegraphists and printers, the only soul
In Fleet Street, they, its only consciousness?
Perhaps the bricks remember. Who can tell
When filthy fog comes down and lights are out,
Machinery still, and traffic at the ebb,
If idle streets with time to meditate
Resent enforced passivity? I think
The admirable patience of the bricks
May fail them of a Sunday. Imagine it:
To be for ages unalterable brick,
Sans speech or motion, nameless in a wall
Among a million bricks alike unknown!
I think the splendid patience of the bricks
Gives out, in darkness and foul weather, even
To the length of envying the wonderful
Exalted destiny of Saturn's belts;
And then I long to tell them, if I could,
How much more happy their condition is
Than that of rubbish revolving endlessly
In agonies of impotent remorse
About the planet it deserted. Thus
Should I exhort them: – 'Bricks, beloved bricks,
My brethren of the selfsame ether bred,
I hold it very beautiful of you
To think so handsomely of Saturn's rings
Your old companions in the nebula;
But I can tell you and I'll make you know,
Your fate is not inferior to theirs.
These seeming jewelled zones that shine so bright
Are the mere wreck of matter, broken bits,
Detached and grinding beaches of barren rock
Hung up there as a menace and a sign;
Circular strips of chaos unredeemed,
Whirling in madness of oppugnant powers.
Whether his rings are Saturn's own attempt
Abnormal and abortive, a brilliant ninth
Consummate moon to utter, or likelier still,
A leash of runaway material tides
That mutinously left their native orb
In molten youth to show all other stars

The real and only way to shine, and failed
Inevitably, being immature,
They are, beyond all doubt, unhappy zones,
Forlorn, remorseful, useless and ashamed.
Most beautiful, I grant you; beautiful
And useless, like all art: their fate it is
To be an agony of beauty, art
Unutile, unavailing, misconceived.
But you, most genial, intellectual bricks,
Most dutiful and most important, you
Are indispensable, an integral
Component of the world's most famous street.
Within your wholesome and convenient bield   lodging
The truest miracle is daily done.
Never forget that men have tamed and taught
The lightning; clad it in a livery known
As news; and that without your constant aid
Our modern, actual magic, black and white,
Momentous mystery of telegraphy,
Resounding press, accomplished intellects
And pens expert would be impossible.
Take down the walls your myrmidons compose,
And Fleet Street, soul and body, ceases – fog
Unoccupied, wind, city sunshine sparse
And pallid claiming all the room that now,
Enclosed, accoutred, functioned, named and known,
Serves as the Dionysius' ear of the world.
Honour and excellence and praise are yours;
Be satisfied; be glad.'

                    But all the bricks,
O'erburdened and begrimed, in chorus sighed,
And as one brick, 'Upon my cubical
Content, and by our common mother, I
Had rather shine, a shard of chaos, set
In Saturn's glistering rings, the exquisite
Enigma of the night, than be the unnamed,
Unthought-of copestone or foundation-stone
Of any merely world-distinguished street.'

Applauding the ambition of the bricks,
I felt, I also, I would rather share
Dazzling perdition with material wreck
Suspended in majestic agony
About the withered loins of some undone
Wide-circling planet for the universe

To see, than live the dull life of a baked
Oblength of tempered clay, year in year out   (oblong length)
Unnoticed in a murky mundane street;
But recollecting that the bricks were bricks
And not a planetary wonder, what
Event soe'er awaits the world and time,
I reassured them: 'Gallant souls,' I cried,
'Noble and faithful bricks, be not dismayed!
I hear the shapeless fragments that make up
Aesthetic marvel in Saturn's girdles sigh
Disconsolately, as they chafe and grind
Each other, – *Such an enviable fate*
As that of any single solid brick
In Fleet Street, London, well and truly laid,
A moulded, tempered necessary brick
In that most famous faubourg of the world,   suburb
Exceeds our merits! Could we but attain
The crude integrity of commonplace
Cohesion even in the most exhausted, most
Decrepit, ruinous, forgotten orb
In some back alley of the Milky Way
How happy we should be! Remember, bricks,
Neither success nor failure envy spares:
Use envies art; art envies use. These moods
Will come; but regular bricks like you transcend
Them always. Be courageous; be yourselves,
Be proud of your telluric destiny.'   earthly
With that the bricks took heart. 'Why, so we are,'
They said, 'the ear of England! Let us be
Old England's ear!' And revolution beat
In smothered cries and muffled fusillades
Upon the trembling tympanal; empires
At war thridded the sounding labyrinth
With cannon, loyal peoples through the sea
And through the air by auditory nerves
Electric from the quarters of the earth
And from a hundred isles, their homage sent
With whispered news of aspirations, deeds,
Achievements to the Mother of Nations, she
Whose ever vigilant clairaudient ear
Is Fleet Street.

Vernacular Scots Poetry

Vernacular Scots verse thrived for at least thirty years on either side of the turn of the century, and although there was no single outstanding poet in this period, many good poems were written which remain popular and widely recited to this day. From the anonymous authors of the Bothy ballads, to academically educated writers such as Sir Alexander Gray, these poets adopted a popular voice, whose vigorous and expressive Scots used all the resources of comedy, sentiment and irony to speak for a way of life which hadn't changed for a hundred years. Such linguistic and social stability was particularly notable in the North-East of Scotland, and a significant number of these poets came from that region, or adapted its distinctive local dialect. (See MacGillivray, Jacob, Murray, Angus, Rorie, Taylor, Caie, Gray, Young and Cruickshank.) MacDiarmid discussed many of these writers in *Contemporary Scottish Studies* (1926), and not always in complimentary terms, but the best poems of the vernacular tradition showed an awareness of mortality, or that hint of strangeness in the familiar domestic world, which did, in fact, prepare the ground for his own early lyrics.

Local newspapers were a frequent platform for such verses, where thousands of poems were published every year. (As late as the 1930s a new poem by Charles Murray put the *Aberdeen Press and Journal* through two extra editions.) Then writers with a stronger literary historical sense, such as Lewis Spence, began to echo the Scots of the makars, heralding MacDiarmid's cry of 'Back to Dunbar!' and the rise of what came to be known as the modern Scottish literary renaissance.

Of course, the late nineteenth-century 'Kailyard' tradition of sentimental and nostalgic versifying was still in view, and perhaps the vernacular tradition was a way of holding on to certainties at a time of increasing insecurity and modernity. Certainly hard times and the First World War cast a shadow over some of these poems, and things were not to be the same after 1918. On the other hand, Tom Leonard's *Radical Renfrew* anthology has noted that colloquial verse in the central belt and the industrial west was not afraid to address the hardships and the political inequities of living and working among factories and crowded city streets, a theme which MacDiarmid did not approach until his poetry of the middle thirties, and then in a different genre and a different voice.

Anonymous: The Bothy Ballads

The old Border ballad tradition survived until present times among the singers and tale-bearers of the North-East of Scotland, but the same region also produced a huge store of songs which dealt with everyday rural working life in the late nineteenth and early twentieth centuries. The area was noted for large farms (farm-towns) which were worked with teams of horses. In a labour-intensive market, workers – both men and women – were hired (fee-ed) on a seasonal basis, living in the bothy – a bunk-house building near the farmer's more substantial house. Exploitation was common enough, but the workers could move on to better conditions at the end of the year. A tradition of sturdy independence grew up, along with hundreds of songs which told of the hardships and joys of a daily routine, often salted with complaints or warnings about specifically named farms and farmers.

Drumdelgie

There's a fairmer up in Cairnie,[1]	
Wha's kent baith faur and wide,	
Tae be the great Drumdelgie	
Upon sweet Deveronside.	
The fairmer o' yon muckle toon	farm
He is baith hard and sair,	
And the cauldest day that ever blaws,	
His servants get their share.	

At five o'clock we quickly rise	
An' hurry doon the stair;	
It's there to corn our horses,	feed
Likewise to straik their hair.	comb
Syne, after working half-an-hour,	Then
Each to the kitchen goes,	
It's there to get our breakfast,	
Which generally is brose.[2]	

We've scarcely got our brose weel supt,	
And gi'en our pints a tie,	bootlaces
When the foreman cries,	
'Hallo my lads! The hour is drawing nigh.'	
At sax o'clock the mull's put on,	(water driven) threshing mill
To gie us a' strait wark;	
It tak's four o' us to mak' to her.	handle the corn straw
Till ye could wring our sark.	shirt

1. Parish by the River Deveron, near Huntly in Aberdeenshire. Drumdelgie is indeed the name of a farm there.
2. Oatmeal mixed with boiling water or milk, savoured with salt and butter.

And when the water is put aff,
We hurry doon the stair,
To get some quarters¹ through the fan   winnowing machine
Till daylicht does appear.
When daylicht does begin to peep,
And the sky begins to clear,
The foreman cries out,
'My lads! Ye'll stay nae langer here!'

'There's sax o' you'll gae to the ploo,   plough
And twa will drive the neeps,   cart turnips
And the owsen they'll be after you   oxen
Wi' strae raips roun' their queets.'   straw ropes; ankles
But when that we were gyaun furth,   going
And turnin' out to yoke,   start work
The snaw dank on sae thick and fast   drove
That we were like to choke.

The frost had been sae very hard,
The ploo she wadna go;
And sae our cairting days commenced
Amang the frost and snaw.
But we will sing our horses' praise,
Though they be young an' sma',
They far outshine the Broadland's anes   (a rival farm)
That gang sae full and braw.

Ye daurna swear aboot the toon   farm
It is against the law,
An' if ye use profanities
Then ye'll be putten awa'.
O, Drumdelgie keeps a Sunday School
He says it is but richt
Tae preach unto the ignorant
An' send them Gospel licht.

The term time is comin' on   end of contract
An' we will get our brass   money
An' we'll gae doon tae Huntly toon
An' get a partin' glass
We'll gae doon tae Huntly toon
An' get upon the spree   go skylarking
An' the fun it will commence
The quinies for tae see.   lassies

---

1. Eight bushels of grain.

Sae fare ye weel, Drumdelgie,
For I maun gang awa;
Sae fare ye weel Drumdelgie,
Your weety weather an' a',
Sae fareweel, Drumdelgie,
I bid ye a' adieu;
I leave ye as I got ye –
A maist unceevil crew.

The Road to Dundee

Cauld winter was howling o'er muir and o'er mountains,
   And wild was the surge on the dark-rolling sea,
When I met, about daybreak, a bonnie young lassie,
   Wha asked me the road and the miles to Dundee.

Said I, 'My young lassie, I canna weel tell ye,
   The road and the distance I canna weel gie;
But if ye'll permit me to gang a wee bittie,
   I'll show you the road and the miles to Dundee.'

At once she consented, and gave me her arm;
   Ne'er a word did I speir wha the lassie micht be,   ask
She appeared like an angel in feature and form,
   As she walked by my side on the road to Dundee.

At length, wi the howe o Strathmartine behind us,
   And the spires o' the toon in full view we could see;
She said, 'Gentle sir, I can never forget ye
   For showing me so far on the road to Dundee.

'This ring and this purse take to prove I am grateful,
   And some simple token I trust ye'll gie me,
And in times to come I'll the laddie remember
   That showed me the road and the miles to Dundee.'

I took the gowd pin from the scarf on my bosom,
   And said, 'Keep ye this in remembrance o' me.
Then bravely I kissed the sweet lips o' the lassie
   Ere I parted wi' her on the road to Dundee.

So here's to the lassie – I ne'er can forget her –
   And ilka young laddie that's listening to me;
And never be sweer to convoy a young lassie,
   Though it's only to show her the road to Dundee.

J. Logie Robertson, 'Hugh Haliburton' (1846–1922)

Born in Milnathort, Robertson worked as a schoolteacher in Edinburgh for most of his life, producing useful editions of Dunbar, Ramsay, Burns, Scott and James Thomson. Well known as 'Hugh Haliburton', he produced poems of his own and versions of classical poetry in Scots – *Horace in Homespun* (1882).

The Lang Whang Road[1]
(A miner's wail from Flanders, 1916)

I'm a miner lad fra Mid-Calder Braes,
   In a bog i' the Laigh Countree,   *Low*
An' I'm howkin here in a woman's claes   *digging; (in a kilt)*
   Whaur I never aince thocht to be.

O, there's naething here for your lugs to hear,   *ears*
   Nor a sicht for your een to see,
But a burstin' shell, wi' a stink like hell,
   An' the pole o' a poplar tree.

Noo, that's a thing that is ill to thole;   *hard to endure*
   But its better to fecht than flee,   *fight*
And I'll stick it here like a brock in a hole   *badger*
   Since better it mayna be.

But the far-flung line o' the Lang Whang Road,
   Wi' the mune on the sky's eebree,   *eyebrow*
An' naething but me an' the wind abroad,
   Is the wuss that's hauntin' me.   *wish*

It's a dream that lifts my heart abune
   The swamp that's surroundin' me –
The Lang Whang Road, an' the risin' mune,
   An' the nicht wind wanderin' free.

I'm thinkin' lang, but I'm thinkin' o'd,   *of it*
   An' the howp that's uphaldin' me,   *hope*
Is a Setterday yet, near the Borestane Road,
   Wi' a dog's nose nudgin' my knee.

---

1. Lit. 'Long Chunk': traditional name for the old road from Edinburgh to Lanark, between Balerno and Carnwath.

Oh, the witchin' curve o' the Lang Whang Road
   Is a sicht for an exile's ee –
At the gloamin' hour, wi' the winds abroad,
   If the Lord wad favour me.

Pittendrigh MacGillivray (1856–1938)

A member of the Royal Scottish Academy and a well-known sculptor (he created the statue of John Knox at St Giles), MacGillivray was born at Port Elphinstone, Inverurie. He contributed to the early modern renaissance in 1922 with the collection *Bog Myrtle and Peat Reek*, whose Scots derives from his native North-East.

Mercy o' Gode

i

Twa bodachs, I mind, had a threep ae day,	old men; dispute
Aboot man's chief end –	
Aboot man's chief end.	
Whan the t'ane lookit sweet his words war sour,	one
Whan the tither leuch out his words gied a clour,	other; wallop
But whilk got the better I wasna sure –	
I wasna sure,	
An' needna say.	

ii

But I mind them well for a queer-like pair –	
A gangrel kind,	tramp
A gangrel kind:	
The heid o' the ane was beld as an egg,	
The ither, puir man, had a timmer leg,	wooden
An' baith for the bite could dae nocht but beg	for food
Nocht but beg –	
Or live on air!	

iii

On a table-stane in the auld Kirkyaird,
   They ca' 'The Houff',[1]
   They ca' 'The Houff',
They sat in their rags like wearyfu' craws,

---

1. Actual name of a cemetery in Dundee. Lit.: a burial ground; can also mean a meeting place, a rowdy pub, or a shelter.

An' fankl't themsel's about a 'FIRST CAUSE',   entangled
An' the job the Lord had made o' His laws,
    Made o' his laws,
    In human regaird.

iv

Twa broken auld men wi' little but jaw –   talk
    Faur better awa
    Aye – better awa;
Yawmerin' owr things that nane can tell,   moaning away
The yin for a Heaven, the ither for Hell;
Wi' nae mair in tune than a crackit bell –
    A crackit bell,
    Atween the twa.

v

Dour badly he barkit in praise o' the Lord –   (the grim-faced one)
    'The pooer o' Gode
    An' the wull o' Gode';
But Stumpie believ't nor in Gode nor man –
Thocht life but a fecht without ony plan,   fight
An' the best nae mair nor a flash i' the pan –
    A flash i' the pan,
    In darkness smored.   smothered

vi

Twa dune men – naither bite nor bed! –   food
    A sair-like thing –   painful
    An' unco thing.   strange
To the Houff they cam to lay their heid
An' seek a nicht's rest wi' the sleepin' deid,
Whar the stanes wudna grudge nor ony tak' heed
    Nor ony tak' heed:
    But it's ill to read.   hard to tell of (or to interpret)

vii

They may hae been bitter, an' dour, an' warsh,   grim; dull/spiritless
    But wha could blame –
    Aye – wha could blame?
I kent bi their look they war no' that bad
But jist ill dune bi an' driven half mad: badly treated
Whar there's nae touch o' kindness this life's owr sad   too
    This life's owr sad,
    An' faur owr harsh.

viii

But as nicht drave on I had needs tak' the road,
    Fell glad o' ma dog –   very
    The love o' a dog:
An' tho' nane wad hae me that day at the fair,   (hire me)
I raither't the hill for a houff than in there,
'Neth a table-stane, on a deid man's lair –   grave plot
    A deid man's lair –
    Mercy o' Gode.

Violet Jacob (1863–1946)

Violet Kennedy-Erskine came from a family which had held lands near Montrose for 400 years. She married an army officer and lived in India before returning to the North-East. She wrote short stories and novels, as well as the poetry which she dedicated to her beloved local county as 'songs of Angus'. With their sense of female loss and betrayal in a richly rural setting with a hint of the supernatural, some of these poems anticipated the spirit of MacDiarmid's early lyrics.

The End o't

There's a fine braw thistle that lifts its croon   brave
    By the river-bank whaur the ashes stand,
An' the swirl o' water comes whisp'rin' doon
    Past birk an' bramble an' grazin' land.   birch
But simmer's flittit an' time's no heedin'   summer's left
    A feckless lass nor a pridefu' flow'r;
The dark to hide me's the grace I'm needin'.
      An' the thistle's seedin',
        An' my day's owre.   over

I redd the hoose an' I meat the hens   tidy up; feed
    (Oh, it's ill to wark when ye daurna tire!),   difficult; dare not
An' what'll I get when my mither kens   knows
    It's niver a maiden that biggs her fire?
I mind my pray'rs, but I'm feared to say them,   afraid
    I hide my een, for they're greetin' fast;   weeping
What though I blind them – for wha wad hae them?
      The licht's gaen frae them
        An' my day's past.

Oh, wha taks tent for a fadin' cheek?   *pays heed to*
    No him, I'se warrant, that gar'd it fade!   *made*
There's little love for a lass to seek
    When the coortin's through an' the price is paid.
Oh, aince forgotten's forgotten fairly,
    An' heavy endit what's licht begun,
But God forgie ye an' keep ye, Chairlie,   *forgive*
    For the nicht's fa'en airly   *early*
        An' my day's done!

Craigo Woods

Craigo Woods, wi' the splash o' the cauld rain beatin'
    I' the back end o' the year,
When the clouds hang laigh wi' the wecht o' their load o' greetin'   *low; weeping*
    And the autumn wind's asteer;   *astir*
Ye may stand like ghaists, ye may fa' i' the blast that's cleft ye
    To rot i' the chilly dew,
But when will I mind on aucht since the day I left ye   *remember anything*
    Like I mind on you – on you?

Craigo Woods, i' the licht o' September sleepin'
    And the saft mist o' the morn,
When the hairst climbs to yer feet, an' the sound o' reapin'   *harvest*
    Comes up frae the stookit corn,   *(stacked sheaves)*
And the braw reid puddock-stules are like jewels blinkin'   *toadstools*
    And the bramble happs ye baith.   *conceals*
O what do I see, i' the lang nicht, lyin' an' thinkin'
    As I see yer wraith – yer wraith?

There's a road to a far-aff land, an' the land is yonder
    Whaur a' men's hopes are set;
We dinna ken foo lang we maun hae to wander,   *how long; may have*
    But we'll a' win till it yet;   *get to*
An' gin there's woods o' fir an' the licht atween them,   *if*
    I winna speir its name,   *ask*
But I'll lay me doon by the puddock-stules when I've seen them,
    An' I'll cry 'I'm hame – I'm hame!'

The Helpmate

I hae nae gear, nae pot nor pan,   *possessions*
    Nae lauchin' lips hae I;
Forbye yersel' there's ne'er a man   *besides*
    Looks roond as I gang by.

And a' fowk kens nae time I've gied   everybody knows
  Tae daft strathspey and reel,
Nor idle sang nor ploy, for dreid   fun; for fear
  O' pleasurin' the deil.

Wi' muckle care ma mither bred   great
  Her bairn in wisdom's way;
Come Tyesday first, when we are wed,
  A wiselike wife ye'll hae.   sensible

The best ye'll get, baith but an' ben,   (in every room)
  Sae mild an' douce I'll be;   sweet
Yer hame'll be yer haven when
  Ye're married upon me.

Ye'll find the kettle on the fire,
  The hoose pit a' tae richts,   properly arranged
And yer heid in the troch at the back o' the byre   water-trough
  When ye come back fu' o' nichts.   drunk

The Water-Hen

As I gaed doon by the twa mill dams i' the mornin'
The water-hen cam' oot like a passin' wraith,
And her voice ran through the reeds wi' a sound of warnin,
    'Faith – keep faith!'
'Aye, bird, tho' ye see but ane ye may cry on baith!'

As I gaed doon the field when the dew was lyin',
My ain love stood whaur the road an' the mill-lade met,
And it seemed to me that the rowin' wheel was cryin',   turning
    'Forgie – forget,
And turn, man, turn, for ye ken that ye lo'e her yet!'

As I gaed doon the road 'twas a weary meetin',
For the ill words said yestreen they were aye the same,   painful; still
And my het he'rt drouned the wheel wi' its heavy beatin'.   hot heart
    'Lass, think shame,
It's no for me to speak, for it's you to blame!'

As I gaed doon by the toon when the day was springin'
The Baltic brigs lay thick by the soundin' quay
And the riggin' hummed wi' the sang that the wind was singin',
    'Free – gang free,
For there's mony a load on shore may be skailed at sea!'   dumped

When I cam hame wi' the thrang o' the years ahint me   crowd; behind
There was naucht to see for the weeds and the lade in spate,   in flood
But the water-hen by the dams she seemed aye to mind me,   still; remember
      Cryin' 'Hope – wait!'
'Aye, bird, but my een grow dim, an' it's late – late!'

Charles Murray (1864–1941)

Born in Alford, Aberdeenshire, Murray emigrated to South Africa in his 20s where
he worked as a mining engineer, eventually becoming Secretary of Public Works to
the government. He returned frequently to the North-East and retired there in 1924.
His collection *Hamewith* (1900), went through several editions and made him a well-
known local figure. 'Dockens Afore his Peers' is in full Aberdeenshire dialect.

A Green Yule

I'm weary, weary houkin', in the cauld, weet, clorty clay,
    But this will be the deepest in the yaird;
It's nae a four fit dibble for a common man the day –   planting hole
    Ilk bane I'm layin' by is o' a laird.
Whaever slips the timmers, lippens me to mak' his bed,   (dies); depends on
    For lairds maun just be happit like the lave;   covered; rest
An' kistit corps are lucky, for when a'thing's deen an' said,   coffined
    There 's lythe, save for the livin', in a grave.   shelter

Up on the watch-tower riggin' there's a draggled hoodie craw   crow
    That hasna missed a funeral the year;
He kens as weel's anither this will fairly ding them a',   beat
    Nae tenant on the land but will be here.
Sae up an' doon the tablin' wi' a gloatin' roupy hoast,   hoarse cough
    He haps, wi' twistit neck an' greedy e'e,   hops
As if some deil rejoicin' that anither sowl was lost
    An' waitin' for his share o' the dregie.   funeral feast

There's sorrow in the mansion, an' the Lady that tak's on   takes over
    Is young to hae sae muckle on her han',   much
Wi' the haugh lands to excamb where the marches cross the Don,   river; exchange
    An' factors aye hame-drauchted when they can.   agents always self-interested
Come spring, we'll a' be readin', when the kirk is latten oot,
    'Displenish' tackit up upon the yett;   'Closing-down sale'; gate

For hame-fairm, cairts an' cattle, will be roupit up, I doot,   auctioned off
    The policies a' pailined aff an' set.   fenced off

Twa lairds afore I've happit, an' this noo will mak' the third,   covered over
    An' tho' they spak' o' him as bein' auld,
It seerly seemed unlikely I would see him in the yird,   surely; earth
    For lang ere he was beardit I was bald.
It's three year by the saxty, come the week o' Hallow Fair,
    Since first I laid a divot on a grave;   turf
The Hairst o' the Almighty I hae gathered late an' ear',   harvest; early
    An' coont the sheaves I've stookit, by the thrave.   stacked; (12 sheaves)

I hae kent grief at Marti'mas would neither haud nor bin' –   not be controllable
    It was sair for even unco folk to see;   strangers
Yet ere the muir was yellow wi' the blossom on the whin,
    The tears were dry, the headstane a' ajee.   aslant
Nae bairns, nae wife, will sorrow, when at last I'm laid awa',
    Nae oes will plant their daisies at my head;   grandchildren
A' gane, but I will follow soon, an' weel content for a'
    There 's nane but fremt to lay me in my bed.   strangers

Earth to earth, an' dust to dust, an' the sowl gangs back to God:
    An' few there be wha think their day is lang;
Yet here I'm weary waitin', till the Master gies the nod,
    To tak' the gait I've seen sae mony gang.   road
I fear whiles He 's forgotten on his eildit gard'ner here,   aged
    But ae day He'll remember me, an' then
My birn o' sins afore Him I'll spread on the Judgment fleer,   load
    Syne wait until the angel says 'Come ben.'   Then; come into the house

There noo, the ill bird 's flaffin' on the very riggin' stane,   topmost (on roof)
    He sees them, an' could tell ye, did ye speer,   ask
The order they will come in, ay, an' name them ilka ane,   each
    An' lang afore the funeral is here.
The feathers will be noddin' as the hearse crawls past the Toll,
    As soon 's they tap the knowe they'll be in sicht;   rise
The driver on the dickey knappin' sadly on his mull,   tapping; snuffbox
    Syne raxin' doon to pass it to the vricht.   reaching; carpenter

The factor in the carriage will be next, an' ridin close   manager
    The doctor, ruggin' hard upon his grey;   tugging
The farmers syne, an' feuars speakin' laich aboot their loss,   feu-holders; low
    Yet thankfu' for the dram on sic a day.
Ay, there at last they're comin', I maun haste an' lowse the tow   loosen the rope
    An' ring the lang procession doon the brae;
I've heard the bell sae aften, I ken weel its weary jow,
    The tale o' weird it tries sae hard to say.   destiny

Bring them alang, the young, the strang,
   The weary an' the auld;
Feed as they will on haugh or hill,   hollow
   This is the only fauld.   fold

Dibble them doon, the laird, the loon,   plant; boy
   King an' the cadgin' caird,   beggarman
The lady fine beside the queyn,   girl
   A' in the same kirkyaird.

The warst, the best, they a' get rest;
   Ane 'neath a headstane braw,
Wi' deep-cut text; while ower the next
   The wavin' grass is a'.

Mighty o' name, unknown to fame,
   Slippit aneth the sod;
Greatest an' least alike face east,
   Waitin' the trump o' God.

Dockens Afore his Peers

(Exemption tribunal)[1]

Nae sign o' thow yet. Ay, that's me, John Watt o' Dockenhill: thaw
We've had the war throu' hant afore, at markets ower a gill.   fully discussed
O ay, I'll sit, birze ben a bit. Hae, Briggie,[2] pass the snuff;   move up
Ye winna hinner lang wi' me, an' speer a lot o' buff,   waste time; ask; nonsense
For I've to see the saiddler yet, an' Watchie, honest stock,   type
To gar him sen' his 'prentice up to sort the muckle knock,   make; mend; clock
Syne cry upo' the banker's wife an' leave some settin' eggs,
An' tell the ferrier o' the quake that's vrang aboot the legs.   vet; duck; wrong
It's yafa wedder, Mains, for Mairch, wi' snaw an' frost an' win'
The ploos are roustin' i' the fur, an' a' the wark's ahin'.   furrow; behind
Ye've grun yersel's an' ken the tyauve it is to wirk a ferm,   know; labour
An' a' the fash we've had wi' fouk gyaun aff afore the term; bother; going; contract's end
We've nane to spare for sojerin', that's nae oor wark ava',
We've rents to pey, an' beasts to feed, an' corn to sell an' saw;   sow
Oonless we get the seed in seen, faur will we be for meal?   soon; where
An' faur will London get the beef they leuk for aye at Yeel?   look; Yule
There's men aneuch in sooters' shops, an' chiels in masons' yards,   cobbler's; chaps
An' coonter-loupers, sklaters, vrichts, an' quarrymen, an' cyaurds,   shop servers;
To fill a reg'ment in a week, withoot gyaun vera far,   /slaters; carpenters; tinkers

1. During 1914–18, workers essential for the war effort, or the physically unfit, could be declared exempt from conscription.
2. Farmers were often called by the names of their farms, hence 'Mains', 'Gutteryloan', etc.

Jist shove them in ahin' the pipes, an' tell them that it's 'War';
For gin aul' Scotland's at the bit, there's naethin' for't but list.　　at the point of decision
Some mayna like it vera sair, but never heed, insist.
Bit, feich, I'm haverin' on like this, an' a' I need's a line　　chattering
To say there's men that maun be left, an' ye've exemptit mine.　　must
Fat said ye? Fatna fouk hae I enoo' at Dockenhill?　　What
It's just a wastrie o' your time, to rin them throu', but still –
First there's the wife – 'Pass her,' ye say. Saul! had she been a lass
Ye hadna rappit oot sae quick, young laird, to lat her pass,
That may be hoo ye spak' the streen, fan ye was playin' cairds,　　yesterday; when
But seein' tenants tak' at times their menners fae their lairds,
I'll tell ye this, for sense an' thrift, for skeel wi' hens an' caur,　　skill; calves
Gin ye'd her marrow for a wife, ye woudna be the waur.　　her like; worse
Oor maiden's neist, ye've heard o' her, new hame fae buirdin' squeel,　　daughter;
Faur she saw mair o' beuks than broth, an' noo she's never weel,　　/boarding school
But fan she's playin' ben the hoose, there's little wird o' dwaams,　　Where;
For she's the rin o' a' the tunes, strathspeys, an' sangs, an' psalms;　　faint spells
O' 'Evan' an' 'Neander' baith, ye seen can hae aneuch,
But 'Hobble Jennie' gars me loup, an' crack my thooms, an' hooch.　　thumbs
Weel, syne we hae the kitchie deem, that milks an' mak's the maet,　　kitchen maid
She disna aft haud doon the deese, she's at it ear' an' late,　　(sit down on) the bench
She cairries seed, an' braks the muck, an' gies a han' to hyow,　　hoe
An' churns, an' bakes, an' syes the so'ens, an' fyles there's peats to rowe.　　makes
An' fan the maiden's frien's cry in, she'll mask a cup o' tay,　　/sowens; sometimes; barrow
An' butter scones, and dicht her face, an' cairry ben the tray,　　wipe
She's big an' brosy, reid and roch, an' swippert as she's stoot,　　fat; agile
Gie her a kilt instead o' cotts, an' thon's the gran' recruit.　　petticoats
There's Francie syne, oor auldest loon, we pat him on for grieve,　　then; overseer
An', fegs, we would be in a soss, gin he should up an' leave;　　faith; mess
He's eident, an' has lots o' can, an' cheery wi' the men,　　diligent; skill
An' I'm sae muckle oot aboot wi' markets till atten'.
We've twa chaps syne to wirk the horse, as sweir as sweir can be,　　lazy
They fussle better than they ploo, they're aul' an' mairret tee,　　whistle
An' baith hae hooses on the ferm, an' Francie never kens
Foo muckle corn gyangs hame at nicht, to fatten up their hens.　　How much
The baillie syne, a peer-hoose geet, nae better than a feel,　　cowman; poorhouse brat, fool
He slivvers, an' has sic a mant, an' ae clog-fit as weel;　　drools; stutter
He's barely sense to muck the byre, an' cairry in the scull,　　scoop basket
An' park the kye, an' cogue the caur, an' scutter wi' the bull.　　pasture cows; feed calves
Weel, that's them a' – I didna hear – the laadie i' the gig?
That's Johnnie, he's a littlan jist, for a' he leuks sae big.
Fy na, he isna twenty yet – ay, weel, he's maybe near't;
Ower young to lippen wi' a gun, the crater would be fear't.　　Too; entrust
He's hardly throu' his squeelin' yet, an' noo we hae a plan　　schooling
To lat him simmer i' the toon, an' learn to mizzer lan'.　　measure
Fat? Gar him 'list! Oor laadie 'list? 'Twould kill his mither, that,　　What; make
To think o' Johnnie in a trench awa' in fat-ye-ca't;　　what-do-you-call-it

We would hae sic a miss at hame, gin he was hine awa',   far
We'd raither lat ye clean the toon o' ony ither twa;
Ay, tak' the wife, the dother, deem, the baillie wi' the mant,   stutter
Tak' Francie, an' the mairret men, but John we canna want.   do without
Fat does he dee? Ye micht as weel speir fat I dee mysel',   What; do; ask
The things he hisna time to dee is easier to tell;
He dells the yard, an' wi' the scythe cuts tansies on the brae,   digs the garden; ragwort
An' fan a ruck gyangs throu' the mull, he's   hayrick
          thrang at wispin' strae,   busy bundling straw
He sits aside me at the mart, an' fan a feeder's sell't   beef animal
Tak's doon the wecht, an' leuks the beuk for fat it's worth fan fell't; when slaughtered
He helps me to redd up the dask, he tak's a han' at loo,   tidy; desk; (card game)
An' sorts the shalt, an' yokes the gig, an' drives me fan I'm fou.   pony; drunk
Hoot, Mains, hae mind, I'm doon for you some sma' thing wi' the bank;
Aul' Larickleys, I saw you throu', an' this is a' my thank;
An' Gutteryloan, that time ye broke, to Dockenhill ye cam' –   went broke
'Total exemption.' Thank ye, sirs. Fat say ye till a dram?

                                                                    March, 1916

Walter Wingate (1865–1918)

Born at Dalry in Ayrshire, Wingate worked as a mathematics teacher in Hamilton
and published his verse in numerous newspapers.

The Dominie's Happy Lot

The Dominie is growin' grey,   Schoolteacher
   And, feth, he's keepit thrang   busy
Wi' counts and spellin' a' the day,
   And liffies when they're wrang.   smacks on the palm with a strap or cane
He dauners out at nine o'clock,   saunters
   He dauners hame at four –
Frae twal to ane to eat and smoke –   twelve to one
   And sae his day is owre!   over

   Oh! Leezie, Leezie, fine and easy
      Is a job like yon –   that one
   A' Saturday at gowf to play,   golf
      And aye the pay gaun on!

And when the burn comes doun in spate.   flood
   And troots are taken weel,   trout
To tak' a day he isna blate,   shy
   Syne marches aff wi's creel.   Then
His garden, it has ne'er a weed,
   His tatties are a' soun',   potatoes
The laddies needna fash to read   bother themselves
   As lang's they delve his grun'.

   Oh! Leezie, Leezie, fine and easy
     Is a job like yon –
   Weel or ill he's maister still.
     And aye the pay gaun on!

When winter days are cauld and dark,
   And dykes are deep wi' snaw,   fieldstone walls
And bairns are shiverin' owre their wark,
   He shuts the shop at twa;
And when it comes to Hogmanay,   New Year's Eve
   And fun comes roarin' ben,   into the house
And ilka dog maun tak' a day,   every; must
   The Dominie tak's ten!   (days holiday)

   Oh! Leezie, Leezie, fine and easy
     Is a job like yon –
   To stop the mill whene'er you will,
     And aye the pay gaun on!

And when Inspectors gi'e a ca',
   He tak's them roun' to dine,
And aye the upshot o' it a' –
   'The bairns are daein' fine!'
And sae the 'Board' come smirkin' roun',
   Wi' prizes in their haun';
And syne it's frae the end o' June   then
   Until the Lord kens whan!

   Oh! Leezie, Leezie, fine and easy
     Is a job like yon –
   Sax weeks to jaunt and gallivant,
     And aye the pay gaun on!

David Rorie (1867–1946)

Rorie studied medicine at Aberdeen and Edinburgh. He became an authority on the folk lore of mining while working as a colliery surgeon in Fife. He served in the RAMC during the First World War and went back to Aberdeen to work as a GP.

The Pawky Duke

There aince was a very pawky duke,   *artful*
    Far kent for his joukery-pawkery.   *Well known; doubtful antics*
Wha owned a hoose wi' a gran' outlook,
    A gairden an' a rockery.
Hech mon! The pawky duke!
    Hoot ay! An' a rockery!
For a bonnet laird wi' a sma' kailyaird   *small landowner; kitchen garden*
    Is naethin' but a mockery!

He dwalt far up a Heelant glen
    Where the foamin' flood an' the crag is,[1]
He dined each day on the usquebae   *whisky*
    An' he washed it doon wi' haggis.
Hech mon! The pawky duke!
    Hoot ay! An' a haggis!
For that's the way that the Heelanters dae
    Whaur the foamin' flood an' the crag is!

He wore a sporran an' a dirk,
    An' a beard like besom bristles,   *broom*
He was an elder o' the kirk
    And he hated kists o' whistles!   *church organs*
Hech mon! The pawky duke!
    An' doon on kists o' whistles!
They're a' reid-heidit fowk up North
    Wi' beards like besom bristles!

Then ilka four hoors through the day   *each; hours*
    He took a muckle jorum,   *big glass*
An' when the gloamin' gathered grey   *twilight*
    Got fou' wi' great decorum.   *drunk*
Hech mon! The pawky duke!
    Blin' fou' wi' great decorum!
There ne'er were males among the Gaels
    But loo'ed a muckle jorum!   *loved*

1. See Scott, 'Caledonia stern and wild …': 'land of the mountain and the flood'.

His hair was reid as ony rose,
    His legs was lang an' bony,
He keepit a hoast an' a rubbin'-post   band of retainers; (for cattle)
    An' a buskit cockernony!   well-dressed (beribboned) coiffure
Hech mon! The pawky duke!
    An' a buskit cockernony!
Ye ne'er will ken true Heelantmen
    Wha'll own they hadna ony!

An' if he met a Sassenach,   non-Scot (Gaelic: Southerner)
    Attour in Caledonia,   Abroad; Scotland
He gart him lilt in a cotton kilt   made; sing
    Till he took an acute pneumonia!
Hech mon! The pawky duke!
    An' a Sassenach wi' pneumonia!
He lat him feel that the Land o' the Leal   Loyal (the afterlife)
    'S nae far frae Caledonia!   Is not far from

He never went awa' doon Sooth
    To mell wi' legislation,   concern himself
For weel he kent sic things to be   such
    Unfitted for his station.
Hech mon! The pawky duke!
    An weel he kent his station,
For dustmen noo we a' alloo   allow
    Are best at legislation!

Then aye afore he socht his bed   always before; sought
    He danced the Gillie Callum,   (sword dance)
An' wi's Kilmarnock owre his neb   (bonnet); nose
    What evil could befall him!
Hech mon! The pawky duke!
    What evil could befall him?
When he cast his buits an' soopled his cuits   threw off; flexed; ankles
    Wi' a gude-gaun Gillie Callum!   good-going

But they brocht a joke, they did indeed,
    Ae day for his eedification,
An' they needed to trephine[1] his heid   trepan
    Sae he deed o' the operation!   died
Hech mon! The pawky duke!
    Wae's me for the operation!
For weel I wot this typical Scot
    Was a michty loss to the nation!

---

1. Trepanning: antique medical practice, a hole drilled in the skull to relieve pressure and excitability.

Marion Angus (1866–1946)

Brought up in Arbroath, where her father was a minister, Marion Angus moved to Aberdeen when he died, to look after her sister and an invalid mother. She did not start to write poetry seriously until she was in her 50s, publishing her first collection in 1922. Influenced by the ballads, her best work has a terse and eerie quality.

Ann Gilchrist

As I gae by the Bleedie Burn
    Whaur's nayther leaf nor tree,
Lat me nae hear Ann Gilchrist's feet
    Nor sicht her evil e'e.   eye

As I gaed by the Bleedie Burn
    Tae the witches' howff I cam' –   den
Ann Gilchrist's in among the whin   gorse bushes
    Seekin' a wandert lamb.

She's ta'en it frae the thorny buss,   bush
    Syne thro' the moss and fern   Then; boggy moorland
She's croonin' it and cuddlin' it
    As gin it were a bairn.   if; child

An' I wuss the whins wis nae sae shairp   wish
    Nor the muckle moss sae weet,   big; wet
For wha wull gie Ann Gilchrist fire
    Tae warm her clay-cauld feet?

The Blue Jacket

When there comes a flower to the stingless nettle,
    To the hazel bushes, bees,
I think I can see my little sister
    Rocking herself by the hazel trees.

Rocking her arms for very pleasure
    That every leaf so sweet can smell,
And that she has on her the warm blue jacket
    Of mine, she liked so well.

Oh to win near you, little sister!
    To hear your soft lips say –
'I'll never tak' up wi' lads or lovers,
    But a baby I maun hae.

'A baby in a cradle rocking,
   Like a nut, in a hazel shell,
And a new blue jacket, like this o' Annie's,
   It sets me aye sae well.'   suits

The Fiddler

A fine player was he ...
'Twas the heather at my knee,
The Lang Hill o' Fare[1]
An' a reid rose-tree,
A bonnie dryin' green,
Wind fae aff the braes,   from off; hills
Liftin' and shiftin'
The clear-bleached claes.   clothes

Syne he played again ...   Then
'Twas dreep, dreep o' rain,
A bairn at the breist   child
An' a warm hearth-stane,
Fire o' the peat,
Scones o' barley-meal
An' the whirr, whirr, whirr,
O' a spinnin'-wheel.

Bit aye, wae's me!   But always
The hindmaist tune he made ...   last
'Twas juist a dune wife   spent woman
Greetin' in her plaid,   weeping
Winds o' a' the years,
Naked wa's atween,   walls
And heather creep, creepin'
Ower the bonnie dryin' green.   Over

Alas! Poor Queen

She was skilled in music and the dance
And the old arts of love
At the court of the poisoned rose
And the perfumed glove,
And gave her beautiful hand
To the pale Dauphin
A triple crown to win –
And she loved little dogs
      And parrots

1. A distinctive hill to the north of Banchory and west of Aberdeen.

And red-legged partridges
And the golden fishes of the Duc de Guise
And a pigeon with a blue ruff
She had from Monsieur d'Elboeuf.

Master John Knox was no friend to her;
She spoke him soft and kind,
Her honeyed words were Satan's lure
The unwary soul to bind.
'Good sir, doth a lissome shape
And a comely face
Offend your God His Grace
Whose Wisdom maketh these
Golden fishes of the Duc de Guise?'

She rode through Liddesdale with a song;
'Ye streams sae wondrous strang,
Oh, mak' me a wrack as I come back
But spare me as I gang.'
While a hill-bird cried and cried
Like a spirit lost
By the grey storm-wind tost.

Consider the way she had to go,
Think of the hungry snare,
The net she herself had woven,
Aware or unaware,
Of the dancing feet grown still,
The blinded eyes –
Queens should be cold and wise,
And she loved little things,
       Parrots
       And red-legged partridges
And the golden fishes of the Duc de Guise
And the pigeon with the blue ruff
She had from Monsieur d'Elboeuf.

Lewis Spence (1874–1955)

Born in Dundee and educated at Edinburgh, Spence worked as an author and
journalist writing many articles and essays committed to the renaissance of Scot-
tish literature and identity in the mid-'20s. Fascinated by ancient civilisations,

mythology and the occult, he produced many books, including accounts of Mexico and Peru, North American Indians, legends of Brittany, Celtic lore, the Druids and Atlantis. His poetic output in Scots was quite small, but influential in its time because it looked back to the language of the Makars.

The Queen's Bath-house, Holyrood[1]

Time that has dinged doun castels and hie toures,	struck
And cast great crouns like tinsel in the fire,	
That halds his hand for palace nor for byre,	holds
Stands sweir at this, the oe of Venus' boures.	reluctant; offspring; bowers
Not Time himself can dwall withouten floures	dwell/survive
Though aiks maun fa' the rose sall bide entire;	oaks must fall; remain
So sall this diamant of a queen's desire	
Outflourish all the stanes that Time devours.	
Mony a strength his turret-heid sall tine	lose
Ere this sall fa' whare a queen lay in wine,	shall
Whose lamp was her ain lily flesh and star.	
The walls of luve the mair triumphant are	
Gif luve were waesome habiting that place;	If; woeful
Luve has maist years that has a murning face.	mourning

The Firth[2]

Yon auld claymore the Firth o' Forth,	Highland broadsword
Yon richt Ferrara[3] o' the North,	
Upon whase steel the broon sails scud,	
Staining the blade like draps o' bluid,	
Lies drawn betwixt the North and South,	
A sword within the Lyon's mouth.	
And in yon fell chafts shall it lie	fierce jaws
Sae lang as there is Albanie,	(ancient name for Scotland north of the Forth)
Stapping the roar o' meikle jaws,	blocking; big
Point tae the hert and hilt to paws	
O' yon auld rampant,[4] girning baste	snarling/complaining beast
Wha o' cauld steel luves best the taste.	

Like tae a watter on a wab	cobweb
Woven wi' silks o' gowd and drab,	
Scamander on a palace wall	(the river at ancient Troy)
Shone never mair majestical,	
And like a castel sewn in soye	silk

1. A small tower-lodge at Holyrood Palace in Edinburgh, it is associated with Mary Queen of Scots, her loves and her tragic fate.
2. The poet looks to the roofs and battlements of Edinburgh from across the estuary of the River Forth.
3. Town in Italy famed for the skill of its swordsmiths.
4. See the heraldic lion rampant of Scotland's royal flag.

The turrets o' the Scottish Troy
Atowre that meikle moat rise up   above
Like weirds abune a witch's cup –   omens
A wondrous ferlie frae the sea   strange thing
Warth a hale warld o' poesie!   Worth

Rachel Annand Taylor (1876–1900)

Born in Peterhead and educated in Aberdeen, Taylor became a scholar of the Italian
and French Renaissance. Her poems were published in the first decade of the century.

The Princess of Scotland

'Who are you that so strangely woke,
    And raised a fine hand?'
Poverty wears a scarlet cloke
    In my land.

'Duchies of dreamland, emerald, rose,
    Lie at your command?'
Poverty like a princess goes
    In my land.

'Wherefore the mask of silken lace
    Tied with a golden band?'
Poverty walks with wanton grace
    In my land.

'Why do you softly, richly speak
    Rhythm so sweetly-scanned?'
Poverty hath the Gaelic and Greek
    In my land.

'There's a far-off scent about you seems
    Born in Samarkand.'
Poverty hath luxurious dreams
    In my land.

'You have wounds that like passion-flowers you hide
    I cannot understand.'
Poverty hath one name with Pride
    In my land.

'Oh! Will you draw your last sad breath
  'Mid bitter bent and sand?'
Poverty only begs from Death
     In my land.

J. M. Caie (1878–1949)

Born and educated in the North-East, Caie was a lecturer in agriculture who became a senior civil servant in the Department of Agriculture. His poems come from his upbringing in the country around Fochabers in Banffshire. 'The Puddock' has long been a favourite recitation piece for schools.

The Puddock

	Frog
A puddock sat by the lochan's brim,	small loch
An' he thocht there was never a puddock like him.	
He sat on his hurdies, he waggled his legs,	haunches
An' cockit his heid as he glowered throu' the seggs.	rushes
The bigsy wee cratur' was feelin' that prood,	stuck-up
He gapit his mou' an' he croakit oot lood:	
'Gin ye'd a' like tae see a richt puddock,' quo' he,	
'Ye'll never, I'll sweer get a better nor me.	
I've fem'lies an' wives an' a weel-plenished hame,	stocked
Wi' drink for my thrapple an' meat for my wame.	throat; belly
The lasses aye thocht me a fine strappin' chiel .	fellow
An' I ken I'm a rale bonny singer as weel.	
I'm nae gyaun tae blaw, but the truth I maun tell –	going; boast; must
I believe I'm the verra MacPuddock himsel'.'	
A heron was hungry an' needin' tae sup,	
Sae he nabbit th' puddock and gollup't him up;	
Syne runkled his feathers: 'A peer thing,' quo' he,	ruffled; poor
'But – puddocks is nae fat they eesed tae be.'	what; used

Sir Alexander Gray (1882–1968)

Born in Dundee, Gray worked for the Civil Service before becoming a Professor of Political Economy at Aberdeen and then Edinburgh. He translated songs and ballads from Danish and from the German of Heine into Scots. He wrote his own poetry in both English and the north-east Scots of his boyhood.

The Three Kings[1]

There were three kings cam frae the East;
    They spiered in ilka clachan: *asked; village*
'O, which is the wey to Bethlehem,
    My bairns, sae bonnily lachin'?'   *laughing*

O neither young nor auld could tell;
    They trailed till their feet were weary.
They followed a bonny gowden starn,   *star*
    That shone in the lift say cheery.   *sky*

The starn stude ower the ale-hoose byre
    Whaur the stable gear was hingin'.   *equipment*
The owsen mooed, the bairnie grat,   *oxen; cried*
    The kings begoud their singin'.   *began*

December Gloaming

In the cauld dreich days when it's nicht on the back o four,   *dreary; after 4 p.m.*
I try to stick to my wark as lang as may be;
But though I gang close by to the window and glower,   *stare darkly*
        I canna see.

But I'm sweir, rale sweir, to be lichtin' the lamp that early;   *unwilling*
And aye I wait whiles there's ony licht i' the sky.
Sae I sit by the fire and see there mony a ferly   *strange thing*
        Till it's mirk oot-by.   *outside*

But it's no' for lang that I sit there, daein' naething;
For it's no' like me to be wastin' my time i' the dark;
Though your life be toom, you can aye thank God for ae thing, –   *empty*
        There's aye your wark.   *always*

But it wadna be wark I wad think o', if you were aside me.
I wad dream by the ingle neuk, wi' never a licht;   *chimney side*
The glint o' your een wad be licht eneuch to guide me
        The haill forenicht.   *evening*

I wadna speak, for there's never nae sense in speakin';
By the lowe o' the fire I wad look at your bonny hair.   *gleam*
To ken you were near wad be a' that my her't wad be seekin' –
        That and nae mair.

---

1. Heinrich Heine (1797–1856), *Die heil'gen drei Kön'ge aus Morgenland*.

W. D. Cocker (1882–1970)

Cocker was born in Glasgow and worked there as a journalist on the *Daily Record*, but his poems mostly evoke the Stirlingshire farms of his mother's family.

Dandie

Come in ahint, ye wan'erin' tyke!	Come to heel; dog
Did ever a body see yer like?	
Wha learnt ye a' thae poacher habits?	
Come in ahint, ne'er heed the rabbits!	
Noo bide there, or I'll warm yer lug!	stay; ear
My certie! ca' yersel' a doug?	My oath
Noo ower the dyke all' through the park:	wall; field
Let's see if ye can dae some wark.	
Way wide there, fetch them tae the fank!	sheep-pen
Way wide there, 'yont the burn's bank!	
Get roon' aboot them! Watch the gap!	
Hey, Dandie, haud them frae the slap!	gap in wall
Ye've got them noo, that's no sae bad:	
Noo bring them in, guid lad! guid lad!	
Noo tak' them canny ower the knowe –	knoll
Hey, Dandie, kep that mawkit yowe!	maggoty ewe
The tither ane, hey, lowse yer grip!	other; loosen
The yowe, ye foumart, no' the tip!	polecat; ram
Ay, that's the ane, guid doug! guid doug!	
Noo haud her canny, dinna teug!	carefully; tug
She's mawkit bad; ay, shair's I'm born	
We'll hae tae dip a wheen the morn.	sheep-dip a few
Noo haud yer wheesht, ye yelpin' randie,	be quiet; rascal
An' dinna fricht them, daft doug Dandie!	
He's ower the dyke – the de'il be in't!	
Ye wan'erin' tyke, come in ahint!	

Mrs M. C. Smith (1869–?1949)

M. C. Edgar was the daughter of the minister at Burns's one-time parish of Mauchline in Ayrshire. She was born in Kirkcudbrightshire, and moved to Dulwich in London when she married.

The Boy in the Train

Whit wey does the engine say *Toot-toot*?
    Is it feart to gang in the tunnel?   *afraid*
Whit wey is the furnace no pit oot
    When the rain gangs doon the funnel?
What'll I hae for my tea the nicht?
    A herrin', or maybe a haddie?   *haddock*
Has Gran'ma gotten electric licht?
    Is the next stop Kirkcaddy?

There's a hoodie-craw on yon turnip-raw!   *hooded crow*
    An' sea-gulls! – sax or seeven.
I'll no fa' oot o' the windae, Maw,
    It's sneckit, as sure as I'm leevin'.   *latched; living*
We're into the tunnel! we're a' in the dark!
    But dinna be frichtit, Daddy,
We'll sune be comin' to Beveridge Park,
    And the next stop's Kirkcaddy!

Is yon the mune I see in the sky?
    It's awfu' wee an' curly.
See! there's a coo and a cauf ootbye,
    An' a lassie pu'in' a hurly!   *cart*
He's chackit the tickets and gien them back,
    Sae gie me my ain yin, Daddy.
Lift doon the bag frae the luggage rack,
    For the next stop's Kirkcaddy!

There's a gey wheen boats at the harbour mou',   *quite a number of*
    And eh! dae ye see the cruisers?
The cinnamon drop I was sookin' the noo
    Has tummelt an' stuck tae ma troosers ...
I'll sune be ringin' ma Gran'ma's bell,
    She'll cry, 'Come ben, my laddie.'   *into the house*
For I ken mysel' by the queer-like smell
    That the next stop's Kirkcaddy![1]

---

1. Kirkcaldy was famous for its linoleum factories which left a distinctive smell along the Fife coast. The locals were sensitive about it.

Andrew Young (1885–1971)

Born in Elgin and educated in Edinburgh, Young became a minister of the United Free Church before moving to Sussex and taking orders with the Church of England. He wrote numerous volumes of poetry, and visited Scotland often as a keen mountaineer and botanist.

Culbin Sands[1]

Here lay a fair fat land;
   But now its townships, kirks, graveyards
Beneath bald hills of sand
   Lie buried deep as Babylonian shards.

But gales may blow again;
   And like a sand-glass turned about
The hills in a dry rain
   Will flow away and the old land look out;

And where now hedgehog delves
   And conies hollow their long caves   rabbits
Houses will build themselves
   And tombstones rewrite names on dead men's graves.

Helen B. Cruickshank (1886–1975)

Born near Montrose in the North-East and educated there, Cruickshank worked as a civil servant and spent most of her life in Edinburgh. As secretary of Scottish PEN she befriended many of the poets of the Scottish Renaissance, offering particular support to Hugh MacDiarmid and his family when times were hard for them in the 1930s.

The Ponnage Pool

... Sing
Some simple silly sang

1. Extensive dunes on the Moray Firth coast, between Nairn and Forres, where a sandstorm buried a village and the surrounding fields in 1694.

> *O' willows or o' mimulus*
> *A river's banks alang.'*
>   Hugh MacDiarmid

I mind o' the Ponnage Pule,[1]   remember
The reid brae risin',
Morphie Lade,
An' the saumon that louped the dam.   jumped
A tree i' Martin's Den
Wi' names carved on it;
But I ken na wha I am.   know not

Ane o' the names was mine,
An' still I own it.
Naething it kens
O' a' that mak's up me.
Less I ken o' mysel'
Than the saumon wherefore
It rins up Esk frae the sea.

I am the deep o' the pule,
The fish, the fisher,
The river in spate,
The broon o' the far peat-moss,   moorland where peat is cut
The shingle bricht wi' the flooer
O' the yellow mim'lus,
The martin fleein' across.   housemartin

I mind o' the Ponnage Pule
On a shinin' mornin',
The saumon fishers
Nettin' the bonny brutes –
I' the slithery dark o' the boddom   bottom
O' Charon's[2] Coble   flat-bottomed salmon fishing boat
Ae day I'll faddom my doobts.   fathom (understand)

---

1. Place name (lit.: a pond or dam) on the river North Esk by Hillside where the poet was born. Morphie Lade and Martin's Den can be found there too; also the Craigo Woods of Violet Jacob's poem.
2. Charon: ferryman who carries the dead across the river Styx to the underworld.

Edwin Muir (1887–1959)

After working small farms in the Orkney Islands, the Muirs moved to Glasgow when Edwin was 14. Within a few years disease had killed both parents and two of his brothers. Edwin was to be marked by the experience for the rest of his life. He later wrote that he was 'really born in 1737 ... then in 1751 I set out from Orkney for Glasgow. When I arrived I found that it was not 1751 but 1901, and that a hundred and fifty years had been burned up in my two days' journey.' Largely self-educated, Muir moved to London to work as a writer and critic, and married Willa Anderson with whom he translated Kafka. The couple travelled in Europe before and after the war, returning to Scotland in the 1930s and then in the 1950s when Muir was appointed as warden of Newbattle Abbey, an adult education college outside Edinburgh where he befriended a student called George Mackay Brown. Muir underwent analysis and kept a dream notebook whose timeless images reappear in *An Autobiography* and a number of his poems.

Childhood

Long time he lay upon the sunny hill,
   To his father's house below securely bound.
Far off the silent, changing sound was still,
   With the black islands lying thick around.

He saw each separate height, each vaguer hue,
   Where the massed islands rolled in mist away,
And though all ran together in his view
   He knew that unseen straits between them lay.

Often he wondered what new shores were there.
   In thought he saw the still light on the sand,
The shallow water clear in tranquil air,
   And walked through it in joy from strand to strand.

Over the sound a ship so slow would pass
   That in the black hill's gloom it seemed to lie.
The evening sound was smooth like sunken glass,
   And time seemed finished ere the ship passed by.

Grey tiny rocks slept round him where he lay,
   Moveless as they, more still as evening came,
The grasses threw straight shadows far away,
   And from the house his mother called his name.

Merlin

O Merlin in your crystal cave
Deep in the diamond of the day,
Will there ever be a singer
Whose music will smooth away
The furrow drawn by Adam's finger
Across the meadow and the wave?
Or a runner who'll outrun
Man's long shadow driving on,
Break through the gate of memory
And hang the apple on the tree?
Will your magic ever show
The sleeping bride shut in her bower,
The day wreathed in its mound of snow
And Time locked in his tower?

The Enchanted Knight

Lulled by La Belle Dame Sans Merci he lies
   In the bare wood below the blackening hill.
The plough drives nearer now, the shadow flies
   Past him across the plain, but he lies still.

Long since the rust its gardens here has planned,
   Flowering his armour like an autumn field.
From his sharp breast-plate to his iron hand
   A spider's web is stretched, a phantom shield.

When footsteps pound the turf beside his ear
   Armies pass through his dream in endless line,
And one by one his ancient friends appear;
   They pass all day, but he can make no sign.

When a bird cries within the silent grove
   The long-lost voice goes by, he makes to rise
And follow, but his cold limbs never move,
   And on the turf unstirred his shadow lies.

But if a withered leaf should drift
   Across his face and rest, the dread drops start

Chill on his forehead. Now he tries to lift
   The insulting weight that stays and breaks his heart.

The Return of the Greeks

The veteran Greeks came home
Sleepwandering from the war.
We saw the galleys come
Blundering over the bar.
Each soldier with his scar
In rags and tatters came home.

Reading the wall of Troy
Ten years without a change
Was such intense employ
(Just out of the arrows' range),
All the world was strange
After ten years of Troy.

Their eyes knew every stone
In the huge heartbreaking wall
Year after year grown
Till there was nothing at all
But an alley steep and small,
Tramped earth and towering stone.

Now even the hills seemed low
In the boundless sea and land,
Weakened by distance so.
How could they understand
Space empty on every hand
And the hillocks squat and low?

And when they arrived at last
They found a childish scene
Embosomed in the past,
And the war lying between –
A child's preoccupied scene
When they came home at last.

But everything trite and strange,
The peace, the parcelled ground,
The vinerows – never a change!
The past and the present bound
In one oblivious round
Past thinking trite and strange.

But for their grey-haired wives
And their sons grown shy and tall
They would have given their lives
To raise the battered wall
Again, if this was all
In spite of their sons and wives.

Penelope in her tower
Looked down upon the show
And saw within an hour
Each man to his wife go,
Hesitant, sure and slow:
She, alone in her tower.

The Wayside Station

Here at the wayside station, as many a morning,
I watch the smoke torn from the fumy engine
Crawling across the field in serpent sorrow.
Flat in the east, held down by stolid clouds,
The struggling day is born and shines already
On its warm hearth far off. Yet something here
Glimmers along the ground to show the seagulls
White on the furrows' black unturning waves.

But now the light has broadened.
I watch the farmstead on the little hill,
That seems to mutter: 'Here is day again'
Unwillingly. Now the sad cattle wake
In every byre and stall,
The ploughboy stirs in the loft, the farmer groans
And feels the day like a familiar ache
Deep in his body, though the house is dark.
The lovers part
Now in the bedroom where the pillows gleam
Great and mysterious as deep hills of snow,
An inaccessible land. The wood stands waiting
While the bright snare slips coil by coil around it,
Dark silver on every branch. The lonely stream
That rode through darkness leaps the gap of light,
Its voice grown loud, and starts its winding journey
Through the day and time and war and history.

Scotland 1941

We were a tribe, a family, a people.
Wallace and Bruce guard now a painted field,

And all may read the folio of our fable,
Peruse the sword, the sceptre and the shield.
A simple sky roofed in that rustic day,
The busy corn-fields and the haunted holms,
The green road winding up the ferny brae.
But Knox and Melville clapped their preaching palms
And bundled all the harvesters away,
Hoodicrow Peden[1] in the blighted corn
Hacked with his rusty beak the starving haulms.
Out of that desolation we were born.

Courage beyond the point and obdurate pride
Made us a nation, robbed us of a nation.
Defiance absolute and myriad-eyed
That could not pluck the palm plucked our damnation.
We with such courage and the bitter wit
To fell the ancient oak of loyalty,
And strip the peopled hill and the altar bare,
And crush the poet with an iron text,
How could we read our souls and learn to be?
Here a dull drove of faces harsh and vexed,
We watch our cities burning in their pit,
To salve our souls grinding dull lucre out,
We, fanatics of the frustrate and the half,
Who once set Purgatory Hill in doubt.
Now smoke and dearth and money everywhere,
Mean heirlooms of each fainter generation,
And mummied housegods in their musty niches,
Burns and Scott, sham bards of a sham nation,
And spiritual defeat wrapped warm in riches,
No pride but pride of pelf. Long since the young
Fought in great bloody battles to carve out
This towering pulpit of the Golden Calf,
Montrose, Mackail, Argyle,[2] perverse and brave,
Twisted the stream, unhooped the ancestral hill.
Never had Dee or Don or Yarrow or Till
Huddled such thriftless honour in a grave.

Such wasted bravery idle as a song,
Such hard-won ill might prove Time's verdict wrong,
And melt to pity the annalist's iron tongue.

1. John Knox, radical reformer and Andrew Melville, the 'father' of Scottish Presbyterianism. Alexander Peden, an
   extreme Covenanter, was a self-styled prophet, pamphleteer and propagandist for 'Holy war'.
2. James Graham, Marquis of Montrose, supported the Covenant, but his moderation eventually drew him to the cause
   of King Charles I. He was hated by the more extreme supporter of the Solemn League – Archibald 'King Campbell'
   the eighth Earl of Argyll. Montrose 'lost'; Argyll 'won', but both men were executed in the end. Hugh Mackail, a
   leading young Covenanter, was captured after the Pentland rising in 1666, brutally tortured and put to death in
   Edinburgh in 1666. He died like a martyr.

Scotland's Winter

Now the ice lays its smooth claws on the sill,
The sun looks from the hill
Helmed in his winter casket,
And sweeps his arctic sword across the sky.
The water at the mill
Sounds more hoarse and dull.
The miller's daughter walking by
With frozen fingers soldered to her basket
Seems to be knocking
Upon a hundred leagues of floor
With her light heels, and mocking
Percy and Douglas dead,
And Bruce on his burial bed,
Where he lies white as may   hawthorn blossom
With wars and leprosy,
And all the kings before
This land was kingless,
And all the singers before
This land was songless,
This land that with its dead and living waits the Judgment Day.
But they, the powerless dead,
Listening can hear no more
Than a hard tapping on the sounding floor
A little overhead
Of common heels that do not know
Whence they come or where they go
And are content
With their poor frozen life and shallow banishment.

The Little General

Early in spring the little General came
    Across the sound, bringing the island death,
And suddenly a place without a name,
    And like the pious ritual of a faith,

Hunter and quarry in the boundless trap,
    The white smoke curling from the silver gun,
The feather curling in the hunter's cap,
    And clouds of feathers floating in the sun,

While down the birds came in a deafening shower,
    Wing-hurricane, and the cattle fled in fear.
Up on the hill a remnant of a tower
    Had watched that single scene for many a year,

Weaving a wordless tale where all were gathered
    (Hunter and quarry and watcher and fabulous field),
A sylvan war half human and half feathered,
    Perennial emblem painted on the shield

Held up to cow a never-conquered land
Fast in the little General's fragile hand.

The Interrogation

We could have crossed the road but hesitated,
And then came the patrol;
The leader conscientious and intent,
The men surly, indifferent.
While we stood by and waited
The interrogation began. He says the whole
Must come out now, who, what we are,
Where we have come from, with what purpose, whose
Country or camp we plot for or betray.
Question on question.
We have stood and answered through the standing day
And watched across the road beyond the hedge
The careless lovers in pairs go by,
Hand linked in hand, wandering another star,
So near we could shout to them. We cannot choose
Answer or action here,
Though still the careless lovers saunter by
And the thoughtless field is near.
We are on the very edge,
Endurance almost done,
And still the interrogation is going on.

The Labyrinth

Since I emerged that day from the labyrinth,
Dazed with the tall and echoing passages,
The swift recoils, so many I almost feared
I'd meet myself returning at some smooth corner,
Myself or my ghost, for all there was unreal
After the straw ceased rustling and the bull
Lay dead upon the straw and I remained,
Blood-splashed, if dead or alive I could not tell
In the twilight nothingness (I might have been
A spirit seeking his body through the roads
Of intricate Hades) – ever since I came out
To the world, the still fields swift with flowers, the trees

All bright with blossom, the little green hills, the sea,
The sky and all in movement under it,
Shepherds and flocks and birds and the young and old,
(I stared in wonder at the young and the old,
For in the maze time had not been with me;
I had strayed, it seemed, past sun and season and change,
Past rest and motion, for I could not tell
At last if I moved or stayed; the maze itself
Revolved around me on its hidden axis
And swept me smoothly to its enemy,
The lovely world) – since I came out that day,
There have been times when I have heard my footsteps
Still echoing in the maze, and all the roads
That run through the noisy world, deceiving streets
That meet and part and meet, and rooms that open
Into each other – and never a final room –
Stairways and corridors and antechambers
That vacantly wait for some great audience,
The smooth sea-tracks that open and close again,
Tracks undiscoverable, indecipherable,
Paths on the earth and tunnels underground,
And bird-tracks in the air – all seemed a part
Of the great labyrinth. And then I'd stumble
In sudden blindness, hasten, almost run,
As if the maze itself were after me
And soon must catch me up. But taking thought,
I'd tell myself, 'You need not hurry. This
Is the firm good earth. All roads lie free before you.'
But my bad spirit would sneer, 'No, do not hurry.
No need to hurry. Haste and delay are equal
In this one world, for there's no exit, none,
No place to come to, and you'll end where you are,
Deep in the centre of the endless maze.'

I could not live if this were not illusion.
It is a world, perhaps; but there's another.
For once in a dream or trance I saw the gods
Each sitting on the top of his mountain-isle,
While down below the little ships sailed by,
Toy multitudes swarmed in the habours, shepherds drove
Their tiny flocks to the pastures, marriage feasts
Went on below, small birthdays and holidays,
Ploughing and harvesting and life and death,
And all permissible, all acceptable,
Clear and secure as in a limpid dream.
But they, the gods, as large and bright as clouds,

Conversed across the sounds in tranquil voices
High in the sky above the untroubled sea,
And their eternal dialogue was peace
Where all these things were woven, and this our life
Was as a chord deep in that dialogue,
As easy utterance of harmonious words,
Spontaneous syllables bodying forth a world.

That was the real world; I have touched it once,
And now shall know it always. But the lie,
The maze, the wild-wood waste of falsehood, roads
That run and run and never reach an end,
Embowered in error – I'd be prisoned there
But that my soul has birdwings to fly free.

Oh these deceits are strong almost as life.
Last night I dreamt I was in the labyrinth,
And woke far on. I did not know the place.

The Horses

Barely a twelvemonth after
The seven days war that put the world to sleep,
Late in the evening the strange horses came.
By then we had made our covenant with silence,
But in the first few days it was so still
We listened to our breathing and were afraid.
On the second day
The radios failed; we turned the knobs; no answer.
On the third day a warship passed us, heading north,
Dead bodies piled on the deck. On the sixth day
A plane plunged over us into the sea. Thereafter
Nothing. The radios dumb;
And still they stand in comers of our kitchens,
And stand, perhaps, turned on, in a million rooms
All over the world. But now if they should speak,
If on a sudden they should speak again,
If on the stroke of noon a voice should speak,
We would not listen, we would not let it bring
That old bad world that swallowed its children quick
At one great gulp. We would not have it again.
Sometimes we think of the nations lying asleep,
Curled blindly in impenetrable sorrow,
And then the thought confounds us with its strangeness.
The tractors lie about our fields; at evening
They look like dank sea-monsters couched and waiting.

We leave them where they are and let them rust:
'They'll moulder away and be like other loam'.
We make our oxen drag our rusty ploughs,
Long laid aside. We have gone back
Far past our fathers' land.
                                        And then, that evening
Late in the summer the strange horses came.
We heard a distant tapping on the road,
A deepening drumming; it stopped, went on again
And at the corner changed to hollow thunder.
We saw the heads
Like a wild wave charging and were afraid.
We had sold our horses in our fathers' time
To buy new tractors. Now they were strange to us
As fabulous steeds set on an ancient shield
Or illustrations in a book of knights.
We did not dare go near them. Yet they waited,
Stubborn and shy, as if they had been sent
By an old command to find our whereabouts
And that long-lost archaic companionship.
In the first moment we had never a thought
That they were creatures to be owned and used.
Among them were some half-a-dozen colts
Dropped in some wilderness of the broken world,
Yet new as if they had come from their own Eden.
Since then they have pulled our ploughs and borne our loads,
But that free servitude still can pierce our hearts.
Our life is changed; their coming our beginning.

The Cloud

One late spring evening in Bohemia,
Driving to the Writers' House, we lost our way
In a maze of little winding roads that led
To nothing but themselves,
Weaving a rustic web for thoughtless travellers.
No house was near, nor sign or sound of life:
Only a chequer-board of little fields,
Crumpled and dry, neat squares of powdered dust.
At a sudden turn we saw
A young man harrowing, hidden in dust; he seemed
A prisoner walking in a moving cloud
Made by himself for his own purposes;
And there he grew and was as if exalted
To more than man, yet not, not glorified:
A pillar of dust moving in dust; no more.

The bushes by the roadside were encrusted
With a hard sheath of dust.
We looked and wondered; the dry cloud moved on
With its interior image.
                              Presently we found
A road that brought us to the Writers' House,
And there a preacher from Urania
(Sad land where hope each day is killed by hope)
Praised the good dust, man's ultimate salvation,
And cried that God was dead. As we drove back
Late to the city, still our minds were teased
By the brown barren fields, the harrowing,
The figure walking in its cloud, the message
From far Urania. This was before the change;
And in our memory cloud and message fused,
Image and thought condensed to a giant form
That walked the earth clothed in its earthly cloud,
Dust made sublime in dust. And yet it seemed unreal
And lonely as things not in their proper place.
And thinking of the man
Hid in his cloud we longed for light to break
And show that his face was the face once broken in Eden
Beloved, world-without-end lamented face;
And not a blindfold mask on a pillar of dust.

Dream and Thing

This is the thing, this truly is the thing.
We dreamt it once; now it has come about.
That was the dream, but this, this is the thing.
The dream was bold and thought it could foretell
What time would bring, but time, it seems, can bring
Only this thing which never has had a doubt
That everything is much like everything,
And the deep family likeness will come out.
We thought the dream would spread its folded wing;
But here's a thing that's neither sick nor well,
Stupid nor wise, and has no story to tell,
Though every tale is about it and about.
That is the thing, that is the very thing.
Yet take another look and you may bring
From the dull mass each separate splendour out.
There is no trust but in the miracle.

Hugh MacDiarmid (1892–1978)

Christopher Murray Grieve adopted the pen name MacDiarmid when he first started to write in Scots. A socialist all his life, he believed that there could be no internationalism without small nations, and dedicated his life to the reaffirmation of a distinctively Scottish identity in culture and world politics. The early lyric collections (*Sangschaw* and *Penny Wheep*) were followed by his long poem *A Drunk Man Looks at the Thistle* (1926), a modernist *tour de force* which places him in the company of Yeats, Eliot and Pound. A controversialist and an inexhaustible propagandist for what came to be known as 'The Modern Scottish Renaissance', MacDiarmid returned to English for his later poetry, producing the philosophical masterpiece *On a Raised Beach*; direct political polemic in the *Hymns to Lenin*; and vast and abstruse 'world language' poems (*In Memoriam James Joyce*; *The Kind of Poetry I Want*, etc.), which were drawn together from innumerable linguistic and scientific sources.

The Watergaw

Ae weet forenicht i' the yow-trummle	twilight; cold spell in July (ewe-tremble)
I saw yon antrin thing,	singular
A watergaw wi' its chitterin' licht	broken rainbow; shivering
Ayont the on-ding;	beyond; downpour
An' I thocht o' the last wild look ye gied	
Afore ye deed!	

There was nae reek i' the laverock's hoose	(smoke in the lark's house) signs of life or
That nicht – an' nane i' mine;	/warmth in the sky
But I hae thocht o' that foolish licht	
Ever sin' syne;	since then
An' I think that mebbe at last I ken	
What your look meant then.	

At My Father's Grave

The sunlicht still on me, you row'd in clood	wrapped
We look upon each ither noo like hills	
Across a valley. I'm nae mair your son.	
It is my mind, nae son o' yours, that looks,	

And the great darkness o' your death comes up
And equals it across the way.
A livin' man upon a deid man thinks
And ony sma'er thocht's impossible.

The Eemis Stane

I' the how-dumb-deid o' the cauld hairst nicht   deep dead quiet; harvest
The warl' like an eemis stane   insecure
Wags i' the lift;   sky
An' my eerie memories fa'
Like a yowdendrift.   ground blizzard

Like a yowdendrift so's I couldna read
The words cut oot i' the stane
Had the fug o' fame   moss
An' history's hazelraw   lichen
No' yirdit thaim.   buried (earthed)

The Innumerable Christ

Other stars may have their Bethlehem, and their Calvary too.
      Professor J. Y. Simpson

Wha kens on whatna Bethlehems
Earth twinkles like a star the nicht,
An' whatna shepherds lift their heids
      In its unearthly licht?

'Yont a' the stars oor een can see
An' farther than their lichts can fly,
I' mony an unco warl' the nicht   strange world
      The fatefu' bairnies cry.

I' mony an unco warl' the nicht
The lift gaes black as pitch at noon,   sky
An' sideways on their chests the heids
      O' endless Christs roll doon.

An' when the earth's as cauld's the mune
An' a' its folk are lang syne deid,   long since dead
On coontless stars the Babe maun cry   must
An' the Crucified maun bleed.

Empty Vessel

I met ayont the cairney[1]   little cairn (marking path or summit)
A lass wi' tousie hair   tangled
Singin' till a bairnie
That was nae langer there.

Wunds wi' warlds to swing   Winds
Dinna sing sae sweet,
The licht that bends owre a' thing
Is less ta'en up wi't.   taken up with it

Servant Girl's Bed

The talla spales   candle-wax spills over
And the licht loups oot,   jumps
Fegs, it's your ain creesh   flesh (fat)
Lassie, I doot,
And the licht that reeled
Loose on't a wee   for a moment
Was the bonny lowe   gleam
O' Eternity.

from *A Drunk Man Looks at the Thistle*

I ha'e forekent ye! O I ha'e forekent.   foreknown
The years forecast your face afore they went.
A licht I canna thole is in the lift.   tolerate; sky
I bide in silence your slow-comin' pace.   await
The ends o' space are bricht: at last – oh swift!
While terror clings to me – an unkent face!   unknown

Ill-faith stirs in me as she comes at last,
The features lang forekent ... are unforecast.
O it gangs hard wi' me, I am forspent.   exhausted
Deid dreams ha'e beaten me and a face unkent
And generations that I thocht unborn
Hail the strange Goddess frae my hert's-hert torn! ...[2]

Or dost thou mak' a thistle o' me, wumman? But for thee
I were as happy as the munelicht, withoot care,
But thocht o' thee – o' thy contempt and ire –
Turns hauf the warld into the youky thistle there,   scratchy (disgusting)

Feedin' on the munelicht and transformin' it
To this wanrestfu' growth that winna let me be.   unrestful; will not

1. See the second stanza of the folk song 'Jenny Nettles'.
2. Based on 'The Unknown Woman' by the Russian poet Alexander Blok.

The munelicht is the freedom that I'd ha'e
But for this cursed Conscience thou hast set in me.

It is morality, the knowledge o' Guid and Ill,
Fear, shame, pity, like a will and wilyart growth,   misguided and wayward
That kills a' else wi'in its reach and craves
Nae less at last than a' the warld to gi'e it scouth.   scope

The need to wark, the need to think, the need to be,
And a' thing that twists Life into a certain shape
And interferes wi' perfect liberty
These feed this Frankenstein that nae man can escape.

For ilka thing a man can be or think or dae   every
Aye leaves a million mair unbeen, unthocht, undune,
Till his puir warped performance is,
To a' that micht ha' been, a thistle to the mune.   moon

It is Mortality itsel' – the mortal coil,
Mockin' Perfection, Man afore the Throne o' God   before
He yet has bigged himsel', Man torn in twa   built
And glorious in the lift and grisly on the sod ! ...   sky

There's nocht sae sober as a man blin' drunk.   nothing
I maun ha'e got an unco bellyfu'   very
To jaw like this – and yet what I am sayin'
Is a' the apter, aiblins, to be true.   perhaps

This munelicht's fell like whisky noo I see't.   very
– Am I a thingum mebbe that is kept
Preserved in spirits in a muckle bottle
Lang centuries efter sin' wi' Jean I slept?

– Mounted on a hillside, wi' the thistles
And bracken for verisimilitude,
Like a stuffed bird on metal like a brainch,
Or a seal on a stump o' rock-like wood?

Or am I juist a figure in a scene
O' Scottish life A.D. one-nine-two-five?
The haill thing kelters like a theatre claith   undulates
Till I micht fancy that I was alive!

I dinna ken and nae man ever can.   do not know
I micht be in my ain bed efter a'.
The haill damned thing's a dream for ocht we ken,   all
– The Warld and Life and Daith, Heaven, Hell ana'.   as well

We maun juist tak' things as we find them then,
And mak' a kirk or mill o' them as we can,   (make a church or a mill) do the best
– And yet I feel this muckle thistle's staun'in'   big
Atween me and the mune as pairt o' a Plan.

It isna there – nor me – by accident.
We're brocht thegither for a certain reason,
Ev'n gin it's naething mair than juist to gi'e
My jaded soul a necessary *frisson*.

I never saw afore a thistle quite
Sae intimately, or at sic an 'oor.   hour
There's something in the fickle licht that gi'es
A different life to't and an unco poo'er.   strange power

from *To Circumjack Cencrastus*: North of the Tweed

Cauld licht and tumblin' cloods. It's queer   Cold
There's never been a poet here ...

Shades o' the Sun-King no' yet risen
Are sleepin' in a corner on the straw.
Despair seems to touch bottom time and again
But aye Earth opens and reveals fresh depths.   always
The pale-wa'd warld is fu' o' licht and life   -walled
Like a glass in which water faintly stirs.
Gie owre a' this tomfoolery, and sing   Stop
The movin' spirit that nae metaphor drawn
Frae water or frae licht can dim suggest.
Leid in nae mere Longinian hypsos[1] come   Language; sublimities
But in inhuman splendours, triumphin' wi'
'A dazzlin' disregard o' the soul.'
                              Nocht else'll dae.

Water nor licht nor yet the barley field
That shak's in silken sheets at ilka braith   each
Its lang nap thrawin' the quick licht aboot
In sic a maze that tak's and gies at aince
As fair oot-tops the coontless ripplin' sea.
There's nae chameleon like the July fields;
Their different colours change frae day to day
While they shift instantly neath the shiftin' licht
Yet they're owre dull for this, stagnant and dull;   too
And even your een, beloved, and your hair   eyes

---

1. *Peri Hypsous* (*On the Sublime*), a treatise about literature often ascribed to Longinus, a Greek philosopher of the third century AD.

Are like the barley and the sea and Heaven
That flaw and fail and are defeated by   tell fibs
                    The blind turns o' chance.

Thinkna' that I'm ungratefu', wi' nae mind
O' Deirdre and the fauld o' sunbeams[1] yet,
Or canna find on bracken slopes abune the bog   above
The orchis smellin' like cherry-pie;
Or that the sun's blade cuttin' straightly through
A cloudy sea fails wi' my cloudy hert,
Releasin' it frae self-disgust until I tine   lose
A' sense o' livin' under set conditions
And live in an unconditioned space o' time
Perfect in ilka pulse and impulse, and aince mair
A seven-whistler in Kintyre, or yon broon hill
That's barren save for fower pale violets on
                    A South-leanin' bank.

I've sat amang the crimson buds o' thrift
Abune the sea whaur Buachaille[2] herds the waves;
And seen the primrose nightglow to the North
Owre Moray and the flat sea while the West
Still held a twinkle o' the morning-star,
(For in the Cairngorms simmer nicht and dawn
Come close, but canna thraw the larks' hours oot);
And hoo should I forget the Langfall[3]
On mornings when the hines were ripe but een   raspberries
Ahint the glintin' leafs were brichter still
Than sunned dew on them, lips reider than the fruit,
And I filled baith my basket and my hert
                    Mony and mony a time?

And yet you mind, dear, on the bridal hill   remember
Hoo yon laich loch ootshone my een in yours,   low
Nor wi' the heather could oor bluid compete,
Nor could the ring I gi'ed you when your hand
Lay on the crucifers compare wi' them
Save for a second when the sun seized on't.
Hair of the purple of Strathendrick Hill,
Slant e'en wi' pupils like blue-stane washed wi' rain
And the whites owre white and the hunted look

1. 'Fold of sunbeams': Glendaruel is a remote glen in Argyll above Loch Fyne. In the Ulster cycle of Celtic tales, the
   beautiful Deirdre was raised in seclusion until she could be King Conchobhar's wife. But she eloped to Argyll with
   Naoise and his two brothers. They were persuaded to return to Ireland, but met treachery and tragic death.
2. Buachaille Etive Mor, the big herdsman of Glen Etive, stands at the end of Rannoch Moor, above Glen Coe and Loch
   Linnhe.
3. Woods above Langholm, MacDiarmid's home town.

Here tak' your bairn; I've cairried it lang eneuch,
Langer than maist men wad, as weel you ken.
Noo I'll pipe insteed – what tune'll you hae? –
                                  On Rudha nam Marbh.[1]

In the Children's Hospital

Does it matter? – losing your legs? …
                                  Siegfried Sassoon

Now let the legless boy show the great lady
How well he can manage his crutches.
It doesn't matter though the Sister objects,
'He's not used to them yet,' when such is
The will of the Princess. Come, Tommy,
Try a few desperate steps through the ward.
Then the hand of Royalty will pat your head
And life suddenly cease to be hard.
For a couple of legs are surely no miss
When the loss leads to such an honour as this!
One knows, when one sees how jealous the rest
Of the children are, it's been all for the best!
But would the sound of your sticks on the floor
Thundered in her skull for evermore!

The Skeleton of the Future

At Lenin's Tomb
Red granite and black diorite, with the blue
Of the labradorite crystals gleaming like precious stones
In the light reflected from the snow; and behind them
The eternal lightning of Lenin's bones.

The Seamless Garment[2]

Whene'er the mist which stands 'twixt God and thee
Defecates to a pure transparency
                                  Coleridge[3]

You are a cousin of mine
    Here in the mill,[4]

---

1. 'The Point of the Dead'.
2. Roman soldiers diced for Christ's garment, a cloth 'without seam', at the foot of the cross. It has come to symbolise the coherence and purity of His life.
3. Coleridge's little poem 'Reason' concludes the text of his book *On the Constitution of the Church and State* (1830). The remaining lines read 'That intercepts no light and adds no stain,/There Reason is, and then begins her reign!'
4. Reid and Taylor's woollen mill in Langholm.

It's queer that born in the Langholm
    It's no' until
Juist noo I see what it means
To work in the mill like my freen's.

I was tryin' to say something
    In a recent poem
Aboot Lenin. You've read a guid lot
    In the news – but ken the less o'm?
Look, Wullie, here is his secret noo
In a way I can share it wi' you.

His secret and the secret o' a'
    That's worth ocht.   *anything*
The shuttles fleein' owre quick for my een
    Prompt the thocht,
And the coordination atween
       Weaver and machine.

The haill shop's dumfoonderin'
    To a stranger like me.
Second nature to you; you're perfectly able
    To think, speak and see
Apairt frae the looms, tho' to some
That doesna sae easily come.

Lenin was like that wi' workin' class life
    At hame wi't a'.   *with it all*
His fause movements couldna been fewer
    The best weaver Earth ever saw
A' he'd to dae wi' moved intact
       Clean, clear, and exact.

A poet like Rilke did the same
    In a different sphere,
Made a single reality – a' a'e 'oo' –   *all one wool*
    O' his love and pity and fear;
A seamless garment o' music and thought
But you're owre thrang wi' puirer to tak' tent o't.   *too busy with poverty to pay attention*

What's life or God or what you may ca't
    But something at ane like this?
Can you divide yoursel' frae your breath
    Or – if you say yes –
Frae your mind that as in the case
O' the loom keeps that in its place?

Empty vessels mak' the maist noise
        As weel you ken.
Still waters rin deep, owre fu' for soond.
        It's the same wi' men.
Belts fleein', wheels birlin' – a river in flood,
Fu' flow and tension o' poo'er and blood.

Are you equal to life as to the loom?
        Turnin' oot shoddy or what?   rough cloth
Claith better than man? D'ye live to the full,
        Your poo'er's a' deliverly taught?   deliberately
Or scamp a'thing else? Border claith's famous.   skimp
Shall things o' mair consequence shame us?

Lenin and Rilke baith gied still mair skill,
        Coopers o' Stobo,¹ to a greater concern   Barrel-makers
Than you devote to claith in the mill.
        Wad it be ill to learn   too hard
To keep a bit eye on their looms as weel
And no' be hailly ta'en up wi' your 'tweel'?   twill, a strong cross-woven cloth

The womenfolk ken what I mean.
        Things maun fit like a glove,   must
Come clean off the spoon – and syne   then
        There's time for life and love.
The mair we mak' natural as breathin' the mair
Energy for ither things we'll can spare,
        But as lang as we bide like this   remain
Neist to naething we ha'e, or miss.

Want to gang back to the handloom days?
        Nae fear!
Or paintin' oor hides? Hoo d'ye think we've got
        Frae there to here?
We'd get a million times faurer still   further
If maist folk change profits didna leav't till
A wheen here and there to bring it aboot   few
– Aye, and hindered no' helped to boot.

Are you helpin'? Machinery's improved, but folk?
        Is't no' high time
We were tryin' to come into line a' roon?
        (I canna think o' a rhyme.)
Machinery in a week mak's greater advances
Than Man's nature twixt Adam and this.

1. A local expression from the Tweedside town, meaning 'the best at their trade' (any trade).

Hundreds to the inch the threids lie in,
    Like the men in a communist cell.
There's a play o' licht frae the factory windas.
    Could you no' mak' mair yoursel'?
Mony a loom mair alive than the weaver seems
For the sun's still nearer than Rilke's dreams.

Ailie Bally's tongue's keepin' time
    To the vibration a' richt.
Clear through the maze your een signal to Jean
    What's for naebody else's sicht
Short skirts, silk stockin's – fegs, hoo the auld   faith
Emmle-deugs o' the past are curjute and devauld!   rags; swept away; ended

And as for me in my fricative work   delicate friction of the breath
    I ken fu' weel
Sic an integrity's what I maun ha'e,
    Indivisible, real,
Woven owre close for the point o' a pin
        Onywhere to win in.

The Glass of Pure Water

In the de-oxidation and re-oxidation of hydrogen in a single drop of water we have before us, truly, so far as force is concerned, an epitome of the whole life. ... The burning of coal to move an iron wheel differs only in detail, and not in essence, from the decomposition of a muscle to effect its own concentration.

James Hinton

We must remember that his analysis was done not intellectually, but by an immediate process of intuition; that he was able, as it were, to taste the hydrogen and oxygen in his glass of water.

Aldous Huxley (of D. H. Lawrence)

Praise of pure water is common in Gaelic poetry.

W. J. Watson: Bàrdachd Ghàidhlig

Hold a glass of pure water to the eye of the sun!
It is difficult to tell the one from the other
Save by the tiny hardly visible trembling of the water.
This is the nearest analogy to the essence of human life
Which is even more difficult to see.
Dismiss anything you can see more easily;
It is not alive – it is not worth seeing.
There is a minute indescribable difference
Between one glass of pure water and another

With slightly different chemical constituents.
The difference between one human life and another
Is no greater; colour does not colour the water;
You cannot tell a white man's life from a black man's.
But the lives of these particular slum people
I am chiefly concerned with, like the lives of all
The world's poorest, remind me less
Of a glass of water held between my eyes and the sun
– They remind me of the feeling they had
Who saw Sacco and Vanzetti[1] in the death cell
On the eve of their execution.
– One is talking to God.

I dreamt last night that I saw one of His angels
Making his centennial report to the Recording Angel
On the condition of human life.
Look at the ridge of skin between your thumb and forefinger.
Look at the delicate lines on it and how they change
– How many different things they can express –
As you move out or close in your forefinger and thumb.
And look at the changing shapes – the countless
Little gestures, little miracles of line –
Of your forefinger and thumb as you move them.
And remember how much a hand can express,
How a single slight movement of it can say more
Than millions of words – dropped hand, clenched fist,
Snapping fingers, thumb up, thumb down,
Raised in blessing, clutched in passion, begging,
Welcome, dismissal, prayer, applause,
And a million other signs, too slight, too subtle,
Too packed with meaning for words to describe,
A universal language understood by all.
And the angel's report on human life
Was the subtlest movement – just like that – and no more;
A hundred years of life on the Earth
Summed up, not a detail missed or wrongly assessed,
In that little inconceivably intricate movement.

The only communication between man and man
That says anything worth hearing
– The hidden well-water; the finger of destiny –
Moves as that water, that angel, moved.
Truth is the rarest thing and life

1. Nicola Sacco and Bartolomeo Vanzetti, Italian immigrants and political radicals in America, were arrested in 1920
   for payroll robbery and murder. The case against them was widely held to be unsound and international protests
   followed, but the appeal failed and they were electrocuted in 1927.

The gentlest, most unobtrusive movement in the world.
I cannot speak to you of the poor people of all the world
But among the people in these nearest slums I know
This infinitesimal twinkling, this delicate play
Of tiny signs that not only say more
Than all speech, but all there is to say,
All there is to say and to know and to be.
There alone I seldom find anything else,
Each in himself or herself a dramatic whole,
An 'agon'[1] whose validity is timeless.

Our duty is to free that water, to make these gestures,
To help humanity to shed all else,
All that stands between any life and the sun,
The quintessence of any life and the sun;
To still all sound save that talking to God;
To end all movements save movements like these.
India had that great opportunity centuries ago
And India lost it – and became a vast morass,
Where no water wins free; a monstrous jungle
Of useless movement; a babel
Of stupid voices, drowning the still small voice.
It is our turn now; the call is to the Celt.

This little country can overcome the whole world of wrong
As the Lacedaemonians the armies of Persia.   (the Spartans)
Cornwall – Gaeldom – must stand for the ending
Of the essential immorality of any man controlling
Any other – for the ending of all Government
Since all Government is a monopoly of violence;
For the striking of this water out of the rock of Capitalism;
For the complete emergence from the pollution and fog
With which the hellish interests of private property
In land, machinery, and credit
Have corrupted and concealed from the sun,
From the gestures of truth, from the voice of God,
Hundreds upon hundreds of millions of men,
Denied the life and liberty to which they were born
And fobbed off with a horrible travesty instead
–Self righteous, sunk in the belief that they are human,
When not a tenth of one per cent show a single gleam
Of the life that is in them under their accretions of filth.

And until that day comes every true man's place
Is to reject all else and be with the lowest,

1. A public performance or contest in rhetorical persuasion, sports or music.

The poorest – in the bottom of that deepest of wells
In which alone is truth; in which
Is truth only – truth that should shine like the sun,
With a monopoly of movement, and a sound like talking to God ...

from **The World of Words (*In Memoriam James Joyce*)**[1]

So this is what our lives have been given to find,
A language that can serve our purposes,
A marvellous lucidity, a quality of fiery aery light,
Flowing like clear water, flying like a bird,
Burning like a sunlit landscape.
Conveying with a positively Godlike assurance,
Swiftly, shiningly, exactly, what we want to convey.
This use of words, this peculiar aptness and handiness,
Adapts itself to our every mood, now pathetic, now ironic,
Now full of love, of indignation, of sensuality, of glamour, of glory,
With an inevitable richness of remembered detail
And a richness of imagery that is never cloying,
A curious and indescribable quality
Of sensual sensitiveness,
Of very light and very air itself,
– Pliant as a young hazel wand,
Certain as a gull's wings,
Lucid as a mountain stream,
Expressive as the eyes of a woman in the presence of love, –
Expressing the complex vision of everything in one,
Suffering all impressions, all experience, all doctrines
To pass through and taking what seems valuable from each.
No matter in however many directions
These essences seem to lead.

Collecting up all these essences,
These intimations coming willy-nilly from all quarters,
Into a complex conception of all things,
An intricately-cut gem-stone of a myriad facets
That is yet, miraculously, a whole;
Each of which facets serves its individual purpose
In directing the light collected from every side outwards
In a single creative ray.
With each of these many essences culled
From the vast field of life some part of one's own
Complex personality has affinity and resembles

---

1. MacDiarmid's huge poem sequence, *In Memoriam James Joyce*, contains innumerable references to other languages
   and disciplines. This 'poetry of fact' also works as a kind of collage in which passages culled from other works are
   included in the text.

When climbing on to the ice-cap a little south of Cape Bismarck[1]
And keeping the nunataks[2] of Dronning Louises Land on our left
We travel five days
On tolerable ice in good weather
With few bergs to surmount
And no crevasses to delay us.
Then suddenly our luck turns.
A wind of 120 miles an hour blows from the East,
And the plateau becomes a playground of gales
And the novel light gives us snow-blindness.
We fumble along with partially bandaged eyes
Our reindeer-skin kamiks worn into holes   parkas
And no fresh sedge-grass to stump them with.
We come on ice-fields like mammoth ploughlands
And mountainous séracs which would puzzle an Alpine climber.
That is what adventuring in dictionaries means,
All the abysses and altitudes of the mind of man,
Every test and trial of the spirit,
Among the débris of all past literature
And raw material of all the literature to be.
But all language? A glare like that of an arc-lamp,
No self-deceptions, no quaint hiding-places now,
No groove to get into where one
Can move automatically. Every instant demanding
A new concentration of one's powers,
Breaking completely with all ready-made, mechanical, conventional
      conceptions
Of the conglomerate experience of life, accepted gratefully by laziness and fear,
No shred left us in common now
With those who mistake blind eyes for balanced minds ...

Crystals Like Blood

I remember how, long ago, I found
Crystals like blood in a broken stone.

I picked up a broken chunk of bed-rock
And turned it this way and that,
It was heavier than one would have expected
From its size. One face was caked
With brown limestone. But the rest
Was a hard greenish-grey quartz-like stone
Faintly dappled with darker shadows,

1. The following 13 lines are taken (only slightly rearranged) from John Buchan's novel *A Prince of the Captivity* (1933).
2. Isolated peaks, rising through glacial ice, like islands.

And in this quartz ran veins and beads
Of bright magenta.

And I remember how later on I saw
How mercury is extracted from cinnebar
– The double ring of iron piledrivers
Like the multiple legs of a fantastically symmetrical spider
Rising and falling with monotonous precision,
Marching round in an endless circle
And pounding up and down with a tireless, thunderous force,
While, beyond, another conveyor drew the crumbled ore
From the bottom and raised it to an opening high
In the side of a gigantic grey-white kiln.

So I remember how mercury is got
When I contrast my living memory of you
And your dear body rotting here in the clay
– And feel once again released in me
The bright torrents of felicity, naturalness, and faith
My treadmill memory draws from you yet.

Milk-Wort and Bog-Cotton
To Seumas O'Sullivan

Cwa' een like milk-wort and bog-cotton hair!	Come away eyes
I love you, earth, in this mood best o' a'	
When the shy spirit like a laich wind moves	low
And frae the lift nae shadow can fa'	sky
Since there's nocht left to thraw a shadow there	nothing
Owre een like milk-wort and milk-white cotton hair.	Over
Wad that nae leaf upon anither wheeled	Would
A shadow either and nae root need dern	hide
In sacrifice to let sic beauty be!	such
But deep surroondin' darkness I discern	
Is aye the price o' licht. Wad licht revealed	always
Naething but you, and nicht nocht else concealed.	

from From the Scots Anthology[1]

i
We're a'e clan here; I micht as weel
Ha'e been a Campbell as a MacNeill.

---

1. From a sequence of epitaphs in *To Circumjack Cencrastus*. In xi the poet compares the grave to an abandoned nest, with all the world as an egg in it.

ii
Alas that life is past
Noo I'm a laird at last.   (landowner)

vii
The warld has fadit frae view
As Benbecula used to
And nae seagull follows my curragh noo.   coracle

xi
Here in this forhooied nest   abandoned
To a cauld egg I pit my breast,
And may Eternity dae the rest.
           I canna mair.

William Soutar (1898–1943)

Born in Perth, Soutar served in the Navy during the First World War, before taking a degree in English at Edinburgh University in 1923. He suffered from a progressive spinal disease which kept him at home thereafter, and from 1930 he was confined to bed. He kept diaries, journals and dream books throughout his long illness, selections from which have been published as *Diaries of a Dying Man*. He was a socialist, a pacifist and a Scottish nationalist. Convinced that cultural revival could only come by making the Scots language accessible to children, he wrote 'bairnrhymes', riddles and 'whigmaleeries' with that audience in mind, as well as songs and poems much influenced by the ballad tradition.

The Philosophic Taed

There was a taed wha thocht sae lang	toad
On sanctity and sin;	
On what was richt, and what was wrang,	
And what was in atween –	
That he gat naething dune.	done
The wind micht blaw, the snaw micht snaw,	
He didna mind a wheet;	whit
Nor kent the derk'nin frae the daw,	dawn
The wulfire frae the weet;	lightning; rain
Nor fuggage frae his feet.	rough grass
His wife and weans frae time to time,	children
As they gaed by the cratur,	went
Wud haut to hae a gowk at him	would halt; gape
And shak their pows, or natter:	heads
'He's no like growing better.'	not really
It maun be twenty year or mair	must
Sin thocht's been a' his trade:	since
And naebody can tell for shair	sure
Whether this unco taed	unusual
Is dead, or thinks he's dead.	

King Worm

What care I for kirk or state?   church
What care I for war's alarm?
A' are beggars at my yett: All; gate
I am King Worm.

The Hurdy-Gurdy Man[1]

The hurdy-gurdy man gangs by
And dings a sang on the stany air;   beats; stony
The weather-cocks begin to craw,
Flap their feathers, and flee awa;
Houses fa' sindry wi' the soun'   in pieces
The hale o' the city is murlin' doun.   crumbling
Come out! come out! wha wudna steer   stir/move
(Nane but the deid cud bide alane)   could stay
The habbie-horses reenge in a ring   hobby-horses clatter
Birlin' roun' wi' a wudden fling   Whirling; wooden
Whaur the grass fleurs frae the causey-stane: flowers; cobblestone
And cantl'd asclent the blue o' space,   tilted aslant
Far abune a' the soundin' fair,   above
A swing gaes up into the licht
And I see your face wi' yon look, aye there,   that; still
That swither'd atween joy and fricht.   wavered; fright

Song

Whaur yon broken brig hings owre;   bridge hangs over
Whaur yon water maks nae soun';   that
Babylon blaws by in stour: dust
Gang doun wi' a sang, gang doun.

Deep, owre deep, for onie drouth: too deep; any thirst
Wan eneuch an ye wud droun: Little enough; drown
Saut, or seelfu', for the mouth;   Salt; pleasant
Gang doun wi' a sang, gang doun.

Babylon blaws by in stour
Whaur yon water maks nae soun':
Darkness is your only door;
Gang doun wi' a sang, gang doun.

1. A street musician with a barrel-organ, perhaps heralding a fair or carnival.

The Tryst   Assignation/meeting

O luely, luely cam she in   softly
And luely she lay doun:
I kent her be her caller lips   cool
And her breists sae sma' and roun'.

A' thru the nicht we spak nae word
Nor sinder'd bane frae bane: parted bone
A' thru the nicht I heard her hert
Gang soundin' wi' my ain.

It was about the waukrife hour   wakeful
Whan cocks begin to craw
That she smool'd saftly thru the mirk   slipped away; darkness
Afore the day wud daw.   would dawn

Sae luely, luely, cam she in
Sae luely was she gaen   gone
And wi' her a' my simmer days   summer
Like they had never been.

Lealness   Loyal friendship

Whan a dead man and a dead man meet
Ilka ane cries *Brither!*   each one
They see in the earth o' hands and feet
Their faither and their mither.

They see in the bare bane and bare bane   bare bone
Their faither and their mither:
In their laneliness nae mair alane
Ilka ane cries *Brither!*

They ken, whan loss and a' loss is owre,   know; all loss; over
That they are ane anither: one another
Their stour forgethers and frae their stour   dust assembles
Ilka ane cries *Brither!*

George Bruce (1909–)

Bruce's early poetry echoed the terseness and the austerity which was characteristic of the fishing communities of Fraserburgh, where he was born and brought up on the harsh North-East coast. He worked for many years as a talks producer for the BBC, and his later poetry shows a wittier and more relaxed side to his muse, with a sense of spiritual optimism.

Inheritance

This which I write now
Was written years ago
Before my birth
In the features of my father.

It was stamped
In the rock formations
West of my hometown.
Not I write,

But, perhaps William Bruce,
Cooper.
Perhaps here his hand
Well articled in his trade.

Then though my words
Hit out
An ebullition from
City or flower,

There not my faith,
These the paint
Smeared upon
The inarticulate,

The salt crusted sea-boot,
The red-eyed mackerel,
The plate shining with herring,
And many men,

Seamen and craftsmen and curers,
And behind them
The protest of hundreds of years,
The sea obstinate against the land.

The Curtain

Half way up the stairs
Is the tall curtain.
We noticed it there
After the unfinished tale.

My father came home,
His clothes sea-wet,
His breath cold.
He said a boat had gone.

He held a lantern.
The mist moved in,
Rested on the stone step
And hung above the floor.

I remembered
The blue glint
Of the herring scales
Fixed in the mat,

And also a foolish crab
That held his own pincers fast.
We called him
Old Iron-clad.

I smelt again
The kippers cooked in oak ash.
That helped me to forget
The tall curtain.

Elizabeth Polishing an Agate

My love, you are pulled into a stone.
The skies run into night,
the stone stars are there.
In this lost momentary world
you treasure stone under your hand,
seek out what is most unlike,
smoothing stone like glass

till its fixed hair lines,
finer than Leonardo's line,
mirror stone's permanence.
There are no seasons in a stone.
Lode star it draws you,
you giving your brief warmth
to stone.
Gone, it stays cold.

Why the Poet Makes Poems

(written to my dentist, Dr K P Durkacz
to explain why I failed to keep an appointment)

When it's all done and said
whether he is smithing away by the mad sea,
or, according to repute, silvering them in a garret
by moonlight, or in plush with a gold nib,
or plain bourgeois in a safe bungalow with a mortgage,
or in a place with a name, Paris, Warsaw, Edinburgh,
or sitting with his heart in the Highlands,
or taking time off at the office to pen a few words,
the whole business is a hang-over from the men in the trees,
when thunder and sun and quake and peas in a pod
were magic, and still is according to *his* book, admitting
botany is OK for the exposition of how the buds got there,
geology for how the rocks got just like that,
zoology for the how of the animals,
biology for us kind – but that's not his game:
he's after the lion playing around with the lamb for fun.
He doesn't want to know the how, the why. It's enough for him to say:
That's what's going on. The grass is jumping for joy,
and all the little fishes are laughing their heads off.'

Robert Garioch (1909–1981)

Born and educated in Edinburgh, Robert Garioch Sutherland graduated from university and worked as a schoolteacher in the capital for most of his life. He was captured in the North African desert campaign, and described his experiences in *Two Men and a Blanket*. Determined to write poetry in what he called 'artisan Scots', his first publication was a booklet shared with Sorley MacLean, *17 Poems for 6d* (1940), but he did not become well known until the 1960s. He translated a number of works into Scots, including two Latin tragedies by George Buchanan (*Jepthah* and *The Baptist*), poems by Apollinaire, and numerous sonnets from the nineteenth-century Roman dialect of Giuseppe Belli.

During a Music Festival

Cantie in seaside simmer on the dunes,	Cheerful; summer
I fling awa my dowp of cigarette	butt
whaur bairns hae biggit castles out of sand	built
and watch the reik rise frae the parapet.	smoke
Suddenlike I am back in Libya;	
yon's the escarpment, and a bleizan plane,	
the wee white speck that feeds the luift wi reik,	sky; smoke
dirkins a horror-pictur on my brain.	darkens
And aye the reik bleeds frae the warld's rim	still
as it has duin frae Babylon and Troy,	
London, Bonn, Edinbro, time eftir time.	
And great Beethoven sang a Hymn to Joy.	

Brither Worm

I saw a lang worm snoove throu the space atween twa stanes,	slip
pokin his heid, if he had yin, up throu a hole in the New Toun,[1]	
up throu a crack ye wad hardly hae seen, in an area of stane,	
unkenn'd uplifted tons of mason-wark piled on the soil,	unknown
wi causey-streets, biggit of granite setts, like blank waas flat on the grund,	cobbled;
plainstane pavements of Thurso slabs laid owre the stane-aircht cellars,	/built; walls

1. The New Town of Edinburgh, a civic masterpiece of 18th-century town planning and neo-classical architecture.

the area[1] fifteen feet doun, wi weill-jyned flagstanes, Regency wark. *well-joined*

Nou, in my deeded stane-and-lime property, awntert a nesh and perfect worm.

I was abaysit wi thochts of what was gaun-on ablow my feet, */ventured; delicate*

that the feued and rented grund was the soil of the naitural Drumsheuch Forest,

and that life gaed on thair in yon soil, and had sent out a spy,

thinkin some Friend of the Worms had slockent them with a shoure, *moistened*
  whan I on

my side of the crust had teemit twa-three pails of water, meaning to scrub *emptied*

the place doun wi a besom I had jist bocht. *broom*

Sae a saft, soupple and delicate, pink and naukit craitur

neatly wan out frae atween thae dressed, weill-laid, unnaitural stanes. *escaped from*

I watched, and thocht lang of the ferlies of Naitur; I didna muve; *marvels*

I thocht of the deeps of the soil, deeper nor the sea. I made nae sound.

A rat raxt frae a crack atween twa stanes. *stretched*

I shuik wi sudden grue. He leukit at me, and wes gane. *shiver*

Ane Offering for Easter

Reading a sonnet by Giuseppe Belli,[2]
ye come across, preserv'd in rhyme, some hammy,
lang, thick and phallic Eastertide salami,
regeneration-symbols, sae they tell ye

in a fitt-note, sprecklit inside wi yelly
fat-gobbets, oozy in the sunshine, clammy
(I mind yon fourteen-inchers in Chiami)
wi draps of sweit, suety and smelly.

Nou shairly we wyce folk of Oddanbeery, *savvy; (Edinburgh)*
no in the habit, certainly, of haudin Easter,
the way they dae in Rome, are learie *quick to learn*

eneuch to find our counterpairt. A sudden
thocht has occurred to your auld makar, Garioch:[3]
let's venerate a hame-made mealie-pudden.

Glisk of the Great

I saw him comin out the N.B. Grill, *(North British Hotel, Princes St.)*
creashy and winey, wi his famous voice *greasy*
crackin some comic bawr to please three choice *joke*
notorious bailies, lauchan fit to kill.

Syne thae fowre crousie cronies clam intill *chummy*
a muckle big municipal Rolls-Royce,

1. Tiny sunken courtyard giving access to the basement of a terraced house.
2. 1791–1864, satirical dialect poet from Rome, some of whose many *Roman Sonnets* have been translated by Garioch.
3. 'Garioch' rhymes with 'dearie' in north-east dialect.

and disappeared, aye lauchan, wi a noise
that droont the traffic, towards the Calton Hill.

    As they rade by, it seemed the sun was shinin
brichter nor usual roun thae cantie three   cheerful
that wi thon weill-kent Heid-yin had been dinin.

    Nou that's the kinna thing I like to see;
tho ye and I look on and canna jyne in,   join
it gies our toun some tone, ye'll aa agree.

Heard in the Cougate

    'Whu's aw thae fflag-poles ffur in Princes Street?
Chwoich! Ptt! Hechyuch! Ab-boannie cairry-on.
Seez-owre the wa'er. Whu' the deevil's thon   Pass; water
inaidie, heh?' 'The Queen's t'meet   in aid of

    The King o Norway wi his royal suite.'
'His royal wh'?' 'The hale jing-bang. It's aw in
the papur. Whaur's ma speck-sh? Aye they're gaun
t' day-cor-ate the toun. It's a fair treat,

    something ye dinnae see jist ivry day,
foun'uns in the Gairdens, muckle spates   (Princes St. Gardens) floods
dancing t'music, an thir's t'be nae

    chairge t'gi'in, it aw gaes on the Rates.'   to go in
'Ah ddae-ken whu' the pplace is comin tae   don't know
wi aw thae, hechyuch! fforeign po'entates.'

Heard in the Gairdens

    Wad ye believe it? Eftir thretty year
of steidy wark at twal-pund-ten a week,
on aiverage, that is, I'm up the creek
without a paiddle, got the sack. It's queer

    to gang about lowse: Sinday brings nae fear   free, unburdened
of the morn's morn; nae gaffer, boss nor beak   foreman; headmaster
can touch me ferder. Up in lowe and reik   flame and smoke
gaes my auld siller-howkan masquin-gear.   money-earning disguise

    It's true, I'm telln ye, I hae got my caird
and here it is, aa stamped, my title-deed
til fredome, prievan me the richtfu laird   proving

of my ain life at last: here's the remeid   remedy
for Adam's curse. And nou I drop my guaird,   (work)
bide still in my ain neuk, lift up my heid.   Stay; corner

Lesson

I tuik it in ma heid to gae dounbye Leith Docks,   (the Port of Edinburgh)
eftir hou monie years? I cannae mind,
binna jist coming aff the ship frae Aiberdeen,   except
Saint Sunniva? Thae boats haena made that run for years.

I tuik the samyn gait that Stevenson discryved.   same route; described

I yuistae like ships, but nou they're owre real for me.   used to; too

The samyn gait as he's, binna five-hunner yairds   except for
frae here to Heriot Row; his faither's lichthous tiles[1]
are in his area yet, in some of his neibors' alsweill.

Leith wes a place for merchants, a century sinsyne,   ago
wi weill-appyntit pubs whaur they cuid talk business,
carved wudden alcoves, tables, ye ken the kind of thing,
and I mind the time whan they still had that character about them,
whisky and port and buirdly men wi confident heids.   sturdy
Leith crined in Embro's grup; Scotland in England's;   shrunk/shrivelled
Britain in …? Aweill, Leith's maistly rubble nou.

Stevenson likit ships, he says, while yet a bairn,
and he likit the walk to Leith, past yon stationer's shop,
aye thair yet and whiles wi a theatre in its windae.[2]
While a bairn masel I didnae heed whit ma faither said about ships;
breakwaters and lichthouses wadnae be aa that real to Stevenson.

The Forth Brig is riveted wi plates like a ship yuistae be.
It isnae real to me, even to this day.
The side of a ship in a dry dock is a flegsom thing.   frightening
Hou can a man spend his day near eneuch it to touch?
It wes the bottoms of ships that scunnert ma faither as a laddie,   disgusted
sae he wad aften tell me, the raws of rivet-heids
to be pentit wi red-leid, nae holidays oniewhaur,
the edges of plates hammert ticht wi the caulking-airn,
water ablow his plank, weit waas baith sides of him,   beneath
and the ship's bottom abuin his heid, *le rouge et le noir.*[3]

1. Robert Louis Stevenson's father was a harbour engineer and lighthouse builder, like his father before him.
2. A toy cut-out theatre: see Stevenson's essay, 'A Penny Plain and Two Pence Coloured' (1883).
3. *The Red and the Black*: the title of a novel by Stendhal, referring to the military and the Church. Also the colours of anarchism.

He wes learning nicht-schuil French and takkin an art-schuil cless.
He wad tell me aa this in the Twenties, on a Sunday fresh-air walk
to the end of the West Pier, as guid as a sail, cost naethin.

Sae here I wes, last week, aince mair at the famous corner,
wi Burns's statue, lately Moved On at enormous expense,
Constitution Street, Bernard Street, wi Commercial Street ayont the brig,   beyond
braw, confident names, like the muckle heids of the merchants
snod in their carved alcoves, c.i.f. and f.o.b.,[1]   neat
and Baltic Street aye thair, but whaur's the Baltic tred?
Whaur the Leith merchants? Whaur the tables and cushions?
This is the place aa richt; has memory gane wrang?
Nae sawdust on the flair, tho, jist guid Leith stour.   dust

It's yin of thae near-island pubs, whaur ye glowre at the folk fornenst ye   opposite
owre a neutral space of sinks and glesses and pourin and splairgin.   splashing
I tilt ma pint and a heavy swell rises throu the freith.   froth

Stevenson's faither, he tells us, suffered ae major defeat;
He cuidnae mak Wick Hairbour siccar. This ae failure   secure
is a meisure of the sea's virr he owrecam aawhair else.   energy
Stevenson felt this, maybe later in life,
haean walit by that time words insteid of stanes.   chosen
They were trying a new idea, the last time I saw Wick,
piling concrete calthrops[2] in the newest hole in the waa.   (angular blocks)
Meantime I hadnae noticed something byordnar gaun on,   special
aabody luikan ae airt, at naething that I cuid see.   in one direction
A scrauchin and duntin and yowlin, full blast, wi nae warning,
stertit up at the end of the room, frae a lit-up gless case
switched on, it wad seem, by a lassie in a see-throu pink gounie,
yin of thae go-go girls that I hae heard tell about.
Aweil, she wes nae gret dancer, but bonnie and clean,
and her taes gaed neatly eneuch owre yon dirt-coloured flair,
the same that we strampit about on, in shoon or working-buitts.   shoes
But this wee dance wes just whit ye micht cry an eye-opener.   call
She disappeart ahint the Gents, til some cubby-hole of her ain,
syne cam back in a kinna bathing-suit, aa ticht and trig,   neat
and danced maist eydently up and doun, clawing the air,   eagerly
perfectly douce and assured, as tho she cuid dae it aa nicht,   sweet
like Tchaikowsky whan stumpt for ideas, makkan-dae wi passage-wark.
Syne, for a bit of a cheenge, she gaed roun the bar's peninsula
by whit passage-wey there wes, neatly wan throu.   navigated
The folk lookit on calmly, wi interest, respect and pleisor,

1. Cost/insurance/freight; free/on/board.
2. Lit.: star-shaped iron spikes to be scattered against medieval cavalry.

tho wi the faces of men, had luikit aa day at the side of a ship,
as yon lassie's clean taes acceptit the ordinary stourie flair.

Guillaume Apollinaire,[1] wad ye hae gliskit here
a phantom of Leith haar? Duis it still glimmer thair?   sea-mist

The Big Music   (Gaelic: Cèol Mòr: pibroch)

Victoria Street in London, the place gaes wi the name,
a Hanoverian drill haa, near Buckingham Palace,
near the cross-Channel trains, Edinburgh coaches,
Army and Navy Stores, an ex-abbey, a cathedral,
near the Crazy Gang, the 'Windsor,' Artillery Mansions,
no faur, owre the water, frae the Lambeth Walk,
near the exotic kirk-spire carved wi the Stars and Stripes,
disappointed nou, a frustum, whangit wi a boomb.   broken portion
This great Victorian drill-haa is naethin like Scotland,
binna the unco hicht and vastness of the place.   apart from; unusual
The judges jouk into their tent; the piper treads the tarmac.   duck
His gear lemes in the sunlicht of hunner-and-fifty-watt suns,   gleams
while we in the crowd luik on, MacAdams and Watts wi the lave.   rest
Skinklan and pairticoloured, the piper blaws life in his wind-bag,   Sparkling
aefald, ilka pairt in keeping, the man, his claes and the pipes,
in keeping wi this place, as tho he stuid in Raasay,
Alaska, India, Edinburgh Castle, of coorse, for that maitter,
like a traivler I met in the rain on the Cauld Stane Slap,[2] and him dry;
like the Big Rowtan Pipe itsel, that can mak its ain conditions,   bellowing
as the blaw-torch brenns under water in its ain oxygen-bell,   burns
like the welder's argon island, blawn in the thick of the air,
sae the piper blaws his ain warld, and tunes it in three octaves,
a steil tone grund on the stane, and shairpit on the ile-stane,
like a raisit deil, mair inexorable nor onie ither music,   raised (conjured)
for the piper cannae maister this deevil of the reeds,
binna to wirry him aathegither, and brek the spell.   except
Nou, jaggit as levin, a flash of notes frae the chanter   lightning
slaps throu the unisoun, and tines itsel in the drones,   loses
no jist richtlie in tune; the snell snarl dirls wi a beat,   bitter; vibrates
sae the piper eases the jynts of the drones, and tries again,
and again, and again, he fettles the quirks of his fykie engine,   puts right; fussy
flings the fireflaucht of melody, tined an octave abuin the drones,   lightning
bass drone and twa tenor drones geynear in tune on A,   nearly
wi a michtie strang harmonic bummlan awa on E,   humming
that the piper is ettlan to lock deid-richt in tune wi the chanter,   trying
for the pipes are a gey primitive perfected instrument,

1. French modernist poet. See 'Un fantôme de nuées' in *Calligrammes*, translated by Garioch as 'A Phantom of Haar'.
2. Pass in the Pentland Hills above Edinburgh.

that can fail a fine piper whiles, as his art may fail,
tho it warks in the tradition of the MacKays of Raasay,
guairdit throu generations of teachers and learners and teachers,
and thon piper staunds forenenst us, skeelie in mind and body,   *opposite; skilful*
wi the sowl, a mystery greater nor mind and body thegither,
that kythes itsel by virr of its presence or absence in music.   *reveals; energy*
Yet piper or pipes may fail, whan the piper wad be at his best,
ane of his reeds no jist richt, ae finger no swipper or souple,   *nimble*
the strang rule of the will may falter, and tine the rhythm;
for aa that, comes the time whan the mind, body and sowl
and the reeds, the fowreteen sections, the sheepskin wind-bag
seasoned inside wi honey, or wi some patent concoction,
whan the piper and pipes in sympathy ken that the nicht is the nicht,
as Smooth John MacNab bragged on a very different occasion,[1]
sae the piper, his pipes, judges, the warld at lairge
aa gree, yince, for a wunner, that a piobaireachd is pleyd richt.   *agree*
Nae artist wad hae his medium onie itherweys ordert.
And aa this time my thocht gaes wannerin its lane,   *on its own*
in a three-octave chaos naukit binna its ain harmonics,
a state whaur aa things are possible, and naethin luiks very likely.
Doctor Johnson likit the pipes, we're aye tellt, because he wes deif;
for my pairt, I think, like the Shah, wha likit the first tune best,[2]
he kennd music whan he heard it, whan it garred his nervestrings dirl.   *made*
I mind, yince, masel, I mainaged near eneuch the great drone
to hear a gey guid-gaun piobaireachd, aye, and to smell it anaa:
I cuidnae mak up my mind, wes it Dufftown or The Glen Garioch?
I jalousit a Nor-east maut guffan out, maist musical.   *suspected; malt (whisky)*

Nou, huge, in tune, our stane-and-airn glen   *stone and iron*
dirls three octaves, A in unisoun.   *vibrates/rings*
Straunge hou this music has nae begin or end;
even the tuning, tho nae pairt of the tune,
langs to the music, as duis the tune itsel,   *belongs*
sae that the *urlar*,[3] grund of the hale thing,
taks place insensibly as daith or life.
Pacing fu slawlie, wi steidie meisured mairch,
the piper blaws the lang bare notes of his lament,
a tune that bides lang jist twa steps frae the tap   *stays*
of the chanter's compass, sae heich that it maun faa,
no faur; it rises, syne faas ferder, in dool,   *further; sorrow*
lifts its heid twice: the cadence ends the tune.
The slaw, waesom melody, returning owre and owre,
wi smaa, clever cheenges, that keep our senses keen,

1. On a stealthy raid of the castle on Loch Dochart in 1644.
2. An Eastern ruler is supposed to have preferred the orchestra tuning up (an apochryphal story).
3. The *ground*, the basic musical theme of a pibroch, elaborated in successively more complex variations, until the tune
   returns to its beginning and ends there.

the cadence eith-kennd, airtan aathin in time,   *easily-known; guiding*
comes like sad nicht, that ends ilk dowie day.   *each dismal*
The piper hauds on, wi the siccarness of doom,   *certainty*
fowre centuries of culture ruggan at his hairt   *tugging*
like the michtie pressure tearing throu his reeds,
hauds on til his time, wi the richtness of art,
that is no semplie richt, but we feel that it is richt.
The theme birls slawlie, and aye as it wins roun,
the neist variorum adds on its ain device,
mair short notes and mair, that garr the dirgie daunce;   *make the dirge*
the aureat lament lowes mair and mair wi pride,   *burns*
till there is nae note, but loups it wi the lave,   *jumps; rest*
tho, wi the music loupin, the piper nou staunds still.
Here comes the unco ferlie of the pipes,   *special marvel*
the first of the grace-notes, like a precious stane,
gale-force music, delicately ruled,
a thrawn, strang Clydesdale; the horseman kens the word.[1]
Allanerlie the great Hieland pipe can mak this soun,   *Only*
this rattle of reedy noise, the owretones brattlan thegither, *clattering*
wi maybe a swirlan danger, like musardrie of maut. *whisky dreams*
Piobaireachd adorns tragedy wi maist sensie jewels.   *pithy*
Men, dour as quartz, responsive as quartz to licht,
mak this shairp intellectual and passionat music,
dangerous, maist dangerous, and naethin moderat,
florischan in the warld, a dauntless form of life.

The piobaireachd comes til an end, gin we may cry it end,
the grund naukit again, as tho it had aye been sae.   *naked*
Gin it werenae a competition, wi international rules,   *If*
there seems nae reason why it suidnae stert owre again,
gin the piper has braith eneuch, and there's nae dout about that,
but he neatly thraws the thrapple of the deil in his pipes, *wrings the neck*
that dees decently, wi nae unseemly scrauch.   *dies; screech*
He taks leave of us wi dignity, turns, and is gane.
The judges rate him heich, but no in the first three.

At Robert Fergusson's Grave
October 1962

 Canongait kirkyaird in the failing year
is auld and grey, the wee roseirs are bare,   *rose-bushes*
five gulls leam white agin the dirty air: *gleam; against*
why are they here? There's naething for them here.

---

1. A secret word of power, said to control horses.

Why are we here oursels? We gaither near
the grave. Fergusons mainly, quite a fair
turn-out, respectfu, ill at ease, we stare
at daith – there's an address – I canna hear.

Aweill, we staund bareheidit in the haar,   mist
murnin a man that gaed back til the pool
twa-hunner year afore our time. The glaur   mud

that haps his banes glowres back. Strang, present dool   wraps; scowls; grief
ruggs at my hairt. Lichtlie this gin ye daur: tugs; Mock; if you dare
here Robert Burns knelt and kissed the mool.   clods of earth

Norman MacCaig (1910–   )

Born and educated in Edinburgh, MacCaig has lived and worked in the city all his life, spending each summer in the far North-West, near Lochinver in Sutherland. Conscious of his classical training and his Gaelic roots (his mother came from Scalpay, Harris), he has celebrated the natural world in many collections of poetry which reveal a wry, metaphysically witty and sometimes bleak response to existence, always tempered by a subtle sense of surprise or strangeness at what is to be discovered in the world and in language itself.

Summer Farm

Straws like tame lightnings lie about the grass
And hang zigzag on hedges. Green as glass
The water in the horse-trough shines.
Nine ducks go wobbling by in two straight lines.

A hen stares at nothing with one eye,
Then picks it up. Out of an empty sky
A swallow falls and, flickering through
The barn, dives up again into the dizzy blue.

I lie, not thinking, in the cool, soft grass,
Afraid of where a thought might take me –
This grasshopper with plated face
Unfolds his legs and finds himself in space.

Self under self, a pile of selves I stand
Threaded on time, and with metaphysic hand
Lift the farm like a lid and see
Farm within farm, and in the centre, me.

Still Life

Three apples, if they are apples, and a jug,
A lemon (certain), grapes, a fish's tail,
A melting fruitdish and a randy table:
Squared off from other existences they struggle

Into a peace, a balancing of such power
As past and future use in being Now.

Still life, they call it – like a bursting bomb
That keeps on bursting, one burst, on and on:
A new existence, continually being born,
Emerging out of white into the sombre
Garishness of the spectrum, refusing the easy,
Clenching its strength on nothing but how to be.

Nice lesson for a narrative or for
A thing made emblem – that martyrs in their fire,
Christs on their crosses, fetes and massacres,
When purified of their small history,
Cannot surpass, no matter how they struggle,
Three apples (more than likely) and a jug.

Interruption to a Journey

The hare we had run over
bounced about the road
on the springing curve
of its spine.

Cornfields breathed in the darkness.
We were going through the darkness and
the breathing cornfields from one
important place to another.

We broke the hare's neck
and made that place, for a moment,
the most important place there was,
where a bowstring was cut
and a bow broken for ever
that had shot itself through so many
darknesses and cornfields.

It was left in that landscape.
It left us in another.

Assisi

The dwarf with his hands on backwards
sat, slumped like a half-filled sack
on tiny twisted legs from which
sawdust might run,

outside the three tiers of churches built
in honour of St Francis, brother
of the poor, talker with birds, over whom
he had the advantage
of not being dead yet.

A priest explained
how clever it was of Giotto
to make his frescoes tell stories
that would reveal to the illiterate the goodness
of God and the suffering of His Son. I understood
the explanation and
the cleverness.

A rush of tourists, clucking contentedly,
fluttered after him as he scattered
the grain of the Word. It was they who had passed
the ruined temple outside, whose eyes
wept pus, whose back was higher
than his head, whose lopsided mouth
said *Grazie* in a voice as sweet
as a child's when she speaks to her mother
or a bird's when it spoke
to St Francis.

Aunt Julia

Aunt Julia spoke Gaelic
very loud and very fast.
I could not answer her –
I could not understand her.

She wore men's boots
when she wore any.
– I can see her strong foot,
stained with peat,
paddling with the treadle of the spinningwheel
while her right hand drew yarn
marvellously out of the air.

Hers was the only house
where I've lain at night
in the absolute darkness
of a box bed,[1] listening to
crickets being friendly.

1. Bed set into an enclosed recess in the wall of the living room in old cottages or houses.

She was buckets
and water flouncing into them.
She was winds pouring wetly
round house-ends.
She was brown eggs, black skirts
and a keeper of threepennybits
in a teapot.

Aunt Julia spoke Gaelic
very loud and very fast.
By the time I had learned
a little, she lay
silenced in the absolute black
of a sandy grave
at Luskentyre.
But I hear her still, welcoming me
with a seagull's voice
across a hundred yards
of peatscrapes and lazybeds[1]
and getting angry, getting angry
with so many questions unanswered.

Return to Scalpay[2]

The ferry wades across the kyle. I drive
The car ashore
On to a trim tarred road. A car on Scalpay?
Yes, and a road where never was one before.
The ferrymen's Gaelic wonders who I am
(Not knowing I know it), this man back from the dead,
Who takes the blue-black road (no traffic jam)
From by Craig Lexie over to Bay Head.

A man bows in the North wind, shaping up
His lazybeds,   (old style strip cultivation)
And through the salt air vagrant peat smells waver
From houses where no house should be. The sheds
At the curing station have been newly tarred.
Aunt Julia's house has vanished. The Red Well
Has been bulldozed away. But sharp and hard
The church still stands, barring the road to Hell.

A chugging prawn boat slides round Cuddy Point
Where in a gale

1. Peat cuttings and raised strips of cultivation in the old Highland style.
2. Off Harris in the Outer Hebrides.

I spread my batwing jacket and jumped farther
Than I've jumped since. There's where I used to sail
Boats looped from rushes. On the jetty there
I caught eels, cut their heads off and watched them slew
Slow through the water. Ah – Cape Finisterre
I called that point, to show how much I knew.

While Hamish sketches, a crofter tells me that
The Scalpay folk,
Though very intelligent, are not Spinozas …
We walk the Out End road (no need to invoke
That troublemaker, Memory, she's everywhere)
To Laggandoan, greeted all the way –
My city eyeballs prickle; it's hard to bear
With such affection and such gaiety.

Scalpay revisited? – more than Scalpay. I
Have no defence,
For half my thought and half my blood is Scalpay,
Against that pure, hardheaded innocence
That shows love without shame, weeps without shame,
Whose every thought is hospitality –
Edinburgh, Edinburgh, you're dark years away.

Scuttering snowflakes riddling the hard wind
Are almost spent
When we reach Johann's house. She fills the doorway,
Sixty years of size and astonishment,
Then laughs and cries and laughs, as she always did
And will (Easy glum, easy glow, a friend would say) …
Scones, oatcakes, herrings from under a bubbling lid.
Then she comes with us to put us on our way.

Hugging my arm in her stronger one, she says,
Fancy me
Walking this road beside my darling Norman!
And what is there to say? … We look back and see
Her monumental against the flying sky
And I am filled with love and praise and shame
Knowing that I have been, and knowing why,
Diminished and enlarged. Are they the same?

Two Thieves

At the Place for Pulling up Boats
(one word in Gaelic) the tide is full.

It seeps over the grass, stealthy as a robber.
Which it is.

– For old Flora tells me
that fifty yards stretch of gravel, now under water,
was, in her granny's time, a smooth green sward
where the Duke of Sutherland
turned his coach and four.

What an image of richness, a tiny pageantry
in this small dying place
whose every house is now lived in
by the sad widow of a fine strong man.

There were fine strong men in the Duke's time.
He drove them to the shore, he drove them
to Canada. He gave no friendly thought to them
as he turned his coach and four
on the sweet green sward
by the Place for Pulling up Boats
where no boats are.

Ringed Plover by a Water's Edge

They sprint eight feet and –
stop. Like that. They
sprintayard (like that) and
stop.

They have no acceleration
and no brakes.
Top speed's their only one.

They're alive – put life
through a burning-glass, they're
its focus – but they share
the world of delicate clockwork.

In spasmodic
Indian file
they parallel the parallel ripples.

When they stop
they, suddenly,
are gravel.

Toad

Stop looking like a purse. How could a purse
squeeze under the rickety door and sit,
full of satisfaction, in a man's house?

You clamber towards me on your four corners –
right hand, left foot, left hand, right foot.

I love you for being a toad,
for crawling like a Japanese wrestler,
and for not being frightened.

I put you in my purse hand, not shutting it,
and set you down outside directly under
every star.

A jewel in your head? Toad,
you've put one in mine,
a tiny radiance in a dark place.

Angus's Dog

Black collie, do you remember yourself?

Do you remember your name was Mephistopheles,
though (as if you were only a little devil)
everyone called you Meph?

You'd chase everything – sea gulls, motor cars,
jet planes. (It's said you once set off
after a lightning flash.) Half over a rock,
you followed the salmon fly arcing
through the bronze water. You loved everything
except rabbits – though
you grinned away under the bed
when your master came home
drink taken. How you'd lay your head
on a visitor's knee and look up, so soulfully,
like George Eliot playing Sarah Bernhardt.

… Black Meph, how can you remember yourself
in that blank no-time, no-place where
you can't even greet your master
though he's there too?

In that Other World

They sit at their long table
in a room so long it's a tunnel,
in a tunnel with a green roof
on which sometimes a flower nods
as if to remind them of something.

They talk about everything
except Death, but they don't listen
to each other. They talk, staring
straight in front of them.
And they tremble.

The only time they notice each other
is when Death sweeps past them
with his keys clinking and a long pen
in his hand.

Then they look shyly at each other
for a moment before staring ahead
and talking, talking, trying to remember
what a flower is,
trying to remember
why they are here.

Notations of Ten Summer Minutes

A boy skips flat stones out to sea – each does fine
till a small wave meets it head on and swallows it.
The boy will do the same.

The schoolmaster stands looking out of the window
with one Latin eye and one Greek one.
A boat rounds the point in Gaelic.

Out of the shop comes a stream
of Omo, Weetabix, BiSoDol tablets and a man
with a pocket shaped like a whisky bottle.

Lord V.[1] walks by with the village in his pocket.
Angus walks by
spending the village into the air.

1. The Vestey family own large estates in Sutherland.

A melodeon is wheezing a clear-throated jig
on the deck of the *Arcadia*. On the shore hills Pan
cocks a hairy ear; and falls asleep again.

The ten minutes are up, except they aren't.
I leave the village, except I don't.
The jig fades to silence, except it doesn't.

Small Boy

He picked up a pebble
and threw it into the sea.

And another, and another.
He couldn't stop.

He wasn't trying to fill the sea.
He wasn't trying to empty the beach.

He was just throwing away,
Nothing else but.

Like a kitten playing
he was practising for the future

when there'll be so many things
he'll want to throw away

if only his fingers will unclench
and let them go.

My Last Word on Frogs

People have said to me, *You seem to like frogs.*
They keep jumping into your poems.

I do. I love the way they sit,
compact as a cat and as indifferent
to everything but style, like a lady remembering
to keep her knees together. And I love
the elegant way they jump and
the inelegant way they land.
So human.

I feel so close to them
I must be froggish myself.

I look in the mirror expecting to see
a fairytale Prince.

But no. It's just sprawling me,
croaking away
and swivelling my eyes around
for the stealthy heron and his stabbing beak.

Recipe

You have to be stubborn.
You have to turn away
from meditation, from ideologies,
from the tombstone face
of the Royal Bank of Scotland.

You have to keep stubbornly saying
This is bread, though it's in a sunset,
this is a sunset with bread in it.
This is a woman, she doesn't live
in a book or an imagination.
Hello, water, you must say, Hello, good water.

You have to touch wood, but not for luck.
You have to listen to that matter of pitches and crescendos
without thinking Beethoven is speaking
only to you.

And you must learn there are words
with no meaning, words like consolation,
words like goodbye.

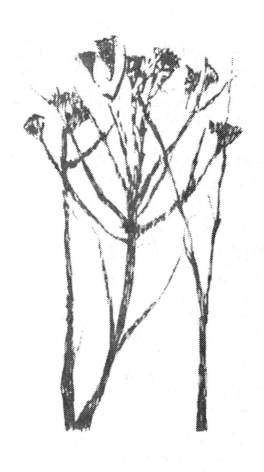

Somhairle MacGill-Eain/ Sorley MacLean (1911–)

Born on the island of Raasay off the east coast of Skye, MacLean has worked as a schoolteacher and headmaster for most of his life. He served in North Africa during the Second World War and was wounded at El Alamein. His poems combine high lyric symbolism with an equally passionate concern for socialism and social justice, most notably in the 1943 volume *Dàin do Eimhir* (*Poems to Eimhir*) in which a

Coin is Madaidhean-Allaidh

Thar na sìorruidheachd, thar a sneachda,
chì mi mo dhàin neo-dheachdte,
chì mi lorgan an spòg a' breacadh
gile shuaimhneach an t-sneachda;
calg air bhoile, teanga fala,
gadhair chaola 's madaidhean-allaidh
a' leum thar mullaichean nan gàradh
a' ruith fo sgàil nan craobhan fàsail
ag gabhail cumhang nan caol-ghleann
a' sireadh caisead nan gaoth-bheann;
an langan gallanach a' sianail
thar loman cruaidhe nan àm cianail,
an comhartaich bhiothbhuan na mo chluasan
an deann-ruith ag gabhail mo bhuadhan:
réis nam madadh 's nan con iargalt
luath air tòrachd an fhiadhaich
troimh na coilltean gun fhiaradh,
thar mullaichean nam beann gun shiaradh;
coin chiùine caothaich na bàrdachd,
madaidhean air tòir na h-àilleachd,
àilleachd an anama 's an aodainn,
fiadh geal thar bheann is raointean,
fiadh do bhòidhche ciùine gaolaich,
fiadhach gun sgur gun fhaochadh.

Dàin do Eimhir XXIX

complex love affair and a troubled conscience about the rise of Fascism in Spain and Europe produced work of rare intensity. MacLean stands with Hugh MacDiarmid as a poet whose work has transformed an older tradition by bringing it into touch with literary modernism and contemporary politics.

Dogs and Wolves

Across eternity, across its snows
I see my unwritten poems,
I see the spoor of their paws dappling
the untroubled whiteness of the snow:
bristles raging, bloody-tongued,
lean greyhounds and wolves
leaping over the tops of the dykes,
running under the shade of the trees of the wilderness
taking the defile of narrow glens,
making for the steepness of windy mountains;
their baying yell shrieking
across the hard barenesses of the terrible times,
their everlasting barking in my ears,
their onrush seizing my mind:
career of wolves and eerie dogs
swift in pursuit of the quarry,
through the forests without veering,
over the mountain tops without sheering;
the mild mad dogs of poetry,
wolves in chase of beauty,
beauty of soul and face,
a white deer over hills and plains,
the deer of your gentle beloved beauty,
a hunt without halt, without respite.

Poems to Eimhir XXIX

Tràighean

Nan robh sinn an Talasgar air an tràigh
far a bheil am bial mór bàn
a' fosgladh eadar dà ghiall chruaidh,
Rubha nan Clach 's am Bioda Ruadh,
sheasainn-sa ri taobh na mara
ag ùrachadh gaoil 'nam anam
fhad 's a bhiodh an cuan a' lìonadh
camus Thalasgair gu sìorruidh:
sheasainn an sud air lom na tràghad
gu 'n cromadh Priseal a cheann àigich.

Agus nan robh sinn cuideachd
air traigh Chalgaraidh am Muile,
eadar Alba is Tiriodh,
eadar an saoghal 's a' bhiothbhuan,
dh'fhuirichinn an sud gu luan
a' tomhas gainmhich bruan air bhruan.
Agus an Uidhist air tràigh Hòmhstaidh
fa chomhair farsuingeachd na h-ònrachd,
dh' fheithinn-sa an sud gu sìorruidh
braon air bhraon an cuan a' sìoladh.

Agus nan robh mi air tràigh Mhùideart
còmhla riut, a nodhachd ùidhe,
chuirinn suas an cochur gaoil dhut
an cuan 's a' ghaineamh, bruan air bhraon dhiubh.
'S nan robh sinn air Mol Steinnseil Stamhain
's an fhairge neo-aoibhneach a' tarruing
nan ulbhag is 'gan tilgeil tharainn
thogainn-sa am balla daingeann
roimh shìorruidheachd choimhich 's i framhach.

Dàin do Eimhir XLII

Fuaran

Tha cluaineag ann an iomall sléibh
far an ith na féidh lus biolaire;
'na taobh sùil uisge mhór réidh,
fuaran leugach cuimir ann.

Air latha thàinig mi le m' ghaol
gu taobh a' chaochain iomallaich,
chrom i h-aodann sìos ri bhruaich
's cha robh a thuar fhéin tuilleadh air.

Shores

If we were in Talisker on the shore   (on Skye)
where the great white mouth
opens between two hard jaws,
Rubha nan Clach and the Bioda Ruadh,
I would stand beside the sea
re-newing love in my spirit
while the ocean was filling
Talisker bay forever:
I would stand there on the bareness of the shore
until Prishal bowed his stallion head.

And if we were together
on Calgary shore in Mull,
between Scotland and Tiree,
between the world and eternity,
I would stay there till doom
measuring sand, grain by grain,
and in Uist, on the shore of Homhsta
in presence of that wide solitude,
I would wait there for ever,
for the sea draining drop by drop.

And if I were on the shore of Moidart
with you, for whom my care is new,
I would put up in a synthesis of love for you
the ocean and the sand, drop and grain.
And if we were on Mol Stenscholl Staffin
when the unhappy surging sea dragged
the boulders and threw them over us,
I would build the rampart wall
against an alien eternity grinding (its teeth).

Poems to Eimhir XLII

A Spring

At the far edge of a mountain there is a green nook
where the deer eat water-cress,
in its side a great unruffled eye of water,
a shapely jewel-like spring.

One day I came with my love
to the side of the remote brook.
She bent her head down to its brink
and it did not look the same again.

Ràinig mi a' chluaineag chéin
a rithist liom fhéin iomadh uair,
agus nuair choimhead mi 'san t-srùlaich
cha robh ach gnùis té m' ulaidh innt'.

Ach bha na glinn is iad a' falbh
is calbh nam beann gun fhuireach rium,
cha robh a choltas air na sléibhtean
gum facas m' eudail ulaidhe.

Calbharaigh

Chan eil mo shùil air Calbharaigh
no air Betlehem an àigh
ach air cùil ghrod an Glaschu
far bheil an lobhadh fàis,
agus air seòmar an Dùn-éideann,
seòmar bochdainn 's cràidh,
far a bheil an naoidhean creuchdach
ri aonagraich gu bhàs.

Ban-Ghàidheal

Am faca Tu i, Iùdhaich mhóir,
ri 'n abrar Aon Mhac Dhé?
Am fac' thu 'coltas air Do thriall
ri strì an fhìon-lios chéin?

An cuallach mhiosan air a druim,
fallus searbh air mala is gruaidh;
's a' mhìos chreadha trom air cùl
a cinn chrùibte bhochd thruaigh.

Chan fhaca Tu i, Mhic an t-saoir,
ri 'n abrar Rìgh na Glòir,
a miosg nan cladach carrach siar,
fo fhallus cliabh a lòin.

An t-earrach so agus so chaidh
's gach fichead earrach bho 'n an tùs
tharruing ise 'n fheamainn fhuar
chum biadh a cloinne 's duais an tùir.

S gach fichead foghar tha air triall
chaill i samhradh buidh nam blàth;

I reached the distant little green
many a time again, alone
and when I looked into the swirling water
there was in it only the face of my treasure-trove.

But the glens were going away
and the pillared mountains were not waiting for me:
the hills did not look
as if my chanced-on treasure had been seen.

Calvary

My eye is not on Calvary
nor on Bethlehem the Blessed,
but on a foul-smelling backland in Glasgow,
where life rots as it grows;
and on a room in Edinburgh,
a room of poverty and pain,
where the diseased infant
writhes and wallows till death.

A Highland Woman

Hast Thou seen her, great Jew,
who art called the One Son of God?
Hast Thou seen on Thy way the like of her
labouring in the distant vineyard?

The load of fruits on her back,
a bitter sweat on brow and cheek,
and the clay basin heavy on the back
of her bent poor wretched head.

Thou hast not seen her, Son of the carpenter,
who art called the King of Glory,
among the rugged western shores
in the sweat of her food's creel.   (a backpack basket)

This Spring and last Spring
and every twenty Springs from the beginning,
she has carried the cold seaweed
for her children's food and the castle's reward.

And every twenty Autumns gone
she has lost the golden summer of her bloom,

'is threabh an dubh-chosnadh an clais
tarsuinn mìnead ghil a clàir.

Agus labhair T' eaglais chaomh
mu staid chaillte a h-anama thruaigh;
agus leag an cosnadh dian
a corp gu sàmhchair dhuibh an uaigh.

Is thriall a tìm mar shnighe dubh
a' drùdhadh tughaidh fàrdaich bochd;
mheal ise an dubh-chosnadh cruaidh;
is glas a cadal suain an nochd.

Ard-Mhusaeum na h-Eireann

Anns na laithean dona seo
is seann leòn Uladh 'na ghaoid
lionnrachaidh 'n cridhe na h-Eòrpa
agus an cridhe gach Gàidheil
dh' an aithne gur h-e th'ann an Gàidheal,
cha d' rinn mise ach gum facas
ann an Ard Mhusaeum na h-Eireann
spot mheirgeach ruadh na fala
's i caran salach air an léinidh
a bha aon uair air a' churaidh
as docha leamsa dhuibh uile
a sheas ri peileir no ri béigneid
no ri tancan no ri eachraidh
no ri spreaghadh nam bom éitigh;
an léine bh' air O Conghaile
ann an Ard Phost-Oifis Eirinn
's e 'g ullachadh na h-ìobairt
a chuir suas e fhéin air séithir
as naoimhe na 'n Lia Fàil
th' air Cnoc na Teamhrach an Eirinn.

Tha an curaidh mór fhathast
'na shuidhe air an t-séithir,
ag cur a' chatha 'sa' Phost-Oifis
's ag glanadh shràidean an Dùn-Eideann.

and the Black Labour has ploughed the furrow
across the white smoothness of her forehead.

And Thy gentle church has spoken
about the lost state of her miserable soul,
and the unremitting toil has lowered
her body to a black peace in a grave.

And her time has gone like a black sludge
seeping through the thatch of a poor dwelling:
the hard Black Labour was her inheritance;
grey is her sleep tonight.

The National Museum of Ireland

In these evil days,
when the old wound of Ulster is a disease
suppurating in the heart of Europe
and in the heart of every Gael
who knows that he is a Gael,
I have done nothing but see
in the National Museum of Ireland
the rusty red spot of blood,
rather dirty, on the shirt
that was once on the hero
who is dearest to me of them all
who stood against bullet or bayonet,
or tanks or cavalry,
or the bursting of frightful bombs:
the shirt that was on Connolly[1]
in the General Post Office of Ireland
while he was preparing the sacrifice
that put himself up on a chair
that is holier than the Lia Fail[2]
that is on the Hill of Tara in Ireland.

The great hero is still
sitting on the chair
fighting the battle in the Post Office
and cleaning streets in Edinburgh.

1. James Connolly (1868–1916), born in Ulster. He came to Edinburgh at the age of 10, spending 18 formative years in
   Scotland before returning to Ireland to become known as a leading Republican and an international Socialist.
2. Lit.: 'stone of destiny', the coronation stone at the site of the ancient kings of Ireland. Connolly was wounded during
   the Easter Rising in 1916 and was executed by firing squad while propped up in a chair.

Curaidhean

Chan fhaca mi Lannes aig Ratasbon
no MacGill-Fhinnein aig Allt Eire
no Gill-Iosa aig Cuil-Lodair,
ach chunnaic mi Sasunnach 'san Eiphit.

Fear beag truagh le gruaidhean pluiceach
is glùinean a' bleith a chéile,
aodann guireanach gun tlachd ann –
còmhdach an spioraid bu tréine.

Cha robh buaidh air ' 'san tigh-òsda
'n àm nan dòrn a bhith 'gan dùnadh,'
ach leóghann e ri uchd a' chatha,
anns na frasan guineach mùgach.

Thàinig uair-san leis na sligean,
leis na spealgan-iaruinn beàrnach,
anns an toit is anns an lasair,
ann an crith is maoim na h-àraich.

Thàinig fios dha 'san fhrois pheileir
e bhith gu spreigearra 'na dhiùlnach:
is b'e sin e fhad 's a mhair e,
ach cha b' fhada fhuaire e dh' ùine.

Chum e ghunnachan ris na tancan,
a' bocail le sgriach shracaidh stàirnich
gus an d' fhuair e fhéin mu 'n stamaig
an deannal ud a chuir ri làr e,
bial sìos an gainmhich 's an greabhal,
gun diog o ghuth caol grànnda.

Cha do chuireadh crois no meadal
ri uchd no ainm no g' a chàirdean:
cha robh a bheag dhe fhòirne maireann,
's nan robh cha bhiodh am facal làidir;
's có dhiubh, ma sheasas ursann-chatha
leagar móran air a shàilleabh
gun dùil ri cliù, nach iarr am meadal
no cop 'sam bith á bial na h-àraich.

Chunnaic mi gaisgeach mór á Sasuinn,
fearachan bochd nach laigheadh sùil air;

Heroes

I did not see Lannes at Ratisbon[1]
nor MacLennan at Auldearn
nor Gillies MacBain at Culloden,
but I saw an Englishman in Egypt.

A poor little chap with chubby cheeks
and knees grinding each other,
pimply unattractive face –
garment of the bravest spirit.

He was not a hit 'in the pub
in the time of the fists being closed,'
but a lion against the breast of battle,
in the morose wounding showers.

His hour came with the shells,
with the notched iron splinters,
in the smoke and flame,
in the shaking and terror of the battlefield.

Word came to him in the bullet shower
that he should be a hero briskly,
and he was that while he lasted
but it wasn't much time he got.

He kept his guns to the tanks,
bucking with tearing crashing screech,
until he himself got, about the stomach,
that biff that put him to the ground,
mouth down in sand and gravel,
without a chirp from his ugly high-pitched voice.

No cross or medal was put to his
chest or to his name or to his family;
there were not many of his troop alive,
and if there were their word would not be strong.
And at any rate, if a battle post stands
many are knocked down because of him,
not expecting fame, not wanting a medal
or any froth from the mouth of the field of slaughter.

I saw a great warrior of England,
a poor manikin on whom no eye would rest;

1. Lannes: Napoleonic general who captured Ratisbon in Bavaria in 1809. MacLennan fought for Montrose at the battle
   of Auldearn, 1645. MacBain penetrated deep into English ranks at Culloden in 1746, killing 14 before being ridden
   down by dragoons.

cha b' Alasdair á Gleanna Garadh –
is thug e gal beag air mo shùilean.

Glac a' Bhàis

Thubhairt Nàsach air choireigin gun tug am Furair air ais do fhir na Gearmailte 'a 'chòir agus an sonas bàs fhaotainn anns an àraich'.

'Na shuidhe marbh an 'Glaic a' Bhàis'
fo Dhruim Ruidhìseit,
gill' òg 's a logan sìos m' a ghruaidh
's a thuar grìsionn.

Smaoinich mi air a' chòir 's an àgh
a fhuair e bho Fhurair,
bhith tuiteam ann an raon an àir
gun éirigh tuilleadh;

air a' ghreadhnachas 's air a' chliù
nach d' fhuair e 'na aonar,
ged b' esan bu bhrònaiche snuadh
ann an glaic air·laomadh

le cuileagan mu chuirp ghlas'
air gainmhich lachduinn
s i salach-bhuidhe 's làn de raip
's de sprùidhlich catha.

An robh an gille air an dream
a mhàb na h-Iùdhaich
's na Comunnaich, no air an dream
bu mhotha, dhiùbh-san

a threòraicheadh bho thoiseach àl
gun deòin gu buaireadh
agus bruaillean cuthaich gach blàir
air sgàth uachdaran?

Ge b'e a dheòin-san no a chàs,
a neoichiontas no mhìorun,
cha do nochd e toileachadh 'na bhàs
fo Dhruim Ruidhìseit.

no Alasdair of Glen Garry;[1]
and he took a little weeping to my eyes.

Death Valley

Some Nazi or other has said that the Führer had restored to German manhood the 'right and joy of dying in battle'.

Sitting dead in 'Death Valley'
below the Ruweisat Ridge
a boy with his forelock down about his cheek
and his face slate-grey;

I thought of the right and the joy
that he got from his Führer,
of falling in the field of slaughter
to rise no more;

of the pomp and the fame
that he had, not alone,
though he was the most piteous to see
in a valley gone to seed

with flies about grey corpses
on a dun sand
dirty yellow and full of the rubbish
and fragments of battle.

Was the boy of the band
who abused the Jews
and Communists, or of the greater
band of those

led, from the beginning of generations,
unwillingly to the trial
and mad delirium of every war
for the sake of rulers?

Whatever his desire or mishap,
his innocence or malignity,
he showed no pleasure in his death
below the Ruweisat Ridge.

1. Alasdair MacDonald: Jacobite chief. This is a reference to Cicely MacDonald's lament, 'Alasdair of Glengarry', with its last line: 'Thug thu 'n diugh gal air mo shùilibh'/'You brought tears to my eyes today'.

Hallaig

'Tha tím, am fiadh, an coille Hallaig'

Tha bùird is tàirnean air an uinneig
troimh 'm faca mi an Aird an Iar
's tha mo ghaol aig Allt Hallaig
'na craoibh bheithe, 's bha i riamh

eadar an t-Inbhir 's Poll a' Bhainne,
thall 's a bhos mu Bhaile-Chùirn:
tha i 'na beithe, 'na calltuinn,
'na caorunn dhìreach sheang ùir.

Ann an Screapadal mo chinnidh,
far robh Tarmad 's Eachunn Mór,
tha 'n nigheanan 's am mic 'nan coille
ag gabhail suas ri taobh an lóin.

Uaibhreach a nochd na coilich ghiuthais
ag gairm air mullach Cnoc an Rà,
dìreach an druim ris a' ghealaich –
chan iadsan coille mo ghràidh.

Fuirichidh mi ris a' bheithe
gus an tig i mach an Càrn,
gus am bi am bearradh uile
o Bheinn na Lice f' a sgàil.

Mura tig 's ann theàrnas mi a Hallaig
a dh' ionnsaigh sàbaid nam marbh,
far a bheil an sluagh a' tathaich,
gach aon ghinealach a dh' fhalbh.

Tha iad fhathast ann a Hallaig,
Clann Ghill-Eain's Clann MhicLeòid,
na bh' ann ri linn Mhic Ghille-Chaluim:
Chunnacas na mairbh beò.

Na fir 'nan laighe air an lianaig
aig ceann gach taighe a bh' ann,
na h-igheanan 'nan coille bheithe,
dìreach an druim, crom an ceann.

Hallaig[1]

'Time, the deer, is in the wood of Hallaig'

The window is nailed and boarded
through which I saw the West
and my love is at the Burn of Hallaig,
a birch tree, and she has always been

between Inver and Milk Hollow,
here and there about Baile-chuirn:
she is a birch, a hazel,
a straight, slender young rowan.

In Screapadal of my people
where Norman and Big Hector were,
their daughters and their sons are a wood
going up beside the stream.

Proud tonight the pine cocks[2]
crowing on the top of Cnoc an Ra,
straight their backs in the moonlight –
they are not the wood I love.

I will wait for the birch wood
until it comes up by the cairn,
until the whole ridge from Beinn na Lice
will be under its shade.

If it does not, I will go down to Hallaig,
to the Sabbath of the dead,
where the people are frequenting,
every single generation gone.

They are still in Hallaig,
MacLeans and MacLeods,
all who were there in the time of Mac Gille Chaluim
the dead have been seen alive.

The men lying on the green
at the end of every house that was,
the girls a wood of birches,
straight their backs, bent their heads.

1. A township on the south-east of Raasay, cleared for sheep-grazing in the 1850s.
2. Pine trees were planted here in the 19th century.

Eadar an Leac is na Feàrnaibh
tha 'n rathad mór fo chóinnich chiùin,
's na h-igheanan 'nam badan sàmhach
a' dol a Chlachan mar o thùs.

Agus a' tilleadh as a' Chlachan,
á Suidhisnis 's á tìr nam beò;
a chuile té òg uallach
gun bhristeadh cridhe an sgeòil.

O Allt na Feàrnaibh gus an fhaoilinn
tha soilleir an dìomhaireachd nam beann
chan eil ach coimhthional nan nighean
ag cumail na coiseachd gun cheann.

A' tilleadh a Hallaig anns an fheasgar,
anns a' chamhanaich bhalbh bheò,
a' lìonadh nan leathadan casa,
an gàireachdaich 'nam chluais 'na ceò,

's am bòidhche 'na sgleò air mo chridhe
mun tig an ciaradh air na caoil,
's nuair theàrnas grian air cùl Dhùn Cana
thig peileir dian á gunna Ghaoil;

's buailear am fiadh a tha 'na thuaineal
a' snòtach nan làraichean feòir;
thig reothadh air a shùil 'sa choille:
chan fhaighear lorg air fhuil ri m' bheò.

Between the Leac and Fearns
the road is under mild moss
and the girls in silent bands
go to Clachan[1] as in the beginning,

and return from Clachan
from Suisnish and the land of the living;
each one young and light-stepping,
without the heartbreak of the tale.

From the Burn of Fearns to the raised beach
that is clear in the mystery of the hills,
there is only the congregation of the girls
keeping up the endless walk,

coming back to Hallaig in the evening,
in the dumb living twilight,
filling the steep slopes,
their laughter a mist in my ears,

and their beauty a film on my heart
before the dimness comes on the kyles,
and when the sun goes down behind Dun Cana[2]
a vehement bullet will come from the gun of Love;

and will strike the deer that goes dizzily,
sniffing at the grass-grown ruined homes;
his eye will freeze in the wood,
his blood will not be traced while I live.

1. The main village on the west side of Raasay; Suisnish and Fearns are neighbouring townships on the southern end of
   the island; the Leac is Rubha na' Leac, a promontory on the bay where Hallaig used to be, overlooked by the hill
   Beinn na Lice.
2. The highest hill on Raasay, a distinctive peak.

Sydney Goodsir Smith (1915–1975)

Born in New Zealand to a Scottish mother, Smith was educated in Edinburgh and Oxford before returning to the city which he was to celebrate so vigorously in many of his poems. Smith's use of Scots evokes the vocabulary of the Makars, but the spirit of his work has an eighteenth-century gusto to it, a wild and learned irreverence, obscene and tender by turns, yet energised, too, by something of Joyce's linguistic invention and a modernist instability. (He wrote *Carotid Cornucopius*, 1947, as a Goliardic prose-extravaganza in the manner of *Finnegans Wake*.) Smith's masterpiece is the sequence of love poems, satires and elegies *Under the Eildon Tree* (1948).

October 1941

Tchaikovski man, I'm hearan yir Waltz o Flouers,
A cry frae Russia fulls this autumn nicht;   *fills*
Aa gousty fell October's sabban in ma room   *unearthly lethal; sobbing*
As the frantic rammage Panzers brash on Moscow toun –   *furious; rush*
An the leaves o wud October, man, are sworlan owre the warld.   *mad*

I' the gowden hairst o Forty-Ane the reid leaves drap, they whorl   *harvest*
Rain-dinged an spin frae the wund-thrawn creak o trees,   *struck; twisted*
Lik tears o bluid they flee wi the airn tanks an drift athort,   *iron; abroad*
Puir shauchlan shroud, the wae battallions o the deid   *shuffling; woeful*
O, *the leaves o wud October, man, are sworlan owre the warld.*

Outby ma winnock raggit branches drune   *window; drown*
As roun the lums o Kiev, Warsaw, an the lave   *chimneys; rest*
O' sunken Europe; throu the wuids, by lochs, ablow the gastrous craigs   *below;*
O' Caucasie, roads slip wi bluid mushed black wi leaves an rain –   */monstrous*
O, *the tears o wud October, man, are sworlan owre the warld.*

Trees greit their tears o bluid, they mell wi the bluid o men,   *cry; mix*
By a daft God's weirdless breith the fey leaves   *idiot; worthless breath; doomed;*
    blawn aa widdershin   *anticlockwise*
In the screich o whup or shell the grummlan wunds o daith,   *whip*
This month bairned you an me, month o breme dualities,   *gave birth to; bleak*
    o birth an skaith –   *harm*
O, *the leaves o wud October, man, are sworlan owre the warld.*

Sune rain wull freeze til snaw an the leaves be stilled
But yet thon oorie Deevil's Waltz'll straik the eastren fields,   weird; strike
Music o fa'an angels sab; maun aye the gray wunds blaw
An the drum o wounds aye dirl throu the smooran snaw?   throb; smothering
Aye, the leaves o wud October, man, are sworlan owre the warld.

Whan Neva's black wi ice an glaizie in the   moon-frost's lily ember
    mune-haar's lilly gleid
An trees drained black o tears, wull then the oorie sworl
Bide lown? Nae, chiel, tho dream ye maun o daw   Stay calm; man; must of dawn
    i the how-dumb-deid   in the dead of night
The leaves o wud October, man, aye sworl across the warld.

A Tink in Reekie   Tinker in Edinburgh

My lass an I in the lamplicht street –
A smirr o snaw on the wind   sprinkling
And she smiled as the ice took her
Lauchan up in my face a tinkler lass
As we left the randie howff   boisterous pub
Bleezan ahint us.   behind

Doomed we were and kent the haill o't –   knew
We that were content wi luve
That ne'er wad ken content
Nor e'er forget
The nicht when mercie drouned
Incontinent.

She was a silent queyne   girl
And she likit the cauld kiss
O' the snaw scuffan her face
As we turnit the corner then
– Ae nicht in Reekie's winter
When luve deed wi's.   died with us

from *Under the Eildon Tree*[1]

xii: Orpheus

i

Wi sang aa birds and beasts could I owrecome,
    Aa men and wemen o' the mapamound subdue;   globe
    The flouers o' the fields,
Rocks and trees, boued doun to hear my leid;   bowed; song
Gurlie waters rase upon the land to mak   rough; rose

1. A tree on the Eildon Hills where Thomas the Rhymer slept and met the queen of Elfland.

A throwgang for my feet. *passageway*
I was the potent prince o' ballatrie,
My lyre opened portes whareer I thocht to gang, *gates; go*
 My fleean sangs mair ramsh nor wine *flying/drunk; heady*
At Beltane, Yule or Hogmanay[1]
 Made wud the clans o' men – *mad*
There wasna my maik upon the yerth *equal; earth*
 (Why should I no admit the fack?)
A hero, demi-god, my kingrik was the hert, *kingdom*
 The passions and the saul –
  Sic was my pouer. *Such*
– Anerlie my ain sel I couldna bend. *Only; self*

'He was his ain worst enemie,'
As the auld untentit bodachs say – *unheeded greybeards*
My hert, a leopard, ruthless, breme, *grim*
 Gilravaged far and near *Rioted*
Seekan sensatiouns, passions that wad wauken
 My Muse whan she was lollish. *lazy*
No seenil the hert was kinnelt like a forest-bleeze … *Not seldom; kindled*
I was nae maister o' my ain but thirlit *enslaved*
 Serf til his ramskeerie wants *irresponsible*
 – And yet I hained but ane in the hert's deepest hert. *kept*

She, maist leefou, leesome leddy *kind-hearted; lovable lady*
 – Ochone, ochone Euridicie – *Alas (Gaelic)*
Was aye the queen of Orpheus' hert, as I kent weill,
 And wantan her my life was feckless drinkin *without her; ineffective*
  Weirdless, thieveless dancin, *Aimless; unconvincing*
   Singin, gangrellin. *vagabonding*
    – And nou she's gane.

ii
The jalous gods sae cast my weird that she *fate*
Was reift intil the Shades throu my neglect. *snatched*
 I, daffan i' the wuids and pools *dallying*
  Wi the water-lassies,
  Riggish, ree, and aye as fain *Mischievous; excited; fond*
 For lemanrie as Orpheus was, *making love*
I never kent o' her stravaigin *knew; wandering*
 Lane and dowie in the fields; *Alone; sad*
Nor that yon Aristoeus loed my queyne. *girl*
 It was fleein him she dee'd
But yet was my neglect that did the deed;

1. Beltane: pagan fire festival at beginning of May, later became a fair-day. Yule: the Christmas season. Hogmanay: New Year's Eve.

Neither was I by her to protect
  Frae the dernit serpent's bane — *hidden; poison*
Green and secret in the raff gerss liggan as she ran. — *rich grass; lying*
– I was her daith as she was life til me;
  Tho I was feckless born and lemanous — *weak; lecherous*
Yet she was mair nor aa the pultrous nymphs — *lascivious*
    O' wuid and burn til me
      – Yet it was I
    That flung Euridicie,
    The aipple of my bruckle ee, — *fallible eye*
      Til yon far bourne — *destination*
Frae whilk, they said, there's can be nae retoure. — *from which*
            Quhar art thou gane, my luf Euridices?'

iii

Ye ken the tale, how, with my lute
  I doungaed amang the Shades — *went down*
  (Gray mauchie Hades, lichtless airt) — *clammy; place*
  And Pluto and the damned stude round
    And grat, hearan my sang; — *wept*
  How, haean wan her manumissioun — *release from slavery*

Frae the Profund Magnifico,
I, cryan her name, socht and found my luve
  Amang thae wearie shadaws,
    Yet tint her in the end — *lost*
    For her a second daith,
    For me a second shame.

        (*The sycophantic gods, ulyied and curlit* — *oiled*
        Reclynan in the bar on bricht Olympus
        Soupan their meridian, outbocked — *noontime drink; belched*
        Their lauchter like a tourbilloun — *tornado*
        At this the latest ploy o' Zeus — *jape*
        The Caird, the Conjuror, the aye-bydan — *Rogue*
        Favourite and darlin o' them aa,
        The Wide Boy – ex officio!
                    – The Charlatan!)

She stummelt on a bourach, outcried 'Orpheus!' — *stumbled; tussock*
– Een, what wey were ye no blind? — *Eyes*
– Lugs, what wey were ye no deif? — *Ears; deaf*
– Hert, what wey were ye no cauld as ice?
– Limbs, what wey were ye no pouerless?
– Hairns, what wey did ye no haud the owerance? — *Brains; keep control*

(And Jupiter, in order til extraict
The maist exquisite quintessence
O' the succulence o' his wee ploy,
And wi his infantile perfectit sense
O' the dramatic, kept this impeccabil
And maikless agonie,   matchless
As a bonne-bouche, til the end.)   delicacy

We werena ten yairds frae the banks o' Styx
The ferrying o' whilk was luve and libertie   which
  – No ten yairds awa!
Our braith was hechlan and our een   panting; eyes
  Glaizie-glentit wi the joy   glitter-sparkling
  Of our twa-fauld deliverance –
And then Jove strak with serpent subtletie: struck
    – Euridicie stummelt.

(Lauchter cracked abune. Jupiter leuch!   above; laughed
– And richtlie sae!
Och, gie the gods their due,
They ken what they're about.
– The sleekans!)   crafty ones

She stummelt. I heard her cry. And hert ruled heid again.
– What hert could eer refuse, then, siccan a plea?   ever; such
    I turned –
      And wi neer a word,
           In silence,
Her een aye bricht wi the joy o' resurrectioun,   still
She soomed awa afore my een intil a skimmeran wraith   swam; shimmering
And for a second and last time was tint for aye   lost forever
Amang the gloams and haars o Hell   shadows and mists
– Throu my ain twafauld treacherie!

'Quhar art thou gane, my luf Euridices!'

iv
  Sinsyne I haena plucked a note   Since then
    Nor made a word o a sang,
    The clarsach and the lyre, the lute,   Highland harp
    'The aiten reed',   pastoral pipe
  Byde untuned in a yerdit kist.   Remain; buried chest
  My taiblets aa are broke, my pens brunt,   burned
    The howff sees me nocht   tavern; not
    Nor the lassies i' the glen.
    The hert in my bosom's deid

For Euridicie is deid
And it was I that did the double deed,
  Twice-bannit Orpheus!   *cursed*

I gang to jyne her in the skuggie airt,   *go; shadowy place*
A convene fou o' dreid for Orpheus' hert.   *meeting; full*

  Aa this will happen aa again,
  Monie and monie a time again.

(*Explicit Orpheus*)

Winter Blues

A high cauld room. Winter.
Put coal to the fire.
It's a while to heat a room   *It takes time*
Even with coal on the fire.

I huddle in a windy nest,
A wee lowe blinkin,   *small flame*
Read stuff I should deal wi,
Dae nocht – o' a lass thinkin.   *Do nothing*

There's food and drink for me here
But nane to provide me.
I sup frae a black bottle
Her face far beside me.   *well beside*

This is nae life for a bard
Lane-sittin, the fire lowpin.   *Sitting alone; jumping*
Wantin her's a half-man: *Lacking*
Less – a dumb shoutin.

Deorsa Mac Iain Deorsa/ George Campbell Hay (1915–1984)

Born in Argyll and educated at Oxford, Hay taught himself to speak Gaelic, writing poetry in all three of Scotland's languages, often in praise of the weather, the sea and the native landscapes he loved so well. Serving in North Africa and the Middle East

Na Baidealan

Neòil iongantach 'gan càrnadh suas
le ruaim ghàbhaidh s tòcadh borb;
turaidean treuna, tùir làn pròis,
brataichean bagraidh, ceò is colg.

Snàgaidh rompa duibhre 's oillt,
's na dealain bhoillsgeach asd' anuas;
slaodar leò an t-uisge glas
'na chùirtein dallaidh trasd' an cuan.

Sud tuinn is tìr air call an dath,
'gan dubhadh as le steall nan speur,
is Arainn bheàrnach uainn fo chleòc –
glòir uamharr e de ghlòiribh Dhé.

Bisearta

Chi mi rè geàrd na h-oidhche
dreòs air chrith 'na fhroidhneas thall air fàire,
a' clapail le a sgiathaibh,
a' sgapadh 's a' ciaradh rionnagan na h-àird' ud.
Shaoileadh tu gun cluinnte,
ge cian, o 'bhuillsgein ochanaich no caoineadh,
ràn corruich no gàir fuatha,
comhart chon cuthaich uaidh no ulfhairt fhaolchon,
gun ruigeadh drannd an fhòirneirt
o'n fhùirneis òmair iomall fhéin an t-saoghail;

630

during the Second World War, he never quite recovered from the violence he witnessed there, finding himself much in sympathy with the fatalism of Arab culture, and with the plight of the poor and the despised.

The Towering Clouds

Wondrous clouds are heaped aloft,
with a dark dangerous flush and a fierce swelling;
strong turrets, towers full of pride,
threatening banners, mist and rage,

Fearful darkness creeps before them,
and down out of them dart the lightning flashes;
they trail after them the grey rain
like a blinding curtain across the sea.

Yonder are waves and land, their colour lost,
blotted out by the torrent from the skies,
and gapped Arran gone from us under a cloak –
it is a terrible glory of the glories of God.

Bizerta

I see during the night guard
a blaze flickering, fringing the skyline over yonder,
beating with its wings
and scattering and dimming the stars of that airt.   quarter
You would think that there would be heard
from its midst, though far away, wailing and lamentation,
the roar of rage and the yell of hate,
the barking of the dogs from it or the howling of wolves,
that the snarl of violence would reach
from yon amber furnace the very edge of the world;

ach sud a' dol an leud e
ri oir an speur an tosdachd olc is aognaidh.

C' ainm nochd a th' orra,
na sràidean bochda anns an sgeith gach uinneag
a lasraichean 's a deatach,
a sradagan is sgreadail a luchd thuinidh,
is taigh air thaigh 'ga reubadh
am broinn a chéile am brùchdadh toit a' tuiteam?
Is có an nochd tha 'g atach
am Bàs a theachd gu grad 'nan cainntibh uile,
no a' spàirn measg chlach is shailthean
air bhàinidh a' gairm air cobhair, is nach cluinnear?
Cò an nochd a phàidheas
sean chìs àbhaisteach na fala cumant?

Uair dearg mar lod na h-àraich,
uair bàn mar ghile thràighte an eagail éitigh,
a' dìreadh 's uair a' teàrnadh,
a' sìneadh le sitheadh àrd 's a' call a mheudachd,
a' fannachadh car aitil
's ag at mar anail dhiabhail air dhéinead,
an t-Olc 'na chridhe 's 'na chuisle,
chì mi 'na bhuillean a' sìoladh 's a' leum e.
Tha 'n dreòs 'na oillt air fàire,
'na fhàinne ròis is òir am bun nan speuran,
a' breugnachadh 's ag àicheadh
le shoillse sèimhe àrsaidh àrd nan reultan.

Meftah bâbkum es-sabar[1]

Is cuimhne leam an Sùg el-Cheamais,
sa' chaifidh dhorcha is sinn a' deasbud,
guth cianail mar ghuth chlag fo fheasgar
a mhol domh strìochdadh do'n Fhreasdal.
'Mo chridhe fhéin, is faoin bhur gleachd Ris,
's gu bheil gach toiseach agus deireadh
air an sgrìobhadh Aige cheana.'

Sgrùd e bas a làimhe 's lean e:

'Do roinn, do mhanadh, is do sgàile,
théid iad cuide riut 's gach àite.

1. Meftah bâbkum es-sabar: 'luchair bhur doruis an fhaidhidinn' – sreath à dàn Arabach.

but yonder it spreads
along the rim of the sky in evil ghastly silence.

What is their name tonight,
the poor streets where every window spews
its flame and smoke,
its sparks and the screaming of its inmates,
while house upon house is rent
and collapses in a gust of smoke?
And who tonight are beseeching
Death to come quickly in all their tongues,
or are struggling among stones and beams,
crying in frenzy for help, and are not heard?
Who tonight is paying
the old accustomed tax of common blood?

Now red like a battlefield puddle,
now pale like the drained whiteness of foul fear,
climbing and sinking,
reaching and darting up and shrinking in size,
growing faint for a moment
and swelling like the breath of a devil in intensity,
I see Evil as a pulse
and a heart declining and leaping in throbs.
The blaze, a horror on the skyline,
a ring of rose and gold at the foot of the sky,
belies and denies
with its light the ancient high tranquillity of the stars.

Meftah bâbkum es-sabar[1]

I remember at Sûq el-Khemis,
while we argued in the dark café,
a voice, melancholy as the voice of evening bells,
that counselled me to be submissive to Providence.
'My heart own, your struggle against It is in vain,
for every beginning and ending
has been written by It already.'

He gazed at the palm of his hand and went on:

'Your portion, your destiny, and your shadow –
These accompany you in every place.

1. Meftah bâbkum es-sabar: 'patience the key to our door' – a line from an Arabic poem.

'An rud a tha san Dàn 's a sgrìobhadh
is gainntir sin a ghlais an Rìgh oirnn.
'S i 'n fhaidhidinn le sealladh ìosal
iuchair dorus ar dubh phrìosain.'

Ghin aintighearnas na gréine lasraich,
is ainneart speuran teth na h-Aifric,
gliocas brùite sgìth nam facal.

A ghliocais mar chluig mhall' an fheasgair,
chan ann dhuinne do leithid!
Oir sgrìobhadh roghainn fo leth dhuinn:
an t-sìth 's am bàs no gleachd 's a' bheatha.

Dh'fhalbh na diasan, dh'fhan an asbhuain?
Thuit na bailtean, chinn an raineach?
A bheil tom luachrach air gach stairsnich?
A shaoghail, tha sinn ann g'a aindeoin;
tha a' ghrìosach theth fo'n luaithre fhathast.

Na iarraibh oirnn matà cur sìos duibh
draoidheachd cheòlmhor fhacal lìomhta,
nithean clòimhteach, sgeòil an t-sìdhein,
ceò no òrain airson nìonag,
òran tàlaidh caillich sìtheil
a' tulgadh a h-ogha 's 'ga bhrìodal –
na iarraibh, ach sgal na pìoba.
Beachdan gnàthach, laghach, cinnteach,
òraid dhàicheil à ceann slìogte,
nòsan àbhaisteach no mìnead,
suaimhneas turban geal na h-Ioslaim,
faidhidinn Arabaich 'ga shìneadh
fo chomhair Allah fo'n bhruthainn shìorruidh,
na iarraibh – tha sinn beò da-rìribh,
agus 'Is fuar a' ghaoth thar Ile
gheibhear aca an Cinntìre.'
Iarraibh gàire, gean is mìghean,
càirdeas, nàimhdeas, tlachd is mìothlachd.
Iarraibh faileas fìor ar n-inntinn.

Siribh an annas ar làimhe
a' bheatha ghoirt, gharbh, luathghàireach,
oir thairg am Freasdal ré ar làithean
roghainn na beatha no a' bhàis duinn.

Blàr-cath' ar toile, leac ar teine,
an raon a dhùisgeas ar seisreach,

'What is fated and has been written
is as a dungeon that the Divine King has locked upon us.
Patience with a down cast look,
is the key to the door of our wretched prison.'

The tyranny of the flaming sun
and the violence of the hot skies of Africa
had begotten the bruised, tired wisdom of these words.

Wisdom like the slow bells of evening,
not for us is your like!
For a choice apart has been written for us:
peace and death, or struggling and life.

Are the full ears gone, and only the stubble remaining?
Fallen are the townships, and up has sprung the bracken?
Is there a clump of rushes on every threshold?
Oh, world, we are here and live on in spite of it;
the hot ember is yet under the ashes.

Do not ask us, then, to set down for you
some musical wizardry of polished words,
soft, downy things or tales of the fairy knowe,
mist or songs for young girls,
the lullaby of some peaceful old woman
as she rocks her oe and gives it fondling talk –   grandchild
do not ask that, but the scream of the pipes.
Nice, conventional, certain opinions,
a plausible oration from a sleek head,
customary ways or smoothness,
the tranquillity of the white turbans of Islam,
the patience of an Arab prostrating
himself before Allah in the eternal sultriness,
do not ask for them – we are alive in earnest
and 'Cold is the wind over Islay
that blows on them in Kintyre.'
Ask for laughter, and cheerful and angry moods,
friendship, enmity, pleasure and displeasure.
Ask for the true reflexion of our mind.

Seek in each new work of our hand
life, sore, rough and triumphant,
for Providence has offered us during our days
the choice between life and death.

The battlefield of our will,
the hearthstone we kindle our fire upon,

stéidh togail ar làmhan 's ar dealais;
an talla a fhuair sinn gun cheilear,
is far an cluinnear moch is feasgar
ceòl ar sinnsre is gàir ar seinne;
an leabhar far an sgrìobhar leinne
bàrdachd ùr fo'n rann mu dheireadh
a chuireadh leis na bàird o shean ann –
b'e sin ar tìr. No, mur an gleachdar,
rud suarach ann an cùil 'ga cheiltinn,
a thraogh 's a dhìochuimhnich sluagh eile.

Tilleadh Uilìseis

Ràinig mac Laérteis,
seal mu'n d'éirich orra 'n là,
Iotaca is tràighean 'oige.

Anns na tràthaibh cianail
mu'n leum a' ghrian, bha 'n iùbhrach àrd
dlùth fo sgàile an t-sean chòrsa.

Bha'n cruinne aosda 'mosgladh,
ag osnaich luchd nan linn a' fàs;
osna air son na gréine
am beul gach dùil roimh'n là;
's an sgùrr a b'àirde air 'ùr òradh.
    Bu chadal da, 's bha'n t-eathar
    gu mear a' breabadh cuip o 'sàil,
    ag cur nam bàgh 's nan rudha eòlach.

An ciar nan coille driùchdach
's nan dùsluinn tiugh thog eòin mu 'n àl
an gearan briste bìgeil;
bha brìdein beul an làin,
is éigh a chràidh aige sa' ghlòmuinn.
Is riamh bu chadal sìthe
do Uilìseas, sgìth o 'fhògradh.
    An déidh gach euchd is faontraidh,
    cleas an naoidhein, rinn e suain
    air a shuaineadh 'na chleòca.

ii
Bu chadal do Uilìseas;
is dh'fhàg iad sìnnt' e air an tràigh,
e fhéin 's a shàibhreas uile comhla.

the field our plough team will awaken,
the foundation for the building of our hands and our zeal;
the hall we found without melody,
and where will be heard, early and evening,
the music of our forebears and the clamour of our singing;
the book where we will write
new poetry below the last verse
put in it by the poets of old
– such will be our land. Or, if there be no struggle,
a mean thing of no account, hidden away in a corner,
which another people drained dry and forgot.

The Return of Ulysses

A short space before day rose upon them,
Laertes' son reached
Ithaca and the strands of his youth.

In the melancholy moments
before the sun leaps up, the high-sided boat
was close under the shadow of the old coast.

The aged world was stirring,
sighing its burden of centuries ever increasing:
a sigh of longing for the sun
in the mouth of every creature before the coming of day;
and the highest peak newly gilded.
   He was asleep, while the boat was prancing,
   kicking foam from her heel,
   weathering the well-known bays and headlands.

In the dark of the dewy woods
and the close set thickets, the birds above their broods
raised their broken complaint of cheeping;
a sandpiper at the lip of the tide
was calling out its hurt in the half-light.
And still Ulysses slept a sleep of peace,
tired from his exile.
   After all his deeds and straying,
   like a little child he slumbered
   wrapped in his cloak.

ii

Ulysses slept;
and they left him lying on the strand,
himself and his riches together.

Bu chadal. Is nuair dhùisg e
cha d'aithnich e a dhùthaich ghràidh,
oir chàirich a' bhan-dia fo cheò i.

B'e sean-chù dall nan cartan
a' cheud bheò a dh'aithnich e,
nuair thill a bheò o cheudan dóruinn.

Gun fhuran i s gun aithne,
'na chùis-bhùirt aig fanaid chàich,
fhuair e cùil 'na àros mórail.

iii
Ag cagnadh 'fheirge, an riochd an déircich
'na dhùn féin, bu ghailbheach
a shùil-fhiar fo 'mhailghean air cuirm nan tòiseach.

'Na dhéidh bu labhar sreang a bhogha,
is b'fhionnar oiteag a shaighdean
feadh an talla air gruaidhean na domhlachd.

Is iomadh misgear uaibhreach a tholladh
is a leig 'fhochaid dheth 's a ghàire,
's a shleuchd 'na fhuil 's a làmhan dearg mu sgòrnan.

Is suirgheach maoth a fhuair a leagadh,
beul fodha, 's e 'sgeith lod fala
measg fìon, feòl', arain chuachan is fhear-feòirne.

He slept. And when he wakened
he did not recognise his dear native land,
for the goddess had put a mist over it.

The old blind dog full of ticks
was the only living thing that knew him,
when he brought his life back from a hundred grievous trials.

Unwelcomed and unknown,
a butt for the mockery of all others,
he found a corner in his lordly dwelling.

iii
Chewing his anger, in the guise of a beggar
in his own dùn, stormy was his sidelong glance   fortified homestead
under his brows at the banquet of the chiefs.

And afterwards, loud was the string of his bow,
and cool was the waft of his arrows throughout the hall
on the cheeks of the throng.

Many an arrogant drunkard was pierced,
and gave over his jibing and laughter,
as he bowed down in his blood with his hands red about his throat.

And many a delicate suitor was cast down,
prone on his face, spewing a puddle of blood,
amongst wine and flesh and bread, amongst goblets and chessmen.

William Sydney Graham (1918–1986)

Graham lived in Cornwall for most of his adult life, but he was born and educated in Scotland where he studied to be an engineer. His long poem *The Nightfishing* (1955) used the sea and the trawlermen's search in darkness as a metaphor for the poet's task. Later poems meditate on Graham's family and his boyhood in Greenock, and develop a long-standing fascination with the nature of verbal creation and the abstractly beautiful difficulties of language.

Listen: Put on Morning

Listen. Put on morning.
Waken into falling light.
A man's imagining
Suddenly may inherit
The handclapping centuries
Of his one minute on earth.
And hear the virgin juries
Talk with his own breath
To the corner boys of his street.
And hear the Black Maria
Searching the town at night.
And hear the playropes caa   turn (skipping game)
The sister Mary in.
And hear Willie and Davie
Among bracken of Narnain
Sing in a mist heavy
With myrtle and listeners.
And hear the higher town
Weep a petition of fears
At the poorhouse close upon
The public heartbeat.
And hear the children tig
And run with my own feet
Into the netting drag
Of a suiciding principle.
Listen. Put on lightbreak.
Waken into miracle.

The audience lies awake
Under the tenements
Under the sugar docks
Under the printed moments.
The centuries turn their locks
And open under the hill
Their inherited books and doors
All gathered to distil
Like happy berry pickers
One voice to talk to us.
Yes listen. It carries away
The second and the years
Till the heart's in a jacket of snow
And the head's in a helmet white
And the song sleeps to be wakened
By the morning ear bright.
Listen. Put on morning.
Waken into falling light.

The Beast in the Space

Shut up. Shut up. There's nobody here.
If you think you hear somebody knocking
On the other side of the words, pay
No attention. It will be only
The great creature that thumps its tail
On silence on the other side.
If you do not even hear that
I'll give the beast a quick skelp
And through Art you'll hear it yelp.

The beast that lives on silence takes
Its bite out of either side.
It pads and sniffs between us.
Now it comes and laps my meaning up.
Call it over. Call it across
This curious necessary space.
Get off, you terrible inhabiter
Of silence. I'll not have it. Get
Away to whoever it is will have you.

He's gone and if he's gone to you
That's fair enough. For on this side
Of the words it's late. The heavy moth
Bangs on the pane. The whole house
Is sleeping and I remember

I am not here, only the space
I sent the terrible beast across.
Watch. He bites. Listen gently
To any song he snorts or growls
And give him food. He means neither
Well or ill towards you. Above
All, shut up. Give him your love.

from 'What is the Language Using Us for?': Second Poem
1
What is the language using us for?
It uses us all and in its dark
Of dark actions selections differ.

I am not making a fool of myself
For you. What I am making is
A place for language in my life

Which I want to be a real place
Seeing I have to put up with it
Anyhow. What are Communication's

Mistakes in the magic medium doing
To us? It matters only in
So far as we want to be telling

Each other alive about each other
Alive. I want to be able to speak
And sing and make my soul occur

In front of the best and be respected
For that and even be understood
By the ones I like who are dead.

I would like to speak in front
Of myself with all my ears alive
And find out what it is I want.

2
What is the language using us for?
What shape of words shall put its arms
Round us for more than pleasure?

I met a man in Cartsburn Street
Thrown out of the Cartsburn Vaults.
He shouted Willie and I crossed the street

And met him at the mouth of the Close.
And this was double-breasted Sam,
A far relation on my mother's

West-Irish side. Hello Sam how
Was it you knew me and says he
I heard your voice on The Sweet Brown Knowe.   (a song)

O was I now I said and Sam said
Maggie would have liked to see you.
I'll see you again I said and said

Sam I'll not keep you and turned
Away over the shortcut across
The midnight railway sidings.

What is the language using us for?
From the prevailing weather or words
Each object hides in a metaphor.

This is the morning. I am out
On a kind of Vlaminck[1] blue-rutted
Road. Willie Wagtail is about.   (the bird)

In from the West a fine smirr
Of rain drifts across the hedge.
I am only out here to walk or

Make this poem up. The hill is
A shining blue macadam top.
I lean my back to the telegraph pole

And the messages hum through my spine.
The beaded wires with their birds
Above me are contacting London.

What is the language using us for?
It uses us all and in its dark
Of dark actions selections differ.

Loch Thom

1

Just for the sake of recovering
I walked backward from fifty-six

1. Maurice Vlaminck (1876–1958), a Fauvist painter notable for his stormy, colourful expressionist landscapes.

Quick years of age wanting to see,
And managed not to trip or stumble
To find Loch Thom and turned round
To see the stretch of my childhood
Before me. Here is the loch. The same
Long-beaked cry curls across
The heather-edges of the water held
Between the hills a boyhood's walk
Up from Greenock. It is the morning.

And I am here with my mammy's
Bramble jam scones in my pocket.
The Firth is miles and I have come
Back to find Loch Thom maybe
In this light does not recognise me.

This is a lonely freshwater loch.
No farms on the edge. Only
Heather grouse-moor stretching
Down to Greenock and One Hope
Street or stretching away across
Into the blue moors of Ayrshire.

2
And almost I am back again
Wading the heather down to the edge
To sit. The minnows go by in shoals
Like iron-filings in the shallows.
My mother is dead. My father is dead
And all the trout I used to know
Leaping from their sad rings are dead.

3
I drop my crumbs into the shallow
Weed for the minnows and pinheads.
You see that I will have to rise
And turn round and get back where
My running age will slow for a moment
To let me on. It is a colder
Stretch of water than I remember.

The curlew's cry travelling still
Kills me fairly. In front of me
The grouse flurry and settle. GOBACK
GOBACK GOBACK FAREWELL LOCH THOM.

To Alexander Graham

Lying asleep walking
Last night I met my father
Who seemed pleased to see me.
He wanted to speak. I saw
His mouth saying something
But the dream had no sound.

We were surrounded by
Laid-up paddle steamers
In The Old Quay in Greenock.
I smelt the tar and the ropes.

It seemed that I was standing
Beside the big iron cannon
The tugs used to tie up to
When I was a boy. I turned
To see Dad standing just
Across the causeway under
That one lamp they keep on.

He recognised me immediately.
I could see that. He was
The handsome, same age
With his good brows as when
He would take me on Sundays
Saying we'll go for a walk.

Dad, what am I doing here?
What is it I am doing now?
Are you proud of me?
Going away, I knew
You wanted to tell me something.

You stopped and almost turned back
To say something. My father,
I try to be the best
In you you give me always.

Lying asleep turning
Round in the quay-lit dark
It was my father standing
As real as life. I smelt
The quay's tar and the ropes.

I think he wanted to speak.
But the dream had no sound.
I think I must have loved him.

Hamish Henderson (1919–)

A founder member of the School of Scottish Studies in Edinburgh, Henderson is well known as a folklorist and a composer of songs such as the 'Barren Rocks of Aden', the 'Freedom Come-All-Ye' and 'The John Maclean March' which have themselves entered the tradition. As an intelligence officer for the Highland divison he served in North Africa and was in the vanguard of the invasion of Italy. His desert experiences gave him his best-known book of poems, published in 1948.

from *Elegies for the Dead in Cyrenaica*

First Elergy: End of a Campaign

There are many dead in the brutish desert,
   who lie uneasy
among the scrub in this landscape of half-wit
stunted ill-will. For the dead land is insatiate
and necrophilous. The sand is blowing about still.
Many who for various reasons, or because
   of mere unanswerable compulsion, came here
and fought among the clutching gravestones,
   shivered and sweated,
cried out, suffered thirst, were stoically silent, cursed
the spittering machine-guns, were homesick for Europe
and fast embedded in quicksand of Africa
   agonized and died.
And sleep now. Sleep here the sleep of the dust.

There were our own, there were the others.
Their deaths were like their lives, human and animal.
There were no gods and precious few heroes.
What they regretted when they died had nothing to do with
   race and leader, realm indivisible,
laboured Augustan speeches or vague imperial heritage.
(They saw through that guff before the axe fell.)
   Their longing turned to
the lost world glimpsed in the memory of letters:
an evening at the pictures in the friendly dark,
two knowing conspirators smiling and whispering secrets; or else

a family gathering in the homely kitchen
with Mum so proud of her boys in uniform:
   their thoughts trembled
between moments of estrangement, and ecstatic moments
of reconciliation: and their desire
crucified itself against the unutterable shadow of someone whose photo
was in their wallets.
Then death made his incision.

There were our own, there were the others.
Therefore, minding the great word of Glencoe's
son, that we should not disfigure ourselves
with villainy of hatred; and seeing that all
have gone down like curs into anonymous silence,
I will bear witness for I knew the others.
Seeing that littoral and interior are alike indifferent
and the birds are drawn again to our welcoming north
why should I not sing *them*, the dead, the innocent?

Second Elegy: Halfaya
(For Luigi Castigliano)
At dawn, under the concise razor-edge
of the escarpment, the laager sleeps. No petrol fires yet
blow flame for brew-up. Up on the pass a sentry
inhales his Nazionale. Horse-shoe curve of the bay
grows visible beneath him. He smokes and yawns.
Ooo-augh,
   and the limitless
shabby lion-pelt of the desert completes and rounds
his limitless ennui.

At dawn, in the gathering impetus of day, the laager sleeps.
Some restless princes dream: first light denies them
the luxury of nothing. But others their mates more lucky
drown in the lightless grottoes. (Companionable death has lent
them his ease for a moment).
   The dreamers remember
a departure like a migration. They recall a landscape
associated with warmth and veils and pantomime
but never focused exactly. The flopping curtain
reveals scene-shifters running with freshly painted
incongruous sets. Here childhood's prairie garden
looms like a pampas, where grown-ups stalk (gross outlaws)
on legs of tree trunk: recedes: and the strepitant jungle
dwindles to scruff of shrubs on a docile common,
all but real for a moment, then gone.

The sleepers turn
gone but still no nothing laves them.
O misery, desire, desire, tautening cords of the bedrack!
Eros, in the teeth of Yahveh and his tight-lipped sect
confound the deniers of their youth! Let war lie wounded!
Eros, grant forgiveness and release
and return – against which they erect it,
the cairn of patience. *No dear, won't be long now
keep fingers crossed, chin up, keep smiling darling
be seeing you soon.*

On the horizon fires fluff now,
further than they seem.

       Sollum and Halfaya
a while yet before we leave you in quiet
and our needle swings north.

       The sleepers toss
and turn before waking: they feel through their blankets
the cold of the malevolent bomb-thumped desert,
impartial
hostile to both.

The laager is one.
Friends and enemies, haters and lovers
both sleep and dream.

Third Elegy: Leaving the City
*Morning after. Get moving. Cheerio. Be seeing you
when this party's over. Right, driver, get weaving.*

The truck pulls out
along the corniche. We dismiss with the terseness
of a newsreel the casino and the column,
the scrofulous sellers of obscenity,
the garries, the girls and the preposterous skyline.   one-horse open carriages

Leave them. And out past the stinking tanneries,
the maritime Greek cafes, the wogs and the nets
drying among seaweed. Through the periphery of the city
itching under flagrant sunshine. Faster. We are nearing
the stretch leading to the salt-lake Mareotis.
Sand now, and dust-choked fig-trees. This is the road
where convoys are ordered to act in case of ambush.
A straight run through now to the coastal sector.

One sudden thought wounds: it's a half-hour or over
since we saw the last skirt. And for a moment we regret
the women, and the harbour with a curve so perfect
it seems it was drawn with the mouseion's protractor.[1]

Past red-rimmed eye of the salt-lake. So long then,
holy filth of the living. We are going to the familiar
filth of your negation, to rejoin the proletariat
of levelling death. Stripes are shed and ranks levelled
in death's proletariat. There the Colonel of Hussars,
the keen Sapper Subaltern with a first in economics
and the sergeant well known in international football
crouch with Jock and Jame in their holes like helots.[2]
Distinctions become vain, and former privileges quite pointless
in that new situation. See our own and the opponents
advance, meet and merge: the commingled columns
lock, strain, disengage and join issue with the dust.

Do not regret
that we have still in history to suffer
or comrade that we are the agents
of a dialectic that can destroy us
but like a man prepared, like a brave man
bid farewell to the city,[3] and quickly
move forward on the road leading west by the salt-lake.
Like a man for long prepared, like a brave man,
like to the man who was worthy of such a city
be glad that the case admits no other solution,
acknowledge with pride the clear imperative of action
and bid farewell to her, to Alexandria, whom you are losing.

And these, advancing from the direction of Sollum,
swaddies in tropical kit, lifted in familiar vehicles
are they mirage – ourselves out of a mirror?
No, they too, leaving the plateau of Marmarica
for the serpentine of the pass, they advancing towards us
along the coast road, are the others, the brothers
in death's proletariat, they are our victims and betrayers
advancing by the sea-shore to the same assignation.
We send them our greetings out of the mirror.

---

1. Mouseion: Academy of Arts and Sciences in ancient Alexandria.
2. Serfs in ancient Sparta.
3. This and the following lines are translated from a Greek poem 'The God Leaves Anthony' by C. P. Cavafy (1868–1933), who saw his native Alexandria as a symbol of life itself.

Edwin Morgan (1920–   )

Having had his university studies interrupted by the Second World War and service in the Middle East with the RAMC, Morgan returned to his native Glasgow where he graduated and went on to become a lecturer and latterly a professor of English litera-ture. Well known as a translator and critic, his own poetry is resolutely modernist in outlook, firmly grounded in Scotland, and yet sympathetic to work in Europe and America. Morgan is experimental, darkly witty and optimistic in his responses to the multicultural and technological surfaces of our modern world, and yet his vision of individual lives who must find themselves alone in such a scene has a lyrical and poignant dimension to it as well.

The Unspoken

When the troopship was pitching round the Cape
in '41, and there was a lull in the night uproar of seas and winds, and a sudden full
   moon
swung huge out of the darkness like the world it is,
and we all crowded onto the wet deck, leaning on the rail, our arms on each
      other's shoulders, gazing at the savage outcrop of great Africa,
And Tommy Cosh started singing 'Mandalay' and we joined in with our raucous
      chorus of the unforgettable song,
and the dawn came up like thunder like that moon drawing the water of our
      yearning
though we were going to war, and left us exalted,
that was happiness,
but it is not like that.

When the television newscaster said
the second sputnik was up, not empty
but with a small dog on board,
a half-ton treasury of life orbiting a thousand miles above the thin television masts
      and mists of November,
in clear space, heard, observed,
the faint far heartbeat sending back its message
steady and delicate,
and I was stirred by a deep confusion of feelings,

got up, stood with my back to the wall and my palms pressed hard against it, my arms
    held wide
as if I could spring from this earth –
not loath myself to go out that very day where Laika had shown man, felt
my cheeks burning with old Promethean warmth
rekindled – ready –
covered my face with my hands, seeing only an animal
strapped in a doomed capsule, but the future
was still there, cool and whole like the moon,
waiting to be taken, smiling even
as the dog's bones and the elaborate casket of aluminium
glow white and fuse in the arc of re-entry,
and I knew what I felt was history,
its thrilling brilliance came down,
came down,
comes down on us all, bringing pride and pity,
but it is not like that.

But Glasgow days and grey weathers, when the rain
beat on the bus shelter and you leaned slightly against me, and the back of your
    hand touched my hand in the shadows, and nothing was said,
when your hair grazed mine accidentally as we talked in a café, yet not quite
    accidentally,
when I stole a glance at your face as we stood in a doorway and found I was afraid
of what might happen if I should never see it again,
when we met, and met, in spite of such differences in our lives,
and did the common things that in our feeling
became extraordinary, so that our first kiss
was like the winter morning moon, and as you shifted in my arms
it was the sea changing the shingle that changes it
as if for ever (but we are bound by nothing, but like smoke
to mist or light in water we move, and mix) –
O then it was a story as old as war or man,
and although we have not said it we know it,
and although we have not claimed it we do it,
and although we have not vowed it we keep it,
without a name to the end

From the Domain of Arnheim[1]

And so that all these ages, these years
we cast behind us, like the smoke-clouds
dragged back into vacancy when the rocket springs –

1. 'The Domain of Arnheim': title of a short story by E. A. Poe, and a painting by Magritte.

The domain of Arnheim was all snow, but we were there.
We saw a yellow light thrown on the icefield
from the huts by the pines, and laughter came up
floating from a white corrie
miles away, clearly.
We moved on down, arm in arm.
I know you would have thought it was a dream
but we were there. And those were trumpets –
tremendous round the rocks –
while they were burning fires of trash and mammoths' bones.
They sang naked, and kissed in the smoke.
A child, or one of their animals, was crying.
Young men blew the ice crystals off their drums.
We came down among them, but of course
they could see nothing, on their time-scale.
Yet they sensed us, stopped, looked up – even into our eyes.
To them we were a displacement of the air,
a sudden chill, yet we had no power
over their fear. If one of them had been dying
he would have died. The crying
came from one just born: that was the cause
of the song. We saw it now. What had we stopped
but joy?
I know you felt
the same dismay, you gripped my arm, they were waiting
for what they knew of us to pass.
A sweating trumpeter took
a brand from the fire with a shout and threw it
where our bodies would have been –
we felt nothing but his courage.
And so they would deal with every imagined power
seen or unseen.
There are no gods in the domain of Arnheim.

We signalled to the ship; got back;
our lives and days returned to us, but
haunted by deeper souvenirs than any rocks or seeds.
From time the souvenirs are deeds.

To Joan Eardley[1]

Pale yellow letters
humbly straggling across
the once brilliant red

---

1. Joan Eardley (1921–1963), a painter noted for her studies of Glasgow slum children in the 1950s and 1960s. Morgan
   owns the painting described.

of a broken shop-face
CONFECTIO
and a blur of children
at their games, passing,
gazing as they pass
at the blur of sweets
in the dingy, cosy
Rottenrow window –
an Eardley on my wall.
Such rags and streaks
that master us! –
that fix what the pick
and bulldozer have crumbled
to a dingier dust,
the living blur
fiercely guarding energy that has vanished,
cries filling still
the unechoing close!   tenement passageway
I wandered by the rubble
and the houses left standing
kept a chill, dying life
in their islands of stone.
No window opened
as the coal cart rolled
and the coalman's call
fell coldly to the ground.
But the shrill children
jump on my wall.

Glasgow Green

Clammy midnight, moonless mist.
A cigarette glows and fades on a cough.
Meth-men mutter on benches,   (meths drinkers)
pawed by river fog. Monteith Row
sweats coldly, crumbles, dies
slowly. All shadows are alive.
Somewhere a shout's forced out – 'No!' –
it leads to nothing but silence,
except the whisper of the grass
and the other whispers that fill the shadows.

'What d'ye mean see me again?
D'ye think I came here jist for that?
I'm no finished with you yet.
I can get the boys t'ye, they're no that faur away.

You wouldny like that eh? Look there's no two ways aboot it.
Christ but I'm gaun to have you Mac
if it takes all night, turn over you bastard
turn over, I'll——'
      Cut the scene.
Here there's no crying for help,
it must be acted out, again, again.
This is not the delicate nightmare
you carry to the point of fear
and wake from, it is life, the sweat
is real, the wrestling under a bush
is real, the dirty starless river
is the real Clyde, with a dishrag dawn
it rinses the horrors of the night
but cannot make them clean,
though washing blows
                   where the women watch
by day
        and children run,
              on Glasgow Green.

And how shall these men live?
Providence, watch them go!
Watch them love, and watch them die!
How shall the race be served?
It shall be served by anguish
as well as by children at play.
It shall be served by loneliness
as well as by family love.
It shall be served by hunter and hunted in their endless chain
as well as by those who turn back the sheets in peace.
The thorn in the flesh!
Providence, water it!
Do you think it is not watered?
Do you think it is not planted?
Do you think there is not a seed of the thorn
as there is also a harvest of the thorn?[1]
Man, take in that harvest!
Help that tree to bear its fruit!
Water the wilderness, walk there, reclaim it!
Reclaim, regain, renew! Fill the barns and the vats!

Longing,
      longing
           shall find its wine.

1. See Matthew 7:16.

Let the women sit in the Green
and rock their prams as the sheets
blow and whip in the sunlight.
But the beds of married love
are islands in a sea of desire.
Its waves break here, in this park,
splashing the flesh as it trembles
like driftwood through the dark.

One Cigarette

No smoke without you, my fire.
After you left,
your cigarette glowed on in my ashtray
and sent up a long thread of such quiet grey
I smiled to wonder who would believe its signal
of so much love. One cigarette
in the non-smoker's tray.
As the last spire
trembles up, a sudden draught
blows it winding into my face.
Is it smell, is it taste?
You are here again, and I am drunk on your tobacco lips.
Out with the light.
Let the smoke lie back in the dark.
Till I hear the very ash
sigh down among the flowers of brass
I'll breathe, and long past midnight, your last kiss.

Absence

My shadow –
I woke to a wind swirling the curtains light and dark
and the birds twittering on the roofs, I lay cold
in the early light in my room high over London.
What fear was it that made the wind sound like a fire
so that I got up and looked out half-asleep
at the calm rows of street-lights fading far below?
Without fire
only the wind blew.
But in the dream I woke from, you
came running through the traffic, tugging me, clinging
to my elbow, your eyes spoke
what I could not grasp –
Nothing, if you were here!

The wind of the early quiet
merges slowly now with a thousand rolling wheels.
The lights are out, the air is loud.
It is an ordinary January day
My shadow, do you hear the streets?
Are you at my heels? Are you here?
And I throw back the sheets.

Glasgow 5 March 1971[1]

With a ragged diamond
of shattered plate-glass
a young man and his girl
are falling backwards into a shop-window.
The young man's face
is bristling with fragments of glass
and the girl's leg has caught
on the broken window
and spurts arterial blood
over her wet-look white coat.
Their arms are starfished out
braced for impact,
Their faces show surprise, shock,
and the beginning of pain.
The two youths who have pushed them
are about to complete the operation
reaching into the window
to loot what they can smartly.
Their faces show no expression.
It is a sharp clear night
in Sauchiehall Street.
In the background two drivers
keep their eyes on the road.

Ellingham Suffolk January 1972

Below a water-mill at midnight
breaking the river Waveney into white
an intricate water-dance of forty-one swans
and one man leaning from the mill window
smokes and broods
ravished and nothing understood.

---

1. This and the following piece are 'Instamatic' poems in which Morgan describes imagined photographs of actual news
    stories.

The First Men on Mercury

– We come in peace from the third planet.
Would you take us to your leader?

– Bawr stretter! Bawr. Bawr. Stretterhawl?

– This is a little plastic model
of the solar system, with working parts.
You are here and we are there and we
are now here with you, is this clear?

– Gawl horrop. Bawr. Abawrhannahanna!

– Where we come from is blue and white
with brown, you see we call the brown
here 'land', the blue is 'sea', and the white
is 'clouds' over land and sea, we live
on the surface of the brown land,
all round is sea and clouds. We are 'men'.
Men come –

– Glawp men! Gawrbenner menko. Menhawl?

– Men come in peace from the third planet
which we call 'earth'. We are earthmen.
Take us earthmen to your leader.

– Thmen? Thmen? Bawr. Bawrhossop.
Yuleeda tan hanna. Harrabost yuleeda.

– I am the yuleeda. You see my hands,
we carry no benner, we come in peace.
The spaceways are all stretterhawn.

– Glawn peacemen all horrabhanna tantko!
Tan come at'mstrossop. Glawp yuleeda!

– Atoms are peacegawl in our harraban.
Menbat worrabost from tan hannahanna.

– You men we know bawrhossoptant. Bawr.
We know yuleeda. Go strawg backspetter quick.

– We cantantabawr, tantingko backspetter now!

– Banghapper now! Yes, third planet back.
Yuleeda will go back blue, white, brown
nowhanna! There is no more talk.

– Gawl han fasthapper?

– No. You must go back to your planet.
Go back in peace, take what you have gained
but quickly.

– Stretterworra gawl, gawl …

– Of course, but nothing is ever the same,
now is it? You'll remember Mercury.

from 'London'

iii: The Post Office Tower

There is no other life,
and this is it.
Gold bars, thunder, gravity, wine, concrete, smoke.
And the blue pigeon London sky
hangs high heat on towers, a summer shower
on trees, its clouds
to swing over cranes
that swing slowly
blue vaguely.
We are drawn to the welder's star.
Ships we
half see.
Glass walls flash new cliffsides, brick-beds
brood with dust, red, grey, grey, blue.
Huge shadows skim the classic terraces.
Hunt sun hunt cloud, one long morning.

And life comes out on the roofs. A breeze
shakes raindrops from bonsai pines,
penthouse terrazzo gleams, dries, washed by heaven
around a fishpool: in dark glasses, a severe white suit
she stands by the marble verge and calls a dog, silently
twenty storeys above the roar.
On a roof southward, broken concrete
between two chimneys blossoms
in a line of washing, an old man
on a hard chair, his hands in his lap,
stares at nothing – linen flowers

tugging to be free. And like some fine insect
poised on a blackened outcrop of stone
a young man mends an aerial far down the central haze,
straddles a fire-escape in ice-blue jeans
and striped shirt, arms bare to the shoulder and his hair
is blown across his arms
as he moves the metal arms
into the path of their messages.
– And all that grace to dwindle to
a faded dressing-gown, a kitchen chair in the sun.
Years in shadows come low
over a penthouse garden dark with weeds,
phones ringing through empty rooms
for ashes thrown on the sea.
But still of life
not in clean waves and airs
the messages most heard
come to the tower
from asphalt and smoke
and break in rings
of strange accident
and mortal change
on the rain wet
silver bars.
It is its own telegrams,
what mounts, what sighs,
what says it is
unaccountable
as feelings moved
by hair blown over
an arm in the wind.
In its acts
it rests there.

The Planets

The planets move, and earth is one, I know.
Blue with endlessly moving seas,
white with clouds endlessly moving,
and the continents creep on plates
endlessly moving soundlessly.
How should we be exempt
or safe from change, we walk
on mercury from birth to death.
A face comes through the crowd, lips move, new eyes,
and the house of roots trembles,

its doors are slack, its windows yawn,
a place not known to be defenceless
undefended. Who wants sedge
at the streak of the kingfisher?
Now you have almost worn out my tape
of 'The Planets', but I don't know yours,
or your sign, though Mars the Bringer of War
is what you play most. We've talked
of Jenghiz Khan, of Christ, of Frankenstein.
I don't know whether you believe
in the fate I can't not believe in,
simply to watch you swinging
in my black vinyl chair,
even bringing war.

Theory of the Earth

James Hutton[1] that true son of fire who said
to Burns 'Aye, man, the rocks melt wi the sun'
was sure the age of reason's time was done:
what but imagination could have read
granite boulders back to their molten roots?
And how far back was back, and how far on
would basalt still be basalt, iron iron?
Would second seas re-drown the fossil brutes?
'We find no vestige of a beginning,
no prospect of an end.' They died almost
together, poet and geologist,
and lie in wait for hilltop buoys to ring,
or aw the seas gang dry and Scotland's coast
dissolve in crinkled sand and pungent mist.

'Dear man, my love goes out in waves'

Dear man, my love goes out in waves
and breaks. Whatever is, craves.
Terrible the cage
to see all life from, brilliantly about,
crowds, pavements, cars, or hear the common shout
of goals in a near park.
But now the black bars arc
blue in my breath – split – part
I'm out – it's art,
it's love, it's rage –

1. Hutton's *Theory of the Earth* (1795) was a key work of geology which established the igneous origin of rocks. See Robert Burns, 'A red red Rose'.

Standing in rage in decent air
will never clear the place of care.
Simply to be
should be enough, in the same city, and let
absurd despair tramp and roar off-set.
Be satisfied with it,
the gravel and the grit
the struggling eye can't lift,
the veils that drift,
the weird to dree.   fate; endure

Press close to me at midnight as
you say goodbye; that's what it has
to offer, life
I mean. Into the frost with you; into
the bed with me; and get the light out too.
Better to shake unseen
and let real darkness screen
the shadows of the heart, the vacant part-
ner, husband, wife.

from From the Video Box[1]

6

my friend and I watched that scratch that scratch video[2]
last night we watched that last night I was
on the black chesterfield and Steve was on the
black chair not that that will interest viewers
interest viewers but I want to be authentic
on the black the black chesterfield just as the sun
went down reddish outside and I could switch
from the set to the sky and back sky and back
and back back there was a squeezed sunset
on the set between gables and a helicopter cut
through the reddish screen like a black tin-opener
while suddenly a crow flew suddenly a crow
a crow flew through the real red outside what we
call the real red and tore it silently it silently
a scratch in air never to be solved scratch
in air Steve said never solved as inside
back went the helicopter to start again
to start again I said those gables don't

1. One of a sequence of poems conceived from the TV programme 'Right to Reply' in which viewers could record their
   own messages in an automatic video-booth.
2. By analogy with 'scratch' record playing which backtracks and repeats phrases by manipulating and reversing the vinyl
   disc.

grow dark those gables don't grow dark
that's what I want to say they don't grow
dark those gables on the set

17

That was so strange last night –
I thought I saw my son
who was lost overboard in a storm
off Valparaiso – five years gone –
I know he was drowned, his body
was washed up on the rocks
and brought back home to Gourock
where I can see his grave.
There are no ghosts. What I saw
in that split-second flash
was an image only a mother
could be sure to be her son,
to have been her son surely
since he was no longer there.
It came in a blizzard of images,
a speeded mosaic of change
in the Americas, I watched
half bored, irritated
by the strident music, ready
to switch channels – then! –
not in his seaman's cloth
but a camouflage jacket,
looking straight at the camera,
his fist in a revolutionary salute,
a letter sticking from his pocket
with writing I saw as mine.
Oh how little we know
of those we love! Perhaps
it was sabotage, not storm,
that sank his ship – perhaps
that broken body after all
was not – oh images, images,
corners of the world seen
out of the corner of an eye –
subversive, subliminal –
where have you taken my son
into your terrible machine
and why have you peeled off
my grief like a decal
and left me a nobody
staring out to sea?

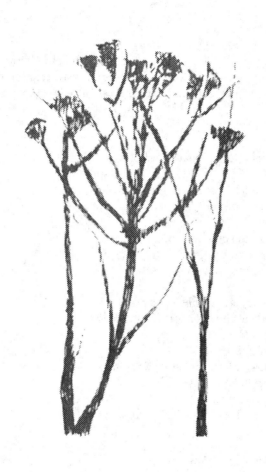

Ruaraidh MacThomais/
Derick Thomson (1921–   )

Born in Stornoway on the Isle of Lewis, Derick Thomson was educated at the Universities of Aberdeen, Cambridge and Bangor and was Professor of Celtic Studies at Glasgow University from 1963 to 1991. As a founder editor of the quarterly *Gairm*,

Pabail

Air iomall an talamh-àitich, eadar dhà sholas,
tha a’ churracag a’ ruith ’s a’ stad, ’s a’ ruith ’s a’ stad,
is cobhar bàn a broillich, mar rionnag an fheasgair,
ga lorg ’s ga chall aig mo shùilean,
is tùis an t-samhraidh
ga lorg ’s ga chall aig mo chuinnlean,
is fras-mhullach tonn an t-sonais
ga lorg ’s ga chall aig mo chuimhne.

Bàgh Phabail fodham, is baile Phabail air fàire,
sluaisreadh sìorraidh a’ chuain, a lorg ’s a shireadh
eadar clachan a’ mhuil ’s an eag nan sgeir,
is fo ghainmhich a’ gheodha,
gluasad bithbhuan a’ bhaile, am bàs ‘s an ùrtan,
an ùrnaigh ’s an t-suirghe, is mile cridhe
ag at ’s a’ seacadh, is ann an seo
tha a’ churracag a’ ruith ’s a’ stad, ’s a’ ruith ’s a’ stad.

Troimh Uinneig a’ Chithe

Nuair tha ’n sneachda mìn seo a’ tuiteam,
a’ streap gu sàmhach ris na h-uinneagan,
a’ mirean air sruthan na h-iarmailt,
ga chàrnadh fhéin ri gàrraidhean
’na chithean sàr-mhaiseach,
is mo mhac ’na leum le aoibhneas,

he has been actively involved in Gaelic publishing all his life. His fine free verse
contains elegiac reflections on the fate of Gaelic, tender love lyrics and quietly barbed
comments on modern culture and politics.

Bayble[1]

On the edge of the arable land, between two lights,
the plover runs and stops, and runs and stops,
the white foam of its breast like the star of evening,
discovered and lost in my looking,
and the fragrance of summer,
discovered and lost by my nostrils,
and the topmost grains of the wave of content,
discovered and lost by my memory.

Bayble Bay below me, and the village on the skyline,
the eternal action of the ocean, its seeking and searching
between the pebble stones and in the rock crannies,
and under the sand of the cove;
the everlasting movement of the village, death and christening,
praying and courting, and a thousand hearts
swelling and sinking, and here,
the plover runs and stops, and runs and stops.

When This Fine Snow is Falling

When this fine snow is falling,
climbing quietly to the windows,
dancing on air-currents,
piling itself up against walls
in lovely drifts,
while my son leaps with joy,

1. Bayble is the poet's home village.

chì mi 'na shùilean-san greadhnachas gach geamhradh
a thàinig a riamh air mo dhaoine:
faileas an t-sneachda an sùilean m' athar,
's mo sheanair 'na bhalach a' ribeadh dhìdeigean.

Is chì mi troimh uinneig a' chithe seo,
's anns an sgàthan tha mire ris,
am bealach tha bearradh nan linntean
eadar mise, 's mi falbh nan sgàirneach,
agus mo shinnsrean, a-muigh air àirigh,
a' buachailleachd chruidh-bainne 's ag òl a' bhlàthaich.
Chì mi faileas an taighean 's am buailtean
air fàire an uaigneis,
's tha siud mar phàirt de mo dhualchas.

Iadsan a' fàgail staid a' bhalaich,
's a' strì ri fearann, 's a' treabhadh na mara
le neart an guaillibh,
's ag adhradh, air uairibh;
is mise caitheamh an spionnaidh, ach ainneamh,
a' treabhadh ann an gainneamh.

Anns a' Bhalbh Mhadainn

Anns a' bhalbh mhadainn bha clàr an fhuinn còmhnard,
bha a' ghaoth aig fois, a strannraich 's a sitheadh
bàthte fon ghilead, gach bleideag 'na tàmh,
càiricht san fhighe mhìn ud mar gheal phlaide.
Chaill sinn na caoraich bha muigh air mòintich
nuair thaom an stoirm ud a-nuas eallach,
is thug sinn a' mhadainn gan dian shireadh.

Thainig stoirm air mo dhùthaich,
sneachda min, marbhteach, mùchaidh:
ge geal e, na creid 'na ghilead,
na cuir t'earbs ann an anart;
dheanadh mo chridhe iollach
nam faicinn air a' chlàr bhàn sin ball buidhe
's gun tuiginn gu robh anail a' Ghaidheil a' tighinn am mullach.

Cisteachan-Laighe

Duin' àrd, tana
's fiasag bheag air,
's locair 'na làimh:
gach uair theid mi seachad

I see in his eyes the elation
that every winter brought to my people:
the reflection of snow in my father's eyes,
and my grandfather as a boy snaring starlings.

And I see, through the window of this snowdrift,
and in the glass that dancingly reflects it,
the hill-pass cutting through the generations
that lie between me, on the scree,
and my ancestors, out on the shieling,   hut on high summer pasture
herding milk-cows and drinking buttermilk.
I see their houses and fields reflected
on the lonely horizon,
and that is part of my heritage.

When their boyhood came to an end
they strove with the land, and ploughed the sea
with the strength of their shoulders,
and worshipped, sometimes;
I spend their strength, for the most part,
Ploughing in the sand.

Sheep

In the still morning the surface of the land was flat,
the wind had died down, its rumbling and thrusting
drowned under the whiteness, each snowflake at rest,
set in its soft fabric like a white blanket.
We had lost the sheep that were out on the moor
when that storm unloaded its burden,
and we spent the morning desperately seeking them.

A storm came over my country,
of fine, deadly, smothering snow:
though it is white, do not believe in its whiteness,
do not set your trust in a shroud;
my heart would rejoice
were I to see on that white plain a yellow spot,
and understand that the breath of the Gael was coming to the surface.

Coffins

A tall thin man
with a short beard,
and a plane in his hand:
whenever I pass

air bùth-shaoirsneachd sa' bhaile,
's a thig gu mo chuinnlean fàileadh na min-sàibh,
thig gu mo chuimhne cuimhne an àit ud,
le na cisteachan-laighe,
na h-ùird 's na tairgean,
na sàibh 's na sgeilbean,
is mo sheanair crom,
is sliseag bho shliseag ga locradh
bhon bhòrd thana lom.

Mus robh fhìos agam dè bh' ann bàs;
beachd, bloigh fios, boillsgeadh
den dorchadas, fathann den t-sàmhchair.
'S nuair a sheas mi aig uaigh,
là fuar Earraich, cha dainig smuain
thugam air na cisteachan-laighe
a rinn esan do chàch:
'sann a bha mi 'g iarraidh dhachaigh,
far am biodh còmhradh, is tea, is blàths.

Is anns an sgoil eile cuideachd,
san robh saoir na h-inntinn a' locradh,
cha tug mi 'n aire do na cisteachan-laighe,
ged a bha iad 'nan suidhe mun cuairt orm;
cha do dh' aithnich mi 'm brèid Beurla,
an lìomh Gallda bha dol air an fhiodh,
cha do leugh mi na facail air a' phràis,
cha do thuig mi gu robh mo chinneadh a' dol bàs.
Gus an dainig gaoth fhuar an Earraich-sa
a locradh a' chridhe;
gus na dh' fhairich mi na tairgean a' dol tromham,
's cha shlànaich tea no còmhradh an cràdh.

from **An Rathad Cian**

14: Is chunnaic mi thu 'na do bheairt

Is chunnaic mi thu 'na do bheairt
an taigh-cùil is glas air:
thainig bodach eòlach á Glaschu
a dhearbhadh dè bh' unnad,
is dh'aithnich e 'n t-slinn 's an crann-snàth,
an t-sliseag-uchd a bha dlùth ri broilleach,
's am maide-teannaidh;
chunnaic e làrach nan cas,
is làrach nam meur air an spàl,

a joiner's shop in the city,   carpenter's
and the scent of sawdust comes to my nostrils,
memories return of that place,
with the coffins,
the hammers and nails,
saws and chisels,
and my grandfather, bent,
planing shavings
from a thin, bare plank.

Before I knew what death was;
or had any notion, a glimmering
of the darkness, a whisper of the stillness.
And when I stood at his grave,
on a cold Spring day, not a thought
came to me of the coffins
he made for others:
I merely wanted home
where there would be talk, and tea, and warmth.

And in the other school also,
where the joiners of the mind were planing,
I never noticed the coffins,
though they were sitting all round me;
I did not recognise the English braid,
the Lowland varnish being applied to the wood,
I did not read the words on the brass,
I did not understand that my race was dying.
Until the cold wind of this Spring came
to plane the heart;
until I felt the nails piercing me,
and neither tea nor talk will heal the pain.

from The Far Road

14: And I saw you as a loom

And I saw you as a loom
in a locked outhouse:
a knowledgeable fellow from Glasgow
came to identify you,
and he recognised the sleay and the beam,
the breast-beam that was close to the chest,
and the beam that the weights hung on;
and he saw the footmarks,
and the finger-marks on the shuttle,

agus na fuigheagan,
is chaidh e dhachaigh agus rinn e sgeulachd ort.

35: An Glaschu
Oidhche Shathuirn air Stràid Jamaica
is feasgar na Sàbaid air Great Western Road,
a' coiseachd 's a' coiseachd anns an t-saoghal ùr;
sìtheanan anns na gàrraidhean,
giobal 's an deoch air ann an doras bùthadh,
an Soisgeul a' tighinn rèidh ás a' chùbainn;
'Eil fada bho nach d'fhuair sibh bhon taigh?'

Is gaoth nan clobhsaichean,
is fasgadh ann an oisinn,
gaoth an iar-'eas le teanga fhliuch,
buntata 's sgadan,
tiormachd na mine an cùl na h-amhach,
glagadaich ann an gàrradh nan soithichean,
a' chailleach a' gearain air prìs an èisg;
'Bi 'g òl ruma 's na bi sgrìobhadh dhachaigh.'

An daorach air Stràid Jamaica,
an traoghadh air Great Western Road,
an Soisgeul anns a' ghàrradh,
sìtheanan anns a' mhuilinn-fhlùir,
a' chailleach anns a' chlobhs,
is tiormachd ann an cùl na h-amhach;
'BHEIL FADA BHO NACH D'FHUAIR SIBH BHON TAIGH?'

36: 'Bheil cuimhn' agad …?'
'Bheil cuimhn' agad …'
– seo air bus ann a Sauchiehall Street –
ars esan, 'an là bha sinn anns a' mhòine …?'
Tha. 'Na mo chuis-bhùirt ann am meadhon Ghlaschu,
ann am meadhon mo bheatha, ann am meadhon Alba,
'na mo shuidh air prugan
a' toirt riamhaichean calcais ás a chèile.
Taing do Dhia gu bheil teine 'na mo bhroinn fhathast.

39: Is chunna mi thu 'na do bhàta
Is chunna mi thu 'na do bhàta
am meadhon na mara,
na lìn ann am pasgadh 's tu feitheamh ri cur.
Shaoil thu gu robh an sgadan pailt
romhad, ga shnìomh anns a' chlàr uaine,
caitean air cur is dlùth,

and the thrums,
and he went home and wrote a report on you.

35: In Glasgow
Saturday night on Jamaica Street
and Sunday evening on Great Western Road,
walking, walking in the new world;
flowers in the yards,
a young fellow, tight, in a shop doorway,
the Gospel coming quietly from the pulpit;
'Is it long since you heard from home?'

And the wind in the closes,
taking shelter in a corner,
a wet-tongued south-west wind,
potatoes and herring,
meal-dryness in the back of the throat,
a clatter in the shipyard,
the landlady complaining of the price of fish;
'Drink rum and don't write home.'

Jamaica Street plastered,
a dry throat on Great Western Road,
the Gospel in the Garden,
flowers in the meal-mill,
the old woman in the close,
and dryness at the back of the throat;
'IS IT LONG SINCE YOU HEARD FROM HOME?'

36: 'Do you remember ...?'
'Do you remember ...'
– this on a bus in Sauchiehall Street –
said he, 'the day we spent at the peats?'
Yes. Making an ass of myself in the middle of Glasgow,
in the midst of my life,
in the midst of Scotland,
sitting on a tuft of moor-grass
teasing out peat fibres.
Thank God I have fire in my belly still.

39: And I saw you as a boat
And I saw you as a boat
in the middle of the sea,
the nets coiled ready for casting.
You thought the herring were thick
in your path, woven on the green,
nap on warp and weft,

ach bha thu ceàrr.
Nuair a sheall thu a-rithist
cha robh ann ach cnàmhan an èisg,
's bha do làmh fuar fon a' phairilis.
Nuair a thug mi sùil eil' ort
chunnaic mi d'ainm sgrìobht ann a litrichean mòra
METAGAMA.

A' Bhan-phrionnsa Diàna

'Nam sheasamh ann an streath
am Buffet an Central an Glaschu,
chunnaic mi a' Bhan-phrionnsa Diàna
'na seasamh air mo bheulaibh anns an loidhne,
seacaid bhèin oirr', 's a falt
cho grinn ann an òrdugh,
boillsgeadh airgid ann,
's an t-sròin cho dìreach,
ard, le casan fada;
còmhradh Ghlaschu a bh' aice,
's thuirt mi rium fhìn
'Nach math
gu bheil a leithid ann dhith
's gu bheil i cho snog 's a thà i,
's nach ro-mhath
gur h-e còmhradh Ghlaschu a th' aice fhathast'.

Tilleadh Bhon a' Bhàs

Nuair a thàinig mi air ais bhon a' bhàs
bha a' mhadainn ann,
bha an doras-cùil fosgailte,
is bha putan dhe na bha 'na mo lèine air chall.

B' fheudar dhomh am feur a chùnntadh a-rithist,
is na leacan,
is dh'fhairich mi blas an ìm ùir air a' bhuntàt'.

Bha 'n càr ag iarraidh peatroil,
's an gaol 'na shuidhe gu stòlda air seuthar,
is tachais anns an iosgaid agam.

'S ma tha thu creidse mar tha mise
gun tuig fear-leughaidh leth-fhacal,
chì thu nach tug mi iomradh
ach air rud no dhà a dh' fhairich mi.

but you were wrong.
When you looked again
there was nothing but herringbone
and your hand cold in paralysis.
When I looked at you again
I saw your name written in large letters
METAGAMA.[1]

Princess Diana

Standing in a queue
in Glasgow Central's Buffet,
I saw Princess Diana
standing in front of me in the line,
wearing a fur cape, her hair
prettily in order,
and with some silver tinting,
a straight nose,
tall, long-legged;
talking in a Glasgow accent,
and I said to myself:
'It's good
there are so many of her,
and that she's as attractive as she is,
and what a bonus it is
that she still talks with a Glasgow accent'.

Return from Death

When I came back from death
it was morning,
the back door was open
and one of the buttons of my shirt had disappeared.

I needed to count the grass-blades again,
and the flagstones,
and I got the taste of fresh butter on the potatoes.

The car needed petrol,
and love sat sedately on a chair,
and there was an itchy feeling at the back of my knee.

And if you believe, as I do,
that one who reads can understand half a word,
you can see that I've mentioned
Only a couple of things I felt then.

1. The *Metagama* was the most famous (notorious) of the emigrant ships to leave Lewis in the early 1920s.

George Mackay Brown (1921–)

Mackay Brown was a mature pupil of Edwin Muir's at Newbattle Abbey, near Edinburgh. Afflicted by tuberculosis in his early years, he went on to take a degree at Edinburgh University before returning to Orkney, the island of his birth, where he has lived and worked in Stromness as a full-time journalist, poet and novelist ever since. His poetic voice is influenced by the archetypal simplicity of the Norse sagas, and he is haunted by a vision of Orkney as a timeless traditional community, at one with a cycle of life which is essentially religious and sacramental.

Ikey on the People of Hellya

Rognvald who stalks round Corse with his stick
I do not love.
His dog has a loud sharp mouth.
The wood of his door is very hard.
Once, tangled in his barbed wire
(I was paying respects to his hens, stroking a wing)
He laid his stick on me.
That was out of a hard forest also.

Mansie at Quoy is a biddable man.
Ask for water, he gives you rum.
I strip his scarecrow April by April.
Ask for a scattering of straw in his byre
He lays you down
Under a quilt as long and light as heaven.
Then only his raging woman spoils our peace.

Gray the fisherman is no trouble now
Who quoted me the vagrancy laws
In a voice slippery as seaweed under the kirkyard.
I rigged his boat with the seven curses.
Occasionally still, for encouragement,
I put the knife in his net.

Though she has black peats and a yellow hill
And fifty silken cattle

I do not go near Merran and her cats.
Rather break a crust on a tombstone.
Her great-great-grandmother
Wore the red coat at Gallowsha.[1]

A Winter Bride

The three fishermen said to Jess of The Shore
'A wave took Jock
Between The Kist and The Sneuk.
We couldn't get him, however we placed the boat.
With all that drag and clutch and swell
He has maybe one in a hundred chances.'
They left some mouthing cuithes in the door.   young coalfish
She had stood in this threshold, fire and innocence,
A winter bride.
Now she laid off her workaday shawl,
She put on the black.
(Girl and widow across a drowned wife
Laid wondering neck on neck.)
She took the soundless choir of fish
And a sharp knife
And went the hundred steps to the pool in the rock.
Give us this day our daily bread
She swilled and cut
And laid psalms and blessings on her dish.

In the bay the waves pursued their indifferent dances.

Haddock Fishermen

Midnight. The wind yawing nor-east.
A low blunt moon.
Unquiet beside quiet wives we rest.

A spit of rain and a gull
In the open door.
The lit fire. A quick mouthful of ale.

We push the *Merle* at a sea of cold flame.
The oars drip honey.
Hook by hook uncoils under The Kame.

1. A 'red-coat' of flame – was burned as a witch.

Our line breaks the trek of sudden thousands.
Twelve nobbled jaws,
Gray cowls, gape in our hands,

Twelve cold mouths scream without sound.
The sea is empty again.
Like tinkers the bright ones endlessly shift their ground.

We probe emptiness all the afternoon;
Unyoke; and taste
The true earth-food, beef and a barley scone.

Sunset drives a butcher blade
In the day's throat.
We turn through an ebb salt and sticky as blood.

More stars than fish. Women, cats, a gull
Mewl at the rock.
The valley divides the meagre miracle.

Love Letter

To Mistress Madeline Richan, widow
At Quoy, parish of Voes, in the time of hay:

The old woman sat in her chair, mouth agape
At the end of April.
There were buttercups in a jar in the window.

The floor is not a blue mirror now
And the table has flies and bits of crust on it.

Also the lamp glass is broken.

I have the shop at the end of the house
With sugar, tea, tobacco, paraffin
And, for whisperers, a cup of whisky.

There is a cow, a lady of butter, in the long silk grass
And seven sheep on Moorfea.

The croft girls are too young.
Nothing but giggles, lipstick, and gramophone records.

Walk over the hill Friday evening.
Enter without knocking
If you see one red rose in the window.

Sea Widow

1

Silence
Did I plead with you to keep from that rock
Where the *Merle* lost strake and mast?
I have dreamed of the white bone under a wheeling flock.
I said, 'On that skerry he'll be cast
This fog or that gale –
A kind story will be over at last.
It is not good for a man to plunder the horizons and bounds of the whale.'
But I said nothing. Love ebbed and flowed. We kept the feast and the fast.
Last night my father came with the funeral ale.

2

Lost Lovers
What if I had turned to greet the tall stranger
With kindness on his face, on the road?
There was one mouth that trembled with desire and danger.
Another suggested a clover ditch for the drift of his seed.
A merchant promised whiteness, a ring, a proper blessing in the precincts of God.
That man was grey and gentle and rich.

I was carried to a door marked with salt, and with tar and weed.

3

What the Fisherman Said
There is no bread like the crust and fragrance
From your hands.

A fisherman dreads a witchlook
On the road to his boat.
Stand well behind me, girl, and always.

Leave that old man
And three thankless brothers.
There are women whose love at last is all for cats.

Spin out of me
Into yourself, the stuff of life, secretly.
Weave it on a sweet loom.

I have not relished ale-house talk
Nor my pipe
With its flame-flowers and smoke and spit,
Nor even Sigurd's fiddle

Since the first kiss among seaweed.
Next morning I woke richer than laird or merchant.

There is nothing to the snow and daffodils and larkrise of you.

Sealed with the brightness of your mouth
How will it be for me now
In the dangerous house of the sea-girls?

Why was this study not ardently taught
Among the globes and inkpots?
Love is better than numbers, seaports, battles.

I will build you a house with my hands,
A stored cupboard,
Undying hearth-flames, a door open to friend and stranger.

I wished once I had not met you.
Sea generations are too long.
It is a net I have folded in your womb.

From strange earth and stones,
A kirkyard on another shore with different names
You came through wind and cornstalks
For the mixing of dust,
For two names to be carved on one stone.
I did not think then
You might lie under it lonely
And I shells, salt, seaweed.

I have put a black streak of tar
Through the ignorant name on the hull
And painted yours there, in red.
Old men, going past, look wicked and young.

4

Wedding Ring
Gold to enclose two lives for ever. There were maybe four
Good rounds, perfect returnings, in that one year,
Four circles of grace.
The rest were pub-stoked lurchings, blood on his face,
Back to my healing or raging hand –
A trudging up from the beach with broken gear,
Or from the merchant's with meagre silver
For his baskets of shifting bronze.

He was lost three days, at the fair, with tinker and miller.
And once
I left him, stone-eared to all his implorings,
His vowing and swearing,
And stayed a month at my father's place.
Four precious restorings
Made all those tatters of time the bridal coat
And sweeter with every wearing.
He left all, house and woman and boat
For a wave that trundled him on past time and space.
The bed, where each day's devious circle closed, is seedless and lonely.
They unweave him, mackerel and gull.
I know the man only
In flecks of salt and grains of sand,
And when through the drifting pools of a child's face
Looks back the skull.

Tea Poems

1: Chinaman

Water, first creature of the gods.
It dances in many masks.
    For a young child, milk.
    For the peasant, honey and mud.
    For lovers and poets, wine.
    For the man on his way to the block, many well-directed spits.
    For an enemy, mixings of blood.
    For the Dragon-god, ichor.
    For a dead friend, a measure of eye-salt.

A courteous man is entertaining strangers
Among his goldfish and willows.
The musician sits in the pavilion door
(His flute is swathed in silk.)
An urn is brought to the table by girls.
This is the water of offered friendship.
Notice the agreeable angle of pouring,
The pure ascending columns of vapour,
The precise arrangement of finger and bowl and lip.
Birds make all about those sippers and smilers ceremonies of very sweet sound.

2: Smugglers

Midnight. Measured musical cold sea circles.
The yawl struck suddenly!
Oars wrapped the boat in a tangled web.
The boy cried out – Smith gagged him with tarry fingers.

It was no rock, not the fearful face of Hoy.
The boat spun back from pliant timbers.
A maze of voices above us then.
Our skipper growled, 'Where's your light?'
(A lantern was to hang in the cross-trees
For half-an-hour after midnight.
In the Arctic Whaler, that had been harped on well.)
'You comm too litt,' a Dutchman said,
The words like a fankle of rusted wire.   tangle
'A sticky ebb,' said Smith
'And it's only twenty-past-twelve. Lower down
Twelve kegs rum, tobacco as much as you've got,
A horn of snuff for the laird. Have you rolls of silk?'
He drew out silver, rang it in his fist like a bell.
Now we could see green-black curves of hull,
Cropped heads hung over the side,
Even the mouth that was torturing the language.
'Fif box tea, bess China.'
With fearful patience our skipper told on his fingers
The smuggler's litany:
Silk, rum, tobacco. The florins chimed in his fist.   (a 2-shilling coin: 10p)
'Rum. Tobacco. Silk. That was the understanding.'
Smith swore to God not he nor any Orkneyman
Would risk rope or irons for women's swill.
He pleaded. He praised. He threatened.
Again the stony voice from the star-web above. 'Tea.
Noding but China tea. For silver. Fif box.'

3: Afternoon Tea
Drank Mrs Leask, sticking out her pinkie.
Drank Mrs Spence, having poured in a tinkle-tinkle of
      whisky (I've such a bad cold!)
Drank Mrs Halcrow, kissing her cup like a lover.
Drank Mrs Traill, and her Pekinese filthied the floor with bits of
      biscuit and chocolate.
Drank Mrs Clouston, through rocky jaws.
Drank Mrs Heddle, her mouth dodging a sliver of lemon.
Drank Bella the tea wife, who then read engagements,
      letters, trips and love
      in every circling clay hollow.

Alastair Mackie (1925–   )

Mackie uses the north-east Scots of his childhood (he was born and educated in Aberdeen) to create a sense of gravity and estrangement in the world he describes. A working-class voice of unforced plain statement makes a memorable match with classical or literary allusion in his work. He lives in Fife and has worked as a schoolteacher for most of his life.

from For My Father
Frank Mackie
Quarryman
(1901–1978)

2

You waitit for me to be born.
I wait for you to dee.   die
I gaed oot for a fill o the sunlicht
alive. Forgot ye in Euripides'[1]

'Trojan weemin''; rape, reek,   smoke
and Troy a bourach o stanes.   heap
A whoor's love-lowe   whore's love-fire
made kinnlin o a haill empire.   kindling; whole

And Hecuba,[2] the donnert auld queen,   decrepit
greetin for her man, his life   weeping
skailin ower the altar steps   spilling out
fae the bleedy sheuch o his thrapple.   ditch; throat

Against that masterpiece, dad,
whit was your life? You werena Priam
or Hector or Ulysses but a blocker,
squarin aff granite fae a quarry-hole.   from

Bleed is clartier than art.   Blood; stickier/dirtier
I canna greet for the Trojan deid,   weep

---

1. Euripides (BC 480–406), Greek poet, author of tragedy *The Trojan Women*.
2. Hecuba: wife to Priam king of Troy, mother to Hector and Paris, the Greeks made her a slave after the fall of Troy.

for the weemin waitin for the lang-boats,
the touzled thraws on a fremmit cooch. — *dishevelled writhings; foreign couch*

Nor did I greet for you. Only, your hirstlin — *wheezing*
oot your life in a ward bed
hung ower me like a spaedom — *omen*
ye wid in time mak true. — *would*

I warstle wi the kennable, — *struggle; knowable*
a death that is near me
in bleed, banes, marra and sinew.
I belang syne to that death. — *thereafter*

I'll never hear that hoast again — *cough*
that waukent me in the sma 'oors, — *wakened; very early hours*
or see ye shauchle to your meat, — *shuffle; food*
sookin life thro your inhaler. — *sucking*

Ane o the spearmen o either side,
a name withoot honour, sung
only by me. May your ess lie — *ash*
quait in the grun, your staney maister. — *quiet; ground; stony master*

from At the Heich Kirkyaird

1: Passin Beinn-Dorain[1]

The bens camp by the road-side. — *mountains*
I see their bald tents forby — *moreover*
on the sky-line hyne awa. — *far away*

The cars birr north.
Or park. The gled — *hawk*
frae his mid-air watch
studies yon file o gollochs. — *beetles*
And fowk get oot and streetch theirsels,
and wyre in to their sandwiches, — *dig in*
tak the view in
and read the news o the world.[2]

It s aa cheenged Duncan Ban;[3]
the aixed wids and the thinned deer — *axed*
and the fowk that traiked wi their tongue — *trudged; language*

1. A mountain between Tyndrum and Bridge of Orchy, the road from Glasgow to Glencoe passes it on the way to Fort William.
2. Also the title of a Sunday newspaper specialising in scandal.
3. Duncan Bàn Macintyre (1724–1812), Gaelic poet, author of *Moladh Beinn Dòbhrain*/'Praise of Ben Dorain', whose form imitates the structure of pibroch.

and their bits o gear   belongings
and ate the saut breid o exile.
Aye, it fair gies the een   certainly; eyes
mair elba-room.   elbow (also a pun on Napoleon's Elba)

Wha s listenin?
Whit's there to listen till?

The muckle lug-hole o the glen   great ear
is cockit still for a music further back,
Moladh Beinn-Dorain,
a pibroch o a mountain,
and you
makkin it wi praise.

The road's a spate o metal.   flood
I pint in homage to the poem   point
as we threidit oor road
thro its themes and variations.

7

There is ae silence for Baudelaire,[1]   one
whaur in his pit-mirk, naethingness   intense darkness
is his grun in aa the airts   ground; in all directions/arts
and he listens in for the wudness   madness
souchin whiles thro his heid.   whispering at times
And ane for Leopardi,[2]
whaur frae the hill-tap
he picturs till himsel
thae silences abeen aa mortal ken   above
and the foonds o stillness   foundations
till aa thinkin fooners   founders
and shipwrack is bliss in sic a sea.

Mine is mair hamely.
I sit on the ashet-rim o this broun pool,   plate (large dish)
its shallas fu o clood shapes and the lyft.   shallows; sky
A Hieland coo stands stock-still
in its black seck o shadda.   sack; shadow
I feel my heid gantin like a joug   gaping open; jug
that drap by drap fills up
wi aa the silence I could haud.   hold

---

1. Charles Baudelaire (1821–1867), French poet and art critic, renowned for his exploration of the darker side of the human spirit, inertia, obsession, aspiration and despair.
2. Giacomo Leopardi (1798–1837), Italian poet with a pessimistic yet compassionate vision of the insignificance of man in the face of an indifferent and infinite nature.

And syne when I was rim-fou   then; rim-full
the spilth was skailt owre Ardnamurchan   overflow; emptied
alang wi bools o sheep dirt, mussel shells,   marbles
the white keel o a seagull,
and the moors, on their heathery mattress
sleepin soond.

12

I sit on this sheep-ruggit boolder.   tugged
My pipe reek gets raivellt in the air   smoke; tangled
and traps in its kinks the lyft,   sky
the sea, the sky-line and becomes them aa.
I sense that Aatumn's in the air this set o day.   condition
I prie it and yet canna prieve it.[1]   taste; prove
It's whit the licht maks wi sleekit watter   glossy/sly
and the gloamin and aathing on this skelp o earth.   twilight; everything; expanse
stane, bush, sheep, tree; and forby, fowk danderin,   also; strolling
the tethert tents, the steekit cars … And yet   fixed/hindered
mair nor aa this either, this faimly the mind
maks oot o the merraige o the senses,
sae that things that are nae a drap's bleed   no blood (connection)
to ane anither are made sib and kin.   related and connected

Inside us we maun hae a clock that tells   must
the cheenge o season to oor haill body,
hair-thin its motions and aa but hidden
as nou when suddenly the first sma whirrs
inside the blood begin, till the 'oor striks   hour strikes
and Aatumn is the time your body tells.

1. Proverb: 'The proof o the pudden's the preein o't.'

Ian Hamilton Finlay (1925–   )

Hamilton Finlay is an internationally respected concrete poet, whose installations have been commissioned and publicly displayed throughout Europe. He spent some of his earlier years in Orkney, but since 1969 has lived in a hill farmhouse at Stonypath in Lanarkshire whose location he has transformed into an extraordinary neo-classical garden landscape with pathways, trees, poems, carved inscriptions and sundials offering a memorable expression of his unique vision. His earlier work is more literary, but still far from conventional, and the same qualities – tender, fierce, gentle and iconoclastic by turns – can be found in the 'zen' animal poems in *Glasgow Beasts* … (1961) or the lyrics in *The Dancers Inherit the Party* (1969), and the many other publications, cards, leaflets and posters of the mid-1960s.

from *Glasgow Beasts, an a Burd Haw, an Inseks, an, Aw, a Fush*

Fox

See me
wan time
ah wis a fox
an wis ah sleekit! ah
gaed slinkin
      heh
an snappin
      yeh
the blokes
aa sayed ah wis a GREAT fox
aw nae kiddin
ah wis pretty good
had a whole damn wood
in them days
hen   (dear)

Minnow

anither
time
ah wis a
minnie
aw

the pond
haw
the shoogly caur   swaying tramcar
gaun   go on
see s   give me
a frond
fir
ma wee jaur

Giraffe

ho
it wis a laugh
been
a giraffe like
ma neck
goat sneckit   got trapped
in this tree
so ah says
haw Sara
an she says whit
way ur ye staunin
aa bandy-leggit?
bandy-leggit
ah says
so help me
get yir
giraffe
free

The Dancers Inherit the Party

When I have talked for an hour I feel lousy –
Not so when I have danced for an hour:
The dancers inherit the party
While the talkers wear themselves out and
        sit in corners alone, and glower.

O.H.M.S.[1]

To my creel and stack-net island
Of the little hills, low and dark,
Her majesty's Government graciously sent
Me an Assistance clerk.

1. OHMS – On Her Majesty's Service, initials on the seal of government officials.

He frowned, 'May I come in?'
– To inspect me, he meant, 'Please do.
I shall sit on this old oil drum
And leave the chair for you.'

'Some questions require to be answered,'
'You must ask me whatever you wish.
– Those things strung on the knotted string
You are staring at, are fish.'

'Fish?' – I thought they were socks.'
He wrote me all down in his book.
O little dark island, I brought him, and after
Did you give me a darker look?

Twice

(Once)

It is a little pond
And it is frail and round

And it is in the wood,
A doleful mood

Of birches (white) and stale
Very old thin rain grown pale.

(Twice)

It is a little pond
And it is brown; around

It (like the eye
Of a cow) soft emerald

Grasses and things
Grow up. The tall harlequins

Sway again
And again, in the bright new clean rain.

Mansie Considers the Sea in the Manner of Hugh MacDiarmid

The sea, I think, is lazy,
It just obeys the moon

– All the same I remember what Engels said:
'Freedom is the consciousness of necessity'.

John Sharkey is Pleased to be in Sourin at Evening

How beautiful, how beautiful, the mill
-Wheel is not turning though the waters spill
Their single tress. The whole old mill
Leans to the West, the breast.

from One Word Poems[1]

The Cloud's Anchor
swallow

The Boat's Blueprint
water

One (Orange) Arm of the World's Oldest Windmill
autumn

Green Waters[2]

Green Waters
Blue Spray
Grayfish

Anna T
Karen B
Netta Croan

Constant Star
Daystar
Starwood

Starlit Waters
Moonlit Waters
Drift

---

1. These poems could have a title of any length, but the 'text' could be only one word.
2. These lines use the names of actual trawlers which were fishing out of Lowestoft, Aberdeen, Milford Haven and other ports.

Mystic[1]

    A litle field is given to every family for
its sepulchres.

    On the slope of the knoll angels whirl
their woollen robes in pastures of emerald
and steel.

    Reproachless children place above the doors
of their houses a picture of their father
and mother.

    And while the band above the picture is
composed of the revolving and rushing hum of
seashells and of human nights,

Whoever desecrates sepulchres is banished.

Saint-Just, Rimbaud

---

1. The poem uses a collage of lines taken, verse about, from Saint-Just's 'Republican Institutions' (prose works found among his papers after his death), and Rimbaud's poetry. Saint-Just (1767–1794) was one of the leaders of the French Revolution, and active proponent of the Reign of Terror. The French poet Arthur Rimbaud (1854–1891) broke all literary and linguistic conventions with his strange and tumultuous images.

Iain Crichton Smith/
Iain Mac a' Ghobhainn (1928–   )

Raised and educated on the Isle of Lewis, Smith went to Aberdeen University and worked as a teacher before becoming a full-time poet and novelist, writing in Gaelic as well as English. His early poetry is driven by an intensely existential response to the physical world combined with a love–hate relationship to the darker rigours of an upbringing in the Free Kirk. In later years a more humorous and relaxed voice has emerged, as well as tender and elegiac poems of strange and almost surreal beauty, often linked to a poignant sense of dispossession or exile.

Old Woman

And she, being old, fed from a mashed plate
as an old mare might droop across a fence
to the dull pastures of its ignorance.
Her husband held her upright while he prayed

to God who is all-forgiving to send down
some angel somewhere who might land perhaps
in his foreign wings among the gradual crops.
She munched, half dead, blindly searching the spoon.

Outside, the grass was raging. There I sat
imprisoned in my pity and my shame
that men and women having suffered time
should sit in such a place, in such a state

and wished to be away, yes, to be far away
with athletes, heroes, Greeks or Roman men
who pushed their bitter spears into a vein
and would not spend an hour with such decay.

'Pray God,' he said, 'we ask you, God,' he said.
The bowed back was quiet. I saw the teeth
tighten their grip around a delicate death.
And nothing moved within the knotted head

but only a few poor veins as one might see
vague wishless seaweed floating on a tide
of all the salty waters where had died
too many waves to mark two more or three.

By Ferry to the Island

We crossed by ferry to the bare island
where sheep and cows stared coldly through the wind –
the sea behind us with its silver water,
the silent ferryman standing in the stern
clutching his coat about him like old iron.

We landed from the ferry and went inland
past a small church down to the winding shore
where a white seagull fallen from the failing
chill and ancient daylight lay so pure
and softly breasted that it made more dear

the lesser white around us. There we sat,
sheltered by a rock beside the sea.
Someone made coffee, someone played the fool
in a high rising voice for two hours.
The sea's language was more grave and harsh.

And one sat there whose dress was white and cool.
The fool sparkled his wit that she might hear
new diamonds turning on her naked finger.
What might the sea think or the dull sheep
lifting its head through heavy Sunday sleep?

And later, going home, a moon rising
at the end of a cart-track, minimum of red,
the wind being dark, imperfect cows staring
out of their half-intelligence, and a plough
lying on its side in the cold, raw

naked twilight, there began to move
slowly, like heavy water, in the heart
the image of the gull and of that dress,
both being white and out of the darkness rising
the moon ahead of us with its rusty ring.

Two Girls Singing

It neither was the words nor yet the tune.
Any tune would have done and any words.
Any listener or no listener at all.

As nightingales in rocks or a child crooning
in its own world of strange awakening
or larks for no reason but themselves.

So on the bus through late November running
by yellow lights tormented, darkness falling,
the two girls sang for miles and miles together

and it wasn't the words or tune. It was the singing.
It was the human sweetness in that yellow,
the unpredicted voices of our kind.

Tha Thu air Aigeann m'Inntinn

Gun fhios dhomh tha thu air aigeann m'inntinn
mar fhear-tadhail grunnd na mara
le chlogaid 's a dhà shùil mhóir
's chan aithne dhomh ceart d' fhiamh no do dhòigh
an déidh cóig bliadhna shiantan
tìme dòrtadh eadar mise 's tù:

beanntan bùirn gun ainm a' dòrtadh
eadar mise 'gad shlaodadh air bòrd
's d' fhiamh 's do dhòighean 'nam làmhan fann.
Chaidh thu air chall
am measg lusan dìomhair a' ghrunna
anns an leth-sholus uaine gun ghràdh,

's chan éirich thu chaoidh air bhàrr cuain
a chaoidh 's mo làmhan a' slaodadh gun sgur
's chan aithne dhomh do shlighe idir,
thus' ann an leth-sholus do shuain
a' tathaich aigeann na mara gun tàmh
's mise slaodadh 's a' slaodadh air uachdar cuain.

———————

You are at the Bottom of my Mind

Without my knowing it you are at the bottom of my mind
like one who visits the bottom of the sea
with his helmet and his two great eyes:
and I do not know properly your expression or your manner
after five years of showers
of time pouring between you and me.

Nameless mountains of water pouring
between me, hauling you on board,
and your expression and manner in my weak hands.
You went astray
among the mysterious foliage of the sea-bottom
in the green half-light without love.

And you will never rise to the surface of the sea,
even though my hands should be ceaselessly hauling,
and I do not know your way at all,
you in the half-light of your sleep,
haunting the bottom of the sea without ceasing,
and I hauling and hauling on the surface of the ocean.

On a Summer's Day

Thus it is.
There is much loneliness
and the cigarette coupons will not save us.

I have studied your face across the draughtsboard.
It is freckled and young.
Death and summer have such fine breasts.

Tanned, they return from the sea.
The colour of sand, their blouses the colour of waves,
they walk in the large screen of my window.

Bacon, whose Pope screams in the regalia[1]
of chairs and glass, dwarf of all the ages,
an hour-glass of ancient Latin,

you have fixed us where we are, cacti able to talk,
twitched by unintelligible tornadoes,
snakes of collapsing sand.

They trail home from the seaside in their loose blouses.
The idiot bounces his ball as they pass.
He tests his senile smile.

The Earth Eats Everything

The earth eats everything there is.
It is a year and a half now since you died.
Your marble tombstone stands up like a book.
The storms have not read it nor the leaves.
The blue lightnings bounced from it.
The ignorant swallows perched on its top.
I have forgotten it over and over.
Life is explainable only by life.
I have read that on paper leaves.

Chinese Poem[2]

1

To Seumas Macdonald,
                              now resident in Edinburgh –
I am alone here, sacked from the Department
for alcoholic practices and disrespect.
A cold wind blows from Ben Cruachan.
There is nothing here but sheep and large boulders.
Do you remember the nights with *Reliquae Celticae*
and those odd translations by Calder?
Buzzards rest on the wires. There are many seagulls.
My trousers grow used to the dung.
What news from the frontier? Is Donald still Colonel?
Are there more pupils than teachers in Scotland?

1. British expressionist painter Francis Bacon (1909–92) made a number of studies of a 'screaming Pope' whose form
   seems to be disintegrating.
2. Compare Ezra Pound, 'Exile's Letter' from Li Po.

I send you this by a small boy with a pointed head.
Don't trust him. He is a Campbell.

2

The dog brought your letter today
from the red postbox on the stone gate
two miles away and a bit.
I read it carefully with tears in my eyes.
At night the moon is high over Cladach
and the big mansions of prosperous Englishmen.
I drank a half bottle thinking of Meg
and the involved affairs of Scotland.
When shall we two meet again
in thunder, lightning or in rain?
The carrots and turnips are healthy,
the *Farmers' Weekly* garrulous.
Please send me a *Radio Times* and a book
on cracking codes. I have much sorrow.
Mrs Macleod has a blue lion on her pants.
They make a queenly swish in a high wind.

3

There is a man here who has been building a house
for twenty years and a day.
He has a barrow in which he carries large stones.
He wears a canvas jacket.
I think I am going out of my mind.
When shall I see the city again,
its high towers and insurance offices,
its glare of unprincipled glass?
The hens peck at the grain.
The wind brings me pictures of exiles,
ghosts in tackety boots, lies,
adulteries in cornfields and draughty cottages.
I hear Donald is a brigadier now
and that there is fighting on the frontier.
The newspapers arrive late with strange signs on them.
I go out and watch the road.

4

Today I read five books.
I watched Macleod weaving a fence
to keep the eagles from his potatoes.
A dull horse is cobwebbed in rain.
When shall our land consider itself safe
from the assurance of the third rate mind?

We lack I think nervous intelligence.
Tell them I shall serve in any capacity,
a field officer, even a private,
so long as I can see the future
through uncracked field glasses.

5

A woman arrived today
in a brown coat and a brown muff.
She says we are losing the war,
that the Emperor's troops are everywhere
in their blue armour and blue gloves.
She says there are men in a stupor
in the ditches among the marigolds
crying 'Alas, alas.'
I refuse to believe her.
She is, I think, an agent provocateur.
She pretends to breed thistles.

Pupil's Holiday Job

The girl who was reading Milton
is at the cash desk in the supermarket.
Her glasses are too large for her pale face.
The bread and milk slide down the same slope
followed by the meat and oranges.
It is possible that there are many worlds –
Lycidas, where are you Lycidas?
You are locked in a school of old paint
you die inside a grille of pale windows.
The bill comes to pounds and pounds and pounds.
A whole week's groceries in front of you
and your pale face has glasses large and round.
Lycidas is floating in the sea
among bouquets and the eternal monsters
with strange names, so Greek, so salt with brine.
Down the slope the bread and cereals pour,
they pour eternally with Lycidas.
He's turning over and over with the cartons
in the sea of everyday with all its monsters.

Speech for Prospero

When I left that island I thought I was dead. Nothing
stirred in me. Miranda in jeans
and totally innocent was standing by a sail

and all the others, happily recovered, talking
in suits made of brine. But to return to

the gossip, the poisonous ring, was not easy,
and many times I nearly tried to turn back
feeling in my bones the desolate hum of the headland,
my creation of rivers and mist.

Still we went on. The corruptible had put on flesh,
the young were hopeful once again, all was forgiven.
Nevertheless the waiters were scraping and bowing,
the rumours beginning, the crowns of pure crystal were sparkling,
the telephones were ringing with messages from the grave
and the thin phosphorescent boys glowing with ambition
in corners of velvet and death.

Still I went on. The ship left its wake behind it
shining and fading, cord of a new birth,
and over by the sail Miranda gazed at her prince
yearning for love.

Goodbye, island, never again shall I see you,
you are part of my past. Though I may dream of you often
I know there's a future we all must learn to accept
music working itself out in the absurd halls and the mirrors
posturings of men like birds, Art in a torrent of plates,
the sound of the North wind distant yet close
as stairs ascend from the sea.

Australia

1
In Australia the trees are deathly white,
the kangaroos are leaping halfway to heaven
but land at last easily on the earth.
Sometimes I hear graves singing
their Gaelic songs to the dingos
which scrabble furiously at the clay.
Then tenderly in white they come towards me,
drifting in white, the far exiles
buried in the heart of brown deserts.
It is a strange language they speak
not Australian not Gaelic
while the green eyes stalk them
under a moon the same as ours
but different, different.

2

Naturally there are photographs of Ned Kelly
in his iron mask in his iron armour.
His iron body hung stiffly in the wind
which blew past the ravens.
In that dry land his armour will not rust
and the hot sun flashes from it
as if it were a mirror, creator of fresh stars.
However dingos leap at it they will not chew him
for he is a story, a poem,
a tale that is heard on the wind.

3

No, you will not return from Australia
however you may wish to do so.
For you have surrendered to its legend,
to its music being continually reborn,
to the eerie whine of its deserts.
Somehow or another it entered your soul
and however much you remember Scotland,
its graves sanctified by God,
its historical darknesses,
you will not return from it.
Its dust is in your nostrils,
its tenderness has no justice,
its millions of stars are the thoughts
of unbridled horsemen.
With blue eyes you will stare
blinded into its blueness
and when you remember your rivers,
the graveyards the mountains,
it is Australia that stands up in front of you,
your question, your love

4

All day the kookaburra is laughing
from the phantoms of trees,
from the satire of nature.
It is not tragedy nor comedy,
it is the echo of beasts,
the bitter chorus of thorns,
and flowers that have names
that aren't easily remembered.
The kookaburra laughs from the trees,
from the branches of ghosts,
but the sky remains blue
and the eyes glow green in the night.

Douglas Dunn (1942–)

Trained as a librarian, Dunn worked in Glasgow and Hull before returning to live in Fife where he is Professor of Poetry at St Andrews University. Themes of personal and national identity feature in his writing which seeks a balance of civilised expression and social concern without losing touch with fiercer Northern roots.

St Kilda's Parliament: 1879–1979 [1]

The photographer revisits his picture

On either side of a rock-paved lane,
Two files of men are standing barefooted,
Bearded, waistcoated, each with a tam-o'-shanter
On his head, and most with a set half-smile
That comes from their companionship with rock,
With soft mists, with rain, with roaring gales,
And from a diet of solan goose and eggs,
A diet of dulse and sloke and sea-tangle,
And ignorance of what a pig, a bee, a rat,
Or rabbit look like, although they remember
The three apples brought here by a traveller
Five years ago, and have discussed them since.
And there are several dogs doing nothing
Who seem contemptuous of my camera,
And a woman who might not believe it
If she were told of the populous mainland.
A man sits on a bank by the door of his house,
Staring out to sea and at a small craft
Bobbing there, the little boat that brought me here,
Whose carpentry was slowly shaped by waves,
By a history of these northern waters.
Wise men or simpletons – it is hard to tell –
But in that way they almost look alike
You also see how each is individual,
Proud of his shyness and of his small life

1. A well-known photograph of the 'St Kilda Parliament' at which all the grown men in the community would meet in the main street every morning to allocate work for the day. The culture could not sustain itself in this most isolated of all the Scottish islands, far to the west of the Outer Hebrides, and the people were evacuated in 1930.

On this outcast of the Hebrides
With his eyes full of weather and seabirds,
Fish, and whatever morsel he grows here.
Clear, too, is manhood, and how each man looks
Secure in the love of a woman who
Also knows the wisdom of the sun rising,
Of weather in the eyes like landmarks.
Fifty years before depopulation –
Before the boats came at their own request
To ease them from their dying babies –
It was easy, even then, to imagine
St Kilda return to its naked self,
Its archaeology of hazelraw   lichen
And footprints stratified beneath the lichen.
See, how simple it all is, these toes
Playfully clutching the edge of a boulder.
It is a remote democracy, where men,
In manacles of place, outstare a sea
That rattes back its manacles of salt,
The moody jailer of the wild Atlantic.
        Traveller, tourist with your mind set on
Romantic Staffas and materials for
Winter conversations, if you should go there,
Landing at sunrise on its difficult shores
On St Kilda you will surely hear Gaelic
Spoken softly like a poetry of ghosts
By those who never were contorted by
Hierarchies of cuisine and literacy.
You need only look at the faces of these men
Standing there like everybody's ancestors
This flick of time I shuttered on a face.
Look at their sly, assuring mockery.
They are aware of what we are up to
With our internal explorations, our
Designs of affluence and education.
They know us so well, and are not jealous
Whose be-all and end-all was an eternal
Casual husbandry upon a toehold
Of Europe, which, when failing, was not their fault.
You can see they have already prophesied
A day when survivors look across the stern
Of a departing vessel for the last time
At their gannet-shrouded cliffs, and the farewells
Of the St Kilda mouse and St Kilda wren
As they fall into the texts of specialists,
Ornithological visitors at the prow

Of a sullenly managed boat from the future.
They pose for ever outside their parliament,
Looking at me, as if they have grown from
Affection scattered across my own eyes.
And it is because of this that I, who took
This photograph in a year of many events –
The Zulu massacres, Tchaikovsky's opera –
Return to tell you this, and that after
My many photographs of distressed cities,
My portraits of successive elegants,
Of the emaciated dead, the lost empires,
Exploded fleets, and of the writhing flesh
Of dead civilians and commercial copulations,
That after so much of that larger franchise
It is to this island that I return.
Here I whittle time, like a dry stick,
From sunrise to sunset, among the groans
And sighings of a tongue I cannot speak,
Outside a parliament, looking at them,
As they, too, must always look at me
Looking through my apparatus at them
Looking. Benevolent, or malign? But who,
At this late stage, could tell, or think it worth it?
For I was there, and am, and I forget.

Washing the Coins

You'd start at seven, and then you'd bend your back[1]
Until they let you stand up straight, your hands
Pressed on your kidneys as you groaned for lunch,
Thick sandwiches in grease-proofed bundles, piled
Beside the jackets by the hawthorn hedges.
And then you'd bend your little back again
Until they let you stand up straight. Your hands,
On which the earth had dried in layers, itched, itched,
Though worse still was that ache along the tips
Of every picking finger, each broken nail
That scraped the ground for sprawled potatoes
The turning digger churned out of the drills.
Muttering strong Irish men and women worked
Quicker than local boys. You had to watch them.
They had the trick of sidewaysbolted spuds
Fast to your ear, and the upset wire basket
That broke your heart but made the Irish laugh.

1. 'Tattie-hawking holidays' allowed Scottish schoolchildren time off to earn money and to help with the potato harvest.
   For travelling Irish families it was a way of life.

You moaned, complained, and learned the rules of work.
Your boots, enlarging as the day wore on,
Were weighted by the magnets of the earth,
And rain in the face was also to have
Something in common with bedraggled Irish.
You held your hands into the rain, then watched
Brown water drip along your chilling fingers
Until you saw the colour of your skin
Through rips disfiguring your gloves of mud.
It was the same for everyone. All day
That bead of sweat tickled your smeared nose
And a glance upwards would show you trees and clouds
In turbulent collusions of the sky
With ground and ground with sky, and you portrayed
Among the wretched of the native earth.
Towards the end you felt you understood
The happy rancour of the Irish howkers.
When dusk came down, you stood beside the byre
For the farmer's wife to pay the labour off.
And this is what I remember by the dark
Whitewash of the byre wall among shuffling boots.
She knew me, but she couldn't tell my face
From an Irish boy's, and she apologized
And roughed my hair as into my cupped hands
She poured a dozen pennies of the realm
And placed two florins there, then cupped her hands
Around my hands, like praying together.
It is not good to feel you have no future.
My clotted hands turned coins to muddy copper.
I tumbled all my coins upon our table.
My mother ran a basin of hot water.
We bathed my wages and we scrubbed them clean.
Once all that sediment was washed away,
That residue of field caked on my money,
I filled the basin to its brim with cold;
And when the water settled I could see
Two English kings among their drowned Britannias.[1]

1. 'Britannia', with her shield and trident, featured on the reverse of the old British penny.

Tom Leonard (1944–   )

Born and educated in Glasgow, Leonard has committed himself to a poetry whose form can stay true to the subtle beat and music of colloquial language as it is actually spoken. Much of his work, and his critical writing, stems from the conviction that the voices of many people are effectively ignored or silenced by education and 'polite' culture.

from 'Unrelated Incidents'

(3)

this is thi
six a clock
news thi
man said n
thi reason
a talk wia
BBC accent
iz coz yi
widny wahnt
mi ti talk
aboot thi
trooth wia
voice lik
wanna yoo
scruff. if
a toktaboot
thi trooth
lik wanna yoo scruff yi
widny thingk
it wuz troo.
jist wanna yoo scruff tokn.
thirza right
way ti spell
ana right way
ti tok it. this
is me tokn yir
right way a

spellin. this
is ma trooth.
yooz doant no
thi trooth
yirsellz cawz
yi canny talk
right. this is
the six a clock nyooz. belt up.

from 'Ghostie Men'

right inuff
ma language is disgraceful

ma maw tellt mi
ma teacher tellt mi
thi doactir tellt mi
thi priest tellt mi

ma boss tellt mi
ma landlady in carrington street tellt mi
thi lassie ah tried tay get aff way in 1969 tellt mi
sum wee smout thit thoat ah hudny read chomsky tellt mi
a calvinistic communist thit thoat ah wuz revisionist tellt mi

po-faced literati grimly kerryin thi burden a thi past tellt mi
po-faced literati grimly kerryin thi burden a thi future tellt mi
ma wife tellt mi jist-tay-get-inty-this-poem tellt mi
ma wainz came hame fray school an tellt mi   children
jist aboot ivry book ah oapnd tellt mi
even thi introduction tay thi Scottish National Dictionary tellt mi

ach well
all livin language is sacred
fuck thi lohta thim

Dripping with Nostalgia

while the judges
in the Snottery Weans Competition
were still licking clean
the candidates' upper lips

the 'Dear Aul' Glesca' Poetry Prize
for the most heartwarming evocation

of communal poverty
was presented to the author of

'The Day the Dug ate ma Ration Book'

hangup

aye bit naw   yes but no

naw bit
aye bit

away
away yi go
whut

mini whut
minimalism

aw minimalism
minimalism aye

aye right
aye right inuff
aye right inuff definitely

aye bit
naw bit

a stull think yi huvty say sumhm

Liz Lochhead (1948–   )

Born in Motherwell, Lochhead went to Glasgow School of Art and worked as a teacher before becoming a full-time poet and playwright in 1978. Her work responds to the trivia of contemporary life with delight and linguistic energy, but there can be personal pain and a feminist edge to her wit as well.

Box Room

First the welcoming. Smiles all round. A space
For handshakes. Then she put me in my place –
(Oh, with concern for my comfort). 'This room
Was always his – when he comes home
It's here for him. Unless of course,' she said,
'He brings a Friend,' She smiled 'I hope the bed
Is soft enough? He'll make do tonight
In the lounge on the put-u-up. All right
For a night or two. Once or twice before
He's slept there. It'll all be fine I'm sure –
Next door if you want to wash your face.'
Leaving me 'peace to unpack' she goes. My weekend case
(Lightweight, glossy, made of some synthetic
Miracle) and I are left alone in her pathetic
Shrine to your lost boyhood. She must
Think she can brush off time with dust
From model aeroplanes. I laugh it off in self defence.
Who have come for a weekend to state my permanence.

Peace to unpack – but I found none
In this spare room which once contained you. (Dun-
Coloured walls, one small window which used to frame
Your old horizons). What can I blame
For my unrest, insomnia? Persistent fear
Elbows me, embedded deeply here
In an outgrown bed. (Narrow, but no narrower
Than the single bed we sometimes share).
On every side you grin gilt edged from long-discarded selves
(But where do I fit into the picture?) Your bookshelves

Are crowded with previous prizes, a selection
Of plots grown thin. Your egg collection
Shatters me – that now you have no interest
In. (You just took one from each, you never wrecked a nest,
You said). Invited guest among abandoned objects, my position
Is precarious, closeted so – it's dark, your past a premonition
I can't close my eyes to. I shiver despite
The electric blanket and the deceptive mildness of the night.

The Grim Sisters

And for special things
(weddings, school –
concerts) the grown up girls next door
would do my hair.

Luxembourg announced Amami night.[1]
I sat at peace passing bobbipins
from a marshmallow pink cosmetic purse
embossed with jazzmen,
girls with ponytails and a November
topaz lucky birthstone.
They doused my cow's-lick, rollered
and skewered tightly.
I expected that to be lovely
would be worth the hurt.

They read my Stars,
tied chiffon scarves to doorhandles, tried
to teach me tight dancesteps
you'd no guarantee
any partner you might find would ever be able to
keep up with as far as I could see.

There were always things to burn
before the men came in.

For each disaster
you were meant to know the handy hint.
Soap at a pinch
but better nailvarnish (clear) for ladders.
For kisscurls, spit.
Those days womanhood was quite a sticky thing
and that was what these grim sisters came to mean.

1. Radio Luxembourg, commercial radio station from Europe that played pop music in the days before the BBC gave it
   air time. Amami is a line of shampoo and hair care.

'You'll know all about it soon enough.'
But when the clock struck they
stood still, stopped dead.
And they were left there
out in the cold with the wrong skirtlength
and bouffant hair,
dressed to kill,

who'd been
all the rage in fifty eight,
a swish of Persianelle a slosh of perfume.
In those big black mantrap handbags
they snapped shut at any hint of *that*
were hedgehog hairbrushes
cottonwool mice and barbed combs to tease.
Their heels spiked bubblegum, dead leaves.

Wasp waist and cone breast, I see them yet.
I hope, I hope
there's been a change of more than silhouette.

Tam Lin's Lady

'Oh I forbid you maidens a'
who wear gowd in your hair –
to come or go by Carterhaugh
for young Tam Lin is there.' [1]

So you met him in a magic place?
O.K.
But that's a bit airy fairy for me.
I go for the specific – you could, for instance,
say that when he took you for a coffee
before he stuck you on the last bus
there was one of those horrible congealed-on
plastic tomatoes on the table ... oh don't
ask me
I don't know why everything has to be so sordid these days ...
I can take *some* sentiment –
tell me how charmed you were
when he wrote both your names and a heart in spilt coffee –
anything except that he carved them on the eldern tree.
But have it your own way.
Picking apart your personal

1. See the Scots ballad 'Tam Lin'.

dream landscape of court and castle and greenwood
isn't really up to me.
So call it magical. A fair country.
Anyway you were warned.

And if, as the story goes nine times out of ten –
he took you by the milkwhite hand & by the grassgreen sleeve
& laid you on the bonnie bank & asked of you no leave,
well, so what?
You're not the first to fall for it,
good green girdle and all –
with your schooltie rolled up in your pocket
trying to look eighteen. I know.
All perfectly forgivable.
Relax.

What I do think was a little dumb
if you don't mind me saying so
was to swallow that old one about you being
the only one who could save him.

Oh I see – there was this lady
he couldn't get free of.
Seven years and more he said he'd sacrificed himself
and if you didn't help him he'd end up
a fairy for ever! Enslaved.

Or worse still in hell without you.

Well, well.
So he stopped you from wandering in the forest
and picking pennyroyal and foxgloves
and making appointments and borrowing money for the abortion.
He said all would be well
If only you'd trust him just this once
and go through
what he was honest enough to admit in advance
would be hell and highwater for you.

So he told you which relatives to pander to
and which to ignore.
How to snatch him from the Old One
and hold on through thick and thin
through every change that happened.
Oh but it was terrible!
It seemed earlier, you see,

he'd been talking in symbols (like
adder-snake, wild savage bear
brand of bright iron red-hot from the fire)
and as usual the plain unmythical truth was worse.
At any rate you were good and brave, you did
hang on, hang on tight.
And in the end of course
everything turned out conventionally right
with the old witch banished to her corner lamenting,
cursing his soft heart and the fact she couldn't keep him,
and everyone sending out for booze for the wedding.

So we're all supposed to be happy?
But how about you, my fallen fair maiden
now the drama's over, tell me
how goes the glamourie?
After the twelve casks of good claret wine
and the twelve and twelve of muskadine,
tell me
what about you?
How do you think Tam Lin will take
all the changes you go through?

Mirror's Song

for Sally Potter

Smash me looking-glass glass
coffin, the one
that keeps your best black self on ice.
Smash me, she'll smash back –
without you she can't lift a finger.
Smash me she'll whirl out like Kali,
trashing the alligator mantrap handbags
with her righteous karate.
The ashcan for the stubbed lipsticks
and the lipsticked butts,
the wet lettuce of fivers.
She'll spill the Kleenex blossoms,
the tissues of lies, the matted
nests of hair from the brushes'
hedgehog spikes, she'll junk
the dead mice and the tampons
the twinking single eyes
of winkled out diamante, the hatpins
the whalebone and lycra,
the appleblossom and the underwires,

the chafing iron that kept them maiden,
the Valium and initialled hankies,
the lovepulps and the Librium,
the permanents and panstick and
Coty and Tangee Indelible,
Thalidomide and junk jewellery.

Smash me for your daughters and dead
mothers, for the widowed
spinsters of the first and every war
let her
rip up the appointment cards for the
terrible clinics,
the Greenham summonses,[1] that date
they've handed us. Let her rip.
She'll crumple all the
tracts and the adverts, shred
all the wedding dresses, snap
all the spike-heel icicles
in the cave she will claw out of –
a woman giving birth to herself.

---

1. The women's movement established a long-running camp to protest the presence of tactical nuclear weapons at an American airforce base at Greenham Common in England. There were many arrests over many years.

Acknowledgements

Thanks are due to the following copyright holders for permission to reproduce the poems in this anthology.

While every effort has been made to trace copyright holders, if the Publishers have overlooked anyone they will be glad to rectify this in any future edition.

GEORGE MACKAY BROWN, 'Ikey on the People of Hellya', from *The Year of the Whale*, 1965; 'A Winter Bride', from *Fishermen with Ploughs*, 1971; 'Sea Widow', from *Winterfold*, 1976; all from Chatto & Windus, London; 'Haddock Fishermen', 'Love Letter' and the three 'Tea Poems', from *George Mackay Brown Selected Poems*, John Murray, London, 1991, all reproduced with the kind permission of John Murray (Publishers) Ltd.

GEORGE BRUCE, 'Inheritance' and 'The Curtain', from *Collected Poems of George Bruce*, Edinburgh University Press, Edinburgh, 1980; 'Elizabeth Polishing an Agate' and 'Why the Poet Makes Poems', from *Perspectives. Poems 1970–1986*, Aberdeen University Press, Aberdeen, 1987, reproduced with the kind permission of George Bruce.

W. D. COCKER, 'Dandie', from *Poems Scots and English*, Brown, Son & Ferguson Ltd, Glasgow, 1979, reproduced with the kind permission of the Publisher.

DOUGLAS DUNN, 'St Kilda's Parliament' and 'Washing the Coins', from *Selected Poems 1964–83*, Faber & Faber Ltd, 1986, reproduced with the kind permission of the Publisher.

IAN HAMILTON FINLAY, 'Fox', 'Minnow' and 'Giraffe', from *Glasgow Beasts …*, Wild Flounder Press, 1961; 'The Dancers Inherit the Party', from *The Dancers Inherit the Party*, Migrant Press, 1961; 'O.H.M.S.', 'Twice', 'Mansie Considers the Sea in the Manner of Hugh MacDiarmid' and 'John Sharkey is Pleased to be in Sourin at Evening', from *The Dancers Inherit the Party*, Fulcrum Press, 1969; 'THE CLOUD'S ANCHOR', 'THE BOAT'S BLUEPRINT', 'ONE (ORANGE) ARM OF THE WORLD'S OLDEST WINDMILL', from *Poems to Hear and See*, Macmillan, 1971; 'Green Waters', from *Honey by the Water*, Black Sparrow Press, 1973, and The Wild Hawthorn Press, all these and 'Mystic' reproduced with the kind permission of Ian Hamilton Finlay.

ROBERT GARIOCH, 'During a Music Festival', 'Brither Worm', 'Ane Offering for Easter', 'Glisk o the Great', 'Heard in the Cougate', 'Heard in the Gairdens', 'The Big Music', 'Lesson' and 'At Robert Fergusson's Grave', all from *Collected Poems*, Macdonald, 1977, reproduced with the kind permission of the Saltire Society.

WILLIAM SYDNEY GRAHAM, 'Listen. Put on Morning', 'The Beast in the Space', 'What is the language using us for? second poem', 'Loch Thom' and 'To Alexander Graham', all from *Collected Poems*, Faber & Faber Ltd, London, 1979, reproduced with the kind permission of The Estate of W. S. Graham.

HAMISH HENDERSON, 'End of a Campaign', 'Halfaya' and 'Leaving the City', from *Elegies for the Dead in Cyrenaica*, Polygon, Edinburgh, 1990, reproduced with the kind permission of the Publisher.

TOM LEONARD, 'Unrelated Incidents: 3', '"right inuff"', 'Dripping with Nostalgia' and 'hangup', from *Intimate Voices*, Galloping Dog Press, 1984, reproduced with the kind permission of Tom Leonard.

LIZ LOCHHEAD, 'Box Room', 'The Grim Sisters', 'Tam Lin's Lady' and 'Mirror's Song', from *Dreaming Frankenstein*, Polygon, Edinburgh, 1984, reproduced with the kind permission of the Publisher.

NORMAN MACCAIG, 'Summer Farm', 'Still Life', 'Interruption to a Journey', 'Assisi', 'Aunt Julia', 'Return to Scalpay', 'Two Thieves', 'Ringed Plover by a Water's Edge', 'Toad', 'Angus's Dog', 'In that Other World', 'Notations of Ten Summer Minutes', 'Small Boy', 'My Last Word on Frogs' and 'Recipe', all from *Collected Poems*, Chatto & Windus, London, 1990, reproduced with the kind permission of Norman MacCaig.

HUGH MACDIARMID, 'The Watergaw', 'At My Father's Grave', 'The Eemis Stane', 'The Innumerable Christ', 'Empty Vessel', 'Servant Girl's Bed', extract from *A Drunk Man Looks at the Thistle, To Circumjack Cencrastus*, 'In the Children's Hospital', 'The Skeleton of the Future', 'The Seamless Garment', 'The Glass of Pure Water', extract from 'The World of Words (*In Memoriam James Joyce*)', 'Crystals Like Blood', 'Milk-Wort and Bog-Cotton' and extract from 'From the 'Scots Anthology', all from *Complete Poems 1920–1976*, Carcanet Press Ltd, Manchester, 1993, reproduced with the kind permission of the Publisher.

SOMHAIRLE MACGILL-EAIN (SORLEY MACLEAN), 'Dogs and Wolves', 'Shores', 'A Spring', 'Calvary', 'Highland Woman', 'The National Museum of Ireland', 'Heroes', 'Death Valley' and 'Hallaig', all from *From Wood to Ridge*, Carcanet Press Ltd, Manchester, 1989, reproduced with the kind permission of the Publisher.

ALASTAIR MACKIE, 'For My Father', from *Back Green Odyssey and Other Poems*, Rainbow Books, 1980; 'At the Heich Kirkyaird: 1. Passin Beinn-Dorain', '7' and '12', from *Ingaitherins*, Aberdeen University Press, Aberdeen, 1987, all reproduced with the kind permission of Alastair Mackie.

RUARAIDH MACTHOMAIS (DERICK THOMSON), 'Bayble', 'When This Fine Snow is Falling', 'Sheep', 'Coffins', 'And I saw you as a loom', 'In Glasgow', 'Do you remember …?' and 'And I saw you as a boat', all from *Creachadh na Clarsaich/Plundering the Harp*, Macdonald, 1982, reproduced with the kind permission of Derick Thomson; 'Princess Diana' and 'Return from Death' from *Smeur an Dochais/Bramble of Hope*, Canongate, Edinburgh, 1991, reproduced with the kind permission of the Publisher.

EDWIN MORGAN, 'The Unspoken', 'From the Domain of Arnheim', 'To Joan Eardley', 'Glasgow Green', 'One Cigarette', 'Absence', 'Glasgow 5 March 1971', 'Ellingham Suffolk January 1972', 'The First Men on Mercury', from 'London: The Post Office Tower', 'The Planets', 'Theory of the Earth', 'Dear man, my love goes out in waves', from *From the Video Box*: '6' and '17', all from *Collected Poems*, Carcanet Press Ltd, Manchester, 1990, reproduced with the kind permission of the Publisher.

EDWIN MUIR, 'Childhood', 'Merlin', 'The Enchanted Knight', 'The Return of the Greeks', 'The Wayside Station', 'Scotland 1941', 'Scotland's Winter', 'The Little General', 'The Interrogation', 'The Labyrinth', 'The Horses', 'The Cloud' and 'Dream and Thing', all from *Collected Poems*, Faber & Faber Ltd, London, 1960, reproduced with the kind permission of the Publisher.

CHARLES MURRAY, 'A Green Yule' and 'Dockens Afore his Peers', from *Hamewith, the Complete Poems of Charles Murray*, Aberdeen University Press, Aberdeen, 1979, reproduced with the kind permission of the Charles Murray Memorial Trust.

DAVID RORIE, 'The Pawky Duke', from *David Rorie: Poems and Prose*, William Donaldson (ed.), Aberdeen University Press, Aberdeen, 1983, reproduced with the kind permission of the David Rorie Society.

IAIN CRICHTON SMITH, 'Old Woman', 'By Ferry to the Island', 'Two Girls Singing', 'On a

Summer's Day', 'Chinese Poem', 'Speech for Prospero' and 'Australia', all from *Collected Poems*, Carcanet Press Ltd, Manchester, 1992, reproduced with the kind permission of the Publisher; 'The Earth Eats Everything' and 'Pupil's Holiday Job', from *Selected Poems 1955–80*, Macdonald, 1981, reproduced with the kind permission of the Saltire Society; 'Tha thu air aigeann m'intinn / You are at the bottom of my mind', from *Modern Scottish Gaelic Poems*, Canongate Press Ltd, 1976, reproduced with the kind permission of the Publisher.

SYDNEY GOODSIR SMITH, 'October 1941', 'Elegy: xii Orpheus', 'A Tink in Reekie' and 'Winter Blues', from *Collected Poems*, Sydney Goodsir Smith, John Calder (Publishers) Ltd, London, © John Calder (Publishers) Ltd, 1975, and reproduced with the kind permission of The Calder Educational Trust.

WILLIAM SOUTAR, 'The Philosophic Taed', 'King Worm', 'The Hurdy-Gurdy Man', 'Song', 'The Tryst' and 'Lealness', from *Poems of William Soutar*, W. R. Aitken (ed.), Scottish Academic Press, 1988, reproduced with the kind permission of The Trustees of the National Library of Scotland.

ANDREW YOUNG, 'Culbin Sands', from *The Poetical Works of Andrew Young*, Secker and Warburg, London, 1975, reproduced with the kind permission of The Andrew Young Estate.

Acknowledgements are due to the following translators of the Gaelic poems in this anthology.

William Neill, who translated poems by Donnchadh MacRaoiridh, Murchadh MacCoinnich, Iain Lom, Màiri Nighean Alasdair Ruaidh, John MacCodrum, Robb Donn, Duncan Ban Macintyre, William Ross, John MacLean and Mary Macpherson.

Professor Derick Thomson, who translated poems by Giolla Crìost Brùilingeach, Aithbhreac Inghean Corcadail, Anonymous ('Brosnachadh addressed to Earl of Argyll on eve of Flodden'), Iain Lom, Sìleas na Ceapaich, Alasdair MacMhaighstir Alasdair, Ann Campbell and Willam Livingston.

Iain Crichton Smith, who translated poems by Mrs MacGregor of Glenstrae, Anonymous ('Thig trì nithean gun iarrraidh, Three things come without seeking'), Iain Lom, Alasdair MacMhaighstir Alasdair, Duncan Ban Macintyre and William Ross.

Ian Grimble, who translated poems by Robb Donn.

William Matheson, who translated the poem by Roderick Morison.

Special acknowledgements and thanks to Joan Macdonald for proofreading the Gaelic texts, and to Jackie Jones, Penny Clarke, Nicola Carr and Marion Sinclair of Edinburgh University Press. 'Of making many books there is no end' – but some are longer than others.